THE DANGEROUS ART C

The Dangerous Art of Text Mining celebrates the bold new research now possible because of text mining: the art of counting words over time. However, this book also presents a warning: without help from the humanities, data science can distort the past and lead to perilous errors. The book opens with a rogue's gallery of errors, then tours the ground-breaking analyses that have resulted from collaborations between humanists and data scientists. Jo Guldi explores how text mining can give a glimpse of the changing history of the past – for example, how quickly Americans forgot the history of slavery. Textual data can even prove who was responsible in Congress for silencing environmentalism over recent decades. The book ends with an impassioned vision of what text mining in defense of democracy would look like, and why humanists need to be involved.

JO GULDI is Professor of History, Southern Methodist University, and Director of the Digital Humanities Minor. Her publications include, as coauthor with David Armitage, *The History Manifesto* (Cambridge University Press, 2014).

THE DANGEROUS ART OF TEXT MINING

A Methodology for Digital History

JO GULDI

Southern Methodist University

CAMBRIDGE
UNIVERSITY PRESS

CAMBRIDGE
UNIVERSITY PRESS

Shaftesbury Road, Cambridge CB2 8EA, United Kingdom

One Liberty Plaza, 20th Floor, New York, NY 10006, USA

477 Williamstown Road, Port Melbourne, VIC 3207, Australia

314–321, 3rd Floor, Plot 3, Splendor Forum, Jasola District Centre, New Delhi – 110025, India

103 Penang Road, #05–06/07, Visioncrest Commercial, Singapore 238467

Cambridge University Press is part of Cambridge University Press & Assessment, a department of the University of Cambridge.

We share the University's mission to contribute to society through the pursuit of education, learning and research at the highest international levels of excellence.

www.cambridge.org
Information on this title: www.cambridge.org/9781009262989

DOI: 10.1017/9781009263016

First published 2023

A catalogue record for this publication is available from the British Library.

Library of Congress Cataloging-in-Publication Data
NAMES: Guldi, Jo (Joanna), 1978- author.
TITLE: The dangerous art of text mining : a methodology for digital history / Jo Guldi, Southern Methodist University, Texas.
DESCRIPTION: First edition. | Cambridge, United Kingdom ; New York, NY, USA : Cambridge University Press, 2022. | Includes bibliographical references and index.
IDENTIFIERS: LCCN 2022043230 (print) | LCCN 2022043231 (ebook) | ISBN 9781009262989 (hardback) | ISBN 9781009262996 (paperback) | ISBN 9781009263016 (epub)
SUBJECTS: LCSH: Historiography–Data processing. | Text data mining–Social aspects. | History–Errors, inventions, etc. | Electronic digital information literacy. | Digital humanities.
CLASSIFICATION: LCC D16.12 .G85 2022 (print) | LCC D16.12 (ebook) | DDC 025.042072/7–dc23/eng/20221116
LC record available at https://lccn.loc.gov/2022043230
LC ebook record available at https://lccn.loc.gov/2022043231

ISBN 978-1-009-26298-9 Hardback
ISBN 978-1-009-26299-6 Paperback

This book is dedicated to my mother, the computer programmer who left punchcards to study painting. She later became an activist for queer rights, anti-racism, and the environment. It is also dedicated to my father, the electrical engineer, the fashioner of microchips, who followed my mother to the art museums. As their love affair developed, both became activists on behalf of anti-racism and the environment. They are role models and leaders in their community; they are also generous parents in every sense.

Early on, my parents taught me an appreciation of complementary ways of knowing as well as shameless enjoyment of play in the pursuit of curiosity. Later, they babysat while I worked on my code, proofread my chapters, and consulted on equations. I feel like I won the lottery many times over.

Contents

Contents

Preface

My studies in literature taught me to look to parables for instruction where formal training fails. Around the world, folktales offer accounts of individuals who have to take up a challenging and dangerous task which is beyond their capabilities. The heroes of these stories are sometimes described as 'fools,' but other times they are portrayed as monkeys. Pondering the question of why data science sometimes resisted collaboration with useful humanists, why humanists sometimes resist useful data methods, and how much I myself had to learn, I found myself looking to these stories for direction.

In the monkey stories, the risk of failure is emphasized. Most monkeys in stories never learn. They have a very hard time learning how to reconcile their desires, hopes, and talents with reality. The Zen Master Hakuin recounts the parable of the monkey who became enchanted with moon's reflection in a pond (Figure 1):

The monkey is reaching
For the moon in the water.
Until death overtakes him
He'll never give up.

The parable is about mistaking an appearance for reality. From the monkey's point of view, the moon has somehow slipped from the sky and is suddenly within reach. The silly monkey can't tell the difference between the real moon and its reflection. He doesn't know that the moon belongs in the sky. Distracted by ambitions that don't make sense, he's meanwhile missing out on other objects that *are* within his reach – flowers, fruit, branches, and water, each in their own loveliness. And frankly, there is a real risk of this monkey dying a nasty death by drowning when he reaches too far and loses hold of his branch.

Hakuin's story warns us to be wary of fantasy, attending instead to the sober methods of knowing what we already have in our possession. This monkey parable offers a reminder equally to data-scientists who open humanities questions without training as well as humanists who unwarily experiment with data science methods. They remind us that enchantment with new questions and methods raises perils. The student who presents a history paper written with artificial intelligence (AI) is liable to find that computers have supplied inaccurate facts. The data scientist who ignores

Figure 1   Hakuin's parable of the monkey who mistakes the moon's reflection for the
moon, as rendered by the Japanese illustrator Ohara Koson, 1927.

the silences that riddle paper archives is liable to have their findings based on electronic data retracted, as may the humanist who applies data science methods without a thorough grasp of algorithms and the ways in which they can be manipulated. When we try to describe human institutions or human lives – the work of history – we attempt to reach for something real. Getting dazzled by a glimpse of possible insight can distract from the hard work of reaching for real facts, and this distraction will almost always land the monkey in trouble.

Sage though the advice is for human readers, Hakuin's warning is pessimistic. The monkey is in a perilous position, almost certain to perish by drowning unless he can learn, which seems unlikely. A happier story, where the monkey can learn, is rare.

I grew up in a landscape scarce on history but flooded with algorithms. I was raised in a company town on the edge of what some chroniclers call the "Silicon Prairie," a windswept and newly developed suburb of Dallas, Texas that is the headquarters of the electronics giant Texas Instruments. The education that I received in the public schools of that technology-obsessed culture was heavily influenced by the ideas of engineers who worked at a corporation that had risen to international success upon the manufacture of the integrated circuit – that is, the hardware that constitutes the brain of all computers and cell phones today. Access to integrated circuits made it possible for the first time to write software programs that made guesses about language and culture, patterned on ideas developed after the Second World War by Claude Shannon, whose theories appear throughout this book. My father, an electrical engineer from a long line of electrical engineers, had studied those ideas in graduate school. He was one of the experts who made integrated circuits cheap and reliable for the first time.

The public education system in the land without history was forged in a truce between old-time Texans, who loved their mythology of Civil War glory, and the mathematical sophistication of newly arrived engineers who had their own reasons to avoid the past. Most serious engagement with history and the classics had been stripped from our textbooks. If my mother appreciated art museums and my father played classical music, there was nevertheless no one prodding me to question the legend of the Alamo, the meaning of the Civil War, or the significance of Juneteenth to communities living just down the road. Like many white Americans of my generation, I grew up ignorant of the fact that a debate was possible or that evidence could be tested. I wouldn't have known where to begin.

Whatever history I stumbled upon, its nuances and implications I had to riddle out for myself, and often clumsily. The relevance of history to data, to electronics, and to everyday life was hardly apparent to my community of origin. Learning more required me to cross enemy lines in the battles of tribe and identity. Even now, when I teach history and code in equal parts in the classroom, I have not forgotten what happened when I first fell in love with history, when all kinds of politics and art were, for me, a kind of forbidden fruit.

My community of origin was a frontier on the leading edge of today's battles over curriculum and the political implications of education. The fact that children in my suburb learned math and code but little history marks out my suburb as an earlier adopter of the in science, technology, engineering, and mathematics (STEM)-focused education in vogue in many places today. Parents who want their children to get ahead stuff their children's schedule full with mathematics tutoring, science, and code. Parents and educators, meanwhile, worry that the arts, humanities, and civics find scant room in the schedule. Conservative parents worry that humanistic instruction can be a pretext for political radicalization. Liberal parents and educators worry that barriers have been erected to keep students from the truth of reality itself. Because of concerns such as these, many public schools across America have also become worlds without history.

My Texan identity had two diametrically opposed components – one comfortable with religion and moral sentiment; the other comfortable in generalizations, numbers, and math. One might have expected these cultures of religion and science to come into conflict, and by the time we were teenagers, they did. By and large, what stopped the potential conflict from ripening was the total lack of historical context with which both sets of ideas were presented.

The public education I experienced was a product of both a local culture devoted to Texan identity and an increasingly international culture wary of politics but steadfast in its faith in the power of science, mathematics, and code. They were excellent classes, in my memory, as were the courses on algebra and calculus. Courses on programming were offered from junior high school forward. They were taught by retired engineers, who were patient and kindly, but possessed a lifetime of experience that tempered abstract instruction with patience, till the student began to feel their confidence growing, recognizable patterns forming in the mind.

History classes, meanwhile, were primarily concerned with the origins and identity of the great state of Texas, and secondarily to American patriotism. Instruction was left to the football coach, who read aloud in a monotone from a textbook. Nobody liked these classes. No one felt they were achieving mastery or beauty. History exams were multiple choice. History questions had right and wrong answers, which one solved by memorizing names and dates, not investigating interpretive strategies. There was little sense that studying the past required mastery of *multiple* histories, each informed by the teller's own perspective, or that working with history required interweaving these contested and often conflicting narratives.

Most parents, mine included, were complicit in this silencing of history, if only by dint of their own educations, which had been focused on earning a living at the expense of a deep acquaintance with art or history. Limited engagement with the past was a way of life, although not an explicit ideology. My mother, the computer programmer, and my father, the electrical engineer, engaged family history largely through the grammar of praise for the virtue of their own parents, teachers, and religious traditions.

Silence about the past meant that politics, history, literature, and art were experienced as disorienting and potentially problematic. Not knowing which battle they were part of, most adults in the town where I grew up faced current affairs with a sense of vertigo rather than the frank judgments of individuals whose sense of history is well formed. The Civil Rights Movement and feminist marches of the 1960s and 1970s left them with a hazy feeling of shame, which they mainly preferred to ignore at the time. Christian duty would later drive my parents to become anti-racist, environmentalist, and gay-rights activists and educators – a story of which I could not be prouder, although that is a tale for another time. No adults that I can remember from my childhoods had stories about either participating in the Vietnam War or of protesting for its end, although I was friends with at least one Vietnamese child whose parents had fled Saigon just before its fall. Neither she nor I had the historical context to put her parents' experience into perspective. We had no sense of the great postwar migrations that had so changed the shape of American cities, nor of the struggles over empire and democracy that punctuated the century. She was a grown adult with several Ivy League degrees and children of her own before she was able to ask her parents questions about what their migration meant to them.

I had equally few tools for making sense of the experiences, identity, and conflicts between the white Americans around me. None of my secondary teachers or Sunday school teachers could speak articulately about the conflicts between Luther and Wesley or Protestantism and Darwin, let alone Marx, Nietzsche, or Freud. There were Irish-American families around me whose ancestors had been Molly Maguires, Jewish-American families whose ancestors had fled the pogroms for Oklahoma, migrants who had fled war in El Salvador and Guatemala, and Kurdish refugees who had fled the aggressions of Saddam Hussein, but I was an adult before I heard their stories. Whether at the dinner table or in the pew, the compass of history I was handed as a young person was a tiny and badly functioning toy. It provided no answers for how to interpret the world around me.

Quantitative learning – not knowledge of history – was the ideal to which my community aspired. It offered truth, a practical skill, and a trustworthy route to earning a living. Nor was it just my family. I grew up in a company town where engineers made radar for the military, with the result that no one's daddy had fought in America's overseas wars. Everyone knew how to code. I myself learned in elementary school. My mother, who was fluent in Fortran and Cobol, had programmed the supercomputers at an insurance firm where her colleagues nicknamed her "super girl." When I asked her how to use the family computer that she had purchased to monitor our finances, she handed me her manual for the programming language BASIC. She told me that the best way to learn was to read it ten times, cover to cover, in succession, even though it would make no sense for the first five readings. I did so. I was ten. Soon I was spending leisured afternoons designing homemade videogames.

When I created videogames, the design toyed with forbidden knowledge. My first project was to code a "which-way-adventure" through the English history section of the family encyclopedia. Starting with the "K" and "Q" volumes of the encyclopedia, I transcribed each royal biography into the green, pixelated screen, wrapping around it an interface that would allow a reader to browse from one biography to related subjects via what would later be known as a hyperlink. My first attempt at history resembled nothing so much as a DIY Wikipedia. Because I had never encountered a critical history, I had no idea what a thoughtful engagement with the content of the articles would look like. All I had was thoughtless reverence for the past: my father loved classical music; my mother loved art; and it seemed natural that my budding interest in history should likewise take the form of thoughtless idol worship. In another sense, however, I was testing my wings. My canon of royals was an attempt to *locate* the stories that had been left out of my elementary school course on Texas history. It would become the first attempt of many.

A child who looks for the lost records of the past can run into many strange alleyways for want of a good guide. Without someone who knows the humanities backward and forward, the only way to learn is by gathering whatever information presents itself. For me, the guide was novelty. I became a compulsive consumer of threadbare volumes of poetry and philosophy from the used book store – the more tattered the better. I set out by studying whatever looked strange from the viewpoint of our company town. Because almost no one knew dead languages in the company town where children learnt to code, I threw myself into Greek and Latin. I read obsessively. I snuck into college libraries and spent hours transcribing poetry and theological arguments, as if working on a plan. There was no plan. My plan was to master the history of the world. The plan was to find out what humans actually were.

In college, guides to this process appeared at last, although they looked very different than anything I had encountered at home. I pored over everything they presented me, throwing myself into reading lists from women's studies, continental philosophy, and Marxist literary criticism. I have no regrets. Under the tutelage of a wide variety of professors, I was drinking in the postwar canon in the way that the designers of "Great Books" curricula had intended modern people should read Aristotle and Shakespeare: as a guide for living. I was interested in learning from books how to meet strangers and apprehend new discoveries. I wanted to profit from the intimate and collective histories that had been denied me as a child.

When I started my graduate studies at the University of California in Berkeley, I entered a place as different from my hometown as one can imagine. If no one in my hometown had a sense of history, everyone at Berkeley seemed familiar with that peculiar dimension of human experience – their awareness of the significance of recent decades even more heightened than at my undergraduate institution. My fellow students all seemed to know when their ancestors had arrived in this country. Many of them could recount the struggles of their parents and grandparents in political battles past. Several had become specialists in local history, too, who could describe, in sumptuous detail, the clashes between protesters and cops in local parks in 1968 – years before any of us were born.

Before long, I too began to discern patterns of time in families and neighborhoods. I learned to interpret the visual clues that marked out evidence of racism in the past, such as the stone archways near campus, in the Berkeley Hills, that marked what had once been gated communities. Those changes, too, could be mapped, documented, collected, assorted, and formed into narratives. They could be used as a compass to plot a direction – how far society had changed in my parents' lifetimes; how far yet it might change within my own.

When I compare the world without history of the dusty plains of north Texas with the graduate lounge at Berkeley, with its high Tudor windows, where endless green tea flows, and graduate students with thick glasses pore over their laptops, I imagine the latter as an outpost of an entirely different way of abstracting the world – a Temporal Cartographers' Society. Members of the Society were and are suspicious of technology. They – or rather *we,* for I was and am a card-carrying member of the guild – can recount with ease stories about how the bioengineered varieties of corn from the Green Revolution of the 1960s put small farmers in India out of business, and how dams built by the British to create irrigation also served to propagate the mosquito and spread malaria.

My path to the Temporal Cartography Society from the world without history took me through a borderland that few inhabitants of either territory know about, a world where computers and humanistic thinking go hand in hand. Already in the 1990s, when I was starting college, only a handful of humanities faculty relied on computational indexes of text, but I had the good fortune to meet a few. As a freshman at Harvard, one of my summer jobs was working on a computational index of Latin poetry for Professor Richard Thomas, who was working on a book about Horace. I worked on the top floor of the Widener Library, in a room from whose window the whole of Harvard Yard was reduced to a miniaturized geometry like a Persian carpet. The room where I labored was attached to the well-upholstered Classics Library, stacked with threadbare volumes. In a supply closet attached to the Classics Library was the only terminal on campus where one could pursue this kind of research. If someone else was using it, I returned to the Classics Library and read Virgil until they were finished. The computer was ancient already: it had a pixelated, green screen like the one on which I had learned to code.

Classical scholars already depended upon digitalized indexes of most known texts from the ancient world to support rigorous comparisons around how classical authors used specific terms. For Professor Thomas, then, I was charged with compiling an exhaustive list of interrelated terms in Horace, cross-referenced with secondary scholarship. Terms could be counted, both by year and by author. The scholar could interpret the usage of a keyword, resting on the assurance that, thanks to the labors of hundreds, they were working with a complete set of references. Compared with the political philosophies we were reading in comparative literature seminars, here was a reassuringly certain kind of knowledge. I quickly learned that Harvard's historical linguists were using these counts of words and their basic components to wring from dead languages the shape of legends never written down and long forgotten. It was as if computational modeling was puzzling ancient rimes out of the very dust of the library.

Encountering talk of text mining for the first time, the reaction of most members of the Temporal Cartography Society is a deep and pensive frown of contemplative puzzlement. Why does one need computers to read books? The same scholars have transitioned over the past twenty years to using electronic catalog systems that make it possible to keyword search thousands of articles, to locate discourses without knowing where to look.

One day in graduate school, I noticed that the electronic catalog systems I had access to were changing. Searching Google for a relatively obscure Scottish laird from the eighteenth century – I turned to Google only in a state of tiredness in the dead of night, having exhausted all the local libraries to which I had access – I had come up dry on a search. In despair, I asked Google, knowing fully well that Google had returned fewer than a dozen hits the last time I had looked. Perhaps some genealogists had more information about the laird's family, I thought, and I could grab place-names or the names of other relatives that I could trace again in archival records.

To my astonishment, Google returned hundreds of hits instead of a dozen. Google Books had launched that very month, untrumpeted and unheralded in the research community. I knew exactly what this meant: the careful counting and tracking of words that had transformed the discipline of the Classics at Harvard and revealed lost epics was now available, for the first time, to people who worked on modern subjects. I knew then that the course of my scholarship was set to change – yet again.

Today, computer scientists devise algorithms that can count words over time and show us which ones are changing. There are even individuals from the land without history who believe that computer-analyzed data about the past equips us with a detector for coming insurrections. For years now, I've taught courses in Python and R, collaborated with statisticians and computer scientists, and spoken at machine learning conferences. I've also continued to work mainly as an archival researcher of history, teaching courses on the history of capitalism, whose curriculum included the evolution of cartographical technology – the use and abuse of compasses, maps, and data.

After 2008, when I was awarded the first "digital history" position in the nation, I began to think about what it would mean to devise keyword queries – and, on a grander scale, how one might develop information infrastructures that would serve popular will and humanistic concerns rather than working at odds with them. In 2012, with the collaboration of designer Cora Johnson-Roberson, I released Paper Machines, an open-source toolkit designed to help my students enjoy distant-reading technologies. In 2014, my second book, *The History Manifesto* (coauthored with David Armitage), discussed the potential effect that digital analysis would have on questions of periodization, graduate student training, and audience in the discipline of history. My current work focuses on how machine learning and statistical approaches can be applied to the history of Great Britain – as it intersects with the history of concepts about property, rent, and eviction.

Today, some defenders of the humanities believe that history, literature, and the teaching of empathy to undergraduates are practices that are best defended when a firm line is drawn between the world of engineers and the world of conversation and reading. I understand why they feel under assault, although I disagree with the remedy. In *The History Manifesto*, David Armitage and I argued that societies face a crisis of "short-termism" that required historians to show the relevance of history to the problems of our era. We urged historians to join public debates about inequality, international governance, and climate change, and we advocated the tools of digital history as one possible approach to modeling historical change on longer scales of time. The book was praised in many other venues, scholarly and public, with translations in a dozen languages. In Europe, it is sometimes referenced as the starting point for both modern digital history and for a practice of History newly engaged in the service of society. The book also raised a major debate in the United States, sparking discussion groups in many departments about the future of the field. In some places, the book was also denounced as a threat to the practice and pedagogy of history.

The criticism had consequences for knowledge-making in the university. The resistance to digital technology visible from History departments in 2014–20 made me fear that my colleagues were rejecting a moment of great opportunity, when the wider university was committing billions of dollars to new hires in digital research – lines that humanities departments sorely needed.

Then the criticism triggered personal consequences. Despite the fact that I had already published a well-respected, archivally driven monograph in my field that had earned me a number of prestigious fellowships, some of my colleagues reacted to my future course of research with trepidation. One can endlessly speculate about why. Whatever the reason, the promise of tenure for my first book – the offer made when I was hired, while the first book was widely available – suddenly vanished. Certain colleagues had experienced a change of heart.

Colleagues presented me with a choice that I would have preferred not to make. I could renounce digital methods and long-term questions, abandon my grants, return to archival work, and, after publishing a new archival monograph, submit my work for tenure review. Or I could choose to pursue text mining, in which case they would not support my case for tenure. Certain senior colleagues advised me to abandon both text mining and long-term studies of history, to return to the archives, and by reaffirming my loyalty to "traditional history," to prove to them that I was still indeed a scholar.

With the blessing of other advisors and mentors, I chose the path that reflected my love of free academic inquiry and my faith in the wider view represented by those colleagues who had voted to support my research. Supported by the generosity of the National Science Foundation – which made serious research possible anywhere – I left my Ivy League post without giving my colleagues a chance to judge my file. I took a place at a small liberal arts school where I was able to pursue my current research so long as external funding lasted. With the guidance of statisticians, data scientists, and physicists, I submitted myself to the task of learning the skills I would need to perform text mining up to a high standard. I kept my conversations with computer science going, and I learned all I could about the promising new work coming from the interdisciplinary outpost called "cultural analytics."

At around the same time, I found myself enjoying a privilege especially rare among historians – the chance to discuss new methods with scholars from across History's many discrete subfields. From their graduate training forward, most historians choose one or two subfields of study whose conferences they attend and for whose journals they review. Very few individuals can spare the time from their own research projects to journey, unimpeded, across the political borders that divide the camp. But because the *Manifesto* touched the field of history as a whole, I found myself invited to keynote conferences in astonishing range of subdisciplines where I was a stranger. In effect, I found myself with a universal passport to visit intellectual historians, historians of conceptual thought, philosophers of history, historians of science and technology, media historians, and historians of political party alike.

I was invited to travel with such liberty because colleagues across the field of History had demands to level with the new practice of text mining. Most could articulate specific fears about the abuses of history in a data-driven age. Quite a few had begun to raise fundamental questions about what a high standard of text mining would look like, capable, for instance, of supporting a technical definition of "event" or "periodization," of what a complete "explanation" looked like and when the language of sciences conflicted with the historical method. I was often out of my depth. Having trained with social and cultural historians, I had to ask foolish questions and start with background reading. I asked questions and took notes. I found myself suddenly in the position of a graduate student with a hundred new advisors, each intent on shaking my arguments. I would have stumbled and given up long ago had not so many of those colleagues offered encouragement as well.

It was becoming clear to me that despite the reaction of some outspoken critics, the discipline of history had not closed ranks against quantitative methods. Rather, history's high standards of reasoning and argumentation had a number of forms, and the discipline was liable to be unsatisfied with any practice of text mining that failed to engage some plurality of its methods and standards of argumentation.

Most practitioners of history wanted, above all, for text mining to engage with a higher standard of truth than early demonstrations had provided. They were alarmed – and rightfully so – at hasty work with text mining published from the information sciences. But most subfields of History could also glimpse certain definite regions where text mining had already offered significance contributions.

I had become accustomed to offering history departments a summation of the most promising arenas where text mining is being deployed – and originally my intent with this work was to publish a book of best practices, combining some of my own strategies with a review of the best work from other digital historians and practitioners across the social sciences and humanities. However, conversations with colleagues have changed the questions that seemed most pressing, making me skeptical of data-driven arguments too tightly tethered to the hypothesis-testing method of the hard sciences. They have solidified my conviction that history's specialization in archives and archival silences had much to offer the world of data science. They have also made me curious about what the fundamental questions of temporal experience – memory, periodization, and event – could do to shape a more intelligent practice of text mining. In the end, I found that though much of my work was about what big data could offer History, the high standards that History could offer data science were equally important.

The precepts for better work with data in Part I of this book may strike as obvious readers in history above the undergraduate level, although they will also set to rest certain minds from humanities departments who worry that quantitative tools will force humanistic readers to abandon our concerns with empathy, historical methods, and an appreciation for the complexity of interpretation. The case studies in Part II, however, offer more to historians and other scholars from the humanities and social sciences. There, I have tried to work out the shape of a study of temporal experience that makes room for humanistic concerns such as the multiplicity of experience and the silencing of subaltern voices, even while holding out the possibility of discovery from new tools. When I look ahead to the future of practice in Part III, I am indulging in individual conjecture about the implications of the trends I see and attempting to answer colleagues' questions about what the shape of research in future History departments and universities might look like. It is here that I extend myself well beyond scholarship and into speculation about the future, a notoriously dangerous occupation, albeit one that is sometimes useful for conversation, and it is in that light that I hope that section will be understood.

Some frank statements about my limits are appropriate here. I have been involved in a decade-long conversation between information scientists and historians. On the best days, text mining for historical analysis feels like a kind of magical undertaking, drawing tigers forth from wardrobes. But I am no magician, and I have stepped into conversations for which no training prepared me. My course of study has been various, and it is often incomplete. I have the impression that my work as a translator working between fields is of value, and it is in the spirit of service that I submit this work, but I readily concede that it will often fall short of perfection. I include some observations about the process and the community behind this work in the Appendix. Leaning on incomplete knowledge, producing a survey of a field which is still growing, I have surely missed many possible methods and questions that are relevant. I barely scratch the surface of the wider fields of which text mining forms a part, although I have elsewhere reviewed some of the wider advances of the digital social sciences, digital humanities, and the field known as cultural analytics. Nor can I tell what the future holds – for the university or for any of the disciplines in which I work. I have no crystal ball, nor time machine, and my algorithms make few predictions. What I present here is mainly the record of ongoing conversations. I hope they may be of use to others.

Hakuin's monkey reminds us that some fears about data may be vague reflections of the truth rather than the truth itself. Colleagues who fear data in the humanities because they are defending their own territory may concoct reasons why text mining represents a threat to humanistic ways of knowing. Sometimes the substance of their attack boils down to a reasonable but personal choice; they themselves do not intend to innovate their methods in a quantitative direction, and they wish that their students should not be pressured to either. Sometimes they channel more abstract concerns by quoting eminent historians of the 1970s on the threat that quantitative methods of yore represented to knowledge based in narrative.

But such fears as these are hazy when compared to more carefully documented abuses of data – for instance the racial bias of algorithms that tilt the price of housing to punish a sector of the population, or the abuse of archives by certain data scientists with the result of false findings. Just as we should look past the glitter of algorithms to the question of historical truth, so too those interested in truth must look past territorial scheming by privileged interests, towards the real threats and abuse of data. It is in the service of that cause that the beginning chapters of this book are dedicated to identifying the real threats and mistakes that plague data-driven history.

The Monkey King

One famous allegory talks about the extraordinary conditions under which monkeys can learn what they don't already know. In the most well-loved monkey story in the world, the Chinese epic *Journey to the West,* the monkey receives the instruction he needs, and terrible suffering is thereby averted.[1] What kind of teachers get through, when instruction seems so liable to fail?

Journey to the West tells us that Sun Wukong, the monkey king, was a great swordsman. He could not be defeated by gods or demons. But he was also conceited – chattering, boasting, overly fond of himself and his talents – and so he never knew when to stop fighting his adversaries. So distracted was he by his delight with weapons that he would forget himself. At the least provocation, he would fly into a fury and hack bystanders to bits. It was simply too much of a risk for ordinary people, so the Buddha imprisoned him in a mountain, sentenced for misbehavior to a term of 500 years.

---

[1] Anthony Yu, ed., *Journey to the West,* 4 vols. (Chicago, University of Chicago Press, 1983).

Figure 2   Sun Wukong, the Monkey King, by Tsukioka Yoshitoshi, 1889.
Brooklyn Museum.

In this story, Sun Wukong is a complex figure who represents both distraction and cunning (Figure 2). An icon of _technology_, his cunning is manifested in his incredible skill with weapons. His imprisonment brings to mind all uses of technology today that merit censure – from the gamification of citizens' internet data by corporations, to the way that the practice of selling data has destabilized democracy, to data science papers built upon a biased use of data, to the racial bias of corporate data, to fears that data-driven disciplines are expanding while support for humanities faculty is dwindling. In turn, some see the faculty who defend older methods of reading – "traditional" historical methods and "close" reading – as similarly armed, self-absorbed, and dangerous – wielding weapons of spite to cut down younger scholars, blocking opportunities for joint hires from the information sciences while faculty lines in the humanities vanish. There are many reasons today why some might see their peers as dangerous monkeys armed with swords – and might even wish them locked away. How, in such a world, can people begin to trust each other, let alone learn from one another's separate intelligence?

What is most surprising about Sun Wukong is that – unlike the monkeys of many other stories – he proves capable of change in the end. That change can be accomplished only with enormous difficulty and the intervention of powerful allies. With proper guidance about what matters, however, even a bully can become a valuable ally.

In the story, the monkey king was eventually freed by Kwan-Yin, the goddess of compassion – but only on one condition. Sun Wukong would have to act as a guardian against ogres and robbers on a dangerous journey. His ward would be a human monk who had just been chosen to carry the Buddhist scriptures from India to China.

Guided by the monk, Sun Wukong changed his ways. He learned to recognize the suffering of others and to control his own destructive impulses. He becomes the monk's loyal friend. The Buddhist scriptures were delivered, and China was enlightened.

Immortal as he was, the monkey king surely felt too proud to walk alongside a humble human as his guard. But the monkey needed the monk, more perhaps than the monk needed the monkey. Like a monkey king, skillful with weapons but overweening with pride, so much of information science today is on a hazardous path. A change of consciousness is no easy matter.

In my travels across interdisciplinary boundaries, I have often felt like a chastened monkey who has foolishly applied data in the wrong way, who needed the conscience of colleagues to wield my weapons or respect the basic principles of humanity. My companions have been philosophers of history, digital humanists, media scholars, historians of all stripes, information scientists, and statisticians, each with their own cautions about how to wield one's weapons well. Many of them have raised caveats about how data science might lead to an abuse of the historical method. Others have feared the abuse of danger and the stifling of stories of vulnerable people. Still others have cautioned me against the reckless use of black-box algorithms without testing what happens inside. The instruction that I have received – and what I attempt to report on in this book – concerns the standards of reliable proof, when historical interventions matter, concerns the modeling of temporal experience, the silences of the archives, and the bias of data.

Data practice today may indeed be a sharp instrument in the hands of a monkey. But most of us who work with data can learn from reviewing retracted papers to respect the many ways that the analysis of the past can go wrong. Data practitioners can learn from historians the significance of compassion for the silenced voices in the archives.

The danger is that the desire to be gods often overwhelms human potential for peaceful coexistence. The urge to slash at data, not realizing that our tools can injure the very meaning we wish to preserve, must be tempered with a broader knowledge base. Without some knowledge of what text is, what human institutions do, or why change over time matters, even powerful AI algorithms will fail to capture the reality of the world around them. A data sector that lusts for predictive algorithms, which sends researchers on a misguided search for the unknowable future, can overwhelm the quest to apply with wisdom the knowledge we already have. The danger is that information science on its own cannot even see what it is missing.

Here we are faced with the problem of a form of technology perpetually in trouble with the god of compassion, with vulnerable lives at stake. Something has to change. The solution is in the companionship of monkeys and monks. Useful innovation is what happens when data scientists and humanists collaborate.

Acknowledgments

In *The History Manifesto* (2014), my coauthor David Armitage and I raised a series of questions about how the new flood of data – associated with social media but also with the digitalization of sources from the past – offers important new opportunities to those who write or teach from the humanities. Since the book's publication, I have continued to learn about what digitalization might portend for the humanities and social sciences, drawing inspiration from experiments in digital literary studies, quantified social science, natural language processing, and informatics. I leaned into many a conversation with humanists who expressed their doubts about their method, and I took opportunities to work with reviewers and editors who pressed me to define the alignment between digital methods and methods from the humanities. This book is the direct outcome of those dialogues: it is the record of a period of learning and growth, my own path through a series of related fields that are increasingly in conversation with each other.

I have attempted to approach those discourses with prudence and humility. I am sure that I have missed much, and that future scholars will build on what they find here; I present this book with the intention of offering a first step in a conversation, not a final plan. Whatever I have learned about this conversation – whether about mathematical descriptions of historical change or about historical theory – is due to the patience and insight of colleagues. As a result, I have many people to thank for bringing me to this conversation, for taking the trouble to educate me, and for their patience with my initial naïveté.

My engagement with the digital humanities was nurtured in many directions – by Adrian Johns and Jim Sparrow, who thought that digital history was ripe for a postdoctoral fellowship in the early days of 2009; by Jan Goldstein, who encouraged me to publish my first digital history article in 2010; by Bethany Nowviskie and Dan Cohen, early pioneers, who hosted inspiring early conferences that brought me face to face with the librarians and younger scholars who would soon become the field's leaders, and which made me want to learn more; by the work of the LiPad and Dilipad groups as well as the Parliamentary Trust, which laid the groundwork for the investigations discussed here by cleaning and linking data and making it freely available. As in so many areas of research, digital history, too, grows only from the labors of many hands.

The same could be said for the problem of theorizing the problem of history, its sources, and its arguments. The orientation to questions of time and history was incubated over three major conferences: one on argumentation and history at George Mason University, Virginia; another on digital history at the Fields Institute, Toronto; and a third on temporality and text mining at the Humlab, Umeå, Sweden. These three conferences, as far as I am aware, were the first such gatherings to bring digital historians together around the charge of explaining their relationship to temporality and causality. I therefore owe the organizers – Lincoln Mullen, Stephen Robertson, Chad Wellman, Ian Milligan, Fredrik Noren, Pelle Snickars, and Erik Erdoff – an enormous debt for helping me understand the themes of this book. My own horizons were also expanded by the members of INTH (the International Network for Theory of History), mainly historians of ideas and philosophers of history, who were generous enough to share their perspectives on periodization with me. Participants in any of those three conferences will find significant chunks of this text a reflection of presentations and conversations over dinner and coffee at those events.

I have been especially moved by the engagement of the reviewers and editors of learned journals in our field over recent years, who gave this project an especial push. Ten years ago, digital engagement was likely to chiefly meet with resistance and sniping from reviewers, but many editors have taken care to position new work for a lively conversation. I benefited directly from the encouragement of editors at *Isis*, *Technology and Culture*, and the *American Historical Review*, which kept me engaged, and especially from the reviewers at those journals who were responsible for pushing me deeper into an engagement with philosophers such as Kosselleck, Erll, and Assman, which at the end of the day has been transformative.

As with many academic undertakings, exercises in digital history rely upon the constant revision, support, and criticism of colleagues to reach a bar of insight, and my work has also benefited enormously from the input of many scholars. In particular, Simon DeDeo, Richard Jean So, Tim Hitchcock, Ted Underwood, Micki Kauffman, Alex Gil, Lauren Klein, Lincoln Mullen, Hoyt Long, Dan Edelstein, Giovanna Cesarini, Nicole Coleman, Ian Milligan, Lara Putnam, Andrew Piper, James Evans, Robert

Chandler, Bethany Nowviskie, Robert Morrissey, Clovis Gladstone, Stefan Tanaka, Melvin Wevers, Ruth Ahnert, Katherine Bode, and Mark Algee-Hewitt made critical history, the digital humanities, information sciences, and digital social sciences into a community, inspired and encouraged me, and taught me how to think about so many of the themes here. Most of them will recognize our conversations duplicated in these pages – with footnotes wherever possible. Many of these individuals became my coaches on statistical methods, coding, and visual presentations; they essentially guided me toward a mastery of another set of methods in which I received no formal training and offered the comradery and cheerleading necessary to keep me going. Richard Jean So, in particular, along with Andrew Piper, Alex Gil, Lauren Klein, and Antoinette Burton, offered invaluable companionship, warmth, and clarity along the way for thinking about what a radical social consciousness wed to data can offer.

Coding required its own support. I owe an enormous debt to Benjamin Williams of the University of Denver Business School, formerly a statistics PhD student in my digital humanities class, whom I paid to teach me and another student how to code one summer, and to Lynne Stokes, chair of the Statistics Department at Southern Methodist University (SMU), who protected and nurtured my collaborations with her department. Shalima Zalsha, a statistics PhD student, has proofread most of the code in this volume. Aren Cambre, PhD, of SMU's Office of Information Technology, has troubleshot many coding problems on demand when I found myself out of my depth. Only by learning from these instructors was I able to make the visualizations in this book, but any errors are, of course, my own. Stephanie Buongiorno was an indefatigable project manager and code consultant; her creative and technical algorithms for understanding agency in the text of the past are cited throughout this book.

Other good conversations from nonpractitioners were just as vital. Pasi Ihalaihnen, Fredrik Norén, Pelle Snickars, and Paul Seabrook formed a seminar to discuss how text mining applies to conceptual history and parliamentary democracy, and lectures and conversations at Dr. Ihalainen's invitation convened and stimulated some of the most esteemed digital historians and social scientists in Europe, including Ruben Ros, Hugo Bonin, and Jani Marjanen. Helge Jordheim and Ethan Kleinberg pushed my ideas about periodization when this project was just coming into formation. Laurence Winnie put Jill Lepore's articles about "disruption" into my hands when they came out and stood in the hallway with me talking about the nuances of data-driven approaches. Jill Lepore herself, over a dinner in Dallas organized by Andy Graybill, told me that she perceived the digital as a danger because of the prediction issue – a short conversation that inspired a full chapter, and really what inspired the "danger" in the title. Graeme Wood's article in *The Atlantic* offered what became the frame for the entire book – how the practice of digital history differs from Peter Turchin's promise of a prediction machine. I have not met most of the non–text-based quantitative historians I mentioned, but I owe their books and articles a great deal for helping me think through the nuances of subfields: E. A. Wrigley, Leigh Shaw-Taylor, Dan Bogart, Walter Scheidel, Geoffrey Parker, and Sam White. Chiel Akker urged me to turn toward them and helped me organize my thoughts about the field. Colleagues from computer science at Brown, especially Shriram Krishnamurthi, helped me recognize the opportunity for a conversation about cross-field experimentation. My colleagues at SMU – especially Ed Countryman, Fred Chang, Stephanie Buongiorno, Lynne Stokes, Ben Williams, Rob Kalescky, Eric Godat, and Macabe Keliher – helped me think through many of the issues in this book, while Andy Graybill and Tom Dipiero ensured that I was able to take the necessary leaves to pursue research. In addition, the current administration has made it possible for me to turn my teaching toward digital methods in support of the new digital humanities minor that I direct.

Institutions shelter scholarship, making room for it and providing the support of archivists; in a digital age, new forms of support are required that fit the hybrid nature of data-driven inquiry. The present book owes a great deal to the patronage of two university chief information officers and one professor of mathematics who believed that an expanding world of data science required professors from all disciplines to have access to the help of data scientists. Michael Hites, Ravi Pendse, and Mark Howison made that work possible on an institutional level.

I have tried my best to reward them with a deluge of citations wherever possible, although surely they each deserve many more references than those in this sparsely annotated book, which is an artifact of ongoing conversations about emergent habits of study rather than a sustained, didactic engagement with texts from a particular moment – it is an artifact, one might say, of oral traditions rather than of written ones, a reflection of a moment when conversations are so sped up in the digital humanities that one frequently learns of new approaches in phone calls and text messages instead of in journal articles. The private conversations and emails that inspired the approaches in this book were so numerous that footnoting them would hamper the printed page. I therefore encourage the reader to imagine the constellation of their names on every page of this manuscript and to watch their names for forthcoming reflections as well as the recent papers noted here.

There are also important omissions in this book. Even in the digital humanities, where we try to be so collaborative, the process of writing and review takes time. News of important and relevant research by Arianna Betti, Jani Marjanen, and Ruben Ross, and new articles by Melvin Wevers and his collaborators, has caught up with me too late to be integrated into this book, although they will undoubtedly be important to later discussions of the fit of text mining with historical analysis.

The Harvard Society of Fellows, the Brown Humanities Center, the National Science Foundation, the Center for Creative Computing at SMU, Neubauer Collegium at the University of Chicago, and the SMU History Department supported the necessary research time to prepare the experiments documented herein; without the encouragement given by then, I never could have made the leap from an archival researcher, and sometimes consumer of digital data, to a coder and investigator that this book required of me. I am grateful to the students of digital history courses at Brown and SMU for their engagement. I am forever in the debt of the many readers and editors who saw previous versions of the text, especially Liz Friend-Smith and Mark Fox, tireless advocates and editors at Cambridge University Press, and including Vinithan Sedumadhavan of Straive.

Even greater than the other debts is the one to my husband, Zachary Gates, who facing my confusion almost always points me towards the real moon in the sky.

Introduction

> Undoubtedly his greatest contributions were in the field of psycho-history. Seldon found the field little more than a set of vague axioms; he left it a profound statistical science.
>
> <div align="right">Isaac Asimov, <i>Foundation</i> (1942)</div>

Danger is implicit even in the metaphor. *Mining* refers specifically to the extraction of valuable metallic ores from the earth, and metaphorically to any process that extracts the rare and valuable content from its surrounding context, usually at the cost of extreme expenditures of labor and at danger to the environment. *Data mining,* a similarly intensive operation with implicit hidden costs, also begins with counting, but includes statistical transformations to test for relationships such as correlation and significance. *Text mining,* a process with all the dangers of the former two categories, mines for value with text as the data. It begins with computational transformations that break up and classify digitalized strings of archival text into units representing constituent words and phrases, and then applies statistical manipulations that enable us to study the kinds of meaningful signals and relationships that trained analysts from the humanities and social sciences would like to detect in the course of reading. With the help of computers, the insights of reading can be carried out over a larger scale.

Text mining is powerful if done right. When rendered as visualizations, the output of text mining offers, at least potentially, an outsized return on investment, distilling shelf miles of text into a valuable, pithy representation of what all those words *meant.* A single visualization might reduce the story of how a single institution's politics have changed over a hundred years. Scholars from the humanities have used text mining to give us a mirror of what stories people have told each other about how Covid is transmitted, and how American novelists present white characters and black characters differently over time.[1]

---

[1] Shadi Shahsavari, Pavan Holur Timothy R. Tangherlini, and Vwani Roychowdhury, "Conspiracy in the Time of Corona: Automatic Detection of Covid-19 Conspiracy Theories in Social Media and

We see an example of this method in Figure 0.1, where word embeddings have been used to show how members of the US Congress talked about the term "slavery" from 1870 to 2010. The *x*-axis is a timeline from 1870 to 2020 (the full length of the dataset), divided into five-year periods. The *y*-axis gives an abstract measure of "similarity" between the keyword "slavery" and words that appeared in the same sentence, paragraph, or debate. Words higher on the *y*-axis appeared alongside "slavery" with greater regularity. The diagram was designed to show the shifting context in which the word "slavery" appeared from one generation to the next.

The big takeaway of Figure 0.1 is that for most of the period since the Civil War, Congress has not talked about race when it has spoken about slavery. Members of Congress used the term "slavery" as a metaphor for a host of other ills they wished to denounce. They classified Mormon polygamy, Naziism, and Bolshevism forms of mental or moral enslavement.

But much less frequently did members of Congress acknowledge that slavery as an institution had wrecked the lives of generations of African-Americans, brought to the United States against their will. Nor did members of Congress talk about the legacy of slavery in modern America. Instead, they associated slavery with developments abroad, especially the "economic slavery" that they associated with communist regimes.

Congress's reluctance to talk about the facts of American history in the chief organ of American democracy persisted for over a century. Only in the 1990s did "racism" and "lynching" become collocates of "slavery" for the first time.

A diagram like Figure 0.1 is designed to dramatize shifts over time, shifts that may be so subtle that they surprise many an American historian.[2] It is not the algorithm alone that renders such an insight obvious. The algorithm has to be deployed by a coder who understands the significance of change over time to patterns of words that appear with other words. Unlocking the mysteries of the algorithm, the category of time reveals how we have lied to each other about our institutions and identity.

There are also many data-driven analyses of text that purport to offer substantive insight – and fail. Such failures of text mining occur when

---

the News," *ArXiv Preprint ArXiv:2004.13783*, 2020; Richard Jean So, *Redlining Culture* (New York: Columbia University Press, 2020);

[2] I am not myself an American historian, but I record the relative surprise of my collaborator, Peter Kastor, with whom I am writing about word embeddings in Congress.

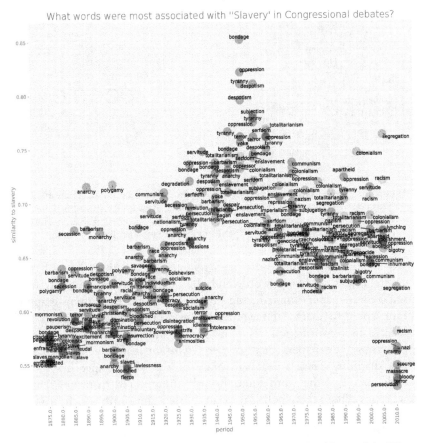

Figure 0.1   Words co-located with the keyword "slavery" in the debates of the US Congress. *X*-axis indicates time; *y*-axis indicates an abstract measurement of "similarity" measuring how consistently the words are invoked together. Detected using Gensim word embedding software.

algorithmic distillations of text are misapplied, with the result of analyses that are empty, biased, or simply false.

Consider the fate of the wordcloud in recent years. The wordcloud (sometimes known as a "wordle" before the arrival of a popular game of the same name) is a visualization where the size of words corresponds to their frequency. In the wordcloud visualization in Figure 0.2, the larger words are at the center, but the words' spatial arrangement is random, a stylistic choice that encourages the viewer's eyes to wander the cloud, free associating along the way.

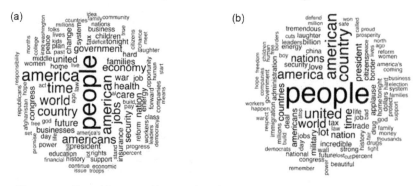

Figure 0.2   Data-driven visualizations that obscure rather than illuminate meaningful differences: Wordclouds for the official speeches of a) Barack Obama and b) Donald Trump during their presidencies. Source: "Presidential Speeches" dataset, https://millercenter.org/the-presidency/presidential-speeches. Visualized by author.

After first appearing as a navigation tool on the photo-sharing website Flickr in 2004, wordclouds became a preferred visualization used by newspapers for reducing political speeches into a pop graphic. From 2004 to 2017, the wordcloud was everywhere. Bloggers and websites used wordclouds as a navigation index. During the Obama presidency, newspapers such as *The Guardian* regularly ran visualizations distilling Barack Obama's State of the Union speeches into a wordcloud. But the wordcloud abruptly disappeared from newspapers and blogs alike when political events tested the limits of the tool to reveal the truth.

As late as the Obama presidency, the wordcloud served the public as an easy tool for rendering complex text into a simple snapshot of a historical moment. In Obama's speeches, keywords such as "freedom," "people," and "journey" loomed large in size, reinforcing Obama's sense of America as a nation at a turning-point in history.[3] Just as importantly, the wordcloud promised to distill into a single visualizable truth the reality of truth in an era of information overload.

Soon after Donald Trump's election, however, the fad for wordclouds began to dissipate. Under a new president, language was being used in a fundamentally new way, but wordclouds failed to do justice to the difference. Indeed, had journalists in 2017 the power to compare all of Trump's speeches from his presidency with Obama's, they would have discovered a

---

[3] "Inauguration Speeches in Wordclouds," *The Guardian*, January 21, 2013, sec. US News, www.theguardian.com/world/gallery/2009/jan/21/obama-inauguration-word-clouds-gallery.

mysterious fact: the two men used *very many* of the same words at the same rate. Both proclaimed their allegiance to the "American" "people" and their "country;" both referenced the "United" "States." Obama talked about the "economy" and "jobs," while Trump talked about "trade" and "jobs." They both referenced "citizens," "families," and "children." Both touted their commitment to "security," to America's role in the "world," and to the importance of the "time" of the present.

The more Trump spoke, the clearer the weakness of the wordcloud became. The word cloud, a tool for showing the most frequent words, did not in its automatic form look for phrases. It could not tell the difference between Obama's "right here in America" – where he intended to create jobs – and Trump's "make America great again," a plea that barely veiled a longing for a time of white supremacy.

In the early years of the Trump presidency, journalists and politicians kept running Trump's speeches and tweets through the visualization, hoping for different results. When that approach failed, one democratic representative in Congress tried a new strategy to capture Trump's abrasive style, creating his own wordcloud generated from a list of the individuals and organizations that Trump had attacked over Twitter.[4] But mainly the wordclouds of 2017–21 continued to backfire. One published wordcloud distilled the keyword "Klansmen" as a word related to Biden, but not related to Trump. In the accompanying article, a journalist reassured his readers that future President Joe Biden had condemned the seeming condoning of the KKK by Donald Trump, who himself never mentioned the Klan by name.[5] By then, it must have become clear: Trump had broken the wordcloud.

By aping his opponents' populist language for nationalist and racial purposes, Trump had produced a close parody of Obama's invocations of patriotism. The result was that Trump's speech was virtually indistinguishable from Obama's – at least in wordcloud form. The wordcloud betrayed how Trump's broadly inclusive language appealed to many American's sense of patriotism, indeed, wooing some voters who had cleaved to Obama, even while carefully encoded dog-whistles summoned hate groups

---

[4] Jessica Estepa, "House Democrat Makes a Word Cloud of Trump Insults," *USA Today*, September 26, 2017, www.usatoday.com/story/news/politics/onpolitics/2017/09/26/house-democrat-makes-word-cloud-trump-insults/705120001.

[5] Ben Schott, "Biden and Trump Go Cloud to Cloud," *Bloomberg*, August 28, 2020, www.bloomberg.com/opinion/articles/2020-08-28/biden-and-trump-nomination-speeches-are-two-clashing-word-clouds.

to his side. For anyone paying attention, the wordcloud might have been trying to tell us something about the political malleability of populist language. For the purpose of explaining to newspaper readers the differences between two presidents, however, the wordcloud was kaput.

Understanding the priorities, values, and falsehoods of president is a matter of no small priority. Reasonable people may reasonably disagree on political values. But newspapers that serve reasonable people try to provide everyone with the same basic facts about the present moment and recent past. The wordcloud vanished because it proved incapable, at least in its automatic form, of generating straightforward facts about Trump that were capable of picking up on the president's many obvious differences from his predecessor.

A world trained on the manipulation of data but ignorant of, or insensitive to, the data's original context will be dangerously cut off from reality. Text mining can aid us by helping humans become more accurate at sifting data at scale. Without the insights of the humanities, text mining falls readily into error: it is a monkey reaching for the moon, guided only by the moon's reflection in a pond, where he will never grasp it.

That we should be interested in accuracy is obvious. Universities have long aspired to be the grounds where children reared in the native bias of their own locale learn to form an acquaintance with a broader reality. Companies that depend on the parsing of language with code should likewise be interested in the forms of hybrid thinking – humanities and mathematics, social science and informatics.

Text mining can be used to paint a portrait of partisan activity in legislative debates, newspapers, and social media sites. It can also support the larger method of using data to locate a discontinuity in time and of learning as much as possible about the distinctiveness of the event relative to other similar disruptions, as well as the individuals, causes, and contexts of disruption.

Once we've turned data to the purpose of understanding how two moments in time differ, we've taken a great step towards reality. We have fit data to the purpose of asking a real historical question. We've provided an instrument that is practically useful for assigning blame and pursuing reform and, even better, for starting to conceptualize the changes that determined the shape of the present.

Why were solutions of this kind invisible to the staff of American newspapers during the Trump years, when the limitations of the word-cloud began to show? They were invisible because text mining for historical analysis was still in its infancy during the Trump years. The place where the new tools would appear was still a no man's land between two enemy encampments.

The No Man's Land Where Better Tools Come From

In the years of the Trump Administration, a vast canyon extended between the experts in quantitative knowledge and that collection of scholars in the liberal arts who study documents for tiny signals of cultural change over time. Let us call these individuals "The Temporal Cartographers' Society." It is they who would face no difficulty parsing the differences between Obama's speeches and Trump's. The Society's ranks include professional historians, literary scholars, and historical sociologists, as well as some of the most talented members of the world of journalism and law. Mainly, they trained in liberal arts subjects, where, if quantitative methods are used to analyze text, they have been introduced (or reintroduced) only over the last two decades.

Those fields have long traditions of struggle and debate devoted to the difficulty of accurately summarizing a thousand letters. Historians' standard of truth, for instance, requires them to carefully reflect on the biases and silences of the documents with which they work, to worry over the circumlocutions and hidden suggestions of text. They also worry over hidden dimensions of change to the historical context in which words are invoked, a problem not easily reduced to the words on the page. As the scholar William Sewell once explained, not only words and ideas, but also new identities structure society over time. The result is the laws of change may work differently in one generation than another.[6] For this reason, historians study the imperfections, distortions, and omissions that riddle records from the past – including circumlocutions like Trump's phrase "make America great again," a phrase that must be unpacked beyond its surface invocation of prosperity for the implied longing for an era of white supremacy and male dominance to surface. The Temporal Cartographer's Society, in other words, has a lot to offer any study that depends on absolute honesty about what we know, what we don't know, and where data has been distorted by the bias of the past.

Traditionally, members of the Temporal Cartographers' Society have lacked tools for generalizing about billions or trillions of words, how those words cluster and change. They have adopted admirably to other forms of work with data – to birth and death rates, or what quantities of nutrition it was possible to buy on a working man's salary, or counting pollen samples

---

[6] Sewell, "Three Temporalities," 245–80.

to chart changing temperatures.[7] Even with data, however, this group tends to be hesitant about over-grand generalizations. They rarely look for laws of historical truth. When they turn to numbers, they examine moments of change with enormous precision.

Generalizations at broad scale are the domain of another group, namely the engineers, mathematicians, statisticians, and computer scientists whose conceptual domain we might call the "world without history," because thinking about cultural and political revolution represents so little of the work done in that domain.

The world without history is the imaginary territory that is home to students of statistics and machine learning. Their labors support the design of computers and the creation of a thousand tools for animating design, medicine, and neuroscience. And some of its scions apply math on the stock market, where they sometimes leverage historical data while promising to predict the future.

The world without history has its own blindspots. In my experience, few computer scientists are exposed to historicist reasoning anywhere in their training. They often lack the broad literacy in the humanities one needs to understand the potential and the limitations of these conceptual models. And this ignorance of computationalists has made trade – let alone conversation – between the world without history and the Temporal Cartographers' Society virtually nonexistent for many years.

The Temporal Cartographers' Society entertains a certain skepticism towards the world without history. Issues of race, gender, the silences of the archive, and the costs of labor highlight the exploitative implications latent in the phrase "text mining," which refers to the process of computationally extracting meaning from digitalized documents. As Kate Crawford has pointed out, the metaphor of "mining" underscores the promise that computational labor will yield precious resources and therefore merits corporate investments.[8] But as historians know, mining industries have also been classical sites of the exploitation of indigenous, ethnic, and other working-class labor, entailing the making invisible of laboring bodies often broken, suffocated, and poisoned by working conditions. Mining industries have also been sites of lasting environmental pollution,

---

[7] Steven Ruggles, "The Revival of Quantification: Reflections on Old New Histories," *Social Science History* 45:1 (October 1, 2021): 1–25, https://doi.org/10.1017/ssh.2020.44; Sam White, Christian Pfister, and Franz Mauelshagen, *The Palgrave Handbook of Climate History* (London: Palgrave, 2018).

[8] Kate Crawford, *The Atlas of AI: Power, Politics, and the Planetary Costs of Artificial Intelligence* (New Haven, CT: Yale University Press, 2021).

as well as the origin point of the fossil economies, dependence on which has produced the carbon emissions of recent centuries, resulting in the climate emergency. To insist on referring to the work of computational history with texts as "text mining" is to testify to the fact that computational enterprises are implicated in potentially exploitative relationships with labor and the environment.

There is a longer story behind the distance between the two worlds as well. In American history departments, many faculty regard with distaste previous encounters with the methods of the world without history. The so-called quantitative turn of the 1960s and 1970s is remembered today as a moment when millions of dollars supported vast research collaborations in history and adjacent social science fields. The Philadelphia Project, a study of social mobility and the American Dream, is remembered chiefly as an expensive disaster whose authors failed to publish meaningful work. More notorious still is Robert Fogel and Stanley Engerman's *Time on the Cross*, which used a data base of life-expectancy to argue that enslaved Americans were treated better than their working-class counterparts in the north.[9] The numbers in Fogel and Engerman's project included 0.7 as the number of times that the average enslaved person was whipped per year at a single plantation in Louisiana between 1840 and 1842.[10] The crudely racist reductionism associated with these projects – which offered a decimal in the spot that could be occupied by tomes on the separation of families of enslaved people, the experience of the body in pain, and intergenerational trauma – still circulates in history departments today as evidence of what can go wrong when the desire for quantitative accuracy overrides humanists' appreciation of the human condition. Even as nearby fields such as political science and sociology have embraced big data, with scholars refining the methods that illuminate the major theories of the field, the refinement of similar tools for dealing with big data in history has only just begun.[11]

---

[9] For the Philadelphia Project, see Luke Blaxill, *The War of Words: The Language of British Elections, 1880–1914*, Royal Historical Society, Studies in History. New Series 103 (Woodbridge; Rochester, NY: The Boydell Press, 2020); Robert Fogel and Stanley Engerman, *Time on the Cross* (Boston, MA:Little, Brown and Company, 1974).

[10] Blaxill, *The War of Words*, 22 n. 9.

[11] For the comparative evolution of political science and history and broader meditation on quantitative methods suited to data, see Gregory Wawro and Ira Katznelson, *Time Counts: Quantitative Analysis for Historical Social Science* (Princeton, NJ: Princeton University Press, 2022). I draw on innovative work from political science and sociology throughout this book, but two books stand out as recent statements about methods in the field: Brandon Stewart, Justin Grimmer, and Margaret E. Roberts, *Text as Data* (Princeton, NJ: Princeton University Press, 2022), and Xiaoling Shu, *Knowledge Discovery in the Social Sciences: A Data Mining Approach* (Berkeley, CA: University of California, 2020).

As recently as the Trump years, historians' warnings about the dangers of quantitative tools and information scientists' patterns of selective study meant that a dangerous and underexplored territory sprawled between the world without history and the domain of the Temporal Cartographers' Society. Few travelers crossed from one domain to the next. Much rarer was a compelling paper embraced by both worlds as the signal of a new field ripe for investigation.

Today, promising things are afoot in this no man's land. Modern "digital historians" who use text mining in their work, for instance Luke Blaxill, readily credit the linguistic turn as the inspiration for their own careful use of wordcount and statistics to discern moments of change in political speeches. The space of "digital history" that applies computational tools to historical problems only now has its first journals – *Current Research in Digital History* was founded in 2018 and the *Journal of Digital History* was founded in 2021. Luke Blaxill's 2020 book, *The War of Words*, is the first historical monograph to use text mining as its major method.[12]

The truth is that scholars in the liberal arts are continuing to profit from and learn from debates about quantitative reasoning in the past, and they have many insights to offer those who work with data. African-American and other postcolonial scholars – especially Jessica Marie Johnson and Roopika Risam – have taken a leading role in describing the possible abuses of quantified perspectives on the experiences of enslaved or otherwise silenced and exploited communities in the past.[13]

Distant reading and the promise of digitalized data have attracted the attention of historians since at least Lincoln Mullen and Keller Funk's "Spine of the American Law" (2016), where legal historians adopted algorithms to detect important turning-points in the history of American case law. Since that point, the range of algorithmic tools for textual analysis available to digital historians has expanded enormously, and a thriving community of digital historians have begun to investigate the best practices of text mining.[14] Researchers in History have begun to apply artificial

---

[12] Blaxill, *The War of Words*.

[13] Jessica Marie Johnson, "Markup Bodies: Black [Life] Studies and Slavery [Death] Studies at the Digital Crossroads," *Social Text* 36:4(137) (December 1, 2018): 57–79, https://doi.org/10.1215/01642472-7145658; Roopika Risam, *New Digital Worlds: Postcolonial Digital Humanities in Theory, Praxis, and Pedagogy* (Evanston, IL: Northwestern University Press, 2019), www.jstor.org/stable/10.2307/j.ctv7tq4hg.

[14] The field of digital history has only just emerged as a proper field, with its first monograph in text mining (Blaxill, *The War of Words*) and the first monograph on using GIS applied to a historical question (Cameron Blevins, *Paper Trails: The U.S. Post and the Making of the American West* (New York: Oxford University Press, 2021).

intelligence (AI) tools to the history field, and my publications have explored a range of different algorithmic approaches. Many of my own technical articles demonstrate positive proof of the effectiveness of natural language processing (NLP) and statistical measures for discovering hitherto unknown historical events in the history of capitalism.[15]

The research is truly "hybrid" in the sense of representing a new undertaking that fits neither into traditional categories of history nor of information science. This research requires scholars to formulate new methods for validating whether and how each AI tool can support the high standard of reasoning required by the history profession.[16] This body of work, as a whole, points the way towards new standards of believability as well as new opportunities for building and measuring historically-significant moments whose traces are embodied in textual data.

The expertise of the new hybrid field is sometimes called the "digital humanities" or "the digital social sciences"; and one corner of it – trained on pattern-recognition in images, movement, maps, video, audio, and text alike – is sometimes described as "cultural analytics."[17] The expertise in text mining

[15] Jo Guldi, "Parliament's Debates about Infrastructure: An Exercise in Using Dynamic Topic Models to Synthesize Historical Change," *Technology and Culture* 60 1 (March 21, 2019): 1–33; Jo Guldi, "The Official Mind's View of Empire, in Miniature: Quantifying World Geography in Hansard's Parliamentary Debates," *Journal of World History* 32:2 (2021): 345–70, https://doi.org/10.1353/jwh.2021.0028; Jo Guldi, "The Algorithm: Mapping Long-Term Trends and Short-Term Change at Multiple Scales of Time," *The American Historical Review* 127:2 (June 1, 2022): 895–911, https://doi.org/10.1093/ahr/rhac160.

[16] Dzovinar Kévonian and Philippe Rygiel, "Connected Ogres: Global Sources in the Digital Era," *Monde(s)* 21:1 (May 11, 2022): 73–79; Jo Guldi, "The Common Landscape of Digital History," *Digital Histories: Emergent Approaches within the New Digital History* (Helsinki: Helsinki University Press, 2020); Ashley S. Lee, Poom Chiarawongse, Jo Guldi, and Andras Zsom, "The Role of Critical Thinking in Humanities Infrastructure: The Pipeline Concept with a Study of HaToRI (Hansard Topic Relevance Identifier)," *Digital Humanities Quarterly* 014:3 (2020). Jo Guldi, "The Measures of Modernity. Word Counts, Text Mining and the Promise and Limits of Present Tools as Indices of Historical Change," *International Journal for History, Culture and Modernity* 7 (November 3, 2019), https://doi.org/10.18352/hcm.589; Jo Guldi, "The Modern Paradigms of Explanation: Significance, Agency, and Writing History in the Era of Climate Change," *Isis* 110:2 (2019): 346–53; Ashley Lee, Jo Guldi, and Andras Zsom, "Measuring Similarity: Computationally Reproducing the Scholar's Interests," *ArXiv:1812.05984 [Cs]*, December 14, 2018, http://arxiv.org/abs/1812.05984; Jo Guldi and Benjamin Williams, "Synthesis and Large-Scale Textual Corpora: A Nested Topic Model of Britain's Debates over Landed Property in the Nineteenth Century," *Current Research in Digital History* 1 (2018), https://doi.org/10.31835/crdh.2018.01; For validation, Jo Guldi, "Critical Search: A Procedure for Guided Reading in Large-Scale Textual Corpora," *Journal of Cultural Analytics* (2018): 1–35, https://doi.org/10.22148/16.030.

[17] The wider field of the digital humanities includes practices such as metadata creation, mapping, network analysis, and the creation of online experiences and games. Cultural analytics focuses on the analysis of data – typically textual, musical, or visual – to produce insights about humanities questions, for instance the nature of cultural bias or the reality of change over time. For the digital humanities more broadly, see Eileen Gardiner and Ronald G. Musto, *The Digital Humanities: A Primer for Students and Scholars* (Cambridge University Press, 2015); for cultural analytics, see

in particular commands a certain corner of cultural analytics, and the problem of historical truth adds another still more specific dimension of concern.

But history is not of concern only to historians. It is also a method embraced across the humanities and social sciences, relevant to law schools and schools of journalism, and useful in practically any endeavor where the investigation of human culture and institutions is at stake. I prefer to refer to the activities covered by this book as "text mining for historical analysis." "Text mining" is a province of research in AI, and there are researchers in computer science and informatics departments dedicated to the question of what makes text mining accurate and robust. Its practices borrow richly from the interdisciplinary cultural analytics community as well as practitioners of text mining who work across the social sciences, especially in political science and sociology. "Historical analysis" marks out diachronic text mining, trained on the modelling of temporal experience in all its variation, from styles of text mining pursued for purposes wherein time does not necessarily factor, for instance modeling fundamental differences between different languages and linguistic groups. Insights derived from historical analysis are relevant to scholars from history, art history, literature, political science, and economics, as well as practitioners at the law and business schools. Robust historical analysis is almost always improved by the insights of history scholars. The phrase "text mining for historical analysis" thus invokes a wide zone where text mining is used for pragmatic reasons. Unlike the phrase "digital history," text mining for historical

---

Lev Manovich, "The Science of Culture? Social Computing, Digital Humanities and Cultural Analytics," *CA: Journal of Cultural Analytics*, May 23, 2016, http://culturalanalytics.org/2016/05/the-science-of-culture-social-computing-digital-humanities-and-cultural-analytics. For a general introduction to the digital humanities, see Johanna Drucker, *The Digital Humanities Coursebook* (London: Routledge, 2021), and the various editions of Lauren Klein and Matthew Gold, *Debates in the Digital Humanities* (Minnesota, MN: University of Minnesota Press, 2004–20). For the long tradition of quantitative measures being used for literary criticism in the past, see Brad Pasanek, "Extreme Reading: Josephine Miles and the Scale of the Pre-Digital Digital Humanities," *ELH* 86: 2 (2019): 369, 375. The digital social sciences, by contrast, have tended to come from departments of sociology and political science and they are experiencing their own revolution in text mining applied to traditional questions motivated by social theory. See Peter Bearman, "Big Data and Historical Social Science," *Big Data & Society* 2:2 (December 27, 2015), https://doi.org/10.1177/2053951715612497; James A. Evans and Pedro Aceves, "Machine Translation: Mining Text for Social Theory," *Annual Review of Sociology* 42:1 (2016): 21–50. The discipline of history has traditionally claimed membership both in the humanities and the social sciences, and typically draws on the methods of both parts of the university. For a general introduction to the variety of approaches used in digital history, including maps, images, and text from the past, see Hannu Salmi, *What Is Digital History?* (London: Polity, 2020). In this book I will invoke the word "humanities" broadly for interpretive issues in contrast to quantitative ones, even though many of the approaches I foreground are of interest to the social sciences or were developed within social science frameworks.

analysis carries no suggestion that computer-driven history will somehow substitute for history by traditional means – a threat that some members of the Temporal Cartographers' Society are all too wary of. Text mining for historical analysis rather sits across the many domains that use text, AI and statistics to produce certain kinds of knowledge, useful to certain purposes.

The hybrid thinking that has emerged in between quantitative and qualitative disciplines combines insights from history with those from information science has the power to catalyze a revolution in smart data. It is *hybrid* rather than merely interdisciplinary because what is produced in the process is more than an adjustment to old conversations. Something genuinely new is being produced where old fields meet, and this hybrid practice has the power to produce insight about large-scale troves of texts, not unlike the hybrid ears of corn that revolutionized industrial agriculture in the middle of the twentieth century.[18] Such a practice as this has a great deal to offer the community of scholars, although it is hard to see text mining replacing the many forms of work with data, documents, and archives that mark the specialty of history. The greatest beneficiaries of a hybrid practice of historical thinking with data are outside the walls of the academy.

Toward a Smarter Data Science

Data science today needs to become smarter in ways that benefit from learning that originates outside the study of data.

In Chapter 1, I tell the story of how my students plotted the trend of mentions of "ignorant women" over the course of debates from Britain's parliament in the nineteenth century. They concluded that women had become more and more ignorant over the course of the century – rather than reasoning as a historian, that Britain's parliament had become more and more biased against women over the course of the same time.

I learned about the dangers of text mining because I welcome students of engineering, statistics, and business, as well as history and literature majors, to my classroom. The gap in the education of a significant

---

[18] As science and technology scholars will note, "hybridization" is, like "mining," a deliberately ambivalent metaphor. Hybrid grains and the industrialized farms they supported drove smaller farmers from business in many parts of the world, helping to produce a global housing crisis and making agriculture overall more vulnerable – even if it was also more productive at scale. A monocrop of hybrid digital history would result in similar imbalances in the name of scale. There is a great deal more to be said that will not be said here. My intention in this volume is to show that hybrid practice can be done in a *more* responsible way, but I also underscore the need for the perseverance of traditional history and the teaching and practice of traditional methods.

proportion of my students is a warning sign. If some of my cleverest students are making those mistakes today, then the titans of industry will be making similar mistakes tomorrow.

The solution to bad graphs and foolish interpretations is, I believe, a return to reality. Reality, in terms of our collective experience with each other, is perhaps only known through stories about our past, and there are many other kinds of stories that only speak to desire, its reflections, and shadows.

This is why hybrid knowledge matters. It's why any university that's teaching data science urgently needs to plan programs of instruction that foreground not only the skills of working with data at speed but also understanding what data means. We *can* use data to discover important trends, recent and older, that give us insights to the subtle changes that are shifting society. But to use those tools effectively, we need smart data and hybrid knowledge, attuned to the latent bias of the data and of algorithm and how to navigate them. Data-driven analysis of language, without a historical method, is apt to produce unusable information. Without help from abroad, the world without history is in trouble.

In spaces like digital history where computationalists and historians meet and ask questions about each other's basic premises, problems tend to emerge that were previously unknown to either field beforehand. When historians consult with algorithms, for example, they tend to move deliberately, reflecting on the fit of each algorithm for each separate stage of analysis. They care about distinguishing the signals of correlation from those of causation. These conversations can be productive of new insight and opportunities for rigor. A truly hybrid research process forces colleagues to submit their unstated hypotheses to careful testing. It requires refraining from hasty diagnoses and cheap answers until the process for arriving at truth meets the standards of fields that have never previously reviewed their terms of agreement.

The birth of new fields where old disciplines meet is a reality of our time. Data science is sometimes presented, in its ideal form, as the application of statistics to big data with substantive knowledge.[19] For this reason, teams of medical researchers work alongside statisticians and memory specialists to produce the field of biostatistics; teams of linguists collaborate with computer scientists and statisticians to produce computational linguistics; and political scientists and social scientists work with

---

[19] Ted Underwood reviews this characterization, which he credits to Drew Conway, CEO of Alluvium, in a blog entry: https://tedunderwood.com/2017/01/29/two-syllabi-digital-humanities-and-data-science-in-the-humanities.

technology experts to produce computational social science. Now, it seems clear, a new field is emerging that engages text mining with the aim of establishing historical truth from the humanities and history in particular.

Hybrid thinking about historical truth has much to offer the rest of the world. It can aid political journalists who are constantly seeking new ways of understanding cultural differences in the electorate. It can support media streaming companies that wish to learn more about who identifies with certain kinds of music, lyrics, and narratives, and what kinds of content leaves them cold. These practices can entertain and educate the general public, which is fascinated by data visualizations that show them aspects of their own experience from unexpected angles. And it can support scholars already dedicated to a careful and critical analysis of *who* human beings are, *what* was changing at any given movement in the past, and *where* culture appears to be heading.

Yet most of the tools from data science today have been developed without consultation with ideas about truth from history or the humanities. Like the wordcloud, they are simplistic approximations of truth where information is lost. Mathematician Cathy O'Neil has documented how bail extension rulings by judge became increasingly racist after the judges were advised by an AI tool whose advice was based on data from racist moment in the past that used data from previous decades. Bias riddles contemporary AI products today.[20] Even GPT-3 cannot be trusted to summarize even relatively simple prose without the service of a trained fact checker.[21] The algorithms designed to correct for bias, meanwhile, rarely go to the root of the problem, because most of them were designed by information scientists who lack a familiarity with how the bias got into the data in the first place. Today's AI is simply not capable of performing

---

[20] Tarleton Gillespie, *The Relevance of Algorithms* (Cambridge, MA: MIT Press, 2014), https://academic.oup.com/mit-press-scholarship-online/book/14976/chapter/169333383; Cathy O'Neil, *Weapons of Math Destruction: How Big Data Increases Inequality and Threatens Democracy* (New York: Crown, 2016); Safiya Umoja Noble, *Algorithms of Oppression: How Search Engines Reinforce Racism* (New York: NYU Press, 2018); Wendy Hui Kyong Chun, *Discriminating Data: Correlation, Neighborhoods, and the New Politics of Recognition* (Cambridge, MA: MIT Press, 2021); Kate Crawford, *The Atlas of AI.*

[21] For my investigations of bias in the historical performance of GPT-3, see "The Dangerous Art of Text Mining," talk at the Alan Turing Institute, London, UK (July 2022), www.youtube.com/watch?v=-V7WZaUk5oA. I've applied it to summarizing my own books, and found that there are errors. Where I set out formal arguments, reviewing the historiography of the field and then stating my own position as a refutation of those arguments, GPT-3 is just as likely to summarize the texts that I'm refuting as fact. It has no preference for my own argument or the evidence I've presented; it will summarize anything. It can summarize them with alacrity and questionable accuracy.

at the rigorous standard of truth that scholars in the liberal arts have long expected of each other.

The cost to society of data science ignoring the liberal arts is enormous. It is represented in quantifiable terms by the lakes of unused textual data that cannot be effectively exploited by today's AI tools. Statisticians estimate that, in 2017, phone users around the world sent 6.8 billion text messages a day.[22] In 2018, the world's population was 86.5 percent literate, and that literate bulk of humanity composed roughly 281 billion emails per day.[23] Indeed, our civilization produces a shocking amount of text every year. Since the advent of electronic systems, such as word processors and webpages, for authoring and sharing text, the amount of text created and preserved in analyzable form has dwarfed earlier numbers. If printed out, the text on the internet itself would consume 136.2 billion pieces of paper.[24] Grand as these figures may be, they are modest compared with the wealth of disposable text that humans generate in the course of continuously communicating, redacting, and recirculating information.[25] One approximation of that number, however, is that the US federal government employees print out about 18 billion pages of documents every year. "Big data just gets bigger and bigger and bigger," wrote Aiden and Michel, reflecting problems of scale from 2013.[26] For want of effective text mining strategies, an ocean of data has gone virtually untouched.

The want of interdisciplinary approaches to text mining that span humanistic questions and quantitative approaches also limits what industry can do with the data it already has. During a conversation with an executive at a streaming movie service, I recently had the occasion to explain the recent successes that define the modern field of text mining

---

[22] Megan Morreale, "Daily SMS Mobile Usage Statistics," *SMSEagle*, March 6, 2017, www.smseagle .eu/2017/03/06/daily-sms-mobile-statistics.

[23] For literacy, see UNESCO Institute for Statistics, uis.unesco.org. For emails, see J. Clement, "Daily Number of E-Mails Worldwide 2023," *Statista*, August 9, 2019, www.statista.com/statistics/ 456500/daily-number-of-e-mails-worldwide.

[24] George Harwood and Evangeline Walker, "How Much of the Amazon Would It Take to Print the Internet?," *Journal of Interdisciplinary Science* 4 (2015): 10–11.

[25] Executive Office of the President, Social and Behavioral Sciences Team, *Annual Report* (2015): 46 (with thanks to J. Nathan Matias), https://sbst.gov/download/2015%20SBST%20Annual%20Report.pdf? fbclid=IwAR1_A_UvH6V5zPzCP1FxJzJB4zsKwp8H7bNcoO3qVIgta5V-EgZsIUtRI9c.

[26] For 18 billion pages, see http://opm.gov/policy-data-oversight/data-analysis-documentation/federal-employment-reports/historical-tables/total-government-employment-since-1962. For quotation, see Erez Aiden and Jean-Baptiste Michel, *Uncharted: Big Data as a Lens on Human Culture* (New York: Riverhead Books, 2013): 11. Aiden and Michel refer to big data in general rather than the problem of text.

in the liberal arts. Curious about my projects, he asked what text mining could do for his own industry and I told him about a dozen new studies from the digital humanities. I explained how scholars in the digital humanities had been counting the underrepresentation of black actors in Hollywood scripts, and observing the structural differences between novels written by women and those written by men.

Because the executive's job was to buy and sell scripts that target the preferences of a wide range of viewers, I offered speculation about how text mining might affect his industry. I imagined that he might do well to hire a digital humanist as these scholars, in recent years, have been modeling the imaginary dimensions of identity and plot, and creating variables that could be measured against the voluminous data the executive had been gathering.

While the company already knew a great deal about which movies were hits and which were duds, a digital humanist could create a model based upon conceptual categories that would explain their viewing behavior and thus offer them movies that best fit their needs. If women stop watching twenty minutes in, for example, near a scene when the men are doing all the talking, a humanist could train an algorithm to recognize the common pattern and its effects on viewing patterns.

The executive agreed. He was thoroughly hooked on the algorithms I described, and he wanted to add them to his business model. But here's the rub, he confessed: he would never be able to sell his bosses on hiring a PhD in literature – a field that has produced some of the finest scholarship on text mining applied to culture. The prejudice against the humanities in Silicon Valley went too deep, he explained.

Creating smart data requires becoming smart *about* data; and if we want the data to provide the most complete reflection of human experience possible, we must try to make a happy marriage between traditional tools of reasoning that have been honed over centuries, and contemporary practices with data.

Having shunned an active collaboration with humanists, Silicon Valley is not nearly as smart as it could be. Big tech needs an engaged, technical conversation about radically improving the way we work with data to model human experience. Many civilizations achieved mass literacy sometime in the nineteenth century; but that didn't mean that every reader could participate in a conversation about hermeneutics. Silicon Valley hires hundreds of computer scientists with basic training in natural language processing, but that doesn't mean they understand what a critical engagement with human experience looks like. If the culture of Silicon Valley added teams of professional humanists to its teams that work on data analysis, this marriage could give birth to a data-driven revolution far more subtle, and far more accurate, than either camp could manage on their own.

For such a thing to happen, however, hybrid thinking across data science and the liberal arts must become routine in the places that drive research innovation – in the universities themselves. The $100 million gifts that have created new schools of information at Cornell University, Harvard, MIT, Stanford, and Johns Hopkins have so far made room for very few scholars with a liberal arts background. The exclusion of the humanities from data science centers up to this point is understandable. It is, after all, only in the last few years that a real watershed has been crossed where the contribution of historical thinking to text mining is visible. Dozens if not hundreds of colleagues have contributed to that effort, some of them members of the Temporal Cartography Society who work with text on paper in dusty archives, and some of them former members who ventured into the no man's land and there met up with a few brave data scientists from the world without history. My modest contribution is to assemble the discoveries of others, alongside a few of my own, into a teachable series of problems about how historical questions can reshape data science into a smarter discipline.

About the Chapters

Part I of this book opens with a catalog of dangers about where contemporary data practices are failing. Drawing on a decade of interdisciplinary research, it lays out best practices of how liberal arts approaches (especially those from history) can make work with textual data more robust. Chapter 1 tours a series of high-stakes disasters from data science, where papers retracted after publication have demonstrated how riddled contemporary data-driven practices are with error. It categorizes the major typology of dangers that lead analysts into trouble, drawing especial attention to insufficient engagement with historical context and fantasies of predictive knowledge that cause analysts to rush toward law-like conclusions without stopping to theorize the work algorithms must do to uncover the logic of the past. Chapter 2 proposes a series of remedies for poor thinking with data, especially care about the provenance of data and an interest in the fundamentals of historical thinking can guide data-driven research processes. The chapter introduces several teams of interdisciplinary analysts whose work forms the inspiration for this book. Their ranks include traditional scholars from the liberal arts who collaborate with information scientists as well as scholars like myself who have trained in liberal arts subjects but sometimes work with data and code. Chapter 3 dives deeper into the problem of treating words with care, explaining how words can act as barriers to interpretive understanding but also keys that unlock powerful analyses of the past. Chapter 4 extrapolates a theory of a research process capable of working between qualitative questions and quantitative tools. It proposes a series of steps for how a "critical" encounter with a digital archive and quantitative algorithm might proceed in such a way as to preserve humanistic concerns with meaning, bias, silence, and perspective. The result is a "critical search" for the past, which can form part of a larger agenda of *re*-search, but which is fundamentally better suited to humanistic questions than searches conducted with out-of-the-box tools like wordclouds. Chapter 5 steps back to the purposes that data scientists sometimes bring to historical data, investigating one of the chief subjects of misunderstanding and conflict between quantitative and qualitative approaches. It asks head-on whether excavations into the past can support a "predictive" theory of the future. Reviewing historians' positions on this subject reveals both numerous objections to predictive thinking with historical data as well as a handful of important opportunities.

Part II of this book explores how ideas from the philosophy of history can help us to study historical change. Drawing on the scholarship of many contemporary philosophers and historians who have wrestled with the problem of how we know about the past, this Part argues that the past is a multidimensional object, in that long-term forces and short-term shifts, experience and memory, all work together to shape the past, their interactions constantly changing. Chapter 6 draws on the philosophy of history to propose a series of categories of temporal experience appropriate as subjects for data-driven modeling.

Next, we consider question of whether mathematics, data, and modeling can expand the analyst's ability to apprehend the multiple dimensions of change in the historic past. To that purpose, I present a concrete series of case studies where I engage datasets around a theory of historical change. In Chapter 7, I deploy a series of text-mining methods to study how the process of memory changed in nineteenth-century Britain. I present multiple possible quantitative approaches that open up different dimensions of the past, and I show how each approach, and each subinvestigation within each approach, adds nuance and complication to our understanding of the past. Chapter 8 discusses algorithms that can be used to detect the distinctiveness of different eras, and explores how those algorithms can be adjusted to highlight the uniqueness of experiences that took place over a day, week, year, or decade. Chapter 9 uses data to study how individuals influence each other. In Chapter 10, I show that algorithms can be used to investigate slow-moving and quick-moving pulses of temporal change at any moment in the past; they can also identify the trends that were at the end of their life, fossils that represented a temporary fad, and other shapes of time that have traditionally been identified through qualitative means. I also theorize what it means to critically adjust an algorithm to a historical question. Chapter 11 introduces theories of "modernization" and suggests several algorithmic strategies for looking at long-term development. At the same time, this chapter proposes important limits to the use of data to revisit the most important questions about modernity, poverty, and marginalization that historians have treated in other ways. In Chapter 12, I investigate a concrete historical question: when and how attacks on environmentalists in the US Congress delayed action on climate change. It argues against the testing of hypotheses in the style of many machine-learning papers, drawing on historical argumentation to propose a process where meaningful insight about the past is the standard of discovery. I also demonstrate, to a degree lacking in the other chapters, what it looks like to work between a data visualization and in-text mentions. Alternating data-driven work with the traditional methods of history makes for a more accurate, nuanced, and robust practice, even when the results are circulated in the form of a data-driven visualization.

In the data-driven case studies of Part II, AI and statistics are a subject for critical inquiry. Of each algorithm, we will ask: Does this approach get us closer to real knowledge, as understood by contemporary historical theories of how memory, temporality, or causality work? How might small adjustments in the parameters of the algorithm or the controlled vocabulary produce different results?

The individual chapters in the Part II will introduce algorithms from vintage statistics such as *divergence*, modern AI approaches to clustering such as *topic modelling*, and machine-learning dependencies such as *word embeddings*. Nonspecialists need not shut the book in alarm; each algorithm will be introduced in accessible language, and the focus of each chapter will remain on the larger question of how hybrid scholarship requires critical thinking about the fit between data, algorithms, and models of historical change.

Some caveats are important. While certain historical "discoveries" are revealed in the middle chapters of this book, I am not primarily concerned in this book with incontrovertible historical argumentation, but rather with a practice designed to combine historical insight with algorithmic rigor. Many of the "discoveries" of data science in recent years merely reproduce standard knowledge; to this end, I am clear where my exercises in data science do the same, although my case studies generally aim for a higher standard of insight. I also emphasize where inadequate data means that the data-driven discoveries in question need to be traced back to archives for the historical explanation to be complete. Chapter 12 looks in greater detail into the notion of "explanation" in history, and how it is that data-driven discoveries can rise to the high standard that historians hold for actual discovery. It is an axiom of the method presented here that data-driven analysis is insufficient for many historical problems. A savvy analyst must apply her skills of skepticism to each phenomenon apparent in the data, validating each discovery by work with the text. Only then can data science rise to the ideal of complete explanation to which historians aspire.

Finally, Part III steps back from detailed engagements with methods to ask what can be accomplished when critical thinking is brought to methods. Chapter 13 looks at how data helped historical linguists to purge centuries of racial bias from their map of the relationships between world languages. It takes a long-term view on the development of disciplines to imagine what our age of reform and data might contribute to other foundational systems of understanding in the humanities and social sciences. Chapter 14 investigates the future of research. It articulates a call for philosophers of history to help us to understand more of the dimensions of the past and for data scientists to use historical understanding to investigate the limits and promise of their models. It envisions a robust future for practices of AI and data science in the future, one where (some) humanists and (certain) historians have an important role to play. It calls on us all to contribute to the collective understanding of where text mining can answer big questions and where traditional research is warranted. Finally, it glances at some public uses of text mining for the purpose of transparency and political reform.

∞

Ultimately, most humanists are already concerned with evidence and analysis. Understanding the past with accuracy and precision is a matter of evidence, and the humanities share this concern for reality with the sciences. Reading the speeches of presidents, comparing novels, studying paintings, or parsing old maps give us evidence, and many humanists pride themselves on their superior talents of attention, comparison, and interpretation.

Text mining can benefit from humanists' careful discernment about the dangers of biased data and the promise of careful categorization of experience. Like other humanistic enterprises, text mining is therefore best pursued with some knowledge of historical context, of the limits of each body of evidence, and the methodological questions suited to those objects in particular.

PART I

Toward a Smarter Data Science

CHAPTER I

Why Textual Data from the Past Is Dangerous

The historian and philosopher Reinhard Koselleck has described what would be required for history to become a predictive science. With a predictive science of history, he mused, it would be possible to generalize about the laws of human experience, as with the laws of physics, even making it possible to predict the future. The problem in getting there, he argued, was the data.

Koselleck described his ideal database: a catalog of the world's historical events, in detail, from catalogs of wars and the deaths and injuries in each battle, down to the thoughts imagined by every human who has ever lived. The database would include a note of each transcription error made in each republication of every text since the dawn of time, allowing the scholar to identify slight rephrasings in the transmission of Aristotle and the degree to which they mattered to the habits of medieval monks. Koselleck's dataset would include "all conceivable singular events of possible histories."[1] He imagines the massive undertaking that would be required of the world's history departments – a single, centralized experiment in collecting data: "In short, all specialized histories would be called upon to deliver their contribution to our common world history."[2]

With such an astonishingly precise and varied array of data, Koselleck conceded, history could indeed become a predictive science. The historian who availed of such a dataset would be able to tell to what degree a difference height, the death of a parent, or childhood events informed the specific cast of mind that made Sigmund Freud different from other members of his family. Koselleck imagines that such a dataset, constructed so as to foreground the principles of singularity and repetition, would allow historians to formulate a truly scientific approach to the past:

[1] Reinhart Koselleck, *Sediments of Time* (Palo Alto, CA: Stanford University Press, 2018), 160.
[2] Ibid., 161.

"We may ask what is specific about all people, what is specific about only certain people, or what is specific about only one single person."[3]

Using this ideal dataset, Koselleck asserts, historians would be able to describe "the migrations, mixing, and melting together of different cultures and units of action – all the way to the economic, ecological, and religious challenges, the rifts and fractures that span across our entire globe and that all cry out for alternative courses of action."[4] Based on data alone, historians would be able to create a totally quantitative approach to the laws that govern human history. Given adequate data, Koselleck argues, historians would have no trouble generating assessments of the "diachronic repeatability of similar kinds of events."[5] They would be able to inspect the "variable interaction between repetition and singularity."[6] Koselleck's philosophy has long revolved around the careful study of "repetition," or the dynamics of change that mark the shifts in the history of ideas and politics. Sufficiently careful studies of phenomena, Koselleck has asserted, might even support a mathematical calculation of what he calls the singularity–repetition ratio – or the distinctiveness of every event.[7]

We live in an era where algorithms are trained to generalize about people all the time. Edward Snowden's testimony confirmed that US security bureaucracy has been reading citizen emails for some time in the search for terrorists. Text algorithms are used to presort college applications at many universities. Textual algorithms also govern which news headlines and websites are promoted first. These mechanized approaches aren't going away. They increasingly represent a filter on what information we receive about the world, and about each other.

As Koselleck's fantasy of a singularity detection algorithm suggests, there are reasons to assume that, given perfect data, computationalists could design a machine to generalize, accurately, about people, their ideas, and the laws of human behavior. Such a machine, Koselleck suggests, might even be able to discern the future.

Of course, the data collection that Koselleck describes is a fantasy. The dataset he describes doesn't exist and could never exist, and that is actually the point of the story in its context. Creating the dataset that Koselleck imagines would require the supernatural powers hypothesized by philosopher Arthur Danto for the character of one of his fables, the "ideal chronicler." In Danto's imagination, an ideal chronicler would be a person

---

[3] Ibid.   [4] Ibid.   [5] Ibid., 168.   [6] Ibid., 160.   [7] Ibid., 168.

who was capable of transcribing every event with preternatural and omni-present knowledge of both observable realities and internal thoughts.[8]

The only problem with these confabulations is that they are, as the authors took pains to emphasize, complete fantasies. As Koselleck himself explained, a dataset such as the one he hypothesized doesn't exist, has never been collected, and in fact defies everything we know about how real historical collections of data come into being. For the majority of the earth's inhabitants, no surviving documentation has come down through the centuries; perhaps, at least for a certain subset of the population, the voluminous logs of "life-casting" on social media today might approximate such a perfect record of experience for a few individuals – but even life-casting is limited to certain segments of the population. And this is Koselleck's point. No prediction machine has ever existed, because no perfect chronicle of the past has ever existed.

Because the record of the past is imperfect, one of the chief places where text mining can go wrong – and where computer-generalized caricatures of terrorists, or college admissions sorting algorithms can produce injustice – is where the data is poor. The data we work with from the past is indeed *almost always* poor in one respect or another. Most professional historians become acquainted with the problems of working with evidence from the past as one of the major points of their training.

Conversely, the data scientist who is trained to work with neat columns of facts is almost never asked to inspect data from the past for evidence of political suppression or prejudice. The world without history lacks an acquaintance with the routine forms of inspection of evidence conducted by professional humanists. There is a real danger of perpetuating bias in data science programs where undergraduates are trained to make calculations without inspecting the data.

Because comparison between events in the past is hard, because the outcome matters enormously, and because data from the past may itself be structured by suppression or bias, text mining is a dangerous art. Those who wish to generalize from wordcounts to grand claims should take heed. For a thousand reasons, the data might be insufficient, misleading, or completely wrong – and we will never know it, unless we look with care.

The chapters in this section set out to offer something like a "ropes course" for students of data who are attempting to think about problems with modeling human experience: they offer a series of challenges, some

[8] Arthur Danto, *Analytical Philosophy of History* (Cambridge: Cambridge University Press, 1965), 148–49.

easy and some difficult, that require critical thinking and interdisciplinary collaboration. But a weekend ropes course doesn't make a mountain climber from a couch potato, and neither will this chapter make a trained historian of a data analyst. What a ropes course *can* do is to introduce those used to engagement with one kind of work to another kind of exercise and team-building. Before we start to play with the data from history, however, we need to agree about the dangers of working with data from the past – what can go wrong and why.

The Quality of Data from the Human Past

This chapter investigates the impediments posed by imperfect and incomplete data. Although these impediments can take many forms, we will focus on the three major dangers researchers often encounter in the digital humanities.

The first danger is that, more often than not, the data of the past may be occluded, that is, closed off from view; historical data has aspects that don't yield to the normal mechanisms of counting prized in data science. By occlusion, I mean the fact that relevant documents are often hidden in separate datasets or archives that have not yet been digitalized, that the structure of where relevant documents exist is a subject of expertise, and that relevant portions of the archive may be invisible even to experts, until serious research into the archive reveals new sources. Failing to acknowledge the occlusions that often hide relevant data means that the analyst may work with gross inaccuracies and distortions that an analysis based in data science alone may never uncover.

The concept of occlusion isn't new to historians, but it may come as a surprise to scholars trained in quantitative disciplines. Having mistakenly assumed that data about the past is complete and reliable, analysts trained on spreadsheets sometimes conclude they have enough information at their disposal to construct historical theories and laws. To detect occlusions, the researcher must pore over historical data with a sensitivity to its sources; one must train one's eye to spotting the inevitable gaps in archival records – and that requires expertise.

A second danger into which quantitative analysis sometimes falls is "dirty data." I will intentionally invoke this term in a nonstandard way to make a point. Traditionally, data scientists reference dirty data to invoke the mechanical distortions that inevitably arise in transmission when an analog record is translated into digital form. Digital humanists have documented how bias in algorithms and in processing affects how text enters into a digital form where computation can be run, for example, raising questions about the dirty data created by optical character recognition (OCR), or the process of machine learning by which computers scan printed documentation of text back into an electronic and digitalized record. Trained on Western alphabets and the products of modern print technology, OCR is biased against non-Western alphabets – a problem that Professor Roopika Risam underscores in her book *New Digital Worlds*, for example.[9] The challenges of working with dirty data from non-Western alphabets, smudged type in newspapers, handwritten correspondence, and premodern manuscripts are the subject of many ongoing collaborations between data scientists and humanists.[10] Other humanists who use text mining have also underscored that cleaning can go too far when the automatic lemmatization of words to their grammatical roots strips away meaning that researchers find valuable.[11] There is no one-size-fits-all solution to these problems, but they comprise part of the general expertise of the digital researcher.

In this book, however, I will argue that even data that appears "clean" – in the sense of having standardized spellings and punctuation – may nevertheless conceal a deeper layer of filth: the racist and sexist biases and other conceptual distortions that belong to historical authors, and which will, as a result, tend to dominate any attempts to model textual records from the past. One cannot underestimate the biases that infuse the data of the past: the recording of history goes to the victors; and even in peaceful times, indigenous people, marginalized people, women, and ordinary citizens have rarely had access to the instruments of recording their own history. Such biases riddle the data of the past, and historians take careful steps not to reproduce them. Data analysts who are untrained in recognizing the bias in their data may stumble into these potholes of misinformation and deliver conclusions that replicate and amplify the most twisted propaganda campaigns of history. With interdisciplinary support, however, dirty data can illuminate the bias of the past in informative ways.

---

[9] Roopika Risam, *New Digital Worlds: Postcolonial Digital Humanities in Theory, Praxis, and Pedagogy* (Evanston, Ill: Northwestern University Press, 2019), www.jstor.org/stable/10.2307/j.ctv7tq4hg.

[10] One valuable overview of the challenges of digital humanities data sets is Eetu Mäkelä, Krista Lagus, Leo Lahti et al., "Wrangling with Non-Standard Data," in S. Reinsone, I. Skadi Fa, A. þÿBakl ne et al., *Proceedings of the Digital Humanities in the Nordic Countries 5th Conference*: (Riga, Latvia: CEUR, October 21–23, 2020), 81–96, http://ceur-ws.org/Vol-2612/paper6.pdf.

[11] Trevor Munoz, Lauren Klein, and Matthew K. Gold, "Against Cleaning," in *Debates in the Digital Humanities* (Minneapolis, MN: University of Minnesota Press, 2019), https://dhdebates.gc.cuny .edu/read/untitled-f2acf72c-a469-49d8-be35-67f9ac1e3a60/section/07154de9-4903-428e-9c61-7a92a6f22e51.

A third danger of text mining is the fantasy to which researchers may submit when confronting the past, for instance, the desire for mastery over the past that motivates the image of a prediction machine. Prediction has motivated many data analysts to haste, and haste tends to compound false assumptions about the past. We will explore in detail the temptation to use material from the past to "predict" the future. We'll review the broad scope of humanists' objections to prediction and touch on the circumstances under which those objections could be removed.

The occlusions and distortions explored in this chapter will be familiar to most humanists, for whom reckoning with the locked rooms of archives, the skew of libraries, and the bias of language is a central matter of training. However, the inherent flaws in texts and archives are more surprising to most data analysts, whose training typically means reckoning with abstracted numbers in spreadsheet format, where one cell looks pretty much like another.

Without taking into account occlusions, dirty data, and time, our laudable inquiry can result in wasted time, meaningless results – and, worse, an undermining of scholarly faith in quantitative approaches of developing theories about human experience. With a greater awareness of the forces that make text mining dangerous, however, a skillful analyst can navigate across perilous bogs and treacherous deserts and proceed with cautious optimism among new observations and stunning analyses.

Danger #1: The Occluded Archive

Occlusions in the archive are all too familiar to practicing historians – but they tend to plague novice historians as they begin to rummage through the archival material. The good news is that an awareness of occlusions in the archive is well understood in the humanities, and history seminars regularly teach students to skillfully navigate occluded archives.

Sometimes the occlusions of the past are technical and institutional. Before the digitalization of archives began, when a historian at Harvard wanted to tell an account of street trees in nineteenth-century America, they had to rout through newspapers on microfiche in the university's main library, navigate over to the agricultural magazines in the science library and then to the fire insurance maps in the map library, and finally to the photographs of trees in the university arboretum.

Through multiple visits over several afternoons, the historian began to reassemble an archive of the suburban world of nineteenth-century America, as represented by the miscellany of contemporary texts documenting a single coherent phenomenon – a stroll down a suburban street, in which pedestrian, street, trees, and sky formed a totality removed from us by centuries. In latter times, when reconstructing the aesthetics of nineteenth-century American cities, the historian would have to piece together a single experience from dozens of different libraries and hundreds of bits of paper, only a few of them taking the form of texts. The archive of the past – "archive," in the singular, again referencing the totality of past experience that a historian might wish to reconstruct – has been mutilated by the flow of time, disassembled into dozens of different reading rooms, which the historian can only reconstruct through shoe leather, patient study, and reassembly.[12]

Sobering labor thus awaits the historian, who must often sift through an overwhelming number of discrete special collections – individual "archives," in the plural, meaning the actual libraries in which fragments of the past are stored – until they locate the material that precisely fits their inquiries. Failing to match one's research question with available data can undermine an entire project. To reassemble the past, the historian must play a game of reconstructing the long and circuitous path of papers – a game also required of contemporary scholars. Today, a certain proportion of that archive might be digitalized; when reconstructing the farmer's experience, for example, one might find digital copies of the newspapers the farmer read; but other material might only be available in their original medium, for instance, manuals and agricultural magazines. If they wish to effectively navigate the past, historians must become familiar with such archival limitations and correct for them.

Often the occlusions of the past are structured by politics. Our documents may be biased; rivals may have destroyed conflicting accounts; or perhaps, only the papers of an elite survived. The servant and farmers and debtors, whose testimony would make the account of the past complete, had neither the luxury nor the schooling to leave many records. Sometimes the violence done to the archives is severe – especially in cases of genocide or other extreme acts of abuse. Consider the case of the research of Harvard historian Caroline Elkins, who discovered an archive that had been deliberately hidden in the name of protecting an empire's reputation. Under the British occupation of Kenya, white settlers seized the land of the native Kikuyu people. Facing the uprising that followed – the Mau Mau Rebellion (1952–60), which preceded Kenya's independence in 1963 – representatives of the British Empire attempted to retain their power by

---

[12] John R. Stilgoe, "Four Mornings, Seven Afternoons," *Harvard Library Bulletin* 6:3 (Fall 1996): 20–27.

turning entire villages into detention camps. Some 1.5 million Kikuyu were subjected to a regime of terror that included the systematic use of isolation, rape, starvation, and torture. The colonizers subsequently destroyed the record of those heinous acts. Only a few copies of the relevant reports that documented these exercises remained, and these were stamped "secret" and locked away in an archive in the British Colonial Office – until they were discovered by Elkins. When Elkins' research brought the issue to trial, a further trove of documents was discovered, stashed in a high-security storage facility by the Foreign Office.[13]

In text-based datasets, such "silences" are often the result of deliberate destruction or obfuscation of documents. They can also be the consequence of collective trauma. Reinhart Koselleck has noted that sudden eruptions of antagonism, such as wars, riots, and genocides, can cause observers to grasp for language. Giving the Holocaust as an example, Koselleck observes, "Indeed, there are events for which words fail us, that leave us speechless, and to which we can (perhaps) only respond with silence."[14] Koselleck believes that the concurrent experience of any war or revolution is liable to leave little trace in the record, because people are busy experiencing the events *out there* in the trenches, not coming back to talk about them in parliament until later. Stunned by experience, otherwise active commentators may become speechless.

Whether the occlusion comes from destroyed documents or collective trauma, historians are trained to confront these silences through the careful comparison of records. Collecting all the necessary evidence to illuminate the silences may require work that simply can't be done in textual datasets. Sometimes the researcher must heroically pursue stray pieces of evidence – like the oral testimony Elkins found in Kenya, which first led her to the Mau Mau rebellion, and the stray folders she found in the British Colonial Office. A professional historian essentially plays the investigative journalist, digging for the story by assembling a plurality of sources, because the text of the past is never shelved in a single library, encyclopedia, or dataset.

The skills of tracking down documents that supply added context can be important for illuminating still more pedestrian issues. Whether or not genocide or the legacy of empire are in play, even the most conscientious libraries and archives can't preserve the past without pieces of information

---

[13] Caroline Elkins, *Imperial Reckoning: The Untold Story of Britain's Gulag in Kenya* (New York: Henry Holt, 2010). See also David M. Anderson, "Guilty Secrets: Deceit, Denial, and the Discovery of Kenya's 'Migrated Archive,'" *History Workshop Journal* 80:1 (October 1, 2015): 142–60, https://doi.org/10.1093/hwj/dbv027.

[14] Koselleck, *Sediments of Time*, 140.

becoming lost and records falling from sight. Indeed, at the Harvard library, the pieces of an ideal archive inhabited different buildings and were filed under separate card catalogs. Special sensitivities are therefore required to guide the researcher toward clues that might illuminate the shadows cast over the past.

The issue of occlusion is different than the issue of bias. When I speak of occlusion, I mean that the archives are quite literally missing something. Archives can be occluded, as with Elkins' archive, because of political deletions. They can also be occluded for historical reasons, for instance, the fact that many women, enslaved persons, and working-class individuals could neither read nor write in periods in the past. They can even be occluded because of a superabundance of other kinds of information that can drown signals in noise, for instance, the Australian newspapers in which, as modeled by Professor Katherine Bode of Queensland University, the original stories by Australian writers needed to be sifted from stories that had been reprinted from authors in Europe and North America.

Without training in the humanities or social sciences, data analysts are especially vulnerable to naïve analysis that doesn't envision data as the product of a moment in time. Aware of the profound eurocentrism of earlier historians, contemporary historians undergo a great deal of training to consider and avoid the pitfalls of naïve analysis. Modern training in the humanities engages extensively with the multitude of inherent problems in using written data from the past – where the perspectives of the dead are not all equally expressed. Simply put, some people are more invisible in libraries, archives, and digital databases than others. From the 1960s forward, this reality became the central focus of historians working through the methods of resurrecting "history from below," which seeks to amend the silences of inherited and biased histories with the actual accounts of the lives of the poor, women, colonial subjects, and other vulnerable populations.[15] Datasets are biased, in part, because the literate and well-connected few influence the writing of history – and if this sounds to the reader like common sense, we must remember that only a few decades ago this was considered a fringe perspective.

Because archives display such bias in their organization, historians and archivists have long considered how to compare the worthiness of different artifacts as accounts of the past. "Reading an archive against the grain," for

---

[15] Tim Hitchcock, "A New History from Below," *History Workshop Journal* 57:1 (March 1, 2004): 294–98, https://doi.org/10.1093/hwj/57.1.294; Antoinette Burton and Tony Ballantyne, *World Histories from Below: Disruption and Dissent, 1750 to the Present* (London: Bloomsbury, 2016).

example, is a deliberate practice of contextualizing elites' descriptions of their actions against accounts of sufferings recorded elsewhere. We see a powerful example of this in Kim Wagner's *Amritsar 1919,* which handles the famous massacre that took place when the British army fired into a peaceful protest, killing over a thousand Indians. As with the Kenyan atrocities decades later, the Amritsar massacre was covered up by British sources and minimized by British writers for generations. Wagner offers his readers a cogent account of how that silencing could happen, despite the existence of myriad local witnesses who took pains to document what had happened, down to photographing the bullet holes left in the walls of streets. Wagner juxtaposes the official parliamentary committee report that excused General Dyer against another source – one gathered by Indian activists, assembling together 150 eyewitness reports of the slaughter of some 1,500 nonviolent protesters. Wagner's careful review of perspectives on the past from multiple sources leaves little room for doubt about the truth of the atrocity.[16]

Data comes from somewhere; it is usually made by human institutions, through human processes, and those have a history. Whether the data is the official archive on British colonial rule, or words in an official government report on events in India, or the text of the records of Congress, or the data about which felons are more likely to become repeat offenders, the data was compiled at a time and a place where rules of knowledge applied. Digitalization is merely "the latest in a parade of ways to make data physical, visible, accessible, and durable," Lorraine Daston writes.[17] Each of those processes offered opportunities for silence and for bias. The fact that the words may have been digitalized does not absolve data scientists from reckoning with the occlusions of the past; it means that data scientists have to deal with matters of politics and history, which are folded into the bias of their data in a profound sense.

What can go wrong when one treats occluded archives as data? If one builds historical narratives from grossly imperfect information, the thesis rarely survives even the gentlest cross-examination.

Even in theoretical work that rises to rigorously peer-reviewed publications, one can often see an abject failure to cross-check across datasets – the kind of work that comes naturally to librarians and historians. While a paper might flawlessly argue its case from within the data, even a cursory

[16] Kim A. Wagner, *Amritsar 1919* (New Haven, CT: Yale University Press, 2019).
[17] Lorraine Daston, "The Sciences of the Archive," *Osiris* 27:1 (January 2012): 156–87, https://doi .org/10.1086/667826.

glance into conflicting datasets might swiftly and disastrously unravel the argument. In a study recently published in the journal *Nature*, for example, researchers studied modern and historical cases of incest in so-called WEIRD (Western, Educated, Industrialized, Rich, Democracies) countries and concluded that prohibitions on incest in Christianity made Europeans cleverer and more open to strangers, astonishingly ignoring enormous databases on incest, researched by European historians, that would have definitively undercut the thesis.[18]

The WEIRD study poignantly illustrates the dangers interdisciplinary researchers face when they fail to ask *lateral* questions about their data and about the adequacy of a given data collection for a particular study. Countless societies around the world have equally rigorous prohibitions against incest; meanwhile, incest was, in fact, regularly practiced within European royal families, as anyone familiar with their family trees can attest.[19]

The study's characterizations of Europe fall apart in other ways. In countless ways, Europeans were, in fact, not particularly "open to strangers," for example, heretics, Jews, Muslims, who were exiled, persecuted, and murdered in ghettos, inquisitions, pogroms, and purges – evidence, one might argue, of a society strikingly *closed* off from "the other."[20]

Without thinking clearly about the way that the rule of violence in the past distorts data, a researcher is in danger of producing caricatures that callously distort the past. We saw a concrete example of this just a few years ago, in the journal *Science,* where several art historians and data scientists published a fascinating study of human migration. The data upon which they built their argument was almost exclusively mined from the work of nineteenth-century European art historians. Because this work unilaterally reflected old-fashioned European perspectives, it was riddled with silences. The voluminous appendices to the article acknowledged these silences, critiqued the antiquated sources, and discussed the limits of the argument.[21] And yet, the spinoffs to the original article – pieces

---

[18] Jonathan F. Schulz et al., "The Church, Intensive Kinship, and Global Psychological Variation," *Science* 366:6466 (November 8, 2019), https://doi.org/10.1126/science.aau5141.

[19] Brian Connolly, Hans Hummer, and Sara McDougall, "WEIRD Science: Incest and History," *Perspectives on History* (May 6, 2020), www.historians.org/publications-and-directories/perspectives-on-history/may-2020/weird-science-incest-and-history.

[20] David Nirenberg, *Communities of Violence: The Persecution of Minorities in the Middle Ages* (Princeton, NJ: Princeton University Press, 1996).

[21] Maximilian Schich et al., "A Network Framework of Cultural History," *Science* 345:6196 (August 1, 2014): 558–62, https://doi.org/10.1126/science.1240064. They write, "Potential sources of bias are addressed in the SM, including biographical, temporal, and spatial coverage; curated versus crowd-sourced data; increasing numbers of individuals who are still alive; place aggregation; location

written for the general public in a plethora of blogs and online magazines with a much wider potential circulation – typically lacked those caveats. The version lacking caveats was amplified through a variety of media and was eventually rendered into data-driven animations that quickly went viral. Mirroring the archaic perspective of the source materials, the animation showed a "video history of human movement since the very beginning of time" in which white missionaries were the first *humans* to visit North America and Asia.[22] In this educational cartoon about human movement, the millions of unfortunate people shipped across the Atlantic through the four centuries of chattel slavery were effectively erased from the human story. Despite being an aesthetically magnificent data visualization, it unapologetically reproduced a brazenly distorted and triumphalist narrative of human history. Even the voiceover presented white migration as the only significant fact of human history, demonstrating a stunning lack of critical engagement. This cultural myopia was not, unfortunately, a harmless oversight, but, rather, the enduring legacy of the colonizer's perspective, a dangerously narrow perspective that perniciously replicates itself again and again, whenever it isn't vigilantly examined.

To extract meaningful answers from data analysis, one must begin by framing questions for the data that take into account the historical context of the time as understood by scholars. From the very beginning of a project, the analyst of electronic data ought to have a sturdy understanding of the institutional and cultural factors that contextualize their subject. One must take refuge in known *facts* regarding historical context, wherever a scholarly consensus already exists – unless the project explicitly aims to question a scholarly consensus. One should also know something about the archives one consults and the particular occlusions with which any given archive is structured.

When wading into the nuances, silences, and unpredictable issues of metadata and reliability, scholars who wish to avoid these dangers must realize that digital archives are dark, not bright; occluded, not readily knowable; and undertagged, underinscribed, and underavailable. By all

---

name changes and spelling variants; and effects of dataset language. Most important, compared with contemporary worldwide migration flux, our datasets focus on birth-to-death migration within and out of Europe and North America." See also "Supplementary Materials for 'A Network Framework of Cultural History,'" https://science.sciencemag.org/content/sci/suppl/2014/07/30/345.6196.558 .DC1/1240064.Schich.SM.pdf.

22 The video is at www.youtube.com/watch?v=4gIhRkCcD4U. See also Alison Abbott, "Humanity's Cultural History Captured in 5-Minute Film," *Nature News*, https://doi.org/10.1038/nature.2014 .15650.

means, one should text mine these inevitably imperfect archives for revelation – but woe upon the data analyst who embarks on text mining without some knowledge of these perils.

Danger #2: The Data about the Past is Dirty in more Ways than One

While the first danger stems from the organization of archives, the second danger involves archives' content, which almost invariably has distortions of its own: dirty data.

Data can be dirty in several senses. When data scientists talk about dirty data, they often simply mean that the data contains transmission errors. We see a basic example of this in Ryan Cordell's transcript of a machine-read version of a nineteenth-century newspaper printing of Edgar Allen Poe's poem, "The Raven": "By the heaven that bends above us, - by the G id we both adore / Tell this soul with sorrow laden if within the distant Aidden / It shall clasp a sainted maiden whom the angels name Lenore / Clasp a rare and radiant maiden whom the angels name Lenore f / Q i-jtb the Raven, 'Nevermore.'"[23] Although the text is readable and analyzable, it isn't *poetry*, or at least not the same poetry it had originally been. Counting machine errors accumulates, however, and eventually results in poor analysis: garbage in, garbage out. Spelling correction algorithms can help as can comparing different versions of the manuscript and, in many ways, the transmission errors and their tentative and imperfect solutions would not be unfamiliar to a medieval scribe.

Although transmission errors are a perennial nuisance in archival studies, I would like to talk about a very different way in which we encounter dirty data – in the form of unconscious bias, falsehoods, editorialization, and many other issues of cultural context that one inevitably comes across in any archive, whether archaic or contemporary.

A glance at the older archives, of course, will reveal bias much more quickly, as we are prone to see contemporary archives through filters similar to the ones that dirty the content. For example, the cultural products of the European powers that engaged the slave trade for three centuries include documents and paintings that glorify coercion and violence. Consider Titian's painting, *The Rape of Europa*, which illustrates Europe's mythological origins in the rape of a helpless young woman,

---

[23] Ryan Cordell, "'Q i-jtb the Raven': Taking Dirty OCR Seriously," *Book History* 20:1 (2017): 188–225.

Figure 1.1   Titian, The Rape of Europa (1560–62). Isabella Stewart Gardner
Museum, Boston.

Europa, who is ravished by the superior power of a god (Figure 1.1). The
painting treats rape as a glorious event. It is a dirty message.

An afternoon in the Louvre or any old museum in Europe will present
the casual observer with enough material of this kind to write a doctoral
dissertation in cultural studies. Likewise, a few hours in our textual
archives will provide the researcher with narratives of power and violence;
many of these narratives are as shockingly brazen as Titian's painting, but
the especially dangerous ones are inconspicuous, slightly attenuated, and
muddied with denials, rationalizations, or distractions.

The surfeit of texts and images excusing violence runs in parallel to the
silence of marginalized people, who rarely produced the content we are
studying – women, laborers, and people of color, whose voices, when they
can be found and text mined, are typically preserved in separate archives.
The archives that protect silenced voices were typically assembled through

the painstaking work of archivists or historians who have indexed, collected, and/or salvaged stray publications from document sales with the explicit intent of collecting a record that would fill in the voices missing from larger collections. Because vulnerable people only occasionally have time to write down their experiences and because those documents don't always survive, the collections in question are usually smaller in scale than the archives of canonical novels and parliamentary speakers, which have been assembled and recirculated widely over time.

In text mining, as with the writing of history, the perspectives of powerful people will tend to dominate every analysis, unless the analyst specifically decides to search for the voices of the powerless. One can read the voices of power against the grain, with critical thinking, but one must do this just as deliberately, triangulating both unspoken justifications for violence and eloquently argued ones against the perspective of people who endured it.

Any data scientist who uses data from human societies is probably working with data contaminated by the biases and silences of those in power – and they must not expect to easily find truth where truth has been systematically excluded from the record.

The "dirtiness" of textual data is implicit not only in the raw data itself, but also in the narratives that our ancestors wove about the past – accounts that are inevitably distorted by the logic of the people who wrote history from one perspective, while erasing others. We learn to understand and interpret the past anew through received myths, told to us by our parents and schoolteachers. When the perspective of those authorities reflects the viewpoint of the British army, the experience of colonized people will largely be erased. If we work on datasets compiled by middle-class clerks working for the welfare authority, the perspective of ordinary poor people vanishes in an instant.[24] In order to see the past anew, we have to free ourselves from the prejudices of the myths that otherwise inform how we interpret every given episode of the past.

I had been teaching undergraduates text mining using the Python programming language for more than one year before I admitted to myself that something was going wrong. In student papers, it became clear that a certain proportion of my undergraduates had followed the directions in the code and plotted the phrase "ignorant women" as a count of phrases

---

[24] For colonized subjects, see Risam, *New Digital Worlds*. For middle-class clerks, see Hitchcock, "A New History from Below."

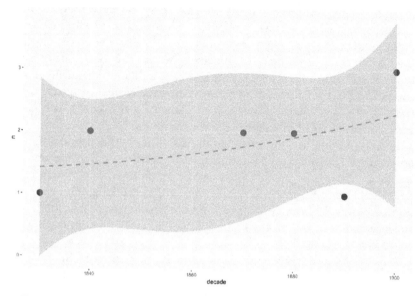

Figure 1.2   Dirty data, an example: The phrase "ignorant women" over time in the
Hansard parliamentary debates. Note the paucity of data points and questionable line of
best fit as well as other problematic aspects of interpretation.
Credit: Stephanie Buongiorno.

spoken in parliament over time, resulting in a graph of a thin dotted line
ticking upward over the century.

Asked to interpret this graph, many students decided that a countable
increase in the two-word phrase "ignorant women" visible in phrase-
counts of parliamentary speeches over the nineteenth century indicated
that women were increasingly ignorant over that time span.

To the trained historian reading the same graph would have led to a very
different interpretation. The phrase "ignorant women" surged at a time
when members of parliament were passing legislation that penalized
women whose employment included sex work. In 1864, the Contagious
Diseases Act held guilty women who gave syphilis to British soldiers, not
the soldiers who paid the women for their work. The upward-ticking
dotted line of references to women on the students' graph shows us that
the prejudice of parliamentarians against working-class women was a long-
term phenomenon, not one that suddenly erupted just before 1864.

In Figure 1.2, I show a plot of the handful of mentions of the phrase
"ignorant women" in *Hansard*. A questionable line of best fit unites them.
But the real hazard here is neither in the paucity of references nor in the

dotted line; it is an interpretive problem. The students have confused representation with reality.

My students were unable to process that the dotted line was an indication of parliamentary prejudice – that members of parliament were increasingly confident in their prejudice against working women – rather than an accurate representation of a fact about women's education. The students demonstrated poor skills at imagining the kinds of people and speeches behind the diagrams we were making together. They also manifested a poor awareness of how to trace points of data back to their original context, or the reasons why doing so might be important. Intelligent data interpretation, in this case, depends on knowledge of the historical context in which the data was produced: it means having someone on the team who is culturally literate enough to understand the bias of data from different sources.

Working with dirty data with the past is a tricky game. At a minimum, it requires a general acknowledgement of biases against women, people of color, and the working class over time, something that is integral to most training in the humanities and social sciences but not to training in engineering or the information sciences. It requires a willingness to look for the evidence of bias in datasets, not treating them as pure representations of a world where some women are actually ignorant. It requires a willingness to go beyond the rush of successfully plotting a graph to ask what the data is and where it will be applied.

This matters because data about the past is being routinely utilized by data scientists today to recommend behavior to judges, police officers, and public school systems. When data from the past is dirty, racially biased data becomes the basis for racially biased recommendations about which neighborhoods to buy, which crimes should get longer sentences, and which individuals should have an opportunity for parole.

Treating biased data with care can also be a matter of realizing that there is a relationship between data about the dead and people who are still alive. Jessica Marie Johnson tells the story of when a CD-ROM of economic data about the slave trade was first presented to an auditorium at Johns Hopkins University. The people of African descent in the classroom, she writes, struggled to make sense of how the raw numbers of individuals transported to different colonies over centuries connected with their knowledge of their ancestors. Johnson argues that the numbers of slaves transported across the Atlantic, like many quantitative numbers used to describe black experience both by abolitionists and slavers in the American past, reduced black experience to an abstraction disconnected from the embodied suffering of individuals who were whipped, raped, torn from their children and parents or lovers, and otherwise dehumanized over the course of entire centuries. Reanalyzing raw counts of births and deaths without thinking about the prejudice and suffering that the data entails, Johnson argues, reflects confusion about what the data is and the extent to which bias is baked into the dataset. The data is dirtied through and through with groans, misery, abuse, silencing, and the defiance of the enslaved individuals who resisted their captors to the point of death. "There is no bloodless data in slavery's archive," Johnson writes.[25]

Dirty data is like some greasy tarnish that covers everything it touches. Dirty data doesn't disappear from datasets with a single act of inspection or a single revelation of new data. The dirty narrative of white supremacy gets everywhere and, wherever it has been, truth disappears and evidence is ignored. The historic origins of slavery, the extent of suffering, the reasons for the outbreak of the American Civil War, the outcome of Reconstruction, and the structural theft of resources from persons of African-American descent would remain contested, subject to study, research, further documentation, and debate, over generations.

Johnson argues that the most relevant research into data about the slave trade today comes not from the crude econometric calculations based on the numbers of slaves transported across the Atlantic, but outside the academy. There, in the community, African-American descendants of slaves looked at the data in detail for themselves. They sought to enliven the data by mapping the slave ship information into stories about families, based on genealogical research being conducted by communities connected over the internet. Johnson's portrait of how the data about slave ships was *used* reminds us that data has a life beyond the academy, where the dirtiness of the data from the past is being held to account. In her article, Johnson begs readers to consider their own accountability to living communities who have a stake in the meaning of data from the past and insight into the ongoing oppression associated with its tarnish.

Using data from the past as if it were clean, not dirty, results in the perpetration of crimes of data prejudice. As Cathy O'Neill has shown in her 2016 book, *Weapons of Math Destruction,* naïve users of apps, such as judges, are therefore being advised to extend the prison sentences for folks of color but not white people – all because of dirty data from the past,

---

[25] Jessica Marie Johnson, "Markup Bodies: Black [Life] Studies and Slavery [Death] Studies at the Digital Crossroads," *Social Text* 36:4 (137) (2018): 70.

which is deployed without consideration of the effects of inflicting racial bias from the past on living communities of people of color.

Naïve modeling of data, that is, lacking a critical viewpoint on the silences in an archive, is almost guaranteed to produce an account of the past that is not merely wrong, but also opens old wounds. Naïve data analysis is bound to silence yet again those voices that had previously been silenced by governments or employers or by other more dominant groups. As long as we know that those voices exist – even if they exist only in the form of secondary sources, rather than data – then *historical truth* requires that any scholarly attempt to explain reality through data-driven models comes with an obligation to consult with studies that bring in the voices of the silenced. Consulting those studies typically requires working beyond the strict limits of data science, as we must look beyond simple metadata, wordcount, and similar statistical or machine-learning methods to arrive at the big picture answers. Data-driven conclusions must be informed by the weaknesses and silences in the database and, at best, researchers can develop measures to explicitly model the silences in the dataset. Meanwhile, the scrutiny applied to what *goes into* the system should also be applied to what *comes out* of it – in other words, those who inspect the results of data-driven studies should be extremely skeptical of any methodological approach that fails to model these silences.

Danger #3: The Pressure of Fantasy

The third distortion of data has to do with the pressure of fantasy: that is, the ideas that analysts bring when they approach digital archives. For analysts used to dealing with spreadsheets, it's easy to forget that archives have occlusions and distortions. Thus the third danger is linked to eagerness, an enchantment with the vast possibilities of this new conceptual toolkit. Faced with unplumbed textual archives and new tools from data science, researchers can easily feel that they are standing on a cliff, looking over an immense vista of potential findings.

Fantasy is a natural human response to the strangeness of the new; it represents the play of the imagination over *what could be*. The storage facilities used for archiving texts in the twenty-first century resemble other-worldly landscapes (Figure 1.3). They are so vast that they have to be cataloged, sorted, and managed by robots rather than humans. Many of the physical records used in the past have been abstracted into metal safe-deposit boxes and magnetic tapes, and the data hoarded there is delivered by robot to the querying hands that type electronic searches. This is still a

Figure 1.3   Library storage as a fantastic landscape. Mansueto Library, University of Chicago.

largely unknown landscape, both in terms of these new robot-managed bunkers and in the arcane meaning of the contents of these boxes.

Fantasy is born out of longings that naturally burst into some concrete articulation. And, of course, our longings grow particularly intense when we enter new landscapes. Like those sea monsters on the margins of medieval maps, marking the limits of terrestrial knowledge, our fantasies explore the blank spaces beyond the edge of disciplinary knowledge. The point of the anecdotal monster, in the hands of John Kirtland Wright, the medieval scholar who first wrote about it, was that naming monsters constitutes a way of understanding geography when one hasn't yet conceived of longitude and latitude.[26] We populate the empty spaces on the map with monsters, with conceptual grotesques that give concrete form to our anxieties and our marvelous remedies for them. Similarly, robot-serviced archives and massive textual datasets are unknown landscapes where the play of imagination runs wild. Scholars and entrepreneurs alike have projected fantasies onto this vast unknown – dreams about a deep

[26] John Kirtland Wright, *The Geographical Lore of the Time of the Crusades: A Study in the History of Medieval Science and Tradition in Western Europe* (New York: American Geographical Society, 1925).

history of human evolution and schemes for predicting human interaction and translating this knowledge into commercial markets.

Large-scale archives do not necessarily provide *complete* datasets. At 63,000 textual works, Project Gutenberg, for example, seems unimaginably vast – until it has been put into perspective. The library of Alexandria had about 540,000 volumes at the time of its destruction in 47 BCE. Project Gutenberg, one of the largest vaults of digital text available to novice data scientists, contains only a tenth of the great library's contents. After the invention of the printing press and the spread of literacy in the early modern world, the volume of our textual archives swelled, but not by as large a factor as one might imagine. How can this possibly be accurate? After careful consideration, we can draw only one conclusion about Gutenberg's digital corpus: *It must be missing a lot.*

Google Books, meanwhile, represents the work of centuries of collecting on the part of dozens of university libraries, and yet it holds only eight million volumes. Can the contemporary world's largest collection of texts be just 15 times larger than the collection of papyrus and vellum at Alexandria? Surely a repository that represents the modern age of literacy, a global population of eight billion people, and five centuries of mechanical printing, distributed over a network of millions of computers and servers, would be at least several hundred times larger than any body of texts that could be shelved within a single library erected in antiquity?

How can we explain this conundrum? While every ship that stopped in Alexandria was required to stay in the metropolitan harbor until any written material on the ship could be laboriously handcopied by a scribe, Google has no so such mandate – and Google Books contains only a fraction of the printed output of the modern era. Drawn from university and public libraries, Google Books reflects rules of curation and biases of its own, especially the pervasive bias toward archiving books to the exclusion of countless forms of printed materials people have used over the centuries, including pamphlets, newspapers, government documents, bills, memos, financial receipts, shipping manifests, private diaries and notebooks, catalogs, surveys, letters, and so on. When historians talk about the variety of ways to access the past, they're usually thinking about special collections curated by libraries, which often hold a greater diversity of paper material than either Google Books or most public libraries. Historians dream about the diversity of collections contained within an imaginary place where one could consult any conceivable textual material from the past: The Archive.

The word "archive" suggests the vastness of the past itself – everything that is archaic. For the historian, the perfect library trip would access the totality of past experience. They may hold this dream with bittersweet fondness, knowing that such an archive may never be realized, as far too much has been forgotten, suppressed, consciously altered, tragically unfinished, carelessly overwritten, and is currently illegible, fragmentary, or missing. Historians talk about the knowledge contained in the archive with the same reverence one often hears when scientists talk about *prediction*. In their respective disciplines, "the archive" and "prediction" represent an ideal form of knowledge: the power we could theoretically harness over time, were our knowledge only complete.

The prophet of computer-based prediction of human societies today is Peter Turchin, a biologist who has claimed in various venues to be in the process of engineering a crystal ball, a predictive model of human society, an "index" that can predict the chance of a revolution in America today. In her book, *If Then: How the Simulmatics Corporation Invented the Future,* the Harvard historian Jill Lepore argues that a fascination with prediction entered the American university in the decades after the Second World War when modern political polling was adopted to presidential campaigns for the first time. During a period of mania for predictive analytics, social scientists at Harvard, Massachusetts Institute of Technology (MIT), and Stanford were enlisted to the cause of modeling sentiment in Vietnam as an aid to US Secretary of Defense, Robert McNamara's, war effort there. As Lepore shows, the efforts in Vietnam were a disaster. They were badly organized, collected little authentic information from Vietnamese subjects, and produced little analysis, let alone advancement, in the field of data analysis.[27]

As Lepore explains, asking academics to supply "prediction" rather than carefully situated data opens the door to an intellectual confidence game in which an advocate for a certain position or product disguises themselves as an expert in stochastic analysis; often the product that they are selling is their "astonishing expertise" itself. Whether they're selling stock market predictions or a telescope into time, the fantasy of mastery over the future can lead otherwise sober people to buy up a swindle.

Deference to humanistic ways of knowing doesn't mean that one can't model society or use data to say interesting things about near-term trends. At Columbia University, historian Matt Connelly's group has experimented with training an artificial chronicler on a list of events, and observing how the artificial intelligence reacts to new information. In the hands of

---

[27] Jill Lepore, *If /Then: How the Simulmatics Corporation Invented the Future* (New York: Liveright, 2020).

thoughtful mathematician such as Kristoffer Nielbo, the measurement of predictive elements is never divorced from the humanistic process of *describing* the present or the past in mathematical terms so that they can then be projected onto the near future in a more meaningful way. Meanwhile, literary scholars such as Ted Underwood and his collaborators have begun applying an analysis of gendered speech in the nineteenth century to contemporary novels en masse, resulting in an analysis that is, in very general terms, predictive of how best-selling and prize-winning novels will continue to talk about gender for at least a handful of years.[28] The predictive experiments of digital humanists or hybrid-knowledge teams tend to fold questions of interpretation into every stage of analysis, casting their work as investigations into the structure of time and the limits of what can be known.

The beauty of these studies is that they seem to work – Nielbo seems to be able, in a limited way, to "predict" which Reddit threads will continue to consume new information and which will perpetuate the same stock of old ideas. But it is also worth noting that Lepore's objections still apply. The ability of any model to generalize about future time depends upon an infinite number of variables remaining unchanged. In most of these studies, "prediction" is essentially a synonym for "extrapolation" – all things being equal, the authors can model present-day discourse and extrapolate what the future will look like. If all things are suddenly different, the old models will necessarily cease to apply.

Fantasy can, at times, be positive and productive. Fantasy can be a healthy response to a deadening atmosphere. By drawing on the energy of suppressed drives, fantasy can give form to and conjure into existence alternate realities that once seemed utopian, but with focus and grit became viable and eventually commonplace. Fantasies might be an essential part of the process of charting out a general direction toward our goal. In the work of Connelly, Nielbo, and Underwood, the play of imagination over historical data has given rise to promising pipelines for modeling contemporary society and generalizing about everyday social change.

As we saw with previous examples of data modeling gone astray, fantasy can become dangerous. It can draw analysts to prepare visions of the past that leave out the experience of non-whites or women; it can harness

---

[28] Joseph Risi et al., "Predicting History," *Nature Human Behaviour* (June 3, 2019): 1–7, https://doi .org/10.1038/s41562-019-0620-8; Kristoffer L. Nielbo et al., "A Curious Case of Entropic Decay: Persistent Complexity in Textual Cultural Heritage," *Digital Scholarship in the Humanities* 34:3 (September 1, 2019): 542–57, https://doi.org/10.1093/llc/fqy054; Underwood et al., "The Transformation of Gender in English-Language Fiction."

attention to superficial generalizations about data, without attention to the archives that have been intentionally suppressed, or biases that deserve critical attention. Because of the dangers imposed on interpretation by fantasies of prediction, robust engagement requires clear steps away from prophecy, and toward actively discerning the *historical facticity* we seek within the data. Engagement may be aided by paying attention to the solid exemplars of new work coming back from the digital frontier. From exemplary practice, the student of data can learn the best practices associated with the new arts of data. They can learn the limits of what we can do with our data, thus avoiding the sea monsters that lurk in the archive's darkest corners.

The Curious Case of *Hansard*: One (Suspect) Record of the Making of the Modern World

Moving from naïve acceptance of databases to a more critical engagement with these archival dangers is fundamental to producing meaningful results. Critical thinking about data is hardly automatic, of course, even among practiced data scientists. But there are specific steps we can take when analyzing a textual archive. In this book, we will explore a methodology for approaching archival text that will help us to extract reliable information from textual data, and answer the big questions: *What changed* and *when?*

The experiments we will discuss throughout this book largely involve a particular dataset, one that invites a great deal of critical thinking: the parliamentary debates of the House of Commons and House of Lords of the United Kingdom in the nineteenth century. The parliamentary debates – the transcripts of which are colloquially known as *Hansard*, after the publisher of the debates in the nineteenth century – offer a sweeping index of Britain's political change. The parliamentary record represents an almanack-like compendium of the concerns of different regions, classes, and ethnicities, as recorded by journalists working in the gallery above the proceedings. The debates were digitized in the 1990s, when more than a century's documents were scanned and translated into digital text with OCR software and made available to the public through a series of governmental projects. Today, scholars and journalists can sift through at least two centuries of proceedings the old way, by reading them, or through the quantitative processes of wordcount known as "text mining."

During the years of my postdoctoral fellowship in digital history when I began my ongoing quest for a relatively clean set of data – corrected for

OCR errors and containing reliably accurate dates and basic bibliographical information – *Hansard* seemed like a natural choice. I found that parliamentary speech, despite varying in length and quantity from decade to decade, was a fairly static genre of recorded data and this consistent format made it a reliable index for understanding the shifting concerns and self-understanding of parliament. It was also a boon for a historian of the *longue durée*, because it covered an substantial period of time that had already been extensively reviewed by other historians: the nineteenth century has been a popular subject of historical writing at least since Thomas Babington Macaulay's *The History of England* (1848). The turning points of the century – urbanization, the industrial revolution, the expansion of the vote to working men, the creation of a consensus around "liberal" values, and the expansion of the British Empire in India and Egypt – have been hotly debated for over a hundred years and contemporary historians have turned to *Hansard* again and again to review what was said or known.

Before *Hansard*, using the traditional toolbox of a historian, scholars spent hours poring over parliamentary speeches, comparing rhetorical flourishes praising the free market against the reality of the starving poor in Ireland, and exposing the callousness of figures such as Britain's prime minister, Robert Peel, who disdained to send them relief. Scholars contemplated parliamentary idealism about the railroad for India in the context of the extractive economy it would bring to the impoverished nation. But even in the well-plowed field of nineteenth-century British history, a text mining resource like *Hansard* is an invaluable tool. Through text mining, one can check the reliability of factual accounts cited by other historians and validate or invalidate historical theories that hinge on the accuracy of events lost within a vast treasury of long-winded antique debates. Even more exciting, a critical search of such a vast textual archive can surprise scholars by directing their attention to previously overlooked discussions, disagreements, and events whose transformative dimensions were not recognized in their own time. Because of the sheer scale of the parliamentary record – a quarter billion recorded words – the careful researcher may still uncover significant new perspectives on the past. *Hansard* thus offers the perfect test subject for exploring whether digital tools could produce knowledge about the past that is *original, meaningful, and true*.

Despite its usefulness, however, we can't forget that, as a reflection of an old imperial power, *Hansard* is also a repository of profoundly dirty data. It's not the case that *Hansard* collects every speech given in parliament during the nineteenth century, an era when voice-to-speech technology did not exist. Mainly, the record we have is compiled from the work of journalists, clerks, and press reports. Many things are left out. One cannot mine the text of *Hansard* with accuracy for variations in sentiment or phraseology because the individual memory and style of the intermediaries intervened.

Hansard is also "dirty" in a second sense: the speeches it records replicated and amplified the prejudices of a violent age. A cursory glance through the speeches of nineteenth-century parliamentarians can shock the modern reader – it abounds with statements about the inherent laziness of the Irish, of Indians, of Roman Catholics. We find a member of parliament speaking about the Maori: "They were inferior to [the British] in actual knowledge of the arts of life ... inferior in warlike prowess. Their notions of religion were so vague that travellers can hardly ascertain their obscure and capricious creed; and in all the arts of government they were deplorably deficient ... they possess ... all the vices of a savage."[29] An intelligent reader today should never take such a reflection as a testament about the contemporary or historic qualities of the Maori – yet a historian could use such a passage to understand a great deal about the *British* and their biases toward the world beyond Europe. In cases like this one, where the textual record displays racial prejudice brazenly stated, counting the speaker's words can be used as one measure of British bias. Even dirty data can be redeemed as a tool of clarifying historical realities, so long as historians carefully read against the grain of the written narrative.

The data of *Hansard* is thus problematic on several levels. The only female voices it archives are from women interviewed in the context of various crises, such as the women who testify about the starvation they experienced in Ireland in the 1840s. Parliament barred female members until 1918 and, until that same year, no woman could even cast a representative vote for that body of lawmakers; thus, the voices of women are categorically *unempowered*. Representatives of the working class, meanwhile, only appear after 1867, when working men in cities got the vote, but even then, the members of parliament as a whole remained far less diverse in class and politics than Victorian Britain itself.

The text of *Hansard* is also deceptive in a fundamentally different way: the text we are mining can often be a wildly inaccurate representation of what actually happened in parliament. The speeches were transcribed before the advent of recording technology and even before the

---

[29] Charles Butler, Speech, in "New Zealand," *Hansard Debates of the House of Commons v.* 81 (17 June 1845).

standardization of shorthand. And not every speech was even transcribed; many were recomposed or paraphrased from a journalist's memory. When the same speech was reported in a different newspaper than *Hansard* – for instance, *The Parliamentary Mirror* – we often find that an entirely different speech was printed. While one can learn a great deal about common perspectives by reading across many parliamentary speeches, one would be foolish to take textual data in *Hansard* as gospel truth regarding any particular speeches, opinions, rhetorical flourishes, or intricate debates, as they're recorded in the parliamentary record.

Despite its shortcomings, however, *Hansard* can be an excellent tool for modeling the history of British political culture, as long as the archive is handled against a strong background in history and critical thinking. We can think of *Hansard* as a pastiche of fragments that collectively reflect a larger political culture: members of parliament regularly read aloud from peasant petitions, newspaper clippings, reports of select committees, and their own precirculated speeches, while other members reacted to these cultural expressions in spontaneous or laboriously crafted speeches of their own. Even when a given speech has been misrecorded by the journalists or transcribers, the text nevertheless represents a body of *plausible* political opinion reflective of its times, deemed worthy of print, and capturing substantive pieces of what was actually debated – even if it is through the lens of careless misapprehensions or emotional distortions. As a cultural artifact, perhaps more than a trustworthy verbatim recording, the "language of parliament" thus offers a mirror for the intersection of four extremely disparate aspects of discourse. Through *Hansard* it offers a record of the aristocratic mind, public opinion via public petitions and newspapers as quoted in parliament, popular will as expressed by representatives of an expanding franchise, and the "official mind" of a vast administration of committees and courts. Despite the limitations of using *Hansard* as a strict proxy for public opinion or even individual performance, the speeches of *Hansard* nevertheless remain an invaluable index of the changing government opinions pulsing beneath both the legislative record and British political culture at large.

Were we to read *Hansard* naïvely – expecting graphs of trends to provide a simple mirror to the history of progress, for instance – we would hazard the risk of outrageous misinterpretation. We would miss all the speeches given by working men, women, and colonial subjects agitating for political power that transpired *outside* parliament. And worse, if we interpret the language of *Hansard* too literally, we might take the jibes and casual prejudice of Britain's tiny aristocratic minority in a Victorian age as reliable evidence of the condition of women, Irish people, or Indians in the past. With a tilt of perspective, however, the outrageous things said by parliamentary speakers against the Maori and other vulnerable populations can be tallied and subjected to analysis.

In other words, vigilantly reading the archive against the grain is not just a tool for shutting down or shutting out the past. It is also generative; it creates new knowledge *about* the past – in fact, some of the most significant studies in the digital humanities take up the problem of reading archives against the grain, for example, Richard Jean So's study of how white authors describe black characters, or the digital literary scholarship that treats the difference between how women are described and men are described in novels from different eras.[30] Reading against the grain is a method for deconstructing the candid utterances of another time, and illuminating the social dynamics from novel perspectives. For example, when we count words and generalize about what *Hansard* says about women, reading against the grain will stop us from blithely accepting the very categories by which parliamentarians in the 1870s might have shelved women; in one box, speakers categorized women who were "respectable," "innocent," "educated," "modest," and "Christian," and in another box, they shunted women who were "unhappy," "wretched," "fallen," "drunken," "miserable," and "masculine." Parliamentary speakers, in other words, routinely categorized women as either saints or whores, placing "educated" women of the elite and middle class into one category and the victims of industrialization into another.

The grammatical word pairs collected in Figure 1.4 demonstrate that the colorful language of saints and whores was not an occasional caricature infrequently deployed while discussing the rights and needs of employed women, elderly women, or women scholars, but an ordinary fact of parliamentary speech in the 1880s. Parliamentarians talked all day long about rich women and poor women, mapping them onto the "innocent" woman and her foil as they went. Such caricatures reflect the mindset of the men who wrote and debated legislation for a society that prohibited married women from owning property until 1870. Contemplating the spread of syphilis among the armed forces in 1862, those same men in had passed laws subjecting prostitutes to bodily medical inspection and

---

[30] Richard Jean So, *Redlining Culture* (New York: Columbia University Press, 2020); William E. Underwood, David Bamman, and Sabrina Lee, "The Transformation of Gender in English-Language Fiction," *Journal of Cultural Analytics* 1:1 (February 13, 2018): 11035, https://doi.org/10.22148/16.019; Eve Kraicer and Andrew Piper, "Social Characters: The Hierarchy of Gender in Contemporary English-Language Fiction," *Journal of Cultural Analytics*, 2019, https://doi.org/10.22148/16.032.

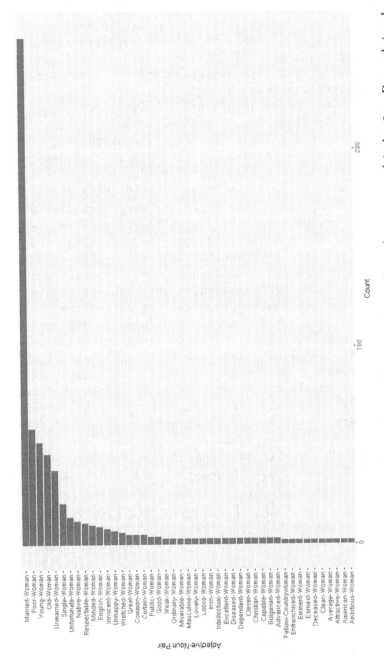

Figure 1.4 Dirty data, an example: Adjectives that modify the noun "women" in parliamentary speech in the 1870s. Data analysis and visualization by Stephanie Buongiorno.

53

imprisonment, while giving broad legal amnesty to the men who visited them – an indisputably misogynistic mindset by modern standards.[31] This language was so commonly and prominently associated with women that the data suggests a habit of mind and, even when the speakers were unconscious of this worldview, it nevertheless structured how parliament reacted, imagined, and governed.

Such an analysis is not news to any scholar of British society of an era that produced Jack the Ripper and his sexually tinged murder spree in the impoverished East End of London. The novelty of detecting misogyny in the 1880s is not the point, however.[32] Rather, my capsule chart of categorizations of women offers a quick sample of how a data-driven analysis that treats dirty data as a *subject* can extract a meaningful, critical analysis of contemporary habits of speech. By studying the taxonomy of virtues and vices, oppressive and offensive as they may be, historians can draw a more precise portrait of the female experience of another time through the actual categories unapologetically imposed upon women by this segment of male society. If the bigotry and nationalism in these examples I've described may be transparent to even a casual modern reader, a great deal of the interpretive work that we must do will not be so brazenly obvious – for example, if we try to read attitudes toward gender, race, poverty, or nationality in chatrooms today, where the biases registered might seem entirely innocent to some analysts. Interpreting the poles of bias in the modern world – the equivalent of the saint–whore dynamic of Victorian Britain – will require some contextual knowledge of British history, as well as critical habits of reading that can prepare us to take with a contemplative grain of salt these antiquated perspectives of British elites toward such groups as women, their colonial subjects, and the working class.

To interpret the bias of textual data, a researcher needs *cultural intelligence*. To develop that indispensable quality in a researcher, or to acquire it for a team, I would suggest three major courses of action:

1. If you are a data scientist, you could enroll in advanced seminars in the English Department or History Department – or seminars in

---

[31] Philippa Levine, *Prostitution, Race and Politics: Policing Venereal Disease in the British Empire.* (London: Routledge, 2003).Judith R. Walkowitz, *Prostitution and Victorian Society: Women, Class, and the State* (Cambridge: Cambridge University Press, 1982).

[32] Judith R. Walkowitz, *City of Dreadful Delight: Narratives of Sexual Danger in Late-Victorian London* (Chicago, IL: University of Chicago Press, 1992).

archaeology, art history, historical sociology, or any field that teachers the skills of reckoning with objects from the past. The seminars you choose should have a heavy emphasis on interpretation and archives – if possible, ones that ask you to handle and interpret multiple sources of different kinds from the past. The skills described in this chapter may seem rarified and acquired only from years of immersive study and, indeed, the best practitioners have often made hefty investments in their own area of specialization – but even a modest inoculation can make a big difference. As with any field, immersion, repetition, and looking at new instances of problems tend to create greater sensitivity and, for this reason, taking several advanced humanities seminars, each of which focuses on techniques of interpretation, may be more helpful than the standard introductory classes where students receive a broad survey of a particular nation or national literature. The point is that skills of interpretation *can be taught,* even to people without a background in the humanities.

2. If you are a data science team, you could enlist a trained humanist to consult with your group, either as a collaborator in the phase of grant writing, or as a paid consultant. The humanist would have to be brought on board during the early phases of constructing the project because of the dangers of occlusion and dirty data. But the humanist's engagement need not end there. The same humanist who helps with occlusions or warnings about dirty data may also have important guidance at the phase of analysis and interpretation. Their sensitivities to interpretive issues may allow them to recognize important findings in the data that look like noise to a data scientist, or conversely, to show that the data scientist's discovery consists of not very remarkable facts that are common knowledge in the field.

3. If the researcher is a trained humanist, then congratulations! You're probably already sensitive to the nuances of interpretation in a certain historical time and place. You're probably also sensitive enough to develop intuitions about data from the present-day. You know about occluded archives and the dirty data of the past and there's no reason not to use the tools of digital analysis to turn your gaze upon them. If you don't code, there are out-of-the-box tools you can use on the web, or you can develop a professional relationship with a data scientist. In later chapters, we will discuss the merits of hybrid knowledge that comes from the meetings of minds, but you are likely to be relatively clear of the dangers that await your data-scientist colleagues.

Conclusion

This chapter has outlined several of the cautions about interpreting historical texts when subjecting them to distant reading. We have argued that the problem of misunderstanding the past is not inherent in working with data, but rather in too hasty a reading of the data, often typified by the fantasy that data alone – without a knowledge of the data's historical context – will satisfy the criteria of interpretation. And we have stressed the need to withstand the pressures in data-centric disciplines to show "predictive" power in the data without first understanding the distortions inherent in the data and remedying them with critical oversight.

A final note: some readers – especially in the humanities – may feel that I have made too cursory an account of these dangers. Any one of the points of discussion made in this chapter – how knowledge was suppressed in the past, what kinds of silences the archives hold – could be continued over pages and even volumes. Indeed, those arguments have been made, with enormous detail, in many of the books cited in the footnotes of this chapter. Articles and books by Tim Hitchcock, Lauren Klein, Chad Wellmon, Lorraine Daston, and Roopika Risam, for example, would offer ideal follow-up texts for any data science class that turned its attention to why data is potentially problematic. Having established the difficulties that those publications treat so well, we will now turn to our central project: to pursue some of the forms of hybrid knowledge that can shed light on the data of the past, including ethnographies of archives and critical archival studies. In the Chapter 2, we will outline a set of precepts designed to guide the practitioner from fantasy to engagement.

CHAPTER 2

From Fantasy to Engagement

Figure 2.1   Sun Wukong receiving the golden crown of obedience from his new master, Tang Sanzang. Japanese woodblock print (nishiki-e) by Tsukioka Yoshitoshi, from his series *The Journey to the West, A Popular Version*, 1865. Museum of Fine Arts, Boston / Public domain.

In China's epic, *The Journey to the West,* the great swordsman Sun Wukong, king of the monkeys, wields his power without regard for humanity until he is imprisoned by the Buddha under a mountain. The monkey king gets a second chance only when the gods choose him to accompany a monk with a mission. Schooled in the teachings of compassion by the monk, the monkey king becomes a steward of learned teachings and a valuable ally to humankind.

Like the monkey king, the data scientist today is a daring if indiscriminate wielder of technology. He races into the swarm of messages, intent upon using the sword of quantitative reckoning to slice through data. But archives, as we have seen, are occluded with the omissions of certain kinds of voices, and the magnification of bias. They attract fantasies about prediction which can lead to false generalizations.

Without compassion and humility, the monkey king will never produce a working analysis. What counsel might Sun Wukong receive from his friend, the monk?

This chapter will explore five precepts that might help an analyst from the World Without History, as they prepare to reckon with the masses of text about human experience present and past:

1. Smart data is data whose origin is specified, where the analysts are aware of shortcomings and delimitations.
2. The building blocks of historical analysis reward inquiry.
3. Critical thinking is most powerful when applied to each part of the research process.
4. Discovery happens where old fields meet.
5. Shibboleths mark out contested areas of practice where interdisciplinary work must proceed with care.

These precepts, of course, are just one door into the mansion of critical engagement with the past. They can't pretend to encompass the entire wealth of ideas from the traditions of the humanities. Instead, they are pedagogical principles that I have found useful in the classroom as a way of bringing students from diverse disciplinary backgrounds into a basic acquaintance with the practice of interpretation.

The precepts move through a series of interpretive problems of increasing abstraction. The first precept – that smart data is data whose origin is specified – asks us to consider that data is always from some other place and time, whose biases and silences may undermine analysis unless the analyst has taken pains to invest in the specific domain knowledge appropriate, that is, an understanding of the historical context of the data, whether that context is 2000 years old or only a decade. The second precept – the primacy of the building blocks of history – urges us to think more expansively about how we observe events, turn them into stories, and generalize about human experience in general. Improperly approached, reckoning with the multiple parameters implied by a changing past will imperil naïve data inquiry. Yet historical concepts such as periodization, causality, and memory can help the analyst to discover linkages and discontinuities that would otherwise be invisible in the data. The third precept – critical thinking – is designed to encourage us to strengthen, through careful inspection, any weak links in the chain of reasoning that links data, analysis, and interpretation. The fourth precept – about interdisciplinarity as the basis for discovering real problems – reminds us that the many fields of university knowledge have all come into existence to discover completely different aspects of the truth of human experience of the world, and each can contribute to the discovery of truth in some respect. The fifth precept gives a starter glossary of terms where interdisciplinary work is particularly challenging, for instance in the consideration of when and how it is appropriate to employ prediction or sampling to historical facts.

The precepts are merely a sample of a wide and deep tradition of critical thought, and do not represent the complete and final word on everything we can learn from the humanities. Each precept simply provides a distillation of one component of the humanities tradition of thinking and engagement. None of them is strictly new – scholars have written about critical thinking since Aristotle; the historical method is as old as Herodotus; and interdisciplinary inquiry into the meaning of sources was familiar to Vico. They are provided as a model of ideas from humanities traditions, brought here into conversation with the work of managing and interpreting data.

This chapter cannot be a substitute for a thorough training in the humanities. Instead, it aims at a cursory introduction, hoping to help data analysts to imagine what sorts of skills, teams, and training might work together to produce a rigorous approach to data about human experience.

Precept #1: Smart Data Is Data Whose Origin Is Specified, Where the Analysts Are Aware of Shortcomings and Delimitations

In Chapter 1, I described the "occlusion" of archives, where certain voices are missing, whether because of government censorship, omission, the ratio of signal and noise, or social delimitations on reading, writing, or publication. The analyst who works with occluded archives gets into trouble, as we have seen, when they treat data as a single morass in which they can track signals and make conclusions, and when they ignore complementary datasets that might allow them to perform a more exhaustive analysis.

The solution to occluded archives is diligence in describing our datasets, their origins, and their limitations. Treating data with care requires data scientists to work with historians, librarians, and other specialists who think about the origins of each dataset. Working with occluded and dirty data requires that, before any other analysis is performed, data science is used to establish the bias of the data in question.

Work with data can reveal the silences and other biases of data from the past. It can be a corrective to occluded archives – archives that are explicitly missing something – and to the dirty data, or bias of data preserved in the records. It can tell us exactly what we are missing, and it can help us to reconstruct those missing stories.[1] One group of scholars, for instance, has used data to study the overrepresentation of white males in the Museum of Modern Art in New York City. Other scholars have used text mining to draw out as many extant details as possible about the lives of women and persons of color in the archives.

Other digital humanities projects have added to our understanding of the violence against African-Americans in the American past by reading traditional archives against the grain – for example in Richard Jean So's critical reading of the archive of novels published by Random House in the years after the Second World War, where he tailored his data analysis to inspect how white novelists wrote about people of color.[2]

[1] For the Museum of Modern Art, see "A Sort of Joy (Thousands of Exhausted Things)," The Office for Creative Research (Spring 2015), cited in Shannon Mattern, "How to Map Nothing," *Places Journal*, March 23, 2021, https://doi.org/10.22269/210323. Thanks to Amalia Levi (via Twitter) for these links and her meditation on how the digital humanities are confronting the occlusion of archives. For drawing out extant details about the lives of women and minorities, see P. Gabrielle Foreman and Labanya Mookerjee, "Computing in the Dark: Spreadsheets, Data Collection and DH's Racist Inheritance," *Always Already Computational: Library Collections as Data*, ed. Thomas Padilla, Laurie Allen, Stewart Varner, Sarah Potvin, Elizabeth Russey Roke, and Hannah Frost, March 2017, 12; Catherine Nicole Coleman, "Managing Bias When Library Collections Become Data," *International Journal of Librarianship*, 5:1 (2020): 12; both cited in Mattern, "How to Map Nothing." See also the powerful meditation on how to use data visualization as a tool of recovery in Lauren F. Klein, "The Image of Absence: Archival Silence, Data Visualization, and James Hemings," *American Literature* 85:4 (2013): 661–88, and the powerful call to use data to enliven stories of the oppressed in Jessica Marie Johnson, "Markup Bodies: Black [Life] Studies and Slavery [Death] Studies at the Digital Crossroads," *Social Text* 36:4 (137) (December 1, 2018): 57–79, https://doi.org/10.1215/01642472-7145658.
[2] For the map of lynchings, see https://eji.org/ and Alex Fox, "Nearly 2,000 Black Americans Were Lynched during Reconstruction," *Smithsonian Magazine*, June 18, 2020, www.smithsonianmag.com/smart-news/nearly-2000-black-americans-were-lynched-during-reconstruction-180975120. For the labor behind the dataset, see Charles Seguin and David Rigby, "National Crimes: A New

These studies prove that data science can be a lens for probing the problems of data from the past. But woe to those who take received data in the form of the database as an innocent record of history, to be mined and interpreted, free of context, and used to advise judges, prisons, university admissions personnel, or public school administrations about what to do next. Before we use data to describe or advise, we must know what kind of data we're dealing with.

I write about the dangers of occluded archives with the authority of experience. A fascination with the possibilities of textual data and an enthusiasm for these powerful digital tools can lead even a professional historian to overstep her training. Ten years ago, when text mining in the humanities was young, I wrote a number of grants in which I outlined an ambitious program of text mining that would encompass all the novels, newspapers, parliamentary debates, and political pamphlets of Victorian Britain, and supply new answers to old questions about the era. In the 2010s, many journalists and scholars, myself included, were enchanted with mass digitalization projects and the possibility of "distant reading" then being formulated by Stanford literary scholar Franco Moretti, which seemed to suggest that new techniques of text mining might shine new light from mass digitalization projects.

Little did I understand back then just how much work would be required to turn the data of the Victorian past into something usable. Years of cleaning text would be required before the first teams that tested the digitalized newspaper archives of Victorian Britain could produce a usable sample of Victorian newspapers, gleaned from only those documents that were most legible to the computer. The pamphlets and occasional papers would require their own cleaning project. Scholars of the newspaper and novel began to raise tortuous questions about when an archive of stories was "complete." Some observers noticed, for example, that the Australian newspapers included an enormous segment of stories republished from the United States; how then could one analyze the "Australian" editorial press of the nineteenth century before first subtracting the American copy from the Australian editions?[3] Through careful consultation with each other, digital humanists were beginning to establish

National Data Set of Lynchings in the United States, 1883 to 1941," *Socius* 5 (January 1, 2019), https://doi.org/10.1177/2378023119841780. For critical history in the archives, see Stewart E. Tolnay and E. M. Beck, "'Racialized Terrorism' in the American South: Do Completed Lynchings Tell an Accurate Story?," *Social Science History* 42:4 (ed 2018): 677–701, https://doi .org/10.1017/ssh.2018.22. For postwar fiction and the Random House archive, Richard Jean So, *Redlining Culture: A Data History of Racial Inequality and Postwar Fiction* (New York: Columbia University Press, 2020).

3 For cleaning and sampling the Victorian newspaper, see Saatviga Sudhahar Thomas Lansdall-Welfare, Justin Lewis James Thompson, and Nello Cristianini, FindMyPast Newspaper Team,

how important it might be to form an intimate acquaintance with the idiosyncratic nature and common occlusions of the archives with which they worked.

For my own research, I resolved to tackle the complex demands of history by taking an enormous step backward. I soon became aware that my working hypothesis, which seemed to follow naturally from the available data and tools, was ultimately drenched in the fantasy of unoccluded archives. Conceding with embarrassment that my original plan was flawed, I took the sage advice of librarians who were knowledgeable about the status and quality of different digitalization projects, and narrowed my research inquiry from *all* digitalized Victorian publications to just the record of Britain's parliament in the nineteenth century. After all, this was an archive whose boundaries had already been mapped by generations of scholars and which was more or less coterminous with the record produced as *Hansard*, the published debates printed by Thomas Hansard.

Hansard is a remarkable archive in that it was both voluminous and essentially complete, which is to say that there is a numbered set of volumes and speeches that corresponds to the speeches given in the halls of Westminster, as collected by the nineteenth-century publishers, whose standards for collecting speeches changed over the century. Setting aside the omissions of the nineteenth-century publisher, the complete publications offer a reassuringly simple standard. A digital replication of this archive can be complete, if transcription was accurate, or incomplete, if the transcription process mangled dates or resulted in lost words. Contrast this satisfying definition of "completeness" with the challenges of defining the complete record of nineteenth-century novels published in English: Do serials published in newspapers but never collected count? What about novels written but never published? What about translations from other languages? Defining where a collection begins and ends is often an inconclusive matter. With *Hansard*, at least I did not have to reckon with the question of whether Australian debates had, by accident, inserted themselves into the British *Hansard*. The archive's boundaries were secure; the occlusions *known*. As we shall see below, however, fantasy – even collective

"Content Analysis of 150 Years of British Periodicals," *PNAS (Proceedings of the National Academy of the Sciences)* 114:4 (January 9, 2017): E457–65, https://doi.org/10.1073/pnas.1606380114. For subtracting the American from the Australian press, see Katherine Bode, "Fictional Systems: Mass-Digitization, Network Analysis, and Nineteenth-Century Australian Newspapers," *Victorian Periodicals Review* 50:1 (2017): 100–38.

fantasies that receive the approval of entire fields of knowledge – can lead even experienced scholars astray.[4]

What saved me from the occlusions in my initial approach? A librarian. At Brown, I worked closely with Brian Croxall, a digital library specialist, who patiently surveyed the datasets I had identified as potentially useful. After careful consideration, Croxall put a pin in my initial ambitions: he flagged most of the data I was prepared to use as having problems of data quality or metadata annotation. It was Croxall who recommended that we start with the parliamentary record, before carefully exploring other records, and keep a close watch on how the data quality, metadata, and archival completeness of one sample compared to the next.

If you are a data analyst working with textual data about humans, well before you begin your analysis, you will need a digital librarian of your own to survey your datasets, their quality, and the "fit" between your data and the questions you propose. To navigate the inevitable occlusions, one should try to work with specialists who know the relevant archives extremely well, and can help identify complementary datasets that may inform one's argument. By working with specialists who know the data and its sources, researchers can develop a better grasp of the conditions that have historically fostered different *kinds* of archives.

In other words, before we begin our analysis, we must first engage the ethnography of datasets and pose questions about the dynamic relationship between society and any given archival medium: "Can I understand the American psyche in the present by looking at Reddit conversations, or will those disproportionately reflect a West Coast, Silicon Valley culture of majority male computer programmers?" Or: "If I want to understand how Americans differ from Australians, should I read newspapers or parliamentary debates, and what is different about the understanding produced in each case?" Or, again: "If the archive I'm using is a file of newspapers, am I prepared to reckon with OCR problems that can typically only be

---

[4] For more on the challenges of "completeness" in parliamentary records, see Sandra Mollin, "The Hansard Hazard: Gauging the Accuracy of British Parliamentary Transcripts," *Corpora* 2:2 (November 1, 2007): 187–210, https://doi.org/10.3366/cor.2007.2.2.187. For other teams which contributed clean data, see Richard Gartner, "A Metadata Infrastructure for the Analysis of Parliamentary Proceedings," in *2014 IEEE International Conference on Big Data (Big Data)*, 2014, 47–50, https://doi.org/10.1109/BigData.2014.7004452. For the technical work of cleaning and topic modeling *Hansard*, see Ashley S. Lee et al., "The Role of Critical Thinking in Humanities Infrastructure: The Pipeline Concept with a Study of HaToRI (Hansard Topic Relevance Identifier)," *Digital Humanities Quarterly* 014:3 (2020). Further work to clean up *Hansard* has been executed since then, but as of the writing of this manuscript, it has not yet been documented; the text mining projects documented in this book began with Ashley Lee's work and the Brown Hansard.

resolved through comparing multiple reprintings of the same text?" As we engage the ethnographic history of each archive, we soon become acutely aware that every archive has its nuances – its palimpsests, its distortions, its silences, and its problems with metadata and reliability.

Does this mean that every team of data analysts needs a five-year professional historian as well as a librarian? Perhaps. But at minimum, one should develop one's awareness of occlusions by interacting with a digital librarian who is aware of broad issues of data quality. Fortunately, most institutes of research these days have at least one librarian trained in both humanistic inquiry and data-driven analysis who is capable of dispensing the sage advice that Croxall gave my team. A digital librarian may be able to flag where data has diverse origins (like American records in the Australian newspapers), where complementary datasets exist (like the Sanborn maps that complemented the photographs of street trees), and where data quality threatens to undermine a project (as in my example of the many archives I decided not to pursue after talking to a digital librarian). Often, a seasoned librarian can keep the digital researcher out of trouble.

A digital librarian can also highlight another aspect of archival occlusion: the metadata, or data around the text, which tells researchers about authors, publishers, places and dates of publication, biographical details, and other significant information. Many databases that are rich in text are nevertheless poorly annotated with respect to metadata. Collections such as Project Gutenberg – a volunteer effort to digitize and archive cultural works – don't necessarily contain much bibliographical information about the authors behind a text or the place of publication. Meanwhile, datasets for the UK parliament and US Congress used by most researchers today have only partial data for speakers' constituencies and political parties. Only recently did one important study annotate the novels of the late twentieth century with the gender of major characters.[5] If even such simple and readily available information hasn't been punched in, one can imagine the volume of metadata that still needs to be correctly annotated – and this is crucial to a leap forward in text mining.

---

[5] For parliament and Congress, I am speaking to my own experience with the Stanford dataset on Congress (https://data.stanford.edu/congress_text) and the Brown Hansard database (see Lee et al.), where my team is currently trying to reconcile party names with the indices provided by Arthur Spirling and other researchers. For a natural language processing (NLP) pipeline to identify the gender of characters as a major recent achievement, see Ted Underwood, David Bamman, and Sabrina Lee, "The Transformation of Gender in English-Language Fiction," *Journal of Cultural Analytics* 3:2 (February 13, 2018), https://doi.org/10.22148/16.019.

Precept #2: The Building Blocks of Historical Analysis Reward Inquiry

To get results, historical analysis does not require digitalized sources or data science. For most historians, counting words – if they use it at all – is only one possible kind of analysis in a larger process of mapping the many dimensions of change in the past. The counting of words may be an extremely peripheral or preliminary step to thinking about the larger set of relationships that govern the origins of world-changing events and their consequences. Most algorithms used in the digital humanities, as of the writing of this book, do little to open up relationships of cause and effect on historical timescales. Even a sophisticated search algorithm, trained to identify words whose meaning has shifted in a very particular way, can only hint at the past.

One strength of the field of history is that it can offer a precise vocabulary of wherein the human knowledge of change consists. In Table 2.1, I list six fundamental building blocks of historical knowledge, drawn from the methodological literature in the history field, which are elaborated in greater depth in the chapters that follow.

The building blocks of historical knowledge represent potential arenas where historians would benefit from contributions to knowledge *from* computer science and statistics. In later chapters, I explore these building blocks of historical knowledge as they intersect with existing studies from scholars working in digital history, staking out the shape of collective expertise in the shape of the algorithms and approaches that promise insight about historical change. I would submit that attention to these building blocks can contribute new research agendas within almost every area of natural language processing. Because one thesis of this book is that digital history is an evolving discipline, which will continue to benefit from collaborations between computationalists and historians, my task in each chapter is less to establish a single best practice around each building block

Table 2.1 *The fundamental building blocks of historical analysis.*

Archive
Change over Time
Event
Period
Influence
Memory

than (i) to validate that current methods from computational disciplines can indeed produce findings of interest to historians and (ii) to explore some of the questions that historians might level about how meaningful, biased, or interpretable the results are.

In this section, I provide a starter glossary of the terms on the list. The glossary is informal and incomplete – informal, because my agenda in this chapter is not a formal review but a series of practical points grappling with history, intended for the consumption of would-be practitioners of "hybrid" approaches to text mining for historical analysis. In the chapters that follow, I offer a fuller discussion of the terms, the intellectual debates out of which they come, and the opportunities that they afford for historical analysis.

The list is incomplete, because the history field and the philosophy of history are vast and lively arenas, whose specialists are dedicated to understanding the complications of chronology in ways that I cannot possibly hope to cover here. It is also incomplete in that I have chosen to list the building blocks of historical understanding that foreground issues of the completeness of data (the "archive") and the representation of data over time ("change over time," "event," "period," and "memory") – issues that can be added to practically any data-driven text-mining project with the result of enhancing the specificity, detail, and insight of the analysis. In focusing on these words, however, I have left out most of the categories that describe the specific subjects of analysis that motivate historical inquiry, data-driven or not, including events in the structure of conceptual thought, change over time in the history of institutions, individual biography, changes to the structure of identity, and so forth. I regard these structures not as inferior (for they motivate most research in history departments today), but as secondary, from a pedagogical point of view, to a discussion of how data science should begin to engage the concerns of history.

Glossary terms

- **Archive.** This is the available remainder of the past, and it is separate from the past as it is lived, being merely a remnant of a far greater number of experiences, events, memories, and experiences never recorded. In the sections on the "occluded archive" and "dirty data" in Chapter 1, we began to consider the problem of archives: finding the data is itself hard, the subject of years of training; and the archive is a repository of – among other things – the biases of the past. Indeed, there are few great historical problems that can be solved in a meaningful way without recourse to multiple archives and deep consideration of what any *specific* archive or dataset misses from totality of possible documents about the past. Consider that even archives as comprehensive and transparent as those used in this book – the annals of the debates in Britain's parliament or the US Congress – are riddled with hidden omissions, literally *missing data,* which may be vital to understanding our historical problem. Some of the missing data is caused by the structure of institutional book-keeping in the past; for instance, it's a fact of institutional history, rather than a natural facet of datasets useful for text mining today, that when one downloads datasets of parliament and congress, one usually is missing the papers of the parliamentary and congressional hearings, which were published and bundled separately, even though members of parliaments and congresses would have access to the reports of these hearings as they sat debating. Other missing data is a reflection of the biases of institutions in the past: for instance, nineteenth-century prejudices resulted in there being no female members of Congress until Jeanette Rankin in 1916. If a student's research project is about women's politics in America, and the student has access only to the congressional debates, the student may be tempted to decide that women had no political activity in America before this date. But historians know that the archives that document women's political activity in the period leading up to women's suffrage are simply *elsewhere,* collected in libraries and archives that came to specialize in collecting those papers. In the case of women's suffrage, some of the documents have been collected by the Library of Congress, which has several provided datasets that can be used for text mining, including detailed transcriptions from the diaries of Carrie Chapman Catt, as well as many published and unpublished articles by members of the movement.[6] But importantly, the Library of Congress dataset is itself far from comprehensive; it is structured around three leading white women in the movement – Carrie Chapman Catt, Susan B. Anthony, and Elizabeth Cady Stanton. The movement for women's suffrage was more diverse in terms of race and class than the papers of these three women might suggest. The archives that survive are often a reflection of the privilege that a writer inherited

---

[6] Susan B. Anthony, Transcription Datasets from Susan B. Anthony Papers (Washington, DC : By the People, Library of Congress, to 2022, 2021); https://www.loc.gov/item/2020445591. Elizabeth Cady Stanton , Transcription Datasets from Elizabeth Cady Stanton Papers (Washington, DC : By the People, Library of Congress, 2021); https://www.loc.gov/item/2020445592. Carrie Chapman Catt and National American Woman Suffrage Association Collection, Transcription datasets from Carrie Chapman Catt Papers (Washington, DC: By the People, Library of Congress, to 2022, 2020), https://www.loc.gov/item/2019667239.

or attained in their own lifetime; while most people in history experienced little privilege, the truth of experience is often hidden. Thus, the most telling documents about the facts of human experience are often those hardest to discover.

A historian who aspired to document all the speeches given by suffragettes, comparing them with the later speeches of women in Congress, would need to assemble her own dataset, scouring newspapers, movement publications, and personal archives for as many available texts as possible. The nature of archives is that one cannot assume that the data that is easiest to find gives the most complete picture of reality in the past.

Knowledge of archives is essential, as a building block of historical knowledge, because failing to understand the bias of each individual archive means missing the implications of each particular set of documents – the congressional debates, after all, tell us something about the public life of the United States, even if they leave out many actors.

Once we understand that the totality of the past is refracted through individual archives, each of which has its own exclusion, there are opportunities for using archives as a tool for understanding the richness, contradictions, and complications of time. For instance: what, we might ask, were the political demands made in the papers of the suffragettes that were *never* heard in Congress? Likewise, each archive has its own temporality – that is, for Congress and the Supreme Court, each would have its own changes, events, periods, and memories that might not be seen in the other; similarly, each party or representative in Congress and each faction or justice in the Supreme Court would likely have its own record of change, event, periodization, and memory.

- **Change over time.** This is the basic unit of analysis in the study of history, a discipline that is largely motivated by understanding the forces that make the present different from the past, or that shaped moments of change in the past. Earlier in this chapter, we glanced at some of the tools used by information scientists to measure aggregate change over time. In the experiments in this chapter, mathematical tools suggested a turning point. But what does the turning point mean? Historians are little content with the raw *assertion* of change over time; we want to know in what details, specifically, an argument about change over time consists. After all, many features of society are often changing at once. Thus, the mandate to model *change over time* means that historians require models of the data that highlight *particularized* strands of change over time, for instance, a group of words whose profile seems to change together.

Much of the study of modern history consists in attempting to identify, isolate and compare major trends of modern societies, for example, the rise of nation-states, bureaucracies, democracy, industrialization, cities, and economic growth. In Chapter 11, we compare inductive and deductive approaches to the description of modernity, and we will see that two approaches (topic modeling and divergence applied to individual words) can produce very different portraits of what it means to be modern. In history, we take delight in the fact that two models contradict each other; it means that we're probably collecting many true facts about what was changing. Indeed, historians are probably less willing to accept a completely positivist account of the *one truth* of what modernity means.

We will explore other tactics for exploring change over time using words, experimenting with different definitions of what it means to "change." In Chapter 10, we will ask: What is the significant change in a recent trend that arises one decade and vanishes the next? Or a lasting trend that persists over time? In Chapters 10 through 13, we will ask: When is describing the short-term dynamics of change sufficient, and when do we need to look over longer horizons? The approaches that I propose are not exhaustive, however, and I make efforts to show that I have barely scratched the surface of possible ways of modeling change over time.

• **Event**. Change over time is punctuated by events. Events are observable moments of historical discontinuity, whether the discontinuity comprises a shift in the names of the individuals involved in an institutions, or the ideas or feelings or values or styles of rhetoric or representation under discussion. Earlier in this chapter, we introduced some naïve approaches to the study of events based on raw statistics. Yet a definitive practice for using text mining to establish a chronology of events remains elusive – offering hybrid practitioners important material for methodological experimentation. Scholars such as Martin Jay have argued for an "eventful" history as one approach to telling stories about the past that emphasize the fundamental mutability of human experience. Discovering little-known episodes of historical change in textual datasets, and adding them together into a portrait of change, is one promising approach to how text-mining can help us to think systematically about *which* events mattered in the past.

Frequently, historical analysis aims to supply an explanation of how an event came to be. David Hackett Fischer defines causal explanation as "an attempt to explain the occurrence of an event by reference to some of those antecedents which rendered its occurrence probable."[7] Fischer goes on to argue that the criteria for accepting a causal explanation are evidence of correlation, evidence of two phenomena being in relationship over time, and a persuasive causal model.

Causal explanation helps us to understand how enormous parts of the human experience are interrelated. Without studying causes and relationships over time, we can only speculate about whether, in the human past, capitalism, slavery, and global climate change had any relationship. With historical analysis, however, we begin to ask: Did the same forces that forged capitalism also actually create the conditions for the spread of slavery? Were the same places that invented the industrial revolution also those that invented the surge of carbon responsible for climate change? In such an analysis, we are doing more than merely naming a series of events in the past; we are starting to analyze how essential one category (capitalism) is to the historical reality of another (slavery). Without historical analysis, we may gather colorful fragments from an archive, but we can't build the complex mosaic that has the enduring face of a well-crafted story about the past.

In Chapter 6, I review the ideas of Jay and Koselleck about "rupture" and "repetition" as potential factors for defining the significance of events. I show why this search for events is both informative and difficult, and I demonstrate how topic models can be used to index the documents of the past in the service of discovering forgotten events. At the beginning of Chapter 12, I demonstrate how another technique, word embeddings, can be used to much the same purpose: the indexing of past speech to create a list of possible events for further research.

- **Period.** Events with a definitive lasting affect may define new eras, or periods, when the everyday realities and rules of the world change in definite ways. In Chapter 8, I investigate the use of statistics to understand the words that are most distinctive of certain decades, years, months, or days in parliament. These exercises raise important questions about what characterizes a period of change – is it a radical break from the past? What about gradual trends? In Chapter 10, I experiment with different quantitative models of change in order to further refine an approach to modeling how one period differs events in the relative past, testing the variety of ways that periodization can be formulated. I consider the problem of what "difference from the past" means – how significant or lasting need these signals of change be?

[7] David Hackett Fischer, *Historians' Fallacies* (New York: Harper & Row, 1970), 183.

I show how mathematical modeling can help us to compare many possible answers to periodization, and why it is useful to accept the plurality of models as potentially valid.

- **Influence.** This represents the modeling of "who changed what": it may be conceived of in the form of the book or individual most quoted or imitated, or the individual, event, or idea that had the power to change how everyone spoke, even if they used their own words. The actions people take in the present may or may not have a meaningful legacy for later actors. Or the legacy we leave may be so subtle as to be imperceptible for years, as with the writing of Emily Dickinson, ignored in her own time but celebrated after her death.

  In Chapter 9, I review some of the leading studies of influence and reconstruct some of them in a minimal example that leads to specific questions about what exactly these measures show and what they (potentially) suppress.

- **Memory.** This represents the working knowledge of the past as it changes from era to era, and as it is passed on through holidays, monuments, references, or anecdotes outside of the formal domain of historical research. In Chapter 6, I introduce the idea that historical events appear differently in the eyes of different viewers, and I draw on Koselleck's argument that the fact of public dissent about how to interpret an event like the storming of the US Capitol on January 6, 2021, reflects the fact that different constituencies have embraced different memories of American history. Memory, the popular reception of the past, differs from the analytic, comparative, and scholarly study of the facts of the past, which is history. In Chapter 8, I return to the scholarly discourse of memory, reviewing Astrid Erll's history of memory in modern culture, before proposing how tools like Named Entity Recognition and controlled vocabularies can help scholars to trace changing patterns of memory in the past.

Speaking of fundamental building blocks of historical analysis is an essential step in translating the concerns of historians into a language where statisticians and computer scientists can engage historical datasets in ways cogent and meaningful to historians. Emphasizing the unique values of historical analysis doesn't mean a "no" to quantification; rather, it is a plea for new forms of quantification that can help us trace the dimensions of these experienced realities.

Indeed, understanding the major building blocks of historical analysis means recognizing opportunities for the complex modeling of change in historical datasets, including modeling forms of change over time that depend upon the interworkings of many kinds of observations at once. Later case studies in this book profile only *one* fundamental of historical analysis at a time – that is, change to memory but not to influence. But scholars of the future may be able to build from validated studies to show how memory and influence interact. For instance, a hybrid quantitative-historian team might become interested in showing the interactions of memory and influence, and they might devise a project to investigate whether and when certain parliamentary speakers were able to use their mastery of the history of recent legislation to propel them to a leadership role. Advances in text mining for historical analysis will come as computer scientists devise tools to help historians to describe archive, change over time, event, period, influence, and memory.

Beyond the sheer wonder of it all, historical thinking has practical use. A journalist wishing to build a tool that measures how congressional debates have changed over the last decade might study the history of the debate, discovering rhetorical turning-points that explain why race is covered in a distinctly new way today. A citizen might appreciate a tool that told them whether their representative in Congress was more or less misogynistic than a decade ago. Companies might want to know *how* they are talked about on Twitter over the course of months, before seeking reasons for any shift in opinion. I myself might seek self-knowledge, and ask how the emotions contained in my emails have changed over the last decade, looking for moments when different tones come to the fore, drawn out by particular relationships and experiences. To organize a story about the events that made a person or an institution is to achieve familiarity with it.

The algorithmic analysis of the past might serve the public in many ways, including the demand for fact-based visualizations of history on demand. From one group's experiments with measuring influence, a watchdog group might build a tool for tracking proposed legislative bills, which could help citizens know when a particular bill was tied to the agenda of a corporate lobby or think tank and when, on the contrary, it had evolved from grassroots conversations detectable in the press or in online conversations. We can imagine another useful example in a news tracker that informs students about the most unusual developments in law, rather than the most canonical ones or the ones linked to influential figures. Whether such data-backed views of history are also *unbiased* is a more problematic question, one to which I will return in Chapter 7, when we consider whether different interpretations of historical events are valid.

A full list of possible experiments that data scientists could undertake with understanding time might include the analysis of influential personalities, the recovery of lost perspectives of ethnic and gender groups, and the analysis of changing concepts and influential stories. The point of proving these dimensions of temporal experience is not to exhaust them, but to notice that the angles of looking at the past are potentially much more varied than that applied by an analysis of "prediction" – even though prediction remains an important concept for describing the motivations for the analysis of the past in quantitative domains. When historians ask about "agency" or "cause and effect," they are probing into the dynamics of social and political relationships that have intrigued philosophers since Hume – a conversation that has been richly developed within the field of the history of philosophy. Where historical building blocks meet quantitative methods a vast arena opens up for experimentation in the data-driven examination and understanding of historical experience. We can treat problems that were once the subject of intuition as mathematical facts, and we can generalize and compare in ways that were once impossible – at least on the level of words in databases from the past – much as an unthinkably vast fishing net might be able to trawl an astonishing swath of the ocean.

To paraphrase this second precept: *the fundamentals of historical analysis reward inquiry.* As we shall see throughout this book, this is true for one major reason – because we are at a point where we can mathematize historical intuition. But as we engage the building blocks of historical analysis, we must take note: this precept in no way counteracts the dangers outlined earlier in this chapter, namely occluded archives, utopian fantasies, and dirty data. Disastrous modeling is still a very real concern and it can only be avoided if data scientists approach their datasets with historical context, a complex understanding of causation, and a profound engagement with the silences in the archive.

Precept #3: Critical Thinking Is Most Powerful When Applied to Each Part of the Research Process

Faced with imponderable archives, scholars need to use tools both to generalize and to narrow. Digital tools are primarily productive for *generalizing* about a corpus, although those generalizations take on a spiraling array of forms.

To understand the causal interactions of the past, even scholars who work with wordcount or quantitative measures typically pair their study of numbers with an equally deep engagement with historical context. Interpreting wordcount requires a deep reading of secondary sources, that is, the books and articles examining that period in history. In best practice, the scholar who uses wordcount is also tracking numbers back to individual texts where the word appears, checking that their surface interpretation of the changing profile of words holds up when they consult the original documents.[8]

By comparing multiple points of view and identifying the bias of each, the historian slowly arrives at a rich and nuanced understanding of an event, from a historian's perspective, as well as a deeper and more intricate sense of how multiple observers understood it when it was unfolding. The description typically includes a great deal of ambiguity – what was said and what it meant, through the eyes of people from diverse segments of an antiquated society. To say the least, the output of a good historical analysis is typically far more complex than a single point on a graph marking some discontinuity. Ultimately, these are not simply points on a graph, but rather the building blocks of a map of a parallel universe. These historical universes will often have extremely different reference points, rhetorical languages, and fundamental structures than our own and, in unpredictable ways, they may even have different cause and effect laws that drive the underlying dynamics of society.

Humanistic research increasingly operates on massive collections where the sheer volume of texts defies indexing by hand and results in an ever-greater reliance upon technologies such as topic modeling as an intermediary between the researcher and archival truth.[9] Scholars such as John Unsworth and Timothy Tangherlini have modeled the fit of the digital within the humanities by focusing on the tasks of collecting data and indexing the patterns to be found within that data.[10] As more researchers turn toward such technological intermediaries, certain agreements about the importance of critical awareness, the conventions of reviewing algorithm findings, and the documentation thereof become absolutely critical, if researchers in the humanities are to function as a community.

---

[8] For more on this best practice, and the use of Keywords in Context as a tool to enable alternation between wordcount and textual passages, see Luke Blaxill, *The War of Words: The Language of British Elections, 1880–1922* (Woodbridge: Boydell & Brewer, 2020), 41–43.

[9] Gheorghe Muresan and David J. Harper, "Topic Modeling for Mediated Access to Very Large Document Collections," *Journal of the American Society for Information Science and Technology* 55:10 (August 1, 2004): 892–910, https://doi.org/10.1002/asi.20034.

[10] John Unsworth, "Scholarly Primitives: What Methods Do Humanities Researchers Have in Common, and How Might Our Tools Reflect This?", in Symposium on "Humanities Computing: Formal Methods, Experimental Practice (King's College, London, May 13, 2000); Timothy R. Tangherlini, "The Folklore Macroscope: Challenges for a Computational Folkloristics," *Western Folklore*, 72: 1 (2013): 7–27.

Throughout this literature, authors have written complex profiles of particular tools. One can find countless journal articles in the digital humanities devoted to a close examination of a given digital toolkit – for example, Lauren Klein introduced the topic model along with the letters of Thomas Jefferson, and Funk and Mullen explained the analysis of textual reuse in the American legal code.[11]

Other authors have engaged particular datasets, since almost every textual dataset embodies its own idiosyncratic biases that can undercut analysis unless they are treated with care. For instance, the parliamentary records that are consulted in most of this book exclude women and the working class for most of the period I study. Meanwhile, the number of words per year explodes over the time period, meaning that raw counts are liable to offer a distortion (almost all numbers go up over the century, even if the words are unimportant). In Google Books, we find that the medical establishment is statistically overrepresented. US publishing networks bias the shape of the output of most nineteenth-century newspaper searches. In recent years, scholars have begun using quantitative methods to peer into what we might call the "hidden dimensions" of temporal change, resulting in an enormous proliferation of strategies, ranging in historical nuance and mathematical sophistication.[12] Any raw wordcount the scholar performs, therefore, is only the beginning of investigations of the relationship between any given textual corpus and temporal experience. It may be useful to put this into formal language: alongside the y-axis of count exist multiple possible z-dimensions that reflect, at minimum, the number of documents in the corpus, the number of working-class or female individuals represented in the corpus, the national origin of the voices represented in the corpus, and the degree to which the corpus represents particular overrepresented power networks.

---

[11] Klein, "The Image of Absence"; Kellen Funk and Lincoln A. Mullen, "The Spine of American Law: Digital Text Analysis and U.S. Legal Practice," *The American Historical Review* 123:1 (February 1, 2018): 132–64, https://doi.org/10.1093/ahr/123.1.132.

[12] For representation in parliament, see Ryan A. Vieira, *Time and Politics: Parliament and the Culture of Modernity in Nineteenth-Century Britain and the British World* (Oxford: Oxford University Press, 2015); for Google Books, see Eitan Adam Pechenick, Christopher M. Danforth, and Peter Sheridan Dodds, "Characterizing the Google Books Corpus: Strong Limits to Inferences of Socio-Cultural and Linguistic Evolution," *PLoS ONE* 10:10 (2015); for US and Australian newspapers, see Katherine Bode, "Fictional Systems," 100–38. I employ the phrase "hidden dimensions" here evocatively to suggest what can be measured by quantitative means but otherwise remain invisible to scholarship. There are certainly other "hidden" aspects of historical experience – including the life worlds of individuals in the past which only occasionally leave a relic on paper or through artifacts – which cannot be addressed by quantitative undertakings. Several studies of temporality attempt to excavate these life worlds, especially that by Michael D. Jackson, *The Varieties of Temporal Experience: Travels in Philosophical, Historical, and Ethnographic Time* (New York: Columbia University Press, 2018).

Data, however, is just the beginning of the problem. When text mining is at stake, there is no *right* algorithm or statistical method for understanding relationships. Every algorithm also encodes biases, however subtle. In the paragraphs below, we will describe two common methods and how each gathers its respective biases – first, modeling the domain of texts as a "galaxy" in which particular systems of affinity emerge, and second, as a "yardstick" with two opposing poles.

In galaxy-type analysis, affinities between texts are represented as clusters, which can be traced by tools such as k-means clustering or topic modeling. In such methods, the algorithm is designed to create *probable clusters* of documents that mirror human discourses of specified lengths, an approach that works especially well for those interested in the discursive nature of a corpus.[13] Humanistic scholars have identified topic modeling with the scholarly reading of "discourses," and defended its logic as compatible with scholarly projects in the humanities.[14] Tools that operate, for example, on the level of figures of speech, analyzing actual phrases or words that appear to cluster together, may be more useful for identifying a *rhetorical* match; they can help us identify similar ways of speaking about an issue, as opposed to a more strictly *substantive* match regarding particular subject fields.[15]

Clusters can be coaxed into generating knowledge of cultural change over time from a body of text. J. P. Cointet and Peter Bearman applied word co-occurrence to the State of the Union, using measures of relatedness to graph converging and diverging themes over time. Statistical analysis allowed them to draw out three major turning points in American history when the themes of presidential politics were vastly realigned. These preliminary measures of relatedness and change over time, in turn, have been rapidly built upon in other ways that suggest how quantitative measures may be used to detect larger patterns of continuity and discontinuity.

---

[13] Timothy R. Tangherlini and Peter Leonard, "Trawling in the Sea of the Great Unread: Sub-Corpus Topic Modeling and Humanities Research," *Poetics* 41:6 (2013): 725–49; Glenn Roe, Clovis Gladstone, and Robert Morrissey, "Discourses and Disciplines in the Enlightenment: Topic Modeling the French Encyclopédie," *Frontiers in Digital Humanities* 2 (2016), https://doi.org/10.3389/fdigh.2015.00008.

[14] Roe and Gladstone winnow the rhetorical from substantive by working only with the nouns in the *Encyclopedie*. Would this strategy work as well in a legal context, when verbs and adverbs govern a field of procedures? Roe et al., "Discourses and Disciplines in the Enlightenment."

[15] Jean-Philippe Cointet, Alix Rule, and Peter S. Bearman, "Lexical Shifts, Substantive Changes, and Continuity in State of the Union Discourse, 1790–2014," *PNAS (Proceedings of the National Academy of the Sciences"* 112:35 (August 10, 2015): 10837–44, https://doi.org/10.1073/pnas.1512221112.

A yardstick-type algorithm, in contrast to a galactic approach, simplifies the corpus according to a fundamentally different metaphor of abstraction. Yardstick-type analysis arranges documents according to their linear proximity to a given pole represented by another body of text – and by including measures from information theory, they impose a spectrum of order onto a corpus.[16] In many fields, *divergence measures* have served as a fundamental metric of difference, where "similarity" and "difference" is ranked by patterns of ordered similarity between two sets of documents. Divergence measures, which have their origins in code-breaking analysis during the Second World War, treat any two texts as a distribution of probabilities and arrive at an artificial number representing the distance, based upon a similar expression of the lexicon as a whole. The flexibility of creating a metric where none previously existed allows the scholar to make structural comparisons in domains where comparison was hitherto available solely on a qualitative basis. Distance measures have thus been used, in conjunction with word embeddings, to measure the likelihood that any given abolitionist newspaper editor was influenced by the earlier work of women abolitionists and editors of color.[17]

Yardsticks have been used, much like galaxies, as tools for approximating historical change over time. Simon DeDeo and his collaborators have used measures of "similarity to the past" and "similarity to the future" to analyze creativity and innovation in a variety of domains, including poetry, physics, and politics. The metric of similarity, in those studies, becomes a measure of cultural influence over a field.

From this brief glimpse, we can get a sense of the bewildering array of uses to which principles of grouping and separation can be put. The variety of examples at hand illustrates that the choice of algorithm does not necessarily determine the quality of the results. Algorithms group and measure, but the numbers and similarity or distance scores that result are applied in a process, the outcome of which is interpreted in terms of other abstractions – difference becomes "change" or "innovation."

---

[16] Alexander T. J. Barron et al., "Individuals, Institutions, and Innovation in the Debates of the French Revolution," *Proceedings of the National Academy of Sciences* 115:18 (May 1, 2018): 4607–12, https://doi.org/10.1073/pnas.1717729115; Sara Klingenstein, Tim Hitchcock, and Simon DeDeo, "The Civilizing Process in London's Old Bailey," *Proceedings of the National Academy of Sciences* 111: 26 (July 1, 2014): 9419–24, https://doi.org/10.1073/pnas.1405984111.

[17] Sandeep Soni, Lauren F. Klein, and Jacob Eisenstein, "Abolitionist Networks: Modeling Language Change in Nineteenth-Century Activist Newspapers," *Journal of Cultural Analytics* 1:2 (January 18, 2021), https://doi.org/10.22148/001c.18841.

Researchers also want to know that the insights provided by the digital tool can be verified in comparison with traditional means of learning about historical corpora. Before adopting new tools, readers first need to be confident that the abstraction associated with the algorithm in question is capable of providing novel insights that fit within a humanities framework – in other words, that a "topic" as quantifiably calculated from word frequency is relatively analogous to the historic "discourses" of communities of knowledge. Most digital history articles to date – including some that I myself have written – conform to this extremely reductive convention of proving that a single tool is useful for understanding the past: they are proof of concept articles. But that convention need not dominate how we publish about the humanities, and it should not reduce our capacities to think in methodologically broad and pluralistic ways about the past.

Researchers in history are also aware that algorithms come from somewhere – they have *histories*. When building, or simply using, an algorithm, we should consider how, as James Dobson has pointed out, an analyst may unwittingly recreate twentieth-century ontologies that group like with like in conceptual categories that can be traced back to the study of eugenics, thus possibly imposing uniformity of gender or race onto the data, when the data itself was characterized by heterogeneous difference and multiplicity.[18] The deeply rooted issues with bias don't simply evaporate by us brushing up on our reading before we start playing with algorithms. A critical perspective on algorithms as tools requires knowing something about the data in question, how the algorithm sorts similarity and distance, and whether there are any alternative versions of algorithms in usage by statisticians that might model the same classification with slightly different prejudices, producing a fresh vantage on the data. In later chapters, I will model a critical research practice by explaining some of the very different results in terms of data that can result from minor adjustments to algorithms. Each mathematical model – even mathematical models that are very similar in composition and intent – produces a different perspective on what historical changes are important, given the same data. A skilled analyst can exploit these differences to produce a more sensitive and nuanced view on historical change over time, but not without first becoming aware about the prejudices attached to each mathematical model.

---

[18] See "The Cultural Significance of K-Nn," in James E. Dobson, *Critical Digital Humanities: The Search for a Methodology* (Urbana, IL: University of Illinois Press, 2019), ch. 4, https://search.ebscohost.com/login.aspx?direct=true&scope=site&db=nlebk&db=nlabk&AN=2098303.

Most of the discussion of algorithms in this book introduces them through summaries of case studies in the digital humanities and sometimes from the presentation of original research. Algorithms come to the fore at three precise points, all of them in the second half of the book, where I will introduce three algorithms in detail: triples analysis (Chapter 7), tf-idf (Chapter 8), and divergence measures (Chapter 9). In each case, I will treat the history of the algorithm, the kind of knowledge it was designed to produce, how it has been used by other scholars, how it can be applied to reveal the dynamics of change over time, how its parameters are adjusted and with what consequences, and what potential forms of bias it contains. The discussions of each algorithm become detailed on the topic of mathematics only for a few paragraphs, which are designed to be read by nonspecialists, but can also be skipped by students of the humanities who are looking for a more cursory acquaintance with the methods and their practical uses.

This book examines what happens as scholars move between questions, tools, texts, and provisional answers. This emphasis on the praxis of investigation marks an adjustment from the strategy typically laid out in journal articles about digital history, the proof of concept article that recommends a single tool for abstracting knowledge. This way of thinking about digital corpora reflects an almost intractable convention in even the best peer-reviewed journals – a convention that, in so many words, presents our working models as ostensible truths, a convention that is fundamentally at odds with more sophisticated historical practice.

Throughout the experiments presented in this book, we will develop a set of ideas about the process of iteratively contemplating the fit between data and analysis that I call "critical search." Critical search is more than just a button we keep pushing until we get results; rather, it's a flexible and extensible set of guidelines for contemplating and bridging the expanse between humanistic thinking and algorithms. Critical search calls for critical thinking at every stage of analysis: in the choice of data, the cleaning of data, the choice of data model, the variety of algorithm, and the reading and interpretation of results. It suggests that the best work with data is by its nature iterative – it cross-checks results by comparing more than one modeling approach and applying several algorithms for each approach.

As an example of how the building blocks of historical analysis make room for future directions in computational research, we might consider a pair of experiments that ask about relationships to temporal change in a very vague way (see Figure 2.2). These charts are inspired by the work of

(a)

(b)

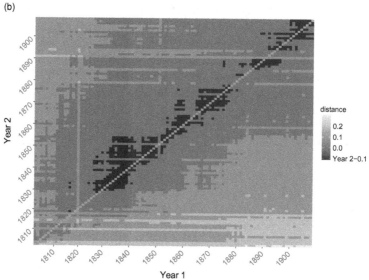

Figure 2.2   Graphs in need of further investigation.
a. How much did each individual year anticipate the future 15−20 years. The highlighted
dot represents the year whose speeches least resembled the lexicon of speeches of 15−20
years in the future according to this measure.
b. Distance between years, measured from Year 1 to Year 2.

two practitioners of hybrid research who have done a great deal to advance my thinking – informatics scholar Simon DeDeo and computationalist Jean-Philippe Cointet. Both DeDeo and Cointet worked in hybrid teams with historians or social scientists who were curious about what scholarship could discover by applying mathematical formulae to measure the raw change of discourse from one year to the next. Later in this book, I will talk about their experiments in greater detail.

For now, let me explain my naïve replication of their studies, intentionally drawing out the promise and limits of measuring "aggregate change over time" as an approach. The subject of both analyses are the parliamentary debates of Great Britain, 1806–1911. Both diagrams in Figure 2.2 use a mathematical measure, "distance" (whose opposite is "similarity," a measure explained in greater detail in Chapter 9 of this book), to compare change to language over time at its most abstract. In theory, both should be able to tell us when the most dramatic breaks of the century occurred.

Figure 2.2a treats one year of parliamentary speech at a time. In this figure, the *x*-axis is the year, and the *y*-axis is distance, the abstract measurement of difference between one year of parliamentary speeches and the complete set of speeches from previous years. If, in a single year, exactly the same subjects were debated as those that had been previously debated, in figures of speech that overlapped with things said previously in parliament, distance for that year would be zero. If wildly new subjects of debate and idioms of speech were introduced in a new year, a complete outburst of novelty, distance would be very high. The diagram suggests that 1820 was the year when speeches in the British parliamentary debates that *least resembled the* future, given a 15- to 20-year window of change. In other words, the changes from 1835 to 1840 would be so dramatic that speakers in 1820 could have little anticipated them – a ruling that makes sense if we consider that, in 1832, the makeup of Britain's parliament was expanded from an aristocratic institution to a middle-class institution. Figure 2.2a also shows a large gray dot highlighting the absolute minimum measurement detected for the dotted "distance from the future," which occurs for the year 1834. The figure suggests that it was in 1832 that the "distance to the future" was at its all-time low for the century – in other words, what was said in 1832 was most like what was said in 1847–1852.

Figure 2.2b treats abstract change over time by measuring each year's speeches in relationship to both relative past and relative future. The *x*-axis is a timeline of years, 1806–1911. The *y*-axis shows the same timeline. The heatmap ranges from pale to dark, where pale represents high distance and dark represents low distance. The resulting heatmap defines each year–year relationship: in the lower right-hand corner, we see a pale patch that indicates that the language used in parliament in 1806–09 was very different from the language used in parliament after the 1870s. Dark triangles spanning 1830 to 1850 suggest that very little changed in what parliament debated or what words it used during this period. Lighter lines suggest moments of innovation in language – for instance, the horizontal discontinuity around 1890–93 and the vertical one around 1820.[19]

The graphs in 2.2a and 2.2b represent attempts to probe and to build upon the significance of sophisticated historical inquiries by colleagues who worked in hybrid labs. DeDeo and Cointet used divergence to measure change in *topic*, a clustering algorithm designed to pick up rhetorical shifts, which has a mixed record when used as a proxy for discourses. To deliberately test the work of statistics by making my data as transparently as possible, I apply divergence to measure not topic but merely lexicon, that is, the set of words used in each year. The goal of this move was to place us on firmer footing when measuring words, as we can trace back a signal of change to individual words at a particular time. From a measurement of the change of lexicon over time, it should be relatively simple to move from the abstract measure of "change" to an index of which words were changing. Once we have a sense of those individual words whose changing probabilities over time are the basis for the computer's measurement, it becomes easier to argue for or against a particular visualization. In other words, the scholar can then "validate" the method of abstract measurement, showing how it works in terms familiar to historians as practitioners. In Chapters 10 and 11, I will explain the results of using similarity measurements to trace a computational measure of aggregate change back to individual words.

The Dangerous Art of Text Mining is designed as a long investigation into a series of experiments that might move the incomplete graphs in Figures 2.2a and 2.2b into more robust inquiries – inspired by critical questions about how far each measure accurately meets an interest in the building blocks of historical inquiry.

The process begins with transparent models of data – in this case, words, not topics. The process then moves to validate how the simple model of change over time works, tracking back the data model to individual words. In another stage still, a researcher might move from the individual words back to mentions of words in the text. In Chapter 4,

---

[19] Cointet et al, "Lexical Shifts."

I will talk about the advantages of a formalized process for slowly validating models and interpreting their results, and I will forward my own ideal model of such a process, which I call "critical search."

For now, I begin my discussion with an incomplete graph, rather than a graph and its interpretation, to underscore the fact that data science applied to historical experience often raises more questions than it answers. We may start with mathematical models of history, but we need to test the alignment between those models and our questions about the past to arrive at useful findings about the past.

Incomplete graphs can, nevertheless, inspire preliminary questions about where we might push the data if we're motivated to engage the fundamentals of historical inquiry. Data has *something* to tell us about events and periods – the problem is understanding how one could build inferences from the discontinuities charged in the two incomplete graphs. Some of the discontinuities portrayed in the visualizations are highly suggestive to those familiar with the history of the parliament, where acts of 1832, 1867, and 1884 broadened who could vote from a tiny, moneyed minority to the middle class and, later, to the working class and to rural laborers. But the timing of the discontinuities in question doesn't match exactly what a historian might anticipate; it isn't a mirror for these three known dates.

To know what to make of Figure 2.2b, we'd want to ask many questions of the data. Upon the basis of which words has the computer determined certain moments of change? Are the words whose usage changed substantive terms like "labor" or "cotton," or abstract words such as "capitalism," or rhetorical words for addressing members of parliament, like "lordship"? From what years does each horizon of difference date? Is high distance assigned to 1884 an expression of change from a period of relatively banal language in 1875, or does it represent a high-water mark of innovative speech overall in the whole period since 1806? A serious process of reflection on the meaning of the charts would require us to determine whether a different algorithm would have returned different words. We would want to look into the significance of the fact that the algorithm employed – the Kullback–Leibler divergence measure – was "asymmetrical," meaning that the measure applied from 1820 to 1821 produces a different number when the years are fed to the algorithm in reverse order, with 1821 before 1820. We'd want to talk to mathematicians and historians to determine if "asymmetrical" measurements are an appropriate proxy for modeling historical change. We would want to determine whether these results are meaningful when traced down to particular words. Finally, we would submit the analysis to common sense and historical understanding, asking questions that challenge the narrative – for instance, whether the measure of 1820 was thrown off by a particularly flamboyant speaker, or by typographical errors in the machine reading of the text.

I will not answer these questions directly – at least not here. I am describing, as I will throughout this book, some of the dead-ends of my research in the process of explaining how I navigated from merely copying the work produced in nearby disciplines to selecting those avenues of research that would pass muster under the critical eye of my fellow historians. Those dead-ends of my research process may yield to others in time, with greater attention to the issues of transparency and the "fit" between domain knowledge in history and mathematical modeling.

My point is that the process of aligning the methods of data science and history is difficult work, where the scholar must often probe diligently in order to progress in a profitable direction. In its raw state, a figure like Figure 2.2 is hardly sufficient for historical interpretation. To become useful, the figure and the process that produced it must both be pulled apart and reexamined as independent projects of smaller analyses which divide up the abstraction "distance" into more familiar components: the shifting use of words, relative horizons of change. As it stands, the diagrams in Figure 2.2 might serve us for the purpose of creating a list of twenty other calculations we would like to make. But we affix meaning to the discontinuities represented in the graph with caution. We don't really know what they mean – not yet.

One of the theses of this book is that meaningful data analysis for understanding change to human institutions requires iterative engagement with the data. Applying an algorithm out of the box is almost never sufficient to produce a meaningful analysis. In later chapters, we will explore the kind of creative process in which hybrid knowledge generates a series of analyses, each leading to more specific knowledge of change over time.

Finding a tipping point in the past, and understanding what it means, might not seem as glamorous as a research project premised upon cracking the stock market. But any new science of text analysis that comes into being will be underwritten by tools for understanding historical experience, such as the ones suggested in this book – influence detectors, watershed detection algorithms, tracers of memory trails, periodization maps, and trend. Future knowledge of text will have to be premised on respect for the study of the archive, because understanding archives precisely and deeply is the domain where careful study of text begins.

Consider another minimal experiment: a basic exercise in finding out something about history, which uses one of the fundamental tools of the digital humanities, a "distance" measurement, to make an educated guess about the course of history over time.

Without going into either the math or the historical question in detail – both will be taken up in later chapters – consider the curious fact: if we switch out three very similar algorithms or formulae for measuring history, we get three very different timelines providing three totally different answers to the question: "When did the event in question happen?" Figure 2.3 shows how three different measures give three different answers to the question: When did parliament debate property during the nineteenth century?

In the visualizations in Figure 2.3, each of which represents the answer to the same question about *when* a revolution in property law occurred, we can, as I've said, see the basic problem that arises for critical analysis: when we try out the three algorithms in question, we get three different results.

The point of this thought experiment is to prove that magic measures, while useful, are only as helpful as the interpretation we can provide of what those magic numbers mean. Critical thinking dictates that we should not accept any single abstract and quantitative answer as final until we have compared different possible measures and their meanings.

In the coming chapters, we will see how critical thinking and computational methods can work together to unpack the problem of interpretation. The approach that I call "critical search" suggests that researchers whose problems involve texts keep revisiting a set of simple questions that strike at the root of the inquiry and illuminate when data about text is interpretable: "Does this algorithm fit my data and my question? Would it be contradicted, or confirmed, by other equally sound algorithms? And if these algorithms produced clear results, would they be credible, far-reaching, replicable, and definitive?"

It is possible to apply a critical lens to the output of any measurement process and to think carefully about whether the results are meaningful in that form, or whether another use of the same process could represent a more legitimate use of the data. As we have seen in this short example, grappling with the results of algorithmic processes, when applied to text and historical questions, doesn't produce a simple answer. Even if we've distilled human relationships or timelines to something as simple as a measure of "distance," that distance metric still has to be interpreted with the same care that we would apply to Rousseau or to the events of the French Revolution.

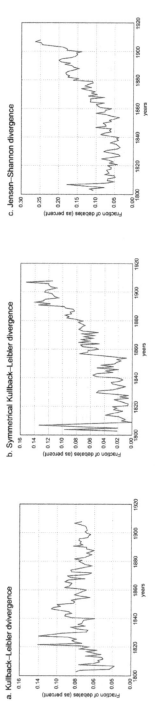

Figure 2.3 Graphs that disagree. The histograms give the number of parliamentary debates classified as the 1% most similar to the Seed Corpus. The *x*-axis gives the year (1800–1910); the *y*-axis gives the fraction of all debates that were classed as 1% most similar to the Seed Corpus within that year. Data analysis and visualizations by Ashley Lee. Previously published in Jo Guldi, "Critical Search," *Cultural Analytics* (2018).

86

The process of critical search works against the pressure of "prediction" and hasty knowledge by folding interpretive questions back into the process of creating knowledge with quantitative approaches. We must not mistake mere mathematization or numbers alone as evidence that this process of critical inquiry is complete. A critical search process isn't finished until we have looked under the hood of each algorithm, each choice about preprocessing the data, each date, and each item in the controlled vocabulary to understand how those choices tilt the results in a certain direction. Through a rigorous process of comparison, real knowledge of relationships and history become possible and the knowledge that is generated can be made more trustworthy.

Precept #4: Discovery Happens Where Old Fields Meet

As the foregoing sections have suggested, we are entering an era in which more and more quantitative algorithms are being developed under influence of the humanist predisposition for understanding the experiential aspects of historical change.

One of the most compelling teams of digital humanists working today is the Lab for Social Minds, run by Simon DeDeo at Carnegie Mellon University, whose algorithmic inquiries into human interactions such as "playfulness," "innovation," "disruption," and "influence" we will inspect in detail anon. DeDeo's team worked to train algorithms to calculate the most "innovative" thinkers in both physics and poetry, as calculated by their playful capacity to take on new topics unexplored by their teachers.[20] Their computations create a new metric that allows the team to make arguments about the structural neglect of underrecognized innovators in each field. Nuanced distinctions about how we model newness – whether conceived of as "playfulness," "innovation" or "modernity" – are newly important because the race to model *change over time* on the basis of textual data has begun in earnest.

One of the strengths of the Lab for Social Minds is that its work routinely involves interdisciplinary teams whose members hail from fields as diverse as literature, history, religious studies, physics, and mathematics. These interdisciplinary composition of these teams means that they have rigorously inspected the abstractions for which they are searching, and the

---

[20] See unpublished talk: Simon DeDeo, "The Data Science of Play," Alan Turing Institute www .youtube.com/watch?v=6v5zCblrCLw. DeDeo references an unpublished paper on *Poetry* magazine by Jenny Huang, previously an undergraduate student at Indiana University, where the Lab for Social Minds began; he also references applications of the same algorithm to papers in physics and fan fiction.

ethnography of the data upon which they work, before beginning quantitative analysis. But that care is not always the rule.

Clear thinking from the liberal arts is important, in part, because the understanding of change over time that is taught in business schools – and amplified in the culture of Silicon Valley – is colored with an ideological bias that tends to see any form of innovation as automatically desirable. In a series of *New Yorker* articles, Jill Lepore has organized a thoughtful and sustained critique of "disruption" as a way of thinking that discards, out of hand, most of the historical context that humanists have found essential when modeling causation In Lepore's estimation, when divorced from careful observation of the past, prediction mostly operates at best as a sleight of hand whereby bad or incomplete data about the past masquerades as a telescope onto the future, with no inconvenient witnesses who can directly contradict it. As Lepore writes in the *New Yorker*:

> The eighteenth century embraced the idea of progress; the nineteenth century had evolution; the twentieth century had growth and then innovation. Our era has disruption, which, despite its futurism, is atavistic. It's a theory of history founded on a profound anxiety about financial collapse, an apocalyptic fear of global devastation, and shaky evidence. ... Disruptive innovation as a theory of change is meant to serve both as a chronicle of the past (this has happened) and as a model for the future (it will keep happening). The strength of a prediction made from a model depends on the quality of the historical evidence and on the reliability of the methods used to gather and interpret it. Historical analysis proceeds from certain conditions regarding proof. None of these conditions have been met.[21]

At the heart of Lepore's argument is a respect for the *nuances* of change, in contrast with an ideologically driven category of "disruption" that classes all change as potential progress, the more the better, even if it destroys ancient or important institutions – for example, the defunding of arts and humanities subjects in public schools.

Lepore's critique is essentially that business school ideology has produced a distorted data science of human behavior that is detached from reality. "Innovation," she reminds us, is just one flavor of (detectable and measurable) change among many. Lepore is lobbying for a study of change

---

[21] Jill Lepore, "What the Gospel of Innovation Gets Wrong," *New Yorker* (June 16, 2014), www .newyorker.com/magazine/2014/06/23/the-disruption-machine. Lepore's insights caused Christensen to fundamentally revisit the use of historical evidence in his theory: Clayton M. Christensen, Michael E. Raynor, and Rory McDonald, "What Is Disruptive Innovation?" *Harvard Business Review* (December 1, 2015), https://hbr.org/2015/12/what-is-disruptive-innovation; "Clayton Christensen Moves on from the Dissing of Disruption," *Financial Times* (October 3, 2016), www.ft.com/content/46bab022-83f7-11e6-a29c-6e7d9515ad15

that models different categories of experience, and change whose nature takes the appearance of a different quality or of different intensity depending on who observes it. Another name for this rich model of change over time that Lepore invokes, of course, is the study of history.

The surest path to a richer definition of historical change is that which begins with a deeper conversation with experts on historical change, that is, with the humanists and social scientists who have reflected on the protests of eighteenth-century peasants alongside the ideas of French parliamentarians and the works of art produced by famous painters. Over recent decades, theorists of change in the humanities and social sciences have plumbed the question of whose actions *made* the French Revolution: Bureaucrats like Turgot? Philosophers like Rousseau? Or peasants in Brittany? Over the course of the twentieth century, complex questions about agency arose as historians have revisited questions of this sort, motivated by the example of more recent events in Russia, China, and Mexico. Their answers have varied enormously, but together scholars began a larger conversation that weighed available evidence on conversation with theories of agency and collective action, now and in the past. Scholars carefully considered such nuances as whether a peasant living before the French Revolution *could* have considered themselves an actor in a collective revolution in the same way as did a Russian worker in the age of Lenin, who had access to Marx's historical philosophy of a proletariat revolution.[22] Every peasant petition is held up as the possible source that inspired Rousseau to draft an examination of the nature of liberty.

If we reject the business school fascination with "innovation," a richer data science might be capable of mirroring disagreement, dispute, and the genesis of new ideas (to name only a few of the thousands of humanistic subjects of inquiry that present alternatives). A reality-based data science would necessarily entail training algorithms to learn about the intention of speakers and writers, to map their influence upon one another, but also patterns of dissent, difference, and the contestation of the civic good. As we shall see later in this book, influence and dissent are both criteria that are yielding to quantitative analysis today. But they are also themes that fill books on the theory of history and the richness of those volumes should push us beyond too comfortable an embrace of any one metric for assessing the roots and potentialities of change.

---

[22] William H. Sewell, "Three Temporalities: Towards an Eventful Sociology," in Terrence J. McDonald, ed., *The Historic Turn in the Human Sciences* (Ann Arbor, MI: University of Michigan Press, 1996), 245–80.

We are apt to get only *thin* characterizations of change from an analysis that reduces all forms of new information – confusing or illuminating – into the same category of, for example, "disruption." The alternative to thin forms of organizing data is what we might call a "critical" analysis, a way of looking at the past that considers the multiple forces of a shifting past, the silenced voices in the archives, and the limited capacity of any one dataset to tell the whole story.

There is a real power lying dormant within the studies in innovation and play cited above, but it can only be unleashed when analysts begin to utilize the algorithms of temporal analysis in conjunction with expert studies from disciplines that have a broader perspective on change.

In one meeting, a group of highly interdisciplinary digital humanists were asked to explain what made their pattern of interdisciplinary inquiry success-ful. Many speakers emphasized the importance of consulting with "domain experts" and apprehending the "concepts" that can elucidate a data-driven study. They emphasized that returning to domain experts' concepts at each stage in the research process tends to produce a more robust encounter with data. They also emphasized the importance of researchers' rigorously and critically subjecting their results to analysis by domain experts – even if the domain experts rejected out of hand the worth of the conclusions at stake. Far from naïve data analytics, where the goal is to produce quick results, the agenda of a truly scientific investigation is to borrow from traditional disci-plines in order to deepen our apprehension of reality itself.[23] The goal is to bridge the chasms between departments by encouraging them to working through the problem sets of data science with curiosity in such a way that takes advantage of disciplinary expertise that reckons with human experience, distortion, truth, and change, in all their complications.

Today, interdisciplinary expertise is at the heart of something like a revolution in measuring human behavior over time. Diverse, multidisci-plinary teamwork is a major characteristic of some of the most accom-plished work in this domain. Consider two recent headlines from the world of digital history:

A mathematician predicts future behavior given reading habits

> "Prediction" as a species of accurate history has recently become a theme of study in mathematics. A longtime collaborator with scholars of religion, folklore, and history, mathematician Kristoffer Nielbo has been applying algorithms to trace the dynamics of cultural change on a microlevel in

---

[23] Dong Nguyen et al., "How We Do Things with Words: Analyzing Text as Social and Cultural Data," *Frontiers in Artificial Intelligence* 3 (2020): 1–14.

online communities. Studying conversations on the social media site *Reddit*, Nielbo has observed that some communities take on new topics and keywords more rapidly, and found that one can predict that those communities will continue to amass new topics. He speculates, however, that communities that digest the same subjects of knowledge for a long time may also be those that develop greater cohesion, understanding, and insight in the long run.[24] Using a computer to classify different community styles of learning, in other words, offers a tool to "predict" what those communities will do in the future.

A historian, mathematician, and physicist test the influence of advertisement on articles

In another experiment, a historian of advertising and a physicist teamed up with a mathematician to uncover the logic of causality over historical timescales. With billions of newspaper archives at their disposal, they began to track mentions of words in newspaper advertisements and articles. They trained their algorithms to answer a simple question: When did language appear first in an advertisement and later in articles? The team has borrowed an algorithm from economics – the measure of *Grainger causality,* which can be used to answer the question: Does a given vector of information increase the likelihood of predicting the values of a second vector of information? They were able to categorize one group of commodities where advertisements predict articles, and another group where journalistic articles precede a later wave of commodity advertising.[25]

Headlines such as these demonstrate that something new is afoot. Alongside the experimentation of the Lab for Social Minds discussed above, both experiments suggest the shape of unprecedented levels of interdisciplinary collaboration in the design of a research laboratory. All three experiments followed upon years of building structured opportunities for hybrid thinking, where graduate students from different backgrounds were purposefully assembled, or a historian was embedded within a group of computer scientists during an extended postdoctoral fellowship. For their construction and interpretation, all three experiments required not only fluency with algorithms, but also some understanding of

---

[24] Kristoffer Laggard Nielbo, Peter Bjerregaard Vahlstrup, and Anja Bechmann, "Sociocultural Trend Signatures in Minimal Persistence and Past Novelty," DH2020: Carrefours/Intersections (University of Ottawa and Carleton University, 2020) https://pure.au.dk/portal/en/persons/kristoffer-laigaard-nielbo(aef8887c-d4e9-4270-9031-1a15553f5590)/publications/sociocultural-trend-signatures-in-minimal-persistence-and-past-novelty(9733aa40-d81d-4ded-ae74-cb493e5a8d97).html

[25] Melvin Wevers, Jianbo Gao, and Kristoffer L Nielbo, "Tracking the Consumption Junction: Temporal Dependencies between Articles and Advertisements in Dutch Newspapers" (March 2019), unpublished manuscript, https://hal.archives-ouvertes.fr/hal-02076512.

the dynamics of humanistic questions regarding causality, influence, and social groups. Their success – as thought experiments in the language of computer code that substantially transformed how we look at complex issues in the humanities – suggests a burning need for an interdisciplinary matrix within the university of a kind that has hitherto only been the subject of experimentation at a handful of institutions.

It will have occurred to some readers already that I am using the term "hybrid" in this book in a sense in which other authors might use a more familiar term such as "interdisciplinarity." I prefer hybrid as a description because it is more specific to the kind of aliveness, the ongoing exchanges, that I have in mind as the basis for the genesis of a new field. Hybrid is a term with an agricultural background. It suggests a living synthesis of two living traditions. Interdisciplinarity is too general for what I'm getting at. I can be interdisciplinary in solitude, reading books on art history and writing the ideas into my paper on history. But hybrid teams require ongoing support and thinking between people trained in, and who identify as members of far-flung disciplines. The hybridity of their conversation may come in the coauthorship of papers, or the cosupervision of teams, or in ongoing conversations about the nature of the fields and how they can work together. I look to hybrid teams because those hybrid teams have been responsible for many of the grandest innovations in the space of text mining for historical analysis.

It is also true that individuals who have grown up on hybrid teams have gone on to perform work on their own. I myself began my digital humanities work collaborating with staff data scientists at the Brown Data Science Institute, before collaborating with graduate students from Statistics and Engineering at Southern Methodist University, all the while in conversations with highly respected colleagues at departments of Informatics and Computer Science. More recently, I began to code myself, but my coding – as well as the modeling of how to fit algorithms with data – still requires frequent checking in with colleagues and students. I make no claim to perfection in the models on display here, nor to their execution; they are contributors to an ongoing dialogue. The strength of a field of knowledge, particularly one in development, rests on no single practitioner and no single article, but in all of the rich exchanges.

Hybrid knowledge, in this sense, is not exactly a new concept. In *Figuring* (2021), the writer Maria Popova gives a history of women mathematicians and scientists from the eighteenth through the twentieth centuries. She makes the case that Ada Lovelace was an early initiator of hybrid forms of knowledge, having inherited poetic passions from her father, Lord Byron, as well as an aptitude for calculation from her mathematical mother, Annabella Byron, a gift that was nurtured by tutoring at an early age by the distinguished mathematician Maria Somerville, the popularizer of the French scholar Pierre-Simon Laplace in the English-speaking world. As a teenager, Lovelace would protest against her mother's exclusion of poetry from her logic-based education, arguing the case of "poetical philosophy" or "philosophical poetry."[26] Lovelace's experiments with the hybridization of existing fields sprouted from the aristocratic salon culture cultivated by her mother, where poets and mathematicians rubbed shoulders (even after the exile of Lovelace's poet father). Popova sketches a suppressed tradition of hybrid knowledge – typically occupied by female mathematicians, but often taken up by male writers as well – where mathematics and astronomy became tools for understanding passion, poetry, sexuality, and identity.

Reducing dimensions of historical change to an equation may seem strike some readers as inherently flawed, a crass and implausible abbreviation. Not so long ago, however, Augustus De Morgan, a British mathematician and logician known for a rigorous science of mathematical induction, conceived of probability mainly in terms of *feeling* – that is, the *feelings about our personal or collective future* that evolve from close examination of our personal or collective past. "The word *probable*," wrote De Morgan in 1836, "as commonly applied to a coming event, indicates many different degrees of that feeling with which the mind looks at the prospects of the future, and which depends upon the habits derived from looking at the past."[27] The historian of mathematics, Joan Richards, began meditating on De Morgan's ideas about probability in the year during which her nine-year-old son developed a brain tumor. De Morgan's professed belief, that we are all literally gamblers with fate and time, resonated with Richards as she waited to hear the results of test after test, which seemed likely, each time, to seal the fate of her family.

The mathematics of description can be wrapped around any human experience, from the ephemeral dimension of human emotion to those experiences that are easily quantified. According to De Morgan – one of the key architects of modern probability theory – mathematics should estimate the future through a rich approach to the past, wherein emotion

---

[26] Maria Popova, *Figuring* (New York: Penguin, 2020).
[27] Joan L. Richards, *Angles of Reflection: Logic and a Mother's Love* (New York: Henry Hold, 2001), 18.

and memory count among the descriptors of the past upon which future calculations are based. Probability, therefore, should aspire to become a study of history.

Today, the realm of text mining, where digital humanists consort with mathematicians, has become again an arena where the traditions of imagination and quantification dance together freely. Critical studies in gender and sexuality can be modeled mathematically; the famous Bechdel test of how women's relationships are represented in fiction, for instance, has been quantified by one team of researchers who used grammatical relationships to identify how many scenes in modern novels involved women talking to other women, in comparison with women talking to a man or men.[28]

Such hybrid forms of thought as these have given us the opportunity to leave the realm of fantasy – where one only dreams about patterns that may be found one day – and to enter the realm of *specificity*. The resulting processes offer tools for specifying and clarifying what we know about cultural change over time, about how ideas originate and how they cross-fertilize, which individuals or groups in a culture are responsible for *innovation* or *playfulness,* and perhaps how dissenting groups contribute to a democratic process. Such metrics allows us to rigorously test and challenge generalizations about the past held by previous generations of historians, as digital historian Luke Blaxill does in his detailed review of how wordcount bears up against political historians of British electoral politics in the 1880s.[29] And with such tools, the digital humanities – even in their more realistic form – promise a rich trove of questions of interest to political, cultural, and social theory that become quantifiable and newly objective.

The teams of physicists, mathematicians, and literary scholars sketched here have not exhausted interdisciplinary inquiry. Indeed, they may have barely cracked a domain of reasoning as potentially vast as the traditional humanities, with its broad concern for understanding the essence of consensus and dissent, change over time, and the construction and effectivity of gender, race, and class. All that is required to pursue this new realm is a modest humility before multiple forms of expertise.

---

[28] Eve Kraicer and Andrew Piper, "Social Characters: The Hierarchy of Gender in Contemporary English-Language Fiction," *Journal of Cultural Analytics*, 2019, https://doi.org/10.22148/16.032.

[29] Luke Blaxill, *The War of Words: The Language of British Elections, 1880–1922* (Woodbridge: Boydell & Brewer, 2020).

Table 2.2 *Shibboleths that divide communities from talking about past experience.*

Prediction
Laws of Historical Change
Future Performance
New Data
Test and Training Data
Sampling Data

Precept #5: Shibboleths Mark Out Contested Areas of Practice Where Interdisciplinary Work Must Proceed with Care

The data scientist, thirsty for reward on his investment, springs up at the mention of this exciting new research technology. He is asking a question familiar in business school: "Can computers predict the future?" His friend, the humanist, is already shaking his head, suspecting that abstraction fueled by desire for profit will only produce a distorted mirror of reality.

The word "prediction" is a shibboleth: it sends quantitative practitioners and aspirants for profit in one direction and humanists and scholars concerned with the ethical dilemmas of the present in another.[30] "Prediction" cleaves the community of knowledge into two halves, each of which can only think with half a brain.

If computationalists are to generate useful generalizations about human experience on the basis of data about the past, they must work with historians towards the establishment of trustworthy, transparent models of data that respect historians' carefully honed rules of interpretation of the past. Hybrid knowledge advances by discovering common touchstones. But the reverse of common touchstones for analysis are shibboleths – words that divide communities. In Table 2.2, I give a list of common terms used by data scientists that form a barrier to entry to the extent that it is nearly impossible to marry these terms to historical practice.

---

[30] Leo Breiman has noted that predictive models began to dominate statistical modeling 30 years ago. See Leo Breiman, "Statistical Modeling: The Two Cultures," *Statistical Science* 16:3 (2001): 199–231. For a critique of predictive modeling, see Matthew L. Jones, "How We Became Instrumentalists Again: Data Positivism Since World War II," *Historical Studies in the Natural Sciences* 48:5 (2018): 673–84.

Consider the case of "new data" and its near cousins, "future perfor-mance" and the dividing of data into "test" sets and "training" sets. Why the division of test and training data? The explanation is often given that we want the algorithm to "learn" about data. Implicit in this arrangement is the assumption that algorithms will be used, even as the Google Search algorithm is used, on *new data*. The data scientists who devise a test algorithm today cannot assume that the users of the future will be search-ing the same terms; they want their algorithm to work, no matter what new words emerge in the English language to describe new music genres, identities, or political events. They are interested, therefore, in *future performance*. In the world where data science serves the search engine, the presupposition of *new data* makes perfect sense, and *test* and *training* sets are useful to the degree that they enable a search engine to index as yet unknown shifts in human behavior.

But in history, the phrase "new data" suggests something else entirely. A new archaeological site may reveal a decomposing body that gives us insight into neolithic burial practice, and every few years a new trove of manuscripts appears in every field, subtly enhancing the collection of knowledge. But it is highly unlikely that archivists will reveal an entirely new corpus of novels by Charles Dickens about which scholars did not previously know. It is simply impossible that a new set of parliamentary debates will emerge for the nineteenth century in Great Britain. The nature of history is that the archive is *closed;* revisions to the dataset will be minor. Historians are therefore less interested in the ability of an algorithm to anticipate the patterns in *new datasets* that have not previously been viewed. More relevant are algorithms that deliver surprising findings about the datasets we already have. Because computer science and history evolved working on different sets of data, with different clients, using separate traditions of knowledge-making, many of the assumptions that seem obvious to computationalists may strike historians as naïve.

At best, shibboleths merely seem silly to one part of a hybrid team, and recognizing the shibboleths affords an opportunity for understanding how different audiences may react to research articles. Test and training may describe the computationalist's preferred way of modeling experimentation, interpretation, and insight. But the historian has other ways of describing insight – usually in terms of a detailed narrative of difference from previous historians. A team of researchers can be agnostic about how insight is described, producing quantitative measures of success for computational audiences and discursive descriptions of success for humanist audiences.

At worst, however, computationalist language may introduce unneces-sary noise and even bias into a research process. Here, consider again the shibboleth "prediction." Many computationalists today assume that algorithms that "predict" knowledge are a first step in approximating expert domain knowledge from disciplines outside computer science. Yet among historians, the term "predict" suggests a violation of the fundamental principle of the study of history: the fact that we live in a present, and that we have certain knowledge, through documents and other artifacts, about events in the past – but that we can never have the same certainty about the future. To claim that work on a dataset of congressional debates will help us "predict" the future will strike many historians as a willful violation of the laws of logic and chronology; we can only know as fact the data about the past, and we therefore leave the realm of science when we try to describe facts that don't yet exist. A research project designed around prediction will therefore alienate most historians.

Even worse would be a project that used machine learning to generate "fake" history. Machine learning experts and digital humanists have long experimented with using computers to write alternative Shakespearean sonnets in iambic pentameter. Imagine that GPT-3 or another machine learning algorithm was employed to "predict" an alternative future dataset for 1938–45 on the basis of the data about the historical and factual debates of 1920–37. Such an experiment in parliamentary science fiction might be amusing or intriguing for the literary imagination – and even for those schools of history that engage in "counterfactual thinking" about histories that might have happened. We may decide to introduce metrics to measure how many possible futures might have erupted after 1938. Such an experiment might tell us much about the ability of algorithms to extrapolate events, the availability of algorithms to historical logic, and the historical imagination in general.

Any analysis contrived on the basis of artificial accounts of the past would be an investigation into the bias of algorithms. It would not be historical research. Such an experiment would violate cardinal principles of archival study. We have the *actual* debates for 1938–45. Historians' problem is to analyze the archives that exist for historical facts – not to introduce alternative facts. To the degree that algorithms for "prediction" introduce new bias into the classification of historical fact, they actively undermine the positivism that is part of the historical method.

As we acknowledge, the validity of historians' complaints against certain ways of thinking in the sciences that historians have argued do not translate well into the study of human experience. In identifying and eschewing these shibboleths, we can make room for a hybrid knowledge that benefits from the understanding of multiple fields.

Here is a basic glossary of the shibboleths that I believe should be treated with extreme care in hybrid research projects:

- **Prediction.** This means different things to different communities. Treated as a measure of objective validation in machine learning circles, in history, predictive thinking is usually regarded, with certain exceptions, as a pseudoscientific pursuit violating basic rules of chronology and retrospective analysis. In this book, prediction is treated with kid gloves. In Chapter 5, I review the fascination with turning history into a predictive science since the writing of Isaac Asimov in the 1930s. I introduce historian Reinhard Koselleck's attempts to explicate the standards that historians would require of data for a truly predictive science of history to emerge. On the basis of this rubric, I trace some arenas where predictive thinking in history is plausible and others where historians are likely to discard predictive thinking overall, and I urge historians' insights on readers as a reliable standard for which analyses of the past we can trust. Instead, I advocate *description* as an alternative standard for algorithmic success in engaging data from the past: Does the algorithm accurately describe events historians already know about? If so, the algorithm has been validated, and can be trusted to describe events that historians do not already know about.

- **Laws of historical change.** Laws of behavior are routinely used as one standard of success in the physical sciences. But in twentieth-century debates, Karl Popper and his successors reacted to predictive thinking by challenging the idea that human behavior adheres to knowable laws – a story that I tell in Chapter 5. Generations of historians have renounced the search for laws of historical behavior, and much of modern history involves the demonstration of how wildly supposed laws of human behavior can change from one generation to another. For this reason, the historical principle of *change over time* is regarded as a building block of historical knowledge, while "laws" of behavior are usually regarded as fanciful projections onto the past. If an algorithm can routinely detect past changes that historians have proven through traditional methods, then we can consider that the algorithm is valid, and we can trust the algorithm to detect other, unknown changes.

- **Future performance, new data, and test and training data. These** are terms that evolved in a corporate context where one standard of success is the ability of algorithms to keep up with new data produced by users in real time. Some digital humanists have embraced "test and training data" as the key to transparent modeling and testing of hypotheses. Historians certainly stand to benefit as training data is retailored to their datasets. In the theory of critical search laid out in

Chapter 4, I suggest a model for how iterative engagement with algorithms, data, and questions may work in the context of historical study. In each of the case studies in Chapters 6–11, I model some processes of critical search, shifting out the parameters of algorithms in order to test what I call the "fit" of each algorithm to historical questions. But in historical study, the terms "future data" and "new data" are problematic because each historical archive is, as a rule, treated as a closed container. For the same reasons that "prediction" can cause problems for historical analysis, so too "test" and "training" datasets can cause problem if the model violates the laws of chronology by hypothesizing an alternative future modeled on the bias of the algorithm.

- **Sampling data.** Sampling refers to the process of curating datasets through the randomized or filtered down-sampling of data. The two senses of the word – sampling as filter and sampling through randomization – are often used interchangeably, both in statistics and in certain digital humanities communities. But for historians, the distinction is extremely important. Historians *down sample* particular facets of data all the time – for instance, selecting a few individuals from a cast of hundreds of politicians, and using those individuals for specific and narrow study. I might be able to realistically validate my algorithmic work about how Gladstone's language changed over his career by reading several biographies on Gladstone and reading at length from his speeches to check the work of the algorithm, but I can't realistically provide the same validation and oversight for the thousands of members of parliament in my dataset. Down sampling data is a responsible practice, because it allows researchers to manage the burden of the analytic work required to understand algorithmic analysis.

  Randomized sampling is more controversial in history. Computational researchers routinely randomly sample data from historical datasets to speed their work. I've also heard of computational researchers jettisoning most of their dataset, taking only the first N words of each speech in the parliamentary speeches, so as to create a "normalized" sample of parliamentary speech, where we have an equalized "sample" of data from each speaker. For the historian, jettisoning big data in this way is anathema. The first half of a politician's speech may be contradicted by the second half of their speech. We use counting to get a picture of the full variety of words. Other mathematical processes for "normalizing" long speeches and short speeches may be useful. But randomized sampling of speeches makes little sense when historians look to text mining as an index of *fact.* The allergy to randomized sampling comes from a place of expectation about what it means to search a dataset. When a historian counts the appearance of the phrase "civil war" over each year in the nineteenth century, they expect the number of total counts, not the number of counts in some random sample. If randomized sampling produces some distortion of that count, extreme transparency is merited about why randomized extraction has been used and what may be left out.

There are exceptions to this rule of thumb. Randomized sampling has certain controlled uses in historical practice. Faced with stacks of unindexed, handwritten manuscripts in an archive, traditional social historians may "sample" the data by choosing to read only every tenth page – a technique recommended by Claire Lemercier and Claire Zalc in their textbook on methods, for instance.[31]

But one of the advantages of text mining for historical analytics is that, given a dataset like the parliamentary debates, I don't have to sample the data to reach a scale of information where a human can validate each individual document that has been processed. In general, *filtering* data to concentrate on a few actors or a smaller moment in time is a valid and useful practice in text mining for historical analysis, while *randomized sampling* has little place.

How should a skillful data scientist balance both the warnings embodied by the shibboleths with the opportunities for new knowledge afforded by an understanding of the fundamentals of historical analysis? What does it mean to engage a hybrid form of analysis, remaining steadfastly critical of context and treating data with sensitivity, curiosity, and skepticism? The five precepts outlined in this chapter lay out a starting position, but the rest of the book is dedicated to showing how a thoughtful examination of historical text from the past might proceed. Guided by these precepts, the following chapters will lay out a path through the woods of danger.

---

[31] Claire Lemercier and Claire Zalc, *Quantitative Methods in the Humanities: An Introduction* (Charlottesville, VA: University of Virginia Press, 2019), 38–50.

CHAPTER 3

Words Are Keys and Words Are Barriers

Our culture is awash with text, from emails to text messages, to the reports of governments and corporations and the memos of the past. While the first chapter of this book explored critical thinking with data about the past, this chapter explores the challenges of interpreting a specific kind of data: the data of texts, where much of the analysis rests on the count of words. We are not the first civilization to undertake the exploration of text, and machine learning is merely the newest set of tools in a long parade.

In the era before keyword search, researching the secrets of semantic history required massive investments of time and capital. Centuries before the most basic laws governing the reflection of light were understood, medieval monks were poring over old books and devoting themselves to the careful comparison and examination of the meaning of words over time. In 1230, the Dominican monk Hugo de Saint-Cher prepared the first concordance to systematically index the keywords of the Bible. His labor required the assistance of some 500 monks under his charge.[1] It must have also required vast material resources in terms of the number of sheep slain to produce the vellum for note-taking and for the concordance itself.

Later, in 1884, philologists at Oxford organized a project for a historical dictionary whose entries documented the shifting life of individual words from their ancient origins to the present. The scholars attempted to draft an army of volunteers to "crowdsource" mentions of words from the wild, using a system of postcards and published notes and queries. But the project was ultimately saved not by volunteers, but by a solitary mad genius, imprisoned in a mental hospital after committing murder, with an unlimited appetite for copying passages and then concatenating those passages into word indexes. When finished, a generation after it was

---

[1] "Concordances of the Bible," in John Francis Fenlon, ed., *Catholic Encyclopedia* (New York: Robert Appleton, 1908).

begun, the *Oxford English Dictionary* would stretch to 6,400 pages of carefully indexed words.[2]

Today, algorithms trained on textual data are pinpointing semantic movements in time. Counting words has lately revealed that people in Shakespeare's time spoke of "freedom" as a feeling, a kind of pleasure that could be understood in the context of words such as "happiness" and "friendship." It wasn't until the era of the American Revolution that writers began to oppose "freedom" to words like "tyranny," and reimagined freedom as a set of conditions that could be shaped by governments and nations. Only in the nineteenth century, meanwhile, did writers begin to oppose the condition of "freedom" to "slavery," and write about how freedom was something that could be guaranteed by a "legislature."[3]

We can see semantic changes even over the last few decades that illuminate subtle shifts in society. Careful comparisons of the context in which words were used show, for example, that "intelligent," "logical," and "thoughtful" have been increasingly applied to women since the 1960s.[4] Contextual readings tell us that the term "journalist," once a working-class profession, is today considered an elite employment and that the context of both *jazz* and *techno* have become whiter and more elite over time, while *bluegrass* and *opera* have become more black and poor.[5]

With an algorithm, we can use baseline measurements to identify the exact books and years in which new attitudes appeared. In order to make meaning from the signals counted by the computer, trained historians then need to contextualize that information by considering primary and secondary sources, but the signals themselves are now plentiful in a new way and convey an intense specificity never seen before, providing enormous data for mapping change over time.

This chapter explores the promise and the danger of automated approaches to words. It investigates the rich tradition of looking at the histories of words and changes in wordcount as a source of knowledge

---

[2] Simon Winchester, *The Professor and the Madman* (New York: HarperCollins, 1998).

[3] Sarah Connell, "Word Embedding Models Are the New Topic Models," NULab for texts, maps and networks, July 25, 2017, https://web.northeastern.edu/nulab/word-embedding-model. Connell's blog post represents the preliminary report on research conducted in Ben Schmidt's lab at Northeastern, using a body of texts primarily from North America; it should not be taken as final evidence on the history of these terms nor as a ruling on the meaning of terms in Europe.

[4] Nikhil Garg et al., "Word Embeddings Quantify 100 Years of Gender and Ethnic Stereotypes," *Proceedings of the National Academy of Sciences* 115:16 (April 17, 2018): E3635–44, https://doi.org/10.1073/pnas.1720347115.

[5] Austin C. Kozlowski, Matt Taddy, and James A. Evans, "The Geometry of Culture: Analyzing the Meanings of Class through Word Embeddings," *American Sociological Review* (September 25, 2019) https://doi.org/10.1177/0003122419877135.

about society and culture. It also highlights some of the typical errors that students of data fall into when attempting historical analysis, as well as some of the best models for insight.

Text Has Been Used as Evidence for a Long Time

The work of comparing different documents is supported by rich traditions – eons of careful testing of hypotheses and best practices. In the fourth century, the scholar and, later, bishop Eusebius developed some of the first primitive techniques of hermeneutics, or textual comparisons as a means of interpretation. Eusebius strove to discern the historical truth of Jesus' life by systematically comparing the texts of the four gospels. In 1230, another systematic innovation in textual interpretation appeared: the first concordance, or book indexing the entire Bible, word by word. In the eighteenth century, concordances of the Bible led scholars to formally recognize the multiple meanings of words. Only a century later, in the era of the *Oxford English Dictionary*, did scholars embrace a new insight about language : that the meanings of words shift over time. Twentieth-century humanists who studied the Roman writers Plautus and Ovid frequently began their expeditions by a careful examination of each writer's lexicon and the multiple uses of every word.[6] Describing a writer, or even a culture, by the words they employ can reveal volumes about them – even if they themselves are lacking that self-knowledge.

In his 1976 book, *Keywords: A Vocabulary of Culture and Society,* Raymond Williams explored a methodology that had informed his career as a cultural historian. Through his demystification of methods, Williams opened up an entire field of research. His method of "inquiry into a *vocabulary*" became one of the foundations of cultural history as it was practiced in the 1970s and 1980s.

The conceit of a new method of social history had occurred to Williams when he returned to Cambridge after his four-year hiatus during the Second World War. That interruption in time made suddenly palpable to him that a cultural rift had taken place. In just four years, old patterns of polite speech once preserved at Cambridge had vanished, according to Williams; their former meanings had either expanded or been diluted,

---

[6] For Eusebius and the long history of the concordance, see Michael Stubbs, "The (Very) Long History of Corpora, Concordances, Collocations and All That," in Anna Cermáková and Michaela Mahlberg, eds., *The Corpus Linguistic Discourse: In Honour of Wolfgang Teubert* (Amsterdam: John Benjamins, 2018), 9–34. For Hugo de Saint-Cher, see "Concordances of the Bible," in Charles Herbermann, ed., *Catholic Encyclopedia* (New York: Robert Appleton, 1913).

while new forms of rhetoric and slang had taken their place. All Cambridge was suddenly speaking a new *dialect*. Williams felt that he was encountering something that demanded to be understood and his close attention to language offered an opportunity to unlock the forgotten debates by which class, identity, and nation had been constructed.

Williams asked himself if there were earlier moments of discontinuity in history, other moments when all Britain seemed to learn to speak a new language overnight. He speculated that the cultural rifts of the industrial revolution might have produced this feeling of disorientation, where new words were adopted as people grasped for appropriate ways of describing the shock of the new: a world of machines, factory towns, slums, and working-class politics. In his early books, such as *Culture and Society* (1956) and *The Country and the City* (1975), the historian traced the shifting meanings of a dialectical pair of words, showing the evolution of cultural arguments around which had coalesced new ideas of class, collective action, pollution, and historical change.

In these earlier books, Williams shied away from turning the process of thinking about vocabulary into an explicit method. In his introduction to *Keywords*, he reflected on a feeling of "embarrassment," which he experienced as he attempted to unpack the process by which knowledge is made – it put his book outside the traditional categories of cultural history. As he opened up this discussion, however, he soon found that he was not alone in his methodology or his interest in these patterns. "I found that the connections I was making," he reflected, "were in practice experienced and shared by many other people, to whom the particular study spoke."[7]

There is an expansive agenda in any explication of the process whereby new knowledge is created. The footnotes in Williams offer a breadcrumb trail of the scholar's search through the library, from dictionary to periodicals to biographies and debates. By reading them, the scholar learns about scholarship, about the kinds of inquiry that are possible; this form of instruction was once an essential kind of knowledge passed on in the reading of history. The scholar who wishes to open up scholarly research in a new direction must document one of the most abstract and diaphanous of experiences: the intuitions and perceptions about what is interesting and important that guide any inquiry in the archives.

---

[7] Raymond Williams, *Keywords: A Vocabulary of Culture and Society* (London: Fontana Press, 1980), 14.

Using Words as Data: Commonplace Mistakes

In the age of big data, the searching of keywords offers a way to unlock the past at a magnificent scale. Keyword searching becomes a means for hacking through redundant material, making possible historical works that take on a breadth of time and space unprecedented in the traditions. It suggests fruitful ways for individuals to cut through the jungle of texts now available in digitized archives and it suggests fruitful means of gently shifting historical publications to emphasize the routes through online materials that may benefit future researchers.[8] Working with digitalized archives, the scholar can use the word as an index, looking up passages where the word appears in context. They may test out synonyms and variations of a peculiar phrase. Like a miner tracing a fissure deeper into a cave, the trail may run for a long way. But if the vein is rich, it will eventually yield pure gold. The scholar may find the keystone for an entire chapter.

If one can find the right period and correct phrase, the doors of the historical archives will swing open. But the user of the key must be skillful enough to know which doors *matter* – and as my students typically discover, that knowledge is not as easy to access as the results of a search engine; it comes hard won by a deep immersion with the text.

Searching for words and interpreting too glibly those that turn up in data-driven results can also mire the analyst in a mess. When my students begin their exercises in counting words, one of the most frequent deficiencies is an appreciation of how words change over time and what the limits of keyword search are. One team looks for a series of contemporary American slurs in nineteenth-century British texts, and when they find no evidence of the derogatory racial words applied to Jews and African-Americans by contemporary teenagers, they come to the conclusion that British people had no racial prejudices – an absurd notion about a civilization whose colonial exploits were grounded in the conviction of the "barbarism" and "backwardness" of the nonwhite peoples of the world. Because neither the term "barbarism" nor the term "backwardness" is familiar to a contemporary vocabulary, it seldom occurs to undergraduates to apply them to the past. An anachronistic expectation of how vocabulary works and how it should behave is therefore a barrier to insight.

---

[8] I am grateful to colleagues at the Chicago New Media Conference, November 2008; THATCamp at GMU July 2009 and May 2010; and the Geoinstitute at the University of Virginia Scholars' Lab, May 2010.

Students also sometimes assume that prevalence of words equals significance; in fact, the converse is usually true, as the most frequently occurring words in any corpus are generally the least significant in terms of meaning. The so-called stop words – such as definite articles, prepositions, axillary verbs, and so on – do not generally contain interpretable content when isolated from their grammatical function.[9] As it turns out, the same is true for the words just below the stop words. In parliament, the most frequent words overall are words such as "house," "country," "lord," "bill," and "speaker," words most commonly invoked in reference to the House of Lords or the House of Commons, or when specifying which speaker said what, and which bill would be presented when (Figure 3.1). Similarly, rhetorical terms often tantalize naïve readers, but the prevalence of "noble," "gentleman," and "hon." in the parliamentary debates indicates little about the sentimentality of the Victorian world, and a great deal about contemporary polite conventions of addressing speakers in parliament as "my noble friend" or "my honorable friend" (even if the ensuing speech then proceeded to demolish the logic or reputation of one's colleague). The words were repeated in parliament as a matter of establishing common truths, but, in general, one attempts to wrest *meaning* from them in vain. All that they signify, for the purposes of the analyst, is that parliament spoke about bills and used polite forms of address.

This is one reason why understanding time is so useful to the analyst of text. Compared with nothing, a wordcount gives us nothing. Of much greater interest than raw wordcount is the eruption of a *temporal discontinuity:* the appearance of a totally new word, for instance "telegraph," signals that something has happened. The discussion of a familiar word such as "landlord" in new terms – for instance, accompanied by the word "greedy"– likewise suggests a shift in the political wind. Comparing different temporal moments offers a baseline for comparison.

New words, according to Koselleck , are generally introduced into society to tame the *chaos of experience*. Concepts, in Koselleck's view, typically have a "stabilizing effect" on the experience of history in all its absurdity and pointless violence.[10] Koselleck calls to mind the period of the French Revolution and the early industrial revolution, when new words came into being at a furious pace. Examining how Europe's middle

---

[9] There are exceptional tests for which stop words may have statistically interesting content, for example, patterns of men and women's speech, which are regularly marked by differences in stop words. See Ben Blatt, *Nabokov's Favorite Word Is Mauve and Other Experiments in Literature* (Riverside, NJ: Simon & Schuster, 2017), 32–34.

[10] Reinhart Koselleck, *Sediments of Time* (Palo Alto, CA: Stanford University Press, 2018), 148.

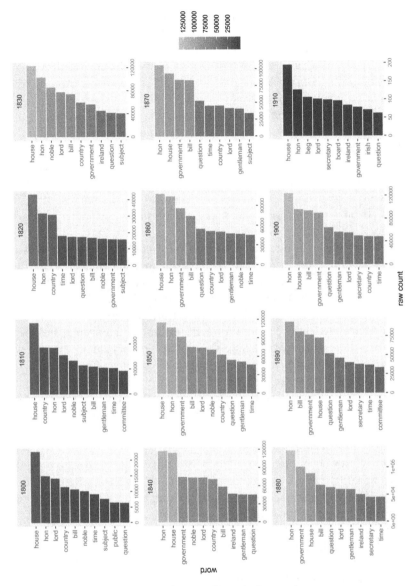

Figure 3.1   A series of meaningless graphs.

classes developed ideas about "progress," "reform," "crisis," and "revolution" in the decades that followed the French Revolution, Koselleck observes that concepts "produced commonalities in language across all political viewpoints," thus creating, from an era fraught with division, the possibility of shared consensus about a common past and future.[11]

Students who are new to text mining can easily miss the flags of significance and often resort to plotting word frequencies over time as an automatic indicator of relevance. Wavering differences – for instance, the one that occurs when the analyst plots the relevance of the word "budget" over the timeline of the nineteenth century – are likely to have little meaning. The variations in the word's appearance may result from a relative rise and fall of financial crises in the state, or they may signal the entrance or exit of particular speakers who possessed a certain rhetorical style, or the habits of the stenographers who recorded the speech. Or such fluctuations may simply be noise. It is the duty of the data scientist to know. In any case, there is no major discontinuity, as there was with "telegraph." The wavering line is not a clear signal of change.

Another barrier to interpretation that often confounds my students is naïvely searching for words that have multiple possible meanings. Trying to understand how discussions of climate have changed on Reddit over recent years, they will search for mentions of "energy," "green," and "climate," generating a guided vocabulary from free association with the terms referencing climate that they might read in the newspaper, and then counting the number of references to these terms as an index of how frequently commenters referenced climate. This snowplow approach to search returns dangerously dirty results – for I might reference energy in the context of talking about my friend's "personal energy," or greenness in the course of describing living room furnishings, or climate while referencing air-conditioning or the social environment at my office.

When students apply an algorithm to a query, and it produces a set of keywords, they encounter an even more difficult challenge: deciding *which* words to interpret and *how* to interpret them. When new to text mining, students tend to grab whichever words are automatically returned by an algorithm, including those that may defy interpretation. Algorithms used to find instances of "new language" in *Hansard*, for example, regularly turn up new rhetorical flourishes adopted from year to year by a new generation of speakers, who might use such conventions as referencing another speaker as "my honorable friend" – material that would only be relevant to a researcher whose interests were explicitly tailored to the rhetorical style of speakers in parliament. Woe to the researcher who sees a rise in the term

---

[11] Ibid.

"friend," and concludes that friendship was on the rise in nineteenth-century Britain!

New students of history who try to pull long-term stories out of wordcounts can easily fall into the mire of poor interpretation, a sticky soup from which it is difficult to escape. These swamps of meaninglessness will not, like the fissure of gold traced into the minds, yield to further investigation. Instead, the traveler who progresses will become muddier, wearied, and eventually, stuck. The best way out is to avoid the swamp altogether, and the way to avoid the swamp is to have a map. In short, before the analyst begins text mining, it is already important to know something about what the text entails: Who wrote these documents and why? What sorts of transformations would one expect to see? Only then will the researcher be canny enough to understand that there is nothing surprising about seeing the word "friend" or "bill" in an archive of parliament. The ideal map is an ethnography of the archive.

Scholars who are serious about the human life of data can spend years engaging just these preliminary questions. In his book, *History in the Age of Abundance?*, Ian Milligan writes about the *Geocities* portal, where many a teenager in the 1990s designed their first webpage. Milligan spends a significant proportion of his book setting up a basic ethnography of the internet in the 1990s, defining terms like "sysop" and "homepage" and contemplating whom this data represented and how. In this work, Milligan is engaging in an exemplary instance of the ethnography of data required to interpret texts. *History in the Age of Abundance?* offers little actual text mining – one gets the sense that Milligan is setting the stage for a later book. What he accomplishes instead is the preliminary step: understanding who was online in the 1990s, whose voices the webpages might capture, how those texts are structured, and what gatekeepers lurked in the folds.[12]

If a team of data analysts can afford to, it would be well advised also to recruit some historian – a graduate student, perhaps, or an outside reader – to perform an ethnography of the datasets it's using, such as the ethnographic work Milligan performed before delving into his text mining project. Not every team of analysts works in league with a historian like Milligan, but ambitious data science teams could certainly recruit a historian to perform an ethnography and bring to the project a greater awareness of the kinds of institutions and individuals that structured the flow of

---

[12] Ian Milligan, *History in the Age of Abundance? How the Web Is Transforming Historical Research* (Montreal: McGill-Queen's University Press, 2019).

text in the past. Archival ethnographies are indispensable for spotting the quicksand in the archive – the deleted narratives and suppressed voices.

Only expert knowledge can contribute a backdrop of understanding against which general conclusions can be drawn about the significance of certain words. For this reason, much of contemporary work in the digital humanities beginning with lists of words inevitably depends on searching not for individual words, but rather wordlists that were prepared for a contemporary context, while being applied to a historical one. The use of a wordlist is typically referred to as using a "controlled vocabulary;" controlled vocabularies may come prepackaged with software or they may be developed by an expert researcher.[13] Controlled vocabularies bring enormous promise to the process of text mining, but they can also contribute dangers all their own.

Expert Input: The Controlled Vocabulary

In many notable studies, controlled vocabularies matched to historically appropriate questions have provided a powerful index of changing historical experience. In the mass data project "Trading Commodities," historian Jim Clifford and his collaborators mined records of Britain's international trade for mentions of fat and soap and demonstrated the previously undetected importance of Central Asia to British trade, before the industry become dominated by Australian sheep in the 1880s.[14] In a study of early-modern gender and employment, a team of Swedish historians and data scientists applied a controlled vocabulary of gendered verbs for work to a corpus of eighteenth-century court records. They discovered thereby that both men and women did almost all the jobs described.[15] In a study of the French Encyclopédie, a group of humanists and data scientists at the

---

[13] Much research in the digital humanities already depends on prepackaged vocabularies prepared by linguists and computationalists, one notable example being Princeton's WordNet thesaurus/ Ingo Feinerer, Kurt Hornik, and Mike Wallace (Jawbone Java WordNet API library), *Wordnet: Wordnet Interface*, version 0.1-14, 2017, https://CRAN.R-project.org/package=wordnet.

[14] Clifford has documented the historical commodity transition here: Jim Clifford, "London's Soap Industry and the Development of Global Ghost Acres in the Nineteenth Century," *Environment and History* 27:3 (2021): 471–97. The methods he used to discover the commodity transition are laid out in a separate article: Jim Clifford, Beatrice Alex, Colin M. Coates, Ewan Klein, and Andrew Watson, "Geoparsing History: Locating Commodities in Ten Million Pages of Nineteenth-Century Sources," *Historical Methods: A Journal of Quantitative and Interdisciplinary History* 49:3 (July 2, 2016): 115–31, https://doi.org/10.1080/01615440.2015.1116419.

[15] J. Lindström, K. Jansson, Rosemarie Fiebranz, Benny Jacobsson, and M. Ågren, "Mistress or Maid: The Structure of Women's Work in Sweden, 1550–1800," *Continuity and Change; Cambridge* 32:2 (August 2017): 225–52, http://dx.doi.org.proxy.uchicago.edu/10.1017/S0268416017000200.

University of Chicago   utilized a controlled vocabulary of nouns that enabled them to detect patterns that showed how the authors evaded censorship by a Catholic authority by disguising their critiques of the church under cover of different nouns.[16] In a similar way, the now-classic digital humanities studies on British modernity made progress by tracking handpicked words associated with particular virtues or cultural domains through the British newspapers and Google Books corpus.[17]

Studies of this kind demonstrate how following a semantic cohort of words can produce new historical insights. Measuring the change of words in a controlled vocabulary enables investigations into the "hidden" dimensions of change, which tend to be – as Ted Underwood has recently argued – otherwise invisible to readers, even as the curvature of the earth remains invisible to the ordinary pedestrian.[18] By studying related sets of keywords, scholars have been able to isolate components of historical change, tracking events and continuity within particular cultural or social spheres of activity.

Yet even while controlled vocabularies can illuminate the past, the wrong controlled vocabularies can also introduce distortions. Many of the vocabularies contributed by computer scientists (as opposed to linguists) are particularly problematic for use on a historical time period or cultural subject other than the one for which they were developed. For instance, one famous sentiment dictionary lists a set of words for feelings and emotional states. The words were crowdsourced from contemporary computer users, who associate the term "socialist" with emotionally charged words such as "fear" and "disgust" – a valence which maps poorly onto exuberant discussions of utopian socialism in the nineteenth century.[19] For these reasons, a visualization like the one in Figure 3.2 is

---

[16] Glenn Roe, Clovis Gladstone, and Robert Morrissey, "Discourses and Disciplines in the Enlightenment: Topic Modeling the French Encyclopédie," *Frontiers in Digital Humanities* 2 (2016), https://doi.org/10.3389/fdigh.2015.00008.

[17] Frederick W. Gibbs and Daniel J. Cohen, "A Conversation with Data: Prospecting Victorian Words and Ideas," *Victorian Studies* 54:1 (2011): 69–77; Dallas Liddle, "Reflections on 20,000 Victorian Newspapers: 'Distant Reading' The Times Using The Times Digital Archive," *Journal of Victorian Culture* 17:2 (June 1, 2012): 230–37, https://doi.org/10.1080/13555502.2012.683151; Saatviga Sudhahar, Thomas Lansdall-Welfare, Justin Lewis, James Thompson, and Nello Cristianini, "Content Analysis of 150 Years of British Periodicals," *PNAS (Proceedings of the National Academy of the Sciences)* 114:4 (January 9, 2017): E457–E465, https://doi.org/10.1073/pnas.1606380114.

[18] Ted Underwood, *Distant Horizons: Digital Evidence and Literary Change* (Chicago, IL: The University of Chicago Press, 2019).

[19] For an example of sentiment analysis designed to work with contemporary sources, see Bing Liu, *Sentiment Analysis: Mining Opinions, Sentiments, and Emotions* (Cambridge: Cambridge University

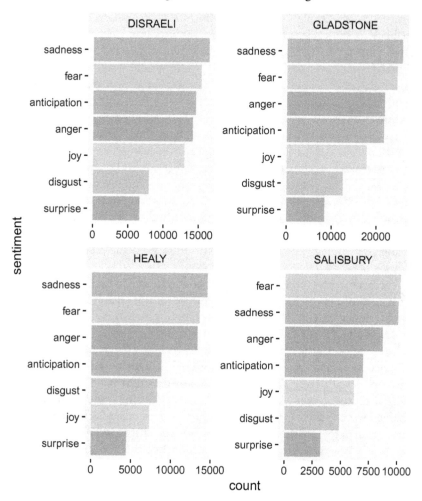

Figure 3.2   An untrustworthy graph.

highly suspect. If we inspect why the computer has ranked speaker Timothy Healy highly for "sadness," we will find that it did so because he was the master of ironically "begging" his fellow speakers to consider

Press, 2015). The coding of "socialist" with fear is part of the NRC sentiment package, whose content was crowdsourced from computer users via Amazon's Mechanical Turk. For the project's origins, see Saif Mohammad and Peter Turney, "Crowdsourcing a Word–Emotion Association Lexicon," *Computational Intelligence*, 29:3 (2013): 436–65; for the map of words and their classifications, see https://saifmohammad.com/WebPages/NRC-Emotion-Lexicon.htm.

the violence of the Irish state. Using a controlled vocabulary designed to study consumer preferences as a map for the emotional valences of Victorian ministers is a recipe for disaster.

The Cure for Error Is Critical Thinking

How is the scholar expected to avoid perils of this kind? By inspecting the results, one word at a time. I offer my students the admirable model of historian Luke Blaxill, who rigorously produces tables showing a sample of every keyword in its original context so that he can make conclusions about the words' meanings that are grounded in reality. Blaxill uses his keyword tables to discard some interpretations out of hand – for instance, he finds that the word "land" was used in too many senses in his corpus for any interpretation to work; his subjects talked about what it took to "land" a vessel as well as the "land" of Ireland or a "land" tax. In exercise after exercise, I ask my students to run code, produce results, and then look back at the text to decide which results are meaningful before they supply an interpretation.

Such studies form a quantitative counterpart to our first approach to studying temporal experience, where we focus upon a single aspect of historical change, and they allow us to study experience related to a particular professional or economic domain. They represent a rigorous means for "checking" the period in which a given phenomenon is supposed to have emerged, correcting for any preconceived opinions that analysts may bring to the data regarding the prevalence of particular figures of speech or concepts. As these methods can be used to robustly examine the chronology of ideas, events, and experiences, a wide range of scholars can benefit from wordcount over time and its variants, including historians who do not consider themselves to be specialists in digital methodology.

My first digital humanities project began with an analysis that tacked back and forth between secondary sources and digitalized primary sources in a search for new information. In 2007, the extent of my digital humanities toolkit was simple word search – using a search box provided in a web portal for accessing texts. The style of digital undertaking that I engaged, which we might call "virtuoso keyword searching," is not typically a matter of building algorithms and programs: it rather depends on a dialectic between open-ended searching and reading, iterative processes that produce finer and finer searches, narrowing the scholar's eye upon more and more precise points on the map. It is also the most common way that historians currently engage digital methods and it typically involves rigorously returning to secondary sources to guide digital inquiries.

I began to investigate the possibilities of using keyword search – at the time, a relative novelty in the scholar's toolkit – because I wanted more details to shape my story. I was trying to tell a rich social and cultural history of how strangers interacted on the new interkingdom highway system – roads and bridges that linked London with her former colonial capitals in Edinburgh and Dublin – which began to be supervised by the state after 1785. I had already dredged, by that time, both the secondary sources and the primary sources available at the Berkeley library. I had read a handful of the published accounts of the Methodist ministers and romantic philosophers who wrote up their travels in that era, but I wanted more detail about ordinary people and their interactions. I wanted to know the *inside* perspective of the ordinary tradesperson or soldier who tramped from place to place, year after year. What sorts of conversations did travelers take up as they walked alongside each other on the road? Who stayed at the wayside inns, where a middling tradesman might be able to pass the night, or at least stop for a pint of ale? Who would you meet if you took a stagecoach in those years and did the characters change if you rode on the outside of the coach in the brisk air – as Keats did, as a medical student – or on the inside with the gentry? Aside from historian Peter Clark's admirable but broad study of the English alehouse, however, there was nothing in this period about the inn and its social life and no authority I could turn to. I would have to compile new data myself.

At this point, I turned to the *Oxford Dictionary of National Biography* (*DNB*) – traditionally, a print reference work, held by libraries in a series of hefty tomes. But the *DNB* had recently been digitized, which made possible a full-text search. After reading a few of the hundreds of entries where "innkeeper" came up in context, I realized that a few were biographies of the famous sons and daughters of innkeepers who went on to fame. Searching for "son of" or "daughter of" and "innkeeper" in proximity with date constraints produced a full list. I began reading and found more patterns: the sons of innkeepers who went on to fame fell in a few professional categories. Some became surveyors, then architects or painters – no great surprise, as the traveling surveyor was among the earliest professions to become mobile in a national sense. There were natural historians and botanists (who overlap, aside from innkeepers, with surveying). A far larger group, however, became famous actors and directors of theatrical spectacles. The explanation seemed obvious: traveling players performed in inns across the country; the stagecoach inn was their major venue. The swirl of strangers passing through the inn left an imprint on the innkeeper's own family. A son of an innkeeper was almost destined to fall in love with the stage, and many did.

Virtuoso keyword searching is also predicated upon a knowledge of all relevant databases: not Google Books alone, but also the databases of periodical literature, government papers, newspapers, and secondary biography, each of which may offer a different angle on the project at hand. My innkeepers turned up nowhere in the other online repositories – the *DNB* alone gave me a trace of their existence. Extracting appropriate information was premised upon having spent a great deal of time with the *DNB* already. The primitive methods I used to parse text into meaningful points of data were unique to the query and the archive: "son of" and "daughter of" appear pro forma in almost all *DNB* entries and I knew that searching "son of innkeeper" would return results, because I had read so many *DNB* entries already. I didn't find everything I needed in the *DNB;* I also reached into Google Books and another resource that had only been digitalized recently, the Old Bailey Archive – the largest repository of criminal trials involving poor people from the eighteenth and nineteenth centuries. I used microfilm collections to examine lawsuits and newspapers. The work was slow; but that slow, iterative examination of the past – thinking and reading, reading and thinking, trying another source or another archive, until another pattern emerges that transforms your understanding of whole – is precisely how historians come to defensible theses about the *truth* of what happened in the past.

The data analyst who goes to a textual database intent upon applying word vectors or topic models misses the opportunities for making the slow connections between documents that live in multiple archives. My early digital humanities experiments mirrored the slow, iterative pace of placing different archives in conversation with each other and developing an interpretation of the documents there on the basis of wide reading, thinking, and reading again.

In each digitalized archive, I tried search after search, adjusting my terms and my scope until new evidence appeared. My queries were informed by outside reading, by feminist theory and urban theory, which kept me curious about what happened in the past when strangers met in public spaces. Often, only after days of trying new patterns, did I find a magic-working query that would unleash a new insight. In the Old Bailey, the key that opened the lock was looking for trials where someone described a crime that they had suffered when they had "asked the way" to the next town – or when they had answered the inquiry of a stranger who "asked [me] the way." Hundreds of cases appeared, each revealing the dangers of traveling alone with strangers: vulnerability to rape, theft, and being framed for someone else's crimes – all real dangers on the eighteenth-century highway.

The stories I discovered in this way were intensely human episodes that revealed much more than ministers' accounts and newspaper stories about what it might have been like to travel the roads of eighteenth-century Britain. Two girls were playing in the street. A traveler promised a trivial gift – a bit of muslin – to the girls if they helped him find the locals' path to circumvent paying a toll at the turnpike gate. The girls showed the traveler the path – a backroad out of sight. As soon as they were alone, the traveler raped them and disappeared.[20]

I knew that stories of this kind were valuable correctives to past histories, in part because other historians have made the case for "recovery projects," the work required to discover silenced voices such as those of women and working-class people, whose perspectives were once routinely neglected by writers and historians.[21]

In my case, it was looking carefully for keywords that unlocked the gate of a kind of cultural and social history to which no one has previously had access. The opportunity paralleled feminist archival recovery projects like Wallach 's, or the "social history" research into the ordinary lives of working-class people, made possible by research into the documentation of religious revivals and working-class organizations of the kind introduced by historian E. P. Thompson in his *Making of the Working Class* in 1963. Just as with that moment, a new archive of experience was suddenly made visible to those asking questions about culture, simply through a change of lens.

Words can be keys, and words can be barriers. What determines the difference is the user's sensitivity to a variety of questions about how language changes, what words mean, the multiple meanings a single word can have, and when a word signifies something of genuine interest or interpretability. Using keyword skillfully, in other words, requires some acquaintance with the traditional interpretative questions associated with the humanities.

---

[20] "Trial of James Barrett," *The Proceedings of the Old Bailey* (July 7, 1779) Ref: t17790707–49.
[21] For the case of recovery made around the Old Bailey, see Tim Hitchcock, *Down and Out in Eighteenth-Century London* (London: Hambledon and London, 2004); *Tales from the Hanging Court* (London: Hodder Arnold, 2006). The phrase "recovery projects" is from Joan Wallach.

CHAPTER 4

Critical Search: A Theory[1]

In previous chapters, we've underscored the dangers that riddle the analysis of data based on human texts about the past, and the relative security conferred by humanistic approaches, cast in broad terms as a four-part strategy: critical thinking about data and algorithms; careful inspection of keywords and their meanings; using the building blocks of historical analysis; and forging a form of hybrid knowledge grounded in the traditional disciplines.

The present chapter dives into the first part of the strategy – critical thinking about data and algorithms – offering a formula called "critical search." In this approach, the researcher investigates the "fit" between data, algorithm, secondary sources, and analysis, recursively iterating through a process until they clearly understand the implications of each choice they have made about how to clean the dataset or which algorithm to use and how.

For algorithms have biases, just as data and archives do. Historical pressures have shaped certain algorithms for certain purposes. James E. Dobson's *Critical Digital Humanities* locates algorithms such as k-means clustering in Cold War ideologies of assimilation.[2] In a recent article in *Isis*, historian of science Stephanie Dick has contextualized the birth of artificial intelligence against the background of debates about rationality and the material limits of early computers.[3] Some scholars focus the critical uses of data visualization in the past, for instance, with scholars

---

[1] A slightly different version of this chapter appeared as "Critical Search: A Procedure for Guided Reading in Large-Scale Textual Corpora," *Journal of Cultural Analytics*, 2018, 1–35, https://doi.org/10.22148/16.030.
[2] James E. Dobson, *Critical Digital Humanities: The Search for a Methodology* (Urbana, IL: University of Illinois Press, 2019).
[3] Stephanie Dick, "AfterMath: The Work of Proof in the Age of Human–Machine Collaboration," *Isis* 102:3 (September 1, 2011): 494–505, https://doi.org/10.1086/661623; Stephanie Dick, "Of Models and Machines: Implementing Bounded Rationality," *Isis* 106:3 (September 1, 2015): 623–34, https://doi.org/10.1086/683527.

such as Lauren Klein, Whitney Battle-Baptiste, and Britt Rusert tracing a nineteenth-century tradition of using visualization methods for critical purposes, citing the work of nineteenth-century educators and reformers such as Elizabeth Palmer Peabody and W. E. B. Dubois.[4] Turning to contemporary problems, scholars have problematized the circulation and exploitation of contemporary data about race by search-driven applications such as Zillow and Google; examples of such scholars are Safiya Noble, *Algorithms of Oppression* (2018), Ruha Benjamin, ed., *Captivating Technology* (2019), and Lauren Klein and Catherine D'Ignazio, *Digital Feminisms* (2020).

Critical data and algorithm studies have become an important frontier for scholars, where interest in the uses of data, visualization, and algorithm to illuminate bias meets critiques of particular processes and forms of data as abstraction and reduction. By understanding the life of information as historically situated between various pressures, all of which potentially distort the historically situated experiences behind data, scholars using a variety of methods have mapped out an important new frontier of understanding the story of how knowledge is made.

Armed with a critical perspective on the past, and with a sense of the diversity and bias of available algorithms, the analyst of historical data will be much better prepared to recognize the silences in the archive – the risk of retelling world history from the perspective of settler colonialism. But the dangers posed by text mining hardly end there – in fact, they multiply at every stage of the research process. No matter what material they're working from, scholars wrestle with the issue of *exemplarity*. Whether they're using hand-selected pages from an archive, or keywords they have personally chosen from a digital corpus, they risk the danger of cherrypicking. Cherrypicked examples leave the analyst's conclusions vulnerable to distortions, which can expose otherwise excellent projects to charges of sloppy analysis or even malfeasance.

In digital research, even seemingly simple queries are plagued with these pitfalls. They can only be addressed by critical thinking at every stage – about what queries we propose, which algorithms we use, and which

---

[4] Lauren F. Klein et al., "The Shape of History: Elizabeth Palmer Peabody's Feminist Visualization Work, www.shapeofhistory.net," *Feminist Media Histories* 3:3 (July 1, 2017): 149–53, https://doi.org/10.1525/fmh.2017.3.3.149; Lauren F. Klein, "Dimensions of Scale: Invisible Labor, Editorial Work, and the Future of Quantitative Literary Studies," *PMLA* 135:1 (January 1, 2020): 23–39, https://doi.org/10.1632/pmla.2020.135.1.23; Whitney Battle-Baptiste and Britt Rusert, eds., *W. E. B. Du Bois's Data Portraits: Visualizing Black America* (San Francisco, CA: Chronicle Books, 2018).

questions we ask of our models. When digital research is approached responsibly, however, it allows the scholar to choose exemplary texts for reading with a precision, clarity, and breadth unavailable to previous generations.

A Case Study in Brief

Consider two different visualizations that offer a reduced answer to a basic question: How did the language of property change in the debates of Britain's parliament from year to year? A scholar who knows the increasing number and length of parliamentary speeches over the century might choose to count keywords over time as a proportion of all words spoken each year.[5] The timeline in Figure 4.1 suggests an eruption of debates about property rights after 1875 – halfway between the signing of the Landlord and Tenant Act (Ireland) of 1870 and the peasant insurrections known as the Irish Land War of the 1880s – followed by an even greater explosion of these "keywords" after 1900. It is based on a raw count of scholar-supplied keywords, a common enough strategy for tracking change in the digital humanities.

The results indicate a discontinuity around 1880, and another one around 1910. At those moments, the yellow bars indicating the discussion of "eviction" explode – suggesting that increasing mentions of tenants and landlords on the floor of parliament may have been driven by discussions of eviction at a time when cases of evicted peasants were being heard on the floor of parliament with great regularity.

On closer inspection, however, we soon find problems with this search – after all, the visualization, as a whole, obscures conflations and exceptions. Searching for the keyword "tenant," for example, pulls in not only results relating to eviction, but also discussions in parliament related to issues with agricultural produce, property taxes, tithes, the franchise, and countless subjects only tangentially related to property; other terms, such as "estate" or "landlord," also cast too wide a net. Another omission is geographical and racial: the absence from this list of any words having to do with Indian or African tenure, as opposed to Scottish, Irish, and English. And thus, however provocative it may be, the visualization tells us very little about exactly what changed when, and the ultimate reasons for these changes.

We can often remedy these limitations, however, with a bit of reflection and some traditional tools available to historians. The researcher

[5] Ryan Vieira, *Time and Politics* (Oxford: Oxford University Press, 2015).

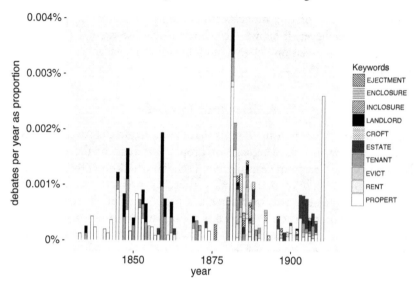

Figure 4.1   Searching for words for property, first iteration.

might enhance the results of Figure 4.1 by turning to another scholarly apparatus that helps us study the shifting usage of individual words – in this case, the *Oxford English Dictionary* (*OED*) – and thereby explore the full variety of historical terms for property. Revising our original search, we follow terms that include local relics of feudal culture (for instance, "udal") as well as the lexicon that grew under centuries of imperialism (for instance, "zemindar"). In this second iteration, using keywords gleaned from the *OED*, we examine the top ten most frequently occurring terms plotted over time.

Revising the search process with this kind of legwork and critical thinking can allow a scholar to ask additional questions of method and interpretation and, at times, it can enormously expand the dimensions of one's thesis. Since the research question in this particular case concerns *displacement*, our search might want to filter out mentions of "rent" or "tenants" pertaining to agricultural commodity prices, household taxation, or the franchise. One way to zero in on our focus is to limit the inquiry to the debates that are likely to be the most relevant – for example, the ten debates in which a given term appears with the greatest frequency – rather than examining every debate that mentions landlords. With a little reflection, we can see why such simple tweaks can be so powerful – by zeroing in on debates that hinge the most on a lexicon of property, we are able to

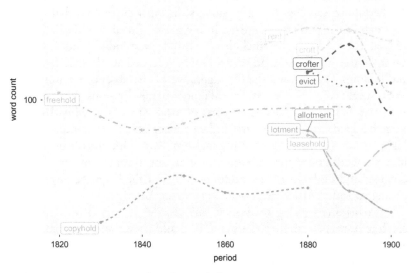

Figure 4.2   Searching for words for property, second iteration.

focus on each given term in discussions that engage them within their most relevant contexts and, thus, we are able to see more clearly how the language around property changed over time.

In its second iteration (Figure 4.2), our research visualization work suggests the prominence of market-related terminology early in the nineteenth century, marked by the use of words such as "freehold" and "copyhold." By the 1870s, however, the market-based discourse of land was giving way to a different conversation about the "leasehold," "tenant" and "rent." These were words that often corresponded to pleas that government recognize what were known as "tenants' rights," the right not to be evicted, for instance, as signaled by discussions of "eviction," as well as the plight of the Scottish "crofter," farmers who owned tiny plots of land and were involved in massive rent strikes in the 1880s. Parliament also debated remedies for these burning issues, such as "allotment" gardening, where regional authorities assigned small plots of land for the use of working-class families. We see all of these terms cresting between 1875 and 1890. The revised search reinforces the impression of an enormous explosion in mentions of tenant–landlord relationships around rent after the Irish Land Act of 1881, along with a corresponding two-to-tenfold increase in the usage of the new terms over the old, within the significant debates of the period.

Like Figure 4.1, Figure 4.2 highlights the eurocentric bias that typifies most debates in parliament – even in the age of global empire. While the original list of keywords included "zemindar/zamindar" and "ryot," a count of the most frequently used words returned no Indian terms for landholding. The missing data is suggestive of the absence of mind with which speakers in Westminster's parliament made decisions about peasant land taxes half a world away, heedless of local terms even while Britain's extractive land taxes plunged the Indian subcontinent into famine. While this iteration has remedied the original problems with British usage over time, we would need further contemplation and research into the lexicon to detect and understand any profound shifts in the language of property relating to India, Africa, the Pacific, or North America .

For a historian trying to recover this broader history of eviction, the search requires a bit more tinkering. One could try yet another iteration of keyword search, this time selecting only the Indian terminology from the *OED*, or perhaps, sampling only those debates with titles explicitly mentioning India, Africa, Australia, or Canada. One might even ask whether term-based search is simply the wrong key to unlock the door of global eviction. To untangle tricky historical quandaries, scholars might have to carefully consider the nature of the document base and contemplate alternative keywords – and even radically different algorithms – that might solve the riddle in unexpected ways.

Working with data is like this. It is not at all atypical for a digital historian to try on half a dozen analyses, switching out different parameters, dissatisfied with each, until the data has been fit to the question. In part, the iterative nature of the inquiry reflects the immaturity of the field of digital history. A decade ago, articles in digital history frequently worked with *only* the titles from various book catalogs because the text wasn't available. Today, a historian might want to work with text, but might reasonably also want to know if the "title" field and "text" field of the parliamentary debates reflect different realities. There are no standardized best practices that guide the scholar beyond common sense.

The point here is that good digital history must be reflective. The trained historian wants to see the real moon, not the moon's reflection. Neither the process of forming a question, nor the interpretation of that question, should ever be *automatic*. Every word in a simple keyword search is open to unpacking; even the commonest words contain stories that unfold in the dimension of time, and every phrase and utterance obscures other word clusters that, in turn, can only be illuminated by further study – including reading from outside the archive itself – and, eventually, by a new round of searches informed by this broadening knowledge. Since one only has so many hours in the day, of course, one must weigh the rewards and the costs of this scholarly legwork, but as a tool for illuminating history, the rewards for this extra-archival work are enormous.

Critical thinking about how the ground upon which historical narratives are built is as old as the Greeks; even Herodotus asked questions about whether myth, epic, and orally transmitted reports were to be taken seriously. Like a good journalist, a historian always validates their sources to see whether all sources agree. When disagreement arises, the historian's job is to ask ask which among them are most trustworthy, what is hearsay, what is the testimony of eyewitnesses, and whether any of the records are clearly copied, falsified, or otherwise motivated.[6]

Thinking critically about the words that go into a digital search lends strength and rigor to our research process. A process of critical engagement allows the scholar to correct for the proclivity to overinterpret a particular chart, that is, the tendency to construct a thesis from a single illustration of discontinuity. Iterative approaches and multiple tools are essential not only for making fine distinctions in complex debates, but as a way to control for the scholar's own subjectivity in encounters with the archive.

A Process for Engaging Machine Intelligence

The two graphs we've just looked at in Figures 4.1 and 4.2 demonstrate not a preconceived trajectory toward some ultimate treatment, but rather the ambling, iterative course of exploration that a scholar might take. Certain truths come into relief on one graph, and other truths emerge from the next graph. Each illustration has its own limitations and these uncertainties and lacunae suggest new research questions and, through a process of winnowing, the scholar must ultimately reconcile all of these heterogeneous findings to the original research project. The succession of charts forms a path through the data, mapping the dimensions of the archive and explaining the findings to the reader. They trace a visual outline of critical thinking as it flows along the contours of critical search.

---

[6] For Herodotus, see Reinhart Koselleck, *Sediments of Time* (Palo Alto, CA: Stanford University Press, 2018), 155. For one version of a procedure for testing sources, see Ernst Bernheim, *Lehrbuch der historischen Methode* (1889). For falsification, see Koselleck, *Sediments of Time*, 154.

The foregoing case study illustrates how multiple measures complement each other, buttress one another, and correct for one another, thereby enhancing the scholar's sense of *what* is being measured and *how* a particular search illuminates and disguises various dimensions of a canon.

Before engaging machine intelligence and negotiating our digital archives, it can be extremely helpful to think through a critically informed strategy, a strategy that is aligned with a sophisticated understanding of how different algorithms evoke their own particular perspectives on textual corpora from the past. We see this play out in the work of Daniel Shore, who vividly demonstrates how a dozen different algorithms produce a dozen different versions of the past.[7] Scholarly work can range from clumsy to brilliant according to a researcher's grasp of how digital algorithms can shift perspectives and open up heterogeneous dimensions of an archive. This range reminds us that no search is complete until all of its aspects – the choice of keywords, the algorithm, the exceptions, and the particular texts taken as exemplary evidence of the result – have been subjected to iterative examination.

This call for ubiquitous critical thinking is at odds with a scientifically empirical and yet limited posture often held by the humanists who embrace these digital tools – a narrow understanding of the perspectival issues inherent in an archive, hidden behind a scientific triumphalism. We often see this posture, for instance, in what we have called "proof of concept" articles, which introduce some bold new tool to a fresh new field. These articles tend to use the language of pure science to stress the correspondence between computerized generalizations and the "objective reality" of the archive, often ignoring occlusions, silences, and uncertainties of interpretation in an eagerness to validate a new method in the field.[8] In so doing and stressing the "discovery" aspect of a new method, these powerful tools typically project a fundamental illusion – emphasizing the unified nature of an essentially heterogeneous reality. As this posture inevitably amplifies the blatant voices in an archive at the expensive of any occlusions, it is unsurprising that readers concerned with suppressed,

[7] Daniel Shore, *Cyberformalism: Histories of Linguistic Forms in the Digital Archive* (Baltimore, MD: Johns Hopkins University Press, 2018).

[8] For instance, Kellen Funk and Lincoln A. Mullen, "The Spine of American Law: Digital Text Analysis and U.S. Legal Practice," *The American Historical Review* 123: 1 (February 1, 2018): 132–64, https://doi.org/10.1093/ahr/123.1.132; Matthew L. Jockers and David Mimno, "Significant Themes in 19th-Century Literature," *Poetics* 41:6 (2013): 750–69; Lauren Klein and Jacob Eisenstein, "Reading Thomas Jefferson with TopicViz: Towards a Thematic Method for Exploring Large Cultural Archives," *Scholarly and Research Communication* 4:3 (2013), www.src-online.ca/index.php/src/article/view/121.

neglected, or forgotten voices might resist such tools. It would be absolutely appropriate for any honest reader to contemplate whether they are instruments of a second-wave imperialism – an imperialism of history, conveniently buttressed by pseudoscientific fact.[9]

We can't consider the specific ways digitally enabled historians engage with macrohistory without considering how each of these approaches comes with its own serious issues of interpretation. To overcome pre-Copernican tendencies, so to speak, we must challenge the illusion of the one true perspective, which is primary, objective, and infallible – we must ask whether these digital tools in "distant reading" are truly designed to illuminate a single, Apollonian, and definitive perspective on an archive or a period of time. In this chapter, therefore, we would like to model a general process that we can bring to critical search which embraces the perspectival nature of algorithms. In the following pages, we will map out a critical, interpretive approach to digital tools based on iteration, focusing on how the various digital tools and the parameters with which they are used each provides its own nuanced perspectival approaches to the vying lexicons, grammar, rhetorical flourishes, euphemisms, ideas, avoidances, oversights, subjectivities, and conceptual constructs of the past. We will model our critical approach to these digital tools in terms of three macrosteps in a process of engagement – choosing a seed text from the secondary literature, winnowing the search results, and then applying ourselves to a focused and guided reading informed by the results of the winnowing.

The challenges of text mining that we have touched upon require more than just another algorithm; they require a new attitude among scholars engaging with digital techniques – a new *sensibility*, embodied here within the phrase "critical search." Critical search, like critical thinking, employs archives from a set of preexisting social and political concerns, brokered through a dynamic attitude of skepticism and curiosity regarding the shifting meanings and hidden voices within any archive, and followed up with an energetic, polymorphous, intellectually open, and robustly careful process of iterative investigation. No single text mining technique – whether topic modeling, keyword searching, or statistical measures – is by itself sufficient for filling out social categories such as, for example, *eviction* – which was referred to over the years under a variety of terms, many of them so general as to be eluding. Such an approach would fit entirely within a strain of historical method that sees historical agency as

---

[9] For instance, Roopika Risam, "Beyond the Margins: Intersectionality and the Digital Humanities," *Digital Humanities Quarterly* 9:2 (2015).

multiple and overlapping and also sees historical interpretation as an endeavor too vast to push through a digital meat-grinder, a process of resurrecting and identifying a dynamic interplay among agents that often defy the names we give to them, within a tangled web of material and social conditions obscured by equally elusive agents and dynamics. This book, therefore, embraces the proposition that digital tools work best when they are generative and perspectival and that, in such circumstances, they can produce visions and versions of the past that function as telescopes do for an astronomer, expanding our capacity to see clearly into the distance.

Critical search, as we are using the term in this book, does not depend on a particular algorithm or set of algorithms, but rather on the incorporation of critical thinking itself into the research process. Critical search suggests how questions of interpretation and scholarly selection permeate the entire process of applying digital tools and discerning their results. In its broadest sense, it is more than a tool – rather, it is a methodological approach, characterized by iterative engagement with a variety of algorithms and tools toward the goal of generating multiple and overlapping perspectives on how lexicons, grammars, and discourses change across various periods of time.

The digitally engaged process of critical search we are exploring here is designed to mirror a traditional history seminar, where students move from an assigned syllabus to a broader set of readings around a topic, followed by the identification of particular case studies for further reading. The student of history typically begins with some process of grouping together reading material based on their interests. Gradually, their reading moves wider, usually by using a variety of prostheses whose nature the student understands well, including a card catalog (or now, more typically, its digitized version), or tasking a research assistant with assembling some primary sources for my next syllabus. If the student does their job well, the base of sources they end up using will be neatly tailored to reflect the research question.[10] Similarly, the social historian is faced with an

---

[10] The virtues of this expansive contextual reading, broad sifting of sources, and synthesis of evidence from different points of view have recently been articulated in the many-authored "Tuning Project" of the American Historical Association; see "AHA History Tuning Project: 2016 History Discipline Core," www.historians.org/teaching-and-learning/tuning-the-history-discipline/2016-history-discipline-core (accessed June 1, 2016). The critical search process proposed here, while crucial to the process of summarizing and dating events in history, is nevertheless fairly irrelevant to many fields in the humanities and information sciences. Critical search, as described here, would be altogether unnecessary for a student of canonical politics who already knows the names of the actors who matter to him. Likewise, a student interrogating the female literary voice may only need to collect fifteen

enormous mass of possible records from which meaning could be extracted and this reality persuasively argues for microhistorical approaches to social questions that follow individual lives and families as microcosms of larger dynamics of gender and class.[11]

As we have shown, critical search, in its broader sense, is an attempt to interpret the range and depth of social experience through a variety of reductive techniques that elicit a multidimensional perspective on the past. In practice, this means discerning when and how it is appropriate to employ digital tools that abstract certain aspects of experience from text or reduce complex historical realities to their most effective quantifiable proxies. Those abstractions and reductions, while only partial views of the whole, can nevertheless shed light on cultural experience and historical change.

A complementary and iterative approach thus provides a powerful antidote to the reductionist tendencies in digital history: when consulting topic models, it pays to use secondary sources to consider which texts to topic model and how to interpret the results; when using keyword search, it pays to use secondary sources to interpret the keyword search. Similarly, when topic modeling, it also pays to reference keyword searches and keywords in context. Complementary and complicating abstractions and simplifications help the historian to convey to the reader the depth and breadth of their understanding of past events and this has always been the challenge and promise of writing history.

---

examples of novels by women to generalize her conclusions. The social historian, however, is responsible for portraying the range of voices related to a particular category, as well as adequately understanding the period for which her query is relevant, ideally by dating the first and peak expressions of her subject. For the literary scholar, mass extraction is irrelevant, and for the sociologist, broad winnowing of the scholarly record is unnecessary. For these reasons, the model of critical search proposed here differs from a more humanistic conception of research, for instance the one formulated by John Unsworth, where the choice and analysis of passages of text from an already constrained sample – rather than the discovery of an appropriate subcorpus from an unreadable mass – is the critical factor under consideration. Unsworth describes a sevenfold list of unordered primitives, comprising "discovering," "annotating," "comparing," "referring," "sampling," "illustrating," and "representing" tasks that are suitable to a small collection such as the Blake Archive on which he was working at the time.

[11] An excellent recent example being Seth Koven, *The Matchgirl and the Heiress* (Princeton, NJ: Princeton University Press, 2016). The opposite approach, of course, also has validity: approaching the official record with the intent of extracting a case of how the assorting and abstracting mechanisms of modern government remade the life of the peasant. "Paradoxically, history from below may be (as mostly it has to be) achieved by examination from above," mused historian Peter Robb on his use of British state records to study the peasants of India. Peter G. Robb, *Ancient Rights and Future Comfort: Bihar, the Bengal Tenancy Act of 1885, and British Rule in India* (London: Curzon, 1997), xxi.

Recently, certain scholars have pressed back against the reductionism of certain quantitative methods, especially the assumption that scholars enter an archive already armed with an exhaustive understanding of the keywords, personal names, places, and dates that matter in a research project.[12] Indeed, recent standoffs over methods and theory have frequently taken the form of scholars insisting that the understanding of historical change depends not merely upon the collection of new facts, but also upon insight into the changing history of human agency and institutions – realizations often opened up through engagement with critical theory.[13]

Critical search   has emerged as a new tool within a contemporary environment marked by polarized positions on issues of technology; some camps insist on critical thinking to the exclusion of new methods, while others focus strictly on the praxis of method. The technologist's perspective emphasizes a reasoned appreciation of the power of algorithms in the humanistic research process. The humanist's perspective focuses upon the multifarious nature of humanistic research, and generally embodies a critique of reductionism and the various other pitfalls of technological dependence. Critical search emerges as an invaluable synthesis of these two divergent perspectives.

The Critical Search Process

So far in this chapter, we have described in abstract terms what constitutes a critical search and how it is different from less dynamic, less iterative approaches to the digital humanities; and we have described in broad brushstrokes the ingredients of a critical search. We will now devote the rest of this chapter to a more nuts and bolts exploration of the critical search, as an ideal toolbox, a refined humanistic research process, and a set of practical, iterative steps that we recommend to practitioners as they engage with text mining.

To put such a dynamic process into words can be dizzying for the newcomer. Critical search begins with a critical reading of the sources,

---

[12] For instance, Nina Tahmasebi and others have investigated more generally the role of a priori knowledge in specifying the insights to be gained from the analysis of texts. Nina Tahmasebi et al., "Visions and Open Challenges for a Knowledge-Based Culturomics," *International Journal on Digital Libraries* 15:2–4 (April 1, 2015): 169–87, https://doi.org/10.1007/s00799-015-0139-1. There also exists a critique of this reductionism from within library science, for instance, Caleb Puckett, "Oh, the Humanities: Understanding Information Behavior to Foster Information Literacy," *Emporia State Research Studies* 46:2 (2010): 33–43.

[13] Ethan Kleinberg, Joan Wallach Scott, Gary Wilder, "Theses on Theory and History," *History of the Present* 10:1 (2020): 157–65. https://doi.org/10.1215/21599785-8221515

which then undergirds algorithmic modeling. All the while, the researcher alternates between scholarly interpretation and computer-aided modeling. Models are made and critiqued, and new models are constructed from this new information. At each stage, these models are subjected to supervision, boundary-making, and guided reading as the scholar inspects the results of each algorithmic model for its accuracy and for any new vantages or insights it may lend to the material at hand. Statistical inspection of the results is performed to reveal any bias implicit in particular models. Before it is turned over to the public, the scholar then documents the state of the project in each of these categories, so that the tentative results of the critical search will not merely be a compelling thesis, but a truly transparent model of the scholarly project in the digital age.

This approach, the critical search, requires a certain amount of energy and determination. It urges researchers to go beyond preliminary reductionist models, such as keyword searching and topic modeling, and to weave together tools from a variety of disciplines – such as statistics, information theory, hermeneutics, critical theory, and critical reasoning – into a process of modeling information whose multiple steps are equally open to inspection. The point of modeling a critical search is to offer reflections on a process of narrowing that is common to traditional research projects and these reflections can guide a vast and unwieldy digital world in which researchers routinely need to constrain a large corpus around a particular question.

Seeding, winnowing, and guided reading – the three essential categories of this process, which we will explore in the coming pages – describe a sequence of research familiar to many professionals who, under the influence of method or theory, constrain and broaden their reading on the basis of their findings. This triplicate process lends a scholar three general stages of opportunity for critical reflection on the search process and can shed light upon exactly how the scholar has engaged algorithms and both the primary and secondary sources – three places where those choices can be usefully documented and described for other practitioners of history. Because the devil is in the details, it will be useful to take a closer look at each category:

Seeding

Before delving into the research, the scholar typically begins by asking a few essential questions: What kind of archive are we using, and which known primary sources, dates, figures, or concepts govern the orientation to that archive? Considering these questions lends itself to a metaphor of agriculture; thinking of these archival elements as seeds, we are inspecting, choosing the most promising, and then planting these keywords, dates, and ideas we have gathered from a variety of other fields. The scholar's choices about which elements to engage always influences the shape of an inquiry: patriarchal words will rarely reveal subaltern attitudes, for instance. In a digital query, the search process is, in most cases, also seeded with a choice of algorithm(s) – a topic model, keyword search, or statistical measurement of significance according to some abstraction. This process, too, will tend to shift the search in one direction or another, lumping or splitting the corpus according to some general mathematical or theoretical concept of discourse, lexicon, or cluster. Carefully documenting and discussing the choice of seeds, whether conceptual, semantic, or algorithmic, is not only a useful step – it is the scholar's first opportunity to make the search process *transparent*.

Broad winnowing

Winnowing, in agriculture, is a necessary stage after the first crops have been harvested; air is blown through the grain to remove the lighter chaff. In a critical search, winnowing should be performed upon the maturing fruit of a first round of searches, as well as each subsequent round. Through a variety of mechanisms, which we will discuss in the pages that follow, the scholar roughly works over the returns of the query to sort signal from noise, sturdy from flimsy, gathering up the promising results and discarding the less clear or less relevant information.

In traditional research, a scholar chooses only particular exemplary texts or characters for close reading. Typically, before these texts are chosen, the scholar accepts some perspective on how unusual the perspective of the texts is – for instance, by reading secondary sources that offer a commentary on the life of the author in their historical context.

In digital research, where an enormous corpus is generally present in every case, a researcher winnows by the algorithm itself being a guide to the most relevant words, documents, or years. In the process of inspecting the "top hits" returned by the algorithm, the research may engage in fine-tuning the parameters on the algorithm or the list of query terms that delimit the search. They may decide to edit out results that cannot be interpreted, such as words that belong on a list of "stop-words" that are exempted from the count. In the process of working through available algorithms and queries, the researcher will likely throw away many false positives or pieces of messy data and, if necessary, try the same search a dozen times with cleaner data and clearer results. As the scholar documents how each specific question or algorithm works with a particular dataset and question, winnowing presents another opportunity for *transparency*.

Guided reading

A researcher only begins to "harvest" results at a mature stage of the research process, turning through the work for evidence of a shift over time, just as a gardener might turn through tomatoes, discarding anything too unripe, too moldy, or bruised. In traditional research, as the primary questions become more and more targeted, a scholar inevitably discards – or sets aside for potential future projects – any episodes irrelevant to the mature query. In digital research, however, scholars must also discern, and keep, any results that might shed light upon some historical question that might be important to the readership. As this requires not only scholarship but, at times, informed assumptions and hunches, the harvesting process is inevitably laden with bias – thus, it presents yet another opportunity for *transparency*, as the scholar documents the reasoning process, explaining what was left out and why and clarifying how much of the results presented is the work of human sorting rather than the automatic detection-work of some algorithm.

We can clearly see that, through this systematic process, critical search humbly models the everyday interventions of traditional research and digital research, dividing them into the course of relatively natural seasons, each of which demands work, affords results, and offers an opportunity for transparent documentation of all the methodological choices the scholar has made along the way.

The process of critical search, however, may be highly eclectic. The steps outlined above are intended only as a useful heuristic – the researcher does not need to follow them, in every case, exactly as they are laid out. Engaging with critical search can take other forms, as long as one understands the essential nature of critical search, which is always an attempt to inquire as deeply as possible into the biases of different digital tools and methods and into the perspectival dimensions of their results, through an iterative process of continual testing and revising with documentation.

To refer to portions of the model as stages or seasons is not intended to delimit or constrain. The resultant process may be either performed simply (in the way that by following a cookie recipe one gets cookies), repeated iteratively, or worked into the flows of inquiry that fork and take on new shapes with each pass.

To divide the stages of the research process in three is merely to discern different actions that are useful in any scientifically robust research process and to signal the many critical junctures where documenting scholarly choice can illuminate the biases that come with every theoretical choice. The choices that are made early in the process, as one reads and winnows, redound upon the next phases of work with data and upon any ultimate argument made on the basis of the data. The entire project will be more useful if each of the inputs to the process – data, query words, algorithms, and their parameters – have been carefully weighed, considered, and documented for future researchers.

In the chapters that follow, we will explore in greater detail what the seasons of research look like in their traditional and digital forms and get a sharper sense of how algorithms themselves – along with their tailored fitting to exploratory data analysis – become part of the model.

The remainder of this book will follow the process of a critical search, inspecting the parliamentary debates of nineteenth-century Britain for evidence of change, guided by theories of history from contemporary scholars. Even though, in practice, provisional technical solutions form part of each stage of critical search, the algorithms presented here are deliberately chosen for their *interpretability*, rather than for their fit as the best algorithm from the continually evolving world of computer science.

What does it mean to have a good "fit" between historical questions and data analysis? "Fit" in dressmaking is about tailoring models to a particular body. There is plenty of discourse in the humanities about the distortions inflicted on desire and the imagination by images of the female body, but that material never handles the gaze of the seamstress or tailor, sometimes a woman herself, whose job is to adjust the model to reality. Fitting a dress involves metrics applied from a basic dress to *this* body, not some ideal body. Dressmakers fit clothes by measuring and realigning to the real body, in contrast to monkeys – who reach for the moon's reflection in the water, cannot fit their image to reality, and risk death by drowning.

Here is what I think such a fitting process looks like, applied to the problem of data and historical change:

1. A modest engagement with digitalized textual archives as indexes of eventfulness in the past to *confirm* known turning points and to *discover* understudied historical events
2. An analytical science that seeks to establish relationships between events, periodicity, change over time, and causal factors and conditions in the past
3. An openness to the principle that specific political problems may require more specific and nondigital solutions

The first item in the list is studying events through confirmation and discovery. Later in this book, we will see what the process of confirmation and discovery looks like. We'll resort to old information science tools, refitting them to historical questions by measuring the distinctiveness of historical periods. We'll turn to tf-idf (term frequency–inverse document frequency), one of the chief algorithms associated with indexing documents for library science since the 1970s. Instead of indexing documents, we'll apply tf-idf to indexing periods of time in order to understand better what distinguishes distant past from near past from recent present. Instead of finding patterns of words at random and squeezing an interpretation from them, our method will be retrofitted to find patterns of change. We'll use this historically retailored algorithm to understand the debates of Britain's parliament in the nineteenth century, taking careful note of what parts of the output are *old* – a "confirmation" that the algorithm works as expected – and what parts are *new* – a "discovery" of possible paths for new research.

The second criterion of a text mining strategy fit to the purposes of history is that it studies the relationships between events. This means that the components of temporal experience – for instance, *memory* and *causality* are foregrounded as objects of research. Later in this book, we'll profile the use of "named entity recognition" to examine what events members of Britain's parliament remembered at different periods in the past. We'll use similarity measures to theorize the causal relationships between different speakers. We'll use simple data strategies like focusing on a small number of phrases and speakers to understand how a particular event unfolded. We'll take every opportunity to think about different possible objects in time, their relationships, and the different algorithms suited to studying each.

The third criterion of a text mining strategy respectful of history is knowing when one's data fails the purposes of an inquiry. As we have seen, dirtiness" of archives that reflect the speech or interests of a tiny minority of white men in power implies real limits on what we can accomplish by text mining. It implies that the evidence for many political experiments in the past is not held within major archives of law, democracy, or the newspaper. This being the case, a totally digital account of the past risks silencing the history of political experimentation. A totally data-driven analysis of language, without a historical method, tends to produce unusable information. Here, again, is a danger that historians are uniquely well poised to help people through – a reason why our teaching is so important. We must know when to stop with the data and when to turn to other ephemera or archives that might tell us about the lives of individuals.

We will get closer to a well-fitted history by coming to history as it is, not some dream history. The process of critical search means moving from questions to algorithms to data, again and again, constantly asking how the question might be framed differently. That critical inspection process is designed to fit the tools of math to the problems of temporal change. We will get closer by consulting with philosophers of history about the problems of periodization, event, and memory. Insight begins when we ask: What is the fit between the methods of data science, the questions of philosophy, and the historical records that we have today?

CHAPTER 5

To Predict or to Describe?

The science fiction writer Isaac Asimov told a powerful fable about what would happen when the records of the past were treated by computers and modeled with math. Although Asimov wrote when the most advanced computer storage was a stack of paper punched with a few dozen holes, he had a shockingly prescient grasp of how intoxicating the power of big data could be. In his Foundation series, his hero, Hari Seldon, is a researcher in the dynamics of human civilization. Combining social observations with the data crunching power of technology, Seldon was able to create a series of potential timelines of the future as uncannily accurate as a crystal ball.

> Gaal sat down and rested his head in one sweating palm, "I quite understand that psychohistory is a statistical science and cannot predict the future of a single man with any accuracy. You'll understand that I'm upset."
>
> "But you are wrong. Dr. Seldon was of the opinion that you would be arrested this morning."

The fantasy of a predictive machine that could foretell the date when civil war would erupt, or when a particular man would be arrested has had a hold on us ever since.

One doesn't have to look far for claims that today's practitioners of data science are actively modeling the past and predicting the future. In the years leading up to 2011, a biologist and mathematician began with textual data compiled by Google – the Google Books portal – to create a tool that reduced vast changes in culture to a squiggly line, charting the rise and fall of single words over two centuries of the human past. Counting the number of unique words in the English lexicon over the last 100 years, the authors were able to show the expansion of unique words since 2000. They also showed that the top 50 individual names, classified by fame, crested in fame in their early lives and then retreated into obsolescence.[1] The tool these scholars produced for the public was called "Google n-grams," named for the one-, two-, or more-word phrases that the tool counted.

The scientists declared that they had invented a new discipline, Culturomics, which would obviate most traditional studies of human experience in the humanities and social sciences. As they recalled in their 2013 memoir, their discovery began with a simple thought experiment. "Wouldn't it be great, we thought, if we had something like a microscope to measure human culture, to identify and track all those tiny effects that we would never notice otherwise?"[2] In comparing their historical research with public health and education research, the scientists implied that history might become a predictive science. At least one scholar proclaimed that the technology offered an analytical tool that could have accurately forecast revolutions in Egypt, Tunisia, and Libya, as well as the location of Osama bin Laden before his capture.[3]

Soon, it seemed as if every talk by a humanities professor employed n-grams to illustrate some point or other. Meanwhile, "culturomics" was mainly shunned by humanists in the university, cutting as it did against most of the self-understanding of the role of humanities subjects into probing human nature. But the promise of prediction never really went away. By 2021, a German text-mining project claimed that it could use novels to predict outbreaks of war in the developing world.[4] Asimov's fable about the power of data-driven analysis to create a science of the future seemed to be taking concrete form.

More recent scientists claim to be honing Asimov's imagined science to the point of a precise instrument. Peter Turchin, an evolutionary biologist who had written influential work in insect ecology, had a theory regarding our own species – that we can accurately measure, and predict, "unrest" in

---

[1] For the Culturomics experiment, Jean-Baptiste Michel et al., "Quantitative Analysis of Culture Using Millions of Digitized Books," *Science* 331: 6014 (January 14, 2011): 176–82, https://doi.org/ 10.1126/science.1199644; Erez Aiden and Jean-Baptiste Michel *Uncharted: Big Data as a Lens on Human Culture* (New York: Penguin, 2013). For a summary of the most historically important findings in retrospect, Nina Tahmasebi et al., "Visions and Open Challenges for a Knowledge-Based Culturomics," *International Journal on Digital Libraries* 15: 2–4 (April 1, 2015), https://doi.org/10 .1007/s00799-015-0139-1: 169–70.

[2] Aiden and Michel, *Uncharted,* 7.

[3] Kalev Leetaru, "Culturomics 2.0: Forecasting Large-Scale Human Behavior Using Global News Media Tone in Time and Space," *First Monday* (August 17, 2011), https://doi.org/10.5210/fm .v16i9.3663.

[4] Philip Oltermann, "'At First I Thought, This Is Crazy': The Real-Life Plan to Use Novels to Predict the Next War," *The Guardian,* June 26, 2021, sec. Books, https://www.theguardian.com/ lifeandstyle/2021/jun/26/project-cassandra-plan-to-use-novels-to-predict-next-war.

human societies through a method of studying quantitative indicators that he dubbed "cliodynamics". Poring over population numbers through the history of revolts in China, Turchin believed that he had found an alignment between population collapse and revolution, which could be applied meaningfully to American history, or to any other stage in human development. After gathering together an enormous database of population growth, violence, and technology in the human past, Turchin believed he had the material to create a "political stress index" that could predict coming conflagrations. In 2020, he proudly told a journalist at *The Atlantic* about his newest prediction: a revolution was set to explode in America in coming years.[5]

Such ideas are highly attractive to investors who want to anchor their bets on the future to data about the past. But if the models and data used by the scientists in question are so vast as they claim, why aren't they predicting election results with accuracy already?

One answer is that history is far more complex that the culturomics or cliodynamics communities have suggested. Only in science fiction are the rules of history reduced to a series of either/or propositions, computable by electronic synapses wired to reduce data into a law that states "whenever this happens, that also tends to happen." Claims of predicting the future have been made before: in the 1960s, psychologists armed with UNIVAC (Universal Automatic Computer) claimed to be able to predict elections and tilt the war in Vietnam; they too failed.[6] Only in science fiction can history be modeled with a simple push of a button.Although he could not have known it at the time, Asimov did a disservice to future generations of readers when he encouraged them to extrapolate sweeping "laws" of behavior from historical analysis. Popular opinions and hunches have often failed to accurately foretell impending collapses – think of Marie Antoinette, on the verge of the French Revolution, laughing about the crowd, or the faithful that gathered in churches to greet the expected Last Judgment in the year 999 as predicted in the Apocrypha. Even while Asimov was working on his novels, historians were busy discrediting the ideas that would so fascinate Asimov's readers.

In the twentieth century, several notable social scientists attempted to stake out the terrain of what a "scientific method" would look like for history and they rejected Asimov's conceit. In 1936, Karl Popper began his

---

[5] Graeme Wood, "The Next Decade May Be Even Worse," *Atlantic Monthly* (November 12, 2020), https://www.theatlantic.com/magazine/archive/2020/12/can-history-predict-future/616993.
[6] Jill Lepore, *If Then*.

project of defining a scientific method for the social sciences by arguing against the fantasy of *determinism*, that is, the idea that history unfolds according to causes that are already established, so that the outcome is already determined and the future can be reckoned from the evidence of the law-like forces of history that run in parallel to the forces of nature. The idea was formulated in a seminar paper called "The Philosophy of Historicism," which he presented at the London School of Economics at a seminar led by Fredrich Augustus von Hayek.

In his seminar paper, which twenty years later would appear as a book of the same name, Popper stressed that historical events are unique, and human behavior unpredictable. Popper took as his aim all those theories that asserted that human behavior could indeed be predicted and followed consistent laws – a line of thinking that he believed to originate with Plato and Aristotle, running through Hegel and Marx into modern ambitions of making "large-scale forecasts" like the ones that ran rampant in Europe of the 1930s: predictions about the certainty of war, the unavoidability of class conflict, or the triumph of one race over others – a category that Popper called "absolute trends." He also thought that they were nonsense, especially when viewed over longer arcs of time.

The "historicism" of Popper's title is, according to Herbert Keuth, specifically the belief that past behavior predicts future behavior.[7] In denouncing prediction, Popper was plotting a revolutionary path for the discipline of modern history that would take it away from the predictive modeling typical of most university disciplines for much of the twentieth century. In this new, nonpredictive history, scholars would come to study events as evidence that society is confronting and rethinking "problems." A civil rights movement is evidence that a society is rethinking race and coming up with new categories, solutions, and ways of being. A women's movement is evidence that a society is rethinking gender. Both are brought into being by people thinking, writing, dreaming, and acting out their experiences. Neither is evidence of anything unavoidable, or anything that could have been seen in advance.

Predicting conflict in general, Popper argued, is impossible, because too many factors feed into the determination of any single war in the past, and modeling a comparison would humiliate the mathematician. Put another way, it would be impossible in Popper's view to construct scientific experiments with history, because conditions have changed since their performance.

[7] Herbert Keuth, *The Philosophy of Karl Popper* (Cambridge: Cambridge University Press, 2005), 196–204.

A scientific method for history, therefore, would require attention to the details that differentiated each new event in its time, as well as a narrative style that highlighted, not determinism, but rather the capacity for *contingency* in history, that is, the complicating causes, unknowable to contemporaries, that burden every human choice with unintended consequence.[8] In the decades since Popper, historians have reaffirmed his analysis: humans, both as individuals and as societies, are unpredictable and it is never possible to narrow the outcome to something knowable in advance.[9]

Popper, Asimov, and Fischer all belonged to an era that was wrestling with the degree to which history was knowable, and to which the tragedies of the past were inevitable. Through different means, all three attempted to imagine a scientific method for history. While Asimov fantasized about a purely logical mechanism for predicting history, the practicing historians tended to work by debunking false principles of history, revealing the ways that untruth had come into common acceptance. As another member of Fischer's generation, Quentin Skinner, complained, "We inevitably approach the past in the light of contemporary paradigms and presuppositions, the influence of which may easily serve to mislead us at every turn."[10] From the wreckage of narcissistic, self-serving categories whose definition once formed a focus of the humanities, the theorists of this era began to formulate a series of questions that help them to identify the elements of history that were suppressed in the past. Alongside Walter Benjamin, whose intellectual flight from the mythologies of the Third Reich was followed by a thwarted attempt at physical escape that ended with suicide, historians began to notice that history was written by the victors and that the perspectives of the illiterate, the indigenous, colonized peoples, women, and divergent sexual subjects frequently vanished in a view of the past grounded in the victors' perspective.[11] Many researchers, such as the historian and literary critic Hayden White, became fascinated

---

[8] Karl Popper, *The Poverty f Historicism* (New York: Routledge & Kegan Paul, 1957), 7–28.

[9] For the transition to predictive modeling in the natural sciences, see Matthew L. Jones, "How We Became Instrumentalists again: Data Positivism Since World War II," *Historical Studies in the Natural Sciences* 48:5 (2018): 673–84; Tal Yarkoni and Jacob Westfall, "Choosing Prediction over Explanation in Psychology: Lessons from Machine Learning," *Perspectives on Psychological Science* 12:6 (2017): 1100–22.

[10] Quentin Skinner, "The Rise of, Challenge to, and Prospects of a Collingwoodian Approach to the History of Political Thought," in Dario Castiglione and Iain Hempsher-Monk, eds., *The History of Political Thought in National Context* (Cambridge: Cambridge University Press, 2001), 181.

[11] Benjamin writes, "Empathy with the victors thus comes to benefit the current rulers every time. This says quite enough to the historical materialist. Whoever until this day emerges victorious, marches in the triumphal procession in which today's rulers tread over those who are sprawled underfoot. The spoils are, as was ever the case, carried along in the triumphal procession." "On the

with the "metanarratives" about the past, once proposed as law-like forces, and how little those claims stood the test of time. Once-supreme assumptions that were commonly discussed by learned historians and social scientists of the nineteenth century – for instance, the superiority of European "civilization" to "barbarity" or the Protestant work ethic – are studied as antiquities of earlier imperial projects. But their assertions are no longer taken as *universal laws*. Well might contemporary analysts in business and technology propose new laws of behavior, Moore's law that computer memory doubles in capacity every twelve to eighteen months being the one that has enjoyed the most renown; professional historians have remained skeptical.[12] Fantasies about the past were being purged in order that the systematic study of historical truth could proceed.

For many of the reasons we've discussed already, the quantitative analysis of past and future can easily go astray. The research program that I have outlined here – careful inspection of the data, respect for the building blocks of the past, interdisciplinary collaboration, and critical thinking through every stage in the process – promises to get us closer to the *lived reality* that data represents; and this is important – even more crucial than "prediction" – when the data is being used to determine the workings of institutions in the real world.

To avoid danger, it is vital that the analysts of textual data be honest about their motivations. The analyst who believes that texts should be used to predict the future would be wise to consider where that ambition came from and to remember how many unhappy accidents have been driven by that fantasy: a view of the future unaccompanied by a knowledge of the territory of human culture.

The Dream of Predictive Social Science

The dream of predictive social science has been with us for centuries. One might say it found its first rigorous articulation, its first manifesto, when

Concept of History" (1940) in Walter Benjamin, *Gesammelten Schriften* I:2. (Frankfurt am Main: Suhrkamp Verlag, 1974), trans. Andy Blunden, in excerpt www.marxists.org/reference/archive/benjamin/1940/history.htm. For the earlier conceit, going back to Thucydides, that history "vindicates" the victors, see Priya Satia, *Time's Monster* (Cambridge, MA: Harvard University Press, 2020), 17–18.

[12] For once-supreme assumptions and one of the major works reviewing the making and unmaking of history in the service of European empire, see Priya Satia, ibid. For Moore's law and other futurist strategies for prediction from a historian's point of view, see Staley, *History and the Future* 8. For skepticism about Moore's law, see William A. Gorton, *Karl Popper and the Social Sciences* (Albany, NY: SUNY Press, 2012), 129, n. 4.

Karl Marx applied a Hegelian conception of history to his analysis of economic injustice. By the mid-twentieth century, however, came the first wave of computers capable of crunching massive amounts of data. Asimov's fictional character, Hari Seldon, the historian who could predict the future with the power of math, was developed in this clime. Seldon was more than a fantasy: he was the reflection, in story form, of the dream life of a generation.

Asimov's fable helped to shape the directions explored by a generation of social scientists. When Asimov was working on *Foundation*, anthropologists, sociologists, and psychologists were still working the old way, reading books, taking field notes, quantifying anything they could measure and piecing their observations together in pursuit of the elusive and possibly apocryphal laws of human behavior. Yet the age of predictive social sciences was already forming in the bud.

Psychology was, perhaps, the first domain to hazard an attempt at a predictive social science. By the early 1950s, a pair of electrical engineers, J. Presper Eckert and John Mauchly, built the mainframe system known as UNIVAC (Universal Automatic Computer). A primitive behemoth, fed with punchcards, UNIVAC correctly predicted an Eisenhower landslide over Adlai Stevenson, while the Gallup poll foresaw him winning by a razor-thin margin. Before long, psychologists at Stanford and Massachusetts Institute of Technology (MIT) had their eyes on how the UNIVAC's successor, UNIAC, could be used for marketing research – for influencing consumptions habits and altering the course of elections. Scholars soon tried to model the desires of peasants in Southeast Asia as a way of speeding an American agenda during the Vietnam War.[13]

Again and again, predictive social science has fallen short of the ideal set for it by science fiction. Predictive social science has looked for laws of human behavior, but it has never evolved anything like a "historical method" – the collection of techniques and guidelines where the origins of a topic are traced and the subject's development is carefully considered through a series of subsequent phases that marked its evolution.

One component of sound historical methods, as we have seen, is the willingness to reckon with data: above all, historians must know where their data comes from. The scholarly concern with accurate data has not always been embraced by scholars who rushed to predict the future.

---

[13] Jill Lepore, *If/Then: How the Simulmatics Corporation Invented the Future* (New York: Liveright, 2020).

Can the Past Predict the Future?

The conversations that we have opened so far – about how to support a rigorous historical analysis of text – require a meeting place between humanities knowledge, and quantitative thinking. But opening up a conversation in that place is no easy matter.

In the   quantitative sciences, the first question researchers ask one another will typically be this: "What are you trying to predict?" But the first attack leveled by members of the Temporal Cartographers' Society against digital work might commence with these words: "Surely, you don't think that we can predict the future?"

Skepticism from each side underscores a fundamental divide between two ways of knowing: one privileging data that provides laws that might predict the future, and one emphasizing the diversity and contingency of debatable social laws in the past. Those who ask humanistic questions using quantitative tools soon find themselves in the middle of a culture war – an epistemological war, even – where even exploratory missteps rapidly become the subject of scorn or mistrust from both sides.

One sign of cultural divides is the existence of a shibboleth, or a word whose usage by one group (and mispronunciation or misusage by another) defines the concepts of insider and outsider. The word "shibboleth" recalls the story from the Hebrew scriptures where the tribes from Gilead used the word as a test of belonging, using it to search out and murder outsiders from the band of Ephraimites, who previously had invaded Gilead but were now on the run. Because the Ephraimites lisped when they said the word "shibboleth," the Gileadites could recognize which individual belonged to their ranks.

Today, the word "prediction" functions as a shibboleth for defining ingroup and outgroup in the quantitative and history-focused disciplines. When scholars invoke "prediction" in everyday speech, they mean different things, but they tend to hold up their own definition of "prediction" as a marker of belonging.

Some analysts invoke prediction as a species of dangerous foretelling of the future. Prediction is the work of prophets and soothsayers. Prediction is also the realm of technocrats who promise to leverage advertising to control the outcome upcoming election. This is the sense in which most historians use the term – whether they are preaching, like Popper, about the fallacies of determinism, or, like Lepore, analyzing the work of the UNIAC machine and the promise of controlling American democracy. Prediction is the opposite of discourse, or listening. It is the opposite of participatory democracy. It stinks of bad logic and authoritarianism.

Other scholars use the term prediction to recall the mathematical certainty of an outcome, like the prediction that an apple will fall to the ground according to the law of gravity. Indeed, some digital humanists in literature use the term as a synonym for modeling or mathematical description.[14] Such scholars mainly invoke the term in reference to extrapolating from one set of data to another. They think of their work as a purely objective exercise in science, not an experiment in prophesy and still less a gesture with political content.

The disparity between the usages of the word "prediction" lies with the unspoken assumptions of both tribes, and that has to do with their orientation to past and future – how specifically those terms are applied to the data. What quantitative scholars imagine "predicting" has nothing to do with prophesying an absolute future. Rather, the analyst trains an algorithm on a sample of data, so that the algorithm performs well. Next, the scholar tests the same algorithm on another sample of data distinct from the original sample, measuring the difference in performance. This difference in performance, in turn, is sometimes used as a marker of raw *difference* between two sets of data.

"Before" and "after" are completely relative in this usage. It isn't necessarily true that the training sample comes from a period chronologically prior to the test sample. The model "predicts" the algorithm's behavior with the second set and the scholar is interested in any failure of the supposed "prediction," which signals a gap between model and reality.[15] The only *pre*-diction – literally, forward telling – involved is the bet that the algorithm in question will be able to accurately interpret the *next* dataset it's faced with. If the algorithm is imagined as a bot, which an analyst will run on social media commentary in some future that hasn't happened yet, the test metaphor suggests that a successful algorithm is one that can "predict" – that is, successfully generate about – future text as yet

[14] For a strong defense of "prediction" from the literary digital humanities, which I would forward as an example of eliding the difference between prediction and modeling, see Ted Underwood, "Critical Response II. The Theoretical Divide Driving Debates about Computation," *Critical Inquiry* 46:4 (June 1, 2020): 900–12, https://doi.org/10.1086/709229. Ted Underwood associates prediction with corpus linguistics, Peter Norvig, and computational linguistic's challenge to Chomskian theory. I will offer a slightly different interpretation of the revolutions in linguistics in Chapter 13 – one grounded in the revisions to earlier laws made possible by "modeling" the archive of language past, as visible in historical linguistics. The variant uses of the term "prediction" in each discipline – and how that word invokes a relative past and future, which is not always the same as the absolute future of what has not yet happened – are beyond the bounds of this book.

[15] Ted Underwood, *Distant Horizons: Digital Evidence and Literary Change* (Chicago, IL: University of Chicago Press, 2019) is filled with examples of the usage of prediction in this sense.

unspoken. Success in computation often means inventing a "predictive" algorithm, which is one that will continue to work in the future, when applied to texts that have not yet been written.

Most of the time, what analysts of culture care about is not prediction, but rather *difference* – a word that has been used since the 1970s to reference philosophers' debates about the nuanced shifts wherein meaning and politics arise.[16] Such a use of "difference" also coincides, to a large part, with ideas associated with Claude Shannon, one of the pioneers of information theory and, thus, of modern computing. Trained in mathematics at the University of Michigan and MIT, Shannon was a polymath who wrote theories that bridged cryptography, studies in automata, and literature. His home office was filled with objects such as a mechanical mouse that was programmed to find its way through a maze and a dry cleaner's ceiling chain, hung with the gowns that he had been awarded along with honorary degrees, that he would turn on when guests visited, so that the gowns' glowing fabrics danced around the room.[17]

Shannon began his work in the environment of the Second World War, where cryptographers on both sides of the Atlantic competed to crack enemy codes and devise unbreakable coding machines. Shannon's algorithms were designed while he was at Bell Labs, studying the components of "noiseless channels." At Bell Labs, his investigation led him to imagine algorithms that would support the efficient encoding of telegraphs, telephone calls, and other messages by eliminating words or letters that added nothing new to a message. He named the measure of pure, novel information, perfectly conveyed, "entropy." The opposite of entropy – or material that contributed no new information – he named "redundancy."[18] By maximizing entropy and minimizing redundancy, Shannon estimated that the efficiency of any encryption could be increased by half.

While many wartime cryptographers, for instance Alan Turing, were fascinated with the possibility of their calculations for supporting a new

---

[16] This use of the term "difference" of course references the word as used by Jacques Derrida of *Différance*.

[17] Robert Calderbank and Neil J. A. Sloane, "Obituary: Claude Shannon (1916–2001)," *Nature* 410:6830 (April 12, 2001): 768.

[18] For Shannon's original formulation of the theory, Claude E. Shannon, "A Mathematical Theory of Communication," *Bell System Technical Journal* 27 (July, October 19848): 379–523, 623–56. For an introduction to information theory and its application to humanities problems, see Simon DeDeo, "Information Theory for Intelligent People" (2015), unpublished manuscript http://santafe.edu/~simon/it.pdf. For more on Shannon and the need for exploration of how classical information theory aligns with humanities problem, see Leif Weatherby, "Critical Response I. Prolegomena to a Theory of Data: On the Most Recent Confrontation of Data and Literature," *Critical Inquiry* 46:4 (June 1, 2020): 891–99, https://doi.org/10.1086/709228.

information age, Shannon was uniquely concerned with framing information as broadly as possible. Turing observed of Shannon: "Shannon wants to feed not just data to a Brain, but cultural things!"[19]

In his published papers, Shannon's meditations on information moved over subjects as diverse as efficiency in transformers and the lexicon of James Joyce. He applied his ideas about measurement to problems including species extinction, contributing one of the lasting indexes for measuring biodiversity. Shannon's ideas about this measurement would later be applied to the precision of lasers and the successful encoding of bits into strings of electrons exchanged across the circuits of microchips to quantum computing.[20] As James Gleick has observed of Shannon's revolution in measurement, he performed the same theorization of information that nineteenth-century natural philosophers performed for the concept of "energy," abstracting information into a universal that could be measured in its pure form in any system whatsoever.

Shannon's theoretical abstractions around information remain powerful in many contexts, offering one standard for the measurement of change over time, influence, or innovation. As a measure of pure "difference," Shannon's algorithm has been used to calculate how different the words in any two documents are. Today, some scholars asking questions about history use Shannon's algorithms to measure the raw difference between two bodies of text, thus extracting Shannon's measure of "entropy" into a measure of raw change over time.[21] More grandly, some scholars have even suggested that "feedback" – an abstraction of Shannon's redundancy or "noise" in the system – constitutes a way of generalizing about the social and economic consequences of disruptions in history, for instance the industrial revolution.[22]

---

[19] James Gleick, *The Information* (New York: Pantheon, 2011), n.p.
[20] The standard history of Shannon's contributions to technology is Paul J. Nahin, *The Logician and the Engineer: How George Boole and Claude Shannon Created the Information Age* (Princeton, NJ: Princeton University Press, 2017). For the Shannon index of biodiversity, Ian F. Spellerberg and Peter J. Fedor, "A Tribute to Claude Shannon (1916–2001) and a Plea for More Rigorous Use of Species Richness, Species Diversity and the 'Shannon–Wiener' Index," *Global Ecology and Biogeography* 12:3 (2003): 177–79.
[21] Patrick Juola, "Language Change and Historical Inquiry," *Humanities, Computers and Cultural Heritage*, 2005, 169; Patrick Juola, "The Time Course of Language Change," *Computers and the Humanities* 37:1 (2003): 77–96; Alexander T. J. Barron et al., "Individuals, Institutions, and Innovation in the Debates of the French Revolution," *Proceedings of the National Academy of Sciences* 115:18 (May 1, 2018): 4607–12, https://doi.org/10.1073/pnas.1717729115.
[22] E. Anthony Wrigley, "The Interplay of Demographic, Economic, and Social History," *The Journal of Interdisciplinary History* 50:4 (February 1, 2020): 495–515, https://doi.org/10.1162/jinh_a_01483. It is interesting to contrast Wrigley's formulation of "feedback" with an older

Textual comparison, of course, is one of the oldest tools in the toolbox of the humanities; it's as old as the bishop Eusebius, who in the fourth century, carefully compared the differences between the accounts of the four gospels in order to establish a more perfect account of the life of Christ. Historians compare documents all the time; comparing eyewitness accounts and official accounts, for example, is one of the best approaches to differentiating historical truth from rumor and hearsay.[23] Good journalists do it; good historians do it; lawyers, of course, review documents and attempt to prove what actually happened, on the basis of comparing many factual accounts. All these professions highlight "difference" in comparing texts, and increasingly, many of them look to wordcount and other computational shortcuts to aid their labors. But none of them refer to their work, however quantitative or general, as "prediction," because that term – however embraced in computational circles as the standard of success – freights the work with undue expectations. The point of serious work that uses the historical method is to establish a consensus about the truth of what happened in the past, not creating a machine that can prophesy patterns in the future.

For scholars interested in time, the word "prediction" evokes implications about the absolute future. The discipline of history defines prediction as the modeling of future events that have not yet taken place, and historians typically circumscribe such work as outside of their practice for extremely specific reasons, even though historians have no trouble with generalizing about cultures past.

The different ways in which words such as "prediction" are used may seem like a trivial matter. But speaking different languages is one of the forces that creates a gulf between the quantitative and qualitative disciplines and which stops the disciplines from being able to talk to each other.

---

generalization from political science, of "resistance," associated with James C. Scott, which was similarly modeled from theories in physics, to describe social processes that resist change. Whereas resistance is framed as a check on progress, feedback, as Wrigley notes, can be either positive or negative. Resistance builds upon data from social and political history, analyzing conflict as a signal of resistance, whereas Wrigley's theory of "feedback" generalizes about mortality, harvest failure, and the burden of household dependents. I extrapolate slightly by referencing Wrigley's notion of feedback in a paragraph on textual analysis, as Wrigley is chiefly interested demographic data, but I reference him because I find his meditation on general metrics of temporality useful to the larger discussion here on prediction, difference, and temporality.

[23] For an example of a sustained comparison between eyewitness and official accounts of the past, see Kim A. Wagner, *Amritsar 1919* (New Haven, CT: Yale University Press, 2019).

The Problem with the Data

Distortions happen where data science is tangled up with the fantasy of prediction, and concerns about the completeness of the archive are forgotten. Consider Peter Turchin's project of distilling quantitative data from history into "laws" about the rise and fall of civilization. Turchin's 300,000-incident-long database – the Seshat database, named for the Egyptian goddess of knowledge – of inventions, warfare, starvation, and protest movements are doubtless *interesting* for history, and the labor required to compile and annotate the events in question is impressive.[24] It's clear that Turchin intended the Seshat dataset to establish a new threshold of facticity about human experience, as revolutionary in our time as the invention of writing was in the past. But is Turchin's dataset vast enough to meet Koselleck's standards for a predictive science?

Many historians believe that, in the past, the publications of philosophers and novelists, and the activities of graffiti writers and peasants who have claimed to have had visions of the Virgin Mary have been among the individuals whose actions precipitated revolution. Such events as these – typically classified as the events of "social" and "cultural" history by historians – have little place in most quantitative databases. Omitting social and cultural data leaves open to question the *robustness* of data represented in any collection supposed to catalog events in general. Another category of analysis usually missing in quantitative data is a sense of the different levels of confidence that historians place in different events. Most historians would argue that there is no such thing as a collection of historical facts devoid of interpretation: the numbers of individuals who died in the Holocaust and Stalinist purges are known with some certainty today only after decades of scholarly debate. In a database like Seshat, which aims to establish an index of historical events based on numbers, historians might wish for something like a confidence score – perhaps, scoring one point for every dozen articles contesting the data published in a scholarly journal.Issues of interpretation – for example, whether cultural and social events count alongside wars, or how confident we are in various numbers – lie at the foundation of the structures on which quantitative history is built. Computers, of course, don't automatically know when an "event" is happening. Humans must tell them what to notice: a collapse in stock prices, a dramatic surge in population, perhaps, or a

[24] Peter Turchin et al., "An Introduction to Seshat: Global History Databank," SocArXiv (September 8, 2019), https://doi.org/10.31235/osf.io/394w2.

war characterized by large numbers of casualties. The actual documents from which those details came are not part of the data: there is no catalog of potsherds or editions of Herodotus given in support of the details.Historians are skilled inspectors of the evidence behind any argument about the past. They scour the various sources for history; like a judge at a trial, they review the testimony of as many observers as possible. Humanists like to know where each piece of data came from. They inspect the details carefully. They command an enormous number of robust facts, whose authenticity they are always questioning. We know the innermost hopes and fears of the Founding Fathers of the United States because their pamphlets and private letters and even diaries have been carefully pored over. We know the differences between the quarto editions of Shakespeare's plays printed in his lifetime and the folio version of his collected works assembled after his death by his actors. Such minutiae are inspected not out of some idolatry of the past, but because scholarly debates about obscure phraseology in the Constitution, or small poetic variations in Shakespeare, can transform our understanding of the author's intentions.Historians don't just take the word of one media pundit or newspaper, when reading of a riot. They arrive at a consensus about historical truth only after rigorous comparison of artifacts, facts, and models of history. They might not reach consensus for a long time. Bringing the same level of curiosity, confidence, and robust inspection to quantitative data is no simple task.In the hands of historians, big data does something different than mere prediction based on a collection of transparent observations. It tends not to produce a single answer – a prediction of when Hari Seldon would be arrested, say, or an insight into a totally unknown event – but rather a complex of models.

The Data Revolution in History and the Promise of Complexity

In the hands of historians, big data does something different than mere prediction. It tends not to produce a single answer – a prediction of when Hari Seldon would be arrested, say, or an insight into a totally unknown event – but rather a complex of models.

Complexity is a result of the vast number of features in play when historians turn their attention to the past. When a dozen scholars of the ancient world gathered to review the Seshat data, they found a provocation that launched them into a deep conversation with earlier generations of scholars. The scholars were interested in structurally reviewing the evidence that a single major philosophical and political revolution shook the ancient world – a moment of social reorganization, from which the great religions of Zoroastrianism, Daoism, and Buddhism emerged. Over half a century ago, the philosopher Karl Jaspers theorized the existence of such a moment in the distant past. He believed that at a particular stage of development, human societies began to organize themselves around a single law, guided by similar expressions of the egalitarian impulses, around the same time. That is, Jaspers believed that most great human civilizations participated in a moment called the "Axial Age."

Some historians of the ancient world have worked directly on Peter Turchin's impressive, comparative index of population, technology, and conflict over time. For the scholars who recently revisited the theory of the Axial Age with Turchin's Seshat data as their guide, big data was an inspiration and a touchstone. But big data alone did not do the heavy lifting. Instead, their chapters describe structured conversations between teams of scholars, established and upcoming, as they debated common terms of reference, turning over the meaning of the data, one civilization at a time. Many ancient philosophies, the experts agreed, contemplated the equality of the human condition and dreamed of a single truth – the Tao of Lao-Tzu, the universal Good of Plato, or the Dharma of the Buddha. But the experts also noticed that the kind of equality and the exceptional hierarchies that typified each society were increasingly divergent.[25]

The scholars' findings did not demonstrate an Axial Age; they showed that different societies changed at different points in their own development. To some observers, however, the collective analysis suggested a threshold in scale, beyond which societies tend to adopt "more prosocial and egalitarian moral principles," in the words of the scholars' conclusion.[26] They theorized that the threshold implied a return to "moral intuitions," hardwired into human behavior at some point in our evolution, which tend to be systematized as a society grows in diversity and scale. But other scholars emphasized that what looked like a "rule" of development in some places, with clearly demarcated phases, looked entirely different in Japan or among the Haudenosaunee. Some stressed that European empires – which might be expected to strive for egalitarian ideals, given the model – actually inflicted extreme oppression on the societies they colonized, "a far cry from the 'universal moral ideals'

---

[25] This process of collaboration is described in detail by Daniel Hoyer and Jenny Reddish in "Introduction," in Daniel Hoyer and Jenny Reddish, eds., *Seshat History of the Axial Age* (Chaplin, CT: Beresta Books, 2019).

[26] Harvey Whitehouse et al., "Conclusion: Was There Ever an Axial Age?" in Hoyer and Reddish, *Seshat History of the Axial Age*, 395.

expected of a post-axial society."[27] Importantly, the scholars' models, once supplied from data, renounced much of the *predictive* theory associated with Karl Jaspers. There was no mathematical law that bound the data about the experience of the ancient world into a series of law-like principles that would have predicted the difference between the philosophies associated with the Persian, Incan, Hawaiian, and Japanese empires. To understand each, a student would have to study the history, not just the data.

In his preface for Hoyer and Reddish's Seshat book, classicist Ian Morris reflected on the experience of collaboration, emphasizing how different the collaborative, data-driven work was from the traditional model of the solitary scholar in his study. Under the influence of data, the conversation became more precise, the points of comparison more nuanced. But Morris emphasized that, while the database allowed scholars to collaborate, it didn't predict a single outcome or law.[28] The scholars who worked on the Seshat project together highlighted a diversity of models of organization and hierarchy, showing that many societies chose a path toward equality even while others were becoming more hierarchical , an argument that runs in parallel to the mainly qualitative evidence of story, architecture, and archaeology collected by David Graeber and David Wengrow. Data about fourteen different civilizations was standardized so that quantitative comparisons were possible and those comparisons (to judge by the scholars' writing) were thrilling to contemplate. But the collaborative study of fourteen different civilizations still produced fourteen different models of historical development.

The fact that models diverge doesn't mean that the models are wrong, or that historians have been asking the wrong questions. Complexity and nuance in modeling are often signs of rigor. Modeling complex data can produce richly descriptive portraits of the past that highlight the diversity of forms of social organization possible. They can also tell us specific stories about the recent past and how we became who we are today.

Turchin's approach is *deductive:* he starts with theories and large categories of data and tries to find laws. The classical model of humanists as antiquarians, by contrast, is *inductive* work: they start by minutely examining the artifacts and from it theorize truths. They may simply describe the chronology of novels written by a single author. They may discern turning points and discontinuities in the past, or argue for the influence of particular individuals, books, or social movements. Chiefly, they describe.

---

[27] Ibid., 401.   [28] Ian Morris, "Preface," in Hoyer and Reddish, *Seshat History of the Axial Age.*

Their claims are grounded in evidence, not asserted because the claims align with some supposed law of how things work.

Some thinkers in the digital humanities have underscored a tension between this sure-footed work with evidence and the generalizations that we tend to make with data, but at the heart of the place where humanists and data meet is a question about whether this data is trustworthy for that project.[29] It's a question of fit. Once we acknowledge that fit is a problem, we can continue making inferences based on limited data and possible theorems. This is a new kind of thinking: *abduction,* tacking between the possibility of inferences about generalizations and the reality of all that is known about bodies of evidence. The approach that Ian Morris describes of the ancient historians at work on the Seshat data operates at the level of abduction. They read theory; they study the sources; they carefully discern which ones are trustworthy. They make inferences. In fact, most humanists today operate somewhere in the zone of abduction, working between overarching theories about human nature, class, race, gender, and time, and the evidence closest to them, to make complex models of society.

The risk of working with deduction alone is that it reifies the data. One assumes that the dataset with which one works houses the complete set of information necessary for the model. Turchin's fascination with predictive laws has led him to propose a singularly narrow set of data as a definitive dataset on the past, where new technology and battles arise constantly, out of nowhere, and unchanging logics of history mark their relationships in defiance of the grand differences of culture and organization mapped out by philosophers of history. The desire to show the existence of historical laws requires strictly subsetted data; conversely, sufficiently narrow data may seem to support laws that don't actually exist. An approach to understanding the past that is grounded not in laws, but in *theory*, requires working with more diverse kinds of data and a richer sensitivity to where the data came from.

---

[29] For the "contradictions" of abstracting sources into data for the purpose of research in the humanities as a "necessary contradiction" that nevertheless requires care, see Miriam Posner, "Humanities Data: A Necessary Contradiction," June 25, 2015: http://miriamposner.com/blog/humanities-data-a-necessary-contradiction. See also Lara Putnam, "The Transnational and the Text-Searchable: Digitized Sources and the ShadowsThey Cast,"*American Historical Review* 121:2 (2016): 377–402, doi:10.1093/ahr/121.2.377; Lauren Klein, "The Carework and Codework of the Digital Humanities," May 2015: http://lklein.com/2015/06/the-carework-and-codework-of-the-digital-humanities. For argumentation, discontinuity, etc. in digital history, see Arguing with Digital History working group, "Digital History and Argument," white paper, Roy Rosenzweig Center for History and New Media (November 13, 2017): https://rrchnm.org/argument-white-paper.

There are datasets that don't rely, as Turchin's does, on proxy data like rough counts of the dead: that is, practices that aggregate text from original sources. Theories penned in the shape of words can almost always have multiple meanings. And historians are familiar with the rules of interpretation, of guessing what this word means, when we can know, and when a speaker deliberately invoked polysemy to signal possibility.

Digitalized collections of text still have shortcomings that require work with care: the digitalized transcripts of the debates in parliament in the nineteenth century – the data used for case studies throughout this book – have errors introduced by computers; they sometimes miss data, due to errors in processing as well as to errors introduced by the journalists and clerks who originally attempted to transcribe the live debates from the gallery above parliament's floor. The transcripts necessarily exclude the voices of women, since neither the House of Commons nor the House of Lords had women members until the twentieth century.

However, those transcripts still offer a diversity of voices, showing different logics of history at work in the same room. There are Irish revolutionaries like Charles Parnell, speaking alongside conservative imperialists like A. J. Balfour. Novelists such as Benjamin Disraeli were also political speakers, and they employed literary style and rhetoric to persuade their fellow members of ideas about the past and visions of the future; we could employ the data to analyze the effectiveness of literary skill as a historical force. Text mining thus offers a portrait of what a rich and complex dataset about the past would look like.

The problem of the data scientist who works with text is not so much one of locating facts – such as the number of dead (multiple numbers were proposed for many important events) – but rather of locating differences of opinion and interpretation. Military events celebrated by one speaker are denounced by another as a massacre. The difference of opinion is the fact. This year, parliament debated how to fight cholera, whether by quarantine or building sewers; that year, parliament debated whether Britain should have an empire, with voices forcefully arrayed on either side. In textual databases, the data *is* a record of varied intention, action, and contestation. Treated with care, textual data offers a complex record of many vying voices. Text mining offers a perfect dataset for doing quantitative history – history with data science – where the digital record of experience is complex, not thin.

In other words, it is an advantage of textual datasets that multiple documents tend to disagree. We can compare multiple models of temporal significance because textual data is so diverse. From the point of view of modeling the past in all its richness, opening multiple windows on the past is highly desirable.

The transcripts of dissent are the perfect material to look at if we want to model a history based not on laws, but on a history that is highly contingent, that is, history in the realm of theory, where we generalize hesitantly on the basis of evidence that needs to be minutely examined. In contrast with Turchin's hypotheses about the specific role of population collapse, a historically informed process of text mining makes few assumptions and gathers a broader assortment of information, casting its trawling net wide across the ocean of empirical data.

Conclusion: The Role of Prediction Today

Accurate methods are important if scholars are to commit to an ethos, like the Hippocratic oath, of doing no harm. When we model the past, we're dealing with the lived reality of cultures. A machine learning algorithm that appears to perform correctly but introduces errors of miscalculation can create untold harm. A biased tool for measuring change in government opinion amounts to a propaganda machine. Too narrow a measure of "playfulness," used by a college admissions office as an algorithm to presort admissions essays, would recreate the profile of a 1950s' boarding school. Not only would these studies be unethical, but the results would also be wrong on a technical level insofar as the quantitative algorithms in question fail to reproduce the complex reality of civic, racial, political, or ideational diversity in the community at large. We do not need a simplistic data science that discerns a single trail through history and generalizes it into the future.

Does history in the age of theory *never* make predictions? Despite the rejection of determinism by historians since Popper, there's no outright ban on prediction as a mode of analysis in the humanities. Historians tend to be wary, however, of the idea that *models* apply to their field – in part because models are frequently used in the natural sciences to establish law-like forces, and the supposed existence of laws of history has been thoroughly discredited.

Nevertheless, legitimate questions about the use of history to predict, or at least advise, political action in the future have intrigued scholars for decades.[30] In general, the critical thinker who examines the applications of

---

[30] Niall Ferguson, *Virtual History: Alternatives and Counterfactuals* (New York: Basic Books, 1999) treats "what if" situations in history; Ethan B. Kapstein, *Seeds of Stability: Land Reform and US Foreign Policy* (Cambridge: Cambridge University Press, 2017) advances a case for "grievance

history tends to delineate the zones of permissible generalizations about the past with care. Reinhard Koselleck, for instance, rejects a mode of linking past to future that he calls "prophecy," whether it comes from astrology, the Bible, or Marx. As an alternative, he proposes a mode called "prognosis," which he counts as a legitimate exercise in historical thought, where the repeatability of experience in the past provides information "directed at singular political, social or economic events in the future."[31]

It is without a doubt true, explains Koselleck, that I can predict when the train is coming this afternoon on the basis of the train schedule printed earlier this year.[32] In this vein, Koselleck reasons that Hitler might have learned from Napoleon and Frederick the Great the ill advisement of starting a land war with Russia in winter.[33] The acknowledgment of general trends is sufficient for a scholar to make a prognosis, in Koselleck's conception. But prediction, Koselleck attests, would require a higher standard of data. The ideal dataset would house a record of each thought and action upon which the course of events might depend – not only, that is, wars and famines, but also books, conversations, and ideas. Only with such an impossible dataset could the *singularity:repetition* ratio be calculated, and could a science of prediction come to rest upon the raw materials of history.

As Koselleck makes clear, whenever we deal in the pure realm of projection, we are necessarily talking about fantasy, not a well-trodden academic realm with its own well-crafted methodology. Koselleck's emphasis on studying repetition and singularity hearkens back to the critical intervention in historical methods developed by the philosopher Karl Popper shortly after the publication of Asimov's *Foundation* series. Popper reacted with horror to the idea that academics might try to predict the future, in part because he knew many who had tried – with disastrous results. In his youth, Popper had worked alongside Marxist organizers who

---

theory" as predictive of the outcome of future US engagements on the basis of the satisfaction of grievances visible in the past.

[31] Reinhart Koselleck, *Sediments of Time* (Palo Alto, CA: Stanford University Press, 2018), 168.

[32] Ibid., 5.

[33] Here is the passage: "After his bloody defeat at Kunersdorf in 1759, Frederick the Great wrote a brief essay about Charles XII of Sweden, whose forces had been decimated exactly a half-century earlier at Poltava by Peter the Great's Russian army. And Frederick deduced an enduring prediction from this: that everyone who advances from western Europe to the east without taking into account conditions of geography and climate will be cut off from his supplies and squander any chance at victory. If Napoleon or Hitler had read this text and had also realized the threatening sequences of actions that were anticipated there, they would have never – under comparable logistical premises – begun their Russian campaigns. They experienced their Poltavas in Moscow and Stalingrad." Ibid., 169.

believed they could predict a revolution on the basis of the level of violence that accompanied their political demonstrations. They urged workers at public gatherings to pursue violence, whatever the consequences, so that they could hasten the revolution.

After attending a rally where the police shot eight of his unarmed friends, Popper began to mull over the logic behind the protest with disgust. Violent demonstrations, he concluded, did not necessarily hasten the revolution; they might simply result in the loss of life. Chastened by these experiences, he began to mull over the criteria for predictability. Two decades later, Popper would publish his theories about why history did not follow predictable laws.[34]

In physics, Popper explained, scientists looked for "laws" like the law of gravity, which applied everywhere. To assert that history followed laws implied the existence of *unchanging principles* that governed human behavior – the domain, perhaps, of psychology. But historians found few such principles; indeed, the study of history revolves around the study of the *differences* that mark human societies, and the events that were unique to each era in the past.[35]

The law that professional historians do not deal in predictive behavior, however, has specific exceptions. We have already seen that Koselleck makes room for a category of "prognosis" where examples from the past can inform the future. Certain professionals use prognosis in a structured way, for example, in business schools, where since the 1970s, students have prepared for the future using the "scenario method" developed at Royal Dutch Shell to review case studies of success and failure in the past.[36] Modern defenders of grievance theory, many of whom move in political, military, and development circles, argue that a sober analysis of social psychology can, at times, effectively *predict* that conflict will arise, a loose claim about the kinds of things that are true of experience.[37]

Popper understood that the fantasy of being able to predict the future can lead to naïve and problematic deference to authority figures. While

---

[34] For an account of Popper's experience of Marxism, his rejection of law-like forces, and his intellectual debts to Marx, see Gorton, *Karl Popper and the Social Sciences.*

[35] Popper, *Poverty of Historicism,* 7–28.

[36] For the scenario method as a use of history to predict the future, and for other applications of the historical method to future studies, see David Staley, *History and the Future* (Lanham, MA: Lexington, 2007). Staley makes clear that the story of how historians grew skeptical of prediction and futurology presented here is in need of complication, and he sets out a rich survey of those historians, such as Warren Wagar, who have engaged futurism directly.

[37] For grievance theory, see Ethan B. Kapstein, *Seeds of Stability: Land Reform and US Foreign Policy* (Cambridge: Cambridge University Press, 2017).

Popper applied his critique to Marxist protesters, we might regard as equally problematic any predictions based on textual data that are generated in support of markets, where data scientists are often expected to produce compelling analytics that foreground opportunities for sales, regardless of their value to society. The grounds are ripe for distortion as business and security analysts have much to gain by promising investors and governments a magical machine for predicting the future. Since so much of modern life is based on an overwhelming number of mutable outcomes, there exist few heads so sober that they aren't turned, at least for a moment, by the promise of a crystal ball.

In the world of professional historians, terms like prediction are approached with the utmost care. Historians tend to bristle at anything that smacks of prophecy, even while historians past and present continue to hazard general rules for how the patterns of time repeat themselves. Leif Weatherby, who has studied the history of information science, warns against prediction as a gauge of success. "After all, no interpretation of cultural artifacts can rely entirely on predictive accuracy," he argues.[38] It is this kind of care that provides the foundation for a clear engagement with data, where the a priori assumptions for creating a certain model can be shared and richly debated.

Historians tend to generalize about past, present, and future only while acknowledging substantive differences between different events. Grievance theory's general prediction that ongoing acts of resistance will follow from the theft of land, by contrast, is fairly amorphous. The existence of grievances about stolen land or racial oppression doesn't predict *when* a revolution will happen; it merely offers a starting precept for taking seriously the *grounds* of ongoing political conflict, a grasp of the social forces at play within an economic reality. Historians prefer to work with data that is nuanced, rich, and diverse enough to support both characterizations of similarity between events as well as statements about their irreconcilable differences.

Unwary deans or provosts may set their universities up for failure in the long term by investing in "predictive" analyses of data, while underinvesting in traditional ways of testing proof from the humanities and social sciences. Supporting data science without supporting the humanistic reasoning that defines a tradition of critical thinking about human experience and institutions is a risky endeavor.

---

[38] Weatherby, "Critical Response I," 891–99

Data science without the humanities lays the groundwork for a naïve enthusiasm for predictive models that simply will not work. Without the humanities, predictive thinking means disengagement with inquiry into the biases and omissions that distort the truth of human experience.

How, then, can a savvy data scientist consult with the traditions of understanding change over time, and thus present a robust approach to the analysis of change over time? While the earlier chapters of this book have surveyed preliminary cautions for dealing with data and tempering expectation, Part II turns to the problem of change over time itself. As we shall see, quantitative approaches have, indeed, been bearing fruit when applied to the description of change over time in textual datasets. By drawing more richly upon traditions in the philosophy of history, future analysis can turn algorithmic methods toward the pursuit of a historical method appropriate for work with textual data.

PART II

The Hidden Dimensions of
Temporal Experience

CHAPTER 6

The Many Windows of the House of the Past

Agreement about recent events is one of the crucial ways that societies come to chart where they are and where they are going. Many times, it is not easy to reach consensus. Consider the anxious chatter over Twitter on the evening of January 6, 2021, as protesters dressed as Vikings and organized into paramilitary groups stormed the US House of Representatives (Figure 6.1). While commentators from every background were piping in – some dismissing events as a joke, others prophesying the collapse of democracy – the professional historians on Twitter were busy at work doing what they do best: comparing available frames for understanding the event and its significance.

Professional historians, whose job it is to discern truth about the past from the detritus of former civilizations, rarely claim to predict the future. But they are more than capable of engaging events like those of January 6 as they unfold. Historians tend to think about new events by comparison with the old, and they tend to move restlessly through the information at hand, comparing multiple vantage points, hesitant to foreclose upon any answers until they have examined the events, their origins and context, and the triggers for more recent developments, as a whole. As John Lewis Gaddis writes in *The Landscape of History*, "Causes always have contexts, and to know the former we must understand the latter."[1]

According to the German historian, Reinhart Koselleck, the significance of every event can be gauged by understanding the degree to which it represents a repetition of similar past events. The individuals who gathered in Washington, DC to protest and derail a democratic election were partially inspired to gather out of an encounter with what historians call "cultural memory" (a subject that we will explore extensively in Chapter 7). Cultural memory is the totality of the popular understandings of the past that are current at any moment in time. How individuals

[1] John Lewis Gaddis, *The Landscape of History* (Oxford: Oxford University Press, 2002), 97.

Figure 6.1   The storming of the US Capitol, January 6, 2021.
CC 4.0 by Flickr user TapTheForwardAssist.

understand their actions has a great deal to do with the previous events that those individuals might use to compare their present undertakings. As Astrid Erll wrote of another era, "If we want to understand '9/11', the actions of Islamic terrorists, or the re-actions of the West, we must naturally look at certain mental, discursive, and habitual paradigms that were formed in long historical processes – via cultural memory, as it were."[2] Just so, we can begin to analyze the events of January 6 by looking at the memories that circulated in the months leading up to the attack on the US Capitol building.

Whether they had gleaned their mental images from elementary school textbooks, documentaries, or television pundits, the individuals who stormed Congress that day came there with preformed ideations of what they were doing, dynamic narratives mined from the logic of protest in the past – as many historians on Twitter pointed out. They may have seen themselves as rebel colonists at the Boston Tea Party (Figure 6.2), or imagined themselves in more contemporary terms, as a conservative rejoinder to the George Floyd marches earlier that year.

---

[2] Astrid Erll, "Travelling Memory," *Parallax* 17:4 (November 1, 2011): 4–18.

Figure 6.2   Boston Tea Party, by W. D. Cooper. In *The History of North America* (London: E. Newberry, 1789). Plate opposite p. 58.
Rare Book and Special Collections Division, Library of Congress.

Protesters are not the only individuals who reason about their actions through thinking about historical precedents. As legal narratives are constructed around their crimes, prosecutors will build cases, quite similarly, from historical paradigms, comparing the mob, its ideological intentions, and its destructive acts with past protests and insurrections, and arguing from legal precedents. Likewise, the vast majority of citizens observing these events as spectators, whether consciously or unconsciously, analyze these events via their own broad or narrow, accurate or misleading, reference points.

Professional historians also scour their reference points to construct narratives, but they bring to this analysis a set of tools that strive for greater breadth and precision – tools that, ideally, are as carefully crafted as the scientific method. As historians watched the events of January 6, they turned to Twitter to discuss the significance of this mob.

Certain British historians speculated about a similarity between the Capitol Hill protest and the Gordon Riots of 1780 (Figure 6.3), when a working-class mob attacked the monuments that represented the British state. Storming every prison in London and the Bank of England, the crowd marched on parliament. When the army later descended upon them, up to 700 protesters were slain. They were a Protestant mob that

Figure 6.3   The burning of Newgate Prison during the Gordon Riots.
Engraving, London Metropolitan Archive.

had been mobilized around a conspiracy theory regarding the undue influence of Roman Catholics in Hanoverian England.

What makes the Gordon Riots apropos as a comparison with the attackers on the Capitol is complex. The Gordon rioters were *seemingly* mobilized against the Catholic minority. But historians today understood the mob as one of the first major instances of political cohesion among working-class Britons, a hungry and desperate people, coming into increasing awareness of their own political power.

In retrospect, the Gordon Rioters seem like a prescient and potentially radical social movement that clamored against the power of a contemporary elite. Some observers have noticed that freed slaves counted among their number. Within a few years, the working-class populations of London would begin to circulate Thomas Paine's *Rights of Man* (1791), a treatise that forcefully argued for a world in which ordinary working men could vote. Is it possible, then, that the January 6 mob also presented the first flush of a disorganized, working-class mob, that will later be re-formed, not around conspiracy theories, but around an aggressive new movement for participatory democracy?

The thought is compelling, but there are also reasons to think that other characteristics – namely, white supremacy – offer a better profile of the mood that launched the attacks of January 6. It was lost on few historians that the sixty-odd arrests of the mainly white rioters were in brazen contrast with the broadcast use of force in the George Floyd protests earlier that year, where some 14,000 protesters had been arrested. As pictures of the Capital police taking selfies with the insurrectionists began to circulate, historians examined the arcana of the mob's outfit, including sweatshirts celebrating Hitler's holocaust and calling for the murder of Jewish people. Historians familiar with the rise of white supremacy groups in contemporary America were quick to point out that a showdown had been brewing for decades, a sense of inevitability having been cultivated quite consciously within right-wing echo chambers and through incendiary "dog whistles" tweeted from the Oval Office itself.

Professional historians also asked careful questions about how we might know when the mob's actions were over. Some noted that Hitler's Beer Hall Putsch, despite being quickly quelled, nevertheless anticipated his rise to power a decade later. Some gathered examples of seemingly failed coups, such as Mussolini's March on Rome, which heralded resurgent movements to come. Carefully thinking through the sequence of such events, historians ruminated over the consequences of downplaying these protests and of ignoring what churns beneath such violent expressions. They were thinking, in part, about what Koselleck – who himself had been drawn into the Hitler youth and spent some years as a Nazi soldier – called the "repetition" of events. Even if this insurrection had, for now, been stopped in its tracks, the march on the House of Representatives, once enacted, could continue to exert a magnetic pull over future events. Even a failed insurrection – whose most aggressive participants were tracked down and charged with crimes, and the president impeached for encouraging it – could have the capacity to inspire further *repetitions*.

Very little has been able to stop such repetitions from happening, especially when they are energized by underlying grievances: for instance, the decline in real incomes in America since 1974, or the perception that American politics is structured so as to prohibit participatory politics from below. With each new protest, the community's language tends to become more refined, as its aims, its urgency, and its historical framing are turned into talking points.

We can consider, again, the Gordon Riots: from a conservative anti-Catholic mob, comes an organized working class, assembled into monster mobs, reciting the history of exclusion of working people from English politics since the Norman invasion, demanding the right to vote, organizing itself around newspapers and housing collectives, and determined at any cost to elect members to parliament. From rowdy beginnings, the mob would gradually come to form the British working class, sowing the seeds of what would become the Labour party whose work to establish modern socialism would eventually sound the death knell for the British aristocracy as it had existed in the eighteenth century. By the early decades of the twentieth century, many British children of working parents attended state-funded schools for the first time, while their parents retired on old age pensions, both enterprises funded by taxes gathered from the rich. Country houses were abandoned because they were too expensive to maintain. The old order crumbled and a new one was born.

To understand what is happening at any given time – say, when the news and social media explode as a mob attacks the Capitol – it's not enough to know the numbers: how many people and when. We also need a sense of what the rioters thought they were up to, where they agreed and disagreed with each other. We need to know if people have always felt this way, or if they only came to these feelings recently as a result of the influence of certain speakers and publications. We need to agree on what people did, what they said, and how new any of these ideas or actions were.

What would it mean to quantify comparisons such as these in terms of language and its change?

In Part I, we thought critically about archives, about the choice of keywords, about the structure of data, and about algorithms, but we have only glanced at the myriad perspectives that historians bring to time itself. The grand categories of influence and agency or cause and effect only scratch the surface of the multiple ways that humans can tell stories about the past. It will become necessary to enter fully into the vast house of windows that comprises history, looking out through each window, in order to glimpse the variety of ways that data promises to transform our conversation.

The chapters that follow investigate how critical use of algorithms can help scholars to discern events over short timeframes and long timeframes. They ask questions about how each era is different from other eras; how each era views the past; the directionality of time, and what we can tell about where history is going. Historical study often begins by asking what was *new* at any given moment in the past, a question that unlocks the potential to study watershed moments in the past when everything changed.

Text Mining as a Key to Temporal Experience

Looking for radical breaks in time is some of the most significant work that historical analysis can accomplish. A significant event is a "watershed," or a "discontinuity." It marks a before and an after. Historian Martin Jay celebrates such events as "radical breaks in the status quo." He writes: "They happen without intentionality or preparation, befalling us rather than being caused by us."[3] Jay has suggested that the canonical "rupture" in history is the events of the New Testament, the discontinuity so widely recognized in the western world that calendars were broken into two metrics, *Before Christ* and *Anno Domini,* in the year of our lord. Koselleck volunteers the conversion of Saint Paul and the French Revolution as events whose canonicity reaches a similar stature.

How unique does an event have to be in order to be significant? Koselleck suggests a mathematical definition: an important event is a "singularity," the like of which has never been seen before. Repeated events like the visit of the mailman or the daily schedule of a commuter train don't count. Jay, meanwhile, makes room for a gray area. A significant event, he argues, doesn't necessarily mean an absolute break with the past; plenty of theologians have discovered "prefigured anticipations" of the work of Jesus in the annals of prophecy documented in the Hebrew scriptures. Nevertheless, "rupture" still remains an adequate descriptor of the event. "No matter how much Christians looked for prefigured anticipations," writes Jay, "the events described in the 'New Testament' were radical ruptures that opened up a future that was very different from the past."[4]

Jay argues that the historian's role is not to provide explanations but to discover genuine events and to provide an encounter with how temporal ruptures generated manifold possibilities that had never previously existed. He explains: "A genuine event in the past only realizes itself in the

---

[3] Martin Jay, "Historical Explanation and the Event," *New Literary History* 42 (2011): 564.
[4] For quotation, see Jay, "Historical Explanation:" 564. For "singularity," see Reinhart Koselleck, *Sediments of Time* (Palo Alto, CA: Stanford University Press, 2018), 4.

possibilities it unleashes in an undetermined future."[5] In part, this means that, for human beings living history in the present, it is almost impossible to assess the abstract importance of an event as it happens; we have to let it work its transformations on us, like falling in love, or the loss of a loved one. We measure how important events were in retrospect through the accumulation of tiny ruptures which later add up to more.

The possibility of *measuring* those tiny changes, however, suggests that shifts can be collected and compared, and events measured against each other, both in retrospect, and – potentially – as history is actually unfolding in the moment. As we shall see, particular algorithms applied to text can help with the tracking of these changes. At their best, algorithms can illuminate an evolving discourse of modernity as *disruption* or patterns in the introduction of new language typical of certain eras.

Applied to text, quantitative measurements offer a robust set of techniques for pinpointing the nature of change over time. The quantitative technique familiar to the largest number of scholars is undoubtedly the wordcount, which many have encountered through the Google n-gram that counts word prevalence over time according to the Google Books corpus. However, wordcount is only one of the many approaches that involve a naïve quantitative analysis of terminology over time, whose depiction of time is reduced to a linear progression against the horizontal *x*-axis.[6]

Perhaps the simplest way of investigating change over time is to control the set of words being examined using controlled vocabulary, a practice that illuminates one *domain* of experience in which change occurred, while leaving the rest of the dataset untouched. In a study of nineteenth-century novels, for instance, literary historians Ryan Heuser and Long Le-Khac were able to detect a significant increase in the mentions of body parts, action words, and other materially specific descriptions as the century progressed and their study corroborated earlier theories about the increasing phenomenological specificity of the nineteenth-century world picture. The precision of their data allowed a definitive revision of the various

---

[5] Koselleck, *Sediments of Time*, 569.

[6] Google n-grams can be found here: http://books.google.com/ngrams. The statement of the developers is this: Jean-Baptiste Michel et al., "Quantitative Analysis of Culture Using Millions of Digitized Books," *Science* 331:6014 (January 14, 2011): 176–82, https://doi.org/10.1126/science.1199644.

For almost a decade, historians have used Google Books n-grams to pinpoint moments of the explosion of a particular discourse, using temporal information extracted from the database as a guide for a closer reading of texts. See Joanna Guldi, "The History of Walking and the Digital Turn: Stride and Lounge in London, 1808–1851," *The Journal of Modern History* 84:1 (2012): 116–44.

timelines offered by literary scholars about when and how the phenomenologically specific novel occurred.[7]

Heuser and Le-Khac hail from a humanities discipline, literature, where scholars entertain theories of temporal change. Their capacity to unpack one theory of change – the theory that Flaubert influenced the development of the novel – contributed to the strength of their work. In other words, as humanists, Heuser and Le-Khac had a "historical method" – an approach to asking *why* something happened: was it because Flaubert was so ahead of his time, or because many authors at once began to write about the experience of the city, something that was changing all around them?

Increasingly, hybrid collaborations between humanists and quantitative specialists are pushing into the domain of historical methods. This frontier is relatively new, even among the ranks of digital humanists who have long consulted digital methods for *other* kinds of humanistic purposes – among them mapping, network analysis, and demographic history. Applications of text mining to history specifically are relatively new as well. History journals and departments have generally been slower than those of literature, for instance, to place digital articles on a regular basis or hire for digital skills. In fact, the first major monograph based on textual analysis appeared only as recently as 2020.[8] Meanwhile, most of the studies in textual analysis applied to historical questions have, with a few notable exceptions, been performed over relatively short periods of time. Although some contemporary historians have theorized propitiously about the place of text mining within a serious analysis of *longue durée* time periods, applications of text mining to data on a temporal scale of a century or more have mostly come from nearby disciplines such as literature or sociology – fields in which questions of temporal experience are typically secondary to theoretical issues of representation or identity.[9]

In interdisciplinary and hybrid spaces, however, computationalists, literary scholars, and political scientists, along with a growing handful of

---

[7] Ryan Heuser and Long Le-Khac, "A Quantitative Literary History of 2,958 Nineteenth-Century British Novels: The Semantic Cohort Method," *Literary Lab Pamphlets* 4 (May 2012), https://litlab.stanford.edu/LiteraryLabPamphlet4.pdf. For the revisionary impact of this argument, see Ted Underwood, *Distant Horizons: Digital Evidence and Literary Change* (Chicago, IL: The University of Chicago Press, 2019).

[8] Luke Blaxill, *The War of Words: The Language of British Elections, 1880–1922* (Woodbridge: Boydell & Brewer, 2020).

[9] Austin C. Kozlowski, Matt Taddy, and James A. Evans, "The Geometry of Culture: Analyzing Meaning through Word Embeddings," *ArXiv:1803.09288 [Cs]*, March 25, 2018, http://arxiv.org/abs/1803.09288; Ted Underwood, *Distant Horizons*; Andrew Piper, *Enumerations: Data and Literary Study* (Chicago, IL: University of Chicago Press, 2019), http://chicago.universitypressscholarship.com/view/10.7208/chicago/9780226568898.001.0001/upso-9780226568614.

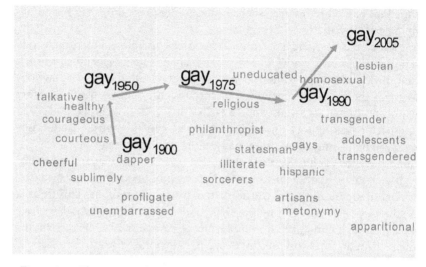

Figure 6.4   Change point detection algorithm, by Vivek Kulkarni. Figure 1 in Vivek Kulkarni, "Statistically Significant Detection of Linguistic Change," *Proceedings of the 24th International Conference on World Wide Web*, 2015.
© International World Wide Web Conference Committee (IW3C2).

digital historians, have begun the process of working with algorithms to make inferences about the experience of time in the documentary record.[10] One exemplary area of research is "change point detection": a body of investigation into historical watersheds as modeled by cultural changes – for instance, the software package for change point detection designed by computer scientist Vivek Kulkarni in 2015 (Figure 6.4).

One of Kulkarni's examples of the algorithm's success was its ability to track in newspapers the shifting context, use, and count of the word "gay" across the twentieth century, as it shifted from a context marked by words such as "dapper" or "happy" to one marked by words such as "lesbian" and "homosexual."[11]   By aggregating three measures of change into one, Kulkarni's algorithm produced a useful measure of change point detection,

---

[10] A useful introduction to several basic new algorithms in this cohort has been provided by Thomas Lansdall-Welfare and Nello Cristianini, "History Playground: A Tool for Discovering Temporal Trends in Massive Textual Corpora," *ArXiv:1806.01185 [Cs]*, June 4, 2018, http://arxiv.org/abs/1806.01185. For the disciplinary range, consider articles by Simon Dedeo (physics/information science), Peter Bearman (political science), Juuola (computer science), and Underwood, *Distant Horizons* (literature).

[11] Vivek Kulkarni, "Statistically Significant Detection of Linguistic Change," *Proceedings of the 24th International Conference on World Wide Web*, 2015.

an aggregate metric of a cultural shift suggested by changes in the context, grammatical usage, and frequency of a word. Given a dataset, the algorithm makes it possible to imagine "automating" the process of abstracting meaningful cultural shifts. The theory of change point detection and related algorithms for detecting "events" on the basis of statistical lexicon change is being applied today by historians who study cultural shifts in advertising and parliamentary debate.[12] Were change point detection applied to a vast lexicon – gathering all words whose meaning changed as much as "gay" did over the twentieth century – it might bring us much closer to producing a new, culturally precise timeline of cultural change based on patterns in the linguistic record.

Kulkarni's intervention stands out, for our purposes, as a potent example of how one can use math to register and measure absolute change. His work provides an algorithm for indexing those words whose meanings changed the most over a given set of years. That linguistic change, meanwhile, provides an important proxy for indexing the emergence of new experiences, which, to follow Wittgenstein, must be named before they can be experienced, compelling the experiencer to use *old words* in a *new sense*. Quantification of language thus provides a robust technique for helping the historian to reach ever-nearer to absolute change in the life-worlds of historical subjects.

How one does the math can affect the outcome in crucial ways and, when applied thoughtfully, it can help us to discern different *categories* of temporal experience, from novel experiences to historical events to raw measures of personal influence. Statistical algorithms have been leveraged against wordcount in the parliamentary corpus to detect "bursts" of new language – a proxy for raw shifts of orientation in the political context.[13] One team studying cultural shifts in advertising has applied another measure of change over time to discern occasions where advertising copy appears to have influenced newspaper copy.[14] Another group applied

[12] Tom Kenter, "Ad Hoc Monitoring of Vocabulary Shifts over Time," *Proceedings of the 24th ACM International on Conference on Information and Knowledge Management*, n.d., 1191–1200; Andrew C. Eggers and Arthur Spirling, "The Shadow Cabinet in Westminster Systems: Modeling Opposition Agenda Setting in the House of Commons, 1832–1915," *British Journal of Political Science* (2016): 1–25.

[13] Andrew C. Eggers and Arthur Spirling, "The Shadow Cabinet in Westminster Systems," 1–25.

[14] Melvin Wevers, Jianbo Gao, and Kristoffer L. Nielbo, "Tracking the Consumption Junction: Temporal Dependencies between Articles and Advertisements in Dutch Newspapers" (March 2019), https://hal.archives-ouvertes.fr/hal-02076512; Melvin Wevers and Jesper Verhoef, "Coca-Cola: An Icon of the American Way of Life. An Iterative Text Mining Workflow for Analyzing Advertisements in Dutch Twentieth-Century Newspapers," *Digital Humanities Quarterly* 11: 4 (January 8, 2017).

metrics of similarity as a raw measure of which speakers in France's Congrès exerted the most influence on other speakers over time.[15] As I have argued elsewhere, such measures are rapidly creating a new mathematics of cultural and social change over time, mathematics capable of detecting and isolating a variety of dimensions of temporal experience, both individual and collective.[16]

As we shall see, recent interdisciplinary collaborations have fomented a tremendous number of new projects which attempt to render into quantitative form traditional questions of temporal experience – for instance, change within discourses, or the influence of particular speakers on others.[17] Most of the articles associated with this movement address data in the form of texts, but algorithmic measurements of time have also been applied to such things as music and images.[18] As scholars embrace the diversity of quantitative applications in the study of temporal experience, they take an important step toward actualizing the theoretical potential represented by the marriage of data science and historical methods. As we shall see, this has the potential to orient scholars toward further cutting-edge research in the digital humanities that is specifically tailored to the interests and questions of historians.

---

[15] Alexander T. J. Barron et al., "Individuals, Institutions, and Innovation in the Debates of the French Revolution," *Proceedings of the National Academy of Sciences* 115:18 (May 1, 2018): 4607–12, https://doi.org/10.1073/pnas.1717729115.

[16] Jo Guldi, "The Measures of Modernity: Word Counts, Text Mining and the Promise and Limits of Present Tools as Indices of Historical Change," *International Journal for History, Culture and Modernity* 7 (November 3, 2019), https://doi.org/10.18352/hcm.589.

[17] For instance, Patrick Juola, "The Time Course of Language Change," *Computers and the Humanities* 37:1 (2003): 77–79; Jaimie Murdock, Colin Allen, and Simon DeDeo, "Exploration and Exploitation of Victorian Science in Darwin's Reading Notebooks," *Cognition* 159: Supplement C (February 1, 2017): 117–26, https://doi.org/10.1016/j.cognition.2016.11.012; Barron et al., "Individuals, Institutions, and Innovation in the Debates of the French Revolution"; Peter Bearman, "Big Data and Historical Social Science," *Big Data & Society* 2:2 (December 27, 2015): 2053951715612497, https://doi.org/10.1177/2053951715612497; Jean-Philippe Cointet, Alix Rule, and Peter S. Bearman, "Lexical Shifts, Substantive Changes, and Continuity in State of the Union Discourse, 1790–2014," *PNAS (Proceedings of the National Academy of the Sciences"* 112:35 (August 10, 2015): 10837–44, https://doi.org/10.1073/pnas .1512221112. Andrew Piper, *Enumerations*; Ted Underwood, *Distant Horizons:*

[18] Matthias Mauch et al., "The Evolution of Popular Music: USA 1960–2010," *Royal Society Open Science* 2:5 (2015): 150081. Melvin Wevers and Thomas Smits, "The Visual Digital Turn: Using Neural Networks to Study Historical Images," *Digital Scholarship in the Humanities*, accessed August 7, 2019, https://doi.org/10.1093/llc/fqy085; Melvin Wevers and Jesper Verhoef, "Coca-Cola"; Taylor Arnold and Lauren Tilton, "Distant Viewing: Analyzing Large Visual Corpora," *Digital Scholarship in the Humanities*, March 16, 2019, https://doi.org/10.1093/digitalsh/fqz013.

The Promise of Topic Models for Examining Aggregate Historical Change

Contemporary scholars have deployed quantitative techniques to tracking discourses in a way that underscores the diversity of simultaneously active threads within a given period. One recent study used a body of computer science work known as "dynamic topic models" – where the "topics" are calculated in relationship to user-supplied periods – to detect a varying range of time horizons, imperial and colonial, that competed with each other in British parliamentary debates.[19] "Unsupervised" techniques of data mining – investigations that are not prompted by any particular vocabulary or set of constraints, of which topic models are one – tend to generate broad-brush overviews that can lend insight about historical change in aggregate.

In that study, the automated detection of different semantic cohorts, each with its own timeline, was able to produce a richer set of timelines than previous scholarship had evinced.

Some of these timelines, in fact, contradicted one another, suggesting a level of complexity and ambiguity in the historical record that might direct the scholar to further research. When used by critical thinkers in a robust way, such case studies suggest how algorithms can support multi-level analyses of historical change that stress the capacity for dissent and divergence.

Figure 6.5 presents a vivid visualization of data based on nineteenth-century geographical images of the forking paths of the Mississippi River – commonly known as a "river network diagram" or "Sankey plot." With poetic economy, the plot translates a complex mathematical model of similarity and divergences into a river with diverging and converging paths. The figure plots the rise and fall of various discourses that historically appeared within the State of the Union address delivered annually by the President of the United States. The *x*-axis is a timeline from 1820 to 1990. The gray river-like bands are populated by topics, or collections of words found to have a statistical probability of coincidence. The names of the topics (e.g. "production & value" or "weapons & air") were assigned by scholars who read the topics. The height of each topic corresponds to the representation of words correlated with that topic in the speeches of the period. Similarity measurements were used to group the topics, whatever their title, into rivers and branches, which were randomly assigned a

---

[19] Jo Guldi, "Parliament's Debates about Infrastructure": An Exercise in Using Dynamic Topic Models to Synthesize Historical Change," *Technology and Culture* 60:1 (March 21, 2019): 1–33.

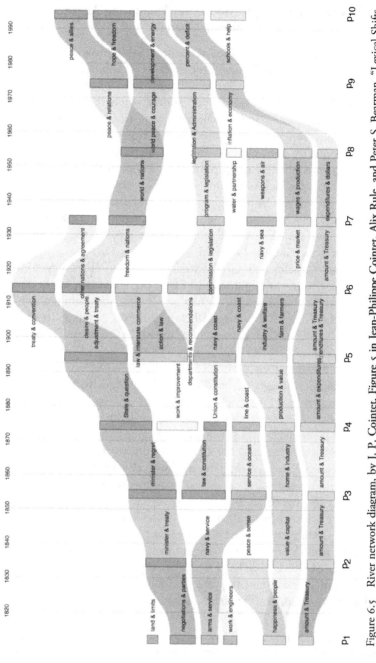

Figure 6.5 River network diagram, by J. P. Cointet. Figure 5 in Jean-Philippe Cointet, Alix Rule, and Peter S. Bearman, "Lexical Shifts, Substantive Changes, and Continuity in State of the Union Discourse, 1790–2014," *PNAS (Proceedings of the National Academy of the Sciences*) 112:35 (August 10, 2015): 10837–44.

different color. Reading the changing titles of a single stream gives an overview of historical change within a constant theme, from "happiness & the people" to "value & capital" to "home & industry" to "production & industry" – changing idioms for talking about the national economy and its purpose, beneficiaries, and means.

This visual history was rendered by the computer scientist Jean-Philippe Cointet in 2015, in conjunction with political scientists Alix Rule and Peter Bearman, who were both attempting to identify *longue durée* periods and short *durée* discontinuities based on a textual database of these annual presidential addresses (Figure 6.5).[20] Because of the highly original set of choices these scholars made about how to represent change over time, the diagram dramatizes the rise of new ways of talking about the nation and the concerns of the president from one historical period to the next. Where the rivers of discourse converge, diverge, begin, and end, the diagram depicts multiple paths within the stream of time, each with its own life. Reaching beyond the simple detection of change points of Figure 6.4, this visualization adds an important element of analysis – it emphasizes the evolution of contemporaneous, parallel discourses, each with its own trajectory.

This novel visual element in Cointet's diagram demonstrates how new themes enter the discourse; how discourses expand and divide; and how they disappear, change, or converge. We can see that a conversation about "land and limits" falls out after the first State of the Union address, and is subsequently replaced by new concerns like "peace and sense," "law and the constitution," and "work and improvement." Many new subjects are fated to become dead ends of history, such as "work & improvement," introduced in the 1870s and quickly abandoned; or the "negotiations & other parties" topic, which was invoked from the beginning and eventually split into two topics – one about parties at home and one about "other nations," which was abandoned after 1930. Some topics split into adjacent rhetorical categories – as we see the "happiness & people" topic fork into "peace & sense" and "value & capital" after 1830. Other subjects, which had once been distinct topics, converge into a single category – as the separate discussions of "waves & production" and "expenditure & dollars" became a singular conversation about "inflation & economy" by 1970. Discourses fork, compete, and die out. Only certain strains remain, and sometimes those themes are transformed utterly.

On a technical level, Cointet's visualization offers one of the hybrid approaches that we described in Chapter 2. By adding measurements of

---

[20] Cointet et al., "Lexical Shifts, Substantive Changes, and Continuity."

similarity to the topics, Cointet is able to capture something of time's geographies: the similarities and discontinuities within the corpus from time period to time period. To the mathematical model of similarity over time that this generated, Cointet applied his form of visualization known as a "river network diagram" or "Sankey plot."

Cointet's analysis uses "similarity" to pinpoint both the moments when a new discourse appears without precedent and the junctures where a discourse splits into two; thus he manages to condense the complexity of political discourse over time as a series of forking paths and dead ends. In the State of the Union addresses, seven years particularly stand out – 1850, 1870, 1890, 1910, 1930, 1970, and 1990 – as moments of rapid experimentation with novel rhetorical themes, or as moments of foreclosure upon older themes.

The visualization's ability to model change and to plot change in a way that renders discontinuities and continuities recognizable in terms of narrative time makes this study so powerful. Instead of presenting a purely mathematical rendering of time, the Sankey diagram suggests how discourses arise and fall away, diverge and converge, in a multivariate timeline of forking paths. It underscores the ability to map time according to particular movements within the record in such a way that particular changes can be isolated, tracked, and compared. In the process of disaggregating the historical record, this produces a forking timeline, even while the x-axis of forward motion and universal measurement still dominates. In this way, it ultimately offers a representation of time that appears, from the historian's perspective, adequate to human experience.

Experiments like this show how we can use quantitative analysis to track the life and death of evolving discourse. Although their short article failed to develop in any detail the theoretical approach I have sketched here, Cointet, Rule, and Bearman offer a first draft of a robust process that, if elaborated, could help scholars rigorously identify the historical moments when a discourse forks off in new directions – indicating those watershed moments when a society produces multiple new distinct and rival ways of talking about a subject previously discussed along a single main thread – and could constitute a quantitatively precise way of identifying moments of dissent and change.

A Dynamic Topic Model of *Hansard*

Before we continue, we should say a few more words about studies along the lines of Cointet, studies that use *dynamic topic models* to study periodicity. Such approaches are often referred to as "unsupervised" methods: as we touched upon in the section "The Promise of Topic Models," they do not require the scholar to supply a list of words, or a special corpus, but rather, can scour a mass database for relevant words, and suggest timelines of events within any corpus of novels, debates, laws, etc. The algorithm classifies words that frequently co-occur with other words into a "topic."

The number of topics, whether ten or 100 or another number, is determined by the scholar, although there are debates about the "natural" number of topics appropriate to corpora of different scales. Traditionally, the scholar hand-assigns a name to each collection of words.

In dynamic topic modeling, the algorithm has a budget for each topic, and the composition of each topic can change according to the expression of different words over time. The algorithm was developed by computer scientists David Blei and John Lafferty in 2016.[21] Dynamic topics have also been successfully applied to the study of changing debates in today's parliament of the European Union over periods of a decade.[22]

To prepare the corpus of *Hansard* for analysis, my lab lemmatized the text of the parliamentary debates, cutting off plural and verb-form endings so that the words roots remained. The data scientists with whom I worked at the time programmed the topic model algorithm was to find the twenty words most statistically significant for 500 topics in *Hansard*. I set to work with my graduate students labeling topics and debating what meaning, if any, we could abstract from this exercise.

A 500-topic model of all *Hansard* in the nineteenth century evidences countless themes familiar to readers of British history, including the transport revolution (one topic on turnpikes, another on railways), the post office and telegraph, and the coming of schools.[23] The multiple topics that concern these events, however, are quite distinct. They range from discussions of plans for urban parks to the governance of London's infrastructure, including bridges, streets, river, and telephone cables. Several concerns are associated with a topic of their own, including eminent domain and the widening of King's Cross (which the computer

[21] David Blei and John Lafferty, "Dynamic Topic Models," *Proceedings of the 23rd International Conference on Machine Learning*, June 2006, 113–20.

[22] Derek Greene and James P. Cross, "Exploring the Political Agenda of the European Parliament Using a Dynamic Topic Modeling Approach," *ArXiv:1607.03055 [Cs]*, July 11, 2016, http://arxiv.org/abs/1607.03055.

[23] Guldi, "Parliament's Debates about Infrastructure." Readers may explore our topic model on their own here: https://eight1911.github.io/hansard/home. There are some discrepancies from the topics described in this article, caused by versioning, stemming, lemmatization, etc.

classifies with the displacement of Scottish crofters). Certain topics – especially ones that are intimately related to the infrastructure of empire – evidence a wider revolution in infrastructure and landscape than is typically described in treatises on urbanization and transport: the rise of shipbuilding, including the construction of yards and docks; private bills specifically for making docks; the role of rail lines and roads around empire in deploying soldiers; naval infrastructures; military and colonial properties; the infrastructure of empire after the Indian Great Rebellion of 1857–59 (especially the construction of barracks for British soldiers around the world); and the spreading of county roads, gaols, and asylums across England and Ireland.

Dynamic topic models not only provide a fascinating glimpse into the quotidian dimensions of the nineteenth-century city, they also illuminate a much broader picture, illustrating how expanding cities required new kinds of agricultural policy, sanitary regulation, and governance of public utilities like water. The topic labeled "Supply of water, food, and meat" (see Table 6.1) shows parliament debating a changing range of subjects – oats and barley in 1800, the shortfall of food in 1810, the water companies in 1820, the Potato Famine in 1840, London's sewerage in the 1850s, demands for gas and meat in the 1860s, the pollution of urban water sources in the 1870s, and meanwhile, from the 1880s, a new conversation about the provision of meat and butter to troops and citizens. The topic also raises intriguing questions for future research regarding the discourse of "want" over time, and implicit relationships between the conceptions of artificial "want" and natural "supply" as they were handled in different generations.

The topic underscores how a discourse about cheap grain motivated not merely a conversation about free trade in the 1840s, but also an expanding array of conversations about the role of government in sanitizing supplies of food and water over the rest of the century. The topic model largely confirms what Chris Otter has called "the nutrition transition," as one of the crucial arenas wherein the poles of debate were constructed for both an ideology of the free market and an ideology of a growing state bureaucracy. In this food-driven process, the pulse of famine and supply symbolized by changing loaf sizes , as regulated by the medieval Assize of Bread, was adjusted into a modern regime of plentiful, cheap food and fat bodies, designed by parliamentary expertise and regulated at a global level.[24] Indeed, the signals tracked in Table 6.1 show a seemingly steady pulse

[24] Chris Otter, "The British Nutrition Transition and Its Histories," *History Compass* 10:11 (2012): 812–25, https://doi.org/10.1111/hic3.12001.

Table 6.1 *Supply of water, food, and meat.*

1800	1810	1820	1840	1850	1860	1870	1880	1890	1890	1900	1900
suppli	suppli	suppli	suppli	suppli	suppli	water	suppli	water	suppli	suppli	water
defici	majesty	water	food	water	supply	suppli	water	supply	supply	meat	boiler
meat	regular	metropolis	want	river	cotton	supply	supply	river	meat	supply	tub
information	rais	commiss	potato	metropoli	water	river	food	companies	troop	food	boilers
contractor	defici	engin	water	metropolis	friday	metropoli	firm	consum	friday	electr	supply
deficiency	food	river	crop	supply	cloth	constant	set	east	contractor	contractor	butter
provid	supply	burdett	defici	companies	gas	metropolis	contractor	birmingham	forag	firm	companies
demand	water	bath	purchas	thame	meat	pollut	seed	boiler	tender	troop	river
contract	furnish	analysi	fever	arm	store	gas	store	thame	sourc	light	stock
oat	demand	metropoli	diseas	thames	demand	companies	manufactur	sanitari	firm	copi	outsid
seed	bills	thames	seed	cloth	price	metropolitan	price	tub	seed	allot	bellevill
surplus	voted	wholesom	indian	drainag	want	lake	cloth	drink	august	store	engin
qualiti	applied	supply	people	quantiti	market	thame	sword	area	defici	tender	joint
company	trust	procur	supply	mowatt	sitting	suffici	articl	boilers	ammunit	lymph	thame
barley	quarter	companies	depend	rifl	contractor	feet	tender	pollut	canteen	ration	arbitr
investigated	ballot	calvert	obtain	sewag	quantiti	obtain	messrs	reservoir	station	beef	corpor
believe	token	defici	quantiti	inhabit	nights	store	drink	cut	qualiti	demand	bulk
supply	quantiti	steam	grain	sewer	food	manchest	furnitur	quantiti	food	liquor	type
want	agricultur	inquir	demand	defici	timber	pure	suffici	purposes	quantiti	tin	metropolitan
compromis	direct	quality	cheap	furnish	estimates	want	ammunit	health	suffici	ammunit	cylindr

Note: Words have been "stemmed" to their likely root form; the lower-case word-stem matched by the computer is shown here.

of parliamentary concern over "food" and its "supply" that, on closer inspection, embodied a transforming conversation – about the price of grain in the 1810s, about the water supply in the 1820s, about the Potato Famine in the 1840s, and about the rights and needs of urban people, over the following decades, regarding the new technology of gas.

As we see in this study, unsupervised methods like dynamic topic modeling can be a powerful tool for illuminating the flow of concepts – marking events like the Potato Famine and the advent of gas technology. Topic models are not, however, self-interpreting – while dynamic topic modeling was able to produce the long table of words in Table 6.1, to make sense of them one must have a great deal of background reading and familiarity with the themes of British history. And topic models have their critics; topic modeling is generally a "black box" algorithm, in that it is difficult to trace words found in the same topic back to the same location in the text. Equally importantly, topic models are highly unstable; the same algorithm run a second time with the same parameters on a body of text will produce a different set of topics. For these reasons, more recent scholars in the digital humanities have tended to prioritize other strategies, including word embeddings. Elsewhere, I have argued that dynamic topic models are chiefly useful for "indexing" the past, and for finding certain patterns that have escaped the notice of trained historians – in other words, they are tools that may be most useful in the hands of trained experts.[25] In Chapter 14, we shall turn to the stakes of "white box" and "black box" text mining, recommending strategies that are most likely to hold up to inspection of the data.

More importantly, the topic model is just one perspective from the house of the past. There is only one x-axis of time. There's no sense of competing timelines or mythologies wrestling with each other, no sense of dissent in the log of change. Nevertheless, dynamic topic models represent one window onto the past. The insights they provide have to be checked against other sources of knowledge, but discoveries can be made – and have been made – even through a distorted window.

Modern Theories of History as the New Frontier of Data Science

The hybridization of quantitative tools and historical methods over recent years has produced new approaches marked by the concerns of both fields. Such hybrid approaches can be extremely useful for an analyst who wishes

---

[25] Jo Guldi, "Parliament's Debates about Infrastructure," 1–33.

to describe the rich context of experience within which a particular event took place – for example, a scholar working with the *longue durée* of decades or centuries – as the dynamic topic model excels at identifying the patterns surrounding a particular event, lending even the quotidian dimension a much richer sense of time and place. Such an interrogation of the past enables analysts to step outside a particular set of events and actors and to glimpse some of the strings that move the world – in other words, to see the multiplicity of rhythms, crises, and competing events contextualized within a particular moment in time.

By automating the detection of discontinuities within a corpus, computer scientists have pushed the process of collecting events further than classical studies once allowed. In many of the exercises conducted by information scientists and mathematicians, we can see an engagement with implicit questions about time, such as what in essence constitutes temporal change and how might time leave evidence in a text-based corpus. Few of these studies, however, have explicitly engaged with the wealth of concepts about analyzing time from the discipline of history. Thus, an enormous ocean of theory remains, effectively, untapped by hybrid knowledge, awaiting new investigations. What are these theories of history?

Understanding the raw material of change per se has indeed been emerging for quite some time as one of the holy grails of history. In *Futures Past: On the Semantics of Historical Time*, the intellectual historian Reinhard Koselleck argued that historical ideas gain meaning through *repetition* and *substitution*.

Koselleck suggests that repetition is part of everyday life. "Everywhere one looks, there are phenomena of recurrence: time hurries and time heals, it brings new things and reclaims what can only be discerned from a distance."[26] The mail is delivered at the same time every day; railroad cars depart on schedule, and legislatures meet according to a plan. Repetition often helps to explain a singularity, Koselleck argues: the regular delivery of mail explains how and when I received a letter announcing the death of a friend. Knowledge of repetition is a key to understanding history because it is by *subtracting recurrence* that historians ascertain what is singular in their time. "Only when we know what can repeat itself at any time . . . can we ascertain what is truly new in our time," he writes.[27]

Just as repetition and singularity offer a baseline for analyzing new events, Koselleck argues, so repetition and singularity can illuminate the workings of language. We have already seen how scholars mark

[26] Koselleck, *Sediments of Time*, 115.   [27] Ibid., 116.

discontinuities in the past through the emergence of new language. Koselleck believes that *substitution* marks temporal change that occurs when old ideas are repeated in a new context. Toward the end of the eighteenth century, for instance, the newfangled word "democracy" was increasingly substituted for the old-fashioned term "republicanism." Where the old "republicanism" chiefly signaled independence from a monarch, "democracy" carried radical resonances, such as the belief that all men (and perhaps even women) might one day have the right to vote. Koselleck believes that the gradual *substitution* of the word "democracy" for "republicanism" shows how a changing historical context required speakers to import a new concept. In the world of text mining, scholars have increasingly applied themselves to what we might regard as a Koselleckian standard of interest in change per se – or the absolute truth of historical experience. Teams of historians working with mathematicians and information scientists have been working on metrics designed to abstract the markers of general change from the entire diversity of textual documentation, providing scholars with insights into the markers of pure temporal change.

In our time, many other important historians have also focused upon new innovations that bring refinement and nuance to our understanding of how temporal experience varies with culture and moment, and their insights into the varieties of temporal experience point in a direction wider than that explored by wordcount over time or topic models. They reach past what Koselleck has called the "bipolar" approach of imagining time as "linear" – "an arrow of time that heads in a teleological direction, or toward an open future" – or "recurrent and cyclical."[28] They suggest a world where multiple *different* temporal experiences are happening *at the same time*, and those different temporal registers are mapped onto landscape.

An historian of modern Japanese history, Stefan Tanaka, has emphasized the multiplicity of cultural models for temporal experience, underscoring the tension between modern notions of mechanical, linear time, against older traditions of spatialized and cyclical time, and showing how these different views of time were in operation in Japanese histories of natural disasters.[29]

Some historians identify approaches for studying change in temporal experience: focusing on a single aspect of historical change, for instance

---

[28] Ibid., 3.
[29] Stefan Tanaka, "History Without Chronology," *Public Culture* 28:1 (78) (January 1, 2016): 161–86, https://doi.org/10.1215/08992363-3325064.

transportation, politics, or labor; and focusing on changing experience of time, for instance through the perceived "speeding up" of time with the railway, or the creation and standardization of time zones.[30]

Historians of today have developed approaches for isolating and comparing different experiences of time – even those held within the same frame – and their work will guide our inquiry. Consider how historians today study the past: historians not only argue about separate events in history and their interpretation, they also debate how best to describe the experience of time itself. Manuel De Landa has suggested that modern experience is characterized by different temporalities operating at different scales, while Koselleck has emphasized the cycles of repetition and singularity that punctuate historical time. Scholars also illuminate "temporal experience" – a subject that would include the disorientation of the first railway engineers faced with working across multiple time zones – and "the politics of history" – the idea that our political and cultural identities inform how we understand and interact with the past. Dipesh Chakrabarty and Sumathi Ramaswamy, for instance, have emphasized that different scalar arguments frequently reflect the role of ideology and empire in assembling time into a narrative structure. Meanwhile, Stefan Tanaka has emphasized the multiplicity of cultural models for temporal experience, underscoring the tension between modern notions of mechanical, linear time, against older traditions of spatialized and cyclical time, and showing how these different views of time were in operation in Japanese histories of natural disasters.[31] Still other

---

[30] To the former approach belong a broad range of studies in change that include plotting new transportation corridors as they expand across the map; documenting the changing rates or nature of participation in politics; following the changing language of labor; and analyzing demographic or economic information according to classical statistics applied to time series. For examples, see Gareth Stedman Jones, *Languages of Class: Studies in English Working Class History, 1832–1982* (Cambridge: Cambridge University Press, 1983); James Vernon, *Politics and the People: A Study in English Political Culture, C. 1815–1867* (New York: Cambridge University Press, 1993); James Epstein, *Radical Expression: Political Language, Ritual, and Symbol in England, 1790–1850* (New York: Oxford University Press, 1994); *The Chartist Experience: Studies in Working-Class Radicalism and Culture, 1830–60* (London: Macmillan Press, 1982). To the second approach belong countless modes of chronicling contemporary perceptions of time – classically, those that remarked upon the speeding up of interaction with the machine age. For instance, Stephen Kern, *The Culture of Time and Space, 1880–1918: With a New Preface* (Cambridge, MA: Harvard University Press, 2003); Vanessa Ogle, *The Global Transformation of Time: 1870–1950* (Cambridge, MA and London: Harvard University Press, 2015).

[31] Manuel De Landa, *A Thousand Years of Nonlinear History* (New York: Zone Books, 1997); Koselleck, *Sediments of Time*; Dipesh Chakrabarty, *The Climate of History in a Planetary Age* (Chicago, IL: University of Chicago Press, 2021); Sumathi Ramaswamy, *The Lost Land of Lemuria: Fabulous Geographies, Catastrophic Histories* (Berkeley, CA: University of California Press, 2004); Stefan Tanaka, "History Without Chronology," *Public Culture* 28:1 (78) (January 1, 2016): 161–86, https://doi.org/10.1215/08992363-3325064.

historians have emphasized the contextual nature of experiences of synchronicity, underlining the function of newspapers in producing an imagination of contemporaneity across different times and places. In their review of ideas about time in the German, British, and French traditions since the eighteenth century, Helge Jordheim and Einar Wigen argue that "progress" and "crisis" are modern concepts that, together with universal history and Greenwich Mean Time, have reorganized the multiple experience of history in its various "speeds, rhythms, and durations" into a single global order.[32] Along with scholars of temporality, such as Vanessa Ogle, they have all have offered insight into the cultural and political hierarchies that structure time. Scholarship of this kind underscores how unpacking the cultural conditioning of different experiences of time can lend insight into the varieties of experience often masked by measures of time that highlight, in the historical record, a single unified order of temporality.

I have not sought to plumb the limits of the philosophy of history. Hayden White, the Annalistes, and other theorists of temporal experience may offer still other insights into the structure of temporal experience that could be mined through digital methods. Nor do I mean to foreclose a conversation upon other philosophers of history at work today. The enterprise of understanding the nature and diversity of temporal experience is an evolving concern. Certain of these theorists will be taken up in the pages that follow as the inspiration for work with particular algorithms that offered a "fit" for their understanding of the past. But there are many more algorithms and more philosophers from whose insights scholarship as a whole would benefit.

We live in the house of the past, where many windows open out onto different vistas. Already, the world of the humanities has peered out of many of these windows, and quantitative methods of text mining have flung open others. But many humanists' insights remain untapped. In the remaining chapters of Part II of this book, I will explore what algorithmic work looks like under the inspiration of theories of history.

Each day, I sit in the cell of my mind, the light moving from dawn to gloom, its changing angles illuminating room after room, much like the scene that a viewer might see from the house depicted in the Tan'yu landscape (Figure 6.6). This is progression toward perfection, no upward climb of a mountain toward a goal, this illumination. There's no final achievement, just the rise and set of the sun, day after day. Each shift of the now represents the

[32] Helge Jordheim and Einar Wigen, "Conceptual Synchronisation: From Progress to Crisis," *Millennium* 46:3 (June 1, 2018): 421–39, https://doi.org/10.1177/0305829818774781.

Figure 6.6   Landscape in the style of Kano Tan'yu, 18th century. Freer Gallery.

chance to reflect on the vaulted ceilings in one chamber, or to capture the golden hour for a moment of appreciation or of work.

Throughout this book I have made the case that the past is a multidimensional object: it is more like a statue or a building than a painting; it can't be taken in all at once; multiple perspectives are necessary to apprehend it. If the past is a building, it's structure is partially occluded by the nature of archives: by the fact that certain paper trails have been destroyed, certain narratives suppressed, certain ways of life barely recorded. To reconstruct the whole architecture from this fragmentary record would require laborious study and comparison. Like a house with locked chambers, it has recesses one can never reach – and sometimes, it has great surprises, when what seemed to be a locked door suddenly springs open. Our changing awareness of how different stories from the past affect us doesn't mean that there is no absolute truth. The feeling of the house shifts from hour to hour with the light, just as politics or family dramas cause us to feel moved by a new perspective on Thomas Jefferson or Sigmund Freud. That doesn't mean that my house isn't real, or that you can't come into my house and see the same rooms. It just means that each of us is liable to be more aware, at one hour than another, of one set of experiences rather than another – aware of the resonance of histories of foremothers lost, for example, or of the ravages of slavery, or of stories about the collapse of civilization, or of holocausts past, or of fights for justice. Even in the lives of individual historians, the power of certain stories waxes and wanes from hour to hour as the spaces of our hearts are activated by the moods and politics around us.

The image of the house gives us a way to conceptualize the multiple perspectives of history on a common experience. Just as a house has three-dimensional reality, so with history. person guiding us through the house can direct our attention toward certain rooms, certain pieces of furniture, or particular aspects of the house, shaping our sense of the whole. A house shields some things from view, depending on where one stands. There's an inside and an outside. Inside the house, I have a changing perspective on what's important with the movement of the sun, even as my own personal concerns and interests about history may changing. Outside the house, there's a shared landscape.

The windows of this house also look *out* in all directions, as if gazing upon the common landscapes of our shared past. And no two windows give the same view.

As if I had hung the walls with paintings of the countryside from different nations, each window offers a strikingly distinct scene. Here, the outside world presses close against the window, and I can only see the plants and flowers growing near by the house. There, an enormous vista opens and I see mountains, stacked with layers of bygone eras. They're probably riddled with fossils. One doesn't come to know the situation of the house of the past by looking out through one window, but only by moving through the house, looking out in all directions, and even by exploring those landscapes in detail, outing after outing.

The possibility of different perspectives on the past doesn't mean that the history is an entirely relative subject. With religious belief or sexuality, nowadays we tend to accept that one person's experience may differ profoundly from that of another. Our shared past, by contrast, is like the landscape: we can both explore the same space and find similar experiences there. That's part of history's wonder and power, and one of the reasons that compelling stories about our common past – like the musical *Hamilton* or the history of the Tulsa massacre of 1921 – exert so much power over us. My map might develop the focus on a particular biography or experience where your map has blank spaces, but if our maps disagree about the placement of an ocean or a continent, it's almost certain that something has gone wrong.

To argue that the house of the past has many windows on a shared truth is not to make room for relativism, or for the idea that all stories about the past are equally valid – far from it. History is a social science in that it makes arguments based on evidence, and historians commit to sharing the evidence and arguing over it when questioned.

In recent years, the belief that history is relative has been used to defend racist and antiquated perspectives on our collective past. As I was drafting this chapter, my home state of Texas was debating House Bill 3979. Now passed into law by the state's Republican government, it legislates that public schoolteachers must present their pupils with a "traditional" version of history, shorn of questions about what citizens today owe to any persecuted minority, including the descendants of enslaved African-Americans who labored without compensation.

With politics or religious belief, we might "teach the debate" or relativize difference, encouraging teachers to acknowledge the existence of Judaism and Christianity without choosing a side. But geology, astronomy, physics, and history are not subjects whose truth-value changes relative to the aesthetic or cultural experience of the listener. The sciences and social sciences both aspire to reference a common experience that is grounded in fact. In both the sciences and the social sciences, new accumulations of evidence and theory are reviewed and debated from year to year. Over decades, the teachings tend to change as the result of the accretion of new knowledge.

Historians differ in interest, specialization, and methods. Well might the historian of Jewishness specialize in one area of the map and the historian of Christianity specialize in another. Not all practitioners of cultural history necessarily need text mining to do their work.

But if your map misses an ocean where others have sailed, your readers have a more basic problem. We need a neutral ground where we can examine our evidence and compare our techniques of plotting, or we need to concede that what we're doing is spinning tales, not teaching children about the reality of our common past.

Conclusion

The explosion in new approaches to temporality – both theoretical and quantitative – casts new light on the traditional approaches to character-izing time. As we glance over this theoretical terrain, we can see how different one algorithmic approach is from the next, and how each algo-rithm offers a unique contribution to the study of long-term forces and short-term eruptions of events.

Throughout this chapter, we have seen how algorithms – especially algorithms of distinction – represent a new method for organizing and prioritizing information about the past. We have had a small glimpse of how scholars researching issues that expand over long timespans have successfully applied these methods with sustained rigor and critical atten-tion. One day, such algorithms may be considered a crucial prerequisite for any historian engaging in a serious, self-conscious, and critical account of the *longue durée*. As a window into historical experience at different temporal scales, the quantitative findings here also supply a critically aware historian with the materials for syntheses that acknowledge the diversity of experience and perspectives.

In the following chapters, we will explore a series of algorithms, each of which entertains a slightly different species of questions: How did each era remember the past, and how did these memories change over time? What is distinctive about a given era? What is distinctive about the longer forces and shorter moments of time and what can we make of their organizational principles, their evolving dynamics, and their interwoven relationship to each other? What was trending at any moment and what is trending now? These are the famous existential questions that the painter Gauguin, struck with despair, traced in the corner of one of his canvases: Where have we been? Who are we? Where are we going? Questions such as these may provoke multiple answers, even disorienting ones. But answering them is the beginning of understanding the house of the past and the greater, common landscape in which it sits.

The chapters that follow explore this triptych of time – past, present, and future – through a series of algorithms, each of which opens another window onto some aspect of the past. As we shall see, the "fit" between tool and conception of time is highly specific; an algorithm used to distinguish the specificity of one era from those before and after it works differently from an algorithm used to highlight the memory of the past at work in the present. The surveys of digital tools and historical theory that follow cannot pretend to exhaust the richness of the emerging field, nor to survey the immense riches of historical theories of temporal experiences. They offer, rather, a mere sample of the wealth of insights available to data researchers at the new juncture where digital analysis and historical theory meet, insights worked out partially through a review of famous case studies and partially through an attempt to recapitulate, refine, and invent algorithmic approaches anew.

CHAPTER 7

Of Memory

Beneath every contemporary world, remembrance structures our lives. For religious believers, each eucharist is a new invitation to participate in the Last Supper; every Christmas replays anew the birth of Christ. Freudian therapists ask their clients to narrate the story of their childhood in detail, making connections to present feelings and reactions, in order to undo the compulsive power to repeat the past. In his novels, Marcel Proust investigated the way a churchyard in rural France conjured the memory of families dating back to Charlemagne, and how an instant's meeting with a lover by the Seine might stretch, in memory, longer than months or years of ordinary time. The newness or distinctiveness of each moment in present time; the memories of the past still with the present, and the trends that might determine the future.

Understanding the attitudes of societies toward their own past is hardly tantamount to a "predictive" science. But the discipline of modern history brings layers of subtlety to the understanding of the past, and these distinctions are important to any hybrid undertaking that seeks to "model" historians' expert knowledge into mathematical form. Practitioners of history distinguish between the expert interpretation of history (that is, the totality of past experience), historiography (what scholars have said about the past in previous eras), and memory (the popular or shared impression of historical experience, typically as enshrined in memorials, collective celebrations, and museums)

Indeed, a society's "remembrance" may have at least some bearing on the future: how societies have described their past indicates much about how they see their future. In nineteenth-century British India, the advocates of European colonization cherrypicked anecdotes to suggest that the Mughal Empire deposed by British Empire was characterized by tyranny and violence. It was left to a few anticolonial writers like Ramesh Dutt, one of colonial India's first native civil servants, to famously develop a historical overview of the disasters associated with British rule. For a century after his death, Dutt's history would help others to organize their thoughts about what was wrong with the British Empire. It would become a text that helped to orient colonial resistance.[1] Studies of memory therefore offer a rational place to begin our orientation to the textual data about time.

Historians have long studied how societies artificially concoct historical facts and a sense of the past, whether by donning kilts, staging processions, building commemorative monuments to kings and heroes, or by adopting architectural styles inspired by previous eras like those gothic arches that grace so many government buildings, train stations, churches, and even skyscrapers in London and New York. Costume, ritual, architecture, and museums are common touchstones of this research into what E. J. Hobsbawm dubbed "invented traditions."[2] In short, historians have long accepted that there is a history regarding how people collectively come to remember the past in a certain way, and the patterns of memory can be tracked in text as well as in the city. Are the dynamics of collective memory and forgetting also something that we can investigate through text mining?

A New Science of Memory

In a study of feminist zines from the 1970s and 1980s, Michelle Moravec profiled how later authors contested received wisdom about which original feminist publications counted as "revolutionary," thus demonstrating the palimpsestic nature of historical memory, as the record of what counts as history was rewritten in each generation.[3] Her algorithm works by detecting years mentioned in the text and footnotes, allowing her to group

---

[1] For Ramesh Dutt's view of history, see Benjamin Kingsbury, *An Imperial Disaster: The Bengal Cyclone of 1876* (New York: Oxford University Press, 2018); for the converse view that celebrated empire, see the account of various contemporary "ABCs of Empire" in Antoinette Burton, *An ABC of Queen Victoria's Empire: Or a Primer of Conquest, Dissent and Disruption* (London: Bloomsbury, 2017).

[2] For architecture and memory, see Stuart Burch, *London and the Politics of Memory: In the Shadow of Big Ben* (London: Routledge, 2019), https://doi.org/10.4324/9781315592916. For processions and other rituals, see M. G. Müller (eds.), *Rituals in Parliaments: Political, Anthropological and Historical Perspectives on Europe and the United States* (Frankfurt, Peter Lang: 2006), A. Wood, *The Memory of the People: Custom and Popular Senses of the Past in Early Modern England* (Cambridge: Cambridge, 2013). For memorials, see Peter Sherlock, *Monuments and Memory in Early Modern England* (London: Ashgate, 2008); J. Winter, *Sites of Memory, Sites of Mourning: The Great War in European Cultural History* (Cambridge: Cambridge University Press, 1995); John R. Gillis, *Commemorations: The Politics of National Identity* (Princeton, NJ: Princeton University Press, 1994); Kirk Savage, *Monument Wars: Washington, D.C., the National Mall, and the Transformation of the Memorial Landscape* (Berkeley, CA: University of California Press, 2009).

[3] Michelle Moravec, "Historical Altmetrics: Measuring What Mattered Most in the Past," Workshop on Quantitative Analysis and the Digital Turn in Historical Studies, Fields Centre for Quantitative Analysis and Modeling, University of Toronto, February 27, 2019.

different writers according to different schools of memory and to discern an increasing obsolescence of the past in later writers.

Studies of this kind have challenged the emphasis on forward movement latent in many studies of history. By working in memory, they plot the recursive movements of reflection on moments in the past. Like the nondigital subfield of memory studies, which was pioneered in the 1980s by French historians associated with Pierre Nora, the digital scholars of memory offer an implicit critique of the forward momentum of time as the dominant factor of experience. In so doing, they challenge a prejudice – visible among Enlightenment historians like Thomas Macaulay, but also implicit in many journalistic and professional accounts of today – that handles history as an accumulation of great personalities, ideas, technologies, or other events. Where Jay Winter gestured toward omnipresent acts of memorialization and statuary after the First World War as a component of lived cultural experience, Michelle Moravec today counts dates and allusions to demonstrate an equally powerful force of memory at work in the feminist movements of the 1970s.[4] They challenge forward momentum by showing that new experience is, in many cases, a reiteration of a certain past: for Moravec, 1970s feminist culture made progress by looking backward. Simply counting new words would not capture the element of recursive experience over historical time: but skillfully counting allusions to the past does.

Insights of this kind, about how the totality of history is structured by cultural experiences and psychological repetitions, indeed structure the lived experience of the past. They demonstrate another arena where historians, with our disciplinary sensitivity to the many ways in which humans experience time, can contribute to contemporary data-driven scholarship across all fields, and add a new dimension into the interpretation of change over time.

Moravec's appreciation of recursive time draws on decades of scholarship in the field of history, where specialists in memory studies have fostered an appreciation for the multiplicity of ways that societies look backward and how greatly these habits have changed from one generation to the next. "During the Renaissance, memory of the dead and mindfulness of one's own death receded and gave way to the hope of immortality

---

[4] Pierre Nora, *Les Lieux De Mémoire* (Paris: Gallimard, 1984); Jay Winter, *Sites of Memory, Sites of Mourning: The Great War in European Cultural History* (Cambridge: Cambridge University Press, 1995); Thomas N. Baker, "National History in the Age of Michelet, Macaulay, and Bancroft," in *A Companion to Western Historical Thought*, ed. Lloyd Kramer and Sarah Maza (Malden, MA: Blackwell, 2002), 185–204.

through cultural achievements," records Aleida Assmann, the scholar of memory in western culture. "Life after death was no longer exclusively at the discretion of God," she notes.[5] Human chronicles of achievement, like the marble busts of worthies preserved in Westminster Cathedral, became a means for national leaders to establish a collective identity, imbued with values powerful enough to send young men to die in war. "National memory helped to transform territories into nation-states," she writes; "it also introduced a new variety of memorial politics."[6] Assmann explains that the politics of national memory produced the modern memorial landscape that typifies most European and American cities – museums, portrait galleries, national cemeteries, and memorials to unknown soldiers alike. It was national memory, enforced by institutions and crystallized in architectural classicism, claim Wolfgang Welsch and Astrid Erll, that created the fantasy of ethnic nationalism. In the era of nineteenth-century museum building, writes Erll, "cultures are seen as monads, as remaining distinguished from one another. It is such delimiting thinking that generates racism and other forms of tension between local, ethnic, and religious groups."[7]

In the scholarship of the twentieth century, memory studies emerged to catalog the processes of remembering and forgetting particular episodes in collective history – for instance, through statuary and stone memorials raised to national wars, or the cumulative effects of trauma as evidence of the body's capacity to remember past events.[8] Maurice Halbwachs, who introduced the idea of "collective memory," believed that societies used monuments to stabilize a sense of identity.[9] One strand of memory studies has emphasized the contestation of memory: that is, the way that particular groups remember the same events differently, or emphasize different events in the same period. In Chicago, there are two separate memorials to the conflict known as the Haymarket Massacre of 1886. One of them memorialized the police, while one celebrates the slain anarchist organizers of the labor movement, who may have been the unjust target of police

---

[5] Aleida Assmann, *Cultural Memory and Western Civilization: Arts of Memory* (Cambridge: Cambridge University Press, 2011 [1999]), 36.
[6] Ibid., 129.
[7] Astrid Erll, "Travelling Memory," *Parallax* 17:4 (November 1, 2011): 4–18, https://doi.org/10 .1080/13534645.2011.605570.
[8] Pierre Nora, "Between Memory and History: Les Lieux De Mémoire," *Representations*, 1989, 7–24; Jay Winter, Sites of Memory, Sites of Mourning.
[9] Assmann, *Cultural Memory and Western Civilization*, 121.

profiling.[10] In contrast to the theory of history as a series of measurable innovations, memory studies suggests that important events are marked by episodic reiterations of some prior moment in the collective imagination.

The historian Pierre Nora believed that signs and symbols like memorials act as aggressions in battles over memory.[11] The parliamentary speaker or US president may, favoring a certain politics, present a history of the nation as a white, Protestant stronghold. In spinning the narrative of the past in a certain direction, they aren't engaging the courtroom drama of *history,* where scholars argue over sources and the truth of the past. Most often, politicians and celebrities of all kinds don't refer to research or the truth-value of history; they tell stories, which may have political content. When politicians' stories promote a certain form of memory over another, the speaker is legitimizing a version of memory.[12]

Studies of memory thus teach us to read *repetition* as an action with political content. Astrid Erll reports on the enormous volume of stories of atrocities that circulated through Britain and the British Empire after the so-called Indian Mutiny, when resistance by Indian soldiers resulted in disproportionate repression by the British occupiers. The British accounts – based on hearsay – circulated accounts of rape and murder of white women. Despite the lack of substantiation, the "repetitiveness" of the details, copied from one British author to the next, seemed to establish memory as fact.[13]

Michelle Moravec's study, with its sensitivity to recursive thinking about the past, translates the careful concerns of Assmann and Nora into a data-driven question: *Which* feminists did the feminist movement remember at any given time, and *when* was each great feminist forgotten? Following Moravec, we can imagine memory studies as an instructive approach to working with data about collective memory at any scale. It can tell us about how our memories change over the course of a single life – for instance, we could text mine our own email for allusions to personal traumas or successes, asking *how long* the memory of any given wedding or graduation continued to be a touchstone in personal correspondence. We can also ask questions about our collective memory of events and belonging.

---

[10] Lara Kelland, "Putting Haymarket to Rest?," *Labor* 2:2 (May 1, 2005): 31–38, https://doi.org/10.1215/15476715-2-2-31.

[11] Assmann, *Cultural Memory and Western Civilization*, 122.   [12] Ibid.

[13] Astrid Erll, "Remembering across Time, Space, and Cultures: Premediation, Remediation and the 'Indian Mutiny'," in Laura Basu and Paulus Bijl, *Mediation, Remediation, and the Dynamics of Cultural Memory* (Walter de Gruyter, 2009), 109–38.

Earlier, we acknowledged how contested memory of particular events can be. As of the writing of this book, the memory of January 6, 2021, when an armed mob stormed Capitol Hill and forcibly entered Congress, is still vivid in the nation's recent experience. Those events are also being rewritten in significant ways; whereas most news sources and bystanders witnessed a violent mob led by President Trump and filled with his right-wing supporters, some politicians now claim that the mob was led by antifa activists. The methods of memory studies can allow us to analyze millions of pieces of testimony about the mob, asking: Who referred to which events from the past, and did that memory change? An analysis that aggregates divergent memories into a single map of when and how consensus split can offer communities important self-knowledge in a time when memory is contested.

How would such an analysis work? We can experiment with Moravec's method of mapping collective memory at a broader scale by applying it to *Hansard*, the record of parliamentary debates in the British House of Commons and House of Lords. Because *Hansard* represents what was spoken in parliament, it contains many instances of speeches where members of parliament invoked events in the nation's history. Parliamentarians have been both readers and writers of history, often instrumentalizing their accounts of the past in the making of party identity.[14] Some of those events – the Norman Invasion or the English Civil War – had produced winners and losers, whose heirs (real or imagined) referenced the other side's victory with rancor centuries later. In the United States, to recall the Boston Tea Party in a public speech is to

---

[14] For instances of nineteenth-century parliamentarians who wrote histories or historically flavored essays and novels, consider: Henry Parnell, *A History of the Penal Laws against the Irish Catholics* (London: Longman, Hurst, Rees, Orme, Brown, and Green, 1825); William Cobbett, *A History of the Protestant Reformation in England and Ireland: Showing How That Event Has Impoverished the Main Body of the People in Those Countries* (London: William Cobbett, 1829); Benjamin Disraeli, *Coningsby: The New Generation* (London: Henry Colburn, 1844); Thomas Babington Macaulay, *The History of England from the Accession of James II* (Boston, MA: Phillips, Sampson and Company, 1849); Thomas Baines and Edward Baines, *Yorkshire, Past and Present: A History and a Description of the Three Ridings of the Great County of York, from the Earliest Ages to the Year 1870*, 2 vols. (London: William Mackenzie, 1871); William Forsyth, *The Rules of Evidence as Applicable to the Credibility of History* (London: (Published for the Institute), Robert Hardwicke, 1874); Henry Richard, *History of the Origin of the War with Russia* (London: Office of the Peace Society, 1876); William E. Gladstone, *The Royal Supremacy as It Is Defined by Reason, History and the Constitution* (London: J. Murray, 1877); Justin McCarthy, *A History of Our Own Times. A New Edition.* (London: Chatto & Windus, 1882); James E. Thorold Rogers, *Six Centuries of Work and Wages. The History of English Labour* (New York: G. P. Putnam's Sons, 1884); Justin Huntly McCarthy, *Ireland since the Union: Sketches of Irish History from 1798 to 1886* (Chicago, IL: Belford, Clarke and Co., 1889).

reinscribe a history of the collectivity that begins with rebellion against authority; to invoke the Civil War is to recall how much of US history and wealth is bound up with slaveholding. In the United Kingdom, to recall the Glorious Revolution, was typically to reference a period of prosperity that depended upon the exile of Catholics and dissenting Protestants; to recall the Norman Conquest is to reference that Britain's elite trace their privilege to acts of confiscation. It stands to reason that a map of mentions of famous events might be the first step in a digital reading of consensus and dissent about the past.

The Memory of the Past in Parliament: A Case Study

Political leaders invoke and even invent traditions when they allude to historical episodes from the past in the course of making speeches or proposing legislation, and these memorials leave traces in text. Speakers in Britain's parliament began to keep memorials of the past and to refer to precedents in increasingly concrete ways after the 1590s, when a new clerk began to keep a regular, bureaucratic register of the debates that transpired. As historian Paul Seaward has shown, the oral memory of why parliament operated a certain way in the past was committed to written records – in this case, informal notes, the forerunner of the daily parliamentary proceedings that much of this book is dedicated to analyzing via text mining.[15]

The ability to command information about precedent has always been a powerful political tool. References to legislative precedents might have acted as a kind of "points scoring" with one's party. They could also be used to sway political sentiment and it was not uncommon, even in the sixteenth century, for speakers in parliament to reference their memory of previous generations and their habits by way of arguing for a particular precedent, for example that long bills should be shortened.[16] Mentions of particular years therefore frequently appeared in parliamentary speeches when a speaker was casting for precedents. The shifting history of those mentions can tell us a great deal about how the use of the past changed from decade to decade across the nineteenth century.

---

[15] Paul Seaward, "Institutional Memory and Contemporary History in the House of Commons, 1547–1640," in Paul Cavill and Alexandra Gajda, eds., *Writing the History of Parliament in Tudor and Early Stuart England* (Manchester: Manchester University Press, 2018), 211–28, https://doi .org/10.7228/manchester/9780719099588.003.0010.

[16] Ibid., 214–15.

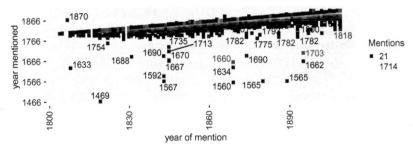

Figure 7.1   Years mentioned in *Hansard* by number (n>20).

The results of an application of Moravec's experiment are shown in Figure 7.1. The graph offers a timeline generated from a dataset of debates from 1806 to 1911, which have been searched for mentions of four-digit numbers from 1066 to 1911 that were mentioned at least twenty times within a single year of parliamentary debate. The mentions of years before 1466 were too few to notice and have been cropped from view; only twice in the century did speakers refer to the Norman Conquest of 1066 by year. Searching for numbers was a hazard. It might have produced references to 1567 bales of hay rather than the year 1567; the narrative that follows explains the results that were discovered when the mentions were looked up and discovered, indeed, to be mentions of years, suggestive of broad political trends of memory.

In effect, the experiment gives what we might call a "double timeline" – a representation of dates memorialized on a certain date in parliament. The dates of the actual speeches are rendered on the x-axis. The y-axis represents another timeline: the timeline of years referenced in the text of speeches, listed from 1466 to 1911. Dots are plotted for each year, with a cutoff of at least twenty references being used. The color of the dots shows how many times each year is referenced: dark dots show a few dozen mentions, like the references to historical years such as 1688. Pale dots indicate historical years that were mentioned hundreds or thousands of times within one year of speeches; typically, pale dots are only recorded for the years immediately previous to the speech. In general, parliamentary speakers were far more likely to mention the events of the previous year or even decade than the previous century. The heavy diagonal line visible from left to right describes references to the current year or years just before it; we see it increasing in intensity over the course of a century that was more self-aware of its past. The diagonal line thickens as the length of recursive memory in those references becomes deeper from 1800 to 1865.

Points above the line typically refer to future dates implied by state relationships to debt; an early reference to 1870 turns out to be a reference to the long loans made on behalf of the East India Company. The points on and immediately above or below this diagonal line are so frequent and dense that much information has been obscured; another rendering of the data would be necessary to probe the dynamics of the points on this section of the graph. I have let the visualization stand as it does because I am more interested in the scattered points indicating the changing patterns of reference in which parliamentary speakers directly named the events of previous centuries.

The scattered, sporadic points of the chart below the diagonal offer an image of the changing shape of political memory in parliament, or at least the structure of references in the past. A few long vertical lines show moments at which a longer span of the past was engaged. The data about how members of parliament referenced the past suggests that speakers focused on relatively recent periods of memory, mainly the hundred years before the speakers lived, references to which cluster as a dark black diagonal with a paler streak running in the middle of it across the top of the visualization.

Speakers in parliament referenced the seventeenth century with partic-ular vividness. A similar horizontal string of references to the 1660s shows memories of the Restoration at work in the nineteenth century, whether through references to the Dutch fleet that sailed up the River Medway that year as a preamble to current naval preparations, or references to Pepys' diary read aloud in parliament in 1902. Particular junctions pop out, such as the importance of 1688 (the date of the England's Glorious Revolution) to the year 1831 (when parliament was debating whether to give the middle class the vote), as ministers made a point of comparing the two revolutions. Vertical lines suggest moments when speakers dove deep into the past, asking questions in 1845 about the meaning of sixteenth- and seventeenth-century legislation.[17]

Most of the time, when speakers hearkened back to memories of the relatively ancient past – for instance the Anglo-Dutch War or the Glorious Revolution – they were attempting to establish a new consensus

---

[17] Almost all of the enumerated dates specify moments of legislation. References to the year 1469 turn out to concern a statute in that year that gave Scottish burghs the right to elect their own magistrates, briefly visited 400 years later to help discern the question of upon what conditions the burgesses of Aberdeen held their posts. The horizontal lines of the 1560s suggest continuous engagement with Tudor policies in the age of Queen Victoria, as speakers looked to precedents of an earlier era, whether for doctrine about the outfits worn by church ministers or a debate over the validity of the title given as the Earldom of Mar.

about a common experience in the past and what it implied for the future. References to the past formed a commonplace of parliamentary debate. When members of parliament or congress invoked past events, they were not simply establishing procedure, they were attempting to inscribe a view of the laws of the past.

But referencing the past didn't always produce consensus. Pepys' diary was read aloud in parliament several times, typically to justify traditions of supporting the Navy; sometimes it was even counterquoted by the opposition to prove that Pepys had been misused. Mr. Croker made such an accusation in 1832. Earlier in the same month, Sir James Graham had previously invoked Pepys to make his case for reorganizing the Victualling Board and other subordinate departments of the Navy under a single administration by the Board of Admiralty. Mr. Croker provoked him, claiming that he could find nowhere in Pepys' published memoirs a reference to the passage Graham had quoted. Croker dared Graham to him to show where his Pepys quotation was coming from. When Croker's request was met with silence, Croker jeered that "this was the first time in the annals of Parliament, that any Member had quoted an authority, without being able and willing to state where the quotation was to be found."[18]

While we are turning up results of parliamentarians bickering over the precedents for new legislation, we're still far short of evidence that would support a capsule view of the uses of *memory* in parliament, as inspired by Moravec. We might consider, therefore, what we learned in previous chapters – that iterative engagement with algorithms might provide clearer answers that would illuminate our view of the data. Perhaps the focus on dates as numbers ("1688" and "1832") is getting in our way. Is there another approach we can try?

One approach might be to notice the important role played by events that were referenced by name rather than by date. Named events such as the First or Second World War frequently serve today as landmarks in political discourse. By the nineteenth century, the writing of popular national histories like Macaulay's formed the context in which historical references to the past were made. Macaulay anchored his history in accounts of the English Civil War, setting the stage for the Glorious Revolution – a course of history that, to Macaulay, proved the superiority of Protestants and the Whig Party over Catholics and the Tory Party.

---

[18] For Graham's case, see "Civil Departments of the Navy," (February 14, 1832): 350; For quotation, see Mr. Croker, "The Navy Civil Departments Bill," House of Commons (February 27, 1832): 766.

Whigs, for Macaulay, represented the advances of democracy and technology over recent centuries and the destiny of Britain as a rational, Protestant world power. Decades later, Benjamin Disraeli would revise Macaulay's account, arguing that Whig history was the history of corruption and that the Tory party had steadfastly defended the traditions of ancient Britain and so could claim to support the poor. When a nineteenth-century speaker in parliament alluded to a prominent historical event – for Macaulay, the Glorious Revolution of 1688 or for Disraeli, the reign of Charles I – they were often making a political argument for unity behind a particular party and its policies in the contemporary world.[19]

In other words, the set of named events referenced in parliament was constantly changing under the influence of a constantly shifting series of political pressures. Text mining allows us to detect and study these shifts, especially where changing references to the imagined past were not so dramatic as Disraeli's revaluation of Charles I. With text mining, the careful study of pattern and repetition can illuminate the changing shape of common aspirations and political fantasy alike.

Parliamentary speakers more frequently referred to events in the past by name rather than by dates, calling upon the "Crimean War" or the "French Revolution." Following this line of insight, we can revisit Moravec's study with a slight adjustment that reveals more information. To find events mentioned by name, it helps to have algorithmic help. A controlled vocabulary would be ideal, but another helpful tool is named entity recognition (NER), or data pipelines that recognize frequent, nonoverlapping sets of strings and then take a guess at whether those frequent phrases refer to people, places, or events. NER works alongside parts-of-speech recognition, where the algorithm begins by breaking the sentence into nouns, verbs, and other parts of speech, identifying the function of each. Once the surrounding grammatical structure of the sentence has been parsed, the software can guess that a capitalized noun phrase like "the Magna Carta" is actually an event, rather than a person, currency, or geopolitical entity (these being some of the other categories for which the NER algorithm searches). The NER algorithm allows the analyst to extract a list of regularly repeated phrases that appear to be "event-like" in terms of how they appear in grammatical structure.[20] To work with this data for the purposes of

---

[19] Dani Napton, "Historical Romance and the Mythology of Charles I in D'Israeli, Scott and Disraeli," *English Studies* 99:2 (February 17, 2018): 148–65, https://doi.org/10.1080/0013838X.2017.1420617.

[20] In this experiment, I applied the NER extractor from the spaCy software package without further adjustments. For spaCy, see spacy.io. The results from spaCy were heavily pruned back to eliminate

understanding history takes patience, because the same phrase can appear referenced by multiple similar phrases; homophonic references have to be compiled by hand through a painstaking process of datacleaning. In addition, many events were referred to with similar language. Everyone knows that the French Revolution happened in 1789, but when the "French Revolution" is mentioned in 1830 or 1848, does that count as a reference to 1789 or to the later dates? What about those occasions when the South African War was referred to as the Boer War or the Second Boer War? A perfect study, meant to probe such questions, would have to include a step of indexing each point of reference. My plan here, however, is not a perfect study but a proof of concept. All mentions of the French Revolution are thrown together into the year 1789; I have counted the Boer War as the Boer War whether it was first or second, feeling justified by the argument that the use of the older term suggests the work of memory. Meanwhile, we can use visualization to unpack the changing pulse of references to the French Revolution, and draw our conclusions from there.

As Table 7.1 indicates, mentions of the Magna Carta, Plan of Campaign, and Crimean War predominated over mentions of any other event-like noun phrases, followed closely by mentions of the Game Laws, French Revolution and the South African War, also known as the Second Boer War (if the first and second Boer Wars are counted together, they surpass mentions of the Game Laws and fall below mentions of the Crimean War – a nice illustration of how the subtleties of counting come to matter). Other colonial wars, railway projects, and Lloyd George's "super-tax," proposed in 1909, are among the highest-ranked event-like noun phrases collected by our process. Far less significant in terms of raw count are the event-like noun phrases that reference contemporary cultural events such as the Great Exhibition (172 mentions), the Paris Exhibition of 1889 (at 28 counts, it was left off of this table), or the American War of Independence (13 counts, likewise missing from the table).[21]

---

phrases such as "the act of 1808" or confused entities ("the civil war" refers sometimes to Prussia, sometimes to England, to Portugal, or America). Because of concerns over accuracy where optical character recognition (OCR) errors were concerned, we used a different algorithm for the counts.

[21] It should be noted that different approaches would produce different figures as well as a different list of events. We have used a matching formula to match near formulae, for instance "French Revolution" and "French Revolutions." The list of events was produced by the spaCy software package, whose named entity extractor attempts to recognize names of events, eras, institutions, and revolutions; it represents essentially a quick-and-dirty attempt to extract information about memory in *Hansard*. The same exercise could be recreated to great benefit using a more exhaustive list of historical events, rigorously checked against inline mentions.

Table 7.1 *Most frequently named event-like noun phrases in* Hansard, *according to spaCy's NER algorithm. Thanks to Stephanie Buongiorno and Alexander Cerpa for data.*

Event Named	Date of Event	Total Mentions
Magna Carta	1215	2,919
Plan of Campaign	1886	2,775
Crimean War	1853	2,614
Game Laws	1389	1,403
French Revolution	1789	1,046
South African War	1899	910
Super-Tax	1910	812
Orange River Colony	1900	799
Great Western Railway	1833	748
Afghan War	1839	664
Thirty-Nine Articles	1563	644
Chinese War	1839	555
Great Northern Railway	1846	477
Great Eastern Railway	1862	379
Sugar Convention	1864	379
Great Southern and Western Railway	1844	352
Kaffir War	1779	317
Zulu War	1879	301
Peninsular War	1807	297
Franco-German War	1871	294
Boer War	1880	243
Abyssinian War	1867	209
Great Southern and Western Railway Company	1844	206
Persian War	1856	206
Great Exhibition	1851	172
Battle of Waterloo	1815	166

From here, we can return to our general question: What can we learn about the history of memory among speakers in Britain's nineteenth-century parliament? The visualized results provide some enticing answers.

In Figures 7.2 and 7.3, we see two variations on the double timeline produced not with an index of years by number, but rather by counting the event-like noun phrases identified by the natural language processing software, spaCy. Figure 7.2 depicts those from the medieval and early-modern past by name; Figure 7.3 depicts those from the nineteenth century. Here again, the x-axis is a timeline of 1806–1911. The y-axis is a timeline of events referred to in parliament by name. A dot is plotted for each group of references to a single event in a single year. Only eight of the most frequently referenced events are shown. A small dark square represents a handful of references; a large pale square represents up to 165 references (Figure 7.2) or 989 references (Figure 7.3) to a single event from the past within a single year. A basic count demonstrates that as memory became political, historical references to certain moments in the past could swell to dwarf other subjects of debate in parliament.

As with Figure 7.1, the double timeline of years, Figures 7.2 and 7.3 are useful for peering into the changing map of memory. A clear hierarchy of memory and political allusions to the past emerges. Out of the eight most frequently referenced event-like noun phrases, only a few memories – the Norman Conquest, the Plantagenets, the Magna Carta, and the Thirty-nine Articles of the Church of England – received sustained attention over the century as a whole. But the most informative conversations are the ones that evidence shifts in collective thinking about the past. Another handful of event-like noun phrases – for instance, the medieval Game Laws – explode at particular moments in time, as if those events erupted into consciousness whenever active political contestations between landlords and poachers brought ancient hierarchies back into view.

One of the most vivid shifts of memory in the nineteenth century concerns the dynamic of nineteenth-century references to two of the major events in the seventeenth century, the Civil War of 1641 (when a Catholic king and his aristocratic supporters were deposed by an army of Puritans sometimes described as yeomen), and the Glorious Revolution of 1688 (which resulted in Protestant monarchs William and Mary II being crowned, without violence, in 1689, establishing the House of Hanover). Discussions of the Protestant establishment created by the Glorious Revolution of 1688 peaked around the time of the Reform Act of 1832, when the middle class got the right to vote. After 1832, however, as the memory of 1688 faded, in its place rose references to the English Civil War, which would be invoked by Victorian historians such as Goldwin Smith as a war by English yeomen against the privileges of the elite. This is not entirely a new insight, of course; the political uses of the memory of 1688 and 1832 have long been the subject of research by historians of the nineteenth century, but the quantitative visualization of references to the past makes clear that there was a turning point when the memory of one event displaced the other.

The visualization also reveals a fact not widely observed in the historical literature – that the first major discussion of the American Constitution transpired during the debates about the 1832 Reform Act. America's loss as

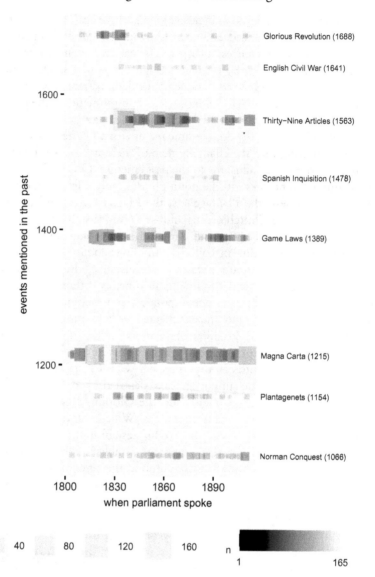

Figure 7.2 Events mentioned by name in Parliament (before 1770). Using a controlled vocabulary of dates mined by spaCy software package and adjusted by author. Thanks to Stephanie Buongiorno and Alexander Cerpa for data.

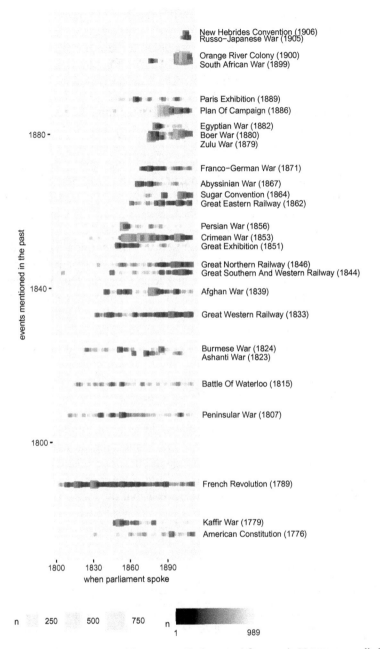

Figure 7.3 Events mentioned by name in Parliament (after 1770). Using a controlled vocabulary of dates mined by spaCy software package and adjusted by author. Thanks to Stephanie Buongiorno and Alexander Cerpa for data.[22]

---

[22] Several of the horizontal lines show apparently anticipatory mentions in advance of the event, which are an aftereffect of working with dirty data that contained several errors where documents' dates were misclassified due to the processing pipeline. I talk about the various iterations of the *Hansard* dataset, including newer versions that eliminate these errors, in the appendix, where I add cautions

a colony had been so painful for the British that it is unsurprising that silence mainly prevailed over the century. But in 1832, the debates over widening the vote and rationalizing parliament gave occasion for several parliamentarians to voice their admiration for the American system of government. Speakers in the House of Lords held up the American Constitution as an example of a document founded upon rational principles based upon a proportional system of representation.[23] The Earl of Falmouth admiringly pointed to the American Constitution as a document intended to stem demagoguery ("the fickleness of the people," as he put it) through the requirement of a two-thirds vote for an amendment to the Constitution.[24] He upheld the sagacity of historical retrospection in America in contrast to the fickleness of the British reform party, whom he accused of being "younger politicians, unused to power, [who] think themselves qualified, when suddenly thrown into office, to write down old Constitutions, and create new ones."[25]

Admiration for the design of the American Constitution did not always imply an endorsement for reform. In the exchange that led up to the House of Lords' endorsement of the new legislation, the Earl of Carnarvon returned to praise the American Constitution – admiring it as a document that guarded against "the changeful spirit of republican legislatures."[26]

The visualization in Figure 7.2 guides us to notice subtler patterns of thought and remembrance as well. References to the Thirty-nine Articles of the Church of England and the Book of Common Prayer form a constant pattern of reference through the century. They offered a coded formula for the superiority of Protestantism and the justification for English influence abroad.

The patterns of Protestant thinking could weave in subtle references to the distant past. The Spanish Inquisition became a regular talking point in the 1820s, as Britons began to debate giving the vote to Roman Catholics (enfranchised in 1829). Looking at the mentions of the Spanish Inquisition in the context of speeches reveals that the Inquisition was most often brought up as a commonplace reference for state terror. Critics of the state talked Inquisition, as critics of the state today might reference

about the preliminary nature of the visualizations shown in this book, as many of them were generated on the basis of earlier data.

[23] The Earl of Haddington, speech, "Parliamentary Reform – Bill for England – Second Reading – Adjourned Debate – Third Day," House of Lords (Wednesday, October 5, 1831), col. 1382.

[24] The Earl of Falmouth, speech, "Parliamentary Reform – Bill for England – Second Reading – Adjourned Debate – Fourth Day" (Thursday, October 6, 1831), col. 70.

[25] Ibid., col. 69.

[26] Earl of Carnarvon, speech, "Parliamentary Reform – Bill for England – Second Reading – Fourth Day," House of Lords (Friday, April 13, 1832), col 378.

Hitler – whether they were discussing the duties paid on malt (1833) or the practice of officials opening secret mail at the Post Office (1845).

To be sure, there are also clear differences between allusions to Hitler today and allusions to the Spanish Inquisition. Invocations of the Inquisition were a form of anti-Catholic bigotry made chiefly by Protestant speakers who associated every local tyranny with an invisible (and technically impossible) conspiracy of papist influence. And every invocation of the Spanish Inquisition in terms such as these helped to solidify the prejudice against Roman Catholics of Protestant listeners and readers of the parliamentary debates.

What is interesting, of course, is that with the help of a quantitative comparison of mentions of the Spanish Inquisition against mentions of other events over the century, we can establish that mentions of the early-modern event were much more frequent than references to other events from around the same time period. We can also understand references to the Spanish Inquisition, the Thirty-nine articles, the English Civil War, and the Plantagenets as a set of historical references that came into alignment around the same time. Why that quadrangle of event-like noun phrases locked into place after 1832, and what work those references to early-modern memories accomplished in the world of nineteenth-century politics, must wait for some future scholar to unpack.

The record of event-like noun phrases that reference the contemporary history of the nineteenth century, shown in Figure 7.3, is denser by far than the earlier record in Figure 7.2. In general, Britain's nineteenth-century parliament talked far more about events since the French Revolution than it did about the ancient past. But in the main, modern events were referred to only for a passing season. With the exception of the French Revolution, historical events – including the Great Exhibition with its massive Crystal Palace, the Peninsular War against Napoleon, and the Persian War – tended to be current within the debating chamber of parliament for a period of between ten and twenty years, before disappearing from regular parlance, after which they might spring back into routine discourse only with great infrequency. Of the many modern events that speakers referenced, only a handful rose to the status of the Magna Carta or French Revolution, and were still frequently referenced after their time. As we see in Figure 7.3, chief among these was the Crimean War, which would form a reference point for discussions of empire and foreign relations for decades to come (again, I note that a fuller interpretation awaits the work of a historian who uses an index like this figure as the start of a project of guided reading).

One obvious pattern that emerges from Figure 7.3 is the working of what Koselleck called "repetition," or the rekindling of old memories when new battles recast previous events. Thus mentions of the "French Revolution" swell in 1830, the date of a French Revolution sometimes called the July Revolution, but also referenced by contemporary speakers as "the Revolution in France;" the phrase calls to mind the earlier French Revolution, which is why we have counted the terms together. Similarly, mentions of the Boer War swell with the outbreak of the South African War, which is not surprising, because we have double-counted the terms. A scholar concerned with how exactly memory changed with these events would be well served to probe deeper than my data allows.

Thus, while at first, the double timeline of events by name may seem promising, the list of events tracked by spaCy also displays shortcomings that should trouble historians. It's not just a matter of data that should be refined in some cases; there are also obvious exclusions. There are no events that overtly seem to concern women, and no events in the modern world that suggest the agency of the working class. Was everything really about railroads and war? We should be suspicious of the data, remembering that one facet of the critical thinking recommended in earlier chapters is the critical examination of controlled vocabularies supplied by a computer.

The spaCy software package is agnostic about vocabularies of events; it is built to detect frequent phrases and to guess that they are events based on their grammatical role in a sentence. spaCy doesn't actually recommend the "Crimean War" as a phrase, or neglect "Chartism." Nevertheless, parliament itself tended to be biased toward events such as wars and revolutions – events, that is, which in theory might destabilize the institutional role of parliament – and entities such as the great railroad companies, whose stockholder lists overlapped with role of parliamentary members and their major supporters. We should not be surprised that parliamentary speakers mentioned working-class Chartists or starving Indians during the Deccan famine less than the Great Western Railway, even if we find it disappointing.

Nevertheless, critical thinking about the experiences of peoples whose voices were underrepresented in the parliamentary debate should lead us to grow curious about another way of peering into memory. spaCy's algorithm for detecting event-like noun phrases has not picked up on references to historical events as memorable as the Irish Famine or Gordon Riots. Knowing when to reject an algorithm is a key part of critical search. In the current case, it is clear that grammar-based algorithmic detection of events is resulting in a biased portrait of memory.

Table 7.2 *Popular experience and acts of resistance in memory.*

Event Named	Date of Event	Total Mentions
Anti-Corn Law League	1836	707
Great Revolt	1857	483
Riot Act	1714	401
Chartism	1838	212
Cotton Famine	1861	156
Irish Famine	1845	153
Paris Exhibition	1889	137
Indian Famine	1630	85
Potato Famine	1845	73
Indian Penal Code	1860	71
Plantation of Ulster	1606	59
Tithe War	1830	51
Gunpowder Plot	1605	50
Peterloo	1819	44
Tichborne Trial	1873	41
Orissa Famine	1866	29
Guy Fawkes	1605	28

We can try counting references to events another way, a more straightforward way, by creating a controlled vocabulary. When using a controlled vocabulary, the scholar simply writes into a spreadsheet a handmade dictionary of events and the various ways to which they can be referred, then writes code to search for and count the items on this list. The resulting code is much simpler than the use of NER, but successful results require more expert knowledge. In this case, I used my knowledge of British history to propose a series of words that might reference events from social history, for instance, "riot," "trial," "famine," "code," "conference," "exhibition," and "commission." I conducted a preliminary search for the most frequent word pairs in which those keywords occur. To the results, I added a list of famous acts of resistance familiar to me as a social historian, scanning an exhaustive list of the most frequent two-word and three-word capitalized phrases in *Hansard* for reference. I then used code to count references to items on this handmade dictionary of events by year.

Using my handmade dictionary of events from social history, I achieved totally different results from those that came from using NER (Table 7.2). The event from my dictionary most frequently referenced was the Anti-Corn Law League, a popular movement founded in 1846 to press for free trade in grain and cheaper bread for the working classes, followed by the Great Revolt in India in 1857, that tremendous signal of Indian hatred of

British rule, the memory of which, distorted by British racism, inspired British atrocities for nearly a century to come. In third place came the Riot Act of 1714, which justified police action every time a public protest erupted

Visualizing the acts of memory that reference the events of social history can bring the lens of memory to a wider set of events than the political memories that we examined earlier. Curiously, almost none of the events collected by the author show up on the chart of modern events by the spaCy software for the simple reason that events in social history were mentioned too few times to make the cutoff of events collected in Figures 7.2 and 7.3.

The double timeline in Figure 7.4 dramatizes the fact that events from social history – that is, the experience of ordinary people, for instance the Irish Famine, with its 1 million dead – were referenced in parliament to a degree dramatically less than events of national consequence like the Crimean War, which saw some 22,000 casualties from across British Empire. The explosion of references to Chartism (1838) and the Rebecca Riots (1839) validates the judgment that an increasing awareness of popular politics was forced upon parliamentary speakers in these years – although both events would also be forgotten relatively quickly in comparison to events such as the Irish Famine (1845), the Indian Great Revolt (1857), or the Plan of Campaign (1886; visible in Figure 7.3). Both parliamentary silence and the persistence of memory about popular politics thus emerge as important questions for research.

Figure 7.4 also can help us to ask: Which events were remembered the longest? The deaths and suffering associated with the Potato Famine were long invoked as an indictment of British rule in Ireland, but references seem to have disappeared as a reference point after the land reform acts of the 1880s. Examining references to this expanded list of events over time reveals that the Great Revolt persisted in memory longer than any other event on record, paralleled only by the French Revolution. Close runners-up included the Potato Famine of Ireland and Scotland (when millions perished because of a fungal blight and the unwillingness of Britain's government to supply welfare), and the Cotton Famine of Lancashire (which is to say, the depression in the British textile industry triggered by the outbreak of the American Civil War). In contrast to these famous topoi of the past, the memory of most massacres, riots, and famines was astonishingly brief – a handful of years at most.

Hand-tailoring a dictionary allows us to make a faceted search that focuses on particular aspects of social history – for instance, the history of

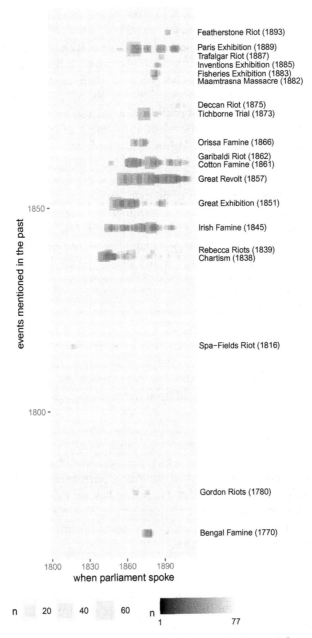

Figure 7.4   Events in social history mentioned by name in Parliament (after 1770), with controlled vocabulary developed by author.

riot. By narrowing our search just to references riots (Figure 7.5), we can see better the way that memories of protests in the past were invoked, or forgotten. Looking at the memory of riots, we quickly see how the Hyde Park riots of 1866 – when working men's vote was on the table – triggered memories of earlier working-class protests such as the anti-Catholic Gordon Riots and the anti-tollgate Rebecca Riots, both of which were tagged by elites as explosions of misrule. We can also see how memory and discourse had changed by 1876, when an outbreak of violence in Ireland triggered no such memories. Again, the significance of these patterns would need to be worked out through guided reading about each of the riots, but what is significant, for our purposes, is the way a series of filtered searches about different aspects of memory can reveal contrasting patterns of memory and of forgetting that otherwise might have remained obscure.

Expanding the list in this way demonstrates the *kind* of iterative refinements that might improve our experiment. The set of events offered here is far from complete or final – and I would love to see this list expanded by a set of historians preparing the names of famous women, colonial subjects, authors, technological inventions, and acts of resistance, including all variations by which those events might be referred to in parliament, which could expand and test this method.

What could we do with more research? A more rigorous study might proceed by recruiting research assistants in history to disambiguate terms that allude to multiple events, allowing us to unpack the references to "The Revolution," which were omitted from the present study, because I could not know whether those allusions indicated "The French Revolution," "The Spanish Revolution," or something else. An enhanced project might also annotate individual laws and commissions, a task that would allow the researcher to conclude which acts of parliament were the most frequently referenced by people living in their aftermath. Such annotations, however, would require a commitment that the author has not made for the present study, which, after all, is not a research project searching primarily for a new view on parliament, but rather a methodological overview of new approaches to the measure of time.

What ought to interest us, then, is speculation about what *might* be possible when such a dictionary exists. With such a dictionary, new frontiers of research might become possible. One could compare parliament's temporal views on the events of Britain's past with rival points of view – for example, the events named in novels, Irish newspapers, or Indian newspapers. Aggregate changes in language could also be measured and compared, for instance, comparative accounts of how contested was

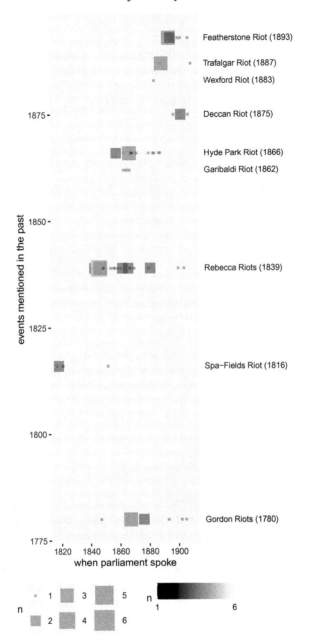

Figure 7.5   Riots mentioned by name in Parliament. Using author's controlled vocabulary.

the memory of the Norman Invasion as opposed to the English Civil War at different moments in parliament. It might even be possible to apply Koselleck's conceit of a "repetition/singularity" measure of historical novelty to each instance where an old event is invoked in a new setting, using the surrounding text to measure whether 1641 is always invoked with the same language, or when that knowledge began to shift in a more singular direction.

Finding the Average Story About the Past

We are only at the beginning of our investigation into how a computer could tell us about consensus and dissent in time. We need not stay here forever, combing over references to individual years or events. Information about how people understand and remember the past is also encoded casually by stray remarks about how things once were and jeremiads about how one day things will be different. Excepting prophets and historians, statements of this kind do not make up the bulk of conversation or discourse. But those occasional remarks, collected digitally, might also offer a portrait of how a society comes to know its past and its future.

Next, we will explore some general tools for identifying the "average" story told about the past. We will use that data to ask which historical realities speakers agreed about, and how their notions of the past changed from decade to decade. We will critically inspect the results of these three processes, linking our conclusions back to contextual knowledge of the time period. We will conclude by highlighting some of the memories that Britons agreed about and disagreed about, and by making some suggestions for the future of memory studies.

"Once upon a time," begins the fairytale. In parliament, too, speakers referenced the past with phrases such as "in bygone times," "in the past," or "for another generation." We searched parliament for explicit rhetorical indicators that a speaker was referencing the past, decade by decade, and found a variation in the frequency of such references as well as the content. When we search for sentences with temporal markers – say, "at that time" or "in times past" – we tilt our search for the average story toward stories that deliberately invoke memory. Stories that begin with the phrase "in times past" rarely reference yesterday, last week, or last month; they tend to reference some earlier memory of years, decades or even centuries in the past.

Suppose we performed such a search and retrieved hundreds of thousands of sentences referencing the past. How could we generalize about their content? One useful approach here is parts-of-speech analysis, a set of tools developed by computational linguists since the 1990s to accurately identify the nouns, verbs, prepositions, and articles of a sentence as well as their grammatical dependencies. The care linguists take to accurately parse sentences means that a computer trained in parts-of-speech analysis knows the difference between the formulation "dog bites man" and "man bites dog." It means that we can call up all the verbs that typically complement female subjects in one decade and compare them with the verbs that typically complement female subjects in another decade.

When we look for *action* relationships in sentences, we can expand from noun-verb relationships into statements about completed action. Instead of looking for descriptions of conditions, such as the hypothetical noun-verb phrase "librarians rock," we're looking for complete actions, such as that encapsulated by the hypothetical, short sentence, "librarians teach citizenship." That is, we're looking for complete action statements, where the sentence tells us not only about the action (teaching) and who benefits (citizens) but also who's responsible for employing them (librarians). A power hierarchy is summarized in three words. It's far more complete and specific – so far as ideas go – than the cheery opinion articulated in the noun-verb phrase, "librarians rock;" "librarians teach citizenship" demonstrates a relationship between two different kinds of people as well as a connecting action. For this reason, mining the triples in a textual database potentially gives a direct route to *relationships* and *actions* – historical or imagined – rather than mere opinion or feeling.

It turns out that the same triples are often repeated, even rewoven with new clauses around them. Counting those triples that were frequently repeated adds up to an index of historical significance, as other scholars have shown; one influential early study that used triples analysis proved that the most frequent triples in American newspaper headlines during the 1960s included "cops beat protesters."[27] Indeed, folklorist Timothy Tangherlini has used grammatical triples to devise a tracker that can identify, follow, and generalize about conspiracy theories developing over social media, because almost any individual on social media who recites some part of the Pizzagate conspiracy theory will repeat the same series of basic formulae about what storytellers claim to have happened: "Tony Podesta has weird art;" "weird art uses a secret language;" "the secret

[27] R. Franzosi, *From Words to Numbers: Narrative, Data, and Social Science* (Cambridge: Cambridge University Press, 2004).

language references pedophilia."[28] Repetition is key to how Tangherlini believes these stories spread and how their wilder claims are validated. Conspiracy theories cohere and gain their trustworthiness – in the eyes of believers – through the repetition of the same grammatical formulations, even if the overall structure of sentences and the alleged details vary considerably. As the first fragments of this narrative – "Tony Podesta has weird art" – are repeated and validated, less-frequent claims about the Podesta connection to pedophilia seem to be validated as well, to those who have been following the online conversation, even when the claims are easy to disprove outside the echo chamber. Our brains are led to believe that the frequent repetition of grammatic fragments in sources inside and out of the echo chamber proves the viability of the echo chamber's story as a whole.

If the power of repetition to compel belief seems spooky, there's also a silver lining. Repetition not only feeds wild fads and disorienting systems of belief – it also drives *analysis*. By counting repeated grammatical structures, researchers can easily pull apart the stories in question, developing algorithmic tools that are trained to quickly sift through the noise and focus on the core, repeated fragments of a set of stories that fill a particular echo chamber. Tangherlini suggests in his articles that such an analysis could help various actors fight misinformation by highlighting truth and dispelling falsehood.

For our purposes, however, repetition in narrative offers another window onto culture as a whole, another tool for understanding what people agree about and disagree about when they talk about their common past. Because of this structure of repetition in how stories circulate, data scientists can use *counting* in the context of triples analysis to identify shared patterns of storytelling or belief in a culture. On a more specific level of analysis, what are we grouping together? We've told the computer to "average out" helping verbs. Consider three hypothetical sentences about the past that would be counted as one:

"In bygone times, in London, they had a right to vote."
"I have learned of the natives of that place that in the past even they had rights."
"We have a right to speak, even as they had, in parliament at that time."

---

[28] Timothy R. Tangherlini et al., "An Automated Pipeline for the Discovery of Conspiracy and Conspiracy Theory Narrative Frameworks: Bridgegate, Pizzagate and Storytelling on the Web," *PLoS ONE* 15:6 (2020).

Following our instructions, the computer will tally all three sentences as the *same* sentence ("they had rights") – even though there are variations in the specific tense of the verb ("had" versus "have had") and the number and nature of rights ("rights" in general versus a "right to vote"). Using the underlying grammatical structure helps us to group together sentences whose sense of action is the same. All three sentences convey the sense that some people ("they") once possessed rights of some kind.

The most frequently repeated sentence level triples in a database represent a grammatical average of the stories that were re-told the most in a given culture. Just as we might take a *statistical average* of the heights of the players on a basketball team so as to study how tall the players are in relationship to the average student on campus, similarly we use triples to take the grammatical average the kinds of stories told about the past in order to understand something about cultural change.

Our triple analysis software builds on three decades of research in computational linguistics since the 1990s, which capitalized on the mid-twentieth-century insights of Ferdinand de Saussure and Noam Chomsky, who first speculated about how sentence grammar could be rendered into a computational process. In the 1990s, a new generation of linguists refined Chomsky's speculations about a "generative grammar" hardwired into the brain into a modern system of "descriptive grammar" that could be replicated by code. This insight allowed researchers at the University of Washington to begin extracting subjects, verbs, and objects – the basic grammatical arc of narrative sentences.[29]

From the triples alone, however, we don't always have all the information we would want about these variations, just as the average height of the basketball team doesn't tell us how tall the team's star is. When the computer detects the triple "we have force" (Figure 7.6, 1870), were the speakers invoking armed forces on the ground in the colonies, or some kind of political force in parliament? If we wanted to investigate what *kinds*

---

[29] It was the University of Washington researchers who called their basic unit of grammatic narrative a "triple." They published their code as Textrunner in 2007; another software package, OpenIE, was published by a Stanford Group in 2015, which compiled linguistically sophisticated rules to produce more accurate results, using "natural logic" to guide the detection of grammatical triples. I owe this history to Stephanie Buongiorno, a digital humanities and computing graduate student. Buongiorno's algorithm is the basis for the triples collected here. It concentrates on accurately parsing the structures of grammatical dependency within each sentence and allows her to mine subordinate clauses within the sentence for grammatical information – thus pulling from the sentence, "I have learned that in the past they had rights," the triple "they had rights" in addition to the vacuous main clause, "I learned that." Buongiorno's algorithm allows us to extract many times over the number of triples that Stanford's software extracts per sentence.

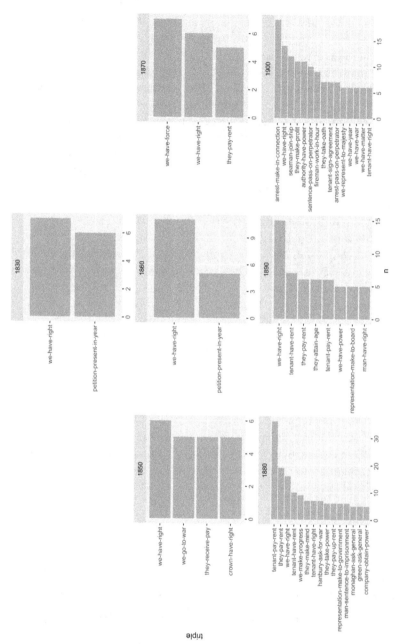

Figure 7.6   Top grammatical triples from sentences that explicitly reference the past (n>2). Based on data analysis by Stephanie Buongiorno. Visualization by author.

218

of rights or force were being talked about, we would employ another technique to drill down further.

Averages are useful, even when they leave us wanting to investigate further nuances another time, and we can find illuminating aspects of the larger story by asking: What was the average story told about the past in parliament during the course of the nineteenth century?

In Figure 7.6, I have instructed the computer to look for sentences that explicitly reference the past through phrases such as "in the past," "in bygone days," or "once upon a time." The resulting common grammatical threads detected by triples analysis paint a picture of how parliamentary speakers invoked a sense of the past. In the past, a "monument [was] erected in [the] church" (1810). They referenced events: a 'person [was] charged with [a] crime' (1820). Sometimes they recalled specific events for which the past gave precedents: the 'city [had] appli[ed] to [the] Treasury for aid' (1820).

How did people use storytelling about the past in parliament? They reminded each other of quantities and interests: the "number [who] voted in the year," "they ma[de] [a] profit' (1900). The past cautioned against extremism; in the past, an "alarm [was] forgot[ten] in [a] week" (1820) The past offered the basis for ideas about comparison, for instance about wages: 'they make in [a] year,' and 'they receive pay' appear in the 1850s.

There is also a great deal of movement as regards which stories people told about the past – the stories they chose to tell changed radically from generation to generation. The biggest story of the nineteenth century was the expansion of storytelling about *rights*. Rights were imagined as having been located in the ancient past; hence the appearance of "rights" in grammatical triples from the 1830s onward. "They had [a/the] right" could be said about one's ancestors who owned common land that was afterward enclosed by local landlords. "They had rights" was reiterated in radical claims of the Chartists who argued that ancient Saxons had had freedoms that had diminished since the Norman Yoke. Sometimes kindred formula appeared: "We [have] ma[de] progress" appeared with regularity starting in the 1880s. "We have power" was the watchword of the 1890s. For most of the nineteenth century, assertions of rights remained some of the top triples referencing the past; variations on the phrase "they had rights" were repeated five times in the 1820s and upward of 30 times in the 1880s.

The past was the ultimate reservoir of a sense of freedom, recalled in the form of rights established in previous generations that provided a template for modern rights. In fact, the *only* substantive grammatical formula about the past that was repeated in the 1810s and 1840s was this: "[a] petition [was] present[ed] in [that] year" (the subgraphs for 1810 and 1840 have been omitted for this reason). The phrase's repetition may indicate that so many peasant petitions to parliament *were* presented in those years – by ordinary people arguing for traditional rights to common land (rapidly being enclosed) and to relief when they were out of work (rapidly being refigured under new ideas about the economy).

The formulations changed, and those identifications of rights mattered: in the 1830s and again in the 1870s – both moments of broadened rights to vote – "we have [a] right," a phrase that was amplified by remembrance that "borough[s] [had[voter[s] in the past," and eventually, by the 1890s, the assertion that in the past a "man [had] rights." But the rights at stake weren't only those of the people. In the 1840s, Members of Parliament asserted that the "party has the [a] right," or even in the 1850s, the 'crown [has a] right.'

Decade by decade, Members of Parliament narrated recent events, churning the present into the past, creating short formulae that encapsulated the dynamics of the times. In 1820, "petition[s] [were] present[ed] in number," and "petition[s] ask[ed] for [a] share," while "[a] person [was] charge[d] with [a] crime." In 1830, as the Chartists began their peaceful assemblies in village greens, where speakers described the right of working men to vote, speakers in parliament discussed what should follow from the "petition [. . .] agree[d] [to] at [a] meeting." In 1840, a "number [of persons] received relief" (nineteenth-century welfare for the poor) while "export[s] show[ed] [an] increase" and the "bank-raise[d] rate[s];" in 1850, "we [went] to war;" in 1870, "they" (probably Irish Catholics, a majority tenant population on an island owned by absentees) "pa[id] rent." In 1880, they remembered that the "company obtain[ed] power" (perhaps the East India Company, with whose charter the British presence in India was first made official). Some debated the conditions under which "[a] man [was] sentence[d] to imprisonment" (for life). In 1900, some described those (motor car companies, land speculators, and other entities to be taxed) who had "ma[de a] profit." That each formula was repeated suggests that these grammatical fragments are not merely one-time formulations, but rather evidence of how and when the experiences of history became statements of collective consensus, acknowledged as fact, and repeated from mouth to mouth – up to thirty times over the course of a decade. Even when speakers disagreed about what to do with those working men who presented a petition for the vote, or the motor car companies making such profits, the whole world acknowledged that petitions had been presented and profits had been made. They did not bother coming into agreement about other fragments of history in the same way; these are the fragments that *lasted.*

We should also acknowledge that this circulation of historical detail from speaker to speaker and from parliament to newspaper was something relatively new and, indeed, scholars of parliament and newspaper tend to point out that these repeated messages signaled something new. In the mouth, the formulae, like religious chants, came to resonate with the ringing authority of truth. Historical knowledge thus displaced the pater-nosters of old, becoming a new oral formula. Once, across Europe, church statuary reminded the passerby of the shortness of life. By the nineteenth century, however, Europe was becoming a world where historical fact was rendered into a shared truth. Ordinary men and women had begun to preach the implications of this message: that ordinary people can, through acts of revolution, effectively remake their world. This message was believ-able, in part, because historical facts about the past – especially about the clamor for rights in the past and the possibility of rights in the future – had begun to appear with increasing frequency in parliamentary speeches and in the newspapers where those speeches were published.[30]

How Much Can Data Tell Us Without Reading?

The method of using triples has sharp delimitations. Formulae that illus-trate how people casually referenced the past from year to year are useful for detecting the slow pulse of cultural change. In our case studies, the evidence points to the increasing importance of ideas about constitutional and human rights in a culture slowly being influenced by the writings of Thomas Paine and Mary Wollstonecraft and the lingering memory of the French Revolution. But we can interpret those formulae so gracefully, in part, because of generations of intellectual historians who have traced the political wars over rights in Britain's parliament.

Sentence grammar also has its limitations and doesn't provide a key to understanding temporality. The number of formulae about the past rises

---

[30] For statuary and memory in the past, see Peter Sherlock, Monuments and Memory in Early Modern England. For an increasing orientation toward a detailed account of the past as a characteristic of modern European societies, see Assmann, *Cultural Memory and Western Civilization.*

with the 1880s and 1890s, but is this because there were more speeches being given every year in those years, or because of the increasing political use of history as a tool for debate? I suspect a bit of both. The number of speeches *was* increasing in those years, but it didn't triple in length, as formulae referencing the past did. But *why* do I know that? The triples referenced don't give enough evidence for me to make a solid interpretation on the basis of the data itself. Rather, it's only because of reading historians of political discourse like Michael Saler's *As If* that I happen to know that from the 1860s and 1870s forward, references to England's gothic past proliferated, anchoring contemporary battles for political rights.[31] It makes sense, then, that the era of "we have a right" became the era of talking about events as they happened as a part of history: political speakers were aware of themselves as heirs to a past, when the struggle for rights was real and they hoped to understand themselves as participants in current political struggles that would be iterated upon in the future.

We have now discussed four different vantages on memory – three of which involve small adjustments to the method of using grammatical interpretation. We have found patterns that, in the main, confirm a general thesis of the increasing importance of past to parliamentary debate, and have found the territory of *rights* to be the subject about which speakers cared the most when they thought forward or backward over time.

For the purposes of serving British history, however, our interpretation is not complete. We would like to know more about each triple – insights that we are likely to glean by following the principles of critical search and indulging in some close reading. We would like to answer some interpretive questions about what the triples meant in context. For instance, repetition of text in a dataset often signifies contestation; people repeat the same phrase because they are challenging each other. Were allusions to the past repeated because of a general consensus about their importance, or were speakers arguing about what happened? Such questions await the scholar motivated to examine attitudes toward past in greater detail.

Our purpose here has been to introduce a possible direction for exploring theories of memory with digital tools. We have inspected how dates, names of events, and grammatical triples can all serve that purpose.

---

[31] Michael Saler, *As If: Modern Enchantment and the Literary Prehistory of Virtual Reality* (Oxford: Oxford University Press, 2011).

The Experience of Time Is Multiple

What will be evident to the reader who has made it this far in the chapter is that this inquiry – like all the others in this book – is governed by the principles of critical search. I have abstained from presenting a squiggle of wordcounts over time and concluding that I understand what happened. Instead, I have refracted the question "How did nineteenth-century people in parliament talk about the past?" through a series of *iterations*. There is no *one* way to glean information about how parliamentarians discussed the past; I found at least three – mentions of years, mentions of dates by name, and temporal markers like "in former times."

Similarly, when producing an "average" portrait of storytelling about the past by abstracting grammatical triples from each sentence, I found another distinct way of drawing the portrait of memory: one by looking for any verbal indicators that the speaker is talking about the past – for instance, what happened "in a bygone era."

The Multiple Worlds of Memory in the Past

In Figure 7.7, the scene is timeless – perhaps it is today, perhaps in the ancient past. We can't really know, and that was intentional. In one sense, the scene is Eden, as symbolized by the figure plucking an apple in the center of the canvas. Around that illuminated body are circled the scenes of everyday life in Tahiti: families watching over a sleeping infant, a child eating an apple, an elder with graying hair; statuary, flora, and ocean. The painting represents different moods of human life: the social pair in the

Figure 7.7   Paul Gauguin, "D'où venons nous? Que sommes-nous? Où allons-nous?" (1897) Museum of Fine Arts, Boston.

lower right-hand corner of the canvas, who look as if they might have just been interrupted; the woman in the background left of center, who stares out at the landscape in a mood of contemplation; the figure in the central ground on the right, who turns away from the viewer; the pair in brown shadows behind her, pressed close in an embrace – are they seeking intimacy, or fleeing fear? Every variety of contemplation is on display, for this is a universalizing image: the painting fuses together the great western origin story of Eden with scenes of daily life in the colonies; it draws together water, earth, and sky; all the phases of life are collected – youth, adulthood, and old age. Sacred time and historic time collapse into one canvas; the stages of human life are all present at once.

In drawing together the ancient world and the contemporary, East and West, birth and death, Gauguin's universalizing image seems to draw together all experience into one reality – even as a great age of globalism shocked Europe from its comfortable belief that such human realms had vanished in the expulsion from Eden.

Gauguin was living through an era of cultural encounters between Europeans and peoples around the globe that exposed the enormous differences of temporal experience among different cultures. In Gauguin's time, many so-called primitive peoples and cultures were producing their own accounts of time and destiny, mainly at odds with European ideas about their past and future. In some places, non-Europeans told epics about their own past; in others, they wrote their own histories, sometimes organized according to their own mythology, as in Sri Lanka, where separatists composed textbooks for schoolchildren organized around a history reconciled with the Vedas.[32] Anticolonial rebellions were erupting across Asia and Africa and anticolonial treatises meanwhile were circulating through London and Paris, persuasive in their indictments of European empire as corrupt and corrupting.

To put it concisely: in this encounter, many Europeans came to feel disoriented in time. Hence, perhaps, Gauguin's questions, which are inscribed in the upper left-hand corner of the canvas and which are also the image's title: "Where did we come from? What are we? Where are we going?" The West had offered facile answers: We came from Eden and are headed to the grave. We came from paganism and are headed toward enlightenment. We came from Europe and will conquer the world,

---

[32] For epics, see Anne Salmond, *Aphrodite's Island* (New Haven, CT: Yale University Press, 2009). For textbooks, see Sumathi Ramaswamy, *The Lost Land of Lemuria: Fabulous Geographies, Catastrophic Histories* (Berkeley, CA: University of California Press, 2004).

converting all subject people into our laborers, servants, and apprentices. In a broad sense, Gauguin's world was in the midst of its own transition, shuffling off various sacred definitions of temporality, where the beginning was known and the end was certain, and opening up the possibility of a new world, where men and women made their own future.[33]

Gauguin's canvas suggests that he was contemplating an alternative set of answers to western doctrines about temporality. His canvas represents a world of basic truths, where we come from babyhood and are going to old age; we come and go through moments of regarding each other with skepticism and engagement, of solitude and conversation. Gauguin's biographers have attributed the uncertainty of his answers to the atmosphere of conflict that marked his personal affairs as he painted: Gauguin had fled to Tahiti to escape his debtors and nurse a series of physical illnesses; while he was there, his daughter died; he had begun to contemplate suicide.[34] Even while he labored on the canvas, the painter must have wondered where he himself was heading. A note of terror marks the canvas, signified by the figure plucking the apple. In Christian mythology, that simple gesture was fated to uncork the many evils of modern existence – self-knowledge, poverty, childbirth, labor, death, and suffering. According to Gauguin, the present and the future collapse into one perpetual Eden, where humans perpetually pluck apples that portend consequences we cannot understand.

Gauguin's confrontation with imperial time in the colonies led him to create a map of time, where birth and death, Eden and modernity, transpire on the same canvas, universalizing the whole into one transcendent experience. In this book, we will be attempting something similar, although our tools are extremely different. Modern theorists of history have grown skillful at drawing out individual motifs or instances of temporal experience and showing their relationships to each other, giving us a precise map of how different peoples in the past have experienced their own history. As I have shown, historians' careful attention to different representations of the past can guide a skillful application of digital tools to textual data.

The quest to understand where we are going and why split open in Gauguin's lifetime and from it splintered a thousand inquiries into the nature of temporality and society. Christian doctrines of the certainty of

---

[33] For Christian sacred time as a theme in Gauguin's thought, see Martin Gayford, *The Yellow House: Van Gogh, Gauguin, and Nine Turbulent Weeks in Arles* (London: Penguin Books, 2006), 99–100.

[34] Wayne Andersen, "Gauguin and a Peruvian Mummy," *Burlington Magazine* 109:769 (April, 1967): 238–43.

perfection were no longer certain. Railway timetables and the reality of time zones forced physicists and mathematicians to contemplate the relative nature of temporal experience. The study of history – already crucial for national politics in the nineteenth century – was becoming more important than ever.[35] Its models are still imperfect, but its demand for temporal modeling have become infinitely more precise in the century and a half since Gauguin produced a record of his temporal bewilderment.

I close this chapter with Gauguin's painting, which I interpret as a partial reflection on Europe's encounter with different temporalities, as seen by one observer, for whom personal time, Biblical time, and imperial time had begun to fold in on each other. I do not propose that Gauguin offers a superior reflection on colonial or Pacific experience. Gauguin's experience in 1897 was one of a broken man, fleeing to a colonized island in poverty and distress. He had rejected all the familiar frameworks – Christian triumphalism, European history painting, and imperialism. He knew that those modes didn't apply to the world he was seeing. Textual databases often contain within them shards of splintered vantages on time, much like the specters of memory recorded in Gauguin's painting. It is the humanist's task duty to parse apart those perspectives and to analyze and compare them.

My training in the humanities taught me to look at an artifact as *multiple*. A painting set in Tahiti by a French painter like the one in Figure 7.7 is not a single object with a meaning that can be distilled into a sentence; it is *simultaneously* an artifact of colonialism, a testament to personal tragedy, a product of a dialogue between a European in the age of colonialism and his native informants, and a piece of evidence – however distorted – about what those colonized people were talking about at a point in time, and work of individual genius documenting one man's struggles with debt, poverty, depression, the loss of his daughter, and the hope of rebirth; and even one man's encounter with a wide collection of western religious myths that order sin, loss, and transcendence within narratives of Eve and the apple. Art's multiple significances mirror the multiple stories we tell ourselves at any point in our lives; art's multiple possible interpretations mirror the multiple voices and misunderstandings and distortions that happen every day in conversation. To pretend to have

---

[35] For railway timetables, see Vanessa Ogle, *The Global Transformation of Time: 1870–1950* (Cambridge, MA; London: Harvard University Press, 2015). For physicists and mathematicians, the culture of time and space, see Peter Galison, *Einstein's Clocks and Poincaré's Maps: Empires of Time* (New York: W. W. Norton, 2004).

"cracked" the account of the past by distilling meaning in one direction is to miss the mystery of the work of art.

As with art, so with history. It makes little sense to reduce the flow of events over a century to a single upward tick of "progress," or a line counting the number of births or deaths, or a line estimating the potential for social grievances. At every given moment, historical experience – like art – consists of multiple conversations about who we are, what we want, where we have been, and where we are going. People who occupy the same historical plane at any given direction are headed in multiple directions, and they jostle with each other.

It follows that with data about texts, stories, and experiences over time, we typically *do not want* a magic number for the index for social disaster, such as the "political stress index" that Peter Turchin has formulated on the basis of his demographic and cultural calculations.

We want the art of counting to reliably reproduce in miniature *one perspective at a time* on how experience has been changing, and we want to be able to compare different perspectives, even as the multiple visualizations of this chapter have done. In many ways, a data-rich visualization, labeled with words that point to other stories, is thus better suited to providing such multiple perspectives than a single squiggle or number, comparing the likelihood of revolution today to that in the past.

Multiple routes through history are typical of the way that most contemporary historians understand historical discourses. When the historians Lincoln Mullen and Keller Funk developed a digital approach to the history of legal codes, they looked to repetition to help them group a congeries of legal codes into the main strands of conversation of the past.[36] Mullen developed the "textreuse" software package, which tracks the probability that one set of words resembles another set of words, thus allowing historians to track the circulation of parts of a legal record across the United States, when court procedure was relatively new and law professors began to draft legal codes in order to standardize judicial practice.[37]

Developing a quantitative practice for understanding textual repetition in the legal codes allowed Mullen and Funk to essentially generate a family tree of legal codes in America, marking out the major traditions, when they

[36] Kellen Funk and Lincoln A. Mullen, "The Spine of American Law: Digital Text Analysis and U.S. Legal Practice," *The American Historical Review* 123:1 (February 1, 2018): 132–64, https://doi.org/10.1093/ahr/123.1.132.k

[37] Lincoln Mullen, "An Introduction to the Textreuse Package, with Suggested Applications," *The Backward Glance* (blog), November 9, 2015, https://lincolnmullen.com/blog/an-introduction-to-the-textreuse-package-with-suggested-applications.

split, and how much they varied from each other. Having a data-driven family tree of legal codes allowed the scholars to perform a close examination of particular turning points in the legal tradition and to examine the most widely circulated parts of the legal code in detail. Quantitatively derived, Mullen and Funk's branching tree of legal history indicates that there was not *one* road through which the law flowed, but *several.*

To conceive of memory as constantly shifting in response to politics also makes a subtle intervention in the literature on memory. When we think about memory in terms of statuary, costume, architecture, religious services, and recurring events, we typically think of acts of remembrance that legitimize present-day institutions by anchoring collective consciousness to an unchanging past. But as modern people interpret the past, the sense of what happened in the past or which episodes of the past matter to the present tend to change as well. Allusions to the past, in print and in speech, anchor present-day consciousness to a set of events in the past that gradually and subtly shifted.

There are many windows on the past and, meanwhile, in an important sense, each historic landscape onto which the windows of the house of the past look refracts its own changing memory of the past that came before it. Text mining gives an important tool for charting the shifting sands of time, for turning some of those wavering currents of memory into graphs and lines. It is as if each decade of a century could be represented by a Gauguin painting in which a different series of past Edens and idols were depicted. As the exercises in this chapter have shown, it is possible to graph each moment in the past as if that moment were a view of a historic vantage on memory.

The process of mapping those shifting sands of memory is not automatic, nor is it easy to perfect, nor is there one ideal method of mapping memory that is self-evidently superior to the other windows on the past offered in this chapter. But text mining nevertheless offers a tool for mapping shifts of consciousness too subtle to talk about in aggregate, which have hitherto remained invisible: transformed into data, the abstract metamorphosis of memory becomes visible at last.

CHAPTER 8

The Distinctiveness of Certain Eras[1]

In the Preface of this book, I described my formative years in a place that I sometimes refer to as "the land without history," a world where children concentrate on coding and science and where argumentation about the historical past is rare. As a child, I delighted in pouring over books of costume history, marveling at the differences between eras that covered and revealed women's necks and ankles. I was experiencing the wonder of periodization — the fact that historical eras encode pronouncedly different rules of culture, such that ideas unthinkable in one generation become routine in another.

Developing and refining our understanding of how eras in the past differed from another is one part of the historical method that comprises the analytical skill of professional historians. Mostly, that work has taken the form of storytelling. The difference between *before* and *after* has been reckoned in terms of story and intuition, not as a mathematical difference, specifiable in terms of wordcount.

It has never been a quantitative pursuit – until now. But the quantitative revolutions that we have examined already have opened the gates of possibility. Many individual components of historical analysis, such as detecting words whose meaning has shifted over time, can be automated. In this chapter, we ask: Can a computer also discern and describe the differences of individual blocks of time? Readers should note that we are in the process of slowly unpacking slightly different approaches to the past. Chapter 7 dealt principally with

[1] *A short portion of this chapter repeats discussions of topic models previously published in* Jo Guldi, "The Official Mind's View of Empire, in Miniature: Quantifying World Geography in Hansard's Parliamentary Debates," *Journal of World History* 32:2 (2021): 345–70, https://doi.org/10.1353/jwh.2021.0028, and Jo Guldi, "The Distinctiveness of Temporal Periods," *American Historical Review* (in press).

differences of time conditioned by *memory,* or what cultures *imagine* to be important as they look backward at their shared past. Instead, this chapter asks: What are the definitive realities that differentiate one decade or year from the next? What is the *reality* of difference between one moment and the next? What traces does historical change leave in the textual datasets of the past, and what algorithms can we use to detect that change?

After discussing these ideas, this chapter will explore some of the statistical tools that have been used for decades already in library science to index new information – in particular, a decades-old algorithm called "term frequency-inverse document frequency" (tf-idf). This algorithm was invented by Karen Spärck Jones in 1973 for the purpose of helping librarians assign new texts with document-specific keywords that could be used in filling out the subject indices of library catalogs. Tf-idf is an excellent tool for understanding what is distinctive to a document and, for that reason, we will deploy it in a slightly adjusted form to find out what is most distinctive to a period of time. We will call this process "term frequency-inverse period frequency" (tf-ipf). Applying tf-ipf to an archive, we can search for the most distinctive characteristics of each period of time – from the decade to the day.

How is such an algorithm useful? In the following pages, we will see that tf-ipf is much more than a parlor trick; more than a tool for dredging up curious tangents and trivia and effluvia of another era – that it can, in other words, support a critical reading of long-term and short-term movements and that it can even satisfy demands for critical thinking about the logic of the past. In the hands of critical practitioners, algorithms can help us check the biases that every researcher brings to the past.

Quantitative findings can help us develop a reliable narrative about the past from lexical building blocks. We will see how, by working on the same material from different perspectives and by putting short-term language into dialogue with long-term trends, this method can support a long-term synthesis that reflects a multiplicity of political and economic perspectives. We will consequently see, in this case, that a distant reading of the *longue durée* supports not only a robust and sensitive review of historical data in the written records of the past, but also the historian's capacity for critical thinking about the many dimensions of historical change.

Beyond the Metanarrative

In the 1970s, postmodern critiques began to challenge the metanarratives that had previously organized history. These overarching narratives often invoked a teleology of progress to explain imperialism and the rise of western nations, and organized history around the tacit assumption that society was guided by unchanging laws – for instance, the ineluctability of class conflict.[2] The high point of critical reflexivity against metanarrative came with the publication of William Sewell Jr.'s 1996 essay "Three Temporalities," wherein the historical sociologist warned social scientists to beware of naïve suppositions that projected familiar patterns of agency and event onto past eras.

In his essay, Sewell lashed Chris Tilly and Immanuel Wallerstein for theories of social conflict that essentially mapped an unchanging law of capitalism onto diverse times and places. He demolished Theda Skocpol's use of narrative, as it presumptuously framed similar conditions around revolutions as dissimilar as those of France, Russia, and China. Such faulty conceptual frameworks, Sewell warned, allowed for a past too closely interwoven with ideas from the present. The results of such a process were "seriously deficient, and actually fallacious."[3] At the heart of his challenge was a plea for scholars to take the *diversity* of past events seriously and not homogenize distinct periods with conveniently overarching stories – to study the past in its lively variety of motive, agency, and structure.

In the last few years, scholars in Sewell's mode might have had good reason to celebrate, for a new era of self-conscious criticality is upon us: the era of the algorithm. Scholars reviewing bundles of evidence for their lively diversity can find an invaluable aid in the growing abundance of digitalized texts and the power of counting words. In his 2019 book *Enumerations,* the digital literary scholar Andrew Piper proposed that, in the past, literary analysis had been distorted by the scholarly habit of cherrypicking

---

[2] Jean-François Lyotard, *The Postmodern Condition* (Minneapolis, MN: University of Minnesota Press, 1984 [1979]), xxiv–xxv. This shorthand account skips the contributions of the *Annales* School and Toynbee, which have been documented elsewhere; see Jo Guldi and David Armitage, *The History Manifesto* (Cambridge: Cambridge University Press, 2014); important addenda to our cursory treatment of the Annales School, which drive home even further the influence of the Annales in raising critical questions about *longue durée* and event, include Peter Burke, *The French Historical Revolution: The Annales School 1929–2014* (London: John Wiley, 2015); Mike Davis, "Taking the Temperature of History," *New Left Review* 110 (March 2018), https://newleftreview.org/issues/ iii10/articles/mike-davis-taking-the-temperature-of-history.

[3] Originally published as a chapter in an edited volume in 1996, the essay was later collected in William H. Sewell, Jr., *Logics of History: Social Theory and Social Transformation* (Chicago, IL: The University of Chicago Press, 2010), 83.

examples. The tastes, biases, and selective memories of previous writers and appointed canons were often heavily reflected in the exempla selected for further study and reading.

Piper's misgivings complemented Sewell's. While both came from different intellectual traditions and recommended different methods, each suggested that a higher bar of objectivity was available for reckoning with the past. As the present cultural moment always imposes an interpretive bias, even knowledgeable scholars cannot unconditionally rely on their biased habits of memory to understand the past. Indeed, in one recent study that compared the caricatures of leading historians with the results of keyword count, scholars were proved to have generalized poorly about the past, using terms such as "enormous" or "considerable" to describe events or figures of speech that were actually sporadic. Historian Luke Blaxill explains that terms of this kind are "inherently opaque" and offer a "poor tool" for knowing the trends of the past, in comparison with wordcount, the strength of which is its ability to represent, accurately and consistently, major shifts of language in the past.[4]

We are entering an age where the rigor dreamed of by Sewell might be best harnessed by applying critical thinking to the algorithm. As we saw in Chapter 7, historians have continued the search for theory that can map the dynamics between long-term forces (such as industrialization) and short-term interventions (for instance, the publication of *The Communist Manifesto*). They have distinguished cultural variances in the experience of time, addressing the workings of memory and trauma in culture and chronicling the forces that synchronized world experience in the modern age.[5]

More recently, in a hybrid world where quantitative measures meet humanistic concerns, other scholars have pioneered a growing body of

---

[4] Luke Blaxill, *The War of Words: The Language of British Elections, 1880–1922* (Royal Historical Society, 2020), 34–35.

[5] For memory, see Astrid Erll, *Memory in Culture* (Basingstoke: Palgrave MacMillan, 2011); for cultural variations in the experience of time, see Stefan Tanaka, "History Without Chronology," *Public Culture* 28:1 (78) (January 1, 2016): 161–86, https://doi.org/10.1215/08992363-3325064; for synchronization, see Stephen Kern, *The Culture of Time and Space, 1880–1918: With a New Preface* (Cambridge, MA: Harvard University Press, 2003); Helge Jordheim and Einar Wigen, "Conceptual Synchronisation: From Progress to Crisis," *Millennium* 46:3 (June 1, 2018): 421–39, https://doi.org/10.1177/0305829818774781; Vanessa Ogle, *The Global Transformation of Time: 1870–1950* (Cambridge, MA; London: Harvard University Press, 2015); for trauma, see Berber Bevernage, *History, Memory, and State-Sponsored Violence: Time and Justice* (New York: Routledge, 2012); Amos Goldberg, *Trauma in First Person: Diary Writing During the Holocaust* (Bloomington, IN: Indiana University Press, 2017).

work translating temporal relationships into the language of code. In their objectivity – and their rigor around the repetitive processes of reading – algorithms are blessedly free from the fatigue and bias that lead humans to project their own personal experience into the past. Incapable of the kind of intellectual shortcuts that come naturally to human beings, algorithms can help scholars to carefully identify moments of change with contextual depth and accuracy. Algorithms can liberate an analysis from unconscious "historicism" – the tendency to impose currently salient themes onto prior events – and thus they can illuminate the historical reality in all its unexpected diversity.

In recent years, many scholars have made compelling demonstrations that algorithmic analysis of text can serve as more than a mere curiosity and can lend itself to robust and pragmatic examinations of worldly concerns. As we saw at the end of Chapter 7, one tool, developed by historians Lincoln Mullen and Kellen Funk for the purpose of analysis of legal documents, analyzed a corpus on the level of a longer passage of text, rather than focusing only on individual words.[6] Mullen developed the "textreuse" software package to determine the probability that a given set of words resembles another specified set of words, allowing historians to track the circulation of parts of a legal record across the United States.[7] This tool enabled Mullen and Funk to perform a close examination of particular turning points in the legal tradition, and to examine the most widely circulated parts of the legal code in detail. From their experiment, we see that a higher-level analysis of such algorithms can, in fact, produce a multilevel timeline of historical change.

This chapter charts a new method for mapping the relationship between the pulses of long-term and short-term change. Very much a love child of our digital age, this method derives its powers of humanistic interpretation from a shift at the level of mathematics. Unlike the more primitive algorithms that simply focus on frequency and average behavior, tf-ipf returns answers that grow richly diverse as we change the scale of aggregation. The algorithm is able to subtly address the concerns of Sewell and Piper, as it applies to a textual archive a quantitative metrics that can generate a more meaningful lexical environment, which is to say, a

[6] Kellen Funk and Lincoln A. Mullen, "The Spine of American Law: Digital Text Analysis and U.S. Legal Practice," *The American Historical Review* 123:1 (February 1, 2018): 132–64, https://doi.org/10.1093/ahr/123.1.132.k.

[7] Lincoln Mullen, "An Introduction to the Textreuse Package, with Suggested Applications," *The Backward Glance* (blog), November 9, 2015, https://lincolnmullen.com/blog/an-introduction-to-the-textreuse-package-with-suggested-applications.

robustly supported characterization of words that are most distinctive of a period. We will explore how an analytic filter can be a powerful lens into the past and how a scholar, observing familiar data through a novel algorithm, can learn significant new things about the past.

Despite the objections of certain humanists that quantitative averages can erase difference, this chapter will articulate a theory of how quantitative measures can, in fact, be retailored to understand distinctiveness, highlight dissent, and raise fundamental questions about political power and access in modern society. We will review evidence from contemporary work on tracking change over time and examine studies that profile a discreet class of experience, such as transportation or politics, and ones that illuminate more abstract tropes, such as disruption. This chapter will argue that, by engaging with the mathematics of distinction, rather than of averages, scholars may pinpoint the material most useful for characterizing the multiple speeds at which contemporary forces worked in the past – how significant social dynamics unfold at diverse velocities – as theorized by postwar philosophers of history, such as Reinhart Koselleck and reformulated more recently by architectural theorist Manuel De Landa.

Finally, this chapter will explore how this species of algorithm can help us formulate a synthesis of long-term forces and short-term change, as we examine the role of dissent in the British parliamentary debates of the nineteenth century. Already familiar to many historians, the material of British parliament provides a useful benchmark for the method's veracity and power. In these case studies, tf-ipf will be applied to the history of the British past via *Hansard*, the record of the British parliamentary debates.

In these case studies, we will engage the mechanisms of critical search, which, as we discussed in earlier chapters, embodies a series of precepts for critically examining each phase in the search process. Following those precepts, we will critically examine the new algorithm and its results, adjusting its parameters to see what it can do with periods of different length – a decade, a year, a month, or even a day. We will examine what the results look like when paired with a controlled vocabulary. We will chart our conclusions about temporal distinctiveness through other visualization techniques designed to help us understand distinctiveness in more familiar ways – as raw wordcount, for instance, or by plotting the occurrence of keywords on the pages of a calendar. Only through such a critical search process will we hazard conclusions about how our measure of distinctiveness aligns with historical methods and questions. Reading the results of tf-ipf, we will be engaging a tool for retrieving "temporal fossils," relics associated with a single moment in the past that disappeared after the moment was gone as, for example, the hoopskirt disappeared with the closing of the Victorian era. Critical search becomes a method for contemplating the shifting boundaries of an era, and for discovering what is most distinctive about a particular era.

Using tf-ipf to guide a careful review of the most distinctive concerns of each period of the nineteenth century, these case studies will demonstrate blind spots in the historical record, that is, an endemic lack of focus among historians of that era upon episodes that occupied less than six months of parliamentary interest. Applying tf-ipf allows historians to discover episodes that were generally overlooked previous generations of historians and to contextualize them in the light of long-term forces. The algorithm can thus encourage historians to look at the past with the scholarly rigor advocated by Piper, while satisfying Sewell's appeal for a systematic approach that unshackles the past from prior assumptions about social structure. In the hands of a critical historian, algorithms can serve as a check on historicism, enabling us to understand past events within in their most authentic context, as a contemporary observer might have experienced them.

Temporal Fossils: Introducing Tf-ipf

In this section, we will take a closer look at how we can use tf-ipf to scour an archive for salient words, and rank them – for any given period of time – in terms of *distinctiveness*.

As the user adjusts the time period – for example, from decade to week – the algorithm returns a new list of temporally distinctive words. Typically, this will show little, if any, overlap between the most "distinctive" words of two adjacent weeks, or between a week and the month that contains it. Its power as an algorithm is in the precision and the nuance with which it can compare components of historical change on varying scales: it can allow the user to discern the slow course of change from decade to decade and contemplate this kind of conceptual inertia in light of the faster clip of ideas that captured the imagination from month to month. When used in concert with traditional tools of a critical historian, it can be tantamount to opening up a complex machine and observing the varying rhythm of each interlocking gear, the utility and sublime significance of each moving part within a previously incomprehensible box of gears.

In mathematical terms, tf-ipf is a simple innovation; its basic structure is cribbed from an algorithm that is already five decades old – the widely used tf-idf. Long familiar to students of the digital humanities and library

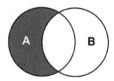

Figure 8.1   Tf-idf showing terms found in A but not in B.

science, tf-idf was developed as a tool for indexing documents within electronic library catalog by identifying the terms most distinctive of any given paper, article, or book.[8] As mentioned at the beginning of this chapter, the algorithm was invented in 1973 by mathematician Karen Spärck Jones and was intended to help librarians assemble catalogs for journal articles by automating the detection of subject-headers. Historically, tf-idf has provided a powerful method of indexing words characteristic of one document, but not characteristic of another document and, as an early incarnation of artificial intelligence, it was able to generate plausible keywords or subject-term indexes for journal articles or books.[9]

Both of these algorithms are special – and for our purposes, quite powerful – because they compare wordcount to produce a measure not of *averages* but rather of *distinctiveness*. The older algorithm was specifically designed to provide a kind of differential calculus, showing the terms found in one set, but not in another set. We can compare the concept of distinctiveness to the Venn diagram shown in Figure 8.1. What is distinctive about circle A is the portion of circle A that does not overlap with circle B.

Tf-idf has traditionally been used to find those words distinctive of certain journal articles, but not of others. Deriving its name from its simple and robust formula, it measures the frequency of any given term within a particular document against its frequency within the corpus overall. Each term-document combination receives a score, which is *high* if the term is highly distinctive of that document and *low* if the term is relatively commonplace across all documents.

The equation for tf-idf (Figure 8.2) ranks term-document combinations with a high score if they satisfy two conditions: the term appears frequently

---

[8] Karen Spärck Jones. "A Statistical Interpretation of Term Specificity and Its Application in Retrieval". *Journal of Documentation* 28 (1972): 11–21, doi:10.1108/eb026526; Julia Silge and David Robinson, *Text Mining with R: A Tidy Approach* (Beijing: O'Reilly Media, Inc., 2017); Gabriela De Queiroz et al., *Tidytext: Text Mining Using "Dplyr," "Ggplot2," and Other Tidy Tools*, version 0.2.2, 2019, https://CRAN.R-project.org/package=tidytext.

[9] Spärck Jones, "A Statistical Interpretation of Term Specificity and Its Application in Retrieval."

$$idf(term) = ln\left(\frac{n_{documents}}{n_{documents\ containing\ term}}\right)$$

$$tf(term) = f_{term\ in\ a\ particular\ document}$$

$$tf \cdot idf = f_{term\ in\ a\ particular\ document} \cdot ln\left(\frac{n_{documents}}{n_{documents\ containing\ term}}\right)$$

Figure 8.2   Equations for tf-idf.

in one particular document (producing a high number in the numerator) and infrequently in the corpus overall (thus producing a low denominator). For instance, if only a handful of documents mention "hoopskirt," but each of these three documents contains several sentences that detail varieties and textures of hoopskirts (thus invoking the term multiple times), then "hoopskirt" would be highly distinctive of those documents. For those documents, the word "hoopskirt" would have a high tf-idf score.

Conversely, the component measurement discounts frequently appearing terms such as definite articles, auxiliary verbs, and prepositions, which will typically have a high score both for the number of times they appear (the numerator) and for the number of documents they appear in (the denominator). A high denominator lowers the tf-idf score to a fraction of what it might be if a frequent word appeared only in one document. Thus, for example, the words "the", "if," and "and," which are found in nearly every document, will be among the lowest tf-idf scores.

The difference-based statistics of tf-idf make it a useful algorithm for indexing words against any aspect of a document base – not only for particular documents, but also for sets of documents produced in a particular period or unit of time.[10]

---

[10] As to the finality of any measurements made with tf-idf, it is important to note that several variations of tf-idf are in use in the information science community, whose variations differ as to how they normalize the scale of difference. The mathematical choice of algorithm will inevitably affect the results; C. D. Manning, P. Raghavan, and H. Schutze, "Scoring, Term Weighting, and the Vector Space Model" in *Introduction to Information Retrieval* (Cambridge: Cambridge University Press, 2008), 100. doi:10.1017/CBO9780511809071.007. ISBN 978-0-511-80907-1. My research group has experimented with variations on tf-idf with different results than the ones presented here; that course of experimentation led to many conversations on the nature of difference and variations produced by algorithms and how they intersect with iterative quests for knowledge in a humanistic and social science context. The resulting theory – which emphasizes the strength of humanists' multiple encounters with documents and its complementarity to iterative, recursive approaches from statistics – is documented in Jo Guldi, "Critical Search: A Procedure for

$$ipf(term) = ln\left(\frac{n_{periods}}{n_{periods\ containing\ term}}\right)$$

$$tf(term) = f_{term\ in\ a\ particular\ period}$$

$$tf \cdot ipf = f_{term\ in\ a\ particular\ period} \cdot ln\left(\frac{n_{periods}}{n_{periods\ containing\ term}}\right)$$

Figure 8.3   Temporally adjusted tf-idf or tf-ipf.

To apply tf-idf to time, one must measure the frequency of a given word within a single period – whether a day, week, year, or decade – against the overall number of periods and also against all other periods in which that word appears.

Figure 8.3 gives an altered equation for a temporally adjusted tf-idf – the modified term that we will revisit throughout this chapter, which, you will recall, I have called "term frequency-inverse period frequency (tf-ipf)." Applying this differential algorithm to time periods, rather than documents, allows a scholar to extract from a corpus the distinctive features of each week, month, decade. While the older algorithm found distinctive words within a document – a powerful tool for librarians who wish to index the key subjects of a book or an article – the new adjustment is a powerful tool for scholars who wish to index the distinctive words, tropes, themes, and rhetorical flourishes of a particular time period.

Applied to the debates of parliament, where the period is set as "day," the tf-ipf algorithm assigns its highest ranking to words used on one day, but not on other days. With this result, the researcher can easily discern which days are most distinctive, as measured against the 10,316 other days in the corpus of 1806–1911, and which words make them so.

As we work through the case studies in the sections that follow, we will see how this algorithm can work as a kind of master-key to many different aspects of time, as the algorithm not only illuminates which words were special on a given day, for example, but also, which particular day was special within a given year or century.

Guided Reading in Large-Scale Textual Corpora," *Journal of Cultural Analytics*, 2018, 1–35, https://doi.org/10.22148/16.030. In the context of that argument, this article should not be read as advocating a final algorithm in tf-ipf, so much as endorsing an approach for studying the dynamics of change characterized by the use of what I call here the "mathematics of distinction," whose exact algorithmic study may take many forms, each of which may provide new nuances.

Applied to a digitalized body of text, tf-ipf allows the scholar to automatically produce a series of keywords adjusted by the desired scope of the temporal period. In the case study we explore in the following pages, only titles to the parliamentary debates were used, and the words that make up these titles were filtered according to a controlled vocabulary of "concerns" relating to political economy, commodities, infrastructure, religion, and social movements.

Before we proceed, we should acknowledge a few limits to this algorithm. The boundaries of periods are assigned by the user, and are not self-generating. This means that the user should approach the corpus with at least a modest familiarity with the historical background. In the case study documented in this section, I divided my data into a range of periods of varying length: 50 years, 20 years, 10 years, 5 years, 12 months, 6 months, 1 month, 1 week, and 1 day.[11] The algorithm is not designed to help a user decide whether the "roaring 1920s" actually began in 1914; for our purposes, the beginning and end of every period comes in canonical lengths: the new decade or half decade, New Year's Day, the first of the month, and so on.

Another limitation of the algorithm is that it fails to pick up on changes in meaning. Tf-ipf will not pick up on words such as "gay," whose cultural significance changed substantially over the period, nor will it rank highly words such as "telegraph," which came into dominance at a certain point and then continued to dominate conversations until the end of period. We met solutions to the former issue – words whose meaning changes over time – in Chapter 6 where we saw the use of word embeddings to pinpoint the changing usage of particular words. We will meet solutions for the latter query – words that come into prominence from nothing – in Chapter 10, when we treat the nuanced application of algorithms. For now, the point is that temporal distinctiveness is only one among a wide variety of algorithmic applications suited to modeling different relationships to temporal change. The usefulness of any one approach depends upon the analyst's skill at examining the relationship between each algorithm, the data, and the analyst's disciplinary questions – an issue of the critical search process that we introduced in Chapter 4.

---

[11] It would be interesting, in the future, to iterate through temporal boundaries of different sizes, testing the "distinctiveness" of each in a search for "ideal" time periods; tf-ipf would provide an ideal method for such an inquiry, although such a project has not been attempted in the work documented here.

Finally, tf-ipf is constrained in its ability to discern multiple meanings of the same word and, if not accounted for with a bit of circumspection, this can produce the false appearance of a trend.[12] In the coming years, in theory, scholars should be able to combine tf-ipf with other algorithms that account for such limitations and create a tool with greater adaptability and sensitivity.

As with the other chapters in this book, we will test our theories on the British parliamentary debates from 1806 to 1911. The *Hansard* archives offer a curated set of high-political documents, whose language shifts dramatically throughout that century, and this set of texts forms the basis for all of the experiments in this book. As we have seen elsewhere, *Hansard* lends itself well to our purposes because it covers a century that has been intensively studied by historians and because it illuminates countless watershed events, including the industrial revolution, the Crystal Palace Exhibition in 1851, the Great Rebellion in India of 1857, and the Second Reform Act of 1867, whose significance as seminal events is broadly agreed upon by historians. Historians trained in the nineteenth century can rattle off names of individuals, places, petitions, and debates that went into the making of each of those events. And they can debate whether any of those events represented the culmination of the decades that preceded it, or a radical break that opened up new changes afterward.

Tf-ipf offers a powerful tool for highlighting the major characteristics that differentiate the different eras that structure a textual database. When we apply it to *Hansard*, dividing the vast corpus into periods of twenty years, the algorithm produces a poignant overview of the long-running political debates that punctuated the century – one that aligns quite closely with the traditional outlines of the era made by British historians (see Figure 8.4). Around 1800, parliamentary debate seems to be dominated by commodities, trade, and industrial and agricultural processes: the "corn trade," "corn distillery," "sugar distillation," "ships registry," "framework," "distillation," and "distillery" – in so many words, the bureaucracy and infrastructure of industrialization. Beside these industrial themes, we see a heightened concern with institutions and civic order, signaled by debates about "seditious meetings" and "blasphemous libel." The next twenty-year

---

[12] In contrast with algorithms designed to disambiguate meanings of particular words (such as topic modeling and change-point detection, both discussed below), tf-ipf will potentially produce errors when confronted by words with multiple meanings (the term "base" could signify either a stop-point in baseball or a military base), while missing related concepts expressed by multiple terminology (an algorithm tracking change in the appearance of the phrase "military base" would miss related changes in the terms "fort" or "outpost").

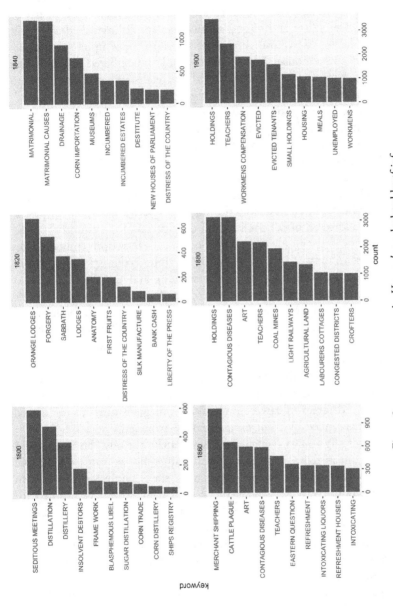

Figure 8.4   20-year concerns in *Hansard* as calculated by tf-ipf.

241

period, 1820–40, lends itself to a quite different characterization. It appears to be a period of church against the enlightenment, whose debates invoke the "Anatomy" Act, the observance of the "sabbath," and "liberty of the press." The 1840s and 1850s, meanwhile, are distinguished as a great era of public works, whose rhetorical eruptions focus upon "drainage," "museums," "new houses of parliament" and "incumbered estates." The 1860s and 1870s appear as the biological era, featuring headlines of debate such as "cattle plague," "contagious diseases," and "intoxicating liquors". During those twenty years, however, we also see a new trend emerging; for the first time, "empire" appears on the top of our list of distinctive words, condensed into a euphemism, the "Eastern Question,"pertaining to war with the Ottoman Empire. The 1880s and 1890s, meanwhile, stand out as the era of industrial socialism, whose debates hinge upon a cluster of words like "teachers," "labourers' cottages," "congested districts," and the plight of the "crofters." In contradistinction to earlier social issues, which parliament had addressed under the heading of "distress of the country" or the plight of the "destitute," the words of this new period embodied an emerging sensibility of collective experience embodied in specific confrontations over the conditions of public servants and the poor. The next period, 1900–10, focuses the interest of parliament even more acutely upon social issues and we see a flurry of terms such as "workmens' compensation," the "unemployed," the "evicted", "small holdings," "housing," and "meals," while continuing the theme of the 1880–90s with its focus upon "teachers."

To fully appreciate the significance of high tf-ipf scores, let us examine a case study that compares tf-ipf scores against raw counts. Figure 8.5 juxtaposes a diagram of raw count against a diagram of tf-ipf for several top concerns ranked by tf-ipf on a twenty-year period.

The diverging results overall are immediately obvious. To understand why these measurements are so radically different, we can examine the starkest contrasts within the two diagrams – for example, the words with an extremely low raw frequency, but a high tf-ipf score. As a term with especially divergent scores, let us consider the word "boycotting," which is the fifth keyword in rank for the period 1880–1900 and yet has the highest tf-ipf score overall for the century. If tf-ipf truly measures "significance" of a term within a period, how can a highly ranked word turn out to have been quite scarce in its period?

The answer to this apparent riddle is that the other terms ranked more highly than "boycotting" in its period – "home rule," the "land league," "eviction," and "crofters" – are fairly distinctive of 1880–1900. But each of

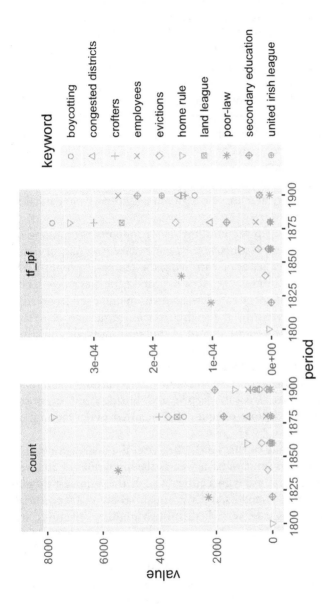

Figure 8.5   Raw wordcount (left) and tf-ipf (right) scores compared, 20-year periodization.

the other terms featured into debate before 1880 and/or after 1920. Boycotting, by contrast, in the British parliament distinctly refers to the practice of "shunning" those individuals who broke with their fellow tenants in the rent strikes of the Irish Land War (1881–86). It was featured in parliamentary debates before 1880 or after 1900. The word "boycotting" is therefore the most *distinctive* term of the period in question, and it receives the highest tf-ipf score. The steep decline of the political concept of *boycotting* – from a defining political movement of the first decade of the century to a political fossil, never again invoked in blatant terms – is representative of exactly the kind of terminology that merits a high score when tf-ipf is applied to temporality: the concept is strongly linked to one era, while being minimally present, or even completely absent, in the following periods. High tf-ipf scores thus potentially suggest that a word is *important* in an ontological sense, the high score signifying some notable shift in collective attention.

After this rudimentary glimpse into how tf-ipf supports the ranking of the terms that are the most distinctive for each twenty-year unit of time, we can observe the consequence of narrowing the temporal period. Each adjustment of the scale – from day to week to year – generates a new set of salient keywords. Each adjustment offers its own unique overview of the century – some characterized by the swiftly concluded debates of a day, others marked by the *longue-durée* tides of twenty-year units. By adjusting the temporal scale through many iterations, we can generate new clusters of distinctive terms that complement and inform one another and, by juxtaposing the resulting variety of timelines and putting them into dialogue with each other, we can deepen and broaden our historical perspective and develop a more complex and nuanced understanding of the past.

When using a technique of this kind, of course, the analyst must still apply a critical sense of its limitations as well as the limitations of archives themselves. To engage responsibly in a critical search, the humanist should appreciate an algorithm's strengths and yet remain aware of its potential blind spots. These can best be remedied through multiple iterations, by adjusting the inputs in a variety of experiments and carefully considering the results.[13] As we shall see in the following pages, this method of comparing temporal scales with the same algorithm can often produce surprising and rewarding results. At shorter horizons of time, for example, we often encounter themes discussed passionately on the floor of

---

[13] Guldi, "Critical Search."

parliament that are relatively unfamiliar to scholars trained in British history, suggesting that this method has revealed a "hidden" dimension of discourse. In the next section, we will explore the fascinating reasons why certain distinctive concerns may remain hidden at one level of periodicity, while the algorithm illuminates them when we begin adjusting the granularities of time.

Revealing Distinctiveness at Different Levels of Temporal Granularity[14]

The experiments contained in this section will reexamine our periodization of the nineteenth century with respect to what Martin Jay called "issues of scale."[15] Reinhart Koselleck, who has reflected on how the structures of repetition work out over different scales of time, has urged historians to contemplate these scalar properties of historical experience. Some of the features of repetition, like birth and death, are structured by what Koselleck calls "biological finitudes," while others have to do with the expectation and experience of a generational cohort, for which Koselleck offers the example of the bourgeois elite in the French Revolution or the Germans who lived for twelve years under Hitler.[16] Of these, he concludes, "We are dealing with social-psychological processes that are constants throughout the history of events."[17] Still other structures of repetition, which Koselleck calls "transcendental," are repeated over generations.[18] Slow-moving repetitions include religious customs or convictions about the operation of justice; among these he classifies most legal history as being the slowest to change among the various studies of history, in part because it deals with the slow coming together of communities, regions, and nations, each making an attempt to reconcile their local law with conflicting ideas of right established by the other.

Thinking about scale allows us to look for evidence of complex changes over time – beyond the simple rise and fall of a word or cluster of words – which can illuminate the simultaneous scales of change operating at every different moment in the past. This chapter will explore a few poignant experiments with time within the archival debates of British parliament and will also investigate how we can design a few powerful algorithms to do this.

---

[14] Martin Jay, "Historical Explanation and the Event," *New Literary History* (2011): 560.   [15] Ibid.
[16] Reinhart Koselleck, *Sediments of Time* (Palo Alto, CA: Stanford University Press, 2018), 8.
[17] Ibid., 115.   [18] Ibid., 9.

One of the marvels of algorithmic thinking is that it can scale – the analyst can count words per paragraph, words per book, words per year, or words per century by adding a single line of code which turns the instructions to count into a loop. Similarly, with tf-ipf the analyst can measure what is distinctive about different quantities of time, from the decade to the year to the day.

Scholars have never had access to a tool so flexible – except, of course, the powerful tool of careful reading. But careful reading is often more difficult when stretched over decades and centuries, while the algorithm can easily produce calculations for comparison between periods of any length.

In the paragraphs that follow, we will observe what happens when we engage tf-ipf to explore the significance of shorter horizons of time. The algorithm allows us to ask the question: What made a particular month or day distinctive in parliament? What were the most distinctive months or days in parliament overall? Because these are questions that no historian has ever been able to ask in a systematic way, even seemingly inconspicuous themes cast remarkable light on the dynamics of the institution.

One facet of the material debated in parliament over shorter timescales is its unfamiliarity – the results of looking at shorter time horizons are less familiar to historians than the material we reviewed in previous sections. When we reduce the threshold from twenty-year periods down to units of six months, many familiar terms are still visible, but the overall results are already significantly less familiar to the historian of the nineteenth century (Figure 8.6). One cluster of terms generated by this method – "wine" (1860), and "sugar" (1910) – suggests unique aspects of widely known historical cases, such as the state's interest in burial grounds and various commodities trades.[19] Other terms – a debate around "bleaching" (1865), "refreshment houses" (1860), "insolvent debtors" (1813), "pillory" (1815), and "dyeing" (1860) – suggest a hitherto unknown story about labor and the economy, as if the events debated over the course of six months, but not over an entire year, for some reason, in the imagination of subsequent historians, had drifted below an invisible threshold of significance.

[19] For burials, see Julie Rugg, "Constructing the Grave: Competing Burial Ideals in Nineteenth-Century England," *Social History* 38:3 (2013): 328–45, https://doi.org/10.1080/03071022.2013.816167. For the wine trade, see John V. C. Nye, *War, Wine, and Taxes: The Political Economy of Anglo-French Trade, 1689–1900* (Princeton, N.J.: Princeton University Press, 2007). For sugar, Sidney W Mintz, *Sweetness and Power: The Place of Sugar in Modern History* (New York: Penguin, 1986), http://catalog.hathitrust.org/api/volumes/oclc/13124498.html, 40.

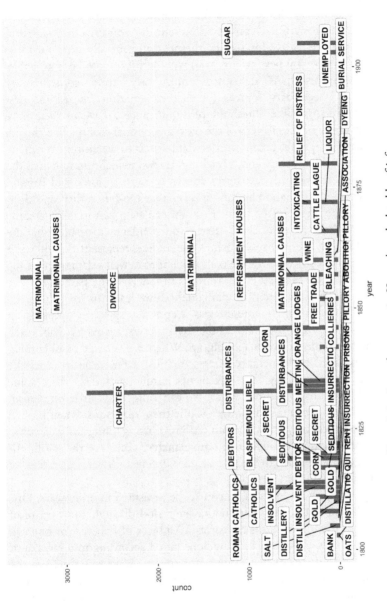

Figure 8.6   6-month concerns in *Hansard* as calculated by tf-ipf.

There are many reasons why an important story could be missed, or hopelessly distorted, because of the way that a historian approaches the material. The invisibility of stories that spanned less than twelve months suggests that historians have projected present-day concerns into *Hansard*, and searching the corpus for specific themes will generally turn our focus away from identifying new events, even when critical material is available. Traditionally, historians depended enormously upon contemporary observers and secondary sources for their orientation toward the past and, thus, an "invisible threshold of significance" may, in fact, have structured many of the silences of the past: a perennial scourge like cholera may be hard to ignore, because sewers had attracted attention over many decades, but the dyeing and bleaching trades, which punctuated the discourse less consistently, are lesser known to most historians of Britain. By condensing information about concerns that took up a disproportionate span of the attention of speakers, tf-ipf can help historians overcome our tendency toward historicism – that is, our tendency to assume that the events valued by historians in previous generations represent the full truth of history. The algorithm offers a complement to Sewell's demand that the historian look past the bias of conventional models of the past.

The invisibility of labor in parliament also leads us to a political question: If parliamentary interest was a currency spent by speakers on the affairs of the rich, what should the dynamics excavated by tf-ipf teach us about the evidence we're looking at? When a given set of unfamiliar events consumed parliamentary interest for just a few months, does the scarcity of interest imply that the events hardly matter? Is there some quantifiable cutoff point from which we can gauge how little interest an event might receive and still matter? While these questions, when pushed to their extremes, may show the limitations of using "interest" as a broad measure of importance, such quantitative analysis can nevertheless illuminate certain aspects of the parliamentary interest as an indication of contemporary politics.

The granularity of time can, of course, be measured in other ways. One can identify top "concerns" within a given period through a raw count of days on which various words appear as a "subject of debate," or one can approximate how long crucial discussions lasted according to a raw count of words, and visualizing the same terms in new ways can elucidate the relationships between different metrics of time. There are, however, distinct advantages of using tf-ipf. This algorithm not only discerns distinctive keywords, but it can rank them according to *how* tightly correlated any given term may be with any temporal window. In this experiment, as we refined the granularity of the search, we were often able to bring more insight to a variety of political agendas. As a general rule, finer granularity, both of time and of language, is often able to reveal hitherto overlooked nuances of debates whose broad outlines are already familiar to scholars.

As for events that consumed parliamentary discourse for a single day (Figure 8.7), it is unsurprising how little we know about topics that received such ephemeral parliamentary interest – for example, the celebration of the Queen's "birthday" (c. 1870), the "Alkali" Acts (c. 1870), and debates about "paving" this or that street (c. 1800–20). That none of these events is immediately familiar and intuitively significant to a historian of Britain suggests that the algorithm has guided us to a new frontier of historical knowledge. We will have to leave it up to future historians, of course, to determine whether such brief parliamentary discussions may, in fact, deserve a much more sustained examination.

We should not be too hasty, therefore, to discard events that originally merited little interest. Parliamentary interest is at best a partial proxy for significance. As often as not, the lack of interest reflects little more than the crass relationship of power and money to a subject that has been predictably sidelined. Monetarily undervalued industries, such as "alehouses" and "plumbers," consumed debate for a single day, for example, while substantial time was allotted to discussing the regulation of the more valuable industries. Parliament devoted a week of debate (not shown) to taxing, regulating, and trading "salt," "guns," "silk," "silver," "newspapers," "paper," "iron," "diamonds," "coaches," "woolens," and "sugar." Meanwhile, it invested sustained interest on the level of months (not shown) to another set of commodities, and brought in debates about "guns" (c. 1825), "copper" (c. 1845), and "lead" (c. 1860). In these examples, a hitherto invisible hierarchy of commodities – and their respective access to parliamentary interest – begins to emerge. The shorter timescales assigned to "pavement" and the relatively longer ones given to "coaches" suggest an unequal representation of the diverse political interests in one debate or another, and on closer examination, this signals an unequal degree of parliamentary attention allotted to local interests (with paving) versus national interests (with coaches). Looking at the debates through different temporal scales, the historian can form a critical sense of which political alliances were able to dominate national debate and for how long.

This hierarchy of power and time is even more visible, in fact, when we turn to social issues. Most of the events of social history that are familiar to the nineteenth-century historian only dominated parliamentary interest for the period of a single month (not shown), including the discussion of

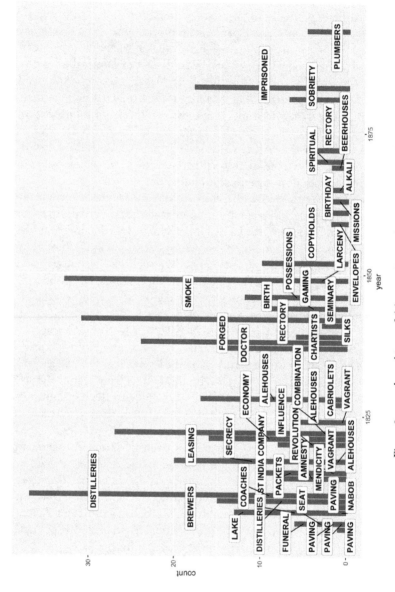

Figure 8.7 1-day subjects of debate in *Hansard* as calculated by tf-ipf.

"interments" (c. 1850), "seditious meetings" (c. 1815), and "popular petitions" (c. 1810).[20] "Crofters" dominated only for a week, as did the "revolution" in France of 1832, the striking workers at the "dockyards" in 1886, and the "yeomanry," "chartists," and talk of the "constitution" in the 1840s.[21] Other concerns important to the popular imagination, meanwhile, only held parliamentary interest for a single day: "vagrant," "mendicity," "beerhouses," and the registration of "plumbers."[22]

Some of these terms may reflect the regulation of commodities – for example, checks on drink and homelessness – but others reflect perennial, unresolved issues of the rights of laborers, whose political organizations were strong enough to present parliament with a charter granting all men the right to vote and yet powerless to see the charter debated on a serious level. Armed conflict eventually led to debates over the rights to land of crofters, whose ancestors had been evicted during the Clearances, but the general exclusion of labor throughout this period produced an irregular pattern of political eruption over the course of the century, which often reappeared in the form of new causes and conflicts. All the while, labor's troubles were never fully investigated; its grievances were never satisfied, and its partisans

---

[20] For interment, see Rugg, Constructing the Grave. For petitions, see R. A. Houston, *Peasant Petitions* (London: Palgrave Macmillan, 2014), https://doi.org/10.1057/9781137394095_2. For seditious meetings, see Albert Goodwin, *The Friends of Liberty* (London; New York: Routledge, 1979), 412; Mary Thale, "London Debating Societies in the 1790s," *The Historical Journal* 32:1 (March 1989): 57–86, https://doi.org/10.1017/S0018246X00015302.

[21] For the much-debated importance of the Chartists in British history, see Iorwerth Prothero, "Chartism in London," *Past & Present* 44 (August 1969): 76–105; I. J. Prothero, "London Chartism and the Trades," *The Economic History Review*, New Series, 24:2 (May 1971): 202–19; David J. V. Jones, *Chartism and the Chartists* (New York: St. Martin's Press, 1975); *The Chartist Experience: Studies in Working-Class Radicalism and Culture, 1830–60* (London: Macmillan Press, 1982); Gareth Stedman Jones, "The Language of Chartism," in J. Epstein and D. Thompson, eds. *The Chartist Experience: Studies in Working-Class Radicalism and Culture, 1830–60* (London: Palgrave Macmillan 1982), 3–58; J. Plötz, "Crowd Power: Chartism, Carlyle, and the Victorian Public Sphere," *Representations*, 2000, 87–114; Antony Taylor, "'The Old Chartist': Radical Veterans on the Late Nineteenth- and Early Twentieth-Century Political Platform," *History* 95:320 (October 1, 2010): 458–76, https://doi.org/10.1111/j.1468-229X.2010.00495.x; Malcolm Chase, *The Chartists: Perspectives & Legacies* (London: Merlin Press, 2015). For discussions of revolution and the constitution, see Gareth Stedman Jones, *Languages of Class: Studies in English Working Class History, 1832–1982* (Cambridge; New York: Cambridge University Press, 1993), James Vernon, *Politics and the People: A Study in English Political Culture, c. 1815–1867* (New York, NY: Cambridge University Press, 1993). For the dockyards, Gareth Stedman Jones, *Outcast London: A Study in the Relationship between Classes in Victorian Society* (Harmondsworth: Penguin, 1976).

[22] In theory, the tf-idf algorithm would also detect an absolute spike over any steady baseline measurement, but in the case of these four terms, interest seems to have indeed been limited to a few days a year, typically not more than one day a month. The section on visualization below ("Checking our Work") illuminates some of the nuances of how the computer's measurement of temporal tf-idf correlates to calendar time.

never managed to summon a sustained inquiry from above. This general pattern has long been understood by British social historians, but the algorithm accurately tracks the pulse of social eruption, organizing diverse political participants into a narrative synthesis ordered by the level of parliamentary interest they were able to demand – a day, a week, a month, five years perhaps, but rarely more. Such an ordering would benefit enormously from a comparison between issues that commanded only short-term attention and those that held parliamentary interest for years or decades – so, we will explore this kind of comparison in this chapter's last section.

In these few examples, the experiment has already given us ample material for observing the dynamics of short- and medium-term change. It vividly demonstrates how different stories emerge from the historical record when we examine different subsections of time – a familiar theme to traditional historians, although one which has not been abundantly engaged through quantitative measures. At the five-year threshold, the abolition of slavery appears, but it disappears again at the ten-year threshold because of a quirk of history – the relative uniqueness of abolition is dwarfed in that larger time period by the relative uniqueness of sabbath observance and dissent.[23] This demonstrates yet again how careful digital scholars must be when counting the top terms of any single period – even a slight adjustment in the beginning and end dates can illuminate certain aspects of the archive while obscuring others. More broadly, however, the anecdote suggests that even so well-plowed an archive as that of Britain's parliamentary debates can hide issues of deep importance that historians have accidentally ignored. The history of British debates about slavery is not, mercifully, one of them today, thanks to scholars who have pursued the history of abolition through a variety of sources, archives, and representations, both microhistorical and macrohistorical, traditional and digital.[24] But if algorithmic overviews easily miss a subject as consequential as slavery, we must soberly consider what other events might lie undiscovered beneath the threshold of regular scholarly attention.

[23] The algorithm might also return a high tf-idf for a spike in the time period relative to a high baseline frequency, but in point of fact, all of the terms in question are relatively unique to the time periods in question.

[24] For traditional interventions that have placed slavery squarely in the center of British history, see Richard Huzzey, *Freedom Burning: Anti-Slavery and Empire in Victorian Britain* (Ithaca, NY: Cornell University Press, 2016); Nicholas Draper, *The Price of Emancipation: Slave-Ownership, Compensation and British Society at the End of Slavery* (Cambridge: Cambridge University Press, 2013); Catherine Hall et al., *Legacies of British Slave-Ownership: Colonial Slavery and the Formation of Victorian Britain* (Cambridge: Cambridge University Press, 2016). For digital projects, see: "Trans-Atlantic Slave Trade," http://slavevoyages.org; David Eltis and David Richardson, *Extending the Frontiers: Essays on the New Transatlantic Slave Trade Database* (New Haven, CT: Yale University Press, 2008).

Attention to Geographic Entities and Ethnic Identities

Thus far, using tf-ipf analysis has helped us to refine our sense of how parliament limited the attention it gave to working-class grievances. But imperial grievances, in contrast, have been almost invisible. Remember that, in the nineteenth century, two-thirds of the world's map was red, that is, indicating countries that were part of the British Empire, and that the British presence in many of those holdings (especially Ireland and India) dated from at least the sixteenth century. But debate time in parliament, as we have seen, was limited. Most members of parliament could not talk about Ireland, China, Canada, and Australia with equal interest, especially with so much unrest on the home front. Is there a way to use the algorithm to highlight how parliament was governing its vast empire, or the fate of Britain's Asian, African, and aboriginal subjects?

We can gaze further into the power of tf-ipf by adding an adjustment to the workings of the algorithm with a controlled dictionary. In this case, we will use a controlled vocabulary of geographic entities and ethnic identities. The vocabulary gathers terms for independent nations (America to Switzerland), ethnicities (Aborigines to Zulus), regional subdivisions and ethnically controlled territories (Algarve to Wituland), empires (Dutch Colonies to Spanish Empire), major islands (Andaman Islands to Virgin Islands), boundaries (Afghan Frontier to Western Pacific), major geographical units (Africa to transatlantic), particular imperial units (Basutoland to Victoria), general descriptions of empire (British possessions to the Crown Colonies), descriptions of Britain (Britannia to the mother country), and general geographical categories (abroad to tropical). That controlled library of 449 unique names offers the basis for counting mentions of geographical entities mentioned in titles of 173,275 unique parliamentary debates from 1803 to 1910.[25] A dictionary structure allows me to classify each entity as ethnicity, continent, or ocean, and as belonging to one or several empires over time.

In the exercise that follows, I have omitted the many variations on references to Britain itself, or the world, the continents, the oceans, British placenames, and Ireland and India (the two colonies spoken about the most in parliament) from the dataset because those entities so disproportionately weight the results that the nuance of other information disappears; instead of producing a timeline of how Britain talked about other

[25] I am grateful to my research assistants, John William Calkins and Stephanie Buongiorno, for their help in refining this vocabulary, and to NSF Grant 1520103, which supported their work and mine.

portions of the world, we would produce a timeline of fashionable ways of referring to Britain and the world, paired with moments when Ireland and India were debated most intensely. Specific Indian and Irish language (for instance, Fenian, Mahratta, and Ceylon) are still present in this dataset, allowing us a sense of how specific references vary over time.

Applied to tf-ipf, a controlled vocabulary of specific placenames outside of Britain allows us to ask: What parts of the world empire did Britain's parliament talk about, and when? Used as a measure of parliamentary interest, our algorithm allows us to examine how parliament balanced the demands of its empire.

Figure 8.8a suggests that, in general, the bulk of parliamentary time devoted to the colonies was spent discussing official responses to wars. Events in the Crimea, Afghanistan, and the Boer War and the accelerating number of foreign engagements after 1880 occupied the majority of parliament's interest as measured in twenty-year periods. The list of place names and peoples in Figure 8.8a would be unsurprising to the analyst familiar with a textbook history of the British Empire over the century.

One may find oneself in less familiar territory, however, when examining which nations differentially occupied the interest of the British parliament within windows of five years. Figure 8.8b presents the results of using tf-ipf scores to develop a timeline of the geographic entities which show a noticeably high mention corresponding to each five-year period of the century. What is surprising about the results is the low profile that most of Britain's colonies assume in the results. In Figure 8.8b, we see that Australia only occupied parliament's imagination for two five-year periods: around 1850, and again around 1900 – far less, at any rate, than the amount of time given the Transvaal, the Crimea, South Africa, or the Boer War. British lawmakers devoted a comparatively negligible amount of time to Tibet (1895) and Nigeria (1900). After 1880, a new trend emerges on the five-year scale – parliament discusses more nations, yet most of these nations occupy a shorter span of parliamentary time. Meanwhile, interest for fifty-year periods peaked in the middle of the nineteenth century, with Fenians, the Crimea, Sardinia, and Queensland predominating. The sense arises from this data of parliament fire-fighting wherever disputes arose in empire, and usually not attending to most of these disputes for very long. In an extended delve into the data published elsewhere, I've used word-counts to show that the data clearly supports and lends specificity to the argument that British Empire was governed in a fit of absence of mind, where Britain's expanding empire meant that each colony received less and

a. 20-year periods

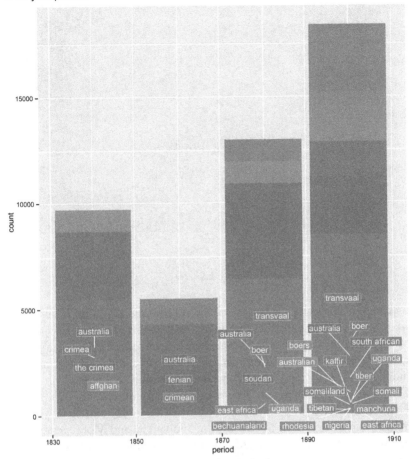

Figure 8.8 Nations, ethnic movements, and geographic regions talked about intensely (shown as "differential interest") for a relatively short period of time. Results show tf-ipf scores, with variation in the "period" variable of the equation, as applied to a controlled vocabulary of entities in the *Hansard* parliamentary debates, 1806–1911.

less attention through the century as a whole.[26] Paired with this finding, the tf-ipf results suggest that the requirement for sustained debate about a place in parliament was military conflict.

[26] Jo Guldi, "The Official Mind's View of Empire, in Miniature."

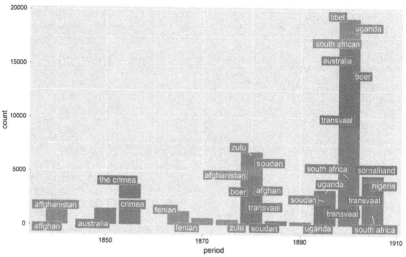

Figure 8.8 (*cont.*)

Another chronology emerges, albeit supporting the same conclusion, when we look at regions that dominated parliament's interest over periods of one month (Figure 8.8c). Napoleonic campaigns ("The Carnatic") suddenly appear, along with crucial moments of military engagement in India ("Mahratta"), and Napoleon III's annexation of the Savoy in 1860. The revolution in Jamaica becomes equally significant, as well as the Abyssinian campaign, the advance on Siam in 1892, and many of the military encounters with the Zulus, the Soudanese, and Montenegro. The one-month chart, in other words, begins to assemble an extremely different list – one suggestive of revolutionary or military engagement.

Measuring the differential interest given to geographic entities and ethnic identities, we can see an emerging hierarchy of how British parliament understood the globe. European powers and the earliest settler colonies, such as Ireland and Canada, rose to the top and were mentioned in high numbers every year. Next come various sites of long-term military conquest, such as Australia, Afghanistan, Crimea, and the Transvaal, which are all spoken about for twenty years at a time. After that, come the originators of colonial resistance, such as the Zulus and Fenians and at the very bottom of the hierarchy are those myriad colonized places given scant interest throughout the century, except when an extreme act of revolution, for example the slave revolt in Jamaica, grabbed parliamentary

c. 1-month periods

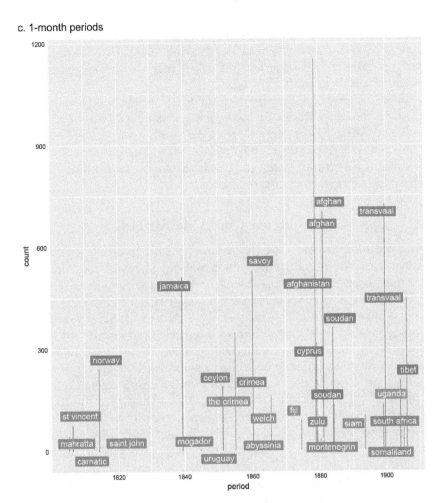

Figure 8.8 (*cont.*)

interest for an instant, before parliament was able, once again, to ignore those regions and the legacy of violence brought to them over the centuries by Britain.

There are many unanswered questions that await further work with this data. Irish and Indian placenames so dominated the results that I removed them from study, but another iteration of the study could be centered specifically on geographies associated with India and Ireland. Alternatively, any of the colonies could be investigated in greater detail. A future iteration over the data might proceed by narrowing the corpus to debates about India or the Zulu, next investigating the distinctiveness of different periods to excavate the changing language used to characterize India. So much remains to be investigated, but we will press on, having signaled the potential usefulness of the method.

Before we pronounce our work in validating the method complete, let us turn from applications to ask a practical question: What exactly is indicated when the computer suggests that Jamaica was debated for one month, or the Afghanistan for five years? How does the computational analysis of the distinctiveness of speech correspond to familiar, human timescales that can be plotted on a calendar?

Checking our Work: Calendar Time

As historians embrace a new generation of metrics such as tf-ipf to help with the classification of period and chronology, they may need complementary tools designed to translate algorithmic results into a usable form, tools that lend themselves to narrative history. Iteratively visualizing data is one of these invaluable tools, as it allows a scholar to distill vast swaths of abstract mathematical metrics into an intuitively lucid format.

Once our algorithm has correlated distinctive words with respect to calendar time, we can illuminate their significance through visualization. A high tf-ipf spike does not necessarily mean that a term is uniquely identified with a particular period; for reasons we might have to consider more closely, the relative importance of the term may not be distributed evenly throughout the period – instead, it might have produced only a momentary spike and then returned to its much lower baseline frequency in the corpus as a whole. Such nuances of measurement are worth studying, as they can represent crucial aspects of the historical period and they can be brought into relief by visualizing frequency over a calendar. These visualizations are an indispensable way to further refine the granulation and explore more subtle characterizations of a period. They can also help us to proof the computer's default categorization by distinguishing spikes from average frequency and, lastly, they can provide important insights into the tempo of a given conversation.

In Figures 8.9 and 8.10 we find debates about "Chartism" and "Railways" mapped onto squares representing the pages of a calendar. Using an organizational form already familiar to most readers, the visualizations highlight those days on which debates titles included the terms "Chartists," "Chartist," or "Chartism." The highlights have been color-

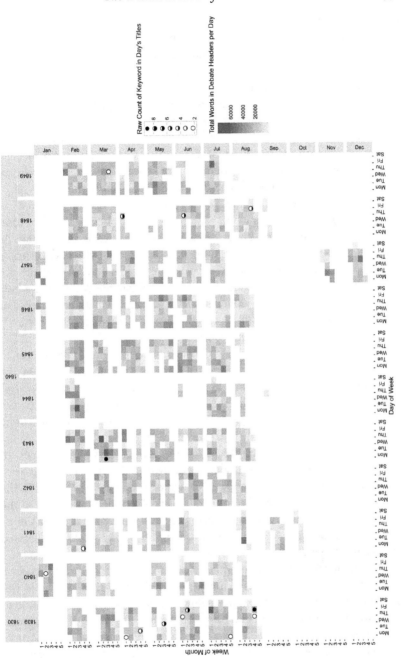

Figure 8.9   Calendar time-series, Chartism/ Chartist: debates with "Chartist" in the title, 1839–49.

coded with circles indicating how many different debates of this kind occurred in a single day, from an empty circle (low) to a full circle (high). As we work through the yearly rows and the monthly columns, and outward to the gray squares that represent a single day within a ten-year period, we quickly translate a great deal of abstract data into theoretical insights, which can be further tested and contemplated through forms of temporal organization familiar to the historian.

In this case study, the algorithm had determined that Chartism was a dominant concern on the level of a day or a week. Figure 8.9 visually organizes this data in a way that lends itself to greater interpretative possibilities by laying out a broad canvas that highlights the entire set of days on which scheduled debates had featured "Chartism" or "Chartist" in their titles. This allows the scholar to check the accuracy of the algorithm and to glean insights from it in an accessible and comprehensive format. As the visualization makes clear, Chartism was typically discussed once a month across twelve sporadic months in the ten-year period. It did not dominate any year in the decade, nor did it dominate the decade as a whole from a parliamentary perspective. It was discussed at relatively infrequent intervals – with the exception of the first week of August, 1839, when it was discussed twice in the same week.

Figure 8.10a, by contrast, shows that railways persisted as a subject of conversation in parliament for much of the nineteenth century. As the visualization demonstrates, there were debates that mentioned "railways" every single month that parliament was in session for 1844–47 – a pattern confirmed by the detailed view in Figure 8.10b. Railways continued to be mentioned more sporadically for the rest of the 1840s, as Figure 8.10a confirms, with a notable uptake in debates around 1879 (not shown in Figure 8.10), although contextualizing this within the dramatic increase of words per year, words relevant to "railways" did not keep up with the proportion of words devoted to other subjects. A detailed inspection of the calendar view, in other words, confirms our naïve interpretation of the tf-ipf result that railways were a term whose *distinctive* period of debate lasted for five to ten years.

Mathematical analysis by itself is, of course, rarely sufficient to produce an interpretation. Contextual knowledge of the historical period is not only a useful corrective, it is often an indispensable interpretative guide to the raw data. Indeed, contextual knowledge informs most of the conclusions proposed here – even as complementary visualizations of time, especially *multiple* visualizations – clarify and deepen that historical perspective, helping a scholar discern exactly what is at stake in the

Figure 8.10   Partial calendar time-series: debates with "Railways" in the title, 1839–56.

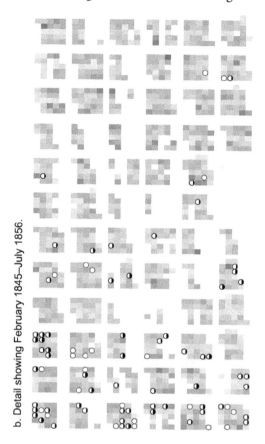

b. Detail showing February 1845–July 1856.

Figure 8.10 (*cont.*)

measurement of time. Iterative engagement with alternative visualizations of the same data, known in the computational literature as "exploratory data analysis," offers historians an important method for untangling the riddle of temporal dynamics. In his review of the ways that naïve visualization practices suggest untruth, one sociologist, Kieran Healy, makes the salient point that iterative visualization can destabilize the hold of bias rather than reinforce it.[27]

[27] Kieran Healy, *Data Visualization: A Practical Introduction* (Princeton, NJ: Princeton University Press, 2019); Kieran Healy and James Moody, "Data Visualization in Sociology," *Annual Review of Sociology* 40:1 (2014): 105–28.

Visualization is, however, one among many approaches that may help us to better understanding the significance of long-term forces and short-term bursts of change. Some of those approaches are critical practices and some come from the realm of other algorithms.

Conclusion

Until now, we have focused primarily on the effectiveness of tf-ipf for producing robust and systematic inquiries into a given period, but the algorithm can also provide a powerful technique for pursuing the relationality among periods of different temporal scales. Almost any juxtaposition will show how the algorithm highlights the differences between timescales. The most distinctive word characterizing a given month in the 1830s, for example, will almost invariably be different than the most distinctive word of the entire decade. By contrast, the most prominent word of January 1830, either by raw count or by proportion, is very likely to be among the most prominent words of the entire decade. Most algorithms of this kind can be applied to scale, but tf-ipf stands out because it highlights *differences* in scale and thereby emphasizes what is *distinctive* about each temporal category. It is a scalar measure of time that, unlike other measures, potentially illuminates the meaning of different time periods, long or short, against one another – what is being measured, in each case, changes according to the level of granularity.

An analogy might help illustrate how this works: We can think of wordcount (and other simple quantitative metrics) as the ideal form of a rectangular grid. One can count all the most frequent words of the century, or just the most frequent words of the decade. As we saw in Chapter 3, the top words are almost always the same, no matter what scale the observer chooses (see Figure 3.1). Indeed, this is how grids work. To an observer standing far away, the rectangle appears small and when the observer comes closer, the grid appears huge, but from any distance, the elemental form is always the same: square upon square.

Wordcount can be a useful tool for history only when the historian introduces measures to plot specific information on the grid, for instance, by working with a controlled vocabulary. If the analyst counts words for technology, they will find different words for technology after the introduction of railway and telegraph. Then again, there may be little variation from decade to decade, after the introduction of these technologies, in whether they are named: they become part of the general vocabulary of things parliament has to regulate.

The usefulness of wordcount depends upon the analyst's introduction of a historical hypothesis in the form of a list of words. The grid only reveals information about historical change over time when tightly controlled constraints are introduced on the dataset in question. We might say that wordcount is therefore virtually useless when used as an "unsupervised" (or automatic) tool for detecting change over time.

In contrast, tf-ipf is like a Persian rug. A great deal of information is woven into its form, which can only be grasped by viewing it from multiple distances – from far away and from up close. From far away, a certain pattern appears, but as the observer comes closer, the major pattern no longer dominates the eye. New patterns slowly appear, minor patterns woven into specific areas of the rug, which were not visible from a distance. As the observer studies the rug on an ever-smaller scale – or conversely, focuses in on other regions at the same or different scales – new patterns constantly emerge, giving the observer an ever deeper and broader appreciation of the narrative woven into the rug as a whole. The minor patterns may occasionally repeat, of course, in various portions and at various scales, but generally, for the patient observer, the rug will offer distinct patterns that only emerge with a comprehensive, multidimensional examination of the entire tapestry.

Just so, tf-ipf reveals a one pattern of macro-level change over time when the viewer is looking at generalities over the century, like what differentiates each period of twenty years. Tf-ipf reveals quite another pattern of micro-level change when the viewer implements the algorithm to look at the specific differences from day to day, week to week, or month to month. One may introduce a controlled vocabulary – as we did in the section above, "Attention to Geographic Entities and Ethnic Identities." But the capacity of the tool to tell a different story at distant scale and close scale is not dependent upon the analyst arriving with a hypothesis. The Persian rug-like variation of results, as the analyst changes varies the period of inquiry from month to decade, as revealed by tf-ipf, is a feature of historical time itself. With tf-ipf, we are using math to directly get at the fact that change looks different over a week and over a century.

Humanists sometimes associate quantification with generalizing: that is, producing a median or mean value that can be talked about as typical of the experience of the whole, and this is generally done by graying out difference and eliminating outliers. Indeed, historians of statistics, such as Ian Hacking and James Dobson , have demonstrated the linkage between quantitative practices for averaging and the political utilization of statistics. Hacking, for instance, profiled Quetelet's search for "*l'homme moyen*," or "average man," as a mathematized version of the concept of natural law, which would be recast by Durkheim and Galton into programs for recognizing the common traits of racial groups, criminals, or the insane – with the intent of identifying, controlling, and eliminating those features of groups considered to be "dangerous" to society.[28] More recently, Dobson showed that, in the postwar period, new statistical algorithms such as k-means clustering emerged for the specific purpose of generalizing about the normal.[29] As Jill Lepore and others have suggested, the mathematics of averaging lent itself to programs designed for social control and often the stifling of dissent – a feature of postwar polling that was already evident to many observers in the 1960s and 1970s.[30]

Studies of this kind have been the bread-and-butter of critical theories of state control for several decades, and rightly so, as they have opened many eyes to the use and abuse of data and their possible implications for the contemporary world. Nonetheless, it would be disastrous for the future of scholarship to uncritically embrace a social theory that asserts that quantification per se is tantamount to abuse – any more than language, history, geography, social psychology, or any other potent mode of structuring social ideas is a priori abusive. Likewise, it would be misguided to associate quantification only with broad generalizations about averages – even if that has been its major application for 200 years, generalization is only one use of mathematics in the realm of social theory. One can also use mathematics to identify and describe outliers, to generalize about exceptions, and to highlight the heterogeneity of the social and historical fabric. The politics of mathematics is not inherent in the numbers – as with any powerful tool, the political dimension emerges from how such a tool is deployed, and this includes the question of who wields it, upon whom, and with how much mastery, care, and critical awareness of its strengths, limitations, and potential ramifications.

Tf-ipf is not designed for averaging, but rather for identifying the most distinctive traits of time periods. As we saw earlier in the discussion of the phrase "seditious meetings," tf-ipf typically does not give a high score to

---

[28] Ian Hacking, *The Taming of Chance* (Cambridge: Cambridge University Press, 1990).
[29] James E. Dobson, *Critical Digital Humanities: The Search for a Methodology* (Urbana, IL: University of Illinois Press, 2019).
[30] As Jill LePore has argued, by the era of the Vietnam War, statistical models seeking to generalize about social groups were programmed into IBM's new supercomputers by cadres of behavioral scientists seeking to generalize about the consumption patterns and opinions of individuals by gender, race, and class, their research feeding the new industries of advertising, political polling, and international development. Jill LePore, *IfThen* (New York: W. W. Norton, 2020).

the most frequently spoken words, nor to those words that are very average or common within a period: instead, the algorithm typically produces the set of words that are *exceptional* overall, and yet are *distinctive* of a particular time period. In other words, the algorithm does not focus on generalizing about words, as much as identifying the words most exceptional within a given category. As a rule of thumb, we can typically say that averages *dissolve difference*, while tf-ipf *highlights differences*.

When examining parliamentary debates, tf-ipf can be a powerful political antidote to methods that rely on generalization. Rather than glaze over the unspoken political hierarchies within an archive, the algorithm tends to dramatically draw them out. As we have seen, there is an inherent politics to the pulse of change in *Hansard*, and this is not lost on the algorithm. The political interests who can only claim parliament's interest for a single day are entirely different from those who regularly demand it for a week. In the context of parliament, "differential interest" can serve as an indispensable proxy for the degree of power exerted by any particular lobby. It allows historians to assess and compare otherwise incomparable abstractions, drawing them into the same narrative: the abolition of slavery, a major debate over five years, received more sustained interest than the parliamentary debate wrangled here and there by the Chartists; the Crimean War had more sustained interest than vagrants.[31] Tf-ipf thus can work as an aid to scholars who would read into their synthesis of the past an account of the exertions of power and the hierarchies on political exchanges thereby imposed. By employing tf-ipf, scholars may fold into their analysis of long-term and short-term forces a political critique that reveals (institutional) time as a reflection of hegemony.[32]

---

[31] More about the differential interest granted by parliament to different imperial territories, and the stakes of that attention for improvement or surveillance, is the subject of another article. Jo Guldi, *Journal of World History* (forthcoming).

[32] Some caveats about the applicability of tf-ipf are crucial here. It is not clear that tf-ipf would support a similarly critical reading for any kind of corpus whatsoever. In the case of parliament, the hours of debate were restricted, more so in the era before 1867; at any rate the ability to dominate debate over months or years can be judged a pure representation of political power in a very real sense, in that expressions of a certain concern evidence consensus at a broad scale of the fundamental importance of the matter at hand. Differential interest similarly measures power wherever access to a publication is similarly constrained. Thus, for instance, it could be applied to measure the significance of inclusion of a concern in a newspaper or other periodical. But it is by no means clear that tf-ipf would register power in the same way if it were applied to a publication whose proliferation was theoretically unlimited – such as the mass-market novel – where persistence of a lexicon over time may suggest a different kind of dynamic.

Some readers have suggested that the term "interest" is more appropriate than the term "attention," which I have applied otherwise.

As the algorithm lends itself to an expansive political critique, depicting temporal experience on varying scales, this brings us to several pivotal questions: Can such a method therefore support a synthesis of the *longue durée?* Would such a synthesis have the capacity to teach us anything new, or to make use of the analytics of power – one of the peculiar merits of applying the algorithm to an institution with limited publishing resources?

An outline of British history in the nineteenth century that relied upon algorithmically produced visualizations would radically differ from the outline of the table of contents in any extant book of British history. For example, the twenty-year events indexed in Figure 8.4 would suggest a narrative that weaves through a diverse set of relatively underprivileged issues: "seditious meetings," "Orange lodges," "matrimonial clauses," "merchant shipping," and "holdings." This peculiar synthesis begins with a story of bureaucratic anxiety, and tightening control, the gag orders around fears of Jacobinism in the early decades of the century.

The long-term view quickly changes from suppression to reform. After 1820 and for the rest of the nineteenth century, most of the differential interest in parliament was devoted to an inquiry into aspects of the Orange lodges related to inspecting and remedying imperial racism in the era of the Catholic Relief Act. We see a similar divergence in focus in each of these other salient topics: the Matrimonial Clauses Act of 1857 legalized divorce and protected a woman's right to property; the Agricultural Holdings Act of 1875 and 1883 and the Crofters' Holdings Act of 1886 provided the first protections for working people against eviction; and the Small Holding Act of 1903 made possible a land redistribution program designed to reverse the economic imbalance of colonization and protect working-class interests by limiting rents. A synthesis supported by Figure 8.4 would offer us a portrait of an age of liberalism, persistently working from era to era to gradually extend the pleasures of privilege to the many, reversing the exclusions of the past, and it would thus endorse the long-term view of progress suggested by fin-de-siècle historians such as Élie Halévy and Sidney and Beatrice Webb.

Cautions aside, tf-ipf offers a potential measure of how particular concerns in parliament were experienced as temporal phenomena. Some of these concerns were pressed with enough political clout behind them to endure over time. Other concerns – for instance the causes associated with labor – commanded attention for only a day or week at a time. The measurement and ranking of concerns allow a scholar to robustly revisit the sequence of events in nineteenth-century Britain according to a new index – one that ranks subjects from the entire range of professional, political, and economic spheres – according to how much repetition they were able to command in parliament.

Yet before we embrace this narrative of progress, which seems to be supported by algorithmic data, let us recall that part of the flexibility of tf-ipf is that it supports another reading of the century as a whole. An alternative synthesis, focused on the pulse of short-term causes that failed to command sustained interest in parliament, appears in the studies we saw in Figures 8.6 and 8.7: the repeal of the Corn Laws, the banning of intoxicating liquors, cheap grain and sugar, not too much liquor. A synthesis organized around short-term subjects tells its own kind of narrative – the story of parliament's short-lived concern for truly radical reforms such as those of the Chartists, or the crofters' plea for land redistribution in Scotland. The algorithm lends itself to a framework for analyzing change over time that identifies exactly which labour causes parliament treated in a similar way – distillers, bleachers, dyers, Chartists, crofters, and miners.

In effect, this synthesis tells a narrative of pauper causes and princely causes, showing the stark divides of access between political issues that might otherwise look the same in terms of access and merit. Using the algorithm reveals how the short-term and relatively narrow victories of labor were mooted for days or weeks, alongside grander liberal causes like Catholic Emancipation that were consistently championed on the floor of parliament over the course of years. By using parliamentary debate as an index of when labor politics reached a national debate, such an approach would complement the many fine studies of labor rhetoric in the archive and rather than using wordcount, it might benefit even more from using tf-ipf as an index of exactly which labor language in parliament was distinctive of each moment.[33]

An even greater synthesis becomes possible when we marry these different narratives, illuminating the portrait of long-term forces in Figure 8.4, for example, with the diagnostic of short-term episodes in Figures 8.6 and 8.7. An analyst working with both sets of data can narrate a complex story about how the chokehold on parliamentary interest by British elites made room for only one or two meaningful reforms per generation – just enough reform, perhaps, to reflect the self-consciousness of a liberal elite, but not enough to undo the pattern of racial, sexual, and class exclusions with which modern historians understand the era of British liberalism.

---

[33] The language of labor politics – especially the use by labor leaders of the image of the "Norman Yoke" and the cause of "the Constitution" – contains well-known chestnuts for British history Mark Goldie, "The Ancient Constitution and the Languages of Political Thought," *The Historical Journal* 62:1 (March 2019): 3–34, https://doi.org/10.1017/S0018246X18000328.

In helping the scholar to organize systematically the themes of parliamentary debate into long-term forces and short-term change, tf-ipf almost inevitably illuminates an historical period through the lens of multiple temporality described by Manuel De Landa, who emphasized that a complex collocation of slow-moving forces and fast-moving forces are simultaneously at work at every moment in human experience. By quantitatively abstracting the varying tempos of historical change from a textual database, tf-ipf provides the historian with material that differentiates the multiple kinds of change that are simultaneously at work at any given moment.

The sense that there are different layers of experience changing at the same time – some developing slowly over decades or centuries, others changing quickly over days – has been noted by many philosophers of history. "Historical times consist of multiple layers," writes Koselleck."[34] Like the geological strata of stone that became recognized in the eighteenth century as repository of fossils from ages past, Koselleck imagines history as layers of sediment deposited in a bygone era. The experiments in this chapter similarly highlight how different subjects taken up in parliament unfolded according to a different tempo, some commanding long months of debate and others mere days. The metric of tf-ipf gives us the opportunity to examine the different kinds of events that might have felt like cataclysms to contemporaries, depending on the temporal scale of the observer.

Some readers may, perhaps, be disappointed that the results of the method do not radically upend our portrait of the nineteenth century – at least in its broadest outlines. One cannot, however, expect thousands of historians, over the centuries, to be completely wrong in every general aspect of their discipline. But even so, as we focus our studies upon smaller timeframes, the quantitative survey can, in fact, upend many portions of the historical canvas. This method can be a powerful way to investigate the multitude of open questions, especially those quandaries involving lesser-known events in the history of empire – the controversy over "hypothec" in the 1860s, for instance, a lesser-known alley in the vast city of British social history and property law. Hypothec governed the experience of farmers in Scotland and Ireland, commanded the attention of lawyers, and commanded interest equal to the governance of usury or cotton weavers earlier in the century and yet, despite the countless pages historians have devoted to that period, no sustained inquiry into the politics of

[34] Koselleck, Sediments of Time, 4.

hypothec reform has been carried out. Similarly, there are tempting questions about parliament's relationship to teachers in 1870–1910, to refreshment houses in the 1860s, and to monasteries in the 1850s – material whose parliamentary significance could be relatively quickly ascertained through the application of a variety of algorithms trained on semantic cohorts alongside close reading of the passages where they appear.[35] As I have argued elsewhere, however, a canny rule of research suggests an 80/20 rule of insight, where promising research typically leaves 80 percent of the findings of a field undisturbed, while contributing at most a 20 percent revision of content.[36] For scholars who wish to track long-term dynamics and their relationship to short-term change, the most fundamental requirement of any method is its capacity to highlight new subjects for research and new approaches for synthesis.

The long-term views of history presented in the case study in this chapter have been multiple: they vary by the length of period consulted, but also by the controlled vocabulary used. Rather than forcing the analyst to ventriloquize a single metanarrative, the algorithm allows us to present a series of refracted vistas on the past, each of which raises new questions about how we interpret parliamentary interest and the data involved.

Even the aggregate view of the *longue durée* woven from this data is hardly binding. Tf-idf is one algorithm for distinctiveness among a galaxy of other possible algorithms, each of which implies slightly different measures of difference. In Chapter 9, we will submit the question of distinctiveness to another round of interrogations, revealing vast differences among the questions we can ask about change in the past. Critical search and iteration are guiding principles that bring critical awareness to bear on every stage in the research process, ensuring that the data of the past are not, at any juncture, abandoned to automatic thinking and unreflective assessment.

It is too early, perhaps, to say whether the experiments in this chapter will bring us to a genuinely revolutionary synthesis for British history, but we can say with certainty that these new methods – once they have been rigorously tested and validated by well-churned archives like *Hansard* – will

[35] The payoff for British history, or even British parliamentary history, is provocative in minor ways, suggestive in terms of new chronologies and hierarchies, but hardly revolutionary. Nor would we expect a distant reading to overturn the consensus of tens of thousands of students of history who have worked on British history, often with the help of the parliamentary debates, over the past century.

[36] Jo Guldi, "Parliament's Debates about Infrastructure: An Exercise in Using Dynamic Topic Models to Synthesize Historical Change," *Technology and Culture* 60:1 (March 21, 2019): 1–33.

be a powerful tool for illuminating significant dynamics when they are applied to relatively unknown archives. Tf-ipf and similar algorithms may, in fact, be especially rewarding for historians of temporal geographies that have not yet been substantially mapped – for instance, those trying to make sense of the pulse of experience over the past fifty years of American history – or for historians studying major turning points in the ongoing evolution of internet repositories such as GeoCities, Reddit, and Usenet.[37] The controlled vocabulary of speakers' concerns, place names, and political classes may not be particularly useful for drawing out original insights, but contemporary linguistic packages such as WordNet will do a fine job. These methods of comparing words differentially linked to particular time periods, depicting a dynamic lexicon moving across different temporal scales and different kinds of vocabulary, allow a researcher to begin classifying periods, discerning major turning points without essentializing any single x-axis as an embodiment of historical truth.

Before concluding this chapter, we should take a moment to briefly say a few words about periodization, which can be a thorny matter even when the boundaries of historical eras are marked using traditional methods. A conscientious approach to periodization, watershed, and causality must grapple with two building blocks of historical time: multiple temporality and the trajectory of modernity. In particular, considering multiple temporality may help us to recover lost voices in the archive. Even when it is advanced as cogently and carefully as possible, however, some historians argue against periodization altogether, viewing it as a western and elitist conceit that projects an invisible metric system on the past, when experience is multiple, cyclical, or haunted by ghosts.[38] These problematic aspects should therefore be engaged, even when our method discerns events and dynamics that lend themselves nicely to periodization.

Recovering lost perspectives on the past may require profiling the insights of individuals who were ahead of their time and disregarded during their lifetimes. In the chapters that follow, we will further explore these subjects, turning first to the measurement of individual influence in history.

---

[37] This point about the horizons of digital history is frequently made in Ian Milligan, *History in the Age of Abundance?: How the Web Is Transforming Historical Research* (Montreal: McGill-Queen's University Press, 2019).

[38] Tanaka, "History without Chronology"; Joshua Kates, "Against the Period," *Differences* 23:2 (2012): 136–64.

CHAPTER 9

The Measure of Influence

Focusing on the chronology of events described in a dataset can provide valuable insights into change over time, but text mining also enables us to peer into the relationships between individuals over time. How forward looking were they? Who took risks in any set of relationships? Focusing on individuals can allow us to highlight act of bravery or clarity (or even conformity) that help create consensus in the world of communities like parliament, the institution that provides the major dataset we explore in this book. In the pages that follow, we will explore how algorithms can be applied not only to study moments in time, but also to compare individuals.

Modernity is frequently imagined as a product of particular individuals "leading" the future through the power of their imagination. This conceit is, itself, a romantic image; "Poets are the unacknowledged legislators of mankind," as Percy Bysshe Shelley put it. While we might reject a model of modernity based solely on the agency of privileged leaders, no account of history would be complete without some account of the agency of individuals. Recent work by hybrid teams of historians and information scientists has explored how the power of individuals to influence their peers shows up in textual datasets. We will borrow from this study, using the algorithms embraced by other teams – divergence measures – to deepen our analysis of modernity. Some of the most exciting experiments with modeling time on the basis of text mining derive from an expansion of divergence to understand the contributions of individuals to innovation in general.

An Information Theory of Innovative Individuals

A key case study that focused on individuals was conducted by a team who used divergence measures to distinguish the speakers around the time of the French Revolution that were most "novel" (in that their words were regularly different from those widely used in the past) and speakers who were most "transitive" (in that they employed words that were distant from those that would be spoken in the future.)[1]

We will investigate divergence measures in greater depth in Chapter 10, but for now, suffice it to say that divergence measures are often introduced as measures of "similarity" or "distance:" they are useful for grouping different documents as "more similar" or "more distant." What is being grouped with what, however, is subject to carpentry by a skilled data scientist. The practitioner of text mining isn't compelled to measure which novels are similar to which novels and which parliamentary speeches are most similar to which parliamentary speeches. Data science also allows the text miner to compare novelists with novelists and speakers with speakers. The data scientist may compare years with years. And the data scientist can even compare speakers with their individual past and individual future, or individual speakers with the collective past and the collective future, relative to the time of the speaker. In this way, divergence measures allowed the French Revolution team to locate personages who were ahead of the curve of time or behind it – the *influencers* and *laggards* of political speech.

Statistical categorization allowed the French Revolution team to create metrics of speech that have never before been used. These metrics were based on divergence measures of individuals speaking at any given point of time in relationship to the collective past and collective future. They allowed the team to measure each speaker's "innovation" – their resemblance to speeches yet to come – versus "irrelevance" – their resemblance to speeches from an earlier time. "Innovation" here provides a measure of raw influence: a speaker with high influence is a person who used language that would be taken up by others after they spoke. A person with high innovation and low irrelevance was introducing concepts that had never been heard before.

In this chapter, I will recreate the French Revolution study with data from *Hansard*, and investigate what happens when we measure influence in British parliament. For the purposes of this book, I am more interested in "breaking" algorithms by critically examining their results than getting a perfect picture of the nineteenth century. Accordingly, I will take a slightly more literal approach than the French Revolution team. The original team

---

[1] Alexander T. J. Barron et al., "Individuals, Institutions, and Innovation in the Debates of the French Revolution," *Proceedings of the National Academy of Sciences* 115:18 (May 1, 2018): 4607–12, https://doi.org/10.1073/pnas.1717729115.

combined topic models and divergence measures as a means of approximating a study of who shared which ideas. Instead, taking a critical search approach, I will test what can be known by one algorithm at a time. I will track which *words* used by speakers were taken up by other speakers, and then review the information to see if this simpler version of the solution also produces rational results.[2] In this minimal example, I will apply divergence measures directly to speakers' output as bags of words to measure which speakers were introducing new language, a language that may have taken the form of novel concepts, proper nouns, or rhetorical flourishes. I will survey the results of this process, moving from what the minimal measure suggests about speakers to time periods to the language itself that seems to be influencing the model. In each case study, I test the results against what I know about history, raising questions about how to interpret the algorithm's findings. In a more expanded version, I would then return to the measure of innovation applied to topics to compare the results, but I will leave that work to another author, instead moving into speculation about what we hope to gain by modeling personal and group influence in history, and how different approaches to the problem may expand the field.

What does the data say about who influenced whom?[3] As we can see in Figure 9.1, plotting the interactions of speakers in *Hansard* reveals a long, bullet-shaped clustering of speakers along the diagonal line that represents a space equidistant from innovation and irrelevance.

The shape of the mass of speakers alone suggests that almost all speakers in parliament were willing to make compromises. The bullet shape tilts close to zero in the lower left-hand corner of the plot. The lower left-hand

[2] I give the measures the names "innovation" and "irrelevance" – rather than "novelty" and "transitoriness", for example, or even "redundancy" – to stress the potential *political virtue* (innovation) associated with distance from the past, and the potential *political cost* (irrelevance) of distance from the future. I use the same divergence algorithm used by the original team – partial Jensen–Shannon Divergence (JSD) – to rank speakers as markedly "innovative" when their lexicon is closer to the language spoken in the ten years following their speech. A speaker who uses words that wouldn't be in use a decade later is classed as "irrelevant." The classification of "irrelevant" speech against "innovative" speech primarily serves as a simple index of how language was changing in the aggregate over a time period.

[3] It should be noted that, to a greater degree than the rest of the data used in this book, the data about speaker names in *Hansard* is highly inconsistent: the several Lord Wynfords and Mr. Gladstones and Lord Chancellors have been run together, and inconsistent spelling and punctuation plague the data. Every claim made about habits of innovation in parliament is tentative at best. Even more than the case studies presented throughout this book, the data in this chapter is presented purely as a model of the kinds of questions that historians might ask with better data.

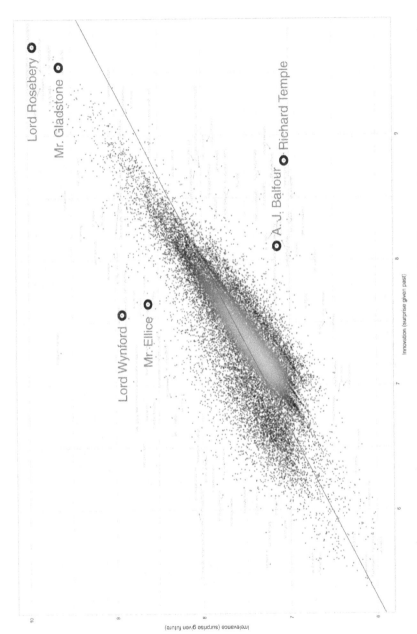

Figure 9.1 Speakers in relationship to irrelevance and innovation. Searching the parliamentary debates of Great Britain, Brown data.

quadrant of the plot holds data points representing speakers who took relatively few risks; they were neither innovative nor irrelevant.

The midpoint of the chart, where the bullet is thickest, tilts under the diagonal line. Points in this region represent speeches that were relatively more innovative and relatively less irrelevant; in other words, these data points represent speakers who took big risks and whose risks matched the choices of lexicon made by speakers who spoke after them. The speakers represented by data-points in this region – for instance A. J. Balfour and Richard Temple – are speakers who tried out a few new words that were later taken up by their peers.

The French Revolution team proved that one of the uses of a diagram of this sort is to identify outliers whose words exerted influence over other speakers. The points on the lower edges of the bullet toward the lower right-hand corner are those individuals who were exceptionally more innovative and less irrelevant than their peers – individuals who spoke words that other people repeated. In the French Revolution study, this is where we find Robespierre. In parliament, this category includes Richard Temple, Lieutenant-Governor of Bengal, who, as Famine Commissioner for the Government of India after 1876, presided over millions of deaths during a horrific famine, and A. J. Balfour, who was responsible for bringing the battering ram to Ireland to help with the eviction of families too poor to pay rent and who later became British prime minister from 1902 to 1905. The leaders who set the road for others to follow were also sometimes the most vicious.

The diagram in Figure 9.1 can also help us think about failed experiments and eddy currents of irrelevance. Clustered toward the upper left-hand corner are speakers who were exceptionally irrelevant: their words might represent idiosyncratic concerns from local politics, or even novel and even radical concepts, but in any event, no one paid attention to them. The names of these speakers are less familiar to posterity; they include Lord Wynford (a famous womanizer) and Mr. Ellice (a merchant turned advocate of the Reform Act of 1832 that enfranchised the middle class).

In the upper right-hand corner are the speakers who tried bravely, again and again. Half the time, their words were taken up; half the time, their words were discarded by the listener. They played a game of high risks and high rewards. Here we find Mr. Gladstone (leader of the Liberal Party and prime minister, 1868–74, 1880–85, 1886, 1892–94) and Lord Rosebery (imperialist liberal and prime minister, 1894–95).

An interesting facet of influence that the plot reveals is the difficulty faced by people with truly new ideas. Individuals in parliament who had the most radical politics were also, quite frequently, the ones who were least able to shift the language of their peers. For example, take Isaac Butt, the Irish radical who is not highlighted in Figure 9.1. If he were highlighted, Butt would appear in the midst of the dense cloud near Mr. Wynford and Mr. Ellice, who are indicated by labels. He is solidly in the upper left-hand quadrant of the highly irrelevant and only moderately innovative, and he's not even very distinctive in his irrelevance.

Any characterization that renders Isaac Butt as the middle of the middle of anything should raise eyebrows. Butt spent his career in parliament pressing the cause of the Irish peasant and he left a powerful legacy behind in a set of concerns taken up by later Irish members of parliament. Butt's long-term legacy might have been pronounced (Ireland, after all, ultimately opted to leave Britain), yet he was unable to alter the mainstream language of parliament, which remained dedicated to Britain's empire.

Butt's case should alert us that there are potential issues inherent to the vocabulary that we are using to describe what is being measured. The radical who insists on alluding to peasant troubles with rent in every speech for a decade and who was remembered by Irish activists long after his career ended is not ranked as "innovative" here, for he fails the test of changing the language used by his peers in Britain's parliament. That hardly means that Butt was irrelevant to world history, or even technically to parliament. But the difference between *algorithmic* innovation and *actual* innovation here should draw our attention again to what is being measured: we are looking at aggregate bodies of words, and raw words, not words or groups of words as approximations of ideals. We are looking for words, not actions. The measures we are using can be informative, but only so long as we remain vigilant about their limitations at describing historical reality in its fullness.

We have performed a minimal example of someone else's measurement here in order to grasp directly how the measure works, to see the algorithm in action on the level of words. In a fuller investigation, we would want to follow up by modeling innovation and irrelevance in relationship to topics, not lexicon, as the original research team had done. A higher-level analysis might show us Isaac Butt in another role. Overall, the minimal example of modeling lexical influence shows Britain as a relatively conservative body during the nineteenth century, one where very few speakers are introducing new words, names, or locations to frame concepts or set agendas. It is not really possible without the topic-level analysis to compare speakers in the British and French scene, but that is not really the point of this minimal investigation.

Our model of lexical innovation suggests a relatively conservative model of innovation. I would expect the results of our foray into modeling influence to differ from the results of the French Revolution team in certain ways. In the French example, speakers were measured over a handful of the most dramatic years of the French Revolution. Clear leaders like Robespierre distinctly emerge from the data as the radicals who stood out for presenting new idea after new idea; the distinctive quality of the French Revolution, after all, is the heat of novelty, expressed in the regularity of new proposals for issues ranging from the formal recognition of rights to the renaming of months.

Nineteenth-century Britain, meanwhile, saw plenty of political change, but its experience was more conservative than that of the French Congrès in the era of the Revolution. Leaders like Gladstone were famous for building modern political parties, which were not so much hotbeds of radicalism and novelty as powerful unions stamped by consensus around key political platforms. The parliamentary annals over the nineteenth century offer a longer series of speakers and years, and the *longue durée* of a century offers a different insight than the short *durée* of a decade in the French Revolution. In the *longue durée* perspective of the data on parliament, we see speakers like Gladstone, who served for sixty-one years (from 1833 to 1894) and who held radically different roles during his tenure, from a novice representative for Newark to prime minister.

We begin to understand the limitations of our method. Any rating of Gladstone in terms of "innovation" or "irrelevance" would necessarily average out Gladstone's multiple roles, reducing the differing incarnations of an individual into a single point of data. A short-term speaker who authored many fiery speeches might be automatically classified as more irrelevant than Gladstone. By starting with a minimal example and measuring how the algorithm works on lexicon before we work on topic, we gain a more nuanced sense of how the algorithm prioritizes certain kinds of speakers. We learn important cautions about what to think about when implementing the algorithm on new data.

Generalizing about Innovation Over Time

Was parliament's tilt toward innovation at the level of lexicon expressed evenly from decade to decade? We can break down the data by decade to answer this question.

Figure 9.2 demonstrates a gradual drift toward innovation – away from the replication of the language of the past – in each individual decade until

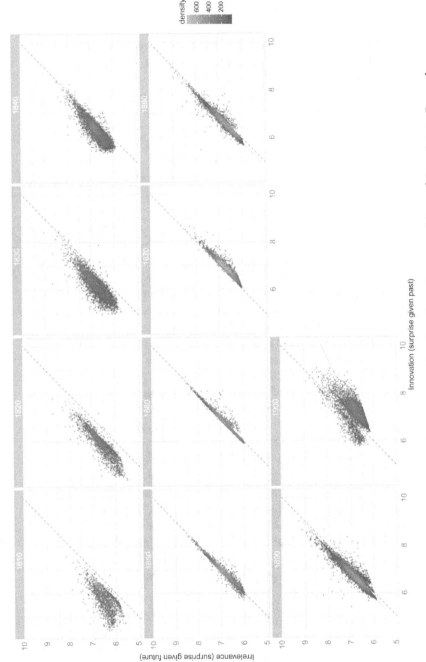

Figure 9.2   The drift of innovation over a century. Searching the parliamentary debates of Great Britain, Brown data.

1870 For the first few decades of the century, the bullet shape of the mass of speakers floats above the diagonal line, suggesting a conservative tendency to recycle the same old words. That conservative tendency seems to have persisted until around 1840, which is what we would expect, given the 1832 Reform Act's assault on parliament as an institution of aristocracy. At that point, the willingness of speakers to introduce new words began to expand. The evidence shows a marked trend toward innovation from 1840 to 1870. Speakers in each decade until 1870, it seems, were conscientiously trying to create a new language of reform, of liberalism, or of conservativism – a movement that historians would traditionally associate with middle-class and popular movements for reform, party formation, the Tamworth Manifesto, and the circulation of debates in newspapers.[4]

Indeed, the growth of newspaper circulation after the expansion of the franchise in 1867, as described by Ryan Vieira, would suggest that MPs might have been incentivized to further distinguish themselves, through new language and party positions, for their increasingly attentive constituents.[5] But in fact, the opposite seems to have been true. After 1870 – perhaps, as a result of the constant pressure to manufacture more speeches – there was a retarding effect on the language of parliament; words spoken in 1880 and 1890 were overall close to those of 1870 and 1880. By contrast, the lexicon of 1850 is classified as much more innovative than the lexicon of 1840.

On a certain level, much of this was already clear to specialists. What we have gleaned from this aggregation of trends is already obvious to most political historians: from the vantage of any given year, the fate of the future is largely determined by which party is in power . Thus, the future mapped out by Gladstone's government was quite different from that of the Marquess of Salisbury. On the other hand, however, aggregate comparisons of language have never before available to the professional historian on such a scale. Glancing over them allows the scholar to define the long-term stakes of short-term victories. For instance, the Conservative idiom of gentility mapped out by the language of "honourable gentlemen," was clearly trending in 1889, but it might not be remembered in 1890. Conservatives of the 1880s were more influential, however, in ultimately

---

[4] Matthew Cole and Helen Deighan, *Political Parties in Great Britain* (Edinburgh: Edinburgh University Press, 2012), 77–79.

[5] Ryan A. Vieira, *Time and Politics: Parliament and the Culture of Modernity in Nineteenth-Century Britain and the British World* (Oxford: Oxford University Press, 2015), http://search.ebscohost.com/login.aspx?direct=true&scope=site&db=nlebk&db=nlabk&AN=1003234.

effectuating those institutional forms that had comprised so much of their speech: a greater role for governance of the colonies through secretaries, the oversight of boards for domestic government, and the importance of the treasury. As quantifiable lexical terms, these institutional pieces would be statistically ascendant over the whole second half of the century and, indeed, beyond (from 1852 to 1911).

Another caution we should take with an approach that highlights individuals is to remember that individual lexicons are never static – that individual speakers, just like society itself, adjust their lexicons over time. As a remedy for this linguistic complexity, divergence measures can easily be applied to an individual speaker's lexicon in order to show, for instance, how Gladstone changed his idiom over a particular question.

Indeed, it is the possibility of abstract aggregation that promises to be instructive to the historian who wishes to synthesize trends and moments of political reorientation in modern textual corpora. Moments of political identity-making that have come down through the historiography (for instance, the Tamworth Manifesto of 1834) may be checked against quantitative measures of the imprint they have left upon the political lexicon of those they influenced. When we apply measures of influence and innovation to speakers' words, we deal in large and general comparisons. In contrast to keyword measures and topic modeling – which provide indices, respectively, of how and what was talked about – information theory stands out as a tool for abstracting change itself.

Because it enables us to abstract the difference between any two dates within any one corpus, information theory enormously helps the synthesizing historian to characterize large swaths of time. If land had been made an issue for parliament in the 1870s, then colonial secretaries and government boards were made an issue in the 1880s. The measure of irrelevance and innovation thus allows a scholar to paint with a broad brush and characterize the contributions of any given event or decade to the "modern" language of British politics that was ascendant in parliament during the period 1852–1911.

Language that Influenced Others

But how is the computer assigning these categories? We can also dive into the data to understand which words factored into the algorithm's calculations of "innovative" and "irrelevant." In this simplified model of influence, we will only look at shared *words* rather than topics or other clusters of words. Because we have two categories of speakers – innovative ones and irrelevant ones – we can ask the computer to tell us which words were most typical of "innovative" and "irrelevant" speakers, decade by decade.

The method is to draw a diagonal line through the middle of the bullet, separating the more innovative speakers of the time from the more irrelevant speakers. In Figure 9.1, the diagonal appears as a dotted line transecting the bullet, and such a line allows us to generalize. Above the diagonal are the speakers whose ideas weren't taken up a decade later, and below the diagonal are speakers whose ideas were taken up a decade later. We use a line of best fit – in this case, a line of least mean squares.

When we subdivide the dataset into decades, plotting the speakers and a diagonal line for each (not shown), we can use the method of generalization about innovative and irrelevant speakers to focus on the lasting trends contributed by speakers in each decade of the nineteenth century. A marked conservatism and aristocracy are clear in the language of the earliest set of speakers. In 1806–09, the words "lord" and "nobl-" were on the rise and discussions of Irish Catholics and the constitution were on the wane, put to flight by a tide of anti-Bonapartism (data not shown). Any decade-long slice of time we examine will present extremely different images of the future: in 1840, discussions of anti-slavery and sugar were mounting; in 1870, anti-landlord politics and the discussion of Irish tenants, and discussions of education and government boards were on the decline.

Now it bears notice that the computer's judgment merits closer inspection by humans. For the 1850s, our measure of "irrelevance" and "innovation" show the words "education," "Catholic," "vote," and "poor" going out of favor, while another cluster of words are coming into favor, including "war," "import," "India," and "tax" (data not shown). According to this logic, the marked shift from conversations about the Poor Law and Catholic representation to debates on the Crimean War and the Indian Land Revenue and Great Rebellion, represented an altogether innovative way of talking about *empire* – an idiom classified as more lasting, in the model of the computer, than the Irish debates over Home Rule and Land Reform in the 1880s (Table 9.1). Many human readers of this analysis might be surprised. In Ireland, Protestant and Catholic violence endured as a matter of international political concern through at least the Belfast Agreement of 1998. Here, again, we learn to treat all models as limited to the precise data and questions that are served to the computer. The computer's reckoning of "innovation" relative to a decade of time isn't a fair reckoning of how relevant Victorian debates about Ireland and India were relative to the twentieth century. It is important to remember that we have no magic metric of absolute historical significance, merely a measure of the relative

Table 9.1 *Words favored by innovative and*
irrelevant speakers in the 1880s.

Irrelevant Speakers	Innovative Speakers
Tenant*	Hon*
Lord*	Gentleman*
Earl*	Secretari*
Ireland*	Sir*
Landlord*	Govern*
Majesti*	Board*
Nobl*	Balfour*
Law*	Matter*
Bill*	Polic*
Land*	Smith*
Colonel*	Gladstone*
Ship*	Chief*
Rent*	Friend*
King*	Sexton*
Hous*	Chancellor*
Lordship*	Speaker*
Country*	O'Connor*
Class*	India*
Minist*	Treasuri*
Parliament*	District*

transmission of certain words among parliamentary speakers over a decade. What we learn from the exercise is that "Ireland" was trending less than India by the end of the 1850s – a finding that is not altogether surprising, given the relative decline of urgency about Irish politics after the Famine and in the era of the Indian Great Rebellion.

Similar caveats should structure our interpretation of the trends visible in the 1880s, another moment when, according to the computer, the focus on Ireland was waning, too. This finding comes as a great surprise to historians of India familiar with the events of the Irish Land War (1879–86) and Plan of Campaign (1886–91), both of which left lasting legislation on the history of property law and colonial governance in Ireland. The computer-identified "trend" makes sense, however, if we understand, again, that the data is not a marker of absolute historical relevance of words in the 1880s, but merely a marker of the relative spread of terms. Ireland was a "trendy" political subject in 1880, but it was relatively less so a decade later, as a new Conservative government grew more interested in police and India, but not in Ireland, tenants, and the price of rent – suggesting that the political

Table 9.2 *Words favored by innovative and irrelevant speakers, 1806–1911.*

Irrelevant Speakers	Innovative Speakers
Friend*	Secretari*
Bill*	Beg*
Hon*	Board*
Law*	School*
Learn*	Weir*
Object*	Chief*
Person*	Lord*
Respect*	Lieuten*
Time*	Jackson*
Church*	Scotland*
Measur*	Awar*
Vote*	Local*
Parliament*	Ireland*
Lordship*	Disraeli*
Power*	Heali*
Everi*	Educ*
Subject*	Answer*
Proceed*	Counti*
System*	Gentleman*
Establish*	District*

concept of "rent" was closely linked to the temporality of Ireland. The divergence measures also highlight the rise of "courtesy" language marked by the use of formal titles such as "honourable," "sir," and "gentleman" to invoke other speakers (see Table 9.1). It is worth underscoring once more that the trends identified by this particular model are short-term ones; part of the beauty of the model is that the horizon of "trend" can be adjusted by the researcher relative to their curiosity.

Suppose we were to rewrite our model to aggregate decade-based irrelevance or innovation over the course of the century – one possible approach to modeling the long-term trends of the nineteenth century. If we examine change over the course of the entire century, it is those who embrace politeness who seem old-fashioned. The most forward-looking members of parliament spoke a language that engaged the colonies and education (see Table 9.2). They talked about schools, education, and local administration more generally. They debated policies everywhere, but especially policies in Ireland. By contrast, those who were highly irrelevant were liable to debate the church and to speak of learning and law.

More generally, over the course of the century, the language of parliamentary courtesy changed. The innovative were liable to invoke a language of cross-examination, both "begging" the listeners for their attention and asking for "answers." The irrelevant speakers, as a general rule, were given to a lexicon of institutional power, with references to the "establishment," to the "church," to "parliament" itself and its "proceedings," to the "system," and to the "law" (see Table 9.2). They were punctiliously polite, above all, to their fellow representatives, referring to another member as "my honourable friend." In short, they were speakers in the thrall of a passing system that accomplished important work early in the nineteenth century. By the century's end, that establishment was being replaced both by a new style of inquiry into facts and realities and by a new set of civil institutions such as boards and commissions.

One weakness of modeling the entire collection of words over time – as opposed to clusters of words grouped in topics or other vectors, or as opposed to a controlled vocabulary – is that the raw and unsupervised results may tell the analyst more about superficial fluctuations in the style of rhetoric than about substantive change. "Progress" is relative, as is "influence." The case studies here aren't isolating some magic formula for winning friends; they're simply documenting the trends of what language parliamentary speakers used from decade to decade. We are back at a question of interpretation that requires us to resort to critical thinking about the data and the algorithm, and their capacity to produce meaning.

One must use a great deal of care in interpreting markers of progress as defined by these quantitative metrics. In the 1880s, the most influential speakers in parliament – at least according to the limited definition of influence we have established – were those advancing an imperial agenda associated with the Conservative party; thus, those who were debating Turkey, Egypt, and the Transvaal. They were the most novel in that they were proposing a wider sweep of empire than ever before and were using jingoistic and patriotic terms in new ways. The same voices would look hopelessly outmoded to Marxist and subaltern critics of their own time, as well as to their descendants in the 1930s or 1950s. In other words, we are easily led astray if the measures of modernity described here are taken as a metric of "progress" or "truth," rather than simply of local victory. Novelty, or innovation, as defined by the measure of closeness to later texts, is a local, not a universal, measure of influence over a measurable period of time – in this case, a decade.

The measure of *modernity*, as we have called the innovation and irrelevance metrics, is designed to capture growing influence, rather than to dramatize polarized views. Meanwhile, the mapping of the most influential strain in politics at any given time obviously masks all sorts of politics that truly mattered historically, both in terms of social experience beyond parliament and in terms of policies beyond the ten-year window tested in these examples. Political or moral consensus, progress, and divergence resist these simplified metrics, which capture shifts in rhetoric as much as they capture substantive effort.

Without question, the measurement of innovation has not been exhausted. But we have modeled here some glimpse of what it might mean to tack between a study of influential *individuals* and changing *language*. We have also shown that changing language is sometimes rhetorical – indexing new styles of politeness – and is sometimes linked to institutions, such as the relative decline of church and aristocratic power and the rise of public education and the civil service. We have shown that a gap exists between the modeling of influential language and the capacity of infective ideas. We have sketched out frontiers that future researchers will undoubtedly explore.

Conclusion: Future Horizons for Research

In this chapter, we have examined a variety of approaches to understanding influence, including foregrounding individuals and diving into the dynamics of speaker language. We have highlighted the limits of the current approach as well as avenues for future research. As such, the tool of divergence offers important approaches for those who would try to interpret less-well-understood time periods – even if the tools are still fairly limited and reduce "innovation" to a choice of words or topics, and average or distill individual lives with their enormous variation down to a single point of data.

Modernity has sometimes been imagined, especially by historians of ideas, in terms of a succession of great minds contributing *new understanding*. In the 1960s and 1970s, new schools of intellectual history destabilized the "great chain of being" with an argument about "moments" of innovation where groups of people introduced new concepts. Historians nowadays tend not to take for granted that the "innovator" is an individual: perhaps innovation is born of networks – as Bruno Latour imagined – or generations; or perhaps, it is forged out of political pressure. This conceptual shift among historians, envisioning collectives rather than unusual individuals, as the catalyzing agents of change, illustrates just one possible aspect of refining the search for innovations.

There are many adjustments that one could try in order to illuminate the power of networks. Adding metadata about individuals (whether their school or geographical background, or their party membership, cohort, or profession) would allow scholars to expand theories of influence to measure groups rather than individuals.[6] Adding information of this kind would enhance the analyst's ability to draw connections and constrain searches: How did influence work within the Conservative Party? What words or topics suggest influence across the parties? With added information, measurements of innovation may become even more exact.

On the other hand, some researchers may want to know more about the individual contributions that were shared and passed on. The case study examined in this chapter examines word influence in a modest way. But we could drill down into the data for insights such as which speakers introduced new words that were then repeated by other speakers within a few days – a preliminary pass through which, for instance, suggests that the Marquess of Salisbury introduced debates about the Sudan ("the Soudan") in the 1880s, while William Harcourt was first to introduce discussion of rape.[7] Or one could refine the data further to investigate which speakers tended to introduce topics related to foreign affairs, local affairs, abstractions, or oppression.

Scholars might also trace influence through the rhetorical strategies found in the debate text, with some caveats about the unreliability of the reported debates. For example, a researcher might track referents to each speaker (there are many: "Gladstone", "my friend the honourable member for Westminster. . ."; "the previous speaker"; "my honourable friend" is usually the previous speaker). Who was named the most? Who was named the most in a mood of refutation, or of praise? The references might potentially offer a quantifiable measure of "respect," both indexing who gave the most effusive respect (ironically or sincerely) to other speakers, as well as who received the most references (whether hostile or adulatory) from others.

More generally, the problem of influence is not necessarily played out in language spoken in public and, in many cases, influence is not even consciously *acknowledged*. Some forms of influence may be played out in

---

[6] Arthur Spirling has begun to collect this material for parliament. I am grateful for the suggestion of school background and profession to Peter Winship, Southern Methodist University Law School.

[7] For the data about the Sudan and "rape," I reference a jejune experiment of my own, applying burst-detection algorithms to speaker relationships. Both my code and the data are too raw to merit further discussion here. For burst detection, see Andrew C. Eggers and Arthur Spirling, "The Shadow Cabinet in Westminster Systems: Modeling Opposition Agenda Setting in the House of Commons, 1832–1915," *British Journal of Political Science*, (2016): 1–25.

unconscious ways that are only visible in the aggregate. But another exten-sion of the study here might identify the person who generated the most memes in parliament: in other words, the speaker whose felicitous phrases routinely became "commonplaces," following the pattern of the research of Clovis Gladstone.[8] Gladstone's algorithm is built to detect phrases that are recycled in new documents. It would support the detection of memes developed by one speaker and quoted (with or without attribution) by other speakers on the floor. Such an algorithmic operation should allow us to track, for instance, which speakers quoted Gladstone's language supporting "the masses against the classes," his famous aphorism for supporting the working masses of Britons against the middle classes, or "good government at home," his famous solution for the problems of foreign relations.

Or again, some speakers might have less facility with minting witticisms than did Gladstone, while still retaining the power to shift the mood of the room. Suppose that, after certain speakers, the sentiment in the room always changes – becoming more enraged in some cases, or happier in others. Such a speaker (or group of speakers) might be looked upon as "provocative" if they always make people enraged, or "conciliating" if the speeches that follow them are generally happier than the ones before. Or perhaps, there's a more complex pattern whereby the speakers of the opposite party become enraged, while the speakers of their own party become happy. After some speakers, the topic generally changes – perhaps, because they invariably offer a new way of looking at things, or perhaps, on the contrary, because they offer a conveniently familiar way of looking at things.

There are still other directions in which researchers could push if their goal is to discover the life of *ideas*. Experimentation with controlled vocab-ularies or topic models (as with the original French Revolution team) would capture the intellectual trends better than my simplified model does. Recent work in sociology allows digital scholars to specify particular genres of language within which terms have specific meanings, thus setting up the parameters for measuring increasing levels of abstraction or concreteness within particular disciplines (such as "agriculture" or "law").[9] It also seems plausible that some speakers had the power to shift both emotion and ideas together, and future scholars will surely try to find them.

---

[8] Literary scholar Clovis Gladstone has generated a sliding matrix to find permutations of several word phrases in his "Commonplaces" app, which looks for figures of speech that were recycled through the literary record of the eighteenth century. Demo: http://commonplacecultures.uchicago.edu; Code: https://github.com/ARTFL-Project/Commonplaces.

[9] Peter McMahan and James Evans, "Ambiguity and Engagement," *American Journal of Sociology* 124:3 (November 1, 2018): 860–912, https://doi.org/10.1086/701298.

Finally, we might grow curious about the evolution of particular speakers over the course of individual careers. There is also a general problem of "averaging" at stake when ranking individuals by their relative innovativeness over the course of an entire lifetime. The speaker who drives debate for a decade, but then follows the course set in his youth for the rest of his life is classified by the algorithm according to an average place in the tide of innovation. Individual idiosyncrasy, the unique patterns of innovation over the course of an individual life, is therefore obscured. A more nuanced approach to this kind of problem is described in Andrew Piper's *Enumerations*, in which the author proposes an array of tools for modeling poetic innovation over the course of a lifetime, including writers who explore new topics, writers who keep the same topic but explored new kinds of grammatical constructions throughout their career, and hybrids of both. Similarly diverse models of political subject-matter, language, grammar, mood, and rhetoric could be equally rewarding for the study of political innovation: Which speakers used the same rhetorical style but adopted new politics? Which speakers kept the same politics but began to apply it to new regions in the world?

Studies such as those explored in this chapter point the way to a more sensitive study of novelty, much of which will require narrowing a research question around the particulars of certain kinds of experience. As scholars examine influence and change over time, they make their way closer to a theory of causality and become more capable of accurately identifying the actors and conditions responsible for major moments of change.

CHAPTER 10

The Fit of Algorithms to Temporal Experience

Miguel De Landa, who is known chiefly as a theorist of architecture, speculates that some forces in history move slowly, as mountains are folded or islands sculpted out of lava, each moving at the scale of eons. Stone and rock are slow-moving, even when sculpted by human hands. The streets and major buildings of a city, for instance, may endure for centuries; think of Rome, where the Pantheon is still a functioning church. Even ideas, when fossilized into doctrine, can last for centuries. As with those old buildings, pieces may chip off and may be replaced with modern adjustments and adornments, but even here, the change is slow.

Other historical forces and cultural phenomena, De Landa argues, transform rapidly. People change the cut of their clothes and their figures of speech from year to year and, in comparison, their fluctuations are as fluid and rapid as the movements of water and fire. Fireworks explode in the sky, making flowers out of sparks, before fading, only seconds later. Similarly, trends on Twitter might flourish for an instant, diverting the attention, but the exchange disappears moments later, leaving barely a trace behind.

Historians understand vying dynamics of long-term and short-term development as an important component of explanation. When we tell the history of science, we don't just talk about alchemy and other curious theories that arose and then dissipated. Can algorithms tell us about these varieties of distinctiveness, the *lasting* discoveries contributed by each period of time, as well as what contributions any two eras share? The short answer to both questions is yes – given an appropriate archive. The longer answer is that there are many ways to measure how much one era overlaps with another one in the past, and measuring trends of this kind responsibly involves us in the nuances of how different algorithms model time.

In previous chapters, we have reviewed a series of approaches for detecting references to a relative past in a textual dataset. We have explored tools for finding what is most "distinctive" about periods of time ranging from the day to the decade. We have intensively investigated the parameters of each algorithm. We've shown that it is possible to use such an algorithm to think about the relationship between long-term trends and the short-term currents of change. We have employed controlled vocabularies to narrow our examination of trends onto problems such as how much time Britain's parliament dedicated to each region of the world and which speakers spoke words picked up by their colleagues. We have found interpretable results. But parliamentary attention and the use of fashionable language aren't the same as introducing words with the power to *endure*. We haven't asked questions about whether some ideas *last* longer than others and how to sort words that signify *lasting shifts* from words that *flicker out* after a moment in time.

Are there algorithmic approaches that can highlight the obdurate power of some ideas and the changing fascination typical of others? In earlier chapters, we noted that part of the critical search process also requires the analyst to compare *different* algorithms that might serve similar processes – urging that only by comparing algorithms do we truly begin to understand what it means to translate mathematical analysis into humanistic language, or humanistic concerns into mathematical claims. In this chapter, we will reflect critically on what it means to propose a mathematical "answer" to the question of how time changed.

As we explore the hidden dimensions of temporal experience in this chapter, we will squeeze our capacity for critical thinking even harder and see whether we can tweak our definition of a distinctive event to include a Steinem or a Linnaeus. This will involve diving even deeper into the workings of relevant algorithms. We will begin our investigation of algorithms with term-frequency inverse document frequency (tf-idf), one of the primary algorithms for studying the distinctive characteristics of two sets of data – which in the case of text mining means which *words* have *counts* that are distinctively higher for one set of documents. In Chapter 8, we applied the tf-idf algorithm to studying the distinctiveness of particular periods, tweaking the original tf-idf equation to produce term-frequency inverse period frequency (tf-ipf), a formula for showing which words are most distinctive of a given decade, year, week, or day in parliament.

In this chapter, we will examine the fact that tf-idf/tf-ipf can be applied to the study of change over time in a number of different ways. Whereas in Chapter 8 we used tf-idf to study the words most distinctive of each day or decade in parliament against the rest of the data as an undistinguished whole, in this chapter, we will use tf-idf to study which words were most distinctive of each decade *relative* to the documents that came before or after that moment in time. These mathematical approaches make it possible to distinguish mathematically the words that mark out short-term trends, long-term trends, last gasps of a fading idea, and ideas that marked discourse for a short period before vanishing from the historical record.

In the name of investigating some of the variety of possible kinds of temporal distinction, I propose five approaches that might be useful to a historian attempting to analyze time:

- **Period distinctiveness**, or the distinctiveness of each period compared to every other period. We calculate this measure, and all measures, using the count of each word relative to the counts of other words, inside and outside the period. We separate our dataset into two periods – Period P represents all the words spoken in one decade, for instance 1850–59, whereas Period Q represents words spoken in all other time periods in the dataset – that is, everything from 1806 to 1849 and 1860 to 1911 combined . Algorithmic analysis produces a measure for each word of how "distinctive" the term is of Period P relative to Period Q. In the examples that follow, we will examine the list of words that are ranked as most "distinctive" of certain decades as an index of the "temporal fossils" of a moment; these are words that came into usage in one decade before disappearing, rarely to be seen again.

- **Absolute historical novelty**, or the distinctiveness of each period relative to previous periods, which is more likely to evidence dynamics of long-term change than other models. To create this measure, we calculate how "distinctive" each term is of Period P relative to Period Q, which is modeled as all years that came before this period. For instance, we might model all the words frequencies from Period P, 1850–59, against the word frequencies from Period Q, 1806–1849. We use statistics to rank the terms that are most distinctive of Period P in comparison with Period Q. In the examples that follow, we examine the list of words ranked as most "distinctive" according to this measure as an index to "historical novelty," or the words that indicate neologisms or totally new concepts or idioms for parliament as a whole during any given period.

- **Historical trends**, or short-term change relative to the immediate past, measured against the immediately preceding decade. To create this measure, we calculate the distinctiveness of each term in Period P relative to the immediately preceding period, Period Q. For instance, we might measure the word frequencies of Period P, 1850–59, against the word frequencies of Period Q, 1840–49. In the examples that follow, we examine the list of words ranked highly by this measure as an index to "trends," or words that were not part of speech at the same rate in the previous decade, even if they had been previously discussed at some other time.

- **Typical speech**, measured an index of the typical speech of the period such as the average measure of distinction for the period, that ranks words that are neither very distant to other periods nor exactly the same. To produce this measure, we average all other term-period scores for Period P and find the words whose score is closest to this average score. In the examples that follow, we examine the results of this process, entertaining the idea that such a score gives us an index of a changing notion of "average" speech – neither what is trending nor what is disappearing, but average speech relative to other temporal trends, or what might have been most familiar to speakers of all generations.

- **Last gasps**, or those words in each period that are most distinct relative to all the periods that came subsequently. We measure the distinctiveness of each term for Period P relative to all data from the years that follow, which we classify as Period Q. For instance, we might measure the word frequencies of Period P, 1850–59, against the word frequencies of Period Q, 1859–1911. We use statistics to rank the terms that are most specific to Period P, and the highest-ranked terms are those terms that were spoken much less in parliament in the years following 1859 relative to 1850–59: they were the "last gasps" of idioms, concepts, or other words, whose significance declined markedly in the period that followed.

In the sections that follow, the results of using these five categories of analysis will be minutely examined. Carefully reading and comparing the words classified as "distinctive" of each measure of change, we will validate that the algorithms can indeed help scholars to extract and interpret the forces of long-term and short-term change for each period in the past.

Because distinctiveness algorithms can help us to compare any two sets of documents, they represent one of the most useful approaches historians have to make sense of past and future: for any given decade, month, year, week, or day, the distinctiveness algorithm can tell me whether *these* words are closer to the previous or successive period of time. They can even help us to identify which days of time sound the most like moments in the distant past or the distant future.

Why might historians care about such measurements? They might care because measuring whether a set of concepts was only recently introduced or not is the nearest index we have to a revolution in intellectual or political history. Indeed, in two famous studies from data science applied to history – a paper on modeling change in the State of the Union addresses, discussed in Chapter 2, and a paper about influence in the French Congrès, discussed in Chapter 9 – the operative tool for understanding relationships over time was measures of similarity and difference, which represent part of the broader family that distinctiveness algorithms are part of.

In both the State of the Union and French Congrès papers, researchers applied measurements of similarity and difference over time to pull out invisible abstractions about how particular speeches and speakers were oriented in the time. In the grandest version of the researcher's conclusions, similarity holds the key to understanding raw influence over time. Drawing upon the State of the Union and French Congrès papers, I set out to examine more carefully the idea that some individual speeches – and indeed words – might be *closer to the past* or *closer to the future*. I also considered that it was possible to apply the measure in ways that extend in complicate the categories used by the original researchers. After all, there are many varieties of experience that fall outside of the model of simple past/future, and these have to do with the *scale* of proximity. If my words are framed as a response to what colleagues have spoken about over the last year, I might be responsive to recent trends (*near to the short-term past*) while still being radical with respect to the speakers who dominated Congress a decade ago (*far from the long-term past*). Indeed, there are many versions of the past, not one.

The idea that mathematical modeling might hold such a key to understanding the dynamics of historical change over time is compelling – but historians may rightfully be wary of ceding control over interpretation to an algorithm without closer knowledge of its inner workings. For this reason, the rest of this chapter takes a more minute approach to equations than other chapters in this book, explaining each variable that forms part of the tf-idf algorithm. We will also investigate the fact that there are several mathematical approaches to the problem of how one period differs from another. We will compare tf-idf, the classic "distinctiveness" algorithm, to two other mathematical approaches: one called "divergence," conceived of as measuring the "absolute distance" between two sets of documents, rather than pure exclusion; and one called "log-likelihood," conceived of as a probabilistic estimation of the likelihood of each word in two sets of data. The three mathematical approaches produce slightly different answers to the same question: How does one period differ from another period? A robust toolkit mathematical toolkit for detecting the difference between any two sets of documents requires a critical perspective on why a single algorithm is favored.

Understanding multiple mathematical approaches underscores the fact that there is no *one* correct interpretation of the past – even given a single set of data and a precise question like which words are most significant for one period of time. Mathematics gives us precise answers, but it also shows that multiple perspectives on the past are still plausible. In the discussion of these different algorithms, we will entertain the fact that each algorithm displays a "bias" towards a specific understanding of difference. A historian can put these "biased" approaches into dialogue with instructive results. In other words, when statistics supports the examination of historical change, statistics can give us very precise descriptions of change over time, but the historian's skill of critical thinking about historical context is still crucial for engaging the reality of multiple, equally valid interpretations of the past.

The approach laid out in this chapter embodies a "critical search" process applied to algorithms: it leads us through the process of comparing different ways of applying the same algorithm, as well as examining the bias introduced by favoring one algorithm's results over others. Algorithms don't have a simple *natural application* to questions of textual interpretation and historical analysis; rather, they have many possible "fits" with different humanistic questions. It is only in the context of such a critical approach, I believe, that quantitative work can truly support humanistic questions. With critical thinking, algorithms, can provide us with rich comparisons about how we might model the past differently, helping us to meticulously document the value of each new theoretical framework.

Looking over the results in the detail with which we pursue it – down to the precise words classified as "distinctive" of a period by five different definitions of temporal distinction according to three different algorithms – gives analysts an opportunity to engage the work of modeling with a critical eye. As we shall see, detail is what draws the scholar's eye to both the promise and the challenges of the approaches profiled in this chapter.

Tf-idf Revisited

As we noted in Chapter 4 on *critical search*, using algorithms with care requires respect for the fact that algorithms themselves have histories.

Table 10.1 *Contingency table for term frequencies.*

	Period P	Period Q	Total
Term frequency of w	a	b	a+b
Term frequencies of others except w	c	d	c+d
	a+c	b+d	N=a+b+c+d

Distinctiveness algorithms are a big family, and each algorithm operates via a model that creates a "gate" that bars certain words and allows others via slight differences in the mathematical formalization of how similarity and distinction are defined.

In this chapter, we will dive into the mathematics of the algorithm in order to specify how tf-idf differs from its near cousins, log-likelihood and divergence. To illustrate the approach, we will walk through the equation, explaining how it applies to a keyword that we are searching for, w, in our document collection. Imagine that we have divided our document collection into two stacks which represent two time periods, Period P and Period Q. The equation produces a score ranking how "distinctive" term w is of Period P.

The tf-idf of term w within Period P, given two periods, can be defined as:

$$tf - idf = \frac{tf(w, P)}{idf(w, \{P, Q\})} = \frac{f_{w,P}}{\log \frac{D}{n_w}},$$

– where $f_{w,P}$ is the term frequency of word w in Period P, D is the total number of documents, and n_w is the number of documents where the term w appears.[1]

The same information is summarized in a simplified way in Table 10.1 and the equation below it, which may make the algorithm above more accessible to readers without a mathematical background.

We see in the simplified view that the equation depends on taking the word frequency of each word in Period P and Period Q. The frequency of word w in Period P is given as a (in the equation the same information is given as "$f_{w,P}$" – the frequency of each term, w, in period P). Another variable, b, is how often the term appears in Period Q. The other variables,

---

[1] Note that there are various ways to define term frequency and inverse document frequency. See C. D. Manning, P. Raghavan, and H. Schütze, *Introduction to Information Retrieval* (Cambridge: Cambridge University Press, 2008). Many thanks to statisticians Ming Zhang and Charles South for the explanations of the equations in this chapter.

c and *d*, are the count of all other words (excepting word *w*) in periods P and Q. Here, we entertain the case where there are only two periods – which is true for all of the examples in this chapter. $\mathbb{I}(a > 0)$ is an indicator function, which is equal to 1 if a>0 and 0 otherwise.

$$\log \frac{\frac{a}{D}}{\mathbb{I}(a>0)+\mathbb{I}(b>0)},$$

Some measures, like tf-idf, essentially have an either/or definition of distinction: a word is "distinctive" of this set of documents, according to the measurements of tf-idf, if that word appears almost nowhere else. Other distinctiveness algorithms, such as log-likelihood, have a more generous definition of distinctiveness; they will rank as "distinctive" of my document a word that I use a great deal, even if the word also appears elsewhere quite frequently. Later in this chapter, we will compare tf-idf with two of its cousins – partial Jensen-Shannon divergence (JSD) and the log-likelihood ratio.

The following experiments have been standardized to facilitate the comparison of different methods. We will compare the results of each of these processes to those of tf-idf, investigating how the measure of the mainstream, what is absolutely new and what is trending, and the temporal fossil, all produce different windows on the past. In each case, we will be working on the scale of decades, setting aside the questions of temporal granularity that we have explored previously. We will strip our results of the controlled vocabularies of parliamentary business, world geographies, and ethnic identities that produced such compelling results in previous case studies. Instead, we will be peering into the raw output of the algorithms, asking: What hidden dynamics of change does each algorithm illuminate?

Period Distinctiveness, or the Distinctiveness of Each Period Compared to Every Other Period

The first of the approaches we're profiling in this chapter is tf-idf, the algorithm that we adjusted in Chapter 8 to measure the distinctiveness of particular periods. In Chapter 8, we established that distinctiveness can be used to classify words that are essentially "temporal fossils" of a certain period – they are used in a single decade but were not highly relevant before or after. For the results in Figure 10.1, I've used a slight adjustment to the process we used in Chapter 8 to select the word. Whereas in Chapter 8 we used a controlled vocabulary of some 3,000 words

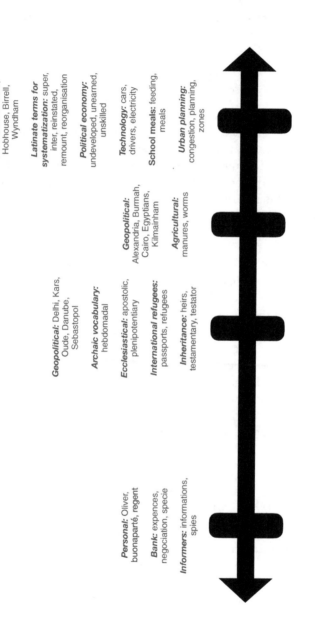

Personal: Oliver, buonaparté, regent

Bank: expences, negociation, specie

Informers: informations, spies

Geopolitical: Delhi, Kars, Oude, Danube, Sebastopol

Archaic vocabulary: hebdomadal

Ecclesiastical: apostolic, plenipotentiary

International refugees: passports, refugees

Inheritance: heirs, testamentary, testator

Geopolitical: Alexandria, Burmah, Cairo, Egyptians, Kilmainham

Agricultural: manures, worms

Personal: Haldane, Hobhouse, Birrell, Wyndham

Latinate terms for systematization: super, inter, reinstated, remount, reorganisation

Political economy: undeveloped, unearned, unskilled

Technology: cars, drivers, electricity

School meals: feeding, meals

Urban planning: congestion, planning, zones

1810   1850   1880   1900

Figure 10.1   Temporal fossils: The words most distinctive of four periods (1810–19, 1850–59, 1880–89, 1900–09) as measured against all other periods in the corpus (1806–1911), ranked by tf-idf. Using SMU Hansard.

preselected from the full list of vocabulary to highlight those aspects of language that look most like concerns or subjects of political debate, here we have used no controlled vocabulary.

The results of this method are more specific as to personal and geographical names than the results in the preceding chapter. In their messiness and variety, the full vocabulary detected by tf-idf tells us much more about how the algorithm is modeling time.

In 1810–19, the cast of characters are that of the Napoleonic Wars and the Regency; there is "Oliver" the spy, the "Buonaparté" partisans of Napoleon, and the regent himself; in 1850–59, the Indian provinces involved in reports of the Great Rebellion in India are on display ("Delhi," "Kars," "Oude") alongside references to Crimean geography ("Danube," "Sebastopol"); in 1880–89, the stage has shifted to the Egyptian, Burmese, and Irish frontiers of empire ("Alexandria," "Burmah," "Cairo," "Egyptians," "Kilmainham"); and in 1900–09 the characters who appear are the leaders of late debates about liberalism and empire ("Haldane," "Hobhouse") as well as the designers of new imperial policies ("Birrell," "Wyndham").

We also see certain idiosyncrasies of parliamentary rhetoric go in and out of fashion – the 1810–19 habits of writing "expences" and "negociation" would soon be subject to a spelling reform; in 1850–59, parliamentarians referenced weekly meetings with the Greek borrowing "hebdomadal"; 1880 shows relatively few such rhetorical idiosyncrasies, while in 1900–09 an entire wealth of neologisms entered parliamentary use, apparently a fashion for the abstraction of managerial processes via the free application of Latinate prepositions and reduplicative or negative prefixes ("inter," "super," "reinstated," "remount," "reorganization," "undeveloped," "unearned," "unskilled").

Having dispensed with geographical, personal, and rhetorical fashions, this measure leaves us with the temporal fossils that distinguish each period, which more or less correspond to those we saw in Chapter 8. 1810–19 is the era of debates over the bank ("expences," "specie"), and a campaign of spying that targeted working-class organizations ("informations," "spies"). 1850–59 appears as the era of debates over the church ("apostolic," "plenipotentiary"), citizenship ("passports," "refugees"), and the laws of inheritance ("heirs," "testamentary," "testator"). 1880–89 appears as the era of debates over agriculture ("manures," "worms"). 1900–09 appears as the era of governing the machine age ("cars," "drivers," "electricity"), of school meals ("feeding," "meals"), as well as the classification of the abstract arenas of land necessitated by land-use planning ("congestion," "planning," "zones").

The timing and list of most of these categories will come as no surprise to historians of nineteenth-century Britain. The fact that the results are little surprising serves to validate the method as a whole, even while the details help us to understand what is highlighted and suppressed by each method – a theme that I will draw out as we move from application to application. Nonetheless, as we saw in Chapter 8, strategies of this kind often raise some historical mysteries, even on a well-read corpus like the *Hansard* parliamentary debates. Why the rage for "chicory" in 1850? Who was the "wiseman" of the same decade?

In previous chapters, I took pains to look up many historical mysteries and provide at least a provisional answer to why they appeared, thus validating that the techniques of digital history are capable of delivering new results even in the well-plowed sphere of British history. In the current chapter, pursuing the algorithm, we will mainly leave historical insight to some later interpreters. Suffice it to say that a few of the artifacts generated by inquiries with tf-idf direct the reader to new information. The 'screw' that was so novel in the debates of the 1850s according to absolute historical novelty, Table 10.2 row 2 refers to the "screw propeller," adopted in naval vessel, which was referred to by some speakers as an invention equal in importance to the electric telegraph.[2] The role of 'cloture' that differentiates the 1880s from other periods is already known to historians of parliamentary procedure as the new invention of cutting short the long-winded speeches that Americans call 'filibusters,' which contemporary MP's had begun to associate with the tyranny of minorities over the democratic process.[3] The rise or fall of the occurrence of the word indicates that an event of some significance occurred. Yet questions of interpretation remain at the fore. Before the end of the chapter, we will meet another measure of distinctiveness that reveals that the words "cheer" and "laughter" were published more frequently in Hansard in the 1900s than in the previous decade. Did the 1900s have more "cheer" and "laughter" overall than previous decades, or did the journalists who recorded the parliamentary debates merely cite affectual rituals with greater regularity in that decade – and if that's the case, why did they?[4] While

---

[2] Debate on "Screw Propellers," House of Commons (May 15, 1855).

[3] Kari Palonen, "Fair Play and Scarce Time: Aspects of the 1882 Procedure Reform Debates in the British Parliament," in Kari Palonen, José María Rosales, and Tapani Turkka, eds., *The Politics of Dissensus: Parliament in Debate* (Santander, Spain: Cantabria University Press, 2014), 329–345.

[4] 'Cheer' and 'laughter' are ranked as distinctive of the 1900s according to log likelihood measurements of distinctiveness; see Table 10.4.

overall familiar to a historian, the timeline suggested by tf-idf presents moments in the history of the century that are surprising given the published record of the past: these moments may be interpreted either as evidence of the shortcomings of the measure, or as evidence of events overlooked by historians that call for further study.

Professors of British history or their classrooms might engage the methods on view in this chapter by engaging in a simple exercise. For each of the words and numbers listed in Table 10.2, they might ask: of what historical event are these words a reflection? And: what is genuinely novel here; do any of these words or numbers help us to identify historical events of which historians were previously unaware, or to understand historical events in a new way?

If the game of looking up words produced by the algorithm seems jejune, one might usefully remember the promise that came packaged with the algorithm: *the words produced by this process are guaranteed to be of historical significance of one sort or another;* they are genuinely new to this corpus at the time mentioned, and they are numerous enough to indicate some historical trend. *What* exactly "chicory" or "hebdomadal" signal is another question, and it is a matter for the craft of historical interpretation, not for the elucidation of mathematical models.

Dynamics of Long-term Change, or the Distinctiveness of each Period Relative to Previous Periods

When we measure absolute change from all historical periods in the past, we are literally taking half the measure of distinctiveness in general that we saw in the previous section, and subsetting just the words that are distinctive from the past. The measure gives us a glance at *absolute historical novelty* – the words that were new in parliament in any given decade. In Figure 10.2 and Table 10.2, we see two views of the words elevated by this measure. In 1810–19, discussions of banking are fundamentally new ("cash, circulation, coin, currency, gold, payments"), as are discussions of the growing populism visible from the working classes ("classes," "Manchester," "meeting," "meetings," "petitioner," "petitions"). In 1850–09, subjects of historical novelty include details about empire which were introduced in the 1850s but may have been talked about past 1859 ("Madras," "Hong Kong"). In 1880–89, we see the Irish Land War in greater detail ("boycotting," "crowd," "crofters," Donegal," "highlands," "leaseholders") – terms that would remain part of debate for the

Table 10.2 *Results with Tf-idf: Using scores between each period and all other periods to understand change over time, with duplications filtered.*

Name	Measure	1810	1850	1880	1900
Period Distinctiveness	Difference from All Other Periods	1806, 1809, blasphemous, buonaparté, controul, disaffected, expences, genoa, grady, informations, lottery, negociation, oliver, quin, regent, retreat, specie, spies	abjuration, apostolic, aylesbury, balaklava, bennett, berkeley, chicory, crampton, dalhousie, danube, delhi, dovor, dundas, enniskillen, gallantry, halls, hebdomadal, heirs, incumbered, juvenile, kars, leonards, lucan, malins, nominees, oude, panmure, partnership, passports, plenipotentiaries, plenipotentiary, principalities, proctors, raglan, redcliffe, refugees, rothschild, sadleir, sebastopol, sewers, siege, spooner, stratford, testamentary, testator, thesiger, torrington, unrestricted, vernon, wiseman	affirmation, alexandria, andrew's, arabi, assheton, barclay, bayonets, berber, biggar, bondholders, bradlaugh, broadhurst, burmah, cairo, callan, candahar, cell, clifford, clôture, conybeare, depositions, dufferin, egyptians, evelyn, forfarshire, harman, harrington, holmes, horncastle, illingworth, jesse, kenny, kilmainham, manures, molloy, peter, raikes, randolph, reporter, roche, rossendale, saunderson, swore, toxteth, venue, warren, warton, wolff, woodstock, worms	1900, 1902, applicant, austen, banbury, birrell, bona, botha, cars, commonwealth, congestion, critics, depot, drivers, electricity, feeding, granite, guillotine, haldane, hampshire, hobbhouse, inter, lyttelton, macedonia, mckenna, meals, nottinghamshire, planning, regulars, reinstated, remount, remounts, reorganisation, retaliation, rosyth, sinclair, socialism, substitutes, super, tibet, undenominational, undeveloped, unearned, units, unskilled, vendor, walton, worcestershire, wyndham, zones

	1850, 1851, 1852, 1853, 1854, 1855, 1856, 1857, 1858,	1880, 1881, 1882, 1883, 1884, 1885, 1886, 1887, 1888,	1901, 1903, 1904, 1905, 1906, 1907, 1908, 1909,
Absolute Historical Novelty	allies, american, apprehended, capital, cash, circulation, city, classes, coin, commercial, community, confined, crime, currency, distinguished, distress, expense, favourable, gold, inhabitants, inquire, issued, liberties, list, magistrates, maintained, manchester, meeting, meetings, notes, payments, petitioner, petitions, population, protestant, reduction, religious, repeal, respectable, restriction, roman, show, signed, society, sovereign, speaker, statute, suspension, temporary, wellington		
Change from All Previous Periods	admirals, audit, burial, camp, canon, carlisle, civilisation, commissariat, convocation, crimea, disraeli, exceptional, fleets, gibson, granville, henley, herbert, hong, inch, inland, kong, madras, malmesbury, marry, pakington, papal, pictures, probate, procedure, requirements, retrospective, russians, screw, seymour, tiverton, trained, walpole, whiteside, wife's, wore	allotments, bethnal, boycotting, camborne, chaplin, churchill, closure, crofter, crofters, crowd, dillon, donegal, fergusson, fowler, girl, gorst, healy, highlands, jackson, khartoum, leaseholders, lothian, macdonald, matthews, miners, monaghan, morley, nationalist, northampton, paddington, policemen, rack, ritchie, sexton, soudan, stanhope, suakin, tanner, thanet, tunnel, tyne	academic, advisory, afforestation, akers, betting, brewery, cathcart, cd, craig, crewe, destroyers, dreadnoughts, driver, gravesend, hotels, indentured, landless, laundries, lessor, montgomery, motor, motorists, organise, peking, personnel, pit, plots, policies, possibilities, recruited, residential, runciman, shetland, shortage, somaliland, stepney, storage, strachey, tuberculosis, underlying, unemployment, untenanted

Table 10.2 (*cont.*)

Name	Measure	1810	1850	1880	1900
Trends	Change from Immediately Previous Period	20, adoption, advanced, alarm, ancient, arose, article, bullion, colonies, constitutional, continent, corpus, death, depreciation, discretion, doctrine, economy, efforts, employment, especially, gentleman's, habeas, houses, human, imposed, labour, libel, magistrate, manufactures, market, marquis, met, names, peculiar, persuaded, portion, prevailed, prevented, revolution, secure, severe, silver, spoken, standard, statements, ten, thanks, town, twenty, william	adultery, allied, annexation, balances, campaign, cardinal, chancellors, commanders, commissioned, conferences, contingent, deductions, depositors, director, divorce, examinations, founders, garrison, generals, infantry, ladies, licence, lyndhurst, mutiny, neutral, neutrality, officials, organisation, peerages, persian, plymouth, polling, recruiting, recruits, reformatory, scholars, scripture, secrecy, serjeant, sinking, stamps, suitors, superannuation, ticket, trustee, turks, volunteer, volunteers, wills, woolwich	antrim, armagh, bail, baring, bolton, boycotted, caithness, cameron, cardiff, clark, conversion, cruisers, drummond, electric, ellis, fitzgerald, furniture, george's, gibson, hanover, inverness, kerry, labouchere, lighting, lloyd, longford, nationalists, northcote, o'brien, o'donnell, orangemen, outdoor, patrick, pier, preston, redistribution, riots, seed, sligo, someone, starvation, strand, stuart, tithe, trafalgar, unionist, webster, wicklow, wolverhampton	bible, bonus, buller, cadets, cargo, conscription, coolies, cowper, deck, douglas, earl's, eighteen, eighty, exchanges, flogging, flour, gloucestershire, grocers, gulf, hop, hops, indians, irrigation, japanese, kennedy, meal, minister's, mounted, nineteen, ninety, persia, persian, primate, protectionist, purchases, redvers, reformers, settlers, seventeen, seventy, sheridan, sixteen, smoking, somersetshire, tariffs, thirteen, trees, tydvil, vehicles, wife's

Typical Speech of Period			1851, 1862, 700, adoption, age, aright, asia, autonomy, beneficent, birkenhead, bodmin, butt, carries, cemeteries, cheaply, considers, contains, contemplates, defining, exactly, facilitating, fired, fore, fraction, group, hearted, junction, ministry, minutes, neighbourhood, overtime, passenger, patients, pleaded, pleasure, practising, printed, provoke, reductions, representation, salmon, signs, simplify, slaughter, speaks, stopped, substantial, taxed, today, wales	
Words of Average Distinctiveness	100, 25, 40, abolition, accede, accomplished, advantageous, ample, argued, articles, create, criminal, declare, deemed, disturbances, documents, doubts, erroneous, escape, ex, exceed, fixed, freedom, habit, habits, happened, injured, intentions, james, loyalty, owed, prayer, preferred, prerogative, pretence, principally, privilege, proposing, propositions, recourse, remark, restoration, sanction, sending, sheriff, solely, step, substance, supplies, viscount	20, 25, accepting, adhere, admirably, advice, africa, alarm, amounted, annum, appropriation, arrears, ashamed, attendant, benefices, capture, chapter, circumstance, communicate, containing, criminal, critical, dear, deserved, destroyed, endeavour, erect, fide, gradually, handed, happened, justices, minor, obligation, parishioners, promises, purchases, purely, pursuits, rapid, reasonable, redemption, remaining, respectable, salary, simple, sovereigns, twelve, weather, westminster		85, abatements, anywhere, batteries, break, bull, chelmsford, clay, communicate, considerations, considers, contain, coronation, crews, defined, dimensions, drew, ealing, egyptian, exact, face, freights, gorst, handing, infectious, lane, leaders, liabilities, lot, omission, ordering, outdoor, oxford, prescribed, publish, quantities, quotation, recommendation, securing, sharp, sittings, speculative, stock, students, technically, thank, theory, thomas, unfairness, yourself
Difference from All Future Periods	enquiry, expence, gent			
Last Gasps		1837, 1838, adverting, alma, amicable, anxiously, assuredly, baltic, bowring, bullion, calamities,	1899, african, answered, battalions, beer, belfast, birmingham, boroughs, cape, colonel, contracts,	

Table 10.2 (*cont.*)

Name	Measure	1810	1850	1880	1900
			canton, ceremony, confided, connexion, devolved, diemen's, divorces, duncombe, ellenborough, emanated, encumbered, endured, et, functionaries, funded, harry, hogg, hume, inglis, inkerman, jew, jewish, jurisprudence, kidderminster, legion, legislatures, lucknow, mather, midhurst, mighty, monteagle, persevered, phillimore, revolt, sepoys, stonor, synod, thence, valour	characterized, childers, cholera, civilization, civilized, clads, clarke, coercive, cognizance, creditor, criticize, dundalk, dungarvan, ejectment, emigrants, enfranchisement, enterprize, excellency, granville, hartington, innocence, ipswich, khedive, northbrook, oaths, organization, organized, plunket, realize, realized, recognize, recognized, recollected, remedial, reporters, rylands, sympathize, sympathized, wilfrid, zululand	convention, corporation, corps, denominational, dr, farms, hoped, insert, inserted, justices, landlords, lease, letters, magistrates, managers, manchester, militia, o'clock, objected, page, premises, profit, rents, river, sell, showed, subsection, sunday, teacher, transfer, transvaal, urban, urged, ventured, volunteer, volunteers, william, wished, yeomanry

Source: Hansard Parliamentary Debates of Great Britain, all words with counts > 200 and more than one letter

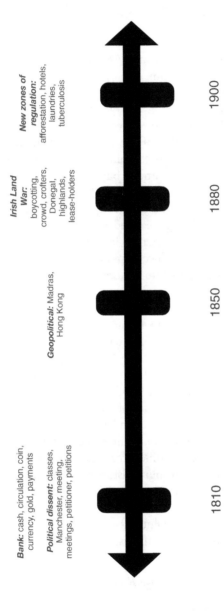

Bank: cash, circulation, coin, currency, gold, payments

Political dissent: classes, Manchester, meeting, meetings, petitioner, petitions

Geopolitical: Madras, Hong Kong

Irish Land War: boycotting, crowd, crofters, Donegal, highlands, lease-holders

New zones of regulation: afforestation, hotels, laundries, tuberculosis

1810   1850   1880   1900

Figure 10.2   Historical novelty: The words most distinctive of four periods (1810–19, 1850–59, 1880–89, 1900–09) as measured against all data from each period's relative past (back to 1806), ranked by tf-idf. Using SMU Hansard.

next decade or more, which is why they were excluded from the Period Distinctiveness measure. In 1900–10, new topics of debate include a grab-bag of new zones for government regulation: "afforestation," "hotels," "laundries," and "tuberculosis."

Some degree of overlap between rows 1 and 2 in Table 10.2 should be expected. Period Distinctiveness and Absolute Historical Novelty both depend on measurement from the past; in the case of Period Distinctiveness, distance from the past is combined with distance from the present. In Table 10.2 we have avoided overlap by simply avoiding duplicating any words found in row 1 when it comes to row 2.

Nevertheless, the near overlap of the results between rows 1 and 2 in Table 10.2 offers a good reason to think carefully about what is being measured. Indeed, there are distortions built into the dataset by way of a simple fact: the dataset has a beginning (1806) and an end (1911) that limit how much we know about historical change towards the data's edges. In 1810–19, distinctiveness is being measured against only a few years of scantily recorded debate. Indeed, the dataset begins only in 1806. The measure of distinctiveness for 1810–19 produces virtually the same answers for Period Distinctiveness (row 1) and Absolute Historical novelty (row 2). The opposite is true at the other edge of the century, in 1900–09, when there are relatively few debates in the relative future of 1910–11. The measure of Absolute Historical Novelty for 1910–11 in Figure 10.2 is measured only against a handful of debates, and the novelty of certain terms has been overrated. What we see here is an issue of "edge effects," or the warping of the measures of time at either end of the dataset. We shall say more about the distorting power of the beginning end of datasets in the conclusion to this chapter.

Thinking about the precise contents of the words elevated by our measure of historical novelty can help us to understand what the measure in its present state does and doesn't do. Unlike the "temporal fossils" in the previous section, that were in fashion for a brief period of time but then disappeared, the indicators of absolute historical novelty usually remained in circulation for some time – whether for another decade or for the remainder of the century. With greater nuance to this measure, it would be possible to detect the terms related to absolute historical novelty that remained in circulation till the century's end – that is, the *lasting contributions*.

Trends, or Short-term Change Relative to the Immediate Past

With a third measure, we look for short-term trends. A short-term trend is distinguished from a long-term trend by the length of the measure. Here,

I'm searching for novelty that shows up when a single decade is compared with the decade immediately previous (Figure 10.3)

In 1850–59, the search for short-term trends shows us a handful of words about political and military trends that might well have appeared first with the Napoleonic Wars but been renewed with the Crimean War ("annexation," "balances," "campaign," "chancellors," "garrison," "generals," "infantry," "neutral," "neutrality," "serjeant," "volunteer," "volunteers."). Another set of words refers to the law of marriage as it relates to women, likely alluded to in the debates over Married Women's Property. ("adultery," "divorce," "suitors"). 1880–89, the method reveals terms that were previously used for a variety of welfare topics, but which appeared with renewed vigor in debates about the Irish Land War ("redistribution," "riots,"). In 1900–09, the trends include the new formula of writing out words less than a hundred, mentions of ethnicity that I assume to be labor around the edges of an expanding empire ("coolies," "Japanese," "Persia," "Persian").

By comparing these words with the words from the previous section, we find that we have an index whether each of these terms had a history before 1880; in the case of "redistribution," the term has a history of political debate in the earlier half of the century, but then underwent a revival after 1880, which results in the high ranking according to a measure of short-term trends but a low ranking in terms of absolute historical novelty.

Again, edge effects matter. There is an enormous overlap between this approach and the approach of historical novelty from the previous section, and that overlap is especially visible at the edges of the dataset, that is, for the periods 1800–09 and 1900–09. For the period 1900–09, there is no difference at all between these two approaches, and we would expect a total overlap between the first columns of row 2 and row 3 of Table 10.2. But for the middle of the century, searching for short-term trends means searching for what is distinctive in 1850–59 from 1840–49, as opposed to a search for long-term change, where novelty in 1850–59 is measured against the preceding half century since 1806.

An Index of the Typical Speech of the Period, or Words That Are Neither Very Distant to Other Periods nor Exactly the Same

A very different measure than the previous, average tf-idf is a tool for finding those words that are neither burning with the fire of intellectual change nor totally in a state of overlap from one moment to the next. Statistician Bill Blatt has used similar measures to sample the difference between the textual style of literary figures, noting that each author

Crimean War:
annexation, balances,
campaign, chancellors,
garrison, generals,
infantry, neutral,
neutrality, serjeant,
volunteer, volunteers

Marriage Law: adultery,
divorce, suitors

**Social conflict over
ownership:**
redistribution, riots

Geopolitical:
Coolies, Japanese,
Persia, Persian

1850   1880   1900

Figure 10.3   Short-term trends: The words most distinctive of four periods (1810–19, 1850–59, 1880–89, 1900–09) as measured against the period immediately previous to each, ranked by tf-idf. Using SMU Hansard.

preferentially uses a specific set of relatively rare words that operate almost like a fingerprint to their identity. With the measure of average tf-idf, the "flavor" of each period is on view.

The reading of the words in Figure 10.4 looks like a catalog of temporary virtues; they are general enough that they could well appear in other moments of the past, but they are tilted towards one era. In 1800–09, "freedom," "prayer," and "habit;" in 1850–59, "capture," "ashamed," "obligation," and "promises;" in 1880–89.

Using average tf-idf or any other such average is more of an art than a science, in distinction to the other measures, where we may say with certainty that a word ranked distinctive of one period against others appears preponderantly in that time. An *average* tf-idf score suggests that the word-period combination is meaningful – but meaningful in comparison to what? In a serious investigation of these trends, the researcher would be best served by counting "freedom," "prayer," and "habit" over the parliamentary debates; in fact, none of these terms has a numerical profile that is particularly remarkable for the period.

Last Gasps, or Those Words in each Period That Are Most Distinct Relative to All the Periods that Came Subsequently

This measure detects what is disappearing. It is the inverse of the measure of "historical novelty." Here, instead of measuring the distance of each period from the entire relative past, we measure the distinctiveness of each period relative to the entire relative future (Figure 10.5).

In 1850–09, a cultural shift betokened by the fact that such values as the "amicable," "ceremony," and "valour" appeared almost never again after 1859 – the sign, perhaps, of a vanishing aristocratic culture? After 1880-89, consensus about "civilization" and the "civilized" seems to have vanished from parliament's debates about empire. After 1889, the euphemism "ejectment" was generally replaced by the more direct phrase "eviction," after a spate of evictions of Irish peasants was problematized by the events of the Land War. Most references to years follow a common pattern; the years of a decade and immediately preceding it are among the most distinctive of each period by any measure. But the measure of "last gasps" helps us to notice how some years lingered in the imagination, for instance 1837, the year of Victoria's coronation, which remained a regular reference through the 1850s.

Here is material mainly unfamiliar to the historian. The disappearances of ideas and the finalization of certain debates is all but impossible to

Enlightenment order: freedom, prayer, habit

Interior states of order: capture, ashamed, obligation, promises

1810

1850

Figure 10.4   Typical speech: The words most distinctive of four periods (1810–19, 1850–59, 1880–89, 1900–09) as measured by an average tf-idf score for the period, when measured against all other periods in the corpus. The results of this measure do not appear to be meaningful. Using SMU Hansard.

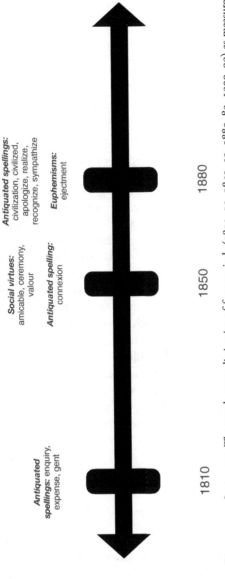

**Antiquated
spellings:** enquiry,
expense, gent

1810

Social virtues:
amicable, ceremony,
valour

Antiquated spelling:
connexion

1850

Antiquated spellings:
civilization, civilized,
apologize, realize,
recognize, sympathize

Euphemisms:
ejectment

1880

Figure 10.5 Last gasps: The words most distinctive of four periods (1810–19, 1850–59, 1880–89, 1900–09) as measured against all data from each period's relative future (up to 1911), ranked by tf-idf. Using SMU Hansard.

detect, no matter how sensitive the reader, via conventional approaches. Investigating the closure of debates offers a compelling project for future conceptual research.

Some of the findings are trivial. In 1810–19 the only trend disappearing are those spellings that were on the cusp of being readjusted – "enquiry" and "expense" – along with "gent" as an abbreviation for "gentleman." The antiquated spelling "connexion" disappears after 1859. Similarly, certain spellings still used in 1880–89 would never again be printed ("apologize," "realize," "recognize," and "sympathize").

Edge effects appear again. There is simply not enough data in 1910–11 for the list of "last gasps" from 1900–09 to be meaningful.

Analysis of Tf-idf

Each separate application of tf-idf to long-term difference, long-term and short-term past, average present, and futurity highlights some aspects of historical experience while suppressing others. In the name of making visible these tensions, I give two different representations of the work of the tf-idf algorithm. I show the words described in the prose, hand-gathered from a list of the top 200 words by each method, in Figures 10.1–10.5. There is, as we shall see, a great deal of overlap between the results of the different measurements. By moving between these figures, the reader can easily compare each application of tf-idf, witnessing the overlap between approaches as I comment on it.

While there is overlap, each application of tf-idf produces a genuinely different model of the distinctiveness of each historical period. I gather the top 50 words returned by each method in Table 10.2, subtracting all words that have been already displayed in the previous rows, such that the terms that appear in 'period distinctiveness (row 1) have already been deleted from rows 2–5. Thus there is no overlap, and Table 10.2 serves to highlight the novel contribution of each measure to a sense of temporal distinctiveness.

Comparison with Partial JSD Divergence

Divergence measures are a broad set of tools used for comparing two arrays. These tools date back to the Second World War when cryptographers at Bletchley Park – among them a mathematician named Solomon Kullback, who was later employed by the US National Security Agency – were developing techniques for testing strings of encoded German that mirrored the patterns of Germany grammar, patterns which, without this knowledge, seemed like random noise. Kullback's tools for deciphering noise would be taken up after the war by Claude Shannon, who had been working for the AT&T company, which was in the process of perfecting audio quality in the telephone. Shannon developed a measure of "telephony" or audio quality, distinguishing how much of a given conversation conveyed through the phone was *information* and how much was *noise*.

Digital humanists still use divergence algorithms derived from the work of these forebears of the information revolution. Although the algorithms known as "Kullback–Leibler" and "Jensen–Shannon" each employ slightly different formulae, they are both potent tools for matching what mathematicians call "distance" between two texts. All matches of distance start from similar bases: high counts of the same unusual features signify overall similarity. If A exhibits an unusual feature which B lacks, that disparity gives one sign of distance. If the algorithm assigns high scores to many of the words from Periods P and Q, then we can say that the two documents are highly distinct.

Distance measures are more subtle than pure distinctiveness measures like tf-idf. While divergence measures can be used to compare two periods of time, part of their beauty is that they not only measure the *quantity* of change from era to era, but also allow the scholar to identify the particular words whose *proportions* changed the most. A distinctiveness algorithm like tf-idf might not pick up on a subtly increasing proportion of a term which was used frequently in one decade but whose usage was amplified in the next decade. A divergence algorithm would pick up on this change. As the partial JSD score gives us an index of words whose relative frequency is greater in Period P than Period Q, this information can be used to characterize the cultural forces that were trending at any moment in time. If Tf-idf works like a Venn diagram – finding anything said after 1850 but not before 1850 – partial JSD works more like a graduated scale, finding the trends that appear before and after a given date.

Applied to the problem of modernity, divergence measures allow scholars to accurately measure any two strings of information and detect how much is "lost." In the 1990s, Patrick Juola, a professor of computer science at Duquesne University, initiated some of the earliest experiments in text mining to understand historical change, leveraging divergence to measure the text of *Time* magazine in the 1950s with that of *Time* magazine in each subsequent decade. The more information was "lost" from the original sample, Juola argued, the greater the evidence of cultural change.

In the digital humanities, recent work has made enormous strides toward understanding temporality by deploying measures of this kind. Measurement of topic frequency in the State of the Union speeches in the United States, for example, defined four moments of discontinuity.[5] Tim Hitchcock and Simon DeDeo examined lexicon change in the records of the Old Bailey and found that "violence" was the semantic category of terms whose counts underwent the most significant transition over time, with descriptions of violent crime undergoing a marked decrease over the course of the eighteenth and nineteenth century.[6] More broadly, a budding industry of keyword counting and statistical comparison has made preliminary approaches to both intellectual history and the genesis of the nineteenth-century novel.[7] In the context of parliamentary debates, divergence measures have been used to highlight the relationship between individual speakers and change.[8] In the paragraphs that follow, this chapter will emulate that work by focusing on individual speakers, with some meditations on the promise and limits of that method.

In the following experiments, we will be using a partial JSD measure. In their paper on the French Revolution, Alexander Barron's team broke up Shannon's original equation into two halves – one to measure distance from the aggregate past and one to measure distance from the aggregate future. They called the resulting halves of the equation *partial* because it represents one part of Jensen–Shannon's original equation. In the example that follows, we will work with the halves of this pulled-apart equation, inspecting the results of measuring Period P against its relative past and future.

The Partial JSD (*pJSD*) between documents P and Q – with respect to term *w* as presented in Table 10.1 - can be written as

[5] Jean-Philippe Cointet, Alix Rule and Peter S. Bearman, "Lexical Shifts, Substantive Changes, and Continuity in State of the Union Discourse, 1790–2014," *PNAS (Proceedings of the National Academy of the Sciences)* 112:35 (August 10, 2015): 10837–44, https://doi.org/10.1073/pnas.1512221112.

[6] Simon DeDeo et al., "Bootstrap Methods for the Empirical Study of Decision-Making and Information Flows in Social Systems," *Entropy* 15:6 (June 5, 2013): 2246–76, https://doi.org/10.3390/e15062246; Sara Klingenstein, Tim Hitchcock, and Simon DeDeo, "The Civilizing Process in London's Old Bailey," *Proceedings of the National Academy of Sciences* 111:26 (July 1, 2014): 9419–24, https://doi.org/10.1073/pnas.1405984111.

[7] Peter De Bolla, *The Architecture of Concepts: The Historical Formation of Human Rights* (New York: Fordham University Press, 2013); Matthew Lee Jockers, *Macroanalysis: Digital Methods and Literary History* (Urbana, IL: University of Illinois Press, 2017); Dan Edelstein, "Intellectual History and Digital Humanities," *Modern Intellectual History* 13:1 (2016): 237–46.

[8] Alexander T. J. Barron et al., "Individuals, Institutions, and Innovation in the Debates of the French Revolution," *Proceedings of the National Academy of Sciences* 115:18 (May 1, 2018): 4607–12, https://doi.org/10.1073/pnas.1717729115.

$$pJSD(P\|Q) = KL(P\|R) = KL\left(P\|\frac{P+Q}{2}\right),$$

where $KL(P\|R)$ is the Kullback-Leibler Divergence between two distributions associated with documents P and R, which is defined as

$$KL(P\|R) = p(\text{term } w \text{ in } P) \log_2\left(\frac{p(\text{term } w \text{ in } P)}{p(\text{term } w \text{ in } R)}\right).$$

Thus, a large partial JSD is associated with a wider distance between two documents, which implies that two documents are distinct with respect to the chosen word.

Using the counts of word w for Period P and Period Q laid out in the contingency table in Table 10.1, the equation can be simplified this way:

$$\frac{a}{a+c} \log_2 2 \frac{a/(a+c)}{\left(\frac{a}{a+c} + \frac{b}{b+d}\right)}$$

Applied to the question of periodization, the general chronology produced by using JSD matches that from the other measures – the Bank of England and popular rebellion emerge as the chief issues of 1810–19; the Crimea and Indian Rebellion show up for 1850–59; and Ireland and Egypt are at the top of the list for 1880–89.

The most important contribution of partial JSD is in the use of the average partial JSD score for each period to identify the speech typical of that period. Here, the ranking is more accurate than tf-idf.

Unlike with average tf-idf, the average JSD scores seem to be valid. For each term, there is at least a small relative rise for each of these terms in the data, even if other decades show renewed interest in them. The method suggests that a scholar could usefully peruse the thousand words ranked by JSD for the period, using free association to detect a variety of cultural trends that might otherwise escape notice.

The eighteenth-century vocabulary classified as 'last gasps' shows other dramatic changes that were not so visible through tf-idf. The vocabulary of the era 1810–9 includes references 'nature' and 'liberty' and moves through a language of enlightened, cognitive comparison, embodied by the terms 'consideration,' 'cause,' 'concluded,' observed,' and 'principles.' By 1850, the rational language of the eighteenth century has been replaced by a public discourse of embodied emotion and public respectability constructed by the avowal of terms such as "faith," "feelings," "felt," "honour," "manner," "opinion," "religion," and "spiritual." Also noteworthy is the fact that the term "Jews" appears as a "last gasp" of the same period, suggesting that parliamentarians were reluctant to reference the identity in debate after the election of Benjamin Disraeli, the nation's first (albeit only) person of Jewish descent in that role (whether attacks on the Jewish people in Britain likewise diminished after 1859 is a matter for closer reading of the debates alongside other sources).

Other results of partial JSD (Table 10.3) are surprising. The most "distant" word for practically every comparison between eras were also the most common words in English – "the," "of," "to," "that," etc. (see row 1). Even more generous than log-likelihood, JSD overlaps with tf-idf and log-likelihood, but also includes a wider variety of the common words often classed as "stop words" and therefore excluded from data analysis ("so," "he," "has"). Comparisons of stop words have been shown to be useful for several purposes in text mining, for example in author identification, where patterns of usage of even very frequent words vary by author in a telltale fashion.[9]

I propose that JSD represents the best strategy for projects that revolve around detecting changes in "average" speech – or for any project that requires measurement of more subtle phenomena through the whole of the stack of words, not merely the words that score as most distinctive of a period.

Comparison with Log-Likelihood

Log-likelihood was introduced in 1993 as a more sensitive alternative to another formula, Chi-Squared. The improvement consisted in log-likelihood's sensitivity to scarce observations.[10] Applied to time, log-likelihood is valuable for its ability to identify slight trends represented by minor differences in number.

A large LL indicates that the evidence from the observed documents supports the hypothesis that the probabilities of catching term w are different in Period P and Period Q. In other words, the two documents are distinct with respect to term w. Using word counts for Period P and Period Q, we can calculate LL scores using the equations below and then use the ranking of words to generate additional insights.

Using the counts of word w and the totals of all other words in Period P and Period Q again produces a score (the "log-likelihood ratio") which

---

[9] Ben Blatt, *Nabokov's Favorite Word Is Mauve and Other Experiments in Literature* (Riverside: Simon & Schuster, 2017), ch. 3.

[10] Ted Dunning, "Accurate Methods for the Statistics of Surprise and Coincidence" 1993). *Computational Linguistics*, 19(1):61–74.

Table 10.3 *Results with Partial JSD. Using scores between each period and all other periods to understand change over time, with duplications filtered.*

Name	Measure	1810	1850	1880	1900
Period Distinctiveness	Difference from All Other Periods	against, all, an, and, any, as, bank, be, been, but, by, catholics, conduct, could, country, every, from, had, he, him, himself, his, house, however, it, its, might, ministers, most, no, not, of, on, our, petition, present, situation, so, subject, such, that, the, their, them, this, those, to, was, were, which	ooo, and, at, believed, but, by, church, could, country, court, earl, government, great, had, he, her, his, house, india, law, learned, lord, measure, might, most, noble, now, of, opinion, our, parliament, russia, said, should, sir, subject, such, tax, that, those, thought, to, upon, war, was, were, which, with, would	act, action, amendment, are, asked, case, chief, committee, cork, do, egypt, for, gentleman, government, has, have, hon, ireland, irish, is, land, landlord, landlords, matter, member, members, mr, order, out, police, prime, question, regard, rent, right, said, say, secretary, sir, tenant, tenants, the, there, very, we, whether, will	africa, am, amendment, are, ask, beg, board, can, clause, council, county, do, education, get, going, has, have, if, in, is, land, local, matter, may, my, on, out, point, put, regard, school, schools, secretary, south, tax, there, these, think, this, under, value, very, view, war, we, what, whether, will, work
Long Term Trends / Absolute Historical Novelty	Change from All Previous Periods	allies, american, buonaparté, capital, cash, circulation, city, classes, coin, commercial, constitution, crime, currency, distress, expense, gold, inhabitants, inquire,	1853, 1854, admiralty, austria, believe, chancellor, commission, company, control, courts, crimea, deal, derby, desirable, despatch, directors, doubt, east, emperor,	1881, able, about, absolutely, accept, anyone, attorney, because, belfast, cases, commission, connection, deal, debate, desire, district, division, dublin, fact, general,	1903, answered, authorities, authority, aware, because, cases, coal, conditions, cost, councils, deal, dealing, district, districts, estate, estates, figures, holdings, kind,

Table 10.3 (*cont.*)

Name	Measure	1810	1850	1880	1900
	Change from Immediately Previous Period	issued, king, list, magistrates, maintained, meeting, meetings, notes, paper, payments, peace, petitioner, petitioners, petitions, population, prince, protestant, punishment, reduction, regent, religious, repeal, respectable, show, signed, society, sovereign, state, statute, suspension, wellington, years	entirely, exchequer, expenditure, form, general, income, indian, large, legislation, london, men, militia, minister, policy, position, proposal, questions, quite, reference, referred, regiments, russian, sea, second, sent, shall, troops, turkish, vote, words	give, information, kind, know, league, lieutenant, like, made, make, mid, minister, northampton, over, position, proposal, quite, rents, rule, scotland, section, shall, sub, take, understand, vote, way, words	know, licences, like, london, make, men, money, new, number, over, per, position, possible, proposals, purchase, quite, railway, really, scheme, section, small, state, take, training, transvaal, understand, up, way, words, years
Short-Term Trends		advanced, alarm, ancient, apprehended, arose, article, bullion, civil, community, confined, constitutional, continent, corpus, crown, death, depreciation,	1849, 1850, 1851, 1852, 1855, admiral, adultery, although, arrangement, arrangements, black, business, chancery, civil, constantinople, contract, crown, departments, divorce, ecclesiastical, fleet,	1880, 1882, 1883, 1884, 1885, 1886, 1887, answer, arrears, balfour, before, bradlaugh, certainly, charge, charges, coercion, constabulary, crimes, criminal, crofters, donegal, egyptian,	1899, 1900, 1901, 1902, 1904, 1905, 1906, 1907, business, chinese, colony, come, compensation, congested, corps, denominational, fifteen, fifty, force, forty, fourteen, horses, increment,

discretion, distinguished, doctrine, economy, especially, evil, favourable, human, imposed, individual, individuals, libel, liberties, magistrate, manchester, manufactures, market, met, names, peculiar, persuaded, prevailed, prevented, restriction, revolution, severe, speaker, standard, statements, temporary, ten, thanks, twenty, william

force, important, jurisdiction, late, liability, marriage, metropolis, military, moment, move, namely, national, oath, officer, offices, oude, ought, oxford, public, reading, regiment, salaries, salary, sebastopol, services, soldiers, sum, well, wife

evictions, gentlemen, healy, inquiry, inspector, lothian, magistrate, night, north, o'connor, oath, officials, parnell, place, prison, resident, see, sexton, solicitor, soudan, speaker, speech, statement, taken, wish

instruction, licence, licensing, managers, many, military, motor, particular, problem, provided, regular, regulations, sixty, stock, subsection, suggested, teaching, ten, thing, thirty, twelve, twenty, unemployed, valuation, volunteers, whole, yeomanry

80, abstract, admission, adopting, advance, advantage, annually, applying, april, burghs, cavalry, charged, charter, clerk, code, complain, considerably, consolidated, countrymen, enough,

accrue, adduced, apology, apt, benevolent, chaplains, characteristic, compliment, contain, contradiction, cry, degraded, enfield, enthusiasm, exceedingly, fought, hardships, honestly,

53, acute, appearing, assisted, attract, awarded, coloured, competent, constituting, contradict, daly, declarations, detriment, elect, enfield, favourite, guilt, healthy, hopeless, influences,

350, 54, abominable, absorbed, accuse, agreed, announce, capture, cargoes, challenge, chances, characterised, deciding, desiring, determining, dockyard, ears, ease, enforcement, extravagance, flag,

Typical Speech of Period   Average

321

Table 10.3 (cont.)

Name	Measure	1810	1850	1880	1900
	Difference from All Future Periods	existing, express, finally, hands, happened, hearing, hesitate, inquired, miserable, opportunities, passage, pressure, pursue, reach, receiving, relieve, returning, sort, sources, subjected, succeeded, superior, task, turn, unless, unwilling, utterly, wait, went, worst	hot, imputed, incorrect, indians, instruct, loyalty, lunatic, midst, mistake, notice, occurrences, occurring, owed, passions, progressive, publicly, recurrence, reject, reproach, rulers, scholars, sectarian, selecting, subscribed, trader, treaties, tribute, undoubted, universal, victory, woman	injuries, intellect, language, lasting, lbs, lights, mind, minded, occurrence, offers, possesses, protecting, quit, rapid, registrars, representations, revival, rifle, risen, safety, selling, servant, stages, strangers, suppression, tells, travel, treat, violent, woolwich	gibson, guaranteed, letting, lodge, neighbourhood, outdoor, permanently, profitable, proves, recalled, redemption, reformer, roll, seniority, shillings, stay, stone, straits, strengthened, strenuous, struggling, successfully, summary, tempted, thursday, warders, willingness, worcester, yield
Last Gasps		alluded, appeared, called, cause, circumstances, conceived, concluded, consequence, consideration, considered, contended, danger, enemy, europe,	1848, appeared, austrian, baron, bills, bishops, canning, character, clarendon, confidence, consequence, consideration, considered, convicts, entertained, europe, faith, feelings, felt,	1878, 1879, accepted, allow, allowed, arrested, attention, below, boycotting, campaign, canal, chair, chairman, churchill, colonel, conservative, constable, dillon, discussion, dr,	accepted, agreement, areas, available, basis, battalions, clear, concerned, consider, date, days, development, difficult, elementary, evicted, facilities, farm, future, largely, limit, lines, method,

farther, felt, former, highness, indeed, liberty, must, nature, necessary, necessity, never, nor, object, observed, occasion, own, period, person, principles, proceeding, proper, respecting, rose, same, security, sentiments, still, subjects, than, though, thus, till, too, whom, whose, without

honour, intended, intention, jews, letter, manner, mode, must, napier, oaths, object, objection, objections, occasion, opinions, peel, period, pope, religion, required, robert, rome, same, sanction, session, spiritual, subjects, thus, transportation, whom, without

edinburgh, fair, fowler, gangway, glad, gordon, holding, intimidation, john, jury, lincolnshire, michael, months, offence, official, past, pointed, prisoners, randolph, reasonable, recognized, redistribution, responsible, sitting, something, telegram, trial, used, withdraw, word

ordinary, outside, owner, owners, past, perfectly, premises, procedure, provide, provision, reasonable, responsible, sale, scottish, secondary, something, spent, staff, stage, steps, suggestion, surely, teacher, total, used, week, why, word

Source: Hansard Parliamentary Debates of Great Britain, all words with counts > 200 and more than one letter

ranks the difference of two Periods in terms of the word w. The log-likelihood ratio builds upon the divergence ideas we investigated in the last section, quantifying the divergence between two periods, but specifying how that divergence relates to the word w.

The log-likelihood value LL can be written as

$$LL = -2\log\lambda = -2\log\frac{\mathscr{L}\left(\widehat{p}_1,\widehat{p}_2|H_0\right)}{\mathscr{L}\left(\tilde{p}_1,\tilde{p}_2|H_a\right)} = 2\sum_{i=1}^{2}\sum_{j=1}^{2}O_{ij}\log\left(\frac{O_{ij}}{E_{ij}}\right)$$

where p_1 and p_2 represent probabilities of term w appearing in Period P and Period Q, and $\widehat{p}_1, \widehat{p}_2$ and $\tilde{p}_1, \tilde{p}_2$ are maximum-likelihood estimates (MLE) of probabilities p_1 and p_2 under two competing hypotheses such that, in our case, $\widehat{p}_1 = \widehat{p}_2 = \widehat{p}$ and $\tilde{p}_1 = \frac{a}{a+c}$, $\tilde{p}_2 = \frac{b}{b+d}$. Let O_{ij} represent each value in ith row and jth column of the table, and p_1 and p_2 represent probabilities of term w appearing in Period P and Period Q.

We can break down the equation to make it simpler to understand, again considering the raw word counts for word w in Periods P and Q found in Table 10.1. The frequency of word w in Period P and Period Q are a and b in the table, and they correspond to O_{ij} in the equation. We use the sum of a and b over the number of words in the corpus ($\widehat{p} = \frac{a+b}{N}$) to calculate E_{ij}.

We can also write out a simplified version of the equation of LL, using the contingency table found in Table 10.1 and assuming that a or b are relatively small, as follows:

$$LL = 2\left(a\log\frac{aN}{(a+c)(a+b)} + b\log\frac{bN}{(b+d)(a+b)}\right)$$

Applied to decades in the parliamentary debates (Table 10.4), log-likelihood gives a broader picture of the 1850s, where evidence of the Crimean War is present but does not dominate ("Russian," "'Austria,'" "Turkey'"). There are fewer personal and geographical names, and more diverse words surface, including the debates over the price of wheat and sugar ("corn," "price, sugar" in long-term trends, "food," "prices," and "wheat" in short-term trends), welfare ("distress," "petition" and "petitioners" among long-term trends, "employment," "labour," "labourers," "slave," "slavery," "trade," "unions," and "workhouse" among short-term trends), and questions of industrialization and the railroads ("company" and "board" in long-term trends; "consumption," "importation," "labour," "manufacturing," "manufactures," "markets," "railway," and "railways" among short-term trends).

Table 10.4 *Results with Log Likelihood. Using scores between each period and all other periods to understand change over time, with duplications filtered.*

Name	Measure	1810	1850	1880	1900
Period Distinctiveness	Difference from All Other Periods	allies, are, bank, bill, board, bullion, catholics, coin, conduct, constitution, could, country, do, education, enemy, expence, farther, from, gent, gold, government, had, has, he, highness, his, hon, is, land, local, matter, member, members, ministers, notes, observed, of, petition, petitioner, petitioners, position, prince, regard, schools, secretary, situation, such, their, was, will	1848, 1849, 1850, 1851, 1852, 1853, adultery, amendment, are, ask, asked, austria, beg, county, crimea, directors, divorce, earl, emperor, had, has, he, her, india, ireland, irish, is, land, learned, local, lord, matter, napier, noble, prime, roman, russia, school, secretary, section, sub, tenants, tiverton, turkey, upon, war, whether, which, will, work	1880, 1881, 1882, amendment, asked, chief, church, coercion, cork, corn, country, egypt, egyptian, evictions, gentleman, government, had, healy, hon, ireland, irish, is, landlord, landlords, league, lordships, lothian, matter, member, members, mid, ministers, mr, noble, northampton, o'connor, parnell, police, prime, rent, rents, right, roman, secretary, sir, tax, tenant, tenants, twenty, whether	1899, 1901, 1903, 1904, africa, am, amendment, answered, are, ask, beg, board, can, church, congested, county, do, education, had, has, have, he, her, his, increment, is, land, learned, local, measure, might, motor, of, school, schools, secretary, section, south, subject, think, transvaal, upon, war, was, we, were, whether, will, work, would
Long Term Trends / Absolute Historical Novelty	Change from All Previous Periods	am, army, as, can, catholic, chief, commander, corps, corrupt, corruption, defence, does, duke, evidence, force, gentleman, have, her, his,	army, baronet, board, clarendon, company, constantinople, corn, could, derby, despatch, distress, government, his, indian, individual,	action, am, anyone, are, arrears, balfour, baronet, belfast, board, can, catholic, catholics, connection, could, deal, division, do, gangway, has, have, he, his,	area, authorities, authority, baronet, believed, clause, coal, conditions, conduct, could, council, councils, deal, does, elementary, england,

Table 10.4 (*cont.*)

Name	Measure	1810	1850	1880	1900
		in, it, law, laws, learned, letters, majesty, may, me, military, militia, mr, my, note, officer, regular, service, shall, she, sir, spain, spanish, testimony, that, this, to, upon, us, we, witness, york, you	individuals, laws, may, militia, ministers, my, officers, people, petition, petitioners, poor, portugal, position, price, regard, regiments, relief, russian, said, schools, sea, service, sir, situation, spain, sugar, their, think, tithe, tithes, troops, turkish, university, was, we	holdings, its, land, laws, lieutenant, local, measure, might, of, officials, order, petition, regard, section, sub, subject, such, their, think, those, transvaal, treasury, was, we, were, which, will, work	estates, figures, get, going, him, holdings, house, however, law, licence, licences, licensing, managers, matter, mode, motion, noble, now, parliament, persons, petition, prime, problem, regard, scheme, sir, subsection, such, tax, their, this, training, unemployed, value
Short-Term Trends	Change from Immediately Previous Period	000, abuses, and, any, appears, bar, beg, cannot, case, cavalry, charges, civil, conversation, discipline, earl, examination, forward, further, house, idea, india, influence, invasion, ireland, john, king, lie, lordships, majesty's, men, officers, ordered, peace, people, poor,	1839, 1841, 1842, agricultural, agriculture, bill, canada, chancellor, clause, consumption, council, countries, court, departments, duty, employment, exchequer, food, guardians, hon, importation, imported, indies, labour, labourers, landlords, manufactures,	1868, 1869, 1871, 1873, abolition, ameer, army, ask, attorney, ballot, be, bishop, bishops, campaign, constable, constabulary, county, cries, dublin, education, england, europe, general, her, however, india, militia, mutiny, oath, officers, our, oxford, people, religious, reserve, russia, school, schools, scottish, she, ship, solicitor,	12, 1886, 1888, 1889, 1891, 1892, 1893, army, bill, cheers, chinese, denominational, earl, egypt, english, fifteen, fifty, forty, fourteen, grand, guardians, hear, honourable, horses, ireland, irish, laughter, lordships, militia, minister, northampton, parish, parishes, relief, right, scotch, silver, sixty,

	1812	1847, 1854, 1855	1878, 1879, 1883, 1884, 1885, 1886, 1887	1898, 1905, 1906, 1907, 1908
Average	practices, price, punishment, right, says, shew, should, state, the, think, those, time, trade, troops, were	manufacturing, markets, measure, measures, military, navigation, prices, produce, protection, railway, railways, repeal, slave, slavery, tariff, they, trade, union, unions, wages, west, wheat, workhouse	system, treaties, treaty, turkey, university, war, women, would	sugar, ten, territorial, thirty, tithe, twelve, twenty, viscount, vote, wales, welsh, yeomanry
Typical Speech of Period	1812, against, alluded, amendment, ask, asked, cash, castlereagh, circulation, clause, commission, conceived, corpus, currency, deal, depreciated, depreciation, distresses, enquiry, former, france, guineas, habeas, him, himself, however, indeed, individual, individuals, its, libels, marquis, might, millions, motion, nature, our, payments, peninsula, persons, petitions, proposal, royal, seditious, sentiments, subject,	1847, 1854, 1855, action, africa, aggression, austrian, baltic, believed, bishop, bowring, can, canton, chancery, chief, christian, church, commissariat, convicts, crown, district, do, ecclesiastical, get, grey, have, jew, jews, law, lordships, marriage, maynooth, now, oath, of, outside, oxford, pakington, pope, postmaster, rent, sardinia, south, subject, tax, that, thought,	1878, 1879, 1883, 1884, 1885, 1886, 1887, bank, beg, boycotting, canal, churchill, clergy, colonies, constitution, courtney, crime, **crofters, dillon, eviction, forty, fowler,** gordon, hicks, honourable, labouchere, matthews, michael, minister, organization, paddington, petitioners, proposition, protestant, recognize, redistribution, reform, religion, repeal, sexton, situation, soudan, stanhope, strand, suakin, sugar, ten, thirty, twelve, your	1898, 1905, 1906, 1907, 1908, agreement, appeared, areas, aware, bonus, cannot, chief, clubs, consequence, estate, evicted, feelings, felt, **former, france, housing, justice, laws, legislature, london, majesty, may, milner, minerals, ministers,** opinion, opinions, organisation, outside, point, postmaster, president, proposals, proposition, purchase, realise, respect, secondary, teachers, that, thus,

Table 10.4 (*cont.*)

Name	Measure	1810	1850	1880	1900
Last Gasps	Difference from All Future Periods	suspension, wellington, whether, which 1797, 1807, 1811, america, appeared, church, circulating, commissioners, concluded, contended, cost, county, danger, department, europe, every, evil, exertions, get, indemnity, irish, legislation, libel, liberties, lordship, measures, mint, most, norway, parliament, period, person, petitioning, police, portugal, president, publications, question, respecting, resumption, say, security, shewn, sweden, talents, there, till, treasury, very, work	transportation, way, wills 1846, accept, am, bank, belfast, canning, catholic, cattle, conditions, conduct, connection, cork, councils, country, deal, does, egypt, feelings, figures, going, however, landlord, legislature, members, might, mode, most, mr, oaths, opinion, opinions, order, out, parliament, parties, point, police, principle, proposal, proposals, proposition, respect, scheme, special, such, teachers, tenant, those, treasury, vienna	6d, africa, agriculture, answered, area, authority, believed, british, budget, cannot, colonial, conditions, congested, council, councils, court, crimes, denominational, did, districts, does, emigration, exchequer, gallant, going, hear, henry, him, labour, learned, licences, london, lords, magistrate, majesty's, managers, motion, my, said, secondary, south, taxation, this, trade, training, value, view, voluntary, wished, you	trade, treaty, untenanted, view 1909, 1910, age, and, anderson, asked, believe, budget, census, chamber, commons, constitution, constitutional, country, declaration, did, election, exchanges, finance, german, germany, hereditary, in, king, last, lieutenant, lords, me, mr, my, our, party, peers, pension, protestant, reform, resolution, resolutions, said, say, sovereign, suffrage, tariff, the, thought, us, veto, women, you, your

Source: Hansard Parliamentary Debates of Great Britain, all words with counts > 200 and more than one letter

Applied to our five categories of temporal distinction, log-likelihood performs equally well to tf-idf for most of the categories, but with significant differences in how it models distinctiveness. In general, the measure is less exactly, and more generous; it will rank as highly distinctive a word that preponderates in the 1850s numerically but also appears less frequently in other decades – hence the relative paucity of personal names. Log-likelihood forms a very useful complement to tf-idf. There is an added benefit to using log-likelihood over tf-idf in the category of "typical speech of the period." With log-likelihood, an average score as an indicator of relative significance works well. With tf-idf, we found average tf-idf to be virtually meaningless, but average log-likelihood accurately identifies vocabularies that surged during particular periods, for example, "sentiments" in 1810–19 and "transportation" in 1850–59.

In its generosity, however, log-likelihood results in certain observations of questionable historical significance. The measure suggests intriguing minor variations in speech, for example, the preponderance of the third-person plural ("we") after 1850 (according to long-term trends) and the use of "has" and "have" in the 1880s (by the same measure). We find that the 1880s are classified as the last decade where female pronouns such as "she" and "her" dominate (according to short-term trends) – a ranking that seems to be accounted for by a dearth of female pronouns in the 1890s. In general, log-likelihood scores seem to be inaccurate to the point of unusability for the most frequent of words.

Analysis: What Does Working with Multiple Approaches and Multiple Algorithms Show Us?

The observations that I have made in this chapter result from a detailed and highly qualitative review of the results of five different measures of time and three algorithmic variations applied to problems of temporal distinction. In general, we find a striation of approaches from "stricter" (tf-idf) to "more generous" (log-likelihood, partial JSD) in terms of how the model interprets the boundary between one period and another. As a result, we can recommend tf-idf for the interpretation of absolute novelty or difference of one period from others, but log-likelihood and JSD for historians interested in more subtle trends. The approaches may be complementary, and use of two algorithms can compensate for what is left out by any single one on its own.

Those observations have turned up specific caveats – for instance, the unusability of average tf-idf, but the relative usefulness of average log-likelihood scores. They also draw the user's attention to problems resulting from edge effects in datasets, such as scores that are skewed by being too close to the beginning or end of the dataset. These latter problems are easy to theorize after the fact as a mathematical model. But there is no rival to actually looking at output on the level of words, and reviewing the results in bulk, as the source of judgment on how a given algorithm works and when and how its results may be trusted. My research shows warping at edges due to little information; past/future can't be trusted. This is the most damning; it should make us skeptical of certain arguments written on the method. For example, consider one study of music history that pronounced the Beatles the most influential musical group on the basis of measures of tone topics, where the Beatles were also the group at the beginning of the dataset, and therefore had the most chance to be ranked as influential over time, in comparison with any later set whose entire plausible field of influence was much shorter.[11] All the measures we have reviewed in this chapter are skewed in the sense that "the aggregate past" against which change is measured in 1900 is a far larger corpus than that in 1806–09, when words are measured against only one year (1806). A great deal is arbitrary about the divergence measure as executed. The results of this bias in the measure would tend to make the results for the second half of the period less accurate. We can correct for this skewing, however, by changing the window of measure from the entire past previous period to the immediate period before that in question.

Looking at the results in detail also raises red flags about the generalizations to which measures of temporal change have been put by some hybrid teams. Many of the measures rank as highly significant variations in spelling, in the occurrence of personal names, in the usage of stop words (i.e. short words often algorithmically eliminated from keyword counts), and in rhetorical terms. When counts of words from those categories are agglomerated into a measure of aggregate change, it is unclear what we are measuring – but the fact that the instances of "Disraeli" or "connexion" in the debates vary does not offer compelling evidence of meaningful change in the history of ideas.

In other words, the work in this chapter offers an important check on the naïve measurements of turning points presented in the second chapter of this book. Such an analysis suggests positive recommendations for the practice of digital history. The use of controlled vocabularies can correct

---

[11] Uri Shalit, Daphna Weinshall, and Gal Chechik, "Modeling Musical Influence with Topic Models," *ICML* 2 (August 10, 2013): 244–52, www.jmlr.org/proceedings/papers/v28/shalit13 .pdf.

for much of the variation in rhetoric and spelling that threatens to throw off measurements.

Overall, my review suggests the plausibility of the research technique for understanding the distinctiveness of time – with the caveat that edges cannot be trusted and that the whole is warped, and that numbers suggesting discontinuities over time can only be trusted with the careful use of a controlled vocabulary.

More broadly, such insights suggest the importance of looking at the words themselves, carefully, and over the course of many comparisons, in order that the analyst truly understand what has been measured and what has been left out. Digital history requires a higher standard of review than that which has traditionally been offered in the pages of scientific articles. The validation of historical texts requires looking at least at words, as performed here, and preferably at words in context; otherwise, the risk of the analyst substituting a mathematical slight-of-hand for actual insight is too great.

The foregoing exercises illustrate the value in validating plausible measures of text mining with reference to texts that are well understood by scholars. Only by testing possible measures with reference to historically familiar events in relevant corpora can scholars prove or disprove the usefulness in a historical and political context of measures developed in another context. By following the instructions of critical search and putting the results of a data-driven analysis into conversation with historical results, we learn that average tf-idf is less instructive for periodizing the flow of time than divergence and peak tf-idf. We also learn to talk in concrete terms about the ways in which different measures are appropriate to different understandings of time: one to trending, one to identifying fossils unique to a particular moment.

Divergence measures and tf-idf complement each other by highlighting different aspects of change over time. Whereas divergence measures highlight those terms that were trending at any given moment of time, tf-idf highlights those terms which were introduced for a period and afterward abandoned. Divergence thus highlights the dynamic aspects of historical change, while tf- idf highlights waymarkers that were unique relative to a moment in time. The two measures form useful complements to each other that can be used in conjunction to highlight different aspects of change over time.

Carefully comparing different algorithms and their results, as we have done, allows the analyst to parse different components of time, discerning algorithms useful for indexing from those that discern trending words and, again, the fossils unique to one period but not from others. The results of the process above illustrate an exercise in asking about the fit between particular algorithms and particular perspectives on the past.

One final limit on the methods of this chapter should be given as a warning. There exists a real possibility that the discontinuities documented in experiments of this kind can only really be explored or understood through critical search, that is, through research propositions that take seriously the existence of a shared social reality in its totality, including archives that have never been digitized, voices that were never written down, and people and ideas that only show up as a distant reflection of truth in the archive. At this frontier, where technology and humanist thinking come together to understand how events are related to each other, it is crucial, in my opinion, that researchers take seriously the possibility that events that are not documented in the language of parliament may nevertheless shift language and concepts: that is, a war on another continent only briefly alluded to, or riots in the street, or a shift in an educational system, might each have restructured the language of parliament, creating reconfigurations that cannot easily be traced by relying on text mining alone.

In a full critical search process, we'd want to trace relevant words back to in-text mentions, especially drawing attention to the conceptual setting of each word by the speakers who employ it most in each period. We'd also want to continue the process of asking about the limits of our archive, and why we may need sources outside the parliamentary debates to understand phenomena expressed in the debates. In Chapter 12, we will turn to the question of how to trace algorithmic indices back to an original historical context, and why continued engagement with archives may remain important. First, however, in Chapter 11, we will share a few more remarks about strategies for understanding long-term trends – and their limits.

CHAPTER II

Whither Modernity[1]

If we engage multiple approaches to the past and understand the past through many lenses, surely we should be able to say something about where history is headed. Are we moving toward progress or away from it? We might not be able to predict the future in any specific way, but we can predict the general sketch of a better future if we tack toward the best examples of initiatives from the past, while avoiding the worst disasters. Such, at least, is the approach set out by many contemporary futurists – for example, Roman Krznaric, who turns toward the past in his book, *The Good Ancestor*.[2]

The vision of history that Kznaric sets after is one inspired by popular approaches to long-term history like those of Steven Pinker and Yuval Harari, authors who have emphasizes the evidence for improvement. Pinker has caused controversy with his views on the role of science and reason in improving the world, as well as his views on the nature of human progress. Harari has argued that the rapid changes brought about by technology have created a new kind of progress, one that is not linear but rather a complex, unpredictable web of human development. Drawing on these thinkers, Krznaric advises "deep-time humility," or a reverence for the timespans of geophysical and biological evolution of the cosmos, alongside a "cathedral thinking," or an attitude of intentional planning for the future we want to create. Unfortunately for Krznaric, the views of Pinker and Harari on the future of humanity and technology are seen by professional historians as overly optimistic and directly contradicted by available evidence.

---

[1] The latter half of this chapter duplicates an article published elsewhere: Jo Guldi, "The Measures of Modernity: Word Counts, Text Mining and the Promise and Limits of Present Tools as Indices of Historical Change," *International Journal for History, Culture and Modernity* 7:0 (November 3, 2019), https://doi.org/10.18352/hcm.589

[2] Roman Krznaric, *The Good Ancestor: A Radical Prescription for Long-Term Thinking* (New York: The Experiment, 2020).

The evangelists of progress tend to leave out more disturbing events in the history of the world, for instance, the story of how Europeans systematically undermined ship-building and other industries in India, which were then the most developed in the world.[3] As Priya Satia has insightfully remarked, stories of this kind have been easy to leave out because the tradition of praising the history of progress began with European politicians arguing that Europe could bring "civilization" to places starkly behind in every form of advancement and innovation – a narrative that required omitting the accomplishments of nations outside of Europe. [4]

The fact of contrary evidence has nevertheless not stopped believers like Krznaric from going in search of data to support their theory of progress. For Krznaric, data about the human past provides the material for an "intergenerational solidarity index," which he believes can help leaders to choose a future for the good of all. The metrics for Krznaric's "index" include data about primary education, child mortality, wealth inequality, forest depletion, and carbon emissions. Human history also supplies patterns for long-term collaboration toward these ends in the form of grand centralized projects of the past – for instance the building of the pyramids or the Great Wall of China, the creation of the US's New Deal or the UK's National Health Service, and the organization of the Mormon missionary system and the Svalbard Global Seed Vault.

The subject of this chapter is whether and how it is possible to reckon where modernity is going. As we have seen in many previous chapters, information from an entire century can be distilled into a visualization. This chapter will return to two algorithms we have seen previously – topic modeling and divergence – to press the account of how algorithms can help an analyst to generalize about change over time.

In Chapter 1 we established that one of the major dangers of text mining is the pressure of fantasy – the belief that we can, on the basis of data alone, revise known understandings about the past. As we saw in Chapter 1, a number of leading papers published in *Nature* and elsewhere attempt to render a simple mathematical answer to one of history's great questions. The press release headlines derived from these articles proclaim that one variable has revealed all: the existence of incest explains Western economic success, or a tendency away from violence over the long-term

---

[3] For the undermining of the Indian economy, see Uday Singh Mehta, *Liberalism and Empire: A Study in Nineteenth-Century British Liberal Thought* (Chicago, IL: University of Chicago Press, 1999); Rajani Sudan, *The Alchemy of Empire: Abject Materials and the Technologies of Colonialism* (New York: Fordham University Press, 2016).

[4] Priya Satia, *Time's Monster* (Cambridge: Harvard University Press, 2020), 14.

suggests how modern society is fundamentally different from those in the past. Sometimes those generalizations are helpful, but more often, the analysts fall into traps such as ignoring the shape of the archive and how it biases the question's answer. Thus, an enormous caveat must be offered to any attempt to revise long-term narratives, or to weigh in on the question of human progress: it is a dangerous undertaking that is not advisable without ample background reading.

As previous chapters have established, part of the power of algorithms is their ability to reduce vast swaths of information to a reduced form. Topic models and other algorithms can create a spontaneous "index" for a volume of documents, making it possible to count expressions of a certain discourse. Approaches to the *longue durée* may be more reductive or more expansive. A century may be represented not as a line of progress, but as a number of trends, each of which can be examined through constituent concepts, particular events, and biographical sketches. An index of the past may open up new perspectives. Or an index of this kind may help us to put together what we know about the past into a new aggregate narrative.

It is less clear, for instance, that such an index can, or should, contribute to settling scores in the debates about world progress such as those between Pinker and his critics. For the details of experience – the lives of laborers, prisoners, women, and slum-dwellers – show up very little in an overview of the century from the point of view of parliament. And that is why the field of social history, with its command of rare and scattered archives, exists: to enhance our understanding of the details of the human condition and so to pose a counterweight to naive conjectures like Pinker's about the reality of progress.

This chapter aims to demonstrate two approaches to collapsing long-term change – one via topic model and one via divergence. It will begin with one of the algorithms introduced in Chapter 10 – partial JSD (Jensen–Shannon divergence) – to show a trivial century-long sweep, looking in detail at the words ranked by the algorithm to discuss the merits and challenges of such an approach. It will then pivot to a more detail-driven approach, a survey of the century in topic models, to advocate for how "indexing" the trends of the century via topic can support an analysis that scales from the century-long overview back to particular case studies.

We will see that such an approach produces a reading more complicated than a simple yes/no verdict on progress. By the chapter's end, I will show that digital history can also support a survey of a century that is made up of individuals, events, people, and concepts, and that supports a closer examination.

Fantasizing about Modernity

Priya Satia argues that the desire to project "progress" onto current events became a temptation at a precise moment in the historical past. When Europeans became dedicated to expanding their colonies overseas, they committed themselves to a doctrine of progress so heartily that they wound up falsifying their own records. In short, Europeans got good at *cheating* with their history, suppressing accounts of abuse, corruption, and racism that reflected poorly on them, while overinflating accounts of the peacefulness, economic bounty, and social progress introduced by western missionaries.[5]

It should be evident that we can only use the past as a light to reckon with the future if our data – and our analysis – are solid. Hence the *danger* of trying to calculate the progress made by a civilization through a self-contrived index – whether it be Roman Kznaric's "intergenerational solidarity index" or Ray Kurzweil's data on the history of technological invention, which he used to argue that humanity was approaching a "singularity" when human consciousness would be uploaded to a technological cloud.[6] Indices where evidence is compiled to serve a single argument about the past tend, by definition, to eschew data that would complicate the story.

Progress may be a compelling construct – but it is also an *ideology*. Already in the eighteenth century, writers associated with the Scottish enlightenment such as David Hume and Henry Home Kames came to believe that they were participating in a verifiable and historical trajectory of progress that would immortalize them among future generations; many of them also developed habits of ignoring accounts of women's experience or the experience of non-Europeans in their accounts, a biasing of the evidence that helped to substantiate their theories.[7] Even the most eloquent writings from this period look naïve even to the most conservative contemporary promoters of Western progress today.

While crucial, the question of where modernity is going is one of the most difficult subjects of history to accurately investigate. It is one of the zones where the problems of dirty data – or the received biases of the past – are most treacherous, and where unchecked fantasies are most liable to

---

[5] Satia, *Time's Monster*.
[6] For "singularity," see Ray Kurzweil, *The Singularity Is Near* (New York: Penguin, 2005).
[7] Silvia Sebastiani, *The Scottish Enlightenment: Race, Gender, and the Limits of Progress* (London: Springer, 2013).

twist the evidence. It is one of the areas where critical thinking about our questions, data, and algorithms is most crucial. False results are everywhere. Easy measures of influence may turn out to be distortions arising from the absence of known actors in the textual record, or mathematically contorted narratives generated from the arbitrary measurement of a period's beginning and end.

Professional historians also have opinions about the trends that govern recent centuries. Historians use the term "modernity" to invoke the aggregate, long-term changes to society that have accrued with the rise of democracy, industrialization, science, and capitalism. Modernity meant an era of immense freedoms, where ideas about the equality of men and women were mooted and came to structure modern institutions, but also an era of enormous hypocrisy, genocide, and theft. While we fit algorithms for tracking modernity to the data of the nineteenth century, we can use historians' theories about modernity as a kind of baseline for subjects of interest, informing which questions we put to the data and how we interpret the results.

Trajectories of the Modern: Topic Modeling the Main Directions

Asked to reflect upon modernity, many scholars might counter broadbrush trends with a series of concrete domains where modern transformations definitively transformed every aspect of life for most Europeans, Britons, and Americans in the period from 1540 to 1911: transport and communications; urbanization; concepts of equality or rights and ideas about democracy; science and medicine; the investigation of race, gender, and class as explicit categories defining the individual's place in society; the ejection of colonized and indigenous people from the land; and industry and manufacture on a new scale.[8]

There is ample evidence that computers can track trends of this kind. In Chapter 3, we saw how a "topic model" can help to periodize transformations like those of the post office and telegraph, delivering an index of dominant discourses for a given body of text.[9] Each topic indexes a set of frequently associated keywords, and is assigned a probability number,

---

[8] For the notion of "modernity" in the history of Britain, see Simon Gunn and James Vernon, *The Peculiarities of Liberal Modernity in Imperial Britain* (Berkeley, CA: University of California Press, 2011); Miles Ogborn, *Spaces of Modernity: London's Geographies, 1680\n1780* (New York: Guilford Press, 1998).

[9] David M. Blei, Andrew Y. Ng, and Michael I. Jordan, "Latent Dirichlet Allocation," *Journal of Machine Learning Research* 3:4/5 (2003): 993–1022; John W. Mohr and Petko Bogdanov,

ranking the proportion of the corpus assigned to that topic. The words can then be used to measure change over time.

A 100-topic model of parliament (shown in Table 11.1) gives an overview of "subjects debated" that roughly resembles the table of contents of a book of British history.[10] The vast majority of the language indexed by the topics has nothing to do with the so-called modernization processes; it rather pertains to the way that bills and other subjects of debate are introduced, the ordering of speakers, budgets of various offices of government, the business of war, taxes and how taxes will be assessed, and other administrative concerns of parliament. The modernization processes make up only 38.9 percent of parliamentary speech.

Of that 38.9 percent urbanism is the clear leader – it consumes 9.2 percent of speech, dedicated primarily to conversations about museums, other buildings, parks, infrastructure, and utility companies. Issues of identity come next, with an emphasis on the administration of welfare for the poor in the so-called poor law, debates over the legality of divorce and married women's property, and conversations about wages, hours, and working conditions, mainly related to coal and factories – famously, British legislation was required to outlaw the employment of children younger than nine in 1833.

Using these top words as a guide, we can chart the topics over time in a hasty manner, giving us a general sense of the rise and fall of events over time. The first attempt looks as it should look: the trend lines distinctly rise over the course of the century (Figure 11.1).

There are, however, some first reasons for caution in the interpretation of Figure 11.1. A careful eye will spot a discrepancy from the numbers in the Table 11.1; where "urbanism" was the dominant topic overall in the table, it is the "colonies" that dominate in the figure. The difference is likely due to the nature of topic modeling algorithms and how they measure discourse. Topics can be hard to work with because they are

---

"Introduction – Topic Models: What They Are and Why They Matter," *Poetics, Topic Models and the Cultural Sciences*, 41:6 (December 1, 2013): 545–69.

[10] It is, of course, possible to have different scales of topic modeling: the 4-, 20-, 100-, and 500-topic models and their uses. A great deal of debate has been expended in computer science and the digital humanities about the "ideal" scale of a topic model, typically defined as the scale at which the topics are most stable. For the humanist asking the critical question of what different scales teach us, stability is less important as an ideal than investigation. My investigations into topic modeling at different scales are documented in Jo Guldi and Benjamin Williams, "Synthesis and Large-Scale Textual Corpora: A Nested Topic Model of Britain's Debates over Landed Property in the Nineteenth Century," *Current Research in Digital History* 1 (2018), https://doi.org/10.31835/crdh.2018.01.

Table 11.1 *Topics relevant to some classic definitions of modernity, excerpted from 100-topic model of parliament, 1806–1911.*

Topic name	Proportion of corpus	Top 20 words
Urbanism		
buildings and parks	0.03842	building house works park public site accommodation plan commissioner room erect build work make place purpose ground provide office survey
museums	0.01215	museum art national gallery work science collection picture public royal british exhibition kensington library academy institution purchase book society present
London's infrastructure	0.02786	london city metropolis metropolitan road public street district bridge mile thames river corporation vestry toll traffic board town improvement inhabitant
water and other utility companies	0.01401	water bill supply private house company bills corporation order standing orders london committee case power public gas promoter companies tramway
urbanism	0.09244	Section total
Democracy		
boroughs and voters	0.01267	borough franchise county vote town members representation bill number constituency population reform member place voter class qualification large house give
popular petitions	0.02731	petition petitioner present house sign state pray receive person subject prayer complain signature member petitions inhabitant read individual hear allegation
reform of parliament	0.01581	people house reform measure parliament constitution country power member principle change present ministers great opinion question bill political influence give
	0.05579	Section total
Science		
hospitals	0.02963	medical case hospital health officer asylum vaccination death lunatic child disease report state sanitary attention die make patient surgeon inquiry
contagious animal diseases	0.01333	cattle disease animal meat agriculture market country council slaughter butter farmer foreign privy food plague case importation order authority restriction
	0.04296	Section total

Table 11.1 (*cont.*)

Topic name	Proportion of corpus	Top 20 words
Transportation and communication		
railways as publicly traded companies	0.03172	railway company line trade public companies great make capital director interest power board train shareholder traffic share canal western mile
shipping companies	0.02227	ship vessel trade port board british shipping merchant shipowner sea seaman case carry liverpool steamer foreign navigation owner mercantile cargo
	0.05399	Section total
Colonies		
Canada, Australia, and New Zealand	0.02088	colony canada colonial government colonies governor council land assembly australia zealand crown british island state legislature canadian province imperial legislative
South Africa	0.02087	south africa transvaal government war state colonies secretary cape british sir colonial colony native boers african lord natal majesty chinese
colonial secretaries, the East India Company, and colonial governors	0.02352	india government indian state native secretary council east company governor sir lord bombay directors revenue british bengal control madras question
	0.06527	Section total
Gender, race, and class		
poor law unions	0.01886	poor law union relief parish workhouse guardian guardians pauper board case person give commissioners act power child labourer district unions
employment	0.02705	work hour men labour trade workman employ employer wage factory mine employment home case day accident coal act week child
marriage and divorce	0.01222	woman marriage law child wife case husband marry sister man divorce person lady age contract question party state mother family
unemployment and relief works	0.02013	distress people relief work government district money emigration employment land condition state country give make population labour poor food relieve
	0.07826	Section total

computational representations of discourses, rather than mere lists of keywords. The twenty words for each topic listed in Table 11.1 are merely an abstraction – in reality, each topic is as long as a vector of all of the

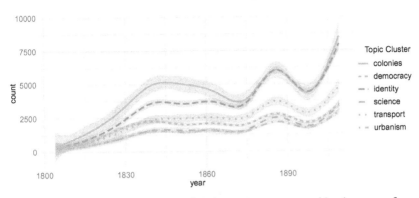

Figure 11.1   Six major categories of modernization, as measured by the count of each topic's top twenty words in the parliamentary debates of Great Britain, SMU data: raw count.

unique "tokens" (words or word-roots) in the corpus. Thus, the top hundred words classified by the topic model as signals of "urbanism" might appear more frequently than the top hundred words classified by the topic model as signals of "empire" – even though the reverse might be true for the top twenty. A naïve interpreter might rush to the conclusion that cities are more "important" than empire or vice versa; the data only supports fairly limited reflections upon when and how a given category dominates over another: text mining, in this sense, remains a *dangerous art*.

Beyond this, however, there are still more reasons for caution. We shouldn't be too hasty in claiming that the 39 percent of *Hansard* represented by the modernization topics represents their *dominance* and we shouldn't assume that the image in Figure 11.1 proves that the modernization topics were growing in their dominance over time. The figure seems to suggest that the top twenty words for each topic – the ones listed in Table 11.1 – were consistently rising over the course of the period as a whole, in such a way that we can easily claim that they dominated the later part of the century.

Figure 11.1 thus masks the historical context of the debates because the number and length of speeches delivered in parliament also went up dramatically over the century, as newspapers and an expanding vote meant more pressure on members of parliament to speak. If we measure the topics as a *proportion* of all debates, rather than as a raw count, we see that the numbers of each topic actually went down over the century (Figure 11.2).

We can find a simple enough way to reconcile the contradictory diagrams. Speakers may have talked more and more about the six great modernization processes – colonies, democracy, identity, science,

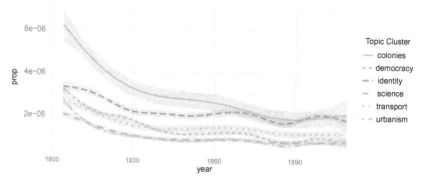

Figure 11.2   Six major categories of modernization, as measured by the count of each topic's top twenty words in the parliamentary debates of Great Britain, SMU data: proportional count.

transportation, and urbanization – over the course of the century, but those processes took up a smaller and smaller proportion of parliamentary speech. As always, we should look at our findings in tandem with a critical search, an indispensable hedge against too eagerly accepting methods that conveniently validate existing theories.

The larger point returns us to one of the precepts of critical search – because the experience of time is multiple and varied, any distillation of the flow of history into a single line or trajectory is vulnerable to reductionism. One solution to this conundrum is to juxtapose multiple computational approaches that unlock a multiplicity of possible interpretations and, from this accumulation of iterations, it should become clear, in every case, that a single algorithm provides only one perspective on the past.

The six institutions of modernity share a unanimous perspective on at least one crucial matter – that parliament, toward the end of the century, talked more and more about those institutions and that it talked more in general. The sections that follow will attempt to unpack various dimensions of how parliament talked about where it was going and they will explore how, by engaging in a variety of algorithmic approaches, we can measure where, in fact, it was going.

The "Average" Story About the Future

In parliamentary speech, how did thinking about the past compare with thinking about the future? We can apply the same process and compare what people saw when they looked backward with what they saw at the same moment of time when they looked forward.

In speech that carries temporal markers – phrases such as "one day," "in times to come," or "in the future" – people perform the work of referencing the future. For the results in Figure 11.3, I have again grouped together sentences based on their core grammar, irrespective of tense or construction.

One instructive finding is this: people talk about the future in the same way that they imagine the past. "They [will] have right[s]," "we [will] have right[s]," and "person[s] [will] have right[s]" became the dominant grammatical structures that were repeated when people in the 1830s talked about their future. At the same time, some of those speakers talked about rights as something people had enjoyed in the past. Those speakers made an argument that future rights were possible because of the existence of precedents, such as the Magna Carta. Speakers in parliament thus made claims that persons in the past "had rights." Their hopes for the future caused them to look back to the past for resources.

As the nineteenth century went on, the future also started to be crowded with speculation and desire. In the 1850s, there are hardly any references to the future. By the 1890s, however, references to the future are nearly twice those of a decade before. "We look to [the] future," which appeared for the first time in a speech in the year 1862, became a common construction in the 1880s.

What did they say about the future? We've had a hint from the most frequent triples, shown in Figure 11.3. But we can also touch on the flavor of forward-thinking idioms by examining the full list.

Future speech is the key of prophesy and only a few times every year did someone engage in speculation about what would or should happen. Sorting parliamentary speeches just for these acts of prognostication can therefore give us a distillation of a century in the key of the future, as we can see in Figure 11.3:

> They looked for a more democratic future to come: "[The] votes [of electors should be] take[n] by ballot," proclaimed the liberals who decried corruption and supported broadened rights to vote in the 1860s; "School[s] [will] receive grant[s]," urged the advocates of public education. References to the future also changed with technology: in the 1870s, members of parliament began to describe a world where "we receive telegram[s]" on a regular basis.

> They spelled out the implications of the policies they endorsed: "Corn [will be] import[ed] into [the] country," warned MPs speaking about the need for the repeal of the Corn Laws (1840s). They also spoke in abstract terms

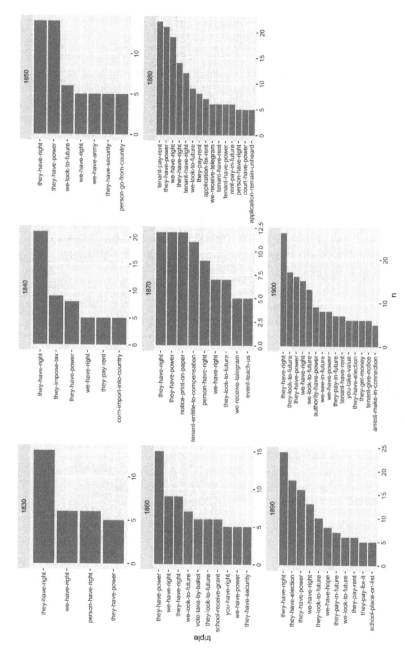

Figure 11.3 Grammatical triples that appear in the context of explicit references to the future (n>4). Searching the parliamentary debates of Great Britain, SMU data: proportional count.

about what they hoped for from this future, holding up the reasons why "they/we look to [the] future" (for lower prices on grain, for young men in the navy, for the recovery of Canton) (1850s), touching on what "event[s] [will] teach us" (that wars could come at any moment) (1870), proclaiming that "we have hope" (for avoiding violent conflict in Ireland) (1890), and sharing what "we see in [the] future" (1900) (some foretold evils in the future of South Africa).

Yet the temporal markers only take us so far. In Figure 11.4, I dispense with temporal markers, and just ask when members of parliament invoked the *future tense* in their verbs, telling us what they *will do*. As the poet Audre Lorde noticed when she was called upon to teach English as a second language to students at a local community college, some of the poetry of language adheres in its grammar. Through verb tense, we organize past, present, and future and the mystery of grammar allows us to perform mental acrobatics of time; past and future can collide within the same sentence. Lorde writes of the epiphany she carried into the grammar classroom: "Tenses are a way of ordering the chaos around time."[11]

The future tense triples often give us more specifics than the triples from sentences where the future was explicitly called upon. Here are their basic characteristics, as shown in Figure 11.4:

Members of parliament discussed specific trends in terms of prices and demographics: the "price will be low" (1840), argued the advocates of free trade for the consequences of their proposals; in the 1860s, as members were debating the reforms that would eventually give a right to vote to working-class men for the first time, members preached that the working "class will have a majority" in coming years.

They made promises and prognostications about the future in general: "we will give protection" (1840); "we will give security" (1860); "we will give assistance" (1860); "we will go to war" (1870); "we will let you" (1890); "we will support you" (1900).

They laid out the course of reforms: "we will reduce [the] duty" (1840); "we will permit upon dominion" (1860); the "cost will be small" (1880); "councils will have control" (1890); the "inspector will visit [the poor law] union" (1890), the "child will attend school" (1890); the "[agricultural] holding will vest in [the] tenant" (1900); "man will pay tax" (1900); and [the local] "authority will have control" (1900). Such phrases stand in for richer detail, hidden in the reduced frame of the extracted triple. A triple such as "tenant will pay rent" (1890), in the context of a parliamentary

---

[11] Audre Lorde, *Sister Outsider* (Trumansburg, NY: Crossing, 1984), 95.

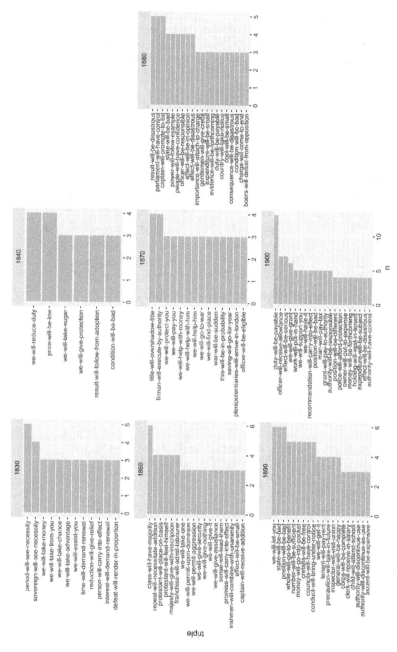

Figure 11.4 Grammatical triples that use the future verb tense (n>2). Searching the parliamentary debates of Great Britain, SMU data: proportional count.

speech, begins a long description of the kind of reduced rents that would be paid by tenants under new legislation.

They preached the peril of their opponents' policies: "the result will be disastrous" (1880); with such a policy, the "consequence will be disastrous" (1880); the "effect will be disastrous" (1880); the "state will be bad" (1890); the "position will be bad" (1900); the "effect will be serious" (1900). Some statements reflect an anticipated battle for interpretation over how history would receive the present: the "country will take notice" (1880).

Much less frequently, they reached around the arc of time, peering into the hoped-for outcomes of their policies in specific terms: the "franchise will admit [the] labourer" [1860]; "Irishmen will combine with unanimity" (1860); "people will have confidence" (1880); "money will go into [their] pocket[s]" (1890); "Cretans will be free" (1890). Sometimes their hopes look naïve in retrospect, such as the claim that "Boers will desist from opposition" (1880).

What is most striking is the gradual increase in both the quantity and specificity of these terms over the century, from a high of three in the 1850s to a high of twelve in 1900. They speak with increasing concreteness about the world that they imagine and its effect both on constituents (the children going to school, the tenant laborer fitted with a mortgage to the land he tills) and on persons in the colonies and around the world (the Irishman, the Cretans, the Boers).

Measuring Raw Change with Divergence

A final metric for understanding modernity is *divergence*. We met divergence measures in Chapter 10, where we introduced partial JSD as the legacy of codebreaking practice in the Second World War. The algorithm can be used to score most highly the words in one set of documents whose frequencies are most different from those of the words presented in another set of documents. In simple terms, partial JSD offers a raw test of *difference*.

In Table 11.2, partial JSD is applied to search for words that are more likely to appear in *Hansard* from 1852 to 1911 than from 1803 to 1851. This produces a list that evidences trends such as the decline of feudal institutions ("nobl-," "house"), the evanescence of a language of consensus based on universal standards ("law," "motion," "country"), and the disappearance of an eighteenth-century language of allusion to the informed public ("respect-," "learn-," "public," "opinion").

Table 11.2 *Words more likely to appear in* Hansard *in 1803–51 and 1852–1911, according to partial JSD.*

Words More Likely in 1803–51	Words More Likely in 1852–1911
Noble	Government
Country	Secretary
House	Board
Measure	Matter
Lord	Bill
Ministers	Amendment
Corn	Hon
Subject	Local
Baronet	Question
Petition	Gentleman
Laws	Position
Stated	Clause
Duty	Schools
Learned	Land
Poor	Deal
Respect	School
Law	War
Motion	Education
Persons	Beg

The list also suggests other sweeping historical changes, including the expansion of state institutions to serve a democratic nation ("school(s)," "education," "board," "secretary"), the contestation of local against national politics ("local" in the later period as opposed to "country" in the earlier one), the rise of a language of democratic advocacy ("beg," "position," "clause," "question," "deal," "bill"), and the consequent rise of contestations of the ownership of estates by different public and private authorities ("land").

In short, divergence suggests another aspect of modernity already well known to historians – the disappearance of aristocratic institutions and the arrival of a modern bureaucracy. Goodbye to the minor nobility and their sense of duty; hello to war, councils, and boards. This is a story that would make sense to Max Weber and to other scholars who have observed the massive shift of institutions between feudal Europe and the present day. That watershed, we learn, must have been highly palpable in the nineteenth century, so distinct was the difference between the language of the first and the second halves of that epoch.

Notably, the other tests of modernity that we have proposed – six processes of modernization and an increasing orientation toward an imagined future where rights are protected – seem little in evidence in this visualization. Those other processes may be in the data, but they haven't risen to the top. The mutual definitions of modernity we propose here are thus compatible, even while utterly distinct.

A broad perspective of meaning and interpretation in the past will rightfully humble the scholar and suggest sobriety and caution when approaching new tools from information theory. New measures provide ample tools for glimpsing aggregate trends over time, but multiple tools can present very different – and entirely complementary – answers to the question of where the century was going.

Conclusion

In a sense, each of the foregoing chapters attempted, little by little, to crack the problem of measuring time: first by focusing on the problem of the dirty data of the past; second, by focusing on the research process, in general, and the need to triangulate results; third, by dramatizing how the choice of algorithm tilts the results; fourth, by raising fundamental questions about the scale of inquiry, and how the results are inflected thereby; and lastly, by exploring how the analyst's sense of modernity biases the results of data. Considering the inevitable realities we face when measuring time, the most auspicious approach is, perhaps, to always examine the past with a sturdy embrace of the multiple perspectives at work behind those seemingly simple questions of what changed and how, and whose voices mattered and why. Case studies allow us to identify the limitations of any of these approaches and to determine how a critical search might best engage the precise nature of the data and phenomena in order to deliver credible and significant results.

The case studies in this chapter suggest that the problem of measuring "modernity" – even when grounded in empirical data – brings scholarship face-to-face with interpretive issues. "Modernity" cannot be meaningfully and essentially identified by an adjacent "future" represented by some arbitrary cutoff date – as 1890 functioned, at least tentatively, in the foregoing study, in its observable relationship to its previous and subsequent decades. This problem of arbitrary baselines is, indeed, a significant issue insofar as it prejudices the causal inferences found by quantitative measures. This has, in fact, been apparent in most of the currently published work on influence using similar methods, including a study of music that identified the Beatles as the most influential music group of the postwar era.[12] If 1850, or any other date, is used to establish a baseline measure of historical change over time, then scholars must be explicit about the fact that they are measuring the relative tendency of discourses to converge at a particular point of time, which is, of course, not the same as the *zeitgeist*, although it may reflect a partial dialectic or even a process of conservative backlash that Adorno identified as a "negative dialectic." Baseline measures, therefore, may be useful for establishing raw "influence," or for comparing degrees of change. But in essence, these data return us to another question: What exactly is meant by "modernity," which has a rich literature in concept history and the analytics of periodization behind it.

While the studies demonstrate the auxiliary need for critical theory and suggest that data is not enough to foreclose the elusive definition of modernity, this does not by any means invalidate the power of the foregoing measurements, or the applicability of data to questions of historical change. Keyword-based measures of innovation illuminate many of the dynamics that shaped policy: empire, education, and environment were ineluctable as subjects of government in the modern period, and those who kept those subjects in their sites were liable to cut a trend in policy that would be copied by others. A critical consideration of the centrality of theories of modernity and the multiple possible definitions of modernity can direct us to a new frontier of digital research, where future researchers might plausibly consider how data-driven tests might be used to illuminate theories of multiple periodization. More specifically, theories of agency might be used to identify the evidence of multiple kinds of influence at work in the archive.

Data-driven research is a frontier that will be satisfied not by more math alone – it will have to include an ongoing search for the best algorithms to "fit" questions about agency, influence, change, and modernity that have been raised outside the world of data. This is a domain in which students of concept history and social theory have an invaluable role, arguing and tinkering alongside the scholars of algorithms and statistics.

Comparing different approaches offers a sound basis for a critical examination of the process of searching historical and cultural data and only a circumspect, well-rounded approach can elevate this from a theoretical curiosity and establish it as a new frontier for data-driven research. Each

---

[12] Uri Shalit, Daphna Weinshall, and Gal Chechik, "Modeling Musical Influence with Topic Models," in *ICML* 2, 2013, 244–52, www.jmlr.org/proceedings/papers/v28/shalit13.pdf.

tool exhibits a particular bias and generates a perspective on the nature of modernity that is extremely contingent upon how the question was framed and upon methodological choices, algorithmic approaches, and the process of managing sources. This chapter thus encapsulates one of the directives of critical search: the mandate to investigate the juncture between algorithms and concepts – in this case, the concept of "modernity" itself.

The foregoing case studies suggest a number of new insights into the problem of modernity and they bring us closer to that delicate methodological fit, where we employ the algorithms with circumspection, without rushing too quickly to assign a *direction* to modernity. Earlier in this chapter, we documented the rise in raw counts of words related to empire – urbanization, industrialization, and other facets of modernity – even as those words decreased as a proportion of words spoken overall in parliament. In statistical measures of divergence, we looked at a tool that could be used to compute, overall, the trends of the century, although as we also saw that the measure must be approached with caution.

Modernity, in a broad sense, is in the eye of the beholder: how the analyst thinks about the problem of modernity, in terms of institutions, grammatical or rhetorical innovations, or reflexive senses of the future, absolutely determines the results of an algorithmic analysis. To return to the Gauguin canvas we encountered in Chapter 7: the art of text mining is, perhaps, on its most dangerous ground when it attempts to give *single* answers about the direction of history, a field haunted by legion impulses and actions, where opportunity and interpretation are always multiple.

For one last demonstration of what it means to move between an overview and a microview, grounded in sources, I will next move to one smaller arena of the twentieth-century debate over government and markets – the attacks on environmentalists as unscientific, irrational, and elitist that marked congressional discourse in America since the 1970s. In Chapter 12, I will pivot to show how examining trends of speech may take us from century-long questions down to particular words, individuals, and episodes in history.

CHAPTER 12

Attacks on Environmentalists in Congress[1]

In Chapter 2, I introduced the concept of "explanation" as core to what historians do: they *explain* what changed and why, rather than proposing and testing models or positing laws of human experience and predicting future outcomes. In many case studies I've shown how computers can help us specify different accounts of "what happened." Many of the preceding chapters are thus organized around a lens on temporal change, for instance the problem of how we represent the past and when representations of the past changed. I've also opened inquiries into why change happened, including the work of influence.

Most of the time, however, practicing historians don't want to merely regard a lens on time or ask about different kinds of forces that exert change: they want to know a specific *what, why,* and *how.* In this chapter, I will attempt to bring together a *what, why,* and *how* in a familiar and common-sense form, using computers to answer the questions: What changed in congressional discussions of climate change? How did this change happen? Why has American politics been riddled with attacks on environmentalists, even after scientists had presented the data of climate change? Who was responsible?

The method that I will apply in this chapter, word embeddings, offers several possible elements to the student of historical processes. Word embeddings can be used to detect many kinds of historical forces, but one of their best virtues is to accurately demonstrate the changing contexts in which certain words have appeared in historical debates. Paired with wordcounts, word embeddings are ideally suited to tracking discontinuities and changes to the life of public discourse. In other words, the words — as

[1] Portions of this chapter have been previously published in Jo Guldi, "The Climate Emergency Demands a New Kind of History," *Isis* 113:2 (2022): 352–65. In its current form, this chapter benefited enormously from the attention of the Davis Seminar on Environmentalism at Princeton University, November 2022, and especially to conversations with Lawrence Glickman, David Avrom Bell, Yair Mintzker, and Kevin Kruse.

representations of concepts that circulated in Congress and outside of Congress – are part of the "how" of collective meaning-making, of how cultures and politics gets shaped – and thus part of the work of a larger cultural history.

Beginning with a distant overview of the word embedding, this chapter will offer many possible hypotheses about how the speeches of members of Congress about the environment and environmentalists changed over time. Indeed, each of these investigations could be a separate chapter. Historians often find such diverging paths in the course of their research. The one they choose is the one they think matters the most – the one with the fullest "explanatory" power for society as a whole.

It is with the principle that history can explain things in mind that I will present the many possible histories available in a single word-embedding model of twentieth-century congressional speech about the environment. From many possible projects, I will select one for greater scrutiny: the moral discourse about environmentalists as irrational – a discourse that appeared in the 1970s, which persisted and grew through the 1990s and 2000s. That this discourse is the one with explanatory power for our society should be obvious, as it was in those years that a definitive climate science of global warming was established, its evidence presented to Congress. Because certain speakers in Congress had already developed an attitude of mistrust toward environmentalists, they had little problem persuading the American public that warnings about significant and costly climate change should be ignored.

The remainder of the chapter outlines the methods I used to follow through with an investigation of who developed the attacks on environmentalists, when and why. In accordance with the principles laid out in previous chapters, my methods alternate between data-driven overviews, guided reading, and iterative engagement with the data. Reading the output of the word-embedding model in detail, I reviewed the individual terms that form the changing moral discourse for the word "environmentalist," that is, selecting words such as "kook" and "despoil" that carry an extremely sentimental connection. From there, I plotted some of the most frequent sentimental words and bigrams that described environmentalists over time. I looked for the key speakers and measure their contributions as a proportion, identifying Senator Ted Stevens as an early shaper of the discourse. Moving ever closer to the primary sources, I used the computer to pull all of Ted Stevens' speeches in which he used the phrases "extreme environmentalist" or "radical environmentalist" to fan the flames of distrust of environmental movements and environmental science.

Reading these speeches in the traditional way, it became apparent how Stevens' career-long advocacy of the Trans-Alaska Pipeline led him to weaponize speech against his opponents in a way that anticipated the 1990s' Republican revolution associated with Newt Gingrich and other Republican speakers, where use of attack-oriented phrases would become routine. Stevens' speeches also show a shift from "extreme" to "radical" in the years after 2001, when protecting America's oil was counterposed to the work of "radical" environmentalists and "radical" Islamists, both of whom were equally identified as potential terrorists. Negative attacks of this kind – leveled over decades – systematically undermined an appreciation of scientific research about the environment, climate change, and the public good.

The history that I will offer in this chapter takes a winding path through different analytic approaches, including word embeddings and simple counting of words by year and by speaker, ending with a careful reading of phrases in context. Importantly, in this chapter, the focus shifts from algorithms and their fit with an abstract conceptualization of temporal experience, to the problem of historical interpretation per se. Along the way I will share some reflections on the role of *explanation* in historical study – that is, the fundamental purpose of historical research in explaining discontinuities over time – which is to say, the sometimes hidden questions of "what matters" that guide students of history as they select material for investigation. In this chapter, each data-driven approach is subordinated to the problem of answering a historical question about climate change. In this way, this chapter represents most fully what a digital history project might look like in the hands of analysts of meaning like historians, journalists, or lawyers, whose priority is typically to understand what changed and how. I will also use this chapter to clarify, concretely, the limits of what computers can accomplish and also to make pronouncements about when an analyst with a respect for truth would return to archives, rather than computational records, for answers.

A Short History of Climate Change via the Congressional Debates

Word embeddings are a representation of every word in a corpus. In the current project, I began with tracing how members of Congress employed the word "environmentalist" between 1970 and 2010, according to transcript of speeches recorded in *The Congressional Register*. Digital historians have borrowed from linguists an appreciation for how subtle differences in word form reveal the layered beliefs, norms, and ideas that make up culture.[2] The choice of "environmentalist" as the target for this project came from trial and error in a process of investigating similar cognates. "Environmentalist" is a more specific term than *environmental* or *environment*, which can pertain to learning environments or work environments; one would need further refinements to make sure that a study in words collocated with "environment" coincided with speech about pollution or climate change. The abstract noun, "environmentalism," was another possible candidate for research. A neologism first employed by *The Washington Post* in 1966, searching for "environmentalism" would capture all sorts of political argumentation related to the environment on a highly abstract plain.[3] But a quick comparison of the results for "environmentalist" suggested that the latter term – referring to the individuals who supported environmentalism – would capture a more heated and rapidly changing discourse than a search for any of the other related terms.

The term "environmentalist" promised to reveal some of ways that members of Congress employed political rhetoric to tilt belief towards their side. As Allitt explains, the protection of the environment was a subject of broad political consensus through the 1960s and even the 1970s, when the early leadership of the Environmental Protection Agency included Republican politicians such as William Ruckelshaus and Russell Train, and John Quarles.[4] Allitt dates the beginning of the end of bipartisan operation behind environmentalism to 1973, the date of the Alaska Pipeline Bill, but also to the identification of environmentalism with the hippies at Berkeley's People's Park, the proliferation of environmental advocacy groups and environmentalist intellectuals who questioned the primacy of economic growth. Allitt believes that a culture of "mistrust" began to erupt with the debate over the Trans-Alaska Pipeline, as oil was painted as a deadly contaminant by one faction but embraced as the least among various evils by other environmental groups. The sparks of mistrust were fanned into a flame, Allitt writes, during the OPEC crisis, when oil prices surged due to the restriction of oil by the Organization of the Petroleum Exporting Countries (OPEC).[5]

Compelling though this account is, it gives us little sense about the longer story about how speakers in Congress spoke about environmentalists in the four decades between 1970 and 2010. As Table 12.1 reveals, as

---

[2] On the importance of investigating linguistic variations, see Pim Huijnen, "Digital History and the Study of Modernity," *International Journal for History, Culture and Modernity* 7 (October 31, 2019), https://doi.org/10.18352/hcm.591, especially 998–99.
[3] Patrick Allitt, *A Climate of Crisis* (New York: Penguin, 2014, 60.   [4] Ibid., 67, 73–75.
[5] Ibid., 72–98.

Table 12.1 *A sample of words and two-word phrases ranked as similar to the keyword "environmentalist," according to Word2Vec, 1970–2009.*

1970	1975	1980	1985	1990	1995	2000	2005
ecologist	conservationist	conservationist	conservationist	conservationist	conservationist	conservationist	conservationist
conservationist	environmentalism	preservationist	preservationist	preservationist	greenpeace	interest_group	environmentalism
preservationist	preservationist	interest_group	logger	greenpeace	sportsman	oil_industry	greenpeace
ecology	outdoorsman	lobbyist	environmental	environmentalism	forester	environmental	environmental
environmental	industrialist	organized_labor	spotted_owl	interest_group	environmentalism	logger	sonoran_desert
environmentalism	environmental	watt	sportsman	biologist	sierra_nevada	cash_cow	interest_group
strip_mining	obstructionist	logger	pacific_northwest	natural_resource	cattleman	mining	global_warming
coal_industry	ecology	environmental	interest_group	environmental	logger	pressure_group	organized_labor
consumerism	consumerism	forester	chemical_industry	food_processor	environmental	pollute	libertarian
environment	ecologist	interior_secretary	rancher	northwest	biologist	oil_company	wildlife
conservation	forester	sportsman	forester	pacific_northwest	ranching	environmentalism	enthusiast

early as 1975–79, certain speakers in Congress were already associating the word "environmentalist" with a politics of opposition, invoking heated terms such as "obstructionist" alongside more moderate debates about conservation and the preservation of species. But the terms invoked alongside "environmentalist" did not stay stable; the references diverged to include the "spotted owl," "greenpeace" and "libertarians."

As we shall see, one strength of word embeddings is the ability to tackle both short-term and long-term dynamics in the changing nature of discourses, allowing the historian reader a practical shortcut through some of the painfully close work with words and algorithms that we undertook in Chapters 10 and 11. I therefore wondered if tracing the context in which environmentalists were invoked in Congress might open a window to understanding who, when, and how members of Congress began to systematically dismiss environmental concerns.

Dividing the corpus into five-year periods, I applied a word-embeddings model to find the terms that most frequently co-occurred with "environmentalist" in the debates of both houses of Congress published as *The Congressional Register*. The result was a long table of the words collocated with "environmentalist," ranked from most prevalent to least (Table 12.1). A first glance at this table gives a timeline with certain familiar terms for wildlife and political interests, giving a faint outline of how discourses and arguments about the environment changed over the course of four decades.

Like most computerized output, Table 12.1 represents only a sliver of a much larger computational model. The table shows us the top eleven words associated with the keyword "environmentalist" for each five-year period of Congress, although the full "embedding" model for each five-year period is a list of words as long as the number of unique words in that period.

My method was to study how members of Congress talked about the term "environmentalist" over time by reading deeply – rather than by taking a superficial glance at Table 12.1. My first step, therefore, was to consult the top hundred or thousand words from the embedding model, reading a table too long to include with the materials with this chapter. That longer data set gives a much denser set of information about how discussions in Congress changed. The names of animals, theoretical solutions, and industries came and went from period to period. To understand what words are doing, one has to read all of them. So I read and read, scrolling down and down an endless grid of comma-separated values in Excel, reading and thinking about what this abstraction of changing discourses told me.

In the paragraphs that follow, I will offer a series of potential historical arguments that an analyst could build on a "distant reading" of congressional speech about environmentalists. Each is a miniature story about the shifting concerns of science, the arguments about how energy policy should shift, the economic interests that seemed most relevant to members of congress, and the moral discourse about environmentalism voiced by politicians. Each of these sublists was generated by a human – myself – through the process of scanning hundreds of keywords that were identified by the algorithm as part of the discourse around the word *environmentalist*, clustering words by hand, and from those words formulating historical hypotheses in the form of narratives for further testing and inspection. Not every hypothesis that emerged directly reflects onto the question of oppositional politics in Congress – and indeed, the many possible hypotheses that follow represent other research stories that might be productively followed in another project.

What Happened to the Environment? A Series of Historical Hypotheses Formulated on the Basis of Reading Word Embeddings

In the decades since we realized that we were losing Earth, members of the US Congress filled the air with the names of endangered creatures, like some perverse anti-Adam designated to name the world out of existence. They spoke of carp, coyote, the tussock moth, and whooping crane in 1975–79; caribou, sea turtle, snail darter, black bear, spotted owls, white pine, and peregrine falcon in 1980–89; kangaroo rat, desert tortoise, warbler, antelope, prairie dog, bobcat, shrimp, mountain lion, and grizzly bear in 1995; and sea otter, bighorn sheep, mule deer, salmon, and polar bear in 2005.

Even while they did nothing to regulate carbon, members of Congress intoned an invocation of a mythical world that they hoped to chant into being through words alone. Already in 1975, members of Congress called upon "alternative energy" and "renewable resources" to free us from the fear of climate change. They promised strategies that would "mitigate" harm to the environment. Members of Congress seemed to believe that their efforts would purge the world of pollution. In 1985–89, they were hopeful about geothermal energy, reforestation, and research into soil erosion, fertilizer, and new approaches to wastewater. They were wary of the "downstream" consequences of pollution. By 1995, advocates of environmentalism in Congress had added a new vocabulary to their debates, one concentrating on "sustainability" and "responsible" approaches. These questions would be persistent frames for the energy crisis into our own day. Only with the millennium came a marked shift toward discussing the dangers of atmospheric carbon, which was on the agenda at last. In the mouths of speakers was a newly utopian vocabulary of cleanliness, compromise, and futurity. By 2005, congressional speakers began to speak about a "cleaner" future, referencing the "long run," looking for "solutions," turning to carbon "sequestration," and asking questions about "biomass," "solar," "wind," and "nuclear" energy. They began to acknowledge a real threat of "global warming" in the future.

Above all, members of Congress named their constituents, whose moneyed interests they hoped to represent: the "timberland" industry and "ranching," zones in which "landowners" were sovereign. As a sign of this transfer of authority from Congress to the new owners of the land, *regulation* was rarely mentioned, except to denounce it as "red tape."

An account of everything that happened also does not necessarily help us to prioritize the *most important* thing that happened. The list of words I have presented are the result of critical thinking, applied to a careful reading of the context for the word "environmentalist" in the transcripts of the US Congress since 1960 as modeled by word embedding. But even a careful description does little to answer the question of what changed in Congress, why Congress delayed acting on the science of climate change to limit carbon emissions, or who was responsible. It may answer the question *what happened,* but not *why* or *how.*

Historians have a word for an account of change over time that never rises to the status of a meaningful explanation. They call such a descriptive account a "chronology," a setting in order of the chronology of what came first and what came later. A chronology may offer the starting point for many interesting research projects, for instance a paper probing the success and failure of campaigns to save endangered creatures. But in packaging the mere chronology of new interests and language as potential progress, our story does a profound disservice to the understanding of the recent failures of government around climate change that scholars and journalists have established as one of the weightiest tragedies of our time. In fact, historians already know that we need explanations of congressional passivity.

The stakes of understanding why the US Congress delayed action on the science of climate change, which has changed little since the 1960s, are enormous. For environmental historians and journalists concerned with recent failures of government to respond to the science of climate change – including Naomi Oreskes and Eric Conway, David Wallace-Wells, Nathaniel Rich, and others – the crucial historical fact of the last half century is the scientific community's growing awareness of how life on earth is imperiled by a changing climate. The next most crucial fact is the unwillingness of national governments to act on this scientific consensus, especially salient in the failure of the US Congress.[6] The delays of the relatively recent past – that is, of the years since 1968 (the earliest scientific consensus around climate change) or 1988 (the year when the data was first presented to Congress) – have exponentially raised the cost of dealing with climate change for future generations.[7]

Focusing on what matters is what distinguishes the work of *mere chronology* – such as that demonstrated in the narrative experiment of the first pages of this chapter – from *historical explanation,* where a historian gives an account of the most significant change and why it happened. Is it possible for a scholar to move from a list of words, like those recounted above, toward explanation? This chapter will argue that it is – to a point. Skillfully modeling an explanation from text requires the analyst to intelligently move between different models of language and counting. Modeling an explanation *well* also entails the historian's knowing when to stop.

From Chronology to Historical Explanation: Seeing through Data to What Matters

When is a description of historical change sufficient for an explanation? In his 1970 magnum opus *Historians' Fallacies,* David Hackett Fischer argued that the work of history was essentially concerned with the explanation of

---

[6] Some readers will object that there is no rule that *intervention* is the law of governments, and that looking for why Congress failed to respond is therefore motivated by a false premise. Historians have answers for this. In his model of bureaucracy since the nineteenth century, British historian Oliver MacDonough formulated a theory of how governments in modern countries respond to crises: first by investigating, then by formalizing solutions, and then by passing laws to enact those solutions, a process that he believes was already way as an implicit response to disease, poverty, etc., in the nineteenth century. Oliver MacDonagh, "The Nineteenth-Century Revolution in Government: A Reappraisal," *The Historical Journal* 1:1 (January 1, 1958): 52–67, While American historians have long maintained that America had been a small-government nation for many years, that opinion has been revised by certain authors, especially William J. Novak, "The Myth of the 'Weak' American State," *The American Historical Review* 113:3 1 (June 1, 2008): 752–72, https://doi.org/10.1086/ahr .113.3.752.

[7] For the chronology of climate science, consensus, and the presentations of scientists to various branches of the US government, see Naomi Oreskes and Erik M. Conway, *Merchants of Doubt: How a Handful of Scientists Obscured the Truth on Issues from Tobacco Smoke to Global Warming* (London: Bloomsbury, 2011), ch. 8. For 1988 and Congress, see Charles C. Mann, *The Wizard and the Prophet: Two Remarkable Scientists and Their Dueling Visions to Shape Tomorrow's World* (New York: Knopf Doubleday, 2018), 326–27. Mark Stander Bowen, *Censoring Science: Inside the Political Attack on Dr. James Hansen and the Truth of Global Warming* (New York: Penguin, 2008).

events and their outcomes in the past and that a high standard of explanation required historians to adopt high standards for which events were meaningful. Remodeling the work of the discipline on contemporary ideas about explanation in physics, Fischer asserted that a "complete" explanation, or successful work of history, could be defined by two complementary halves: one that identified a major event, which he conceived of as an *explandum,* or something that needed to be explained; the other, the causal forces that explained why that shift should have happened at that time, which Fischer dubbed the *explanans.*[8] More recently, some historians, for instance Lynn Hunt, have favored "how?" as an equally important question to Fischer's "why?" Where asking *why?* seeks to assign causal agency to individuals or environmental factors that combine to produce a new historical experience, asking *how?* gets at the richness of the many processes of ideation, identity-making, and the exchanges of symbols by which meaning is made. The words themselves in the embedding offer a partial answer to *how?* – that is, they tell us about the discourses around the environment that circulated in Congress. With more specificity about how each word was used in argument and speech, we would quickly arrive at an understanding of how politicians formulated words into ideas, beliefs and norms about nature, the economy, and how Congress should respond to news of climate change. To follow the question *how?,* we can use word embeddings like an old-fashioned card catalog, tracing a subject keyword back to individual speeches, and then interpreting them. To understand *why* some actors formulated their words into a discourse about spotted owls, or about radical elites and their investment in environmentalism, we must trace the words back to individual speakers and formulate hypotheses about why they might have launched such an argument at such a time.

I am attracted to Fischer's language of an "explanation" that can be divided into an *explanans* (explaining factors) and *explananda* (a temporal experience to be explained), although it may seem old-fashioned to some readers, because Fischer participated in the kind of "translation" process that I lay out in Chapter 2, when I sought to clarify the shibboleths of data-science language that make clear thinking about the past difficult. Fischer's understanding of "explanation," borrowed from contemporary physics, offers a corollary to what I called, in the introduction, the search for "meaning," and so it stands as one possible standard for asking "Which historical research projects matter?" If the standard for successful text mining is historical meaning, explanation is a decent candidate, because

---

[8] David H. Fischer, *Historian's Fallacies* (New York: Harper Collins, 1970).

it asks first *what* happened in the past that must be explained, whether the explanatory factor is construed (narrowly, with Fischer) as "why" or more broadly (with Hunt) as "how."

What is the role of new methods, for instance text mining, in guiding discernment about which events and explanations matter? Just such an approach lends itself when we have an encompassing set of data about some discrete archive in front of us, for instance in the distillation of twentieth-century trends provided above. Being able to catalog the archive as a whole offers the opportunity to identify each of the individual changes or shifts demonstrated in the historical material and to organize them into the main events and causal mechanisms that Fischer favored as the material of history. Computational approaches may guide and even enhance such an endeavor by availing the analyst of a consistent approach to a wider swath of sources taken from a longer duration than are typically studied. But the matter of historical explanation is essentially narrative in nature. Narratives about the meaning of change in the data are *built on top of* observations made about the past – whether those observations are constructed atop legal treatises in the archive, one lawsuit at a time, or on the basis of a series of visualizations and tables carefully honed with the help of computational statistics about words and their change over time.

First *Explanandum*: A Shift in the Moral Vocabulary for Discussing Environmental Issues

One of the things that matters in the history of political apathy around climate change is the attitude toward climate science, which was dismissed both in Congress and in the press, as Oreskes and Conway have shown, as a species of alarmism that needed to be subjected to further peer review. The word embeddings model described above can tell us more about attitudes toward environmentalists – but only if we go looking for them.

As we have seen throughout this book, producing meaning from text mining often requires a step where the analyst reads the results and submits them to a critical judgment that is not computational. Reviewing the output of the word embedding model *by hand* – not via any automated process – I made choices to focus on a question of "explanation" aligned with the writings of Oreskes, Wallace-Wells, and others. I wanted to understand not the entire panoply of environmental interests or terms in which biodiversity had been framed in the past. I wanted to understand why the US Congress had failed, once presented with the data, to respond. It occurred to me, in reading the word embeddings results, that many of the words and phrases co-located with the keyword "environmentalist" were terms of reproach. These terms that indicate moral judgment, whether the judgment of environmentalists that corporations were "despoiling" nature, or the judgment of conservatives that environmentalists were "kooks" distracted by nonsense. Other terms are more difficult to interpret without close reading, for instance "alike" and "overly," modifiers that suggest a grouping function applied to minimize other points of view, which could at least in theory have been used by either left or right.

Some readers will wonder why I pursued this step by hand rather than by algorithm. Data scientists might have systematized this step of analysis with a sentiment analysis algorithm. But it can be a mistake to count sparse data rather than looking for oneself. Sentiment analysis algorithms developed to interpret Amazon reviews are notoriously ill-matched to textual data from other times and places. Working with the relatively sparse language of attacks on environmentalists, I wanted more hands-on control on the words – skipping some sentimental terms and identifying others, based not on pure sentimentality but on what I was learning about the gradual formation of an attack on environmentalists after 1970. Therefore, I proceeded by hand.

Hand-selecting terms containing moral judgment from the first 500 terms in the word-embedding vector for each five-year period produces the results in Table 12.2. The resulting index of the moral terms invoked in debates about environmentalists reveals three major moments of tension where the vocabulary of moral dispute expanded relative to other periods: one in 1970–79, another in 1990–95, and a third in 2005–09. At these three peaks, the debates in which environmentalists were invoked were suddenly more vivid. Parties accused each other of being "selfish" or of "alarmism." They described other participants in the debates as being "critic[s]," "opponent[s]," "idealogue[s]," and "populist [s]." In the temporal valleys between these peaks – especially 1985–89 and 1995–99 – the range of terms for moral judgment leveled in debates associated with the keyword "environmentalist" appears to have noticeably dwindled. The environment might have been discussed, but the language grew less heated, and when moral judgment was applied, it was less vivid.

These three moments of charged language also illustrate that members of Congress often engaged the question of the truth of climate change on the level of rhetorical defenses and attacks. In the 1970s, those advocating for the environment were more likely to talk of "despoliation" condemning the "selfish[ness]" of the "unconcerned," talking "vehemently," "avidly," and "bluntly" about the facts, with their opponents dismissing them as

Table 12.2 *The moral discourse associated with the word "environmentalist," US Congress, 1970–2009.*

1970	1975	1980	1985	1990	1995	2000	2005
pollute	unconcerned	ardent	esthetics	alike	elitist	cash cow	enthusiast
vociferous	overly	combative	scenic	extremist	despoil	pollute	populist
despoilation	vociferous	supporter	avid	ideologue		backer	alarmism
loudly	vehemently	intensely		overzealous		dupe	advocate
bandwagon	death_knell	vociferous		adamantly		despoil	alike
alarmist	irreconcilable	naysayer		elitist		kowtow	pristine
adamantly	selfish	recreation		academician		elitist	pander
kook	extremism	outcry		supporter		demonize	frenzy
zealot	despoil			pollute		extremist	activist
howl	vociferously			stirred up		special interest	cozy
crazy	opponent					pristine	denier
selfish	lock_up					advocate	hardheaded
vigorously	gullible					ardent	populism
retort	uninformed					alarmist	dirty
hesitant	promoter					vilify	zealot
vehemently	spout						lover
critic	alike						rabid
crusade	pressure_group						vociferously
quibble	overzealous						alarmist
unconcerned	special_interest						
	yell						
	howl						
	nuisance						
	angry						
	virgin						
	ruining						
	mighty						
	pollute						
	liberal						

"vociferous," "alarmist[s]," "howl[ing]," or "whin[ing]," "crazy" "zealot[s]" and "academician[s]," driven on a "crusade" because of "quibble[s]." The attitudes described are sometimes dismissive of environmentalists, but the dispute reveals a historical fact: at three points in history, members of Congress are actively debating how seriously they should take the facts presented to them by science.

The affective descriptions of environmentalists died down in the 1980s, but resurged again in the 1990s. By 1990, the picture shifts from a debate over how seriously to take fact to assertions of a conspiracy. Environmentalists are condemned as "elitist" "academician," "stirred up" by "ideologue[s]," while environmentalists spoke of "join[ing] forces" and finding "common ground." The difference between the parties is on the one hand, a dismissal of environmentalism as an elite conspiracy, and on the other hand, a plea for cooperation. This apparent rift grows in force and tone over the following two decades, in which environmentalists are described routinely as "rabid" "zealot[s]," "alarmist[s]," "elitist[s]" and "extremist[s]" who "demonize" the opposition, "vilify" industry, spreading "alarmism" and "frenzy." Even as science corroborated the importance of rapid action, political rhetoric was undercutting science as a hysteria secretly planted by elite special interests.

Certain elements of this picture stay the same over time. Advocates of environmentalism meanwhile connected with positive feelings that did little to underscore urgency: they talked about themselves as "advocate [s]," "lover[s]" of the environment, who were "ardent" in their feelings. They talked about the fossil fuel industry as "dirty" interests," "big business," and "right-wing" "denier[s]" of facts.

But behind the constants, what begs to be explained is the change. Why, after 1989, when the science of atmospheric climate changed caused by carbon emissions was presented to Congress for the first time, did key speakers return to a language of dismissal? When, exactly, did the language of elitism erupt, and who made the charge of an elite conspiracy of environmentalists and why? We are able to ask questions of this specificity only because closer inspection of the word embedding model has led us to an apparent discontinuity.Although word embeddings tell us little about word-count – and so the scale of engagement – they produce an effective window into the changing color of discourse. For the purposes of explanation, they offer an important issue to be explained: they show us three events, corresponding to the three peaks of diversity in moral language around environmentalism. We have thus identified an *explananda* – a series of apparent events to be explained by delving into *why* and *how* the language changed.

Specifying the historical change in question and beginning to understand the explanatory causes behind it has drawn us to the limit of what the word embedding model for "environmentalist" can shows us. We will need to turn, instead, to alternative approaches, partially to be supplied by alternative methods of counting, and partially by secondary sources. We can nuance the findings above by adopting a different approach, one where the numbers are more transparent and thus easier to cross-check – an approach that I firmly recommend for the practice of digital history.

The word embeddings are an example of "black box" machine learning, which is to say that the algorithms behind their analysis are only open to limited inspection and adjustment. Generally speaking, the words associated with "environmentalist" by the model are located in speeches about environmentalism, and rigorously inspecting the in-text mentions of words in the context of debate supports the similarities proposed by the model. A more rigorous approach than the one taken here would corroborate the in-text word associations suggested by the model, confirming the interpretive sense with which each word was applied – something that I have not done in this brief demonstration, in part, because as an outsider to American political history and environmental history, I am less qualified to do so than other interpreters will be.

In text mining for historical analysis, we can complement black box machine learning with instances of "white box" machine learning through easily interpretable quantitative analysis of words over time. White box text mining – characterized by transparent quantitative data rather than black box algorithmic analysis – has recently been called for in the medical sciences, where some practitioners have advocated a preference for clear analyses where numbers can be traced, debated, and understood. A concrete example of cross-checking with transparent or white-box methods would be to count words that appear in the same sentence or phrase as the term "environmentalist" – a perfectly transparent measure which shows a dramatic rise from 1965 to 2009 in negative references to environmentalists articulated by speakers in Congress. I have performed my counts with the help of code, but counting keywords in context in a digitalized text is an approach within the grasp of most historians and, thus, this method also has the benefit of being accessible and therefore replicable within the broader community of practicing historians. It is to the results of such a count that I now turn.

First Explanatory Factor: Who Imagined an Environmentalist Conspiracy and When?

The terms used by speakers in Congress to cast a negative imputation on environmentalism have fallen and risen in number, diversity, and frequency over recent decades, from a low of five uses per slanderous term for the five-year period 1985–89, surging to a high of fifteen such remarks in 2005–09 (Figure 12.1), the last period for which we have data. Two-word phrases, for example, "radical environmentalist," have had an even more marked surge, from a handful of references in 1970 to eighty instances of the phrase spoken in the period 2005–09.

The negative words most frequently associated with "environmentalist" have changed. The dominant form of denouncing environmental advocacy – as "overzealous" (four counts in 1970–74), "rabid" (frequent 1980–99), and "antibusiness" (1975–99) – experienced a marked decline; all three terms all but disappeared from the political lexicon by 1995.

After 1980, however, a new set of terms began to appear with regularity when environmentalism was invoked: "liberal," "activist," "crazy," and "extremist" (data not shown). The two-word phrases "radical environmentalist" and "extreme environmentalist," meanwhile, surged after 1985, the former term witnessing exponential growth in its use from 1995 to 1999 (Figure 12.1). It remains for historians of party politics to investigate whether this rhetoric was the work of a few individuals, an organized campaign, a shift in worldview that responded to trends in the media, and/or a spontaneous cultural phenomenon.

What the numbers illustrate, beyond a doubt, however, is a focused political trend hostile to environmentalism, not simply characterizing environmentalism as one possible economic concern among others (for instance the economic interests of coal miners), but rather tarring environmentalism as the invention of privileged special interests, that is, the "liberal" and the "wealthy," who show up after 2000 in the phrases "liberal environmentalist" and "wealthy environmentalist" as rhetorical figures whose presence in political storytelling suggests a hidden conspiracy of the elite. Together, the negative terminology suggests how dismissive language was applied to those who took up the science of climate change. Environmentalism was painted as a dangerous and radical political position, not a rational position in accord with science.

The data does not tell us a new narrative, of course, so much as it adds specific details about the timing of a political shift, the role of Congress as a rhetorical battleground, and a political style of disengagement that can be

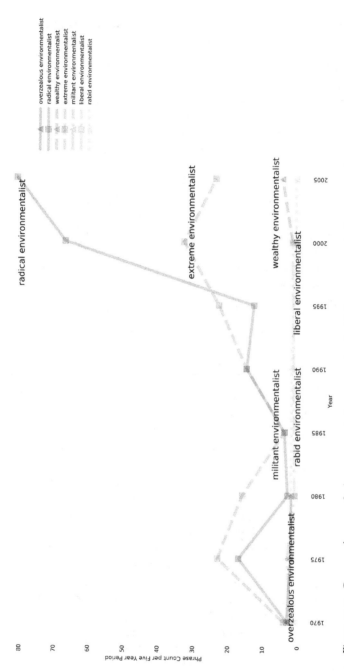

Figure 12.1 Raw wordcounts of select two-word phrases associated with "environmentalist" spoken in the US Congress, 1970–2009.

tracked in discourse today. Identifying the shift complements what we already know from Oreskes and Conway about concerted campaigns to cast doubt on scientific evidence.

Second Explanatory Factor: Changing Attitudes Toward the State

Word embeddings can also give us a portrait of wholesale retreat from the embrace of state as actor to the advocacy of the work of the free market. Generally speaking, this trend matches the consensus of intellectual historians who attribute trends in postwar political culture to the influence in economics departments and law schools of Friedrich Hayek, Milton Friedman, and other proponents of markets who urged the retraction of the power of the state.[9] Word embeddings simultaneously corroborate the account of growing faith in market power, while amplifying our understanding of what happened, when and why. Armed with a new analysis, historians may wonder whether the influence of immediate postwar debates was as important, where Congress was concerned, as later debates that transpired during the Cold War.

Consulting an embedding model for the keyword "administration" reminds us that a century ago debates over the administrative work of the government typically referenced a variety of roles – "ministerial," "departmental," "subordinate," "clerical," "regulatory," "supervisory," ""managerial," "investigative," and "enforcement" – of which bureaucracy was composed. In 1875, people imagined the work of government bureaucracy as an "organism," whose "centralization" required the "subordination" of a number of units working through coordination toward the same end. They also frequently referenced the values for which government bureaucracy strived, articulated in 1875–1905 in concepts such as "talent," "trust," "completeness," "faithfulness," and even (from 1915) "redistribution."

The lexicon that binds together trustworthy administration, managerial oversight, and virtue reflects an ideology associated with the thought of Max Weber, who imagined modern bureaucracies like the Post Office as the outcome of a centuries-long project of social and political evolution from clan behavior to court to nation-state.[10] The vocabulary employed by

---

[9] Angus Burgin, *The Great Persuasion: Reinventing Free Markets since the Depression* (Cambridge, MA: Harvard University Press, 2012), Daniel T. Rodgers, *Age of Fracture* (Cambridge, MA; London: Belknap Press, 2012).

[10] Max Weber, *Politics as a Vocation* (Philadelphia, PA: Fortress Press, 1968); Max Weber, *Economy and Society* (Berkeley, CA: University of California Press, 1968).

speakers in the US Congress through the 1960s suggests that they many were enthusiastic believers in Weber's conception of the state.

Discussions of government in Congress little referenced "private enterprise" before 1925, and through much of the twentieth century, discussions of the function of government in Congress were characterized by discussions of the role of different arms of government: the federal government against the local or municipal government; the duty of the government to "maintain" certain standards; the question of national debt, money, and government payments, and the problem of fighting corruption.

We can use word embeddings to do more than to simply supply a list of words that form the context of a keyword at a point of time. We can also look for clues about when new words came to form part of a discourse. In Figure 12.2, a dark shade indicates words that were used in the context of the keyword "government" from the nineteenth century forward. A lighter shade indicates new words that were paired with the keyword "government" to form a new discourse in more recent years.

A dramatic shift of shade around 1965–79 signals how the language of representatives in Congress transitioned from extolling the virtues of bureaucracy to the virtues of the unfettered market. During this time, negative references to the state began to proliferate in the form of allusions to "totalitarian state(s)," "oligarchy," and "red tape," while positive allusions to market principles began to abound with references to "private corporation(s) or "free enterprise."

The long-term rise of anti-statism in twentieth-century US is not new to the historiography. Historians such as Lawrence Glickman have mapped out how the phrase "free enterprise" began to circulate among popular conservative authors in the 1950s as a "common sense" antidote to the expanding state of the New Deal.[11]

What word embeddings add to such an account is a data-driven, objective view allowing us to pinpoint when and how the debate over state and market played out in Congress. Drawing directly on speech in Congress, the word-embedding chart indicates that a shift toward speech about the free market occurred in the 1960s and 1970s as a response to the Cold War. In contrast to Glickman's claim that the language of free enterprise (and with it, the rhetoric of markets versus the state) "changed little" from the 1920s to the 1980s, word embeddings allow us to pinpoint

---

[11] Lawrence B. Glickman, *Free Enterprise: An American History* (New Haven, CT: Yale University Press, 2019), 8.

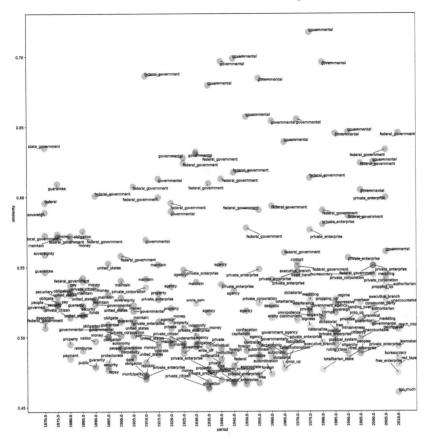

Figure 12.2 Words most similar to the keyword "government" in the US Congress, according to a word embeddings model.

an instructive shift in congressional speech.[12] Only from 1965, that is, the height of the Cold War, did members of Congress begin regularly to philosophize about the difference between "despotic," "totalitarian," "dictatorial," "oligarchic," or "communistic" governments. Speakers equated big government with despotism, bigness, oligarchy, meddling, and corruption, from roughly 1965 forward. The attack on "big government" drew on the language of Hannah Arendt and Barrington Moore, and which contrasted big-government systems with the positive aspects of "constitutionalism" (1965). In other words, it was only in 1965 that "free

[12] Ibid., 11.

enterprise" was weaponized in Congress as a tool for differentiating American's "small government" system from bureaucratic systems of government characterized by expert oversight.

Even more pronounced is the arrival of a new critique of government after 1990. Only then did discussions of government begin overall to dwell on questions of "privatiz[ing]," to discuss government as "intrusive," "unaccountable," or "meddling," as if the only form of administration that Congress could imagine was one characterized not by trust, talent, and responsibility, but by interference. That the turn against government in Congress was inspired by Cold War thinking is indicated by the fact that the language of this position closely mirrored the language of a half-century prior, such that warnings about "tyrannical," "authoritarian," and "communist" styles of government persisted into the 2000s, well after the fall of the Berlin Wall.

In the context of allusions to "environmentalist(s)," the shifting language of state and markets was particularly pronounced. From the 1980s forward, little language of administration appeared in the context of debates over the environment. Allusions to "free enterprise" and "market forces" show up with regularity, suggesting how Republicans leaned on "common sense" reasoning of popular conservatism to reject out-of-hand pleas for an expanded environmental mandate.

The debates of the 2000s over environmentalism were played out in a language totally different from that of the 1970s or 1990s. By 2005, the most common references to government's role in global warming were references to "socialism" and "totalitarian" or "authoritarian" government, sometimes echoing mentions of "Putin" or "Venezuela." It was far more frequent to hear references to the benefits of "private enterprise," "market forces," and "free enterprise." These findings should confirm the observation that a serious, concerted government approach to the problem of global warming has never been undertaken by the US government, as scientific news of global warming reached Congress in a climate of hostility to the federal government wherein leaders were unable or unwilling to imagine an active role for the state.

Four specific components of this trend are worthy of remark. The first is the imagined relevance of private landowners to solving climate change. As members of Congress retreated from a Weberian orientation to a neoliberal one, where private actors are held to be responsible, they began to reimagine the cast of characters concerned with the relationship between government and the environment. In 1970, the major sphere of government was imagined as a national bureaucracy, as epitomized by the new

Environmental Protection Administration (EPA), founded in 1970. By the 1980s, executive concern with environmental protection was marked by allusions to the secretary of the interior. Speakers frequently referenced private actors – for instance "rancher(s)," "forester(s)," and other "land-owner(s)" – as the proper agents for executing environmental reforms. By 2000, when "rollbacks" were under discussion, references to libertarianism and business interests outflanked discussions of the role of the state.

A second component of the trend is the rise of allusions to nongovernmental actors, for instance "Greenpeace" – frequently alluded to in Congress in the 1990s. This trend that matches the recent diagnoses of Stephen Macekura, who has argued that postwar twentieth-century politics embraced government by nongovernmental organizations (NGO) such as the World Wildlife Federation, which, because it was constrained to acting with the nonbinding power of philanthropy rather than the binding power of the state, therefore lacked the power to make effective decisions for the causes it supported.[13] Similarly, Greenpeace, as an NGO, had the capacity to stage remarkable feats of propaganda – for instance, boarding and occupying whaling vessels. But it lacked the regularity power of the EPA. It is worthy of remark that Greenpeace came to the forefront of debate in the 1990s, at a time when federal, not voluntary, action was being called for from the realm of science.

A third component of the trend toward markets is the lack of alignment between these imagined actors and the scale of carbon containment recommended by science. As speakers in the 1990s increasingly imagined the environment as a matter that could be settled by private actors, they were simultaneously involved in tilting the conversation about the environment back in time toward the language of an older scientific consensus about pollution and conservation. Conserving trees and aesthetic landscapes is a matter that can be handled by private actors. But atmospheric carbon, while it sometimes interfaces with issues of agricultural land use, has never been described by scientists as a matter that could be dealt with solely by landowners in the private sphere; state regulation of carbon emissions has always been part of the conversation.

A fourth component of the debate over state and market influence in the environment is the disappearance of references to a memory of a time when the landscape was considered the repository of a common experience. One of the great advantages in a distant reading of Congress is that we can glimpse the common reference point toward past and future that

---

[13] Stephen Macekura, *Of Limits and Growth* (Cambridge: Cambridge University Press, 2015).

structure discussions. Allusions to Cold War language or historical personages not infrequently turn up in the list of words associated by
frequency with a particular keyword. Similarly, in discussions of the
environment and environmentalism, we also see a shift in the historical
references at work in the imagination of speakers in Congress. Rachel
Carson was a frequent referent in 1970–74, her *Silent Spring* a major
touchstone for the need for environmental regulation.[14] From 1970 to
1994, regular references to the seventeenth-century English poet of fishing,
Izaak Walton, stipple discussions of conservation, speaking to a generation
who had grown up reading Walton in English literature courses in college
and for whom ecological conservation seemed rooted in a conservative,
traditional, masculine, and literary approach to recreation. In 1975,
speakers also entertained questions of the "long run" and the danger of
being "shortsighted" – a terminology that would all but disappear in
coming decades. After 1994, however, the historical references disappear,
as if the memory of eras and writers who valued the environment for its
own sake had dried up and were no longer relevant to an era of industry
and global warming. And here the embeddings model presents us with a
historical conundrum: *Why* is it that the historical past disappeared in
environmentalist rhetoric at this point and what are the consequences of
that failure of memory?

Attending to the shift in the discourse of government in Congress can
give us an important contextual hint for understanding the causal forces
that have paralyzed efforts to deal with the climate change emergency,
despite the consensus of atmospheric scientists since 1968 that humanity
had caused a disruption in planetary temperature that would result in
massive displacement and hunger. As Oreskes and Conway have shown,
the evidence on global warming had already been submitted to Congress
by the 1970s and 1980s. However, Congress failed to act, perhaps
distracted by the many campaigns to manufacture doubt seeded by a
handful of scientists on the payroll of big oil and amplified by journalists
associated with the *Wall Street Journal* and other leading American
newspapers.[15]

The history of Congress's language adds another dimension to the
Oreskes–Conway story about manufactured doubt. Even while big oil
attempted to destabilize faith in science, many members of Congress were
increasingly speaking in a language of faith in markets rather than faith in

[14] Rachel Carson, *Silent Spring* (New York: Houghton Mifflin, 1962).
[15] Oreskes and Conway, *Merchants of Doubt*.

bureaucracy.[16] The shift of language indicates that Congress was not, as a body, subjecting the EPA and other arms of government involved with environmental questions to the same probing of responsibility and value that characterized earlier generations' engagements with bureaucracy.

In short, a study of language suggests that members of Congress abandoned idioms of state trustworthiness and expertise just as they were most needed. The crisis of the environment was very much a crisis of the political imagination. To paraphrase Wittgenstein, we can't think or plan when we haven't availed ourselves of the language with which to do so. Similarly, we can't expect a national legislature to plan an organized response to climate change if the only language the legislature speaks is that of business.

Third Explanatory Factor: Naming Names

The changing discourse of government gives us a long-term condition that enabled members of Congress to ignore the case for a needed government intervention to reduce the carbon emissions behind climate change. But that long-term context does little to specify who was responsible for Congress turning a deaf ear to the work of scientists in documenting their rising concern about the science of climate. To understand the personal role of individuals, we need a blunter method: directly counting. We can count the instances of affective slurs against environmentalists documented in Figure 12.1.

The graph in Figure 12.3 identifies three members of the US Congress who between them contributed 60 percent of the phrases shown in Figure 12.1: Ted Stevens, senator for Alaska (1968–2009), Dana Rohrabacher, representative for California (1989–2019), and John Duncan, representative for Tennessee (1988–2018). All three were Republicans. Together with three other speakers – Walter Herger of California, Virginia Foxx of North Carolina, and Orrin Hatch of Utah – this tiny group of Republicans contributed 90 percent of the bigrams shown in Figure 12.1, inflating occasional complaints about "overzealous" advocacy into what amounted, after 1995, to an onslaught of condemnation directed at the advocates of science-based policy.

---

[16] The text of the Congressional debates is Matthew Gentzkow, Jesse M. Shapiro, and Matt Taddy. *Congressional Record for the 43rd–114th Congresses: Parsed Speeches and Phrase Counts.* Palo Alto, CA: Stanford Libraries [distributor] (January 1, 2018): https://data.stanford.edu/congress_text.

Figure 12.3   Speakers of negative bigrams containing the word "environmentalist." Searching the debates of the US Congress for phrases shown in Figure 12.1.

The data represents two clear turning points in the genesis of the anti-environmentalist lexicon. Stevens alone, of this group, began experimenting with negative epigrams targeting environmentalists as early as 1970, as Figure 12.3 shows. Representatives Herger and Duncan began their campaign in 1990, followed soon by a resurgence of activity by Stevens. After the year 2000, they were joined by Hatch and Rohrabacher, with Foxx adopting the lexicon briefly in 2005. As Duncan and Herger led an onslaught of coordinated phrases, Stevens' own use of the negative epigrams began to swell, suggesting that either (i) Stevens renewed his use of a negative vocabulary, charged with enthusiasm by the use of negative vocabulary by his fellow congressmen or (ii) the negative attacks on environmentalists after 1990 represented a coordinated campaign explicitly designed to attack contemporary environmental policy.

    The data from the archive of speeches in Congress can help us to identify major discontinuities in how environmentalism as a whole was talked about after 1960. It can help us to efficiently and cogently compare changing discourses about animals, political lobbies, and economic solutions. It can help us to contextualize the suspicion of centralized government response over the long term. It can even help us to identify a major explosion of slurs against environmentalists in the 1990s and the individuals responsible for that speech. All of these insights represent new contributions to an explanation of congressional inaction. But they are not what Fischer would have us look for – a "complete" explanation that accounts for the multiple causes of institutional change.

Why did six members' use of affective phrases against environmentalists explode during this time period? Why were their speeches seemingly synchronized in their use of these key phrases for a period of time – phrases that do not seem to have been broadly adopted by other members of Congress?

Historians are already aware of one possible context that might explain the explosion in attacks on environmentalists. In 1990, Republican candidates received a memo endorsed by Newt Gingrich entitled "Language: A Key Mechanism of Control."[17] The memo, drawing on the psychological linguistics associated with strategies Frank Luntz, suggested a list of words to Republicans about how to undermine environmentalists from the left. "Read them," exhorted the pamphlet. "Memorize as many as possible." The memo was accompanied by a collection of audiotapes and videotapes on tactics and strategy, drilling Republican candidates in the use of language to create a coordinated message undermining their opponents.[18]

In general, the memo urged candidates to stress the differences between Republican and their opponents by associating Democrats with weakness, red tape, and corruption. Among the words recommended was at least one of the terms whose usage exploded around 1995: "radical."

The members of Congress whose words are represented in Figure 12.1 followed Gingrich's advice in abstaining from an attack on the environment or nature per se, while developing an attack on the "environmentalist" as elitist and radical – that is, potentially corrupt, as opposed to an unbiased servant of science. In doing so, the speakers expanded upon the strategy that Luntz and Gingrich recommended in their memo: attacking environmentalists following this strategy, with the direct aim of undermining political opposition.

We now understand that attacks on environmentalists accomplished a secondary aim as well: undermining demands that carbon emissions be taken seriously in national policy, and ultimately contributing to the destabilization. But the use of data has added specificity to our picture of when and how these attacks took place. Using data gives us a glimpse of

---

[17] FAIR. "Language: A Key Mechanism of Control," (1995). https://fair.org/home/language-a-key-mechanism-of-control.

[18] Daniel Balz and Ronald Brownstein, *Storming the Gates* (Boston: Little, Brown and Company, 1996), 145–46; Julian Zelizer, *Burning Down the House* (New York: Penguin Random House, 2020), 294.

how members of Congress deployed the political strategies associated with Luntz and Gingrich. The data reveals surprising facts, for instance that it was only six representatives who were responsible for 90 percent of the words in circulation and that the explosion of attacks transpired over a five-year period. It shifts our attention from the names that political historians have traditionally equated with the Gingrich revolution in Republican politics – John Boehner, Dick Armey – and directs our attention to a new set of individual members of Congress who were remarkable for their deployment of weaponized language. The data also shapes our sense of chronology; and we learn that the proliferation of a linguistic attack on environmentalist was still contributing to the organization of members' speeches in Congress five years after the release of the memo. The "event" worthy of inspection becomes not the 1990 circulation of Gingrich's memo or even the 1994 class of representatives elected to Congress, who demonstrated greater willingness to deploy Gingrich's tactics, or even the 1995 Republican push to balance the budget so much as an even later onslaught of attacks against environmentalists that the memo seems to have enabled.[19] We can shift our analysis, in other words, from party policy and election cycles to actual *moments* when rhetoric was deployed.

Such an analysis leads to still further questions that might drive towards what Fischer calls a "complete" explanation, or an understanding of how and why the speakers' words changed at the moment when they did. To what factors do we credit the seeming coordination in timing of the individual speakers? Did each of them read Gingrich's article and apply it independently? Or did they share press clippings, meet, and prepare guided memos preparing a strategy that laid out which words to apply to environmentalists and when? We could speculate about the influence of lobbying interests on the six speakers in question, or about the role of news media in recirculating catchphrases and soundbites at the time.

Historians know that a finer-grain approach to truth is almost certainly out there, but importantly, a trained historian would realize that such questions as these represent the time to stop counting – and to return to the gumshoe work of interviewing individuals who were there at the time and poring over archival materials. Whatever the data has contributed thus far, the further answers we seek are not available in the data of the speeches in the *Congressional Record*. A historian committed to understanding the coordinated response of the major speakers in Congress during the 1990s

---

[19] For the significance of the 1994 class and the 1995 push for balancing the budget, see Balz and Brownstein, *Storming the Gates*, 151–57.

would turn to such a step next, using a more specific set of historic records to uncover the psychological, political, or even economic reasons behind the synchronization.

Then again, a committed historian might become curious about the usage of these phrases by particular individuals, especially Senator Ted Stevens, whose use of the phrase "extreme environmentalist" began well before it was adopted by most other speakers and intensified well before the surge of attacks in the 1990s. Data tells us where to look, but a trustworthy interpretation of why and how Stevens began to attack environmentalists requires looking at the phrases in context. While other representatives in Congress began their attacks on environmentalists around 1995, Ted Stevens' anti-environmentalist rhetoric began to take shape long before that of the others, dating from practically the beginning of his forty-year career in the Senate. For the final stage of investigation in this chapter, we will turn to a careful reading of Stevens' use of moralistic phrases about environmentalists.

Fourth Explanatory Factor: Three Moments in Ted Stevens' Career

Senator Ted Stevens was a Republican senator from Alaska who was elected to the Senate in 1968. He was a major proponent of the Trans-Alaska Pipeline, which was completed in 1977 and was a major source of income and employment in Alaska. He served in the Senate for 40 years, becoming the longest serving Republican senator in history and was a powerful voice for Alaska and its resources. Stevens was a key figure in the passage of the Alaska National Interest Lands Conservation Act in 1980, which set aside over 104 million acres of land for protection from development. He also worked to protect the rights of Alaska Native tribes and helped to secure billions of dollars in federal funding for infrastructure projects in the state.

In order to understand the role of attacks on environmentalists in Stevens' career, we may trust the phrases that have surfaced as relevant in our data analysis. But a timeline of wordcounts does not by itself count as a narrative of history. To effectively describe the processes of communication and signaling that normalized attacks on environmentalists, we must do more than count. We must also read and in reading develop a sensitivity to the specific historical contexts – political, economic, and cultural – in which attacks on environmentalists were first leveraged for certain purposes, asking: How did these attacks come to seem normal? In other words, at this point we will move from counting to the practice

I described in Chapter 4 as "guided reading," or careful inspection of prose from the primary-source documents from the past, using data as a guide towards where to start reading.

Data, after all, can point us to the significance of the phrase "extreme environmentalist" as the form of political attack that became routine by 1995, and data can point us to Ted Stevens as among the first and foremost users of this rhetorical approach. Data therefore points to Ted Stevens' speeches in which he uses the phrase "extreme environmentalist" as an important suite of sources that may illuminate the question of why Stevens and others started using the phrase and how that purpose changed over time. But the analysis at this stage is traditional – through the careful reading and inspection of documents. The data we have worked with does not tell us how to interpret those documents.

Stevens Invents the Attack on Environmentalist: The Trans-Alaska Pipeline Debate of 1973–79

The very first appearance of the phrase "extreme environmentalist" appears in a Stevens speech in 1973, as Stevens spoke to introduce the Alaska Pipeline Bill, which would have supported the surveying and construction the Trans-Alaska Pipeline System (TAPS), which called for the construction of a pipeline to transport oil from Alaska's North Slope to Valdez, Alaska. Stevens pressed the economic benefits that the Alaska pipeline would bring in terms of jobs, exhorting his listeners not to be swayed by "a minority of the *extreme environmentalists* of the country" [emphasis mine] who opposed the project.[20]

The Trans-Alaska Pipeline became the defining political event of Stevens' career. His 1973 bill passed in the Senate, but was not approved by the House. Undeterred, Stevens continued to push for the pipeline, introducing a revised bill in 1975. This bill was approved by both houses of Congress, but President Gerald Ford vetoed it. In 1977, President Jimmy Carter signed the Trans-Alaska Pipeline Authorization Act into law. This act provided for the construction of the pipeline and the establishment of the Alaska Pipeline Service Company to manage its day-to-day operations. In 1979, construction of the pipeline began. Senator Stevens was a major advocate for the project, pushing for its swift completion and defending it from potential legal and political challenges. Despite numerous delays, the pipeline was completed in 1977 and began

---

[20] Ted Stevens, Speech, (July 17, 1973).

transporting oil in June of that year. Since then, the pipeline has been a major source of debate in Congress, with members from both parties taking stances on its environmental impact, safety, and efficiency.

Stevens' rhetorical approach to environmentalist lobbies was launched around the battle for the Trans-Alaska. Although Stevens introduced the term "extreme environmentalists" and "extreme environmental groups" in as early as 1973, when the pipeline project was new (Table 12.3). The phrases were weaponized to support a broadly antidemocratic program, designed to limit the powers of grassroots activism as a whole, even while painting Stevens as the advocate of a diverse coalition of working people.

The speech where Stevens first wielded the phrase "extreme environmentalist" in advocating for the 1973 Alaska Pipeline Bill was itself a direct attack on the principle of grassroots democracy wielded through the courts. Stevens proposed to use Congress's power to render the entire project invulnerable to any later lawsuits from activists concerned with the pipeline's environmental or social implications.

The emergency action implied by a bill rerouting the pipeline around the courts was justified, in Stevens' rhetoric, by two contemporary events: first, the 1972 US Court of Appeals ruling on the contemporary environmentalist appeals against the Three Sisters Bridge in Washington, DC, and second, the 1973 OPEC oil embargo. The first – the bridge case – was a left-wing action to avoid the courts, which Stevens leaned on as a justification for his own antidemocratic policies.

The Three Sisters Bridge case (1970) was a conflict typical of the era of Jane Jacobs' campaign against Robert Moses. It pitted various grassroots groups – including African-American neighbors and environmentalists – against representatives of a developmental state who believed that they should have the power to build without limits. The key question was of whether a bridge supporting the George Washington Memorial Parkway would be built, against local citizen protest, through the wildlife area of the Three Sisters islets, as well as through African-American neighborhoods in Arlington, Virginia.[21]

In Arlington, Virginia and Washington, DC, neighbors of the proposed bridgehead weighed in again and again, using public hearings as a vehicle for drawing out the potential social and environmental disruptions that construction would entail. The neighbors who showed up to testify were pioneers of a new democratic forum – the public hearing – which

---

[21] Zachary M. Schrag, "The Freeway Fight in Washington, DC: The Three Sisters Bridge in Three Administrations," *Journal of Urban History* 30:5 (2004): 648–73.

Table 12.3 *Senator Ted Stevens' invocation of "extreme environmentalists" in the 1970s. Emphasis mine.*

Date	Sentence
1973-07-17	The administration has complied with NEPA, and our amendment takes the position that in view of that compliance, a minority of the **extreme environmentalists** of the country should not be able to delay the project. [...] The administration, in the lawsuit brought by the **extreme environmental groups** had been charged with failure to totally investigate the alternatives through Canada. [...] We are asking Congress to substitute its judgment for the judgment of the court in a case brought by **extreme environmental groups**, a small minority of our population, who say they will use the courts by any means possible to delay the construction of the pipeline.
1977-01-31	That was because of a long, drawn-out court fight. brought on by **extreme environmentalists**.
1978-03-21	It is fair that similar consideration be given to the people in Alaska whose employment opportunities would be disturbed if congress accedes to the requests of the **extreme environmentalist** organizations and sets aside almost a third of Alaska.
1978-06-14	In other words, onshore, where we can contain the risks and meet the problem of spills and the problem of runaway wells, the industry has been excluded because of the overzealousness of the **extreme environmentalists**, who are the same people who complain about the fact that the oil and gas industry is now exploring the Outer Continental Shelf. [...] But what they fail to recognize is that there is no other group more responsible for the premature exploration of the Outer Continental Shelf off Alaska than the **extreme environmental** movement that is insisting upon the passage of legislation such as H.R. 39 and which encouraged the withdrawal of all lands in Alaska until the 17d2 problem was resolved.
1978-06-19	For example. I understand now that there are some **extreme environmental** groups that are thinking about extending seaward boundaries off Hawaii 6 miles. To take the position that the oceans out to 6 miles should be managed for the benefit of land use, particularly for a single use concept involving millions of acres of land, is very shortsighted.
1978-08-01	It is one of the basic contentions in the so-called Alaska lands dispute that, as to the extent to which we know the mineral content of these Federal lands in Alaska, that the **extreme environmentalists** want to set aside before that knowledge is gained. [...] I must believe, knowing that Survey and its personnel the way I do, that the Survey has been throttled by those people who have infiltrated the administration from the **extreme environmental** organizations.
1978-08-10	Now, we have in the Department of Agriculture, in my opinion, an **extreme environmentalist cadre** that seems to be responsible to some equally **extreme environmentalists** in the White House. They are not loyal to the Secretary. They are not loyal to the Department.

Table 12.3 (*cont.*)

Date	Sentence
1979-04-26	It is going to be impossible to explain to the American people why this nation is not evaluating its own resources simply to please a special interest group, the **extreme** environmentalists. These groups are as much a special interest group as any other and do not look to balance the overall national interest.
1979-06-04	The administration continues to court the **extreme environmentalist** clique – about 3 or 4 percent of the people – that has infiltrated almost every department and division of the federal government and which continues to delay the development of the energy resources of this country.
1979-06-04	It has become a symbol of the **extreme environmentalists** demand to use land control to prevent rational and reasonable development under stipulations necessary to protect our environment.

contemporary theorists of urban planning believed was capable of eliminating the bias of race and class traditionally associated with urban development and slum clearance in particular.[22]

The case was also a notorious example of expensive, drawn-out public debate over a minor development issue that had played out in Congress's back yard. Over the course of a decade of hearings and debate, a political stalemate emerged around the bridge, involving presidential and legislative offices pitted against metropolitan ones. At the intervention of President Nixon, the Supreme Court of the United States heard the case and returned a Court of Appeals ruling that required metropolitan, local, and state authorities to comply with democratic hearings by citizens from the neighborhood, thus halting construction. Surely no senator who had been in office through the 1960s could have ignored those debates over the highway's path. As a freshman senator, Ted Stevens knew that the bridge was the argumentative hook he needed to win votes to protect another piece of infrastructural development – not a bridge, but a pipeline.

In Stevens' telling, the Three Sisters Bridge case proved that democratic deliberation was dangerous for a developing society. Some sort of bar needed to be enacted against the unchecked "crisis of rising expectations," as contemporary social scientists described it. Failing protections for vital infrastructure, nothing could be built in a dangerously democratic age. Gesturing at the Three Sisters Bridge stalemate, Stevens urged his fellow

[22] John Friedmann, *Retracking America* (Garden City, NY: Anchor, 1973).

senators to approve clauses in the proposed bill that would protect the Alaska pipeline from review in the courts. When Stevens' suggested text for the bill was passed as law in 1973, the Trans-Alaska Pipeline was a new kind of creature: a form of infrastructure utterly immune to protest. It was a piece of infrastructure that could not be called in for hearings or controverted in the courts. The language of Stevens' bill had rendered Congress – and not the courts or local legislatures or public hearings – the sole and sovereign authority capable of revising the pipeline plans.

Stevens' rationale for limiting deliberation was that court fights resulted in unnecessary delays and expenses. Indeed, the Trans-Alaska project had been subject to from hearings and court cases from 1969, before Stevens arrived in Washington as a senator. The legislation of 1973 allowed Trans-Alaska to begin building in 1975, averting further delay. As Stevens recounted the court battles in 1977, the court cases headed off by congressional intervention were a source of enormous and unnecessary expense:

> I stood on the dock in Valdez, Alaska in 1969 and saw the first pipe delivered. That pipe was not put in the ground until 1975. That was because of a long, drawn-out court fight. brought on by *extreme environmentalists*. In my opinion, if it had not been for that court fight, we would have had our gas pipeline completed by 1973 and the gas from our North Slope would have been delivered to what we call the South 48 by 1975. *This was the most expensive delay in the history of the United States.*[23]

In many of Stevens' speeches throughout the 1970s, democratic debate about infrastructure was represented as a potential item of unnecessary expense to the public purse. For Stevens, environmentalist objections to the pipeline were fundamentally motivated by a tactic of "delay" intended to paralyze American access to energy.[24] Stevens did not acknowledge the existence of any rational reason why the community of environmentalists might have been concerned with slowing an oil-based economy.

It was in the context of a rhetorical strategy of describing the pipeline and carbon interests as essential to American industry and warning against democratic pressures that Stevens minted a strategy of calling environmentalists "extreme" and "radical," while Stevens meanwhile pledged himself as the heroic proponent of the Trans-Alaska Pipeline (1973–2008), the Alaskan timber industry (1987–90), the Alaskan fisheries (1994–2000), and the building of roads and highways (1993–98). In contrast to the

[23] Ted Stevens, Speech, US Senate (Jan 31, 1977), emphasis mine.
[24] Ted Stevens, Speech, US Senate (June 4, 1979).

"extreme" beliefs of environmentalists, Stevens routinely cast development as "rational" and "reasonable," polarizing all possible political stances into two opposed categories.[25]

In effect, at the time that he launched his lasting verbal rhetorical attack on environmentalists, Stevens was introducing a procedural innovation designed to short-circuit grassroots activism in general, especially where it attempted to engage the process of the hearing to call into question development. "[T]he extreme environmentalists," he explained in 1979, routinely strategized to "use land control to prevent rational and reasonable development."[26] The only possible solution for such an insidious nuisance, Stevens argued, was to dismantle the options for democratic review. According to the terms of the 1973 Alaska Pipeline Act that installed the Trans-Alaska Pipeline, public review in the courts was banned, leaving Congress alone the sovereign authority with the power to review the pipeline. With this quiet assassination of the democratic hearing, cast as blame on the heads of zealots, Stevens launched his career.

Who were the "extreme environmentalists" of Stevens' speeches? They were environmentalists affiliated with different grassroots efforts to protect Alaskan wildlife and preserve the Alaskan wilderness from development. Their ranks specifically included representatives the Wilderness Society, the Sierra Club, and Friends of the Earth.[27] He mentioned individual biologists and bureaucrats at the EPA as caricatures, rarely using names, except in the case of George Frampton, Assistant Secretary of the interior for Fish, Wildlife, and Parks, and former president of the Wilderness Society, whom Stevens singled out in 1993 as a dangerous example of an "extremist" in power.[28]

Throughout the 1970s, Stevens consistently painted a picture of "extreme environmentalists" as lonesome individuals at odds with the wider consensus of scientists and trained administrators of land use in the Forest Service and Bureau of Land Management. These environmentalists were caricatured by Stevens as those who believed in absolute purity in terms of conservation over a reasonable marriage of economic development and wilderness preservation that could peaceably coexist. The possibility that Stevens' hard-headed protection of the oil economy and the

---

[25] Ted Stevens, Speech, US Senate (June 4, 1979).
[26] Ted Stevens, Speech, US Senate (June 4, 1979).
[27] Ted Stevens, Speech, US Senate (August 10, 1978).
[28] Ted Stevens, Speech, US Senate (June 30, 1993).

forestry industry might have blocked possibilities for the policing of fossil fuels was never acknowledged.

Already by the 1970s, Stevens had begun to paint this environmentalist caucus as misguided individuals who were fundamentally opposed to American economic growth. "It took over an hour for the people on the west coast to get gas, and those lines are going to get longer," he quipped in 1978, reminding his listeners of the centrality of oil to the American economy.[29] The 1973 OPEC oil embargo both justified the Alaska pipeline and became a permanent feature of Stevens' explanations of why the pipeline was crucial to America's economic and political stability.

Gesturing at the centrality of petroleum to the American economy allowed Stevens to make the case that he was the sole ally and defender of working-class interests. Contrasting the working class with the supposedly limited priorities of environmental advocates, Stevens would play up the diversity and need of those parties who stood to benefit from the pipeline. In 1978, he asked his listeners to consider the "people in Alaska whose employment opportunities would be disturbed" by any delay to the pipeline.[30] Later, he presented evidence that the pipeline was supported by veterans, steelworkers, fishermen, oil workers, loggers, mill workers, Jewish interests, African-American interests, all of whom united in supporting the development of Alaska. Similar allusions to working men would populate his speeches through the 1990s and 2000s.[31] By implication, the environmentalists who worked against development were also the enemies of diversity and of the working man.

Stevens emphasized the pipeline's place in a hoary tradition of American infrastructure development. His speeches regularly made references to long-term traditions in American democracy in order to justify the pipeline and government support of industry. The highest good, in Stevens' universe, was the unimpeded economic development of Alaska in general and the Alaskan oil and timber industries in particular, and he allowed no possible negative downstream consequences of this development. Environmentalists, in Stevens' view, were threatening the livelihood of Alaska's oil workers and timber workers, who depended upon the development of the pipeline and the exploitation of the Tongass National Forest for their income.[32]

---

[29] Ted Stevens, Speech, US Senate (April 26, 1979).
[30] Ted Stevens, Speech, US Senate (March 21, 1978).
[31] For instance, Ted Stevens, Speech, US Senate (July 26, 1994): "There are literally hundreds of timber workers and their families who are appealing to us to take some action."
[32] Ted Stevens, Speech, US Senate (June 12, 1990).

Occasionally, through his early speeches, Stevens made room for a conciliatory attitude towards activists of many stripes. As late as 1978, he was still trying to make common cause with environmentalists who lobbied against undersea drilling in the Outer Continental Shelf, even as he pressed the cause of the pipeline.[33] But this attitude of conciliation would disappear over time.

As Stevens' strategy matured, he began to minimize environmentalists rather than making common cause with them. Stevens' rhetoric would increasingly focus on representing the conservationists who opposed the Trans-Alaska Pipeline as an isolated and irrational minority, whose marginalization Stevens routinely pegged with the phrase "extreme environmentalists." Stevens' speeches to the senate would repeatedly insist were no more than a "clique" representing at most "3 or 4 percent of the people."[34] By 2002 his reckoning placed the figure even lower, at 2 percent.[35]

By the late 1970s, Stevens was developing a case that environmentalist agendas were poorly grounded in scientific fact and opposed to the open airing of ideas. In 1978, he accused "extreme environmentalists" of trying to move ahead with a ban on extraction in public lands in Alaska before a United States Geological Survey (USGS) survey was conducted, and he even asserted that environmentalists had intentionally "throttled" the surveying process itself in a quest to shut down information.[36] He went so far as asserting that environmentalist efforts to shut down public lands in Alaska were driving environmentally irresponsible practices off Alaska's coast.[37] By 1987, Stevens was gloating about how environmentalists' whimsical predictions about a loss to the caribou population had failed to play out.[38]

As early as 1979, Stevens had reduced environmentalists' claims about the public good to those of a "special interest like any other," and whose interests were therefore disconnected from "the overall national interest."[39] Stevens also began in this period to refer to environmentalists as the agents of "special interests," implying that money from elites outside Alaska was the primary motivation of environmentalism.[40] In 1993, defining the term

---

[33] Ted Stevens, Speech, US Senate (June 14, 1978).
[34] Ted Stevens, Speech, US Senate (June 4, 1979).
[35] Ted Stevens, Speech, US Senate (April 17, 2002).
[36] Ted Stevens, Speech, US Senate (August 1, 1978).
[37] Ted Stevens, Speech, US Senate (June 14, 1978).
[38] Ted Stevens, Speech, US Senate (June 19, 1987).
[39] Ted Stevens, Speech, US. Senate (April 26, 1979).
[40] Ted Stevens, Speech, US Senate (June 30, 1993).

"special interest" upon the confirmation hearing of George Frampton, Stevens compared Frampton's former standing as president of the Wilderness Society to the interestedness of appointing the president of "a major oil company" to such a position of power.[41] As Stevens had defined environmentalists since the 1970s, they represented an opposite extreme from development. There was no world in which the concerns of the Wilderness Society merely represented the common good.

Stevens also developed, early on, a conspiratorial stance on environmentalists as potential saboteurs who were intent upon deliberately undermining the workings of the state itself, like the Communist spies in a Hitchcock film who masqueraded as ordinary workers until they had dismantled the workings of crucial American machinery. In several speeches, Stevens even suggested that extreme environmentalists had infiltrated the Department of the Interior, where instead of advocating for the public, they were advocating for the minority interests of those groups: "They are not loyal to the Department," insisted Stevens in 1978. "Instead, they come from the various organizations that have aligned themselves in the past with programs aimed at attacking organizations like the Forest Service, and I think it is high time the Senate looked into this situation."[42] In 1979 he repeated the quasi-McCarthyist charge that environmentalists had "infiltrated almost every department and division of the federal government" with the express intent of cutting short America's access to oil.[43] Stevens repeated these charge in 1993 upon George Frampton's appointment to the Department of the Interior, arguing that the radical extremists of the Wilderness Society "are going to try to come in that door of his."[44]

By the end of the 1970s, Stevens' rhetorical style was intensifying into an all-out assault. He launched a major campaign of speeches railing against environmentalism from April to June of 1979, when construction of the pipeline was underway, although subject to a number of political challenges. At this moment, Stevens began to shape claims about environmentalism that would echo in his attacks and the attacks of others over the next two decades: that environmentalists were detached from reality, a small special interest group motivated by the principle of self-enrichment.

[41] Ted Stevens, Speech, US Senate (June 30, 1993).
[42] Ted Stevens, Speech, US Senate (August 10, 1978).
[43] Ted Stevens, Speech, US Senate (June 4, 1979).
[44] Ted Stevens, Speech, US Senate (June 30, 1993).

Stevens as the Pioneer of the Gingrich Strategy: 1974–2000

For five years, from 1982 to 1987, Stevens put down the cudgel of the phrase "extreme environmentalist," turning his attention elsewhere. When it first returned to his diction, in 1987, however, it returned with a concentration that suggested deliberation. The context was a speech on June 19, 1987, upon the occasion of a proposal to protect the 1.5 million acres of the Arctic Wildlife Refuge Coastal Plain. Stevens, of course, wanted not protection, but more investigation and more development.

And so in this context, Stevens turned into a historian, commemorating the tenth anniversary of the Trans-Alaska Pipeline. Four times in a single speech, Stevens invoked the "extreme" politics of his adversaries, denouncing their "dire" predictions of species loss, and providing evidence that in the new regime of the Trans-Alaska Pipeline, the caribou had flourished. Meanwhile, Alaska's oil outputs swelled to 9 million barrels a day, thereby heroically stabilizing America's "energy future" against the "urgency" of threats from the Middle East.[45]

The story that Stevens offered his fellow Republicans in this retrospective history lesson was one about the power of rhetoric. In Stevens' telling, the fight had been a close one – tilted in his favor only by the sudden skyrocketing price of oil under OPEC as well as the single vote cast to break a tie in Congress by then Vice President Spiro Agnew. In other words, it was after 1987 that Stevens spun the tale that his *rhetoric* was the crucial act that had saved the Trans-Alaska Pipeline in the 1970s. When Stevens reminded his listeners of the powerful step he had secured to protect the pipeline's interest, namely, rendering further questioning toothless outside of Congress by officially closing the courts as an avenue of appeal, he was recommending a set of power plays – which included closing down democracy and his own rhetorical style – as one worthy of emulation by the entire Republican Party.

I know of no document that directly connects Stevens' speech of 1987 to the creation of the Gingrich memo, "Language: A Key Mechanism of Control." But as we have already established, the thinking of that memo, delivered to Republicans in Congress in 1990, ran in parallel to a strategy that Stevens had contrived nearly two decades previously, then recast as a moment of heroic rhetoric in his speech of 1987. The evidence suggests that Stevens' memorials of 1987 offered a compelling case of how language could tilt a vote in the Republicans' favor – just

---

[45] Ted Stevens, Speech, US Senate (June 19, 1987).

as Gingrich was looking for strategies that could unify and bolster the power of the Republican Party. In any case, Gingrich soon began urging his followers to use terms like "extreme" to typify their opponents, and no one responded as heartily as Stevens himself, who had been using that strategy for twenty years already (Table 12.4).

Following the issuance of Gingrich's memo, "Language: A Key Mechanism of Control" in 1990, Stevens' attacks on environmentalists remained sporadic but intense. In 1993, during the fight over the development of the Tongass National Forest, Stevens packed modifiers like "extreme" were packed into sentences, with as many as ten such instances of the word "extreme" in a single speech.[46] Stevens had pioneered the modality of rhetorical attacks on environmentalists in the 1970s, and in the 1990s he came to model the use of language to undermine environmentalists' credibility in public.

In the Gingrich era, Stevens continued his assault on environmentalists as poor stewards of scientific facts, while developing an argument that poor science masked a hidden agenda. In 1993, describing a campaign for goshawk preservation as a ruse for battering Alaska's economy, Stevens suggested that environmentalists had purposely undermined Alaskans' efforts at clarifying matters of geography and development. He described the Wilderness Society as the enemy of ground truth. "The Wilderness Society is afraid we will take these people and show them specific sites, make them understand that the site they are looking at is not the same as one 100 miles away or one 1,000 miles the other way," he explained to the Senate.[47] In 1994, he described environmentalists as drawing circles of 70–300 square miles "around every tree that has a goshawk nested in it," even though the environmentalists themselves knew that "the goshawk is not endangered" or even "threatened in our state."[48] Stevens suggested that similar distortions were afoot in efforts to protect wolves, which were likewise thriving in Alaska.[49] In 1998, he argued that conservation efforts conducted under the mantle of protecting bird migration were covertly being used to prohibit routine connection of an air force base by highway. In 2000, he argued that junk science was the basis for a sea lion protection rider on the Labor, Health, and Human Services Appropriations Bill.[50]

---

[46] Ted Stevens, Speech, US Senate (June 30, 1993).
[47] Ted Stevens, Speech, US Senate (June 30, 1993).
[48] Ted Stevens, Speech, US Senate (July 26, 1993).
[49] Ted Stevens, Speech, US Senate (July 26, 1993).
[50] Ted Stevens, Speech, US Senate (November 1, 2000).

Table 12.4 *Senator Ted Stevens' use of modifiers in the 1990s. Emphasis mine.*

Date	Sentence
1990-06-12	The people of my State and I are ready to see these issues settled. Alaskans will not stand aside and let the whims of **extreme environmentalists** destroy the economy of any region of our State. [...] We did set aside 1.4 million acres of the Tongass for wilderness in 1980.
1993-05-18	The mentality that Alaska is somehow a territory or a colony is not there among the **extreme environmentalists**. They believe that Alaskans have no right to use the Federal lands in our State.
1993-06-30	Mr. Frampton promised me he would take a balanced approach to the issues before him if he is confirmed as Assistant Secretary of the Interior for Fish, Wildlife, and Parks. [...] Mr. Frampton comes to us from one of the **extreme environmental** causes of the United States. He has been the president of the Wilderness Society. [...] I am sure that my friends on the other side of the aisle would say that I was being very **extreme**. I want the Senate to know that I think this President has been equally **extreme**. He has picked a person who represents the furthest out position in the environmental argument. the most **extreme person** that I know of. He has to change his position from being an **extreme environmentalist** to a balanced administrator, and that is going to require a great deal of strength and courage and integrity to do so. The **extremely volatile** organizations with whom he has worked are going to try to come in that door of his, as would the colleagues of a president of a major oil company if he were in such a position. They are going to try to pursue their **special interests,** as would the colleagues of the corporate president. Mr. Frampton will have to consider, as I am sure the corporate oil company president would, the national interest and not just the **special interests** of his former colleagues. [...] I do not criticize those people who want to be **extreme environmentalists**. [...] The **extreme environmentalists** want to treat Alaska as a total withdrawal, really. In order to accomplish Mr. Frampton's goals as the president of the Wilderness Society, we would have to withdraw the whole blasted state. [...] I think he represents that **extreme**. [...] I cannot believe that a President would select such an **extremist** [...].
1994-07-26	The Forest Service and the **extreme environmental community** have really just driven a stake right in the heart of the Tongass forest economy. [...] [T]he **extreme environmental community** has contacted every Member of the Senate and urged them to vote against my amendment because, they say, I plan to disturb the Pacfish policy of the Pacific Northwest. Nothing could be further than the truth. [...] The amendment I presented to the committee was not an amendment that dealt with Pacfish, as **the extreme environmental community** has told Members of the Senate. [...] [The executive agencies] deserve much more than they have received at the hands of the **extreme environmentalists,** and the time is going to come when I am going to start making some of these people tell the truth.

The agenda behind such easily contested science, according to Stevens, could not possibly have been the actual defense of real animal populations. Rather, the possibility of contested numbers illustrated that environmentalists, like communist saboteurs, worked for a hidden agenda – the desire for media attention. Stevens cast environmentalists as a creature of the media age, driven by the power of stories rather than the firmness of fact. In a speech in 1981, when Reagan's secretary of the Interior, James Watt, came under fire, Stevens quoted from a leaked emo from an environmental movement that advocated press coverage as their aim:

> Their plan, they say, is designed – and I am quoting from the memo – for "maximum political and media impact." They suggest that actual events be "staged to assure maximum coverage, especially for television cameras." They recommend that the announcement of the petitions be "held in conjunction with your highly photographic rally at which you turn out a nice big throng of club folks and others to cheer at every anti-Watt statement and to conduct a kind of pep rally for your chapter representative as he/she departs." I find it very interesting, Mr. President, that nowhere in the plan do they mention policies or actions with which they disagree. There is no suggestion that those who are participating in this rally make an effort to talk about the issues. There is no attempt to make constructive proposals. This is simply a staged media event, and I hope Congress will see through these tactics.[51]

In Stevens' telling, environmentalism was about show crowds and photo opportunities; Stevens' own brand of developmental governance was about fact, constructive debate, and reconciliation. He made no mention of his own role in outlawing the hearing process that should have been the major vehicle for fact-finding and constructive debate around the Trans-Alaska Pipeline. In contrast to the fickle, volatile environmentalists whose science was so easy to contest, Stevens painted himself as the champion of transparency: "The time is going to come when I am going to start making some of these people tell the truth," he averred in 1994.[52]

Stevens believed that media fanfare was intended to distract the public from the fact that environmentalism, in its most basic form, was a puritanical ideology opposed to economic growth and required absolute reverence for nature divorced from human enjoyment. From June 1990 forward, when the questions over the Tongass National Forest were debated anew, Stevens launched into caricatures of environmentalists

---

[51] Ted Stevens, Speech, US Senate (October 16, 1981).
[52] Ted Stevens, Speech, US Senate (July 26, 1993).

whose "whims" were bent on "destroy[ing] the economy of any region of our state."[53] Again and again he painted environmentalists as the opponents of enjoyment "The Wilderness Society does not like the idea that Alaskans are able to visit and use these lands within the borders of our state," asserted Stevens in 1993.[54] He went on to explain that "in order to accomplish Mr. Frampton's goals as the president of the Wilderness Society, we would have to withdraw the whole blasted state," implying that environmentalism as a whole required a total and unreasonable separation of humans and nature, precluding not only development but even tourism.[55] In 1998 he reminded his listeners that two-thirds of the state of Alaska was already "withdrawn federal land," which he explained in the following terms: "It is there for us to look at, but we can't use it without permission from some bureaucrat who is compelled by a law passed by the extreme environmentalists who come to this floor and say we need to withdraw more, we need to protect this more." [56] Stevens explained that environmentalists were driven by misguided sentimentalism about the old growth forest, which he assured his listeners, "will never be cut."[57] He also referenced "doomsday" thinking and "naysayers and doomsday advocates," casting concerns about climate change as a species of apocalyptic cult.[58] Nowhere did Stevens credit a relationship between deforestation, cheap oil, and global climate change.

Through the 1990s, Stevens increasingly also painted environmentalists as the enemies of democracy – a charge that, as we have seen, could be all the more easily laid at his own feet. Whereas early in his speeches in the 1970s, Stevens had accused environmentalists of infiltrating government offices to undermine the economy, increasingly he also painted environmentalists as enemies of the ordinary enjoyment of citizenship, whose blessings in other states included the enjoyment of public works projects. In 1993, he accused environmentalists of desiring to deprive Alaskans of their natural economic rights, treating Alaskans as denizens of a "colony" rather than "as residents of a full-fledged state," a charge he repeated within months.[59] "The Wilderness Society has a colonial mentality," he quipped,

[53] Ted Stevens, Speech, US Senate (June 12, 1990).
[54] Ted Stevens, Speech, US Senate (June 30, 1993).
[55] Ted Stevens, Speech, US Senate (June 30, 1993).
[56] Ted Stevens, Speech, US. Senate (June 30, 1993).
[57] Ted Stevens, Speech, US Senate (July 26, 1993).
[58] Ted Stevens, Speech, US Senate (October 16, 1981) (second quotation) and (July 26, 1993) (first quotation).
[59] Ted Stevens, Speech, US Senate (May 18, 1993) and (June 30, 1993): "We are here in Congress to represent the people of a State. We must be treated as a State. We are not to be treated as a colony."

"They do not think we should have any rights as Americans."[60] He argued that environmentalists fundamentally opposed Alaskans' involvement in determining the future of land use, even suggesting that environmentalists had conspired to keep Alaska from having access to a regional EPA office.[61] In 1998, he warned his listeners of an environmentalist plot to deny Alaskans highways. Environmentalists, he argued, had taken the attitude that "we need to come up with some way to prevent Alaskans from living."[62]

Stevens' attacks on environmentalists, from in the 1970s to the 2000s, helped to set the pattern that later Republicans would follow. They set the tone for portraying environmentalists as marginalized enemies of the economy. In the 2000s, Stevens would take these attacks to an even further extreme, buoyed by a sound-wave of his fellow Republicans echoing his terms of denunciation.

Attacks on Environmentalists after 2001: Radicals Who Threatened the Nation

It was shortly after September 11, 2001, when Stevens first began to call environmentalists not "extreme" but "radical," a word chosen for its potential to trigger associations with radical Islamism (Table 12.5).

In April of 2002, Stevens faced down a filibuster designed to stop the progress of the Alaska pipeline. Twice, Stevens displayed a poster of General Eisenhower advocating work in oil as essential to military victory again. He framed contemporary oil workers as the equivalent of military labor, a vital sector in staving off potential attacks from suicide bombers, not only directly – by supplying the military with oil – but indirectly, by competing with Saudi Arabia and Iraq for oil money and therefore. According to Stevens, drilling for oil in Alaska was a patriotic act in an age of terrorism because it diverted the ability of would-be sponsor governments to pay for suicide bombers.[63]

Like Stevens' site of speeches delivered from April to June of 1979, the speeches of 2002 were likewise launched in the late spring as Alaskan soil thawed and the construction industry readied itself for more work – that

---

[60] Ted Stevens, Speech, US Senate (June 30, 1993).
[61] Ted Stevens, Speech, US Senate (June 30, 1993).
[62] Ted Stevens, Speech, US Senate (October 1, 1998).
[63] Ted Stevens, Speech, US Senate (April 12, 2002).

Table 12.5 *Senator Ted Stevens' invocations of "radical environmentalists" in 2002. Emphasis mine.*

Date	Sentence
2002-04-08	That promise has not been kept because of the opposition that has come from the **radical portion of the environmental lobbying group** in this city. It is time to put **radical environmentalists** behind us and realize this country is united in trying to fight this war against global terrorism.
2002-04-12	The great environmental organizations – call them the **radical environmental organizations** – opposed the building of the Alaska oil pipeline. As a matter of fact, that pipeline was delayed for over 4 years by litigation brought by these **radical groups** trying to prove everything from we were going to kill the caribou to we were going to destroy the area. [. . .] It was signed by himself and Senator Hatfield – urging that the views expressed by these **extreme radical environmentalists** be ignored because of the great necessity to have that oil because it was a matter of national security. [. . .] We are at war again, and the same **radical environmentalists** are now opposing us moving out into another area of Alaska to explore for oil and gas. [. . .] Should a small group of **radical environmentalists** block the United States from obtaining another source of oil to lead us toward total dependence on foreign sources? At [. . .] What happened to the *New York Times*? Change of management? Yes, another change of management. Maybe they hired one of the **radical environmentalists**, for all I know.
2002-04-15	An interesting thing about it is, if the amendment we have is defeated, the oil industry will not proceed. The steel industry will not proceed. The natural gas pipeline will not proceed. But not one of these **radical environmentalists** will lose their health care coverage. The American steel retirees are going to be the ones who pay the price in the long run. [. . .] The **radical environmentalists** of this country have overwhelmed the Congress.
2002-04-17	The minority of the population – 2 percent – which represents these **radical environmentalists**.

the rhetoric of political radicalism was honed and developed. Stevens was pressing for an extension to the Trans-Alaska Pipeline that would link the lower 48 states of the United States to the Prudhoe Bay oil fields on the North Slope of Alaska. In the midst of these debates, Democrats threatened to stall the pipeline project through the application of the filibuster (see Table 12.4). Stevens countered by introducing a new line of argument: that environmentalists were undercutting the War on Terror by limiting American access to American oil, causing America and the other nations of the world to become dependent on foreign oil.

Conclusion: Using Methods as if Explanation Mattered

Drawing together the insights of our multiple investigations, we began the case studies in this chapter by using word embeddings of the keyword "environmentalist" to survey the many dimensions of how congressional speech about environmental issues changed since 1970, including shifting geographical and biological subjects that captured Congress's imagination during this time. To narrow our study, we used word embeddings to identify a moral discourse of skepticism and disbelief that seems to support an explanation of why Congress failed to act when presented with the scientific facts of climate change. We used word embeddings to identify three moments – 1970–79, 1990–95, and 2005–09 – when a language of hostility and skepticism flared up in Congress. We next applied wordcounts to show that the use of negative phrases attacking environmentalists flared after 1990, the date of New Gingrich's memo on the use of language.

The dates of periods and fact of changing discourse together constitute half of our work of explanation. They offer a precise *explananda*, a fact of temporal change that is potentially meaningful. But they don't yet show the *explanans*, or the explanatory factors of how and why events played out this way.

To show how and why things played out the way they did, we returned to word embeddings for possible explanations, and found that in the 1970s, members of congress were increasingly likely to reference private interests like foresters, rather than experts, as the appropriate organ of land administration. Thus, an intellectual history demonstrates shifting attitudes towards markets and government offers one part of an explanation. We also used wordcount to consider which attacks on environmentalists were most frequent and when they occurred. Data demonstrated that a narrow and more precise series of attacks on environmentalists as "extreme" and "radical" were launched in 1990–95 by a small cohort of six members of Congress who together contributed 90 percent of the measured attacks against environmentalists. Finally, we used keywords in context – a strategy of reading guided by data – to trace the most prolific of those individuals involved in attacking environmentalists, Alaska's Senator Ted Stevens, from 1973, when he entered Congress, through his retirement in 2008, showing how his use of phrases such as "extreme environmentalist" matured in the course of his advocacy for the Trans-Alaska Pipeline and other development projects in the 1970s. We saw that Stevens effectively pioneered Gingrich's rhetorical strategy of using discourse to counter and minimize the ideas of the political opposition, and we also saw how Stevens advocated for his strategy in 1987, before Gingrich's memo, amplifying his use of this strategy after 1990 along with other members of the Republican Party. We finally saw that Stevens shifted his own rhetoric from the language of "extreme" to the language of "radical" in 2001, using language to substantiate his case that environmentalists, like radical Islamists, were potential enemies of the American people, possessed of a dangerous ideology bent on the destruction of the American economy.

What is the role of data in historical narrative laid out in the sections above? Data provides one medium for insight, but humanistic questions about what matters provide answers. Nor is data the only medium I used to produce explanations; careful reading of primary sources was also important. In the critical search process laid out in Chapter 4 of this book, we saw that researchers who employ text mining strategies are well served by attending to each stage in the research process with critical thinking. Previous chapters have demonstrated what it means to make critical inquiries into the bias of an archive, a perspective on temporal experience, or an individual algorithm. But this chapter offers insights about what it means to critically attend to the results of text-based data analysis, counting, and visualization. While data-driven visualizations give us some insight into historical change over time, they represent an enormous information loss. That information loss can be compensated for most efficiently by selecting samples of primary sources to read in depth, as we have done above.

Reading keywords in their original context (the "primary sources" of the historical research project) almost always adds insight, nuance, and detail that data-driven visualizations fail to capture. For proof of this, compare the detail-rich account of court cases, pipelines, and depictions of environmentalists in the section about on Ted Stevens (Tables 12.3–12.5) with the much sparser account of changing words over time in the earlier sections above on word embeddings and wordcount (Figures 12.1–12.3). The visualizations obscure as much as they reveal. The insight that Stevens' use of the language of "extreme environmentalism" changed to "radical environmentalism" in 2001 as part of an attempt to paint environmentalists as enemies of the state emerges not from the data visualizations, but from carefully reading speeches. Carefully reading words in context gives us information about historical change that cannot be deduced from a "distant reading" of dots on a timeline.

At the same time, the visualizations have added specificity to our inquiry. Perhaps a specialist in late twentieth-century American environmental history might have had a hunch that a study of Ted Stevens' speeches might be useful. But even a specialist might not have had the instinct to track how Ted Stevens' references "extreme" and "radical" constituted a pioneering experiment with the Republican strategies later endorsed by Gingrich. The vantage of overall change in the community – including the fact of 90 percent of the attacks on environmentalists coming from only six speakers – was a contribution from data-driven analysis. Data provides an objective metric of who the most relevant individuals were to this rhetorical approach, when the attacks on environmentalists crested, and which language seems to have been the most contagious. For the nonspecialist (like myself), getting context from data visualization provides a baseline of vital information about who said what when and when attacks on environmentalists crested. Even a specialist can receive important guidance about where to start reading from data-driven inquiries of this kind. It is indisputably the case, as this chapter demonstrates, that text mining can complement argumentative questions like the one about the political history of the environment. Through the power of aggregating information about thousands of debates and hundreds of millions of words, word embeddings allow the scholar to generalize.

Alternating between data analysis and careful reading – a part of the critical search process – creates better results than either strategy on its own. Reading Stevens' speeches, we might notice that his phrases for typifying environmentalists include phrases such as "extremist" and "extreme environmental groups," a phrase that was not counted in the original exercises represented in Figures 12.1–12.3. Careful reading of the other speakers' speeches would likely unveil other phrases equally meaningful.

Let it also be understood that the exercise above is merely a demonstration of part of the critical search process. Alternating between careful reading and data visualization could productively continue over several iterations. We could expand our search, using the lemma "extrem-" alongside a search for "environmentalist" in the same speech to gather references to "extremist" and "extreme environmental groups" made by all speakers in Congress, and we could see how the results line up with Figures 12.2–12.3. Knowing as we do from close reading that Stevens switched out the rhetoric of "extremist" for "radical" in 2001, we could search for those words over Congress as a whole, and we could see whether Stevens' rhetorical strategy was copied by others, and whether it was applied to denounce American activists beyond environmentalists, or whether environmentalists held a special status in these years. We would want to redesign our text mining visualizations to include those phrases and to gather the names of other speakers who employed them. If motivated to continue modeling, we could pursue a model of influence via text mining, tracing which other members of Congress in general adopted Stevens' stories about environmentalists "infiltrating" the offices of federal land management.

There is also a great deal more to read. In a fuller study, we would want to go in search of the language of moral judgment, finding those speakers who referenced "kooks" and "ideologues" from Table 12.1 in the context of discussing environmentalist positions. Broader reading would help us to test my assertion, garnered from the word embedding in Figure 12.2, that government was increasingly spoken about in terms of private landholders rather than civil servants. A fuller reading could also follow up on the other speakers from Figure 12.3. Stevens was the most prolific of the six speakers who attacked environmentalists identified in Figure 12.3, so it makes sense to begin reading his speeches. But the speeches of the other five are worth consulting as well. We would want to many relevant speeches carefully at this point, making note of meaningful rhetorical phrases that might have escaped our first pass at text mining.

The results of careful reading may confirm that the other five speakers of Figure 12.3 shared Stevens' strategies of minimizing environmentalists' scientific grounding and insinuating an alternative agenda. Or they may reveal a variety of different rhetorical strategies and political beliefs held by those speakers. The number of speeches identified as part of a trend in Figure 12.3 is relatively small – perhaps threefold the 15,000 words of Ted Stevens' speeches that I aggregated for the purposes of careful reading. Carefully reading those hundred pages of single-spaced prose is within the grasp of even an undergraduate preparing a final term paper. Such a source base – narrowed to the scale where it can be meaningfully read and digested – should certainly be consulted *through actual reading and note taking* by the researcher who would make definitive claims about the past.

If the point of this exercise were to write a definitive, data-driven history of attacks on environmentalists in Congress, reading remains the final gold standard of fact and believable interpretation. Free associations from reading data plotted over time may offer suggestions, but they are also easy to misinterpret. Until we look up the words in context, we don't actually know whether "kook" was a word applied by opponents of environmentalism to environmentalists, or whether liberal advocates of regulation protested that environmentalists were "not kooks." It is reading the words in context, rather than blindly accepting an apparent interpretation of a data visualization, that offers the final arbitration of truth about the past. And yet: the strongest case can be made by data and reading together.

Critical search – the only trustworthy standard for text mining in the humanities and social sciences – is necessarily an iterative process for investigating where meaningful change lies in the past. Iteration is important, because, as we have seen through the preceding sections of this chapter, with each new strategy, the shape of the inquiry and our conclusions about what happened when gently shift. That the analyst is capable of reframing their inquiry according to new insight is usually regarded, in the practice of history, as a satisfying demonstration that the analyst has gravitated towards persuasive evidence on the road to meaningful insight. What I hope to have illustrated in part is the importance of returning to the word embeddings model over multiple queries, not just the most obvious ones: therefore, my approach requires not merely reviewing the most prominent context for words, but also reading deeper into the word embeddings model for what I have called the "moral discourse" around environmentalism; not modeling only the changing context of the keyword "environmentalist," but also returning to word embeddings for information about background context, for instance the twentieth-century changing context of the keyword "government." The work of text mining is iterative and recursive, and it requires not merely a historian giving orders to a computer once, but multiple queries that evolve as the historian's sense of the problem develops.

I have not revisited the data here in creating alternative visualizations, compelling though they would be, because my point in this chapter is to underscore the shape of the research process. When we search for historical understanding about human experience, insight comes from alternating between perspectives – from data-driven visualizations to careful indexing and inspection of the data given another set of criteria, back to reading the text of speeches. There is nothing automatic about this process; rather, assembling facts into a narrative requires the artful skill of the individual skilled in the ancient craft of reading and thinking about the past, no matter whether the modern craftsperson consult data in the midst of their deliberations.

There are also important limits to the method of critical search as laid out here, and the chief one is that we have consulted only a single archive. Though we might look for signals of grand events in Congress and deem them worthy of study because they represent shifts of the political imagination in one of the world's leading powers, not all underlying causes are represented in the corpus of speeches in Congress. Many causes will have to be identified in the secondary literature. I have focused only on Congress in an attempt to elucidate the method. In a more extended study, it would be possible to trace the work of meaning-making around the discourse of environmentalism not only in the pages of congressional debate but also in the newspaper, the courts, and activist pamphlets and social media; indeed, the code used to generate these word embeddings could be applied to corpora of those other text bases without much work; the major labor is that of preparing the data. At certain leading research universities, funds and service positions exist to help researchers with such tasks as these, meaning that a follow-up project would be trivial.

In any case, a hybrid approach is probably the right solution: by using computational approaches alongside conceptual questions, such as the historian's problem of explanation, the analyst can leverage the scalar power of the algorithm against questions that matter. Such an approach requires a commitment to a textual database (the US Congress) and to a series of methods (at minimum, wordcount and word embeddings), as well as a working knowledge of debates over meaning in history and major forces in the twentieth century. The training required almost certainly places this work outside the grasp of the lone data analyst with no training in the humanities.

The most important part of the work is explanation – in the sense of identifying which questions mattered. My case study leans heavily on historians like Naomi Oreskes for the relevant question: Why did Congress not respond to the science of climate change? It then treats word embeddings, wordcounts, and guided reading as stops along the way to providing answers for questions that already exist in the world. Because of this imbalance of computational fungibility with respect to the evidence of *explanandum* and *explanans* as distributed in textual databases, the process of working with historical explanation in a digital setting is best understood as an art. Text mining can support historical explanation, but not automatically. The historical explanation that combines evidence from word embeddings will almost always have to rely on the analyst's understanding of and appreciation for historical context and grand questions of historical change, none of which are provided in computational form.

Regarding text mining as an *art* that requires a sense of *what matters*, engaged with humanists and social sciences, produces a very different research process from a data science paper concerned solely with *proof.* To date, many studies in the digital humanities and social sciences have by and large concentrated on the range and flexibility of applications of text mining to problems of social theory. In general, much classical canon of these articles has taken its form from computer science, which prizes a "methods" article concentrating on the workings of the computational approach, followed by a "proof" that shows reasonable working results when applied to the raw material of data, in this case some historical text. Likewise, most of the articles published by computer scientists such as David Blei and his collaborators, much admired from the digital humanities, take as their organization a paper on mathematical reasoning and computational methods followed by an extremely brief exposition of proof. The proof is typically a short illustration of how the language of some historical corpus changed over time – for example, using dynamic topic models to demonstrate the computer's ability to detect the changing interest of journals entries about neuroscience from the "the brain" (c. 1881) to the "synapse" (c. 2000) over the long twentieth century.[64] But looking for meaning, explanations, and what mattered in the past points us to a more complex kind of work with data. We cannot do that work supported only by a scientific method for testing a single hypothesis about a predictive and unchanging law.

Many digital humanities articles, including ones by the author, have gently adjusted the computer science approach, abbreviating the "methods" section to a short summary of the method and its applications by other scholars, and expanding the "proof" section into a careful summary of evidence, usually summarized with some discussion of how findings derived from computational methods expand findings available from traditional or archival ones.[65] Many articles in the digital humanities

---

[64] For the example, D. Blei and J. Lafferty, "Dynamic Topic Models," *Proceedings of the 23rd International Conference on Machine Learning*, June 2006, 113–20. See also Victor Veitch, Dhanya Sridhar, and David M. Blei, "Using Text Embeddings for Causal Inference," *ArXiv:1905.12741 [Cs, Stat]*, May 29, 2019, http://arxiv.org/abs/1905.12741; David M. Blei, "Probabilistic Topic Models," *Commun. ACM* 55:4 (April 2012): 77–84, https://doi.org/10.1145/2133806.2133826.

[65] I will cite my own work to clarify that I am not attacking other scholars when I describe one of the conventions of the subfield, which has been salutary at an early stage of development. Joanna Guldi, "The History of Walking and the Digital Turn: Stride and Lounge in London, 1808–1851," *The Journal of Modern History* 84:1 (2012): 116–44; Jo Guldi, "Parliament's Debates about Infrastructure: An Exercise in Using Dynamic Topic Models to Synthesize Historical Change," *Technology and Culture* 60:1 (March 21, 2019): 1–33. Other notable examples of the methods-proof organization include Saatviga Sudhahar Thomas, Lansdall-Welfare, Justin Lewis James Thompson, and Nello Cristianini FindMyPast Newspaper Team, "Content Analysis of 150 Years of British Periodicals," *PNAS (Proceedings of the National Academy of the Sciences)* 114:4 (January 9, 2017): E457–65, https://doi.org/10.1073/pnas.1606380114; Kellen Funk and Lincoln A. Mullen, "The Spine of American Law: Digital Text Analysis and U.S. Legal Practice," *The American Historical Review* 123:1 (February 1, 2018): 132–64, https://doi.org/10.1093/ahr/123.1.132; Sandeep Soni, Lauren F. Klein, and Jacob Eisenstein, "Abolitionist Networks: Modeling Language Change in Nineteenth-Century Activist Newspapers," *Journal of Cultural Analytics* 1:2 (January 18, 2021): 18841, https://doi.org/10.22148/001c.18841. This is not, of course, the only genre of presentation in the digital humanities and social sciences; it is, however, the primary model for introducing new techniques of text mining and generalizing about their implications.

have concentrated on exploring the applicability of a single method such as keyword count or topic modeling, harvesting a series of historical trends, and putting those trends into dialogue with the viewpoint of practicing historians. Indeed, some exposition of method is almost necessarily required by articles using new computational tools, so unfamiliar are these approaches to the bulk of readers in the humanities and social sciences.

Yet, as the opening of this chapter demonstrates, questions such as the contrast between chronology and explanation may necessarily require analysts who use computers to entertain questions that are wider than the approach afforded by any one model. Answering such questions well may be a matter of combining background reading and mental arithmetic with concepts, and iterating through computational approaches – in short, a matter of the sheer craft or artistry with which the individual approaches a problem. As I have suggested elsewhere, a thoughtful engagement with digital methods often requires alternating between multiple tools in order to illuminate the blind spots of any given algorithm or data set. It often requires setting the results of computational analysis against context from secondary sources and using the results of text mining as an index for delving back into primary sources.[66]

The final result of text mining, in other words, need not be a visualization that seems to distill meaning into a single frame. The point is that we are after meaning, typically in the form of a historical explanation that defines certain discontinuities over time, characterizes the difference between those events, and supplies some narrative about how those changes took shape and why they matter.

Text mining is simply one step in a process of analyzing the past whose power is superior to any of the automatic data visualizations generated by computer scientists looking for terms of proof. Far more important, for the purposes of valid and trustworthy discoveries about human experience, is how text mining, combined with critical thinking, a knowledge of historical opinion, and an engagement with primary sources, can supply the analyst with a robust, specific map of the shape of change in the past that discloses many events that would have previously escaped the reader's notice.

---

[66] Jo Guldi, "Critical Search: A Procedure for Guided Reading in Large-Scale Textual Corpora," *Journal of Cultural Analytics*, 2018, 1–35, https://doi.org/10.22148/16.030.

PART III

Disciplinary Implications

CHAPTER 13

A Map of World Culture, Purged of Bias

How realistic is it to believe that quantitative measures can be shorn of bias, and thus become a serious tool for understanding culture? Most historians today, including myself, trained to reckon with heady issues of interpretation and aesthetics, retain a degree of skepticism about the capacity of quantitative approaches to capture the reality of human experience. As I have urged throughout this book, that critical distance from quantification is an asset and a strength and yet it need not work to the utter exile of quantitative approaches from cultural analysis. Indeed, the two are already being used together to make grand discoveries about the human past and present.

Historians of my generation are also wary of grand generalizations about culture, knowing how European generalizations about the past recapitulated antique biases and were used to support the atrocities associated with colonization. In the course of confronting the prejudice of the past, scholars have debunked metahistorical narratives that assumed progress. They have deconstructed and problematized classifications of gender, race, and class – categories that themselves came into being in an earlier age.

Yet "universal" stories, which string together macroscopic views of the human past into a single frame, remain compelling, and with reason. Among the long stories of the past that remain compelling for the present is the history of human languages and myths, which distills into a single forking tree of human divergence, migration, convergence, and influence the thousand moments when languages diverge into accents, or into dialects, and then into new languages. The tree, historically, has not been without bias. Trees representing the history of human languages have been used as support for theories of racial superiority of the Aryan tribes, for instance. But the desire to plot the paths of divergence and convergence between languages remains larger than any one of the biases that motivated study in the past.

In a digital age, the study of worldview has returned in a new guise. Quantitative measures, applied in a critical fashion to big data about linguistic change in our common past, have been used to purge earlier generations of bias from the study of historical linguistics. Data scientists can quantitatively calculate the similarity and distance between languages present and past. Quantitative metrics offer a baseline standard for understanding linguistic similarity and those metrics, in turn, are less likely to be influenced by theories of racial superiority than rough estimates of linguistic history of old.

In the study of languages, then, quantitative measures have become an aid to objectivity in the service of purging an entire field of its inherited bias. Stories of this kind are important because they can lend perspective, courage, and caution. In our time, data visualizations built upon statistical analysis seem to offer a magic "key" to world mythologies, capable of synthesizing vast information about the past. Having worked hard to purge their disciplines of the implicit racism of the past, linguists and folklorists are now returning to the old questions about what defines a culture, guided by new, data-driven methods. Under those conditions, research into worldview is bearing new fruit.

A Brief History of the Rise and Fall of Keys to Mythology

It is easy to dismiss the fantasy of a universal key to world mythologies as just another phase of Victorian ideology. The phrase, of course, recalls George Eliot's intentionally ridiculous portrait of Edward Casaubon in *Middlemarch*. In the novel, Casaubon is a didactic scholar who labors intently on synthesizing the stories of all lands, whilst remaining out of touch with the lived experiences of the poor mothers and orphans around his estate who become the focus of his educated and empathetic wife Dorothy Brooke, whom Casaubon tries to reduce to a secretary.[1]

Scholars who are familiar with the story of worldview know that most disciplines in the university at some point in the twentieth century rejected

---

[1] In the beginning, Casaubon's project is presented as enchanting: Eliot describes Casaubon appearing in Dorothea's eyes as an "affable archangel," and his theories of dispersed mythological fragments are "luminous with the reflected light of correspondences." As the story progresses, however, Dorothea becomes disillusioned. What transpires is a sad tale of spousal indifference, born of the consuming project that Casaubon has taken at the risk of engagement with the world around him. So enmeshed in "bitter manuscript remarks on other men's notions about the solar deities" was he, that Casaubon at last became "indifferent to ... sunlight" itself.

master narratives about the hierarchy of languages associated with the racial bias of nineteenth-century European empires. Indeed, reviewing the story of Indo-European language research from the seventeenth through the nineteenth centuries underscores the fact that, in every generation, the study of worldview depends on the technologies and politics systems of its time.

Historically, keys to world mythology have much resembled the fictional Casaubon in their damaging relationship to the world around them. Consider the classic case of a search for shared mythology, the origins of Indo-European linguistic theory. From the seventeenth century, scholars attempted to draw together the languages of the world into a single, branching "tree" representing the historical relationship of world languages to each other.

The search for a key never really ceased. Richard Dawkins' 1976 introduction of the concept "meme" opened the gates of a quasi-scientific study of culture, cultural evolution, which aimed to apply the quantitative laws of genetic prediction to the memes of stories. In the 1980s, Germanic literary scholar Hans Blumenthal pushed in a similar direction, arguing for the "theriomorphic" or animal forms given to angst in classical mythology as an indication of the early role of storytelling for survival in our evolutionary history. By the 1990s, among the sites of the university where the analysis of mythology remained most alive was the subfield of biology known as "cultural evolution," where anthropologists and statisticians used models of diffusion to analyze the spread of memes across tribes. Some of the scholars of cultural evolution became the first scholars to experiment with the tools of latent semantic analysis that became part of the backbone of modern search engines and the digital humanities. As mythology retreated as a subject for the classical liberal arts, it was welcomed as a topic by new fields on the fringe of evolutionary science. What can we learn from the historic search for a key to the kinds of data that defined world culture? What was the promise, and what were the pitfalls of that endeavor?

In its time, Indo-European theory was a triumph of scale. It succeeded two centuries of linguistic theorizing and analysis since the Swiss orientalist Theodore Bibliander, the French scholar Isaac Casaubon, and his son Méric (for whom Eliot's hero was surely named) in which the relationships between Latin, Greek, and the Germanic languages were detailed with new precision. However, no overarching theory linking them into a family tree of evolving concepts over time was possible. Writes George Metcalf, the historian of early linguistics:

There was no general accord on many of the relationships that we consider basic today but that involved a more complicated pattern of relationship. There was, for instance, no proposal that might – even in a modest way – resemble the present Indo-European hypothesis that might account for the similarities that were found among Ancient Latin and Ancient Greek and the Germanic languages ... We must again ask why the age did not seem ripe for such a hypothesis.[2]

To answer his own question, Metcalf catalogues the rival hypotheses that accorded language a "special status," which classified language as a form of sacred object. "There was always the possibility that God had instituted" some particular language himself as the original and divinely ordained means of communication.[3] Candidates for this distinction included Hebrew, but also Dutch and Swedish, defended as the original God-given languages by seventeenth-century nationalists. What was sacred could be neither systematized nor historicized.

Indo-European blasted away so much chaff by providing an overarching theory built nowhere out of such speculation, composed entirely from fact. It also systematized a geographical relationship instead of the diachronic relationships of how Latin evolved from Greek and so on. It was initially proposed in Wittenberg in Germany around 1686 by Andreas Jäger, a Swedish pastor and polymath, who employed a set of genetic metaphors to classify mother-, sister-, and daughter-languages.[4] This metaphor, for Metcalf, became the organizing principle that allowed later enlightenment thinkers to entertain the possibility of historical change within systematic relationships. Just as branches of a family might develop along the lines of separate fates while nevertheless passing on common expressions, so too language "families" might have continued to evolve in different directions, even while the vestiges of shared experience remained visible across enormous distances.

The theory received its validation in the first colonial age of collecting, as gentleman collectors in India turned their profits from the indigo and tea trade to the problem of collecting objects, books, and ideas, inspired by the neoclassical painter Johan Zoffany's theories of universal beauty. Among them was Sir William Jones, graduate of Oxford, linguist, judge, and civil servant for the East India Company, whose time studying Sanskrit at the ancient Indian university of Nadiya armed him with the

---

[2] George J. Metcalf, *On Language Diversity and Relationship from Bibliander to Adelung* (John Benjamins, 2013), 22.
[3] Ibid., 25.   [4] Ibid., 33.

tools of testing current enlightenment theories about linguistic families. Recognizing family resemblances allowed him to formulate a theory of the relationships between Sanskrit, Persian, Latin, and Greek, which later scholars would fill in with a set of common shared cultural practices: patrilineal descent, hospitality, wagons, and a male sky god.[5]

We now understand that the colonial collectors of language helped to culturally justify the colonization of India.[6] Cultural knowledge, including collecting languages and stories, would supply administrators like Jones with the necessary tools to administer Mughal law within a system of courts presided over by English judges.[7] Enraptured as they may have been by the collection of stories and words from other cultures, they worked and promoted their ideas within a deeply racist and exploitative empire. Jones's linguistics studies, for example, helped to inspire similar cross-cultural work on Indo-European shared systems of law, for instance the famous "Village Community" by Henry Maine, which were used to justify the imposition of a systematic bureaucracy onto the *ryots* (peasant cultivators) of south India.[8]

Meanwhile, the linguistic theories that Jones helped to promote – the Indo-European tree of languages (Figure 13.1) – was applied in new context to justify new theories of racial and national superiority. Belief in the determinative effects of linguistically based culture and biologically shared race was the impulse at the heart of nineteenth-century nationalism. Applied as a justification for colonization, these ideas underlay the proliferation of plantation, slave, and coolie culture around the world.

Back in Europe, the tree of languages justified impulses of collecting words and stories that reinforced new theories of the hierarchy of races and nations. With Friedrich Schiller, collecting stories was wed to nationalism – the

---

[5] David W. Anthony, *The Horse, the Wheel, and Language: How Bronze-Age Riders from the Eurasian Steppes Shaped the Modern World* (Princeton, NJ: Princeton University Press, 2010), 15. Biographies of Jones include Thomas R. Trautmann, *Languages and Nations: The Dravidian Proof in Colonial Madras* (Berkeley, CA: University of California Press, 2006); Garland Cannon, *Oriental Jones: A Biography of Sir William Jones (1746–1794)* (London: Asia Publishing House, 1964); Michael J. Franklin, *"Orientalist Jones": Sir William Jones, Poet, Lawyer, and Linguist, 1746–1794* (Oxford: Oxford University Press, 2011).

[6] Perhaps ten years ago, the debate was replayed again, this time as a drama between historians. Historians of empire, such as Maya Jasanoff and Karuna Mantena, revisited the story of Indo-European linguistic theory and disrobed the politics of its origins, although the debate continues, with two women of color (Jasanoff and Mantena) on one hand and, on the other hand, Jones' (white) hagiographic biographer for Oxford University Press, Michael Franklin, defending him as a demolisher of Eurocentrism.

[7] Anthony, *The Horse, the Wheel, and Language*, 7.

[8] Metcalf, *On Language Diversity and Relationship*.

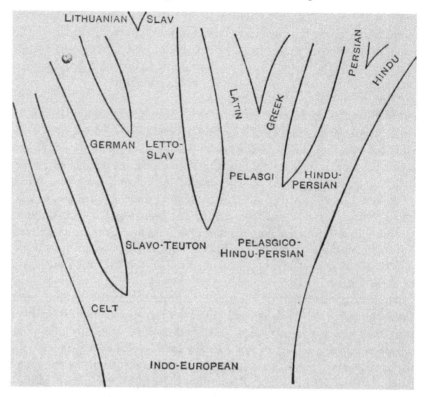

Figure 13.1   A tree of Indo-European languages, from Allg Kieler, Monatsschriften für Wissenschaft uber Litteratur (1853), p. 787, as reproduced by Otto Schrader in *Prehistoric Antiquities of the Aryan Peoples* (1890), p. 73.

stories of the people are the infancy of the nation. And the study of storytelling was launched on an altogether new scale, one that required the Brothers Grimm to trudge the countryside collecting stories. The search for ultimate origins motivated nationalistic fantasies of collecting peasant folktales, including the philosophy of Johann Gottfried Herder and the collections of the Brothers Grimm. National folktale collections were used to fill out the content of national identity, and hierarchies based on folktale-derived ordering lay at the root of racialized practices of medicine, literature, pedagogy, and law.

British Empire is not the only regime that used myth-making to codify a national hierarchy and whitewash its system as an objective study of culture. During the Cold War, American political scientists turned to

contemporary theories of culture to argue for the fundamental irreconcil-
ability of contending political worldviews. Harvard professor Samuel
Huntington's famous essay "The Clash of Civilizations" cites enlightenment precursors to his theory of incommensurable cultures nowhere, buts
its assertion of civilizations destined to clash posits as a starting point the
discrete and separate worldviews of different cultures. After all, if China
and Russia had remained beyond the pale of Indo-European culture for
millennia, only an idiot would imagine those independent cultures would
easily acquiesce to Lockean single-proprietor ownership or the habits of
democracy.[9]

Within a few years of Huntington's article, however, a rebellion transpired. The young anthropologists of the 1970s and 1980s – among
them Clifford Geertz, Marshall Sahlins, and Michael Taussig – took a
new position. Their scholarship was marked by a new attention to political
abstractions such as "gender" and "power," and a rebellion against
Eurocentrism. Instead, they looked with great detail into the cultural
and political context of myths and rituals, frequently coming to understand them as cultural coping mechanisms that evolved in the face of
political repression from above. Myth, in other words, was being revalued
as the people's tool for local resistance, rather than a universal system of
connection. It was being recast as something infinitely specific, that divides
people, rather than as an all-consuming set of practices that unites them.
Similar movements were made in contemporary sociology, religious studies, archaeology, and linguistics.

In linguistics, too, new generations of scholars began explicitly to
articulate the problems with inherited forms of analysis. In the hands of
mythology scholar Bruce Lincoln, Jones' formulation of a single Indo-
European tree of languages justifying European superiority offers another
cautionary tale: that of the "temptation" of finding centers and origins,
where history offers us only evolving discourses. Implicit in his critique is
the suggestion that we look for origin stories as a reflection of our own
prejudices, a process he describes as entering a "recursive spiral, spinning
their own myth while [scholars] sincerely believe themselves to be interpreting others who may even be the products of their imagination."[10]
Scholars of Lincoln's generation committed themselves to the process of
stripping away the bias of generations of scholarship past.

---

[9] Samuel Huntington, "The Clash of Civilizations," *Foreign Affairs* 72:3 (1993), 22–49.
[10] Bruce Lincoln, *Theorizing Myth: Narrative, Ideology, and Scholarship* (Chicago, IL: University of
Chicago Press, 1999).

Linguistics Reassembles Itself

The story of linguistics doesn't end with rebellions against nineteenth-century culture, however. Rather, the case of historical linguistics illustrates how critical insights about empire informed a new moment of data-gathering and research, one that has eventually turned back toward data-gathering, analysis, and visualization.

In the 1980s and 1990s, scholars of languages and mythology began to challenge the Indo-European tree with its implicit tale of shared origins and European mastery. As two observers put it, "historical linguistics stood in disarray as a result of failing to confront implicit assumptions at the heart of its assumptions about linguistic phylogeny.[11]

Even while critical thinking decentered historical linguistics, data offered a way of reassembling the tree, purged of the biases of the past. A new generation of scholars began to argue for a "new gold standard" for comparing languages, which would rest entirely on the measurement of word similarity at different periods of time, casting aside historical conjectures that did not align with rigorous observation. In time, they forged a standard that was designed to measure every layer of grammar and social context around language, including the intermingling of different cultures. In trying to aggregate these factors, the scholars turned to Levenshtein distance (a number that creates a pure "measure" of linguistic proximity), applying this measure to every phoneme.[12] Their measurements carefully blended from corpus linguistics (that is, the sampling of language types within a moment in time) and syntactical information, sociolinguistics, and the history of migration and cultural contact.[13] In other words, as the discipline of historical linguistics has had to come to terms with its "recursive spirals" of myth-making, quantification has offered an antidote to antiquated theories, racial mythologies, and other implicit assumptions embedded in the field from its eighteenth-century origins.

As historical linguists borrowed from statisticians, they were able to return to the search for a phylogenetic tree of language – like the ideal tree that Allg Kieler had sketched in 1853 (Figure 13.1). But if nineteenth-century linguistic trees like Kieler's were mere fantasies born of racial prejudice, a new generation of historical linguistics revisited the idea of the phylogenetic tree, turning to data and measurements. With these

---

[11] Asya Pereltsvaig and Martin W. Lewis, *The Indo-European Controversy* (Cambridge: Cambridge University Press, 2015).
[12] Ibid., 218.   [13] Ibid., 216.

objective tools, they intended to purge their discipline of the prejudices of the past. And that is indeed what happened. The proximity of any language to any other language, dead or living, could be calculated as an exact Levenshtein distance number on the basis of mathematically comparing strings of recorded text. With their newly mathematically correct tree, the scholars could make assessments of profound precision:

> Russian is more similar to other Slavic languages (with an average similarity rating based on forty cognates of 72.5, where 100 means full identity) than it is to modern Romance (37.6) or modern Germanic languages (39.3). In contrast, Norwegian is more similar to other Germanic languages (57) than to either modern Romance (40.8) or modern Slavic languages (39.3). In the comparison of modern Romance languages, Italian is the closest to Latin (63) and French is the most distinct (36).[14]

A revised version of the tree of linguistic families, where mathematics replaces tradition as the basis for similarity, is shown in Figure 13.2.

Part of the power of this story is in the marriage of critical thinking and data implicit in the narrative. The case of historical linguistics offers a model for how hybrid knowledge, produced at the intersection of disciplines, can drive aid a discipline in establishing a ground truth, purged of the biases of centuries past.

Pressing Forward

Had linguistics not gone through a period of critique and directly engaged data on the basis of sources gathered by nineteenth-century imperialists, the tree might look very different than it does today. The story moves from an episode of early-modern theological searches for truth, to trees built of nationalistic narcissism, to trees built out of the imperial search for colonial acquisitions, to a period of pruning back the corrupt narratives of a previous moment, to engaging new sets of data and new measurement in the service of drawing a new tree of languages, purged of the bias of the past.

The search for a key to world languages and stories offers one of the classic cautionary tales of grand ambitions in the humanities and social sciences and how tainted they became by the goals of empires and nations around them. Much scholarly labor was required to purge the traditions of linguistics, history, and anthropology (among other subjects) of that bias.

---

[14] Ibid., 219.

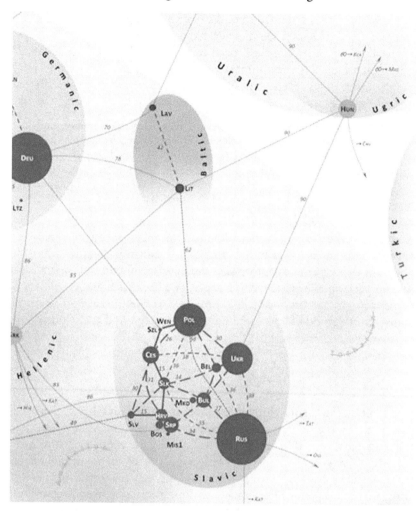

Figure 13.2   A modern tree of languages, supported by data-driven distance measurements. Detail from visualization by Stephan Steinbach, www.alternativetransport .wordpress.com, (CC BY-SA 3.0 AT), based on linguistic work by T. Elms (2008) and K. Tishchenko (2009).

Indeed, reviewing the history of a search to master narratives of the past shows that the past is littered with attempts to synthesize the texts of all nations and times, structured by the technologies available to the people of the past, the political connections and ideologies of their time. The result has been, in some cases, the production of data-driven overviews of history based on outdated fantasies of European supremacy.

Even while the past offers many cautions for would-be discoverers of a key to all knowledge, it also offers encouragement. Almost 200 years later, the attempt to map the languages of the world took the form of drawing a single tree – an endeavor that is still bearing fruit in the form of digitally driven linguistic research. The theories of the past might have been contaminated with outmoded ideology, but generations of scholars across many disciplines labored to recognize the limits of the stories they were telling and to reimagine their research in a new way. Paired with critical thinking about the dirty data of the past, statistics can offer a means of correcting outmoded analyses.

The search for a key thus offers a pattern for thinking about how grand questions regarding human relationships in the past can be approached – partially through critique, partially through data, and partially through the skills of visualization and analysis. The skillful work of combining far-flung forms of expertise made possible new insights, cleansed of the distorting effects of racial bias in the past.

To me, the story of linguistics' phylogenetic tree of languages, shorn of bias, raises the possibility of performing new calculations that would illuminate discrete patterns of history that otherwise might elude our grasp. Divergence measurements can be used to query the annals of Congress or Parliament, asking how often the concerns voiced by working-class, minority, or immigrant groups have made it into legislation. Divergence measurements also open the gates for studies in transnationalism, making it possible to compare speech across many national political traditions with more sophistication than the "clash of civilizations" thesis. Might it be possible to ask, using mathematical models of documents, which texts represented the height of mutual convergence between Russia, China, and the West? Might it be possible to ask which documents from the United Nations or World Bank most accurately reflect the perspectives of multiple cultures? What new frontiers might divergence methods offer the study of the history of concepts? Can the discipline of history use historical linguistics as a model? What would it mean to establish moments in the confluence and divergence of world cultures, using to textual records and mathematical modeling as a tool? In general, digital humanists have hesitated to speculate about such vast projects as the "reform" of a discipline. But digital tools will only come into their own as scholars begin to apply them to the core questions of the field – using memory, periodization, event, and influence to question the lists of key events, crucial memories, periods, and influential individuals who have come down to us from other traditions. If data scientists of the future, following the model of linguists and folklorists, can lend their hands to this study, then hybrid knowledge may as yet lead to new discoveries that purge our prejudices about the past in the places we least expect.

CHAPTER 14

The Future of the Art

This book has argued that a smarter data science can arise from pursuit of the kinds of "hybrid knowledge" that are documented here, where concerns about the bias of data and algorithms from the humanities and questions from historical theory meet mathematical modeling. Once such forms of evidentiary circumspection are in place, computers nevertheless can aid us by being *more accurate* than humans at sifting data at scale. What does that mean for the work of those who would build like data in the future? There are several possibilities.

Historically aware text mining generates a wealth of new possibilities of potential interest to scholars, journalists, and even corporations as they engage with contemporary data about change over time – an approach with a unique set of opportunities and challenges that I briefly address below in the section "A Culture of Audits." What I have elsewhere referred to as "auditing" refers to the practice of gathering up-to-the-moment textual data into databases with the intention of tracking recent change and holding authors accountable for the ethical dimensions of the data, for example, how the representations of people of color have changed over recent decades, or whether speakers in Congress persistently engage or ignore issues of climate change in their speeches. Such audits represent one frontier of research which is in a position to profit from the evolution of a historically sensitive data science of text.

A second frontier involves the democratizing of access to text-based data and its analysis, for example through web-based portals that some countries use to turn democratic deliberation into an arena open to all. Countries like Taiwan are experimenting with such portals to enable a climate of citizen initiative where text mining is used to ensure that citizens can also learn from each other. As insights about historically sensitive text mining come to inform portals of this kind, the designers of portals will have new opportunities to educate citizens about their institutions, their representatives, and how the culture of democracy is changing in our time.

A third frontier is the creation of new research and teaching initiatives. In the research for this book, I have glimpsed a wide swath of new research questions, some of which concern using traditional historical methods to track down questions about the past, others of which involve applying data to new databases, and still others of which involve philosophers of history and data scientists working in collaboration. I will say more about that in the section "Future Horizons for Research in Digital History."

As this book has emphasized, a smarter data science is one that actively profits from new understandings of history being generated by historians and philosophers of history in dialogue with data science. Thus, the success of the first two ventures depends in part on the embrace of the third. Final sections of this chapter ask what sorts of investments, infrastructures, and collaborations might support a rigorous art of text mining, before asking what kind of historians or data scientists might live in this hybrid world.

A Culture of Audits

An even more ambitious version of this last possibility is to use knowledge of text as data as a tool for what I have elsewhere called the "auditing" of institutions, which is to say, using text mining to perform regular counts of words, targeting institutions that are *still* producing new textual records. Parliaments, congresses, newspapers, publishers, corporations, government bodies, universities, their social media feeds, and the textual production of individuals all in theory lend themselves to auditing. Auditing deserves special consideration as a form of text mining distinct from text mining for a closer understanding of historical change in the past, even while these two approaches share many overlaps. When the understanding of change over time is brought up to the present, we are less able to reflect on whether this week's peak of quantitative production also suggests a historical discontinuity from the past, for the sheer reason that change is measured in retrospect. That problem set aside, we are still able to measure a great deal about contemporary institutions and where they are going.

Auditing implies distinct advantages in terms of the self-knowledge of institutions with regard to ethical considerations such as their inclusion of diverse voices and representations from women and minorities. Already, literary digital scholars like Richard Jean So are in the *New York Times*, auditing the racial and gender diversity expressed by American publishing houses.[1] They can count authors – male and female, white authors and authors of color. And their tools also allow them to check how authors *portray* men and women, white authors and authors of color. Scholars such as So are interested in exploration, rather than being thought police. But they've also uncontrovertibly accumulated quantitative evidence of bias in the official literary imagination. From the point of view of individual publishers – for instance Random House, who contributed the data that So uses – this data represents a challenge for reform. So was able to show that Random House effectively included diverse voices only during the tenure of Toni Morrison as an editor.

If So's data was challenging for executives in publishing to read, it also gave them precise tools with which to solve the problem: his tools for tracking both counts of authors by race and depictions of race in publishing give a benchmark for examining how different communities are presented. The findings represented by these metrics apply to the publishers of fiction and nonfiction, the producers of screenplays, and the publishers of newspapers, as well as their investors: they represent data that can be used to actively measure how far aspirations toward diverse representations are being realized.

Such a life of data implies a changing realignment between corporate metrics and the concerns of the academic humanities and social sciences. Auditing institutions is not the active concern of most humanities and social science professors, but the "audit" where text mining strategies meet corporate and government institutions may be where the abstract concerns of literature faculty meet reality in the future. For generations, much of humanities scholarship has taken the form of critical theory. As critical theories about the depiction of race and gender or other identities are translated into metrics, those metrics can be adopted.

If all of this seems like science fiction, there are already examples of how text mining is preparing examinations of leading institutions and discourses, demonstrating their changing patterns of bias and challenging their silences, often with the explicit intent of calling for reform. One example hails from sociology, where Chicago grad student Austin Kozlowski (with professors Matt Taddy and James Evans) used word embeddings to track a century of change to the racial, gender, and class valence of different professions and categories of music. Another example

---

[1] Richard Jean So and Gus Wezerek, "Opinion | Just How White Is the Book Industry?" *The New York Times*, December 11, 2020, sec. Opinion, www.nytimes.com/interactive/2020/12/11/opinion/culture/diversity-publishing-industry.html.

offers an audit of gender and race in the classic British reference work, the *Dictionary of National Biography* (*DNB*), conducted by Carnegie Mellon University literature professor Christopher Warren. The audit revealed that gender biases of an earlier age were at work in today's instrument, such that the #3 employment for which women listed in the *DNB* are identified is "royal mistress."

While these audits haven't been automated such that the analysis is run repeatedly to update results on the basis of more recent publications in the United States or new entries for the *DNB*, they certainly could be. After all, replicability of analysis is one of the virtues of code. Christopher Warren says as much in his article, throwing down the gauntlet for the *DNB* editors to use his study as a shopping list for new articles about women: here is the first audit, expect the next one on a regular basis.[2] Warren's audit is multidimensional. It gives twenty different charts that break down the articles of the *DNB* by period, gender, continent, and employment. Any one of those audits could be automatically repeated, thus producing an index of how far the field of history has come over recent decades, at least as represented by the *DNB*.

A calendared audit gives the analyst – and the public – evaluations that are updated with each new moment in time. As we have seen in the rollout of reactions to Covid, up-to-date information about how a crisis is unfolding is crucial to the public being able to organize an informed response to an emergency. Audits therefore have the potential to accommodate – and perhaps also to activate – *urgent* demands for change.

The promise of automated text-based auditing is instead the creation of something like a ticker for whether my newspaper, my congressional representative, or my city council member has mentioned climate *this week*. Like the sports scores, stock reports, weather maps, and the Covid maps that were published on a weekly or daily basis by most newspapers, automated audits of text can produce knowledge of change up to the moment: a cultural ticker of whether our institutions are still paying attention to our survival. A feature of tickers is that they are read by citizens of broadly diverse professions and identities to inform them about opportunities for immediate action. Covid maps helped school board members, hospitals, university administrators, and ordinary families to plan their level of exposure.

---

[2] Christopher N. Warren, "Historiography's Two Voices: Data Infrastructure and History at Scale in the Oxford Dictionary of National Biography (ODNB)," November 23, 2018, https://doi.org/10.31235/osf.io/rbkdh.

Measuring who is talking about climate this week – and who is silent – similarly would provide a daily view of which institutions or individuals in our society are willing to tolerate sustained engagement with the climate emergency and which are failing. That information, in turn, tells citizens where to direct their gaze, talk, efforts, and money – away, perhaps, from institutions and individuals that have regularly failed to address climate and toward those that outpace their peers in terms of sustained attention. Regular auditing can thus contribute something that long-term history and archival history cannot: it can keep climate change in the public eye, rendering the immediate past subject to inspection and appropriate reaction by a broad diversity of citizens.

Among the most compelling kinds of future research that digital history can deliver, I believe, are those that shape data to help us to tell historical stories about the institutions and cultural patterns that shape our world. That is, data can show us about the reality of the past through the search for turning points. And data can help us track our course as present moments turn into the past through the audit.

If we want to set a high bar for a kind of documentary history that insists on reasserting reality against political illusion, there are few better examples than recent publications from the field of environmental history. Historians have been engaging climate in the mode of litigation for at least a decade, cross-examining the cases of acid rain, the DDT pesticide, air pollution, and the precautionary principle to understand when limits were enforced and when broken. Perhaps the most urgent of these analyses is Naomi Oreskes and Erik M. Conway's *Merchants of Doubt* (2011).

In Oreskes and Conway's account, the discovery of a climate emergency in the 1960s was met with urgent pleas from the scientific community for federal attention and sustained research. By the 1980s, however, a handful of rogue scientists with close ties to the fossil fuel industry began to deliberately distort the analysis of climate change, using doctored graphics and bringing defamation lawsuits against the scientists who tried to argue with them. Weak reporting by the *Wall Street Journal* further undermined the case of truth, with the result that doubt was cast upon the broadcast consensus of climate scientists, whose scientific consensus was routinely thereafter denounced as a "hoax."

By naming names, Oreskes and Conway bring something like a suit of litigation against the *Wall Street Journal* and other interlocutors, underscoring how small acts of distortion have added up to a political crisis of delay. We might call this the "litigative" mode of writing in the humanities. Historians often imagine their work as that of litigants: cross-examining the evidence, putting the documentary record in plain view, and persuading the judge and jury to right the wrongs of the past. In distinction to *litigation,* an *audit* is typically performed on a regular basis. Audits are conducted, producing new analyses, on a regular and cyclical calendar. Traditionally, corporations are responsible for auditing their own accounts on a quarterly basis; the government audits taxes on an annual basis. Audits also have the feature of being flexible as to time: we submit annual taxes, but an official audit by the IRS requires individuals to prepare documentations stretching back into time. Audits are routine, repeatable, and potentially automated on a daily or even hourly basis.

A society that was committed to changing reactions to climate change would surely adopt whatever measures it could to gauge its progress, using those metrics of change as a conscience for making sure its adjustments were keeping up to speed with reality. Our society is launching more of these metrics for carbon emissions and pollution – as well it should. But we can also afford, and should make plans for, similar audits of newspaper copy, legislative debate, corporate reports, and popular culture. How distracted have we been from time-sensitive issues like climate change? Which legislators have chosen to ignore the reality, or have given it lip-service once a year? Only text mining gives us the toolkit to answer these questions with exactitude and nuance and to update the results on a regular basis.

Auditing culture through text mining means making mirrors. Without a mirror, I can't possibly know whether my face is dirty or the part of my hair uneven. Similarly, without the mirror of So's text mining practice, American publishing can't possibly know how prejudiced their choice of books have been, nor can they know whether they're making progress. Without such a mirror, ordinary citizens can't know how much or how little the environment has been talked about in Congress, how women's interests are talked about, or how far we have to go.

Tech Mining for Democracy

A knowledge of shared history can help citizens to understand their democracies by making transparent the archives of democracy's past. As many developed nations seem to face a crisis of democracy unprecedented in recent times, historians like Jill Lepore have provided the American public a new sense of our nation's past, identity, and possible future, grounded in an intimate acquaintance with the artifacts of the past (see Chapter 1 of this volume).

The digitalization of texts, the creation of web-based infrastructure to share those texts, and the creation of a new consensus around the principles of accurate historical text mining all have a role to play in supporting the consensus-building process around our common past that Lepore proposes. Digitalized databases of legislatures, paired with text mining tools, mean the possibility of making the kinds of analyses detailed in this book available to every citizen in a nation. Given access to a series of tools, citizens could browse the history of contentious debates over abortion, climate change, the history of slavery, or labor unions, asking for themselves how much the debate has changed. Given such a portal, citizens could inspect and easily compare how their legislature had shifted over the last six months or six years. They could compare, at a glance, the interests and advocacy of their congressperson to other members of the same party or other members of Congress. Text mining, in other words, would offer ordinary citizens greater clarity and precision upon which to base their political opinions.

Why, one might ask, does the US Congress not have such a portal? And why are most portals of this kind underdeveloped for the purposes of helping citizens understand what is new in a given month, year, or decade, or how their constituency differs from other constituencies in its contribution, or how their current representative differs from representatives of their jurisdiction past? Why is there not such a portal for every state legislature, school board, town council, or university legislature? Without transparent access to the historical transcripts of its institutions and their doings, democracy runs not on information, but on *gossip*. Trustworthy, transparent text mining, built upon the principles of this book, can shift gossip into data-based knowledge.

Access to data does not, of course, necessarily produce a consensus, but text mining tends to be better than humans in reducing many stories to a single view. Agreeing about the past and agreeing about the data we use to make assessments are vital when questions of justice are at stake. As of my writing, America has just witnessed the public work of history in the commission that reviewed the events of January 6, 2021. Much of the commission's work was to ascertain the intent and actions of the protesters. They reviewed these facts through traditional historical means, which is to say, by reading texts and reviewing evidence, one datum at a time. While it is too early to tell if the commission's work will generate a public consensus about recent events, it is nevertheless important that in a time of crisis, Congress still turns to the tools of history to work toward a mutual understanding of truth.

What would happen if a computer programmer were to use Koselleck's machine (see Chapter 1) to try to understand the protests of January 6? A faulty machine learning algorithm, trained on the public writing of the protesters, will tend to generalize. Asked to assemble the texts of the protesters, would the machine learning algorithm match the protesters with the Tea Party (defenders of democracy), the Gordon Rioters (conspiracy-addled protesters for rights), the George Floyd protesters (contemporary calls for justice), or the Ku Klux Klan (perpetrators of terror)? For an automatic machine to get the history equation *wrong* could mean an injustice or a distortion. Depending on who was using the algorithm and why, a false reading of history might mean flooding social media with misinformation, or subjecting the wrong party to surveillance.

The dangers covered in this book, in other words, are just the beginning of why the art of text mining might be dangerous. The visions of the future of text mining outlined below in this subsection are brave futures and they reflect many conversations with data scientists, activists, and scholars over recent years. They also highlight the limits of this book, for they touch on important issues like surveillance and privacy. The ethical life of data has inspired series of volumes already – from approaches that highlight the way that social media acts as an echo-chamber for political discourse, to reporting that shows how trolls have tilted American belief patterns before elections, to questions about the security of data in an era of state surveillance. Adding historical text mining to any of these moral quandaries would further complicate them.

There are reasons for being cautiously optimistic about what text mining can do to educate citizens, to help their voices be heard, to help citizens listen to the voices of others, and to develop a kind of government that responds to citizen demand. In Taiwan, the government has created a zone where any citizen can upload a sample of text giving their opinion of social needs or government initiatives. While the channel is open, back-and-forth commentary is limited so as to discourage trolls. The textual insights are monitored by artificial intelligence software designed by the American company, Pol.is, which groups like text into "opinion bubbles." The interface is organized to create a large-scale collaboration process such that citizen can see what other citizens believe and government and private initiatives can respond. One piece of evidence of the success quoted by Taiwanese information minister Audrey Tang is that in the era of Covid, the opinion bubbles were used to gather citizens' concerns about government information, which in turn fed into the design of the Taiwanese government's application for "contact tracing," or tracking when citizens had been exposed to Covid. As a result of this robust process, citizens in Taiwan received a notification on their cell phones whenever they were exposed to Covid. Was privacy a concern in this government tracking of citizens? It wasn't, in part because citizen concerns about privacy had been gathered using the online portal, organized into discrete headings by artificial intelligence, digested by government bureaucrats, and factored into the design of the initiative.

One of the most compelling features of the Taiwanese model is the recursive element: citizens write what they think the government can do and those statements are organized in such a way that makes obvious areas of agreement, overlap, and disagreement. Data analysis is used in the service of transparency. It holds up a mirror to what citizens are thinking. Whether or not Taiwan has solved the riddle of government transparency for good, the principle that data and text can be used to create mirrors for citizens' knowledge of how their community is responding is a powerful one.

But the Taiwanese interface is not designed to show citizens the history of their nation, or the silences of legislators over the scale of decades. As this book has shown, that information can be analyzed by data, but the analyst has to have a keen sense of the importance of historical change. In the book's Introduction, we saw how members of the US Congress remained silent about the legacy of slavery until the 1990s, even while they used the word "slavery" as a metaphor. What else might citizens learn about themselves if they were given a mirror that showed them not just areas of agreement and disagreement, but also the silences that structured their national and local legislatures in the past?

I envision a future for research, funded by governments and leading institutions, where hybrid teams of data analysts, assembled from the humanities, social sciences, and data sciences, work to develop apps to serve the public by showing it a mirror of its own distant and recent history. Arguably, such portals do not exist – or are not more widespread – because knowledge of historical methods applied to data science is underdeveloped. My principal inspiration in writing this book is to support the development of a historical method for text in data science, so that historians and technologists can come together to support a radical transparency of many kinds.

However, I have also been working myself toward a demonstration of a public-facing portal that makes the kind of analyses described in this book available to anyone, as well as toward a body of work that theorizes the alignment between scholarly research, scholarly data, and public uses of that data, especially on the important frontier of the social experience of the adverse effects of climate change by minority populations around the world. While I worked through the various algorithms profiled in this book, I simultaneously worked with a graduate student and a team of data scientists to produce a first pass at a public-facing apps. The URLs for those apps are available in the appendix. The articles where I have turned to the history of governance to imagine a data-driven infrastructure working for the cause of justice are listed in footnote 1.[3]

Future Horizons for Research in Digital History

This book documents a process of working with digitalized text to study time. Much of the work documented is about validation, or steps that show that an algorithm can reproduce the facts of history as accepted by scholarship. A much smaller portion of the case studies in this book foreground genuine historical discoveries and, even then, most of the work of historical explanation is left incomplete as matters to be pursued with better data, closer readings, or corroboration from archive.

The point of emphasizing validation is to show the kinds of care that are necessary to support a smarter data science. In such a practice of data science, it is the accurate representation of historical change over time rather than the fantasy of prediction that matters. Accuracy can only be supported when the analyst has investigated with sincerity the limits of her data and has considered the bias of her algorithms and the range of historical theories that might elucidate what she is modeling. These forms of evidentiary study have a natural home in humanities and social science fields like history rather than in data science, although they can naturally also be pursued through collaborations that arise between history and other fields.

---

[3] Jo Guldi, "From Critique to Audit: A Pragmatic Response to the Climate Emergency from the Humanities and Social Sciences, and a Call to Action," *KNOW: A Journal on the Formation of Knowledge* 5:2 (September 1, 2021): 169–96, https://doi.org/10.1086/716854. Jo Guldi, "Scholarly Infrastructure as Critical Argument: Nine Principles in a Preliminary Survey of the Bibliographic and Critical Values Expressed by Scholarly Web-Portals for Visualizing Data," *Digital Humanities Quarterly* 14:3 (September 1, 2020), http://digitalhumanities.org/dhq/vol/14/3/000463/000463 .html; Jo Guldi and Macabe Keliher, "Should Governments Have Access to Our Data?," *Public Seminar*, July 20, 2020, https://publicseminar.org/essays/should-governments-have-access-to-our-data; Jo Guldi, "What Kind of Information Does the Era of Climate Change Require?," *Climatic Change* 169:1–2 (November 2021): 3, https://doi.org/10.1007/s10584-021-03243-5. Ashley S. Lee et al., "The Role of Critical Thinking in Humanities Infrastructure: The Pipeline Concept with a Study of HaToRI (Hansard Topic Relevance Identifier)," *Digital Humanities Quarterly* 14:3 (2020).

Algorithmic investigations into memory, eventfulness, influence, and periodization of the kind showcased here could be applied to different databases of text with new results. Indeed, massive experiments in modeling textual data at scale are underway in many parts of the world of digital history, many of them beginning with the text mining of the debates of national legislatures, which have been digitalized in many parts of the world.

Another frontier for research is the modeling of what I have called "eventfulness" in history (following historian Martin Jay; see Chapter 6), when referring to a historical narrative that is driven by the possibility that different events structured the life of different communities. While Jay himself does not use quantitative measures to support his identification and comparison of the meaning of events to different populations, the tools profiled in this book give a series of quantitative bases for examining and comparing the events that garnered the interest of one political community – that of parliamentary speakers. Putting these tools into dialogue with the insights of thinkers like Martin Jay (Chapters 6–8) and sociologist William Sewell (Chapter 8) implies a tool for asking, in detail, which events mattered to different communities and how.

These tools offer the basis for institutional as well as international comparisons. If the debates of America's Congress changed in 1980, did screenplays change then too? Did the judicial rulings of the Supreme Court, which tend to be influenced by the retirement and appointment of new individuals, change on the same pulse and when did these changes synchronize? If the major historic discontinuities of language in the British parliament occurred in 1832 and 1884, are the same moments turning points for the British novel and what did such shifts portend in terms of the content handled by fiction or poetry as opposed to the legislature? Using change-point detection algorithms and other algorithms for modeling change across different corpora, historians have the opportunity to compare moments of change across different institutions.

What can be compared across institutions and nations can also be compared across social groups or individual lives. Andrew Piper's showcase of literary modeling over time in his book *Enumerations* (2018) include exercises intended to investigate the exemplarity of individual writing careers, for example by investigating the individuals whose interests or style changed the most. Applied to parliament, Piper's toolkit would allow historians of politics to investigate the speakers whose interests were the widest over their careers as well as those whose political orientation changed the most over time.

Nor are these quantitative approaches uniquely important to political and intellectual historians who deal in parliamentary debates. Some recent debates in history, including ones in which I have participated, have suggested a firm line between those historians who move in quantitative directions and those who hold steadfast to the micro-analysis of intimate lives, revealing changing attitudes toward gender, race, and class.

Social historians have already embraced many of the techniques of text mining on display here to investigate problems such as those of memory and silence. Were databases that offer insights into women's lives, subaltern, and proletarian lives combined with questions about eventfulness and turning points in the past, the analysts who use text mining would find themselves leading a new era of social history.

Cultural history offers another frontier for text mining research. Recent text mining projects from literature including Richard Jean So's *Redlining Culture*[4] essentially offer a sterling representation of cultural history via text mining, which proves that sustained analysis over a half century is possible with quantitative readings of race in American novels. I wonder, too, about the implications of historical linguistics research, which has investigated the role of metaphors about power. What other commonplace shifts in the life of metaphor could be traced by text mining, revealing a world of imagination at work in parliamentary debates, judicial readings, newspapers, and novels? The studies of influence discussed in this book would allow sophisticated researchers to ask questions about where shifts to the life of metaphor originated, thus laying open the possibility of a more nuanced history of authorship and imagination, where slight adjustments to figures of speech – for instance the broadening meanings of "gay" and "queer" in the twentieth century – are traced back to particular publications, communities, and authors.

Any such research that privileges questions of influences, it will be obvious, must tread carefully on questions of oral and written traditions. Many new metaphors originated in the playful dynamics of social spaces like cafés or dance halls, for instance those that are the subject of histories of queer life by George Chauncey and Nan Boyd. Only for the period of social media in the twenty-first century can text mining systematically investigate the role of space through geotagged archives that reflect the *spaces* where people forge new figures of speech in between social

---

[4] Richard Jean So, *Redlining Culture: A Data History of Racial Inequality and Postwar Fiction* (New York: Columbia University Press, 2020).

interactions with strangers. All the same, a general study of the life of *rhetorical inventiveness* may add important layers to the study of historical change.

In a world of international collaborations, we have still grander opportunities for data-driven comparison and discovery. I have in mind basic questions of chronology, applied to each project: What turning points are suggested by American, British, Australian, and French archives, by the Swedish and Finnish papers? Once we begin with international comparisons, enormous vistas of potential questions swell into view. What turning points occur across all the datasets, and which are unique to only one? Which shifts only seem to matter in metropolitan newspapers, and which shifts are felt most acutely only in the countryside? If the legislatures of different nations are compared with national newspapers or archives of novels and screenplay, which of these legislative systems kept in step with new representations of women in popular culture, and which lagged decades behind?

There are enormous horizons of research to be accomplished by digitalizing the archives of the international institutions as well. We have, from Franco Moretti, a first attempt to model change in the reports of the World Bank, which establishes international economic policy, and from Robert Shiller, we have a stirring new case study in using data to establish the overall consequence of the rise and fall of economic theories.[5] Once international economic narratives are paired with national newspaper and legislative debates that describe the fallout of currency devaluations and other austerity measures on the ground, historians will be in a position to examine, as never before, the *consequences* of economic theory.

International archives also make possible a revisitation of the story of the twentieth century, especially the decline of European empire and the rise of postcolonialism – a topic that is mainly known today through profiles of individual economists and national leaders. But the official documentation of international aid agencies holds material for telling an infinitely more pixilated story of international shifts, one populated with the personal stories of refugees and their lawyers, artists and archaeologists, national farmers' unions, and the scientific researchers of climate. The papers of the United Nations (UN), UNESCO, the UN Human Rights Council, or the UN's Food and Agriculture Organization hold reports on nearly every

---

[5] Franco Moretti and Dominique Pestre, "Bankspeak: The Language of World Bank Reports," *New Left Review* 92:2 (2015): 75–99; Robert J. Shiller, *Narrative Economics: How Stories Go Viral and Drive Major Economic Events* (Princeton, NJ: Princeton University Press, 2019).

nation on the globe. When do those reports move in a synchronized pulse, shifting according to the same metronome of international thought, and when do they follow more national or regional directions? What was the politics of memory like in international governance? What chronology of postcolonialism can we learn from their papers? What turning points mattered in the history of the welfare state? If the data collected in these projects can show analysts how to structure a narrative around turning points of the past, each of which had causes and actors identified, Fischer's criterion for complete argumentation would be satisfied, and digital history would have contributed major new work toward establishing an argumentative understanding of the conditions, causes, and contingency of modernity.[6]

Another possibility is that a conversation about the alignment between the theory of history and the fit of algorithms deserves to be pursued by philosophers of history engaging the concepts on display in this book, or even working alongside data analysts. I have sampled only some of the treasures from the philosophy of history; my investigations of Reinhart Koselleck, William Sewell, and Astrid Erll (Chapters 6–8) deserve to be expanded to encompass the questions about the workings of temporal experience raised by Stefan Tanaka, Helge Jordheim, and Hayden White in Chapter 6, and Joan Wallach Scott (see Chapter 3), to name only a few likely suspects. In this book, William Sewell's theory of eventfulness and Astrid Erll's engagements with memory (see Chapters 6 and 7) serve as inspirations for new investigations that raise questions about which subjects capture the interest of an institution and for how long, about which events endure in memory and which are forgotten. But this book has not had room to investigate how Hayden White's concept of "metahistory" might inspire textual analysis that aims to ask, overall, about the objectivity of different historical windows on the past.[7] The themes of temporality in Chapter 6 stop short of engaging White's concepts of the "synchronic" and "diachronic," and someone else must draw out a method for examining these pulses through archives and finding meaningful ways to extract quantitative data that would support the comparison of facts about text over time. I have referenced Tanaka's questions about circular history, but I have no algorithms in mind for pursuing them. Jordheim's questions about event and periodization, likewise, might lend themselves to the burst

---

[6] David Hackett Fischer, *Historians' Fallacies* (New York: Harper & Row, 1970).
[7] Hayden White, *Metahistory: The Historical Imagination in Nineteenth-Century Europe* (Baltimore, MD: John Hopkins University Press, 1975).

detection algorithms studied by Arthur Spirling or the Granger analyses used by Melvin Wevers in their investigations, but these are not questions that I have had the time to pursue and I must leave them to others.[8] I have raised more historical problems than I have solved in this book, and much of the follow-through does not require digital tools.

Perhaps the most radical challenge that the humanities and social sciences can pose to data science as practiced today is the challenge of white box versus black box studies of text (see Chapter 12). When humanists compare a dozen different translations of Aristotle, they aren't interested in generalizing until they can show exactly which alterations of the original text deviated and why. As this book has emphasized, humanists are masters of evidence. Some humanists tend to be suspicious of black box technologies designed to provide a single translation at the touch of a button, at least when it comes to questions of scholarship; many of us might use Google Translate in desperation on the street in Paris, but we'd cross-check a translation of a line of French poetry with a native speaker before accepting Google's assessment. Meanwhile, a culture of practical usability in Silicon Valley has generated algorithms such as those at work in many machine learning models, where proprietary algorithms, for instance fine-tuned neural nets, model the relationships between documents. Silicon Valley experts may be satisfied with the visual association algorithm that can tell a photo of a chihuahua from that of a blueberry muffin. But a specialist in images is likely to be unsatisfied for the same reason that I would reject Google Translate for my interpretation of Baudelaire.

In medicine, researchers have lately called for a shift from black box to white box measures, meaning the sharing of code and a rich discussion around the algorithmic assumptions behind any pairing of data and analysis. This book has taken a similar position: a text mining practice that can be viewed with legitimacy from the humanities and social sciences, with their historical disciplinary involvement with data, must necessarily be one where we give preference to white box algorithms and the iterative engagement with data and analysis that I have called "critical search." The pursuit of absolute clarity about why one analysis improves upon another offers an important frontier for research from digital history, one that will also be attractive to scholars from science and technology studies.

---

[8] Andrew C. Eggers and Arthur Spirling, "The Shadow Cabinet in Westminster Systems: Modeling Opposition Agenda Setting in the House of Commons, 1832–1915," *British Journal of Political Science* 48 (2016): 1–25; Melvin Wevers, Jianbo Gao, and Kristoffer L. Nielbo, "Tracking the Consumption Junction: Temporal Dependencies between Articles and Advertisements in Dutch Newspapers" (March 2019), https://hal.archives-ouvertes.fr/hal-02076512.

What all such frontiers of knowledge require is the creation of institutions capable of supporting them, whether those institutions become centered in universities, archives, corporations, or government offices. As I have taken pains to show throughout this book, an intelligent data science of textual analysis can only come into being with the support of traditional researchers in the humanities and social sciences.

I know the most about university structures, having spent my research career in them. Many of the universities in which I have worked have suffered from barriers, both structural and psychological, to collaboration between the humanities and data science, such that even when faculty in computer science themselves saw the possibilities, collaborations and innovative work were blocked. It is therefore critical that, as universities pour new funding into research of data, room is made for hybrid scholarship and that departments from the humanities and social sciences have a significant sway in how the course of study and research evolve.

The obvious challenge for any institution that seeks to support hybrid knowledge is to start by including humanists and social scientists in plans for new research ventures such as labs and centers, from which they are often sidelined. While I do not work at an institution that has made room for new investigations into hybrid knowledge in any structured way, I have enjoyed the experience of serving on several committees and ad hoc partnerships that included deans and chairs of departments of computer science, videogame design, and digital art as they reviewed best practices for interdisciplinary research and laid schemes for building a center where text mining would be at the heart of new programs of research that spanned the interests of the humanities and information sciences. Many of the insights in this book first took shape out of conversations in that venue – where Fred Chang, the head of computer science, asked me what the discipline of history hoped to predict, and where Dean Thomas DiPiero inspired us with tales of how new innovation was most frequently taking place today at the meeting place of disciplines.

My communicants dreamed of funding a center that would convene top researchers from computer science, linguistics, history, sociology, and literature, alongside supporting teams of undergraduates, graduate students, staff researchers, postdoctoral fellows, faculty, visiting faculty, and visiting activists, all collaborating in the service of new knowledge. My partners imagined several units participating in the work, some of which would focus on the improvement, testing, and limits of data, while others labored on the building of public-facing portals to "audit" the changing representations of contemporary newspapers, governments, and corporation. Still other teams would pursue problems such as periodization or causality and influence through a careful study of the alignment between the philosophy of history and the modeling of data; others would peer into the black box of machine learning using statistics and attention to interpretive questions to weigh the consequences of decisions about algorithms and data for output. Still others would offer a haven for traditional humanists, mainly working in archives, whose interests intersected with the data-driven problems and who could provide valuable context, insights, and strictures for the work of other teams.

One advantage of an interdisciplinary center, which brought together humanists alongside information workers, over other data-driven centers is the ideal of independent study that digital history inherits from humanistic study. In most humanities programs, undergraduates and graduate students are encouraged from their very earliest classes to write papers, the subject of which is their own choosing. This independence of direction is a hallmark of most kinds of humanistic study and it persists through a student's entire career. As soon as students trained in the humanities learn the basics of code, they are equipped to lead cutting-edge work in most digital humanities disciplines, such is the state of knowledge in the field. From the viewpoint of an interdisciplinary center, students and faculty from the humanities represent a valuable investment not least because they train students to develop new ideas and follow through on them relatively early in their careers.

New Styles of Collaboration

The starting premise of this book is that data science, on its own, applied to text engages in an enterprise riddled with danger and it is liable to produce specious results. The problem cannot be solved simply by the development of a text mining course in a computer science or data science department that students of history or political science or literature take from time to time. The challenge for beginners learning text mining for the first time is that, as this book has argued, the best use of textual analyses is that which is sensitive to historical context. The best course of education for an undergraduate is therefore one that combines the study of basic data science with the study of history. Computer science, data science, statistics, and informatics departments that make joint hires with departments of history, the history of science, sociology, and literature will find themselves better able to offer well-informed courses that teach the entire range of skills necessary to make data science "smart" when it comes to problems of text and change over time.

Teaching tomorrow's data scientists requires a serious working knowledge of the kinds of humanistic research documented in this book. That knowledge is ideally passed on in the form of an in-depth program of study, one that requires not only the skills of data science but also a willingness to intellectually engage problems of bias in evidence and algorithm and philosophical approaches to the multiple dimensions of historical experience.

Some colleagues may feel motivated to develop and offer a curriculum on text mining in particular, separate from the digital humanities curriculum now offered in many schools. The kinds of statistical analyses and code described here can be taught, alongside an introduction to the philosophy of history, in a single one- or two-semester course, although advanced seminars are important for the development of individual research skills. Students who are acquainted with code might be encouraged to perform audits of the historical and contemporary treatment of gender in newspapers, for instance verbs used with female and male personal pronouns. Almost all of this could be done by students with little training, for example by asking them to examine the data output and interpret it.

The challenge for teaching hybrid knowledge is that most of the component skills are currently offered in separate departments, including statistics, the history and philosophy of science, philosophy, history, and literature. A course of study that would familiarize students with the relevant methods can be devised as one track within a minor about the digital humanities, although strictly speaking, many digital humanities curricula emphasize the skills of curation and web creation, of spatial analysis or network analysis, or other skillsets that are extraneous to developing an expertise in manipulating text for knowledge of historical change over time. Making the different tracks of such a program align depends, of course, on the faculty involved being incentivized to keep abreast of new research from a variety of fields, something that may happen occasionally through conferences and seminars, but which is structurally supported at a university level only by the existence of well-funded centers that can sustain ambitious programs of teaching and learning from one funding cycle or one administrative regime to the next.

What of humanists' fears that lab-like collaborations, centered on research, will endanger individual study, long-term engagement with sources and arguments, individual teaching, and the relative creative freedom of individual teachers and students? Some critics of the digital humanities have raised the specter of lab-like collaborations dependent on external funding ending the traditions of scholarly independence in the humanities. And yet, this fear has been overstated.

Ian Morris's expostulation of the work by historians of the ancient world on the Seshat database compiled by Peter Turchin and his collaborators (see Chapter 5) is, I believe, an excellent model for such collaborations. As Morris and the other participants explain, the database was used to inspire questions and comparisons that would have been impossible otherwise. The experience of collaborative engagement offered a welcome alternative to traditions of individual study and writing. But collaboration and solitary writing are ultimately matters of individual predilection, and for most of us they alternate according to some highly personal tempo.

Other kinds of collaborations require deeper learning together as a community, something that comes out of sustained dialogue about the values prized and opportunities offered by different disciplines. As I have been writing this book, I have been giving talks at gatherings of digital humanists where I have promoted the records of the parliamentary debates mined here. In the course of those presentations, I invited many historians and data analysts to join me in a conversation about whether text mining could be used to model the history of democracy and make the annals of democracy more transparent to ordinary citizens. One propitious response came from the historians of European parliamentary debates, several of whom now operate an ongoing bimonthly seminar on text mining, wherein we have investigated the principles of text mining, digitalization, clean data, data analysis, and building infrastructure for the public. Our collaboration has brought historians of political thought together with data scientists from across Europe and the United States. This is one simple model of what hybrid knowledge looks like in action: the familiar space of an interdisciplinary seminar.

Some forms of hybrid research profiled in this conclusion flow nearly automatically via the cut-and-pasting of one set of code onto a new set of texts. Today the debates of dozens of national legislatures are available for download and scholars of those places have a minimum level of labor to overcome to gain access to the kinds of computational data represented in this book, which will likely inspire different insights by different scholars. Many state legislatures and city councils have also posted their debates in a way that is accessible to text mining. The archives of letters, pamphlets, and other documents already digitalized by various archives offer another useful trove. It makes sense for this data to become the subject of investigative seminars in the university and research projects by individual scholars.

One of the virtues of an analysis in code is that it can be applied to other datasets, sometimes with minimal adjustments. This kind of collaboration typically requires a few hours of work from a skilled computationalist ; it is the kind of matter that can be covered by a small departmental or university grant, rather than the in-depth collaboration that requires philosophers and data scientists studying concepts together over a sustained duration of attention. My code for studying the distinctiveness of different periods was subsequently used by a colleague in my department, a China scholar, with minor adjustments that made it possible for him to study the temporally distinctive features of conversations about Hong Kong. A few hours of data reconnaissance from university data science staff allowed him to apply the same code to the debates of the legislature of Hong Kong itself, giving him a new reference point. Some historians or political scientists may adopt such a strategy without themselves learning to code, merely using the data-driven output as an index that gives insight into the turning points and periods that naturally arise from the study of a single institution. The analysis has been replicated on new sources without my friend the China scholar being required to generate the algorithms that produced the original analysis; it was sufficient, in terms of methodology, that he read and understood the original methodological paper that I produced.

There are no behemoth labs here. My friend has not had to become a coder, or even to work with one, except for the dozen emails required to hire a few hours' labor. It has not been required of him to surrender his intellectual freedom, nor to work in a lab, nor to conscript his students to laboratory research. He writes in solitude, as he is accustomed to do, with the addition of a new set of evidence at his disposal.

In many parts of the digital humanities, graduate students and fresh-minted PhDs are actually leading the field, as evidenced by the enormous ferment coming out of particular graduate schools at this moment, much of it driven by original projects for which individual students are lead authors, aided by a team of fellow-students, advisors, and other data experts who help with different parts of the heavy lifting.[9] In the social science traditions in

---

[9] To point to publications by students and recent graduates of .txtlab, Knowledge Lab, etc.: Dan Sinykin, Eve Eve Kraicer, and Andrew Piper, "Social Characters: The Hierarchy of Gender in Contemporary English-Language Fiction," *Journal of Cultural Analytics* (2019), https://doi.org/10.22148/16.032; Dan N. Sinykin, "The Conglomerate Era: Publishing, Authorship, and Literary Form, 1965–2007," *Contemporary Literature* 58:4 (2017): 462–91; Dan Sinykin, "The Apocalyptic Baldwin," *Dissent* 64:3 (July 20, 2017): 15–19, https://doi.org/10.1353/dss.2017.0066; Dan Sinykin, "Evening in America: Blood Meridian and the Origins and Ends of Imperial Capitalism,"

which these papers are published, first-author status for the graduate students indicates that the bulk of the credit has been attributed to the student, rather than to the faculty; thus the publications mark out student labor in such a way that the field can recognize and reward their merit directly by way of jobs, promotion, and other opportunities.

Departments cannot expect to see their own graduate students accomplishing such marvels without support, of course, and supporting graduate research requires the hiring of text mining specialists from the humanities who are actively engaged in new frontiers of research.

Educating the Next Generation of Data Scientists

History departments will become stronger in training students in text mining only when they hire faculty dedicated to innovation around new methods. Ideally, a departmental search would recruit a scholar who has engaged, in some deep and systematic way, the debates over where and how insight is produced by new methods, who could offer the department a regular rotation of courses in new methods, whether using code or by introducing students to a slew of out-of-the-box-tools.[10] In leading departments, there will be room for more than one such specialist – ideally, a range of experts who have familiarity with diverse periods and the digital analysis associated with each approach to or moment in history. Such a forward-looking department might employ a specialist in text mining who works with the European and American products of the age of mass publication, and perhaps a second who works on twentieth- and twenty-

---

American Literary History 28:2 (April 1, 2016): 362–80, https://doi.org/10.1093/alh/ajw006; Sara Klingenstein, Tim Hitchcock, and Simon DeDeo, "The Civilizing Process in London's Old Bailey," *Proceedings of the National Academy of Sciences* 111:26 (July 1, 2014): 9419–24, https://doi.org/10.1073/pnas.1405984111; Jaimie Murdock, Colin Allen, and Simon DeDeo, "Exploration and Exploitation of Victorian Science in Darwin's Reading Notebooks," *Cognition* 159: Suppl.C (February 1, 2017): 117–26, https://doi.org/10.1016/j.cognition.2016.11.012.

[10] Facing this question, some administrators will ask if text mining is best offered through existing structures, for instance in the form of "bridge courses" taught by adjuncts as an appendage to the extant computer science curriculum. The bridge course approach typically asked adjuncts to fill positions offering basic training in wordcount or GIS (Geographic Information Systems). The stopgap nature of the approach resonated with a moment of relative scarcity, when the production of digital history was thinner, when the array of exemplars for each critical method was more sparse, where there was less material examining the historical production of bias in the level of algorithm, data, and practice. Thus bridge courses are rarely sufficient, in most circumstances, to bring a department into conversation with the world of text mining as practiced by digital historians in an age when innovations are being accomplished by professional specialists who have dedicated years of their PhDs to problems of text mining and the fit between new methods and questions at the core of the historical discipline.

first century bureaucracies or online communities, with their gargantuan troves of textual data. A third specialist might be an expert in geospatial analysis familiar with debates about the spatial turn and the archaeology or landscape of some historical period and region, with perhaps a fourth specialist in critical data or algorithm studies and the silences of the archives, a fifth in network analysis, a sixth in big data on the environment, a seventh working on demographic and trade history in the ancient world, an eighth collecting oral histories and curating them through digital means, and a ninth invested in the digital analysis of material objects. Each of these might *also* be a specialist in a particular time and place.

The diversity of data-driven kinds of history practiced in departments is a reality not because of the evangelism of any individual administrator, nor even because of the arguments made on behalf of the digital humanities community – but rather because modern methods and questions about data are already thoroughly interwoven with many subfields, and colleagues have taken pains to recruit faculty who are actively advancing the areas in which they work. Healthy conviviality and pluralism with regard to new methods demand a culture of mutual respect. Departments should not ignore the merits of traditional, nondigital first volumes from their faculty, or expand the requirements for tenure from one book to three because junior faculty have experimented with new methods in public.[11]

What does educating undergraduates in an era of text mining imply for workaday departments of history, which may lack even one specialist in text mining? Departments of history already try to survey history since the dawn of time, featuring specializations in each geographic area of the world and in most periods of time. No department of history will choose to abandon these important subjects by focusing exclusively on text mining. I would hazard that even departments that only make a few modest interventions to their program of study can offer undergraduates a meaningful introduction with text mining that can open eager minds to what historical thinking has to offer to conversations about data.

Integrating text mining within existing surveys of history has a certain advantage: in most standard survey courses, professors of history already introduce students to the problem of biased evidence, to debates over the interpretation of key moments and figures, and thus implicitly to most of

---

[11] For experimental methods and the ways that they are sometimes discouraged, see my discussion of the "culture of delay" in "Scholarly Infrastructure as Critical Argument."

the major issues discussed in this book. Adding a few conversations about text mining or a few data-driven exercises would be sufficient, in many circumstances, to introduce the problem to students and to begin encouraging them to take a critical perspective on text as data, while establishing the perspective that humanities departments have to offer. Adding a few exercises is a task that can be done by most faculty in modern history, with the support of a qualified librarian or other colleague. Today, several public-facing portals place the kinds of analyses performed in this book within reach of undergraduates who do not code: they can still compare topic models of Britain's parliament or investigate wordcounts over time in Google Books. The appendix describes several public-facing portals that make the textual analysis described in this book accessible to students who have no code. Half an hour is sufficient for a librarian or other colleague acquainted with the portal to show students how to manipulate it and to raise important questions of what a compelling use of text mining data for historical explanation looks like. Indeed, it is reasonable to imagine that the entry-level history class of lectures on national or global modernity could include a number of assignments where students use a text mining portal to ask questions about history. For example, students of American history might be asked to examine a word-embeddings model of Congress's debates over the twentieth century as a preliminary exercise in their second-semester introduction to American history, producing a five-page paper as a result of their analysis. The same students might be asked to review a topic model of the World Bank reports when they arrive in the postwar world.

Programs of study that have been focused around science, technology, engineering and mathematics (STEM) disciplines and data science sometimes lack a meaningful appreciation of where those disciplines fall short. For a smarter data science to be possible, it is crucial that the worth of insights from the humanities is recognized and taught.

In Conclusion: Toward the Cyborg Historian

Somewhere between the traditional historian, who works feverishly among yellowing books with the simplest technology available to a medieval scribe, and the cool scientist, who feeds figures and facts into a heartless machine, this book suggests a middle path, part human, and part automaton: a semi-automated system churning electronic cogitations in tandem with the critical oversight of a human theoretician, which is to say, a *cyborg historian*. As Donna Haraway has observed, "By the late twentieth century, our time, a mythic time, we are all chimeras, theorized and fabricated hybrids of machine and organism; in short, we are cyborgs."[12]

The path of the cyborg historian means appreciating the raw processing power of the machine, which can churn through two centuries of parliamentary debates within seconds, and can synthesize the results into any number of patterns – while respecting the unique qualifications of the human expert, who, also within seconds, can not only rearrange salient factual information into a credible narrative, but can glimpse into occluded dimensions and grasp what voices are missing.

Applying algorithms to detect evidence of change within any temporal unit, the cyborg historian explores the archive without abandoning critical theory. This paradigm considers human interpretations a fundamental and inextricable part of the system.

The cyborg has important work to do. A theme throughout this book has been the possibility that by agreeing on a common past we can renew the institutions of democracy. I write during a period when it has become fashionable in certain places in America to point out the flaws of democracy, as if tyranny or meritocracy would make a better substitute. I believe, however, that the better alternative is an educated democracy and that education takes many forms, but the most relevant of them is the self-knowledge of a community. A community should know where it has been. It should know what it agrees on. It should have spaces where it can deliberate. Online spaces help, but they must include some historical perspectives on the debate in order for all members of the community to recognize what they share in common. This is where *history* comes in. It acts as the guide and keeper of archives that are the testimony to where the community has been together. It also acts as the guide to the best practices for modeling representations of change over time that underscore the biases of the past, demonstrate the peculiarities of past generations, highlight discontinuities and breaks with corrupt traditions, and open room for both dissent and the possibility of consensus about what the shared tradition means. In addition, this is where *text mining* comes in – as the toolset that can make those archives radically accessible to inspection and argumentation. What the vulgate editions of the Bible did for Christianity, text mining will do for the records of democracy. As Haraway explains,

---

[12] Donna Haraway, "A Cyborg Manifesto: Science, Technology, and Socialist-Feminism in the Late Twentieth Century," in *Manifestly Haraway* (Minneapolis, MN: University of Minnesota Press, 2016), 7, https://www.jstor.org/stable/10.5749/j.ctt1b7x5f6. The chapter was originally published in the *Socialist Review* in 1985.

"The cyborg is our ontology; it gives us our politics. The cyborg is a condensed image of both imagination and material reality, the two joined centers structuring any possibility of historical transformation."[13]

Throughout this book, I have explored the hazards of text mining. After this brief glimpse, do we feel confident that we can move from fantasy to engagement – for example, could we construct a narrative account of the most important hour in the last decade of Congress? If a true robot historian were built one day, our role in these experiments might simply be to feed our machine algorithm upon algorithm, and then press the button and let our system definitively tells us the most important event of the century. In the meantime, however, our approach must be *hybrid*. It may involve datasets and web portals, but as we have seen, no single visualization can abstract the answer to the question, "What changed over the past ten years?" because the windows of the house of time are many.

I would like to   see hybridization run wild. Computationalists and humanists might work together at making portals in the service of the public, opening up government reports and the reports of fiscal institutions to public scrutiny, and where portals are designed to help users to embrace the rigors of critical search. I would like to see interface designers, artists, and humanists collaborate on the construction of web portals on text that clearly showcase strategies that would submit their research to an iterative process of "guided reading" and "broad winnowing," such that readers of Congressional and parliamentary transcripts could easily navigate – and even debate – the results of iterative algorithmic processes. Critical search, after all, requires that the analyst do more than propose any one of these hybrid algorithms: the results of any one transformation need to be unpacked and inspected so that, at the very least, the analyst can walk an audience through the aspects of change and relationality encapsulated in algorithms designed to produce an understanding of time.

The recommended application of the kind of thinking explored in this book is not prediction, in any specific sense, but rather, further reading of history in the hybrid space where quantitative measures and humanistic concepts meet. The fundamental principle embraced by this book is that understanding time – together with its components of periodization, temporality, and modernity – is only possible with a critical relationship to the digitized records of the past. This requires historians to play with algorithms, analysis, and visualization to disaggregate periodization and meaning in the past. The exercise of text mining the historical record is not

[13] Ibid.

nearly as straightforward as simply running a Google n-gram, or otherwise pushing a button on a computer. It is an art, an art best approached through extensive reading and a long acquaintance with ongoing debates. And it is a dangerous art, whose stakes include fundamentally lying about the past or circulating the lies of previous generations under the imprimatur of big data.

Thus, questions about the future of text mining end up in the past, with questions about the bias of data: How complete is my archive? How biased are my sources? How can I measure words and people so as to most accurately determine what happened? The future of any data science that runs on text must bring historians along with it.

Appendix: Notes on Data, Code, Labor, Room for Error, and British History

Digital enterprises are not *always* collective endeavors, but they *often* depend upon long-term collaborations, where shared labor, data, code, and models make possible new insights. Understanding the contribution of this book is predicated on recognizing the limits of a book written about imperfect data with code still in the process of review, which rests upon the contributions of many hands – both those that directly worked with me and those who forged the infrastructure and ideas that made it possible to explore the interdisciplinary terrain of quantitative work with history. This note acknowledges those limits and aids.

Note on Data

Readers who wish to investigate themes explored here will take interest in any of the following public-facing web tools for exploring the parliamentary debates:

- *Hansard Viewer site*: https://shinyviz.smu.edu/shiny/public/hansard-shiny. This an app developed by engineering PhD student Stephanie Buongiorno on the basis of code written by me. It offers a toolkit for comparing the words of different periods of time, comparing grammatical triples, and viewing word embeddings over time. This toolset was developed in parallel with the writing of this book, and the available tools reflect many of the transformations discussed in detail in this book. The code is open-source and available on Github (https://github.com/stephbuon/hansard-shiny). Analysts who wish to create a rendition of the app using a different textual dataset can do so in an efficient and practical way with minimal support from a coder.
- *Hatori Topic Browser site*: https://brown-ccv.github.io/hatori/page/home. This allows the user to investigate a 500-topic dynamic topic model of the *Hansard* debates – something not provided in the

Hansard Viewer site. Hatori was designed by Poom Chiarawongse, an undergraduate student who worked with my team at Brown.

- *Parliament's own page*: hansard.parliament.uk site (curated by the Parliamentary Trust).
- *Hansard Corpus site*: www.english-corpora.org/hansard/ (curated by a multicorpus team of historical linguists). This is an excellent source for searching for patterns of word collocation.
- *Huddersfield Hansard*: https://pure.hud.ac.uk/en/projects/hansard-at-huddersfield-making-the-parliamentary-record-more-acce. This was designed by literature faculty for public engagement.

It should be noted that each of these portals uses a slightly different version of the corpus, and Hatori alone uses the "Brown Hansard" version of the data upon which most of the experiments in this book were based. Various portals also use different algorithms as a default for a fuzzy search, that is, for multiple-word phrases. As a result, wordcounts from in any of the portals will likely differ from the exact wordcounts delivered here.

Credit for the dataset consulted in this book does not belong uniquely to me. I neither scanned the printed page of the parliamentary debates nor cleaned the data. The original scanning work was done under the aegis of an array of other grants by scholars to whom I am grateful but whom I have never met. Under the direction of an NSF grant in the social sciences, of which I was principal investigator, a series of initiatives was begun to improve the quality of the dataset – although this was a secondary priority next to the basic research undertaken for this book. The energies of data scientists at Brown and Southern Methodist University (SMU) prepared the clean data that was used throughout this book, and Ashley Lee of Brown prepared the topic models consulted throughout.[1] The "Brown Hansard" and its successor, the "SMU Hansard," resulted from multiple, iterative engagements with the digital text, but still has known limitations.[2] The SMU Hansard resulted from data collaborations with

[1] For more on this collaboration, see Ashley Lee, Jo Guldi, and Andras Zsom, "Measuring Similarity: Computationally Reproducing the Scholar's Interests," *ArXiv:1812.05984 [Cs]*, December 14, 2018, http://arxiv.org/abs/1812.05984; see also the wonderful, public-facing web browser developed by our then intern, Poom Chiawongse, "The British Hansard," https://eight1911.github.io/hansard. The NSF IBSS grant also supported ethnology, political mapping, and visual research on three different campuses, as well as my own traditional work in various traditional, paper archives; hence the secondary nature of our data-cleaning effort.

[2] For a detailed discussion on the state of *Hansard*, the pipeline used for cleaning *Hansard*, and the limits of using *Hansard* as a scholarly source, please see Jo Guldi, "Parliament's Debates about Infrastructure: An Exercise in Using Dynamic Topic Models to Synthesize Historical Change," *Technology and Culture* 60:1 (March 21, 2019): 1–33; Ashley S. Lee et al., "The Role of Critical

data scientists at SMU, who worked to standardize the dates and to retrieve data from years that were missing in the Brown Hansard and the preliminary versions of the *Hansard* XML data which we downloaded from hansard.org.uk. The SMU Hansard still has optical character recognition (OCR) errors and inconsistencies, especially in speaker names, as of the writing of this document. The SMU team has not yet published an account of its pipeline development, although its code and a short version of the team's work are publicly published on GitHub (https://github.com/rkalescky/import_hansard_data). Our plan is to release the data for public use after finalizing the quality of speaker names, documenting the creation of the clean data, and publishing a series of first uses of the clean data. We continue this work as part of a larger consortium of scholars who work on congressional and parliamentary data, who regularly share strategies for data quality and analysis, and who intend to continue this work.

Some readers may wish that we had rerun all the code in question with the cleanest version of the data available, so as to share the most authoritative results possible on the past. However, data projects are complex, interinstitutional affairs. Cleaning takes place in stages and those stages depend on the commitments of many parties. We are still awaiting a final version of *Hansard* that would take into account OCR corrections and consistency in speaker names, for example.

Because of the limitations on data quality, all findings in this book must be understood as preliminary. The major purpose of this book is to describe a methodological problem and to forward a general approach to work on humanistic problems that requires algorithms, not to advance a final historical verdict on the lineaments of computational interpretations of parliamentary speech during the nineteenth century.

The energy dedicated to interpreting the results of analysis in this book vary by case study. I have followed my own rule of critical search in many instances of interpretation, tracing visualizations back to the text and contextualizing my findings in terms of secondary research. In other cases, I essentially offer a limited critical search, where I deploy questions about gender, race, class, empire, and the silences of the archive to raise questions about a naïve reading of the parliamentary debates. In general, I have

Thinking in Humanities Infrastructure: The Pipeline Concept with a Study of HaToRI (Hansard Topic Relevance Identifier)," *Digital Humanities Quarterly* 14:3 (2020). Certain other figures in this text were modeled on another version of *Hansard*, the "SMU Hansard," for which Rob Kalescky, PhD, and Eric Godat, PhD, of Southern Methodist University recovered missing pages not available with previous versions of the *Hansard* data, and for which Stephanie Buongiorno led a research team improving data about speakers' names.

attempted to flag in the text of the book whenever there are opportunities for other scholars to return to a subject.

Note on Code

I learned to code because I enjoyed the freedom at SMU to pursue new methodological directions. I do not take this freedom lightly. I had to leave my tenure-track line at another university because colleagues there asked me to surrender digital history in order to continue. Almost all of the new work presented here was analyzed and visualized by me on the basis of the parliamentary debates of Great Britain from 1806 to 1911, recorded in what is commonly known as *Hansard*. Where visualizations were made by other collaborators or on the basis of data analyzed by collaborators, I have noted their work in the caption. My scholarship uses the experience of Great Britain and its empire as an index of larger forces of modernity, for Britain housed the industrial and urban revolutions, an expanding empire, and clashes over the rights of the working class, imperial subjects, and women, in a way experienced by most other places around the globe. Other scholars funded by other grants have used the debates to capture the political dynamics of ingroup and outgroup, as speakers identified themselves with party but also with frontbench and backbench positions over time, and my work builds upon theirs.[3] Digital analysis of parliamentary debate offer a suitable background for any historian working on parts of Britain and its empire on a question of modernity, in which parliamentary dealings, alignments, and debates inform issues of economy, politics, and culture.

A version of Chapter 4 was originally shared as an article in the *Journal of Cultural Analytics,* which requires the sharing of code and data, and as such it can be found there. At another time, I hope to emulate the admirable pattern set by Kieran Healy and Andrew Piper, who have shared the code behind their book and so turned a book of theory into a textbook for a new approach to code.

Many parts of the code thus have been reviewed or are currently in a process of review, after which they will be made public as software packages or textbooks. But this is primarily a work of theory, which meditates on the fit between code, questions, and data.

---

[3] For a mere sample, see "Hansard Archive (Digitised Debates from 1803)," www.hansard-archive .parliament.uk; "Hansard Corpus: British Parliament, 1803–2005," www.hansard-corpus.org; Andrew C. Eggers and Arthur Spirling, "The Shadow Cabinet in Westminster Systems: Modeling Opposition Agenda Setting in the House of Commons, 1832–1915," *British Journal of Political Science,* 2016, 1–25.

Note on Labor

Storytellers and information workers of many kinds today have an opportunity to make real strides in critical investigations of the past. They are typically aided in doing so by collaboration with experts, attention to the data sources they investigate, curiosity about the question of the biases in those datasets, and realism about the purpose of their visualization. Throughout this book, I comment on visualizations made by a great many other people, skilled in data analysis and visualization in ways that I myself am not.

One of the critiques sometimes leveled at the digital humanities is that of depending on *invisible labor*, for many scholars in the humanities guard against any transformation that might disrupt the quiet scholarship of the committed individual, corralling individual imagination and energy into the cooperative enterprise of the laboratory. This book represents no such harnessing of graduate student effort. The labor on it has been compensated by institutional support for full-time data staff and by grant support for part-time research assistants (RAs), undergraduate and graduate, who consulted on particular portions of the project while pursuing their own research. I am very grateful to the RAs who cleaned the lists of nations and cities and concerns referred to as the various "controlled vocabularies" used here, and to Stephanie Buongiorno, my project manager, who supervised their work and coordinated the cleaning of data and sometimes adjustments to the data or the execution of code.

Where members of my lab developed new data (as in Buongiorno's triples analysis) or visualizations, I have acknowledged them by name. If labor is not explicitly acknowledged, then the analysis was principally written and executed by myself.

Note on Room for Error

Throughout this book, I have endeavored to emphasize the limitations on the quality of insights available at present from these undertakings, as a result of imperfect data and coding. I very much regard this book as a preliminary work, authored midway through the task of perfecting data and code, before later publications which may be offered less as a methods book and more as a book about *history*.

We can learn about the challenges of interdisciplinarity from observing recent controversies in the digital humanities in the field of literature, where one scholar fomented a minor "replication" crisis by charging that the leading investigators of the field – who in many cases had been responsible for theorizing new processes, founding new journals, writing grants, and teaching all aspects of work – had not yet achieved the standards of "replicability" expected in fields such as economics, where all the infrastructure for teaching and review has already existed for decades.

I hope to warn my own discipline away from such an adversarial approach, for the sake of making the domain in which I work safe for new scholars. I propose, as a practical measure, the following standard of perfection for an emerging field: one rigorous enough to invite constant improvement, yet not so strict that it penalizes any single scholar for failing at collective standards that can only be realistically accomplished by the labor of many hands. A rigorous contribution to collective standards of knowledge, then, might be one that acknowledges the limitations in the data and code it uses; it might even introduce error, so long as it clearly demarcates the process, algorithm, method, dataset, or interpretation that represents the major novel contribution. A productive critique of such an offering should likewise be specific: not an indictment of quantitative methods as a whole, or of the labor of all of the hands that touched the field, but rather a specific new contribution, for instance, an improved dataset that is more reliable for a particular issue such as the quality of speakers' names.

Some readers may find it ironic that, having authored a 100-page polemical pamphlet – *The History Manifesto* – that found certain recent work in social history wanting in its capacity to influence political debates, I should now protest against "adversarial approaches." I submit that the intention of the polemic and the current work on methods is very different in nature and that I come to the current work humbled by the bitterness that the earlier polemic provoked. That pamphlet was coauthored with the chair of the history department at Harvard in the service of imagining future directions for the discipline as a whole, where our PhD students would be as well armed as possible to win debates with other social scientists about the nature of capitalism or internationalism. But it was often misread as a condemnation of all nondigital work.

Because we struck a prophetic tone toward a number of future trends in which we did not endorse microhistory, some of our readers felt antagonized and further endorsed the apparent cleft between the traditional history and digital practice, eschewing the latter. I have observed that rift with remorse and it is for that reason that this book begins with the apparent rift between traditional history and digital practice and an attempt to discern where that divide is necessary.

In other words, this book is very much a testament to an ongoing dialogue between those historians who remained engaged with questions about how temporality works and where quantitative approaches can go right and wrong. The conversation about history and technology – already mature in the field of science and technology studies – has continued to mature through dialogue with quantitative approaches over the last decade, and this book represents a report on that conversation and a contribution, but not one that stands apart from any of the many communities it seeks to serve. The code and the thinking in this book have been reviewed in journals that asked information scientists, digital humanists, British historians, and historians of philosophy to investigate my arguments. In many cases those reviewers pressed back upon my interpretations or directed me to further reading, and my work improved in that process. The current book thus represents a testimony to a shared endeavor, testifying to the state of the field where it is now.

Thus, even with the well-flagged limitations of the data, and even if some of the unreviewed code supporting the exercises in this book has inevitably introduced some errors into the calculations it has visualized, the book's overall offering is a *process*. That process, put into dialogue with the best standard of data and code available, represents a meaningful and rigorous contribution to a discourse about how history and quantitative analytics engage each other.

My point is not that I have intentionally introduced error, or to excuse myself from responsibility for any errors that are found, but rather to point to the community process as a context for understanding my errors – or the errors of other scholars – as they arise. We are investigating new terrain, as I point out throughout this book, and we must rely on collaborative processes. We iterate over data, code, and processes, and part of productive engagement means flagging our changing standards for perfection as code and data are amended. Such an approach necessarily entails a tolerance for error. Collaborators in computer science and statistics affirm that errors in code or even calculations, while embarrassing, tend not to be career-destroying in those fields where collaboration is expected and new contributions improving the process of working with data are prized.

No author exploring terrain such as this should be held to the standard of perfection in all polymathic pursuits; no one expected Derrida to prepare a scholarly edition of Rousseau to write *Of Grammatology* – and yet that book, at the juncture of linguistics, semiology, classical history, enlightenment, and power relations, provided new food for thought for a generation. It is appropriate that *The Dangerous Art of Text Mining* aspires only to such a standard as Derrida's, because it is a work of theory. Meanwhile other digital history books, for instance Luke Blaxill's monograph, aspire to the standard of monographs, given the tools with which they work, and still others aspire to the standard of the scholarly edition or textbook that aggregates the insights of many scholars into a new form.[4]

In a new field based on hybrid knowledge where many experts collaborate to produce new approaches, we do not work alone. Our insights – as well as our errors – are collateral. To slander collective and individual errors without commending the insights garnered from collective labor represents a misunderstanding of (if not a disservice to) collaborative inquiry as a whole.

Note on British History

New methodological work requires its own treatment. This book therefore has been organized around the problem of the "fit" between text as data and history in general, rather than the questions of British history in particular. Because the book is not concerned primarily with new insights to British historiography, many of the findings will largely correspond to what is already known about the British past, with only a handful of data-driven surprises, but many striking observations that deserve to be followed up on by scholars pursuing more focused questions. Elsewhere, I have argued that *Hansard* is useful for exactly this reason: because it has been widely used and studied, it offers a baseline against which we can test the reliability of our results.

I have attempted to remark, in most of the case studies, where the balance lies between new insight and work that merely validates that the algorithm is functioning correctly by producing results that will look unremarkable to specialists. The reader familiar with British historiography can rapidly identify where the algorithm has replicated widespread knowledge and where the algorithm has found something completely divergent.

For methodological purposes, validation represents a clear indication that an algorithm is working as expected. The canny analyst of text mining hopes that when applied to data that intersects with a subject so well studied as the parliamentary debates, the algorithm will in *most* instances replicate the

---

[4] Luke Blaxill, *The War of Words: The Language of British Elections, 1880–1914*, Royal Historical Society, Studies in History. New Series 103 (Woodbridge, UK and Rochester, NY: The Boydell Press, 2020),

known consensus of hundreds of scholars. If the algorithm *didn't* turn up a nineteenth century marked by industrialization, urbanization, and empire, it would probably mean that the analysis had failed. The best-case scenario is, in fact, something like an 80/20 split, where 80 percent of the results replicate what scholars of British history already know and 20 percent of the findings are new. If my algorithms and process perform at the 80 percent level for replicating British historiography on the parliamentary debates, then we can judge the algorithms to be a success and apply them (with some adjustment and iteration) to other troves of documents that are less well understood – for instance, papers of twentieth-century administrations, or the voluminous text of twenty-first-century social media.

Some readers will be underwhelmed by the conclusions about British history that can be drawn from my visualizations: perhaps, an insight that simply confirms the gender prejudices of parliamentary speakers, or some pedantic insight about the dates of legislation named. Those readers might wonder why we should devote all of this work for so few rewards in terms of new perspectives on history. Elsewhere, I have outlined in greater detail the full scope of my project, one vector of which focuses specifically upon new insights into the British historiography of landownership. That work is already documented in several smaller publications, with further publications to come. It is not chiefly on display here and, even when I offer visualizations that have implications for the historiography of landownership, I have cut out most of my interpretation – saving that for another venue where I can dive into the nuances of historical debate.

Index